UNCHE

UNCHECKED

The Untold Story Behind Congress's Botched Impeachments of Donald Trump

RACHAEL BADE & KAROUN DEMIRJIAN

wm
WILLIAM MORROW
An Imprint of HarperCollins*Publishers*

HarperCollins books may be purchased for educational, business, or sales promotional use. For information, please email the Special Markets Department at SPsales@harpercollins.com.

FIRST EDITION

Designed by Bonni Leon-Berman

Library of Congress Cataloging-in-Publication Data has been applied for.

ISBN 978-0-06-304079-3

22 23 24 25 26   LSC   10 9 8 7 6 5 4 3 2 1

For Alex, Karen, and Ara

. . . and Bill Duryea, without whom we would
probably still be writing

CONTENTS

PREFACE

In November 2019, just a few weeks into the House's high-profile impeachment proceedings against President Donald Trump, we were working the weekend, burrowed deep in the bowels of the U.S. Capitol building in hallways that had become our second home. It was just before a series of blockbuster public hearings were set to begin, and we were staking out the House Republicans' and Democrats' competing practice sessions, hoping to get a scoop about the strategies each side planned to trot out before the cameras.

Karoun, then a national security reporter on Capitol Hill, approached Rachael, who covered congressional leadership, with a bottle of water and a proposition. "Let's write a book together," she suggested. Rachael was already there; in fact, she had just spoken with an agent.

By then, we'd cemented ourselves as the two top reporters on the impeachment beat for the *Washington Post*. Karoun, who had recently returned from a stint reporting in Russia, was the intelligence panel whisperer, giving us inroads to the committee leading the effort to oust Trump. Rachael, who had logged almost a decade covering Capitol Hill, had a deep network of sources within House leadership circles. Together, we had spent hundreds of hours staking out the secure facility in the basement of the Capitol, where lawmakers were investigating whether Trump had abused his office to secure his own reelection. We had tag-teamed chasing members of Congress down narrow halls and hounding them deep into the night for insights into what was going on behind closed doors. We had covered for each other when we needed a break for coffee or food—and even when we needed to steal moments in the bathroom to cry over a bad breakup and a failed round of IVF.

But for all the time we had spent witnessing history in the making, we knew this once-in-a-generation event was moving *way* too fast to fully comprehend. And we weren't alone.

That fall, every time we huddled with editors at the *Washington Post* to talk through our coverage, they often prodded us with questions we couldn't answer: *What do you mean Democrats were only planning two weeks' worth of hearings in a process that traditionally took months? What do you mean investigators wouldn't pursue subpoenas of key firsthand witnesses—and that there wouldn't be any witnesses at the trial?*

At the time, all we knew was that House Democrats felt confident they had the goods on Trump and were eager to move quickly. Yet when the president was easily acquitted a few months later in the Republican-controlled Senate, the fireworks of impeachment faded as fast as they had initially erupted. The simultaneous emergence of a deadly pandemic and the approaching presidential election quickly pulled the public's attention elsewhere.

But the lingering questions about impeachment still remained unanswered. *How could a president who shattered norms so readily just skirt accountability so easily—and emerge even stronger? Why had Democrats pulled certain punches? And did Republicans* really *see nothing wrong with Trump's behavior?* And most of all, *was the outcome as preordained as everyone seemed to think it was?* As we set about writing our book, we vowed to get those answers.

We spent thousands of hours deconstructing everything we had already witnessed and re-interviewing sources, including lawmakers from both parties, Hill staffers, White House officials, and others who had played some role in the impeachment investigation and trial. What we learned from our more than 250 interviews surprised us, even though we were two of the most plugged-in reporters on the impeachment story. And it completely changed our understanding of what had happened.

We discovered that political calculations—not fact-finding—dominated nearly every key decision of Speaker Nancy Pelosi's impeachment strategy. We learned that some House Democrats were sounding dire warnings early on that the party was bungling its case against Trump—and leaving half the nation behind. We found that while Democrats said they wanted bipartisanship, when presented with ways to achieve it, they chose paths that guaranteed the opposite. We also were told about the panic that gripped Trump's key GOP congressional allies in the early days of the impeachment probe—and how they consciously muzzled their scruples in order to ardently defend the president publicly. A clear picture began to form of an impeachment that had been crippled by doubt and exploited by avarice—emboldening the president and weakening the legislative branch.

And then, just as we were finishing our manuscript, it happened again.

The circumstances and the fact of Trump's second impeachment were unprecedented; yet the same problems that plagued the first impeachment hobbled the second one too. Even armed with a better case, Democrats chose expediency over thoroughness in the name of saving the agenda of newly elected president Joe Biden. Republicans who were disgusted by Trump's behavior on January 6 found narrow procedural escape hatches to avoid convicting a former president who still held sway over their political futures. And the result was a further degradation of Congress's oversight authority—and the efficacy of impeachment overall.

This is the never-before-told story of what *actually* happened behind the scenes of the historic impeachments of Donald Trump, when Democrats twice deployed Congress's most powerful weapon against the same president—and failed both times to bring him down. The efforts to oust Trump garnered round-the-clock, obsessive media coverage, dominating headlines and cable news. But the full picture of what transpired on Capitol Hill has never been revealed until now. At a time when congressional oversight was more vital than ever, lawmakers repeatedly fumbled in their bid to rein in a president determined to upend the democratic system, emboldening one of the most divisive and controversial presidents in American history and exposing deficiencies in the constitutional order—particularly regarding impeachment.

The prevailing narrative of these two critical years—from the Democratic takeover in early 2019 to the dramatic weeks after the January 6, 2021, Capitol insurrection—has been overly simplistic. The conventional wisdom in Washington has been that Republicans turned a blind eye to the misbehavior of their party's leader and thus empowered him to greater acts of recklessness. And that Democrats simply couldn't overcome the intransigence of Trump's congressional lackeys, who defended him despite overwhelming evidence of his guilt. But while there is some truth to that narrative, the reality of what occurred, we learned, was far more complex: Trump escaped accountability not simply because his own party wouldn't stand up to him, but because the opposing party was also afraid to flex the full force of its constitutional muscle to check him. Republicans didn't just block and sabotage impeachment—Democrats never went all in, fumbling their best chance to turn the American public away from Trump for good.

Rather, under the leadership of a cautious Speaker, Democrats hesitated when they could have acted decisively following a special counsel's findings that Trump had effectively obstructed justice—and may have even lied to investigators. Instead, they fixated on political concerns, worried that blowback from the populist president could cost them their House majority. Even when revelations that Trump had tried to bully a foreign ally into smearing his 2020 election rival pitched the House into an impeachment investigation, Democrats rushed through an artificially narrow probe, leaving serious allegations against Trump on the cutting-room floor. And they eschewed court fights for firsthand testimony that might have persuaded Republicans of Trump's guilt—or at least attracted more public support.

The result was a half-baked inquiry riddled with holes that Republicans readily and shamelessly exploited to keep their ranks united behind Trump. The Senate's subsequent acquittal vote unleashed Trump to act on his worst instincts with impunity—and ultimately set the stage for his second impeachment. Even after Trump incited a mob to violently attack the Capitol, Democrats once again prioritized political expediency over full accountability, forgoing witnesses during the trial in the name of safeguarding the Biden agenda and bypassing an opportunity to turn GOP voters against Trump when he was most vulnerable. Congress emerged from the exercise riven by bitter partisanship—and left Trump room for a political comeback.

There have been countless books written about Trump and his unprecedented White House. But none has taken a hard look at the Congress that tried and failed to keep him in check, or chronicled the two impeachments that were definitional for his presidency—and for American democracy itself. Our work, in that regard, occupies a unique space in the vast library of Trump-related narratives. It is the only forensic account to date of the critical two years in which a divided legislature was called upon to test the strength of the Constitution's checks and balances—and twice found them, and themselves, to be lacking.

Many political observers believe the country's unbridgeable and toxic partisan divide had doomed the efforts to oust Trump from the very start. There's little doubt that historic levels of distrust between the parties severely worsened their chances of striking the type of bipartisan cooperation needed to confront Trump—the kind that was a hallmark of the Watergate probe that resulted in Richard Nixon's resignation from the presidency. But our reporting revealed key moments when things might have swung a different way.

Few know, for example, that during the first impeachment, one of Pelosi's own chairmen warned her against taking procedural shortcuts that could repel Republicans—loopholes that House GOP leaders readily exploited to keep wavering members of their rank and file in line. Or that a conservative House Republican approached Pelosi on the chamber floor to tell her he was open to impeaching the president—if only she would take the time to run a more complete investigation. Until now, it has never been reported how top House Republicans tried to get the president to cooperate with the probe, only to end up loudly defending a stonewalling strategy they feared would cause long-term institutional damage. Neither has the extent to which Trump's defenders panicked when they first learned that Trump pressured Ukraine to investigate Joe Biden—nor how closely then–Senate Majority Leader Mitch McConnell coached the president's lawyers, shaping their arguments throughout the trial despite his private disgust with Trump's actions toward Ukraine.

Our book reveals how ugly partisan politicking took precedence over serious oversight, in both parties. It shows how Republican leaders grossly misled their own members to whip them into an indignant fervor—while Democratic leaders catered to the demands of politically vulnerable novices over the caution of some of their own investigative chairs. It documents, for the first time, how rank-and-file Democrats began to question the Speaker's judgment, especially when the party turned a blind eye to egregious Trump conduct falling outside the narrow scope of the impeachment investigation. And it details how both parties failed to learn from their mistakes, even after a horde of Trump sycophants laid siege to the Capitol on January 6, 2021, sending Democrat and Republican alike running for their lives.

In painstaking, minute-by-minute detail, we show how Democratic and Republican congressional leaders had a sense of shared purpose during the unprecedented assault, working side by side from a secure location to wrest control of the Capitol back from a Trump-inspired mob. Their successful cooperation—and their shared trauma—could have laid the groundwork for Congress reclaiming its oversight role and demanding accountability from the president all of them believed had incited the attack.

But once again, they missed their moment. Republicans eager to secure their own political futures—or fearful of turning Trump into a martyr—either vocally opposed impeachment or quickly sought to sweep the incident under the rug, leaving GOP voters with the distinct impression Trump did nothing wrong. And Democratic leaders quietly pressured their own prosecutors to abandon their fight for conviction prematurely, to free Joe Biden's fledgling presidency from the shadow of Trump. Even after the first attack on the Capitol in over two hundred years—and the only one ever perpetrated by American citizens—Congress treated its oversight responsibility, and its constitutionally derived power to impeach and convict, as burdens too heavy to bear.

The ultimate result was more than a second acquittal of Trump, permitting the forty-fifth president to contemplate another run for office and allowing Trumpism to grow even stronger. The failed effort exposed the devastating limits of impeachment, Congress's most powerful tool for holding a president to account. Trump's moves to run roughshod over congressional subpoenas and investigations—and Democrats' acquiescence—created a standard of unhindered executive power for future leaders to emulate and exploit. By laying bare the fundamental weakness of Congress's greater oversight power, Trump's two impeachments shook the foundations of the constitutional order that had governed the nation for more than two centuries, throwing the future balance of government checks and balances into doubt and weakening impeachment as a tool for future Congresses.

"No one is above the law," Pelosi frequently said in reference to Trump during this time. Yet if anything, Congress's efforts to hold Trump to account—and the decisions on both sides of the aisle that led to his acquittals—revealed how despite the Framers' best intentions, a president can remain unchecked.

AUTHORS' NOTE

Our reporting is informed by hundreds of hours of interviews with almost every main player in the Trump impeachment sagas, including members of Congress, White House officials, witnesses, lawyers, and staffers who worked on the investigations, impeachments, and trials. They shared notes from House Speaker Nancy Pelosi's leadership meetings and Senate Majority Leader Mitch McConnell's private lunches with senators, text messages of their exchanges with other lawmakers, and firsthand stories of interactions with Trump in the Oval Office.

Given the sensitive nature of what happened—and the continued posturing around such politically contentious events—we conducted our more than 250 interviews on deep background. That allowed our sources to speak frankly and honestly, and permitted us to tell their stories—and those of their bosses and associates—in greater detail than would have been possible had we insisted on full attribution. We did this for the sake of history, to enable people to come forward and ensure our book is as complete, accurate, and unvarnished an account of what occurred as possible.

Sources spoke with us for many reasons. Some talked to set the record straight. Others to contradict narratives they felt were unfair or inaccurate, or refute the spin promoted by their party leaders. Still others talked for their own therapeutic purposes. Many, in fact, were still digesting the chaos of what they had lived through and trying to decipher the conclusions they should draw from two failed impeachments of Trump.

For the facts in our story, we relied on multiple sources. Quotes in the book were described to us by people who were present for the conversations—or multiple people who had been informed about them. We have used italics to indicate a person's internal thinking, according to our reporting, or a more vague recollection of what someone said when our sources could remember the gist, but not the precise phrasing, of certain exchanges.

Major characters in the book have been given a chance to respond to our reporting. Several key lawmakers contested new revelations we unearthed, and for transparency's sake, we included their push-back in the Notes section in the back of the book. We also included explanations of how we determined which account was accurate—and why in certain instances, despite characters' denials, we stuck by our reporting.

We will note that due to the ongoing political sensitivity surrounding this topic, there has already been much interest in rewriting history on both sides of the aisle. Since Trump maintains a firm grip over the Republican Party, some GOP lawmakers have tried to paper over their own private concerns with his actions during these critical two years. Some Republican sources who spent hours with us discussing every twist and turn of these events later came back and asked us not to publish things they told us, fearful of blowback from Trump. Others have tried to downplay the violence of January 6, 2021, whitewashing the riot as a standard protest or a benign tourist sojourn to the Capitol.

Democrats, meanwhile, have tried to paint a rosy picture of being motivated exclusively by the higher callings of the Constitution and their own collective moral conscience, rejecting the suggestions that politics influenced decisions to counter Trump—and their decisions not to—in any way. But time and time again, other Democratic sources revealed episodes where this was not the case, detailing how the politicking going on behind the scenes tripped up the party's oversight work.

When asked about our reporting, some senior Democratic sources threatened to cut off cooperation with us—and in the case of Pelosi's office, chose to disengage from the book entirely after learning that our discoveries challenged the Speaker's preferred narrative. When we sought comment on reporting that had not been sanctioned by her office for release, one of Pelosi's top staffers even cornered certain impeachment aides and lawmakers to angrily accuse them of sharing too much with us. Others, including a top aide in Senate Minority Leader Chuck Schumer's office, reached out to fellow Democrats he assumed had cast himself and his boss in an unfavorable light, seeking to get them to change their story. We did not allow these sorts of intimidation tactics to impact our reporting or the story we tell in this book.

Thanks to our sources—some of whom spent more than twenty hours with us over the course of several months to ensure we accurately represented and reconstructed critical moments—we feel confident in our firsthand accounts of what transpired. We hope you enjoy the book as much as we have enjoyed writing it.

UNCHECKED

PROLOGUE

JANUARY 6, 2021

BOOM!... BOOM!... BOOM!

Congressman Jamie Raskin shot up from his seat, spinning around to stare at the source of the harrowing bangs ricocheting through the cavernous chamber of the House of Representatives. Republicans and Democrats had been ensconced in debate just moments before. But now Capitol Police officers, guns drawn, raced toward the elegant double doors in the back of the room, while other security officials frantically pushed furniture into a makeshift barricade to block the yelling rioters outside from beating down the door.

"Get back! Get back!" the cops yelled at lawmakers milling about in confusion. Amid the unfolding chaos, someone shouted for everyone to remove the circular bronze pins on their shoulders that identified them as members of Congress so the intruders wouldn't target them.

From his crouch at the center of the room, not fifty feet from the doors, Raskin took in the panic spreading around him. In front, the House chaplain had taken over the microphone at the rostrum to pray for their safety. On the floor, scattered between the tiered rows of leather-bound chairs where Congress typically voted and debated, lawmakers struggled to don never-before-used emergency escape hoods tucked under their chairs, setting off an eerie drone of low beeps as their headgear ballooned to protect them from any lurking deadly gases. Others were frantically calling their spouses to say a desperate goodbye.

Raskin's mind was on his family too. Somewhere inside the Capitol were his daughter and son-in-law, and he had no idea if they were safe.

BOOM! . . . BOOM! . . . BOOM!

That morning, before he left for the Capitol, Raskin's youngest daughter, Tabitha, had begged him to stay home. Outgoing president Donald Trump, who refused to concede the 2020 election and claimed it had been stolen, had summoned his followers to the National Mall for a last-ditch protest to object to Congress's certification of the Electoral College results that afternoon. There were already concerns about violence erupting on the streets of Washington and demonstrations at the Capitol.

"Dad, don't go," Tabitha, twenty-three, had pleaded. "Please, stay home."

It wasn't an idle request. The Raskin family was still deep in mourning over the death of their twenty-five-year-old son, Tommy, an ardent humanitarian and Harvard Law student who had killed himself exactly one week before following a battle with depression. Raskin had personally discovered his son's body in their basement and tried to resuscitate him. He later laid his son's suicide note on his dresser as a reminder of the lifelong task his son had laid out for him: "Look after each other, the animals, and the global poor for me. All my love, Tommy."[1]

But Tommy's death had only redoubled Raskin's resolve to be there when Congress finally brought Trump to heel. Plus, he had a job to do: The Speaker of the House had selected him, one of the most progressive members of the caucus, as part of a four-member team to defend the integrity of the election against Trump's allegations of fraud, which his congressional allies were parroting.

"I have no choice. It's my constitutional duty," Raskin told Tabitha. To allay her fears, he suggested she come along. "We'll be inside the Capitol," he had promised. "We'll be safe."

"Constitutional duty" meant something very specific to Jamie Raskin. He was still one of the newer members of Congress, having been elected in 2016 to represent a safely blue district in Maryland. But in some ways he represented a kind of lawmaker who was almost out of vogue. As a professor of constitutional law, he had an almost religious devotion to the idea of checks and balances, the Founders' careful balancing act between the three branches that had succeeded in holding together the republic for more than two centuries. Essential to that equation was Congress's power of oversight, the ability of lawmakers to investigate the executive branch to ensure the proper functioning of government. Nothing had challenged that authority as dramatically as the president who had arrived in Washington in the same election cycle.

Raskin had identified Donald Trump as a threat to the constitutional health of the nation as early as anyone. He saw Trump's refusal to divest from his real estate, golf resort, and branding businesses as a blatant attempt to profit off the Oval Office. He had been appalled by evidence that the president welcomed Russia's help in his 2016 campaign effort—then subsequently sought to obstruct a special counsel's investigation into his actions. When Democrats reassumed control of the House in early 2019, Raskin and a small group of like-minded members immediately began pressing their leadership to utilize Congress's full arsenal of oversight tools—including the ultimate sanction of impeachment—to check and restrain Trump.

But Raskin ran into a problem: House Speaker Nancy Pelosi was

almost as disdainful of aggressive, all-encompassing oversight as he
was a believer in it. And the powerful Democratic leader had surprisingly made the task of holding Trump accountable difficult, if
not impossible.

Pelosi's deep reluctance to police Trump using the oversight
power at her disposal—especially impeachment—boiled down to
one thing: her belief that it was a political boomerang. She feared that
by going too hard after Trump, she would jeopardize her hard-won
majority—and could even land Trump a second term. To Raskin,
however, oversight of Trump was a matter of principle. It was why,
in early 2019, he had launched a guerrilla operation to try to force
the Speaker's hand on impeachment, and why he had buttonholed
her so often to call out Trump's profiting off the Oval Office. It was
why he had urged investigators to leave no stone unturned when
they did finally pursue an effort to oust the president in the fall of
that year—and why he was so dejected when they ignored him and
Trump was acquitted in early 2020.

Raskin had privately blamed himself for the outcome—and
rued that he had not done more to educate his colleagues about
the dangers of letting Trump escape accountability. As he anticipated, Trump had only grown more reckless. He had hamstrung a
national response to a deadly pandemic, fearing that acknowledging the dangers would cripple his reelection campaign. He continued to shatter norms and line his own pockets with government
money. And now, he was blatantly trying to overturn a presidential
election.

For Raskin, the fact that a formality like the certification of the
Electoral College results had turned into a circus of unfounded
Trump conspiracies of voter fraud proved that not aggressively
standing up to Trump had only unleashed him to act on his more
outlandish impulses. The Democrats had held on to power in No-

vember, yes, and they had even regained the White House. But it had come at a terrible price.

Earlier that day, Tabitha and Hank Kronick, the new husband of Raskin's older daughter, Hannah, had watched from the upper balcony as Raskin, wearing a black ribbon of mourning on his lapel, manned the proceedings on the House floor below. He had written his opening speech in the days before Tommy died. When he stood to deliver it, the entire chamber had applauded in a show of support due to the tragedy that had befallen his family.

At fifty-eight, Raskin's usual boundless energy and youthful gait belied his age, even if the wisps of hair around his bald spot did not. He was fit—thin even, thanks to a vegan diet that was inspired by his son, an animal-rights activist. And he was always smiling. Yet when Raskin addressed the chamber, his normally bright face was sunken, his usually sunny personality solemn. With dark circles under his eyes, he spoke with intensity and determination—believing his son would have wanted no less.

"We are not here, Madam Speaker, to vote for the candidate we want; we are here to recognize the candidate the people *actually* voted for," he said. "The 2020 election is over and the people have spoken."

As he settled into his chair to listen to the House debate, Raskin's phone started buzzing. Family members at home, watching on TV as pro-Trump crowds were beginning to mass at the doors to the Capitol, wanted to know if he was okay. Raskin dismissed their concerns. There were few places in the country more fortified than the Capitol, and no chamber in the building more heavily guarded than the House floor.

But shortly after two p.m., his sense of security began to crumble.

In the middle of the debate, as Republicans decried Trump's loss in Arizona, murmurs swept through the chamber—and they had nothing to do with the proceedings on the floor. Looking around, Raskin could see members studying their cell phones and holding up their devices to colleagues. Others had begun to place whispered calls, violating strict House prohibitions against phone calls in the chamber.

Puzzled by the fuss, Raskin pulled up his Twitter account and stopped short at the images he saw on the screen: a cloud of smoke rising over the crowd outside; protesters appearing to beat up police officers as they pushed toward the Capitol; Trump supporters proudly carrying the Confederate flag—and making their way *into* the building.

How did they get in? Raskin wondered frantically. *How many were there? Fifty? A hundred? Were they armed?* Whatever the answer, he knew the once unthinkable had happened: Trump's angry mob had breached the crucible of American democracy.

Looking up from his phone, Raskin turned to his right and caught sight of Congresswoman Liz Cheney, the third-highest ranking Republican in the House, who was sitting across the wide center aisle that divided the two parties. Raskin knew that Cheney, despite her party position, abhorred Trumpism—and that she would be repulsed by this.

"Liz, it looks like we're under new management . . . There's a *Confederate flag* in the Rotunda," he said, holding up his phone for her to see the pictures and blanching at the absurdity of the words escaping his lips.[2] She looked at it, looked back at him, and shook her head in dismay.

"What have they done?" she breathed, smarting as she realized what the intruders were there for—and that her own party was complicit in the chaos befalling the Capitol.[3]

Suddenly, a phalanx of guards whisked Pelosi off the marble dais, where she had been supervising the debate, and out of the chamber. Members who had been murmuring over the images on their phones began openly fretting as they anxiously paced the chamber. The Rules Committee chairman—who had just been shoved onto the dais to take over for Pelosi—vainly banged his gavel to demand order as Democratic members began screaming across the room at their Republican colleagues: "Call Trump and tell him to call this off!"

BOOM! . . . BOOM! . . . BOOM!

A Capitol Police officer rushed to the front, seized the microphone, and confirmed what Raskin already knew.

"We had a breach of the Capitol building," he said, advising members to stay put. "Be prepared to get under your chairs if necessary."[4]

Pandemonium engulfed the room. Tear gas, they were told, had been dispersed in the Rotunda, just down the hall from the chamber. Members, an officer told them, needed to put on escape hoods, located under their seats. Raskin didn't bother. They were like sitting ducks. If a mob broke into the House chamber, an escape hood wouldn't protect them.

Police announced they would bring lawmakers to a secure location to hide. They needed to move swiftly and quietly out the side doors, they instructed. Now.

Raskin froze. If they were evacuating, he needed to find his family—but he had no idea where they were.

As the entire chamber began to move toward a pair of doors on the GOP side of the hall, Raskin found a member of Nancy Pelosi's staff and begged for a Capitol Police escort to locate and rescue his children. The cops volunteered to go find them, but instructed Raskin to head to the secure location with his peers in the meantime. If he hung around panicking, he would only complicate their job and slow them down. They would bring his children to safety.

Fumbling for his cell phone, Raskin called his chief of staff, who assured him she had Tabitha and Hank safely hidden in a side room off the House floor. She had locked the door, shoved the heaviest thing she could find—a bronze bust of a buck—behind it, and hid Tabitha and Hank under a desk. In her hand, she explained, she had a small iron poker from the fireplace in the room. A weapon, just in case.

"Guard them with your life," he told her.

As Raskin joined the stream of lawmakers snaking through the back stairwells and underground tunnels of the Capitol, he could hear the screaming of the rioters down the hall. The president's supporters called out for the vice president's execution for refusing to overturn the election results as Trump had demanded.

"Hang Mike Pence! Hang Mike Pence!"

In the distance, he heard a gunshot. Then, another pack of marauders calling for their next victim in a foreboding taunt.

"Where's Nancy? Where's Nancy?"

As the group of lawmakers ran with their armed police escort, one of Raskin's colleagues pulled up the news on his phone. The echo of the broadcasters' voices filled the spaces as they fled: Someone had been shot. Bombs had been found at the Republican and Democratic headquarters across the street. Eventually, the cops led them to a large committee room—the same elegant space where Democrats had laid out their impeachment case against Trump to the nation, just one year prior.

It wasn't until he was settled in the guarded, secure room that Raskin fully understood what he had escaped—and what was still threatening Tabitha and Hank. Another lawmaker had pulled up a CNN feed on her iPad, where live video showed thousands of

Trump supporters descending on the complex, laying waste to the barriers and pummeling police officers in their path. Hundreds had smashed through windows to enter the marbled halls of the Capitol. Others were tearing apart congressional offices. It was suddenly clear to Raskin that the rioters he had passed in the hallways weren't just a couple dozen rowdy protesters; they were the vanguard of what seemed to be an all-out attack on the Capitol. This was a coup of Congress, Raskin thought. *Trump's coup of Congress.*

He immediately called his daughter.

"We're going to get you out," he told Tabitha.

On the other end of the line, Tabitha's voice sounded lifeless. "When?" she pressed, still hiding under a desk. "We saw them all coming up the Hill, Dad. There are thousands."[5]

For the next forty-five minutes, Raskin kept checking his phone for updates on his kids' whereabouts as he watched the horror play out on his colleague's iPad, frantically alternating between the two as his worries mounted. *What was taking so long?* Finally, an officer interrupted Raskin's nervous reverie.

"Your daughter will be here in a moment," the officer said. A minute later, the doors burst open, and Tabitha and Hank rushed into his arms.

"I promise, it won't be like this, next time you come back to the Capitol with me," Raskin told them through grateful tears.

"Dad," Tabitha said, "I don't want to come back to the Capitol."

Her words hit Raskin like a punch in the gut. American constitutional democracy had been the bedrock of his life's work. Now his own daughter was afraid of the building at the heart of American governance. He had just lost his son. *Was he about to lose his faith in the country too?*

As they huddled together watching the violence play out on a television in the lawmakers' hiding place, Raskin couldn't help but think of the September 11, 2001, terrorist attacks. That morning, Americans didn't know whether the assaults on the Twin Towers and the Pentagon were a one-off attack or the beginning of an all-out war on U.S. soil. Nearly twenty years later, as Trump's die-hard supporters desecrated the Capitol, Raskin was gripped with a similar sense of uncertainty and foreboding. *Was this just one attack? Or a coup that might spiral into civil war?*

Elsewhere in the Capitol, Raskin's friends were experiencing the same sense of doom. Around seven p.m., his phone flashed with a text message from two of them: David Cicilline, a Democrat from Rhode Island, and Ted Lieu, a Democrat from California. Both had helped Raskin push Pelosi to impeach Trump in 2019. From Cicilline's office, where they were hiding during the riot, the pair had cooked up a similar idea: The House should impeach Trump again. Immediately.

"Ted and I are working on a resolution of impeachment," Cicilline's text read, "and we'd love for you to join us."

Raskin thought quickly. No Congress in history had ever tried to impeach a president twice. The tool had been deployed so rarely, in fact, that only two other presidents before Trump had ever faced impeachment charges, while a third, Richard Nixon, outran them by resigning before they could be voted on in the House.

Raskin knew that modern impeachments were complicated, laborious processes—and there were barely two weeks left in Trump's presidency. Yet that day's assault on the Capitol had made it abundantly clear to him that with every additional hour Trump stayed in office, he posed a mortal threat to the survival of the republic. If they did not act, there was no telling what he might do next, Raskin reasoned, determining that he had no choice. *This cannot be the future of America*, Raskin thought.

He called his friends back with a simple reply.

"Count me in."

PART ONE

1

"IMPEACH THE MOTHERFUCKER"

JANUARY 4, 2019

As Nancy Pelosi's black Suburban pulled away from the U.S. Capitol, the newly elected Speaker was fuming.

After eight long years in the minority, the California Democrat had meticulously planned her first twenty-four hours back in power, eager to convey a sense of calm and competence to a country exhausted by the chaos of President Donald Trump. There were speeches to give, press conferences to attend, and television interviews to prepare for, all to project one message: that reclaiming her gavel was not just about checking an unpopular and controversial president, but about fighting for the underprivileged and middle class. That, after all, was why she believed voters had flipped the House into Democratic hands.

But just hours after being sworn in, Pelosi's carefully crafted public relations plan was starting to unravel. The night before, in a dimly lit bar just blocks from the Capitol, one of Pelosi's newly minted members was caught on camera celebrating the Democratic takeover by promising to oust Trump—and punctuating it with a four-syllable expletive.

"We're gonna impeach the motherfucker!" Congresswoman Rashida Tlaib of Michigan yelled to a cheering crowd of progressive activists.

For left-wing Democrats, Tlaib's words were a long-awaited call to arms. For Pelosi, they were a dangerous distraction.

"This is *so* unfortunate," Pelosi had lamented when her team informed her of Tlaib's off-the-cuff remark earlier that morning of January 4, 2019. "It's going to overshadow *everything*."

A few hours later, as her SUV full of security guards and aides turned north, Pelosi, seventy-eight, was still grappling with how to handle Tlaib's outburst. The Speaker was on her way to Trinity Washington University, the country's first Catholic college for women and her alma mater, to pre-tape what she thought would be a softball MSNBC interview about her party's top legislative priorities. The location had been strategically chosen to highlight both how far Pelosi had come over more than a half century in politics, and the milestone Pelosi had just achieved, swearing in the most diverse freshman class in American history, including more than a hundred women.

But now, Pelosi knew all the MSNBC host would want to ask her about was Tlaib's blunder. Turning to her staff as they drove, she insisted they make a plan to steer the conversation away from impeachment back to legislation.

Pelosi, a thirty-two-year veteran of Congress who knew the pulses of Washington better than almost anybody, wasn't wrong. The clip of Tlaib's profanity-laced remarks was already dominating the headlines that morning, leaving little oxygen on the frenetic cable networks for Pelosi's lofty observations about her historic victory. Republicans on conservative channels had giddily seized on Tlaib's outburst as fresh ammunition to accuse Democrats of trying to over-turn the results of the 2016 election. Democrats unlucky enough to have booked interviews on other networks were scrambling to distance themselves from Tlaib's sentiments.

Meanwhile, Pelosi's office phones had been blowing up with calls from moderate Democrats representing districts Trump had won, upset that they were being forced to answer for Tlaib's impeach-ment battle cry. It had hijacked their message of progress through unity, and they were begging the Speaker to push back on the un-folding narrative that Democrats' ultimate agenda was to impeach the forty-fifth president of the United States.

In her kickoff meeting with all the House Democrats in the base-ment of the Capitol that morning, Pelosi had studiously avoided dis-cussing Tlaib's comments. Instead, she gave an upbeat welcome to her rank and file, apprising them on the latest negotiations with Trump, who had decided to shut the government down just before Christmas to try to force Pelosi into funding his border wall with Mexico.

But behind the scenes, Pelosi was already cracking down. She instructed her chairmen and senior members to push back hard on the idea that Democrats were even contemplating impeachment. And to silence Tlaib, she phoned Congresswoman Debbie Dingell, a senior Democrat from Michigan, insisting she have a private word with her new delegation mate to shut her up quickly. Tlaib needed to understand: Now that she was in Congress, she could no longer act like a brash activist.

The Speaker had never hidden her disdain for the president. In private conversations with members over the first two years of his presidency, Pelosi had likened Trump to a petulant child throwing temper tantrums to get what he wanted. Only weeks before, she had questioned whether his obsession with building a border wall

was "a manhood thing for him—as if manhood could ever be associated with him."[1] To Pelosi, Trump was unworthy of the office he
held. The blusterous real estate tycoon and former reality TV star
had been accused of colluding with Russia to swing his election victory, fired his FBI director for refusing to drop an investigation into
the matter, sided with white supremacists marching on Charlottesville, Virginia, and paid off women alleging affairs with him. He had
sought to ban Muslims from entering the United States, attacked
the media as "fake news," and tried to separate migrant children
from their parents to discourage asylum seekers from seeking refuge
in the U.S.

But as far as she was concerned, trying to impeach Trump was a
divisive move that could have potentially devastating political consequences for her new majority. Her party had flipped about forty
House seats thanks to moderates who had campaigned to protect
people with preexisting medical conditions, lower the cost of prescription drugs, and bolster the economic fortunes of middle-class
voters. In Pelosi's mind, impeachment would do nothing but distract
from those pocketbook issues that had put her party back in the
majority.

Pelosi's apprehension about impeachment was not new. In 1998, she
had witnessed how then-Speaker Newt Gingrich's attempt to impeach former president Bill Clinton had backfired. Instead of ousting Clinton for lying under oath about having received fellatio in the
West Wing, the Senate rejected the charges of perjury and obstruction of justice—and in the process, Gingrich's party rejected him.
Gingrich ended up resigning as Speaker after the GOP lost House
seats in what became the poorest midterm election performance
by a party that didn't control the White House in sixty years. And

Clinton ended up enjoying a political lift, as his approval ratings climbed from a pre-impeachment 62 percent to a post-impeachment 73 percent.[2]

Pelosi knew Clinton's impeachment had played out in a Congress far less polarized than the one she was presiding over. And as a party leader who had lost her power, then fought like hell to regain it, Pelosi was wary of deploying a political weapon she could not control. In order for impeachment to be successful, she reasoned, it had to be bipartisan—just like the effort to oust former president Richard Nixon, who vacated his office after both parties turned against him, even before the impeachment vote could take place.

Pelosi's bipartisan standard set a high bar. While most congressional Republicans had only begrudgingly supported Trump's candidacy in 2016, they had fallen firmly in line with the president since his inauguration, so much that most feared even criticizing him in public. Pelosi knew it would take something unfathomably damning to pull Republicans away from the president, and that absent that, it would be folly—or possibly political suicide—to try to impeach him. If they failed, it could end up giving Trump a second term.

On the night her party flipped the House, in a *PBS NewsHour* interview just hours after the first polls closed, Pelosi tried to warn her base against ousting Trump.

"For those who want impeachment, that's not what our caucus is about," Pelosi said. "That is not unifying, and I get criticized in my own party for not being more in support of that—but . . . If [impeachment] would happen it would have to be bipartisan and the evidence would have to be so conclusive."[3]

During her first turn as Speaker, Pelosi had easily put down calls from her party's left flank to impeach then-president George W. Bush over the Iraq War. Even after picketers surrounded her home and slept in her driveway,[4] Pelosi insisted her caucus stay focused on legislating—and she had been rewarded for it: Two years later, Democrats swept the 2008 elections to seize the White House and expand their majorities in Congress, giving Pelosi the political fire-power to pass a landmark health reform law that came to be known as Obamacare.[5]

Now, over a decade later, Pelosi knew holding back demands for impeachment against Trump wouldn't be easy. Tlaib was express-ing a fury that had been brewing on the left since his 2016 victory. In 2017, a few dozen liberal-minded House Democrats had forced a vote to try to impeach Trump over what they considered his displays of bigotry, including his attacks on NFL players kneeling during the national anthem to protest police brutality and his likening of Afri-can and other predominantly Black nations to "shithole" countries.[6] It had failed miserably, with Republicans and even all but a couple dozen Democrats opposing the move[7] thanks in part to Pelosi's ar-gument that it was premature.

Pelosi knew that such demands would continue, but she figured she could once again keep simmering liberal anger at bay. There was a reason that reporters and Democrats whispered that she wielded an iron fist in a velvet glove. Her members respected her leader-ship, and if they disagreed, she could often cajole, manipulate, and, when necessary, scare her caucus into submission.

The first fifteen minutes of Pelosi's MSNBC interview went just as she had planned. Sitting in the center of a large arena-style au-ditorium, wearing four-inch lavender heels and a purple dress, the Speaker commanded the attention of the room as she blasted Trump for shutting down the government over border-wall funding, vowing her party would be the adults at the negotiating table. She touted her chamber's move to pass bills that week reopening the government and vowed to fight to lower health care costs. And she proudly boasted about the diversity of her new conference, the perfect tapestry of a diverse nation.

But then came the question she was dreading. As host Joy Reid mentioned Tlaib's call for impeachment, Pelosi's jaw stiffened, her eyes narrowed, and she cocked her head.

"That is not the position of the House Democratic caucus," Pelosi said flatly. "Impeachment is a very divisive approach to take and we shouldn't take it for anything other than the facts and the law."

Unfortunately for Pelosi, hers wouldn't be the last word on the subject. Her back-channel pressure operation hadn't chastened Tlaib at all.

"I will always speak truth to power," Tlaib wrote on Twitter that day, closing it with a new hashtag: "#unapologeticallyMe."

Talk of impeachment was not going away.

2

"ALL THE SUBPOENAS"

MARCH 24–APRIL 24, 2019

President Donald Trump stood on the tarmac at Palm Beach International Airport and proclaimed victory, a moment he had awaited for more than two years. Flanked by suited Secret Service agents in dark sunglasses, the seventy-two-year-old ex-TV-star president spoke slowly and deliberately to ensure his every word sank in with the reporters standing beside Air Force One. On his lapel, an American flag pin complemented his bright red tie. And beside him, teams of allies and advisors smiled—glee the president did not reflect as he took a more sobering turn before the television cameras.

"It was just announced there was no collusion with Russia, the most *ridiculous* thing I've ever heard," Trump declared indignantly above the noisy hum of the airplane engines. "There was *no obstruction* . . . It was a complete, and *total* exoneration!"

It was Sunday, March 24, and Attorney General William Barr had just revealed that Special Counsel Robert Mueller III had finally completed his twenty-two-month investigation into allegations that

Trump colluded with Russia to win the 2016 election. The probe had cast a pall over Trump's first two years in office, as leaks about the ongoing investigation seeped into the hands of an eager Washington press corps and dominated the cable TV shows, upending the president's efforts to tout conservative policy wins from tax cuts to the booming economy.

For Trump, the entire existence of the probe had been an affront to his ego—an attempt by his perceived enemies to downplay his historic victory over Hillary Clinton. It was why he had fired FBI director James Comey—who had previously rebuffed Trump's private demand for a loyalty pledge—when he had learned of the agency's Russia investigation in early 2017. Only, the result wasn't what he wanted: It had only spurred the creation of Mueller's probe.

"This is the end of my presidency. I'm fucked!" Trump had said when he learned that a special counsel had been designated to probe the issue in Comey's place.[1]

Since then, Mueller had charged several of Trump's closest aides, including his former campaign chairman, national security advisor, and his own personal lawyer, with illegally lying to federal officials. There was even talk that the special counsel—a famed war hero and former FBI director himself—might be narrowing in on Trump's family, or could recommend indicting Trump for obstructing justice. Trump, after all, had tried—and failed—to persuade his own former White House counsel Don McGahn to oust Mueller, a move law enforcement officials viewed as a possible unlawful attempt to disrupt their review.

At the same time, several other criminal investigations were coming uncomfortably close to the president. Prosecutors in New York had all but named Trump as the mastermind of an illegal hush money scheme to silence two women—a porn star and a former Playboy bunny[2]—who had alleged during the campaign that they had had extramarital affairs with Trump. The president's former "fixer" and attorney, Michael Cohen, had also pleaded guilty to related campaign finance violations, tax evasion, and lying to Congress about Trump's plans to build a tower in Moscow[3]—plans that coincided with some of the perplexing praise Trump offered Russian president Vladimir Putin during his 2016 campaign.

Trump had dismissed the special counsel's work as a "witch hunt," echoing a term ex-president Richard Nixon had used to discredit the FBI investigation that eventually helped bring him down. But the more Trump fought, the more the walls seemed to close in on him. In the waning days of 2018, even his closest aides were whispering that he might even be charged with a crime.

And then, something even worse happened: Trump lost control of the U.S. House of Representatives.

The president knew that some Democrats had been threatening to impeach him since he took office. But with Republicans in charge of both chambers of Congress during his first two years, he never had had to take that talk seriously. When Democrats flipped the House, however, his political line of defense had cracked.

The Democratic takeover had come as a shock to Trump—despite warnings from his advisors that his unconventional and norm-shattering ways would almost certainly alienate key swing-district voters. Trump had truly believed that his own personal magnetism would carry the party through the 2018 midterms regardless of what the polls said, just as it had during his 2016 presidential campaign. Instead, the GOP lost about forty House seats.

The day after the election, Trump tried to send a message to Democrats to back off. In a press conference, he threatened retaliation if they used their newfound majority to try to investigate him and his family.

"They can play that game, but we can play it better, because we have a thing called the United States Senate," Trump had said, referring to the chamber still under Republican control. "I'm better at that game than they are."

For a while, Trump had ignored Democrats entirely and sought to channel his energy into churning up plaudits from his base to distract from the midterm shellacking he'd received. Just before Christmas, he pitched the country headfirst into a weeks-long government shutdown against the advice of Republican leaders, convinced a fight for his "big beautiful wall" on the U.S.-Mexico border was exactly what he needed.[4]

But just after New Year's, an incoming freshman lawmaker's words had shaken his focus. When Trump saw Tlaib's "impeach the motherfucker" comments plastered across the screen of his favorite Fox News morning shows on January 4, he did what he had always done when he was most angry: He took his fury to his millions of Twitter followers, writing: "How do you impeach a president who has won perhaps the greatest election of all time, done nothing wrong . . . and is the most popular Republican in party history 93%?"

As congressional leaders piled into the Situation Room later that afternoon for a shutdown negotiation session, Trump was still furious. His aides, worried about Pelosi besting him on national television, had specifically moved the talks to a discreet location where cameras and cell phones were prohibited. They had also sandwiched the Speaker between Congress's top two Republicans, Senate Majority Leader Mitch McConnell and House Minority Leader Kevin McCarthy, hoping to intimidate the formidable woman leading the Democratic Party.

Trump, seated at the head of the long mahogany table, had opened the session by demanding Congress fund his wall—but Pelosi, undaunted, repeatedly shut him down and vowed he wouldn't get a penny. Trump threatened to keep the government closed "for years" if Democrats didn't give him what he wanted. But his bluster only made Pelosi scoff.

At one point, Trump stood in frustration and folded his arms, looming over the seated Pelosi—and suddenly said what was really on his mind.

"Are you planning to impeach me?" Trump had asked Pelosi.

Pelosi was caught off-guard. "We're not looking to impeach you," she replied, though her spokesman later denied she said so.

"That's good, Nancy," Trump responded. "That's good."[5]

Trump had spent the late-March weekend awaiting his fate at his namesake hotel company's glamorous Palm Beach resort, Mar-a-Lago. Barr had given his attorneys a heads-up that a short letter summarizing Mueller's findings was looming. He had added one additional sweetener to ease Trump's nerves: that Mueller had not recommended any additional indictments, meaning Trump was likely home free—at least legally.

But the president had no idea what his aides had revealed to the special counsel in the course of his investigation, nor how Democrats in Congress would react. *Would Mueller's report open him up to an impeachment?*

As he waited, Trump busied himself with a flurry of social engagements. On Friday night, he and his wife Melania threw a thirteenth birthday party for their son, Barron.[6] On Saturday, the president hosted Kid Rock for a turn on the golf course.[7] On Sunday morning, he hit the links again—this time sharing a golf cart with Republican senator Lindsey Graham of South Carolina, his former rival turned top ally.[8]

"Linds," he predicted to Graham that Sunday morning, "it's going to be a good day."

"Mr. President, I hope so," Graham had responded.

A year before, Graham had warned Trump that if Mueller uncovered evidence his campaign had colluded with the Russians, "we're done." Now, as they headed to the airport to fly back to Washington, Graham was relieved: The full 448-page Mueller report hadn't yet been released to the public. But Barr had summarized its findings in a four-page memo to Congress, stating unequivocally that Mueller "did not find that the Trump campaign or anyone associated with it conspired or coordinated with Russia in its efforts to influence the 2016 U.S. presidential election."[9]

Never mind that the same document also warned that Mueller specifically said his report did not "exonerate" Trump. Barr's letter was music to the ears of both men.

"Mr. President, this is about as good as it will get for you or anybody else under these circumstances," Graham said.

It wouldn't take long for Trump to realize that while Mueller's work was finished, his nightmare was far from over. On Capitol Hill, the report would embolden a new crop of investigators who still wanted to see his head roll: House Democrats.

Several days later, Trump upended a policy meeting with House Republicans to go on a tear about Jerry Nadler, the new chairman of the House Judiciary Committee, jeering him for weight loss surgery he had undergone about twenty years prior.

"Fat Jerry!" Trump groused, reaching for an old schoolyard taunt he hadn't used in decades as Republicans in the room uncomfortably squirmed. "I've been battling Nadler for *years*."

The jeering masked the real reason Trump was suddenly so obsessed with Nadler. The New York Democrat was threatening to subpoena Trump's White House—one of several committee chairmen itching to take a swing at him, even while Pelosi sought to pump the brakes. Trump couldn't believe Nadler's audacity. As far as the president was concerned, he had just been legally cleared by Barr and all investigations should end.

Nadler and Trump had been nemeses since the 1980s, when Trump was a young and ambitious developer trying to make his mark on New York City's skyline. Trump had proposed building a "mega-community" along the Hudson River by repurposing a dilapidated rail yard between Fifty-Ninth and Seventy-Second Streets. He dubbed it "Television City," and began mapping out a complex of high-rise apartment towers, television stations, a shopping mall, and a 152-story skyscraper—which Trump predicted would be "the greatest piece of land in urban America."[10]

But area residents wary of congestion and traffic bitterly opposed Trump's glittering dream. To help block the project, they turned to Nadler, their then-thirty-eight-year-old assemblyman who was known for taking down big developers.

Nadler supported the resistance in local lawsuits against Trump's project. And after he was elected to Congress, he personally lobbied the federal government to reject Trump's applications for Federal Housing Administration loans and tucked riders into legislation to keep Trump's project from receiving a dime of taxpayer financing.

Trump was furious.

"If Nadler spent more time in the gymnasium losing weight, he would do the voters a bigger service," he said in 1995, coining the "Fat Jerry" nickname for the congressman who had always struggled with obesity. "He needs to lose about 200 pounds!"[11]

Nadler shot back through a spokesman that at least he "never went bankrupt and had to spend his father's fortune to keep his family's business afloat."

A quarter century later, Nadler was causing Trump problems again. In one of his first moves as chairman, he had fired off eighty-one letters to Trump business associates, allies, and White House aides demanding records in what the president decried as a "fishing expedition." But that, it turned out, was only the start. Trump was furious to learn that even after Barr's letter, Nadler planned to relitigate Mueller's entire report, summoning Trump's own aides up to Capitol Hill to put them on the witness stand.

Trump knew Nadler wasn't alone. Richie Neal, the incoming chairman of the Ways and Means Committee, was demanding he turn over the last six years of his tax returns, alleging tax evasion.[12] Adam Schiff, the new Intelligence Committee chairman, was talking about subpoenaing accountants and banks that had financed his real estate empire on suspicion of possible foreign money laundering.[13] Elijah Cummings, the incoming chairman of the Oversight Committee, had sent an early salvo of fifty-one letters to agencies, departments, and the Trump Organization, as well as a handful of other document demands. The missives sought evidence regarding everything from Trump's decision to overrule his intelligence advisors and dole out security clearances to members of his family, to his lease of a government building just blocks from the White House where he had placed a Trump-branded hotel, a clear conflict of interest.[14]

But Nadler's plan to dig back into Mueller's report in public was perhaps the most daunting. Unlike the special counsel, who had conducted his nearly two-year probe in secret, Nadler was planning to make a public show of every investigative twist and turn on national television. Trump, a former reality TV host, knew and feared the power of a compelling broadcast. In February, his "fixer" Michael Cohen had taken a turn before the House Oversight panel before heading to prison, accusing Trump of cavorting with Russia and lying about his wealth to cheat on his taxes and commit fraud. Cohen had even brandished the checks Trump's son and his chief financial officer had signed reimbursing him for paying the porn star

Stormy Daniels, with whom Trump allegedly had an affair, for her silence during the campaign.

That single hearing had been damaging enough. Trump decided he could not risk any more embarrassment.

When Democrats had flipped the House, Trump had lawyered up to protect himself from Hill oversight. He had hired Pat Cipollone, a partner from the hard-charging corporate litigation firm Kirkland & Ellis, who was well known in GOP circles and came personally recommended by Fox News TV host Laura Ingraham.[15] Cipollone, like Trump, was a firm believer in protecting the power of the executive branch. And as one of his first moves, he doubled the size of the White House counsel's office to prepare for the investigative onslaught.

Cipollone, however, also knew that he was expected to make a good-faith effort to cooperate with some congressional investigations, as was the practice of previous White Houses. It was why he had paid a courtesy visit to Nadler on Capitol Hill in early 2019, vowing to find "reasonable accommodation" for his investigative requests.

"We're not going to agree on everything," he had told Nadler that February, "but you can always call me."

Trump, however, had other ideas. And after Barr's letter, he put his foot down and told Cipollone to comply with nothing.

Trump knew the strategy was guaranteed to pitch the White House headfirst into a series of protracted court fights with Congress. Administrations that ignored congressional subpoenas risked being slapped with lawsuits from the legislative branch, as lawmakers appealed to federal judges to uphold their subpoenas. But for Trump, that was the whole point. The president was counting on the courts' slow pace to grind the Democrats' oversight ambitions to a halt.

As a young real estate developer, Trump had learned a valuable lesson in how to weaponize the court system to exhaust his enemies. When the Justice Department sued him and his father for racial housing discrimination in 1973, they managed to avoid admitting fault by filing a massive countersuit and forcing a settlement.[16] Over his next three decades as a businessman, Trump had liberally used the courts to fight all manner of disputes, dragging associates, corporations, ex-wives, television personalities, a game-show magnate, states, the U.S. government, and even Scotland into court to protect his personal interests.[17] By the time Trump was elected to the Oval Office, he had been a party to over four thousand lawsuits.[18] Now he was ready to repeat that playbook from the highest office in the land—this time to stop the Democrats' investigations.

Trump's brand of stonewalling was unprecedented in both its scope and severity. Heated tug-of-wars between Congress and the White House had cropped up under every administration, as most presidents resented congressional scrutiny—especially when it came from an opposing party. But in the past, the executive branch had made at least some good-faith effort to acknowledge Congress's constitutional right to oversee its activities. During the Obama administration, the Justice Department had battled with House Republicans in court to keep them from questioning Attorney General Eric Holder Jr. in a probe of a gun-trafficking sting operation gone awry.[19] But the administration eventually ponied up documents and key witnesses for the GOP's investigation into a terrorist attack on a State Department outpost in Benghazi, Libya.[20] Former president George W. Bush's White House picked its battles in a similar fashion. Under duress, officials handed over records for investigations into their Hurricane Katrina response and a CIA agent's leaked identity—even as they resisted lawmakers' efforts to investigate suspicious firings of U.S. attorneys.[21]

Trump's resistance to oversight, however, was absolute. By the time the full Mueller report came out in mid-April, Trump had ignored more than a dozen requests for information from Democrat-led congressional investigations,[22] setting the executive and legislative branches on a constitutional collision course for the history books. On April 24, he even stood on the White House lawn and unapologetically proclaimed Cipollone's legal strategy to the world.

"We're fighting all the subpoenas!" Trump vowed shamelessly.[23] And he would.

3

PRESSURE POINTS

MAY 7–21, 2019

Jamie Raskin was fed up. On the night of Tuesday, May 7, the usually easygoing and friendly former constitutional law professor stormed into the Judiciary chairman's office and insisted panel Democrats stop lollygagging and show some muscle.

"We've *got* to get serious about doing something," Raskin told Jerry Nadler sternly. "We've *got* to start talking about impeachment."

The moment had been in the making for a while for Raskin. It had been obvious to him that Trump was using the White House as a moneymaking and branding operation in violation of the Constitution. The appalling findings in the Mueller report, released just days prior, had only solidified Raskin's conviction that Trump had been up to no good.

But now Trump was refusing to comply with *all* their oversight investigations. To Raskin, a man who had dedicated his life to the study of American democracy—and as a member of the House

Judiciary Committee eager to conduct oversight of a president out of control—Trump's stonewalling operation had crossed a line. It was time to start impeachment proceedings, Raskin believed.

Raskin, however, had a problem: Pelosi had been telling her rank-and-file members that impeachment was premature. In an April 22 call with House Democrats, she had implored them to "stick with a program" of what Raskin viewed as slow, seemingly aimless investigating. "We are going to go as fast as the facts take us," Pelosi had said, flatly.

Since then, the "i-word" had become almost taboo among House Democrats. But in Raskin's estimation, Trump's flagrant disregard for their oversight duty had effectively nullified Pelosi's strategy. How were they supposed to follow Pelosi's mandate to "continue investigating" Trump's actions if they couldn't procure any documents or witnesses?

Raskin had grown up with an ingrained appreciation for the levers of American government. His mother was a journalist and his father worked for the late president John F. Kennedy's National Security Council before founding a liberal think tank. Following law school, Raskin found his calling in teaching budding lawyers about the Constitution's checks and balances, settling into a tenured position at American University. He was a wonky professor with an encyclopedic memory who could quote dozens of Founding Fathers from memory. He kept a bust of Abraham Lincoln on his desk, a treasured possession he'd inherited from his grandfather, a Minnesota politician. He even named his first and only son after Thomas Paine, a Founding Father whose writings had helped inspire the American Revolution.

By the time he got to Congress, Raskin had survived stage-three colon cancer, become a vegan, and watched his three children grow into adults following his footsteps into careers in law and teaching.

But the then-fifty-four-year-old congressman was still bright-eyed, gregarious, and eager to pump his colleagues full of the knowledge he'd acquired over a lifetime love affair with the history and laws of the republic. Raskin knew better than almost any of them how American democracy was supposed to work—and it was anathema to him that House Democrats were doing nothing while Trump was thumbing his nose at Congress. The Judiciary Committee had to assert its authority, Raskin had started arguing to his colleagues that May, if they wanted the administration to take their investigations seriously. Otherwise Trump might do something even worse.

Raskin had learned he wasn't alone in his frustration with Trump for disregarding the legislative branch—and with his own leadership's apparent nonchalance. In the opening months of 2019, he had become friendly with three other Democratic members who, like him, served on both the Judiciary Committee and Pelosi's junior leadership team: Joe Neguse, a freshman from Colorado; Ted Lieu, a third-term representative from California; and David Cicilline, a fifth-termer from Rhode Island. All four were lawyers before they ran for Congress in deep-blue districts—and each regularly railed about Trump stymieing the House's efforts to police his actions. They agreed that Mueller's report was teeing up Congress to take up impeachment and run with it, and that Pelosi's vague mandate to "investigate" in the face of Trump's across-the-board blockade was a Sisyphean waste of time.

Together, the quartet had tried to raise the topic of impeachment privately with Nadler's Judiciary Committee aides, buttonholing the chairman's longtime chief of staff Amy Rutkin to demand a meeting of Judiciary Democrats where they could discuss the "i-word" candidly. But over and over again, Rutkin told them no. She and Nadler had personally asked leadership for permission, she explained, and Pelosi "won't allow it."

On that Tuesday, the Trump administration escalated matters by invoking executive privilege to block former White House counsel Don McGahn from turning over subpoenaed records. It was Judiciary's third missed swing in the span of a week. Attorney General Bill Barr already had been a no-show for a hearing the prior Thursday—then subsequently ignored a subpoena for redacted portions of the Mueller report that hadn't been released to the public, as well as underlying evidence that went into writing it. Raskin hit the roof, and with his new allies as reinforcements, marched into Nadler's office to vent his frustrations.

"We can't let them just ignore our subpoenas like this," he argued to Nadler and his aides, complaining that the White House was trampling all over the legislative branch. "It's terrible for the institution. We need to do something to break the logjam and restore the power of Congress."

"We need to have a members' meeting to talk about impeachment," Neguse added. "We understand the communication from leadership is that we can't have this meeting, but this isn't sustainable."

As Raskin and Neguse spoke, Rutkin looked exasperated.

"We're not having this meeting!" Rutkin pushed back. "We're trying to convince leadership, but we're not there yet."

As his ever-loyal longtime chief tried to shut them down, Nadler sat quietly, studying Raskin. The two men were of similar minds: constitutional geeks eager as hell to stop Trump. In fact, Nadler's staff had privately taken to calling Raskin "Jerry Junior," a nod to each one's penchant for debating the ins and outs of precedents and constitutional theory.

Nadler needed none of Raskin's convincing. The short, portly Judiciary Committee chairman, who shuffled through the halls of Congress with a copy of the Constitution in his pocket, knew what his fellow New Yorker was capable of. And he had long believed it was only a matter of time before his longtime rival pitched the nation into a constitutional crisis.

Nadler hadn't liked Trump from the moment he'd met him in the mid-1980s. Trump, who had the confident air of a strapping playboy used to schmoozing politicians, had invited Nadler, the son of a Jewish chicken farmer who had completed his Fordham law degree in night school, to his eponymous tower on Fifth Avenue. When Trump had tried to sell Nadler on his "Television City" project, boasting about how he would build the world's tallest skyscraper and live so far above the clouds he'd have to call the concierge to find out what the weather was like, Nadler was repulsed. It cemented his impression of Trump as a greedy, rich elitist trying to take advantage of the system.

For the first two years of Trump's presidency, Nadler had watched in frustration as the GOP majority turned a blind eye to scandal after scandal emanating from the White House. Nadler couldn't stand it. So when the top Democratic spot on the Judiciary Committee opened up in late 2017, he eagerly pitched himself for the job, promising to do whatever it took—even if it meant potentially impeaching Trump—to bring the rogue president in line.[1] He won—and immediately started making plans to bring Trump to heel. When the Democrats flipped the House, he started putting those plans into action.

"The next two years of your life are going to be hell," he had told his assembled aides in a January 2019 team meeting in his Washington, D.C., conference room, for which he had carted in meat and cheese sandwiches all the way from a New York deli. "We are the 'accountability people,' and it's going to be very, very busy. We have a lot of work to do, and we are not going to shy away from the fights because they're hard. But no matter how hard it gets, keep your eye on the world to come: This guy is *not* going to be president forever."

In February, Nadler hired two outside guns for the express purpose of bolstering his panel's Trump investigations. Norm Eisen, a chatty government ethics lawyer turned prominent watchdog group founder, and Barry Berke, a salty-mouthed white-collar defense attorney from Manhattan, had written a white paper about why Trump deserved to be impeached—arguments they knew had caught Nadler's attention.[2] Within days of coming aboard, the two newcomers had devised a plan to put their new boss's committee at the center of the action with the deluge of eighty-one letters to Trump associates demanding records.

Their aggressive move—which even fellow Democrats likened to a ham-handed, indiscriminate attempt to throw spaghetti at the wall—had landed Nadler in hot water with Pelosi. The Speaker had been adamant that her chairmen not feed into allegations of "presidential harassment" by the GOP, and her handpicked House counsel Doug Letter had even warned chairmen early on to "pick your battles" in terms of probing Trump's misdeeds. Nadler's refusal to listen, however, also triggered an expletive-laden fight between his aides and those of House Intelligence Committee chairman Adam Schiff, who accused Judiciary staffers of duplicating their efforts and infringing on their turf in an attempt to garner attention.[3]

When Mueller's report was released about a month later, Nadler found himself in a similar predicament. While the special counsel had not determined that Trump coordinated his 2016 campaign efforts with the Kremlin, it had uncovered plenty of evidence that the president and his aides were aware of Moscow's activities and welcomed the help. The special counsel had also documented ten instances in which Trump appeared to have tried to obstruct justice. And Mueller was explicit that he had refrained from making a final determination into whether Trump had broken the law only because Justice Department rules shielded sitting presidents from being indicted.

In Nadler's estimation, Mueller's report was as good as an impeachment referral, though the special counsel hadn't mentioned the word once. The lengths to which Trump had gone to stop a federal investigation into his actions, Nadler believed, would have landed any average person in prison. But when he told the Speaker so on a call three days after the Mueller report was released, Pelosi had shut him down. To her, the 448-page report was simply too long and too impenetrable to sell in digestible soundbites to swing voters—and too inconclusive to convince people there were grounds for impeachment. Schiff, who Nadler knew had Pelosi's ear more than any other committee chairman, backed up Pelosi's assessment, arguing impeachment was premature.

With no other options, Nadler had channeled his energy into a new strategy: finding witnesses who might dazzle the public by bringing Mueller's report to life. He knew that in 1973, the case against Richard Nixon went from committee preoccupation to national scandal when the president's men were summoned to Capitol Hill and questioned in nationally televised hearings. If he could similarly get someone like McGahn to say publicly what he had told Mueller about Trump instructing him to fire Mueller, it might lead to impeachment, he thought. So, he fired off his subpoenas—only to have Trump blatantly flout them.

As Raskin and his compatriots argued with his chief of staff in his office, Nadler realized he owed his frustrated members an explanation. Jumping into the conversation, he confessed how he had personally failed to convince Pelosi to begin impeachment proceedings.

The Speaker, he said, is scared to death about impeachment blowing back on her so-called frontliners, her most politically vulnerable members in swing districts. First and foremost, she had a duty to protect her majority, he explained. Plus, he added, Pelosi had a powerful ally: Schiff was making the case against impeachment to other members. And as long as Schiff was a no, Nadler said he would be hard-pressed to change Pelosi's mind.

On the wall above them hung a portrait of Peter Rodino, the late Judiciary chairman who famously shepherded the panel through the Nixon impeachment proceedings. But while Nadler longed to follow in the footsteps of his idol, he knew that it was not the time—and that it was not his call.

"My hands are tied," he told the members, explaining that as a top lieutenant of Pelosi's, he could not go against her in public.

But Nadler suggested there was something else the impatient rank and file could do: Start quietly lobbying their colleagues to build support for impeachment in the caucus, member by member. Until an overwhelming percentage of House Democrats backed impeachment, Pelosi's opinions about it were unlikely to change, Nadler said.

"The way to get her to 'yes' is to get her caucus to tell her this is the right thing to do for the country," Nadler said. "Go talk to your colleagues."

That was all the prodding Raskin and his group needed. As they filed out of the room, they began plotting a way to pressure Pelosi into impeachment. All they would need was the right moment—and the right number of supporters.

The day's last rays of sunlight streamed through a pair of massive windows framed by ornate curtains in Pelosi's conference room as her leadership team filed in for their weekly meeting on the evening of Monday, May 20. A view of the National Mall stretched out to the formidable Washington Monument and the Lincoln Memorial in the distance far beyond, a constant reminder of the weight of the decisions made in that room every day. The large rectangular conference table was adorned with fresh flowers, Ghirardelli chocolates, and nuts, personal touches by a Speaker who demanded elegance and class.

The stately surroundings were familiar to Raskin after several months of serving on Pelosi's leadership team. But as he settled into his chair, he suddenly felt nervous. Nobody shattered Pelosi's world of carefully orchestrated calm without consequence. And yet, that was just what he was about to do.

In the two weeks since the meeting with Nadler in his office, Raskin and his group had devised a strategy to nudge their colleagues into backing impeachment. They decided they would publicly call for an "impeachment inquiry," a phrase that they decided was nuanced enough to let lawmakers embrace the idea of escalating their probes of Trump, but without suggesting that impeachment was a predetermined outcome. The group thought of it as a "half-kiss" that would keep skittish moderate Democrats from running to the Speaker to complain, and allow others to dip their toe into the waters of impeachment without fully committing to dive in.

Nadler liked it for a different reason: His lawyers, Eisen and Berke, predicted enthusiastically that "impeachment inquiry" would pack just enough punch to force Trump's team to take their efforts seriously. Trump wouldn't dare ignore their subpoenas if impeachment was on the line, they reasoned.

Raskin and his friends made a secret pact: The Judiciary Committee had subpoenaed McGahn to testify in person on May 21. If he did not show, they committed to publicly endorse an "impeachment inquiry" together that same day—regardless of what leadership might think.

With that, the four men became the backbone of an unofficial whipping operation to turn Pelosi's Democrats into a pro-impeachment caucus. Each had his role: Raskin, the professor, would articulate the legal and theoretical rationale behind their demands for an "impeachment inquiry," while Neguse, the most gregarious of the lot, would sketch out how the group could add numbers to their ranks. Cicilline was the messaging guru—as head of the Democratic Policy and Communications Committee, he was in fact responsible for helping craft House Democrats' messaging strategy. And Lieu, being a Californian, had the closest relationship with the Speaker, which, they hoped, he could exploit to help persuade her to embrace their efforts.

Dubbed the "four musketeers" by some of their own staffers, the quartet organized themselves on the sidelines of Judiciary panel hearings, during votes on the House floor, and in a steady stream of text messages.

"The real mistake we made was that we did not open impeachment proceedings the day after the Mueller report was released," Cicilline texted his cohorts. "A real missed opportunity."

When libertarian Republican Justin Amash—who would leave the party just weeks later—came out in support of an impeachment probe that month,[4] the group got even more riled up. "Are we as Democrats now prepared to be more conservative than a GOP rep on this issue?" an incensed Lieu texted his colleagues.

The group's campaign was audacious—and not simply because they were plotting to oust a president for only the third time in American history. Their initiative was also extraordinary because of whom they were challenging to pursue it: Nancy Pelosi. Unlike House Republicans, who had developed a habit of openly defying their leaders—and had driven two GOP Speakers from Washington in less than four years—only the rare rank-and-file Democrat dared publicly challenge the seasoned California congresswoman, whose penchant for revenge was fabled. Pelosi demanded loyalty and respect, and loathed surprises. Those who disagreed with her were welcome to air their grievances in private, but not publicly. Those who broke her unwritten code of conduct could find their favored policy ventures mired in limbo and their desired committee or leadership posts suddenly out of reach.

Pelosi had developed a reputation for strong-arming her underlings early on in her leadership career—and holding a grudge if they resisted her will. It was party lore how Pelosi had once barred her nemesis and rival, Congresswoman Jane Harman, from becoming the Intelligence Committee chair in 2006, giving the prized gavel to a more deferential and loyal backbencher with far less experience.[5] John Dingell, the late congressman from Michigan and top Democrat on the House Energy and Commerce Committee, met a similar fate in 2008 for siding too closely with the interests of Detroit-based auto companies at a time when Pelosi wanted to embrace a move toward promoting clean energy. Pelosi, who had supported a failed primary challenger against him, tacitly backed a fellow Californian to take Dingell's gavel.[6]

On the eve of reclaiming her speakership in 2018, Pelosi faced a mutiny from nearly three dozen Democrats demanding new blood at the top of their leadership team. One by one, Pelosi—dubbed "the shark that never sleeps" by some of her members—wooed them with political favors, clinching their defections by promising not to exact revenge for having opposed her. But within weeks, she effectively reneged on that pledge: One of the mutineers, savvy and outspoken former federal prosecutor Kathleen Rice, found Pelosi had taken a Judiciary Committee seat she thought was hers and arranged for it to go to a freshman member.[7]

Raskin had gotten a taste of Pelosi's temper in March, when he pushed back on her suggestion to the *Washington Post* that Trump was "not worth" impeaching. The question wasn't "whether or not the president is worth it," he had told the press. "The question is whether the republic is worth it and whether the public interest commands it and whether there are high crimes and misdemeanors."[8] Soon after, Raskin got a call from Pelosi's chief of staff, who let him know that the Speaker wasn't happy with the quip. *How bad would it be when he challenged her a second time?* He was about to find out.

Sitting in her chair at the head of the table, Pelosi opened the session by complaining that all the impeachment chatter was drowning out Democrats' policy message. The week before, the House had passed a bill ensuring job protections for gays, lesbians, and bisexuals, a major 2018 campaign promise checked off the list. But coverage of the legislation's passing was on "page twenty-six" of the newspaper while impeachment talk dominated the front, Pelosi complained.

When the Speaker paused, Raskin felt someone kick him under the table, a not-so-subtle nudge from one of his fellow "musketeers"—probably Neguse, he thought—to speak up. He cleared his throat.

"Madam Speaker, I think this sounds like a perfect argument for why we need to centralize investigations in an impeachment inquiry," he said, prompting everyone at the table to turn and look at him, askance. An impeachment inquiry, Raskin explained, would allow Democrats to "distinguish between our oversight of the president's high crimes and misdemeanors from all the legislative work that we're doing."

"We need to clear the air and talk about this," Raskin continued, pushing to dispel the taboo surrounding impeachment talk. "We can't become an institution where people ignore our subpoenas."

Raskin had caught the room—apart from the other three "musketeers"—off-guard. Pelosi, in particular, looked distinctly perturbed.

"You want to tell Elijah Cummings to go home?" she asked Raskin, referring to the chairman of the House Oversight Committee, who was one of the most respected members in the chamber and had already made headway in his own Trump investigations.[9] Pitching everything to the Judiciary Committee would cut the legs out from under the other five investigative panels that had been deputized to probe Trump's wrongdoing across his affairs, Pelosi argued. More importantly, she added, other House Democrats did not want to begin impeaching Trump.

"People have different experiences; some people are saying 'no impeachment,' that it would be bad for Democrats in 2020," Pelosi said.

Raskin pushed back. There was plenty to investigate, he said, and Cummings's Oversight Committee could take the lead probing other matters beyond the obvious impeachable offenses.

As if on cue, Pelosi's allies flew to her defense. Connecticut congresswoman Rosa DeLauro started wagging her finger at Raskin. House Majority Whip James Clyburn, Pelosi's third in command, argued that "voters don't want Democrats to spend all their time talking about Trump." Hakeem Jeffries, the House's No. 4 Democrat and a member of the Judiciary Committee, had a more practical concern: Democrats didn't even have a unified oversight message to counter Trump's "no collusion," "no obstruction," and "witch hunt."

"What are *our* words?" Jeffries asked, to sell an impeachment probe to the public?

That was an easy one for Raskin. "Corruption, obstruction, contempt of Congress," he shot back.

The "musketeers" in the room rallied to Raskin's defense. But the meeting split up without consensus, and the topic trailed Pelosi as she descended to the Capitol basement to meet with a larger section of her rank-and-file members. Judiciary Committee member

Steve Cohen lamented that Republicans had impeached Clinton "over sex," but Democrats were doing nothing as Trump was "raping the country."

This time, however, Pelosi was ready with a retort. She pointed to a court ruling from earlier that day, in which a federal judge had rejected Trump's attorney's sweeping claim of executive authority to block a House Oversight Committee subpoena for Trump's financial records.[10]

"Today, we won our first case," Pelosi told the room, trying to signal that impeachment was unnecessary. "We've been in this thing for almost five months, and now we're getting some results."

Later that night, Pelosi summoned Nadler to her office for a grilling, determined to squelch the impeachment uprising. She suspected Nadler was giving his panel members oxygen and knew that if he publicly endorsed impeachment alongside his rank and file, it could trigger a jailbreak among liberals and expose a party schism. She had to separate the Judiciary chairman from his pro-impeachment wingmen and unleash the full force of her top deputies to make sure Nadler got the message.

As he made the plodding trek from his office in the Rayburn House Office Building to Pelosi's Capitol suite, Nadler could anticipate the gist of what he was in for. But the Speaker wasn't the only one losing patience. Since Nadler had huddled with Raskin and his friends earlier that month, the House's grievances against the administration had only continued to mount. White House counsel Pat Cipollone had categorically rejected Nadler's request for documents related to his investigation, dismissing his probe as an illegitimate gambit "to harass political opponents."[11] Treasury secretary Steven Mnuchin had announced he would bar the Internal Revenue Service from complying with congressional subpoenas for Trump's tax returns, though federal statute explicitly gave the Hill's tax panels the right to demand such documents.[12] Trump had even instructed his attorneys to sue his bankers and accountants to keep them from releasing any of his personal financial information to Congress, invoking a lawsuit that rested on a 139-year-old Supreme Court decision that had been overruled many times over.[13]

Nadler firmly believed that Trump's claims of executive privilege and immunity were bogus and that the president was merely making a play for time in the slow-moving courts. Still, that worried him, as he knew how long the courts took to rule on inter-branch disputes. House Democrats had battled the George W. Bush administration for over two years to enforce a subpoena for a former White House counsel's testimony, eventually giving up when the case took longer than the remainder of Bush's presidency. House Republicans had a similarly exhausting experience years later when trying to subpoena President Barack Obama's attorney general Eric Holder, only to have the case settled years after Obama left the White House.

Nadler thought he had come up with a solution: Though the courts were notoriously slow to enforce congressional summonses, they had acted with comparative alacrity during the impeachment probes of Presidents Bill Clinton and Richard Nixon. If House Democrats could simply persuade a judge that there was similar impeachment-fueled urgency around Trump, Nadler thought, they might compel McGahn to testify and the White House to turn over documents quickly.

But once again, Nadler's solution ran afoul of Pelosi. The Speaker wouldn't allow the committee to utter the word "impeachment"— not until the courts enforced Democrats' subpoenas. Yet at the same time, she was dragging her feet in letting Nadler go to court to

sue the Trump administration for ignoring those compulsory summonses. Nadler, in fact, had spent almost the entire month of May
trying to persuade Pelosi to allow his panel to quickly hold Attorney
General Bill Barr and McGahn in contempt of Congress for flouting their subpoenas—a move that would then allow them to start
the lengthy legal process battling for their testimony. But Pelosi
was concerned that such an aggressive step would be interpreted
by the public as a move toward impeachment. And her vulnerable
members hailing from districts Trump won, known as "frontliners,"
didn't want to take such a politically sensitive vote, Nadler was told.

By the time Pelosi summoned Nadler to her office that Tuesday
night, the chairman from New York—who felt Pelosi was tying him
into an investigative knot—was ready for a showdown.

"I'm not saying 'Let's draw up impeachment articles,' but we
shouldn't be afraid of saying the word," Nadler argued to Pelosi.
"We are engaged in mortal combat across the board to get even
bare-bones information from the Justice Department . . . How do
you think we're going to get these people in if we don't say the word
'impeachment'?"

Pelosi, flanked by her loyal leadership deputies, bristled.

"The Democratic caucus doesn't support the idea, let alone the
American public," she shot back. "We're in the majority because of
about two dozen members, and all of the evidence we have in front
of us shows that those people will be taking a profound risk if they
talk about impeachment—if *you* talk about impeachment."

She then turned to her highest-ranking deputies, who all ganged
up on Nadler to tell him his idea was lousy.[14]

As Nadler shuffled out of the Speaker's office that night, he awkwardly ignored questions from a throng of reporters about whether
he supported impeachment. That night, in a hastily organized ten
o'clock phone call, Nadler told the Judiciary Democrats what Pelosi

had said—and encouraged them to keep fighting for impeachment anyway.

The next day, when McGahn skipped his hearing, the "musketeers" called for an impeachment inquiry, taking to Twitter and appearing on television broadcasts to make their case. Within twelve hours, twenty-three other House Democrats had joined them. Over the next two weeks, their ranks doubled to almost sixty, more than a quarter of the House Democratic caucus.[15]

The count would loom over everything Pelosi did in the next four months, as news organizations began a daily tally of how many House Democrats were interested in the president's potential ouster. As the numbers inched ever higher, the pressure on Pelosi grew into an unprecedented battle of wills between a Speaker famous for her unflinching grip on the party and the upstart liberals on the Judiciary Committee, who were determined to force her into endorsing their demands for Trump's head.

4

RELEASE VALVES

JUNE–JULY 25, 2019

The third week of June, Pelosi made her way down to a secure facility three levels deep in the Capitol basement to view classified materials. Her team had summoned the top lawyers for the Judiciary and Intelligence Committees to meet her in the House's Sensitive Compartmented Information Facility, called the "SCIF" for short, to answer any questions she might have as she read. Given what she was about to see, they knew she'd want answers fast.

A few days prior, Attorney General Bill Barr had handed over a trove of previously undisclosed portions of the Mueller report that he had initially refused to show Congress. Jerry Nadler had been itching to get his hands on the files for weeks, and now Pelosi knew why. Tucked inside, away from the eyes of the public, was a suggestion that Trump may have committed perjury. The Speaker was determined to see for herself.

Since the confrontation with Nadler in her office the previous month, Pelosi had launched full-bore into impeachment containment mode. The very next day, she had convened an emergency, mandatory meeting for all House Democrats in the basement of the Capitol, forcing her rank and file to listen as the investigative chairmen, including her ally Adam Schiff, drilled down on a single message: Impeachment was premature. After whipping her members into line, she then sought to distract the media from the "impeachment inquiry" clamor by throwing them some red meat: Walking straight up to a bank of TV cameras, she accused Trump of orchestrating a "cover-up" by stonewalling congressional investigations.

"No one is above the law—*including* the president of the United States," she said indignantly.

Just as Pelosi expected, the video clips of her "cover-up" jab instantly went viral. It was a dramatic and intentional escalation of her careful rhetorical feud with the president, and for a while, it worked in its key objective of giving the media something other than her caucus's impeachment infighting to chew on.

But in the days that followed, support for impeachment in her caucus only continued to rise. By early June, two of her panel chairs and ten of the party's presidential hopefuls had called for impeachment. Even House Majority Whip James Clyburn admitted on CNN that it seemed impeachment proceedings were becoming inevitable, prompting the Speaker's office to yell at his staff and demand he walk the statement back.

Pelosi realized she had a problem. The polls, both public and internal, were unequivocal: Impeachment was a loser with swing voters. Just over a third of the country supported beginning proceedings, and Pelosi believed she could not afford to squeeze her moderate members on those unfavorable odds.[1] Yet with so many Democratic members calling for an inquiry, it was impossible to keep dismissing their demands. It was time, she realized, to "let the air out of the balloon before it pops," as one of her aides described it. She was going to give members a way to blow off steam—but also make sure they knew who was boss.

At Pelosi's first leadership meeting in early June—the first time the group had huddled since Jamie Raskin's interruption—she informed her team that they would adhere to a policy of "legislating, investigating and litigating."[2] They would conduct traditional oversight to check the president, without resorting to impeachment. If the White House stonewalled their probes, they would take the matter to the courts to get them resolved, she directed. And to anyone who disagreed and wanted to talk impeachment, she said with a knowing look directed toward Raskin and Cicilline, "speak for yourself, not the caucus."

Her top allies were at the ready to help put the matter to bed.

"When you say impeachment, it muddles the message," Majority Leader Steny Hoyer said.

"We need to *not* talk about impeachment; people don't care about impeachment," Cheri Bustos, who led the House Democrats' campaign arm, added, pointing to internal party polling showing 33 percent of voters didn't even know who Mueller was.

The Speaker's tactics were effective. A caucus-wide fear of incurring Pelosi's wrath that June made many rank-and-file Democrats think twice about joining Raskin and his group. And even the most gung-ho impeachment enthusiasts lacked the temerity to call Pelosi out by name for trying to quash their efforts. At the same time, secret impeachment supporters like Jerry Nadler refused to publicly endorse the Raskin effort for fear of getting crosswise with Pelosi, even as they privately encouraged Raskin's group to continue to buttonhole members to try to grow their numbers.

Still, Pelosi knew her power was not absolute and that she would have to give the impeachment supporters a consolation prize to reduce the threat they posed. Knowing the core group of rabble-rousers came from the Judiciary Committee, she took a step she had been resisting, allowing Nadler to hold Barr and former White House counsel Don McGahn in contempt of Congress for ignoring subpoenas and prepare to sue for their cooperation.

But in a last-minute bid to dissuade them, Barr offered Nadler a deal: He would let the full Judiciary Committee see "key evidence" that had been redacted from Mueller's report—if the House held its fire. For once, Pelosi and Nadler agreed on what to do: They took the deal. And by the next week, Pelosi was in the SCIF, reading what Barr had sent over.

As Pelosi pored over the redacted pages of Mueller's report, her eyes fell on a passage from the unpublicized section—and she froze. There, in his own words, Mueller was questioning the honesty of Trump's written testimony that "he did not recall 'the specifics of any call'" he had had with his friend Roger Stone regarding Russia's hack of the Democratic National Committee. That claim clashed with other witnesses, Mueller wrote, who testified that Trump did discuss the act of political sabotage with Stone and others. In fact, Mueller suggested that Trump was also encouraging his allies to conveniently forget about his conversations regarding the Russian hack when they spoke to investigators, hinting those who helped cover up unsavory details would be rewarded.[3]

Lawyers around Pelosi chimed in to help her connect the dots. The special counsel, they explained, believed the president had tried to get his associates to lie on his behalf to the special counsel—and may have lied to Mueller himself.

As Pelosi looked up from the pages, a combination of disbelief and devastation was written on her face. She caught Judiciary Committee counsel Aaron Hiller's waiting stare.

"Aaron," Pelosi said, "do you think this is impeachable?"

The assembled panel lawyers all began talking at once. The Speaker silenced them with a flick of her palm.

Turning back to Hiller, she repeated her question: "Aaron, do *you* think this is an impeachable offense?"

The room went silent as everyone turned to Hiller, who didn't hesitate.

"Yes, ma'am," Hiller answered. "I do."

If Pelosi agreed, she did not say. But the knowledge that Trump had tried to obstruct justice so blatantly—actions that almost certainly would have led to criminal charges against any other American—did not make her change course.

On Friday, July 26, a core group of influential freshman Democrats from swing districts were demanding a private word with Adam Schiff, the chairman of the House Intelligence Committee.

It was two days after Mueller had bombed in back-to-back congressional hearings before Nadler's and Schiff's panels, turning a much-anticipated Democratic attempt to showcase Trump's misdeeds into a cringeworthy—and very public—reminder that even legends age. The elderly special counsel had spoken haltingly and oftentimes appeared confused, asking lawmakers to repeat their questions. He had stumbled over his words, at one point even fumbling Trump's name. He had struggled to recall key elements of his own report, including the name of a research firm at the heart of the allegations that Trump colluded with Russia. He couldn't even remember key details of his own biography, such as which president had appointed him to serve as an assistant U.S. attorney in Boston. And he appeared to have regular difficulty determining who on the forty-one-member panel was talking to him.

Within minutes of the hours-long spectacle, the verdict was in: Mueller had been a complete flop. "Dazed and confused" read the banner on the conservative-leaning website Drudge Report.[4] "This is delicate to say, but Mueller, whom I deeply respect . . . does not appear as sharp as he was," tweeted Obama's former top political advisor David Axelrod.[5] "President Trump was probably never going to be impeached by the House of Representatives before the 2020 elections," wrote the *New York Times*, declaring: "The testimony by Robert S. Mueller III . . . makes that a near certainty."[6]

But then the day just got worse: In a private meeting after Mueller's hearing, Nadler had blindsided Democratic leaders by arguing before the entire House Democratic conference that it was time to start drafting articles of impeachment. Schiff, standing next to him, had been horrified by Nadler's freelancing. He and Pelosi had huddled with the Judiciary chair just prior to the conference meeting, and Nadler had said nothing about intending to make such a call to action. Schiff knew Pelosi certainly wouldn't have sanctioned it. In fact, she'd looked as shocked as Schiff, snatching the microphone away from Nadler and adjourning the meeting before anyone else could chime in.

Holed up in his office two days later, Schiff could anticipate what he was in for. The Intelligence Committee chairman knew the members coming to visit him were a no-nonsense bunch of former military and intelligence officers hailing from battleground districts from Denver to New Jersey. They were ex-Marines, Navy helicopter pilots and commanders, nuclear reactor engineers, and CIA officers. Between them, they had two Bronze Stars, a Purple Heart, and had logged multiple tours in Iraq and Afghanistan. Every one of them had come to Congress by flipping a red district blue in the 2018 midterms, composing the vanguard of the new House majority. And they were among the most vocal centrists opposing impeachment, which was why Schiff figured they wanted to talk to him. Everybody knew he was close to Pelosi and that for weeks, he had been helping her tamp down calls for impeachment from the liberal wing of the party.

Within a few minutes of their arrival, Schiff learned he was right. The members were furious at Nadler's call to arms, and they wanted Schiff to put a stop to it.

"We have lost the focus on what's important," Congresswoman Abigail Spanberger of Virginia told Schiff, speaking for the group. "Our messaging is getting lost in the impeachment talk."

Spanberger, a former undercover CIA officer who recruited and trained spies in Europe, represented a district that had been in Republican hands since the early 1970s. She had barely ousted one of the most conservative Republicans in the House, winning by less than two percentage points, and her reelection was already considered an uphill battle.

Since the Mueller report's release, Spanberger's conservative-minded constituents consistently had expressed their disapproval of any move to oust Trump. They buttonholed her at public events in her district and called her office to register their resistance. The pushback at home was so great, in fact, that Spanberger frequently grew annoyed when her liberal House Democratic colleagues would stand up in meetings and declare: "The American people want impeachment!"

"I'm not saying you are right or wrong in what you think we should be doing, but you are most certainly wrong in what you're saying the American people want," she would retort, animatedly explaining what she was hearing back home.

Like her fellow national security freshmen, Spanberger, who drank her morning coffee from a mug that read "Tears of my enemies,"[7] received special leeway from party leaders to operate independently when needed—which she often did. She had pitched herself to voters as a pragmatic workhorse who shunned politically motivated takedowns. The mother of three daughters regularly boasted about bucking the establishment, voting against Pelosi for Speaker and opposing "Pelosi's budget" that would have added $1.5 trillion to the national debt. She frequently touted her work across the aisle, including occasional meetings with the vice president or Trump himself, and her support for GOP proposals like requiring the government to be notified when undocumented immigrants sought to purchase guns.

It wasn't that Spanberger didn't have concerns about Trump. She found his cavalier approach toward Russia's organized election interference alarming. She and Congresswoman Elissa Slotkin of Michigan, a fellow CIA veteran in their national security clique, were disturbed by Trump's frequent attacks on their former colleagues in the intelligence community as "the deep state" working against him—just because they had fingered Russia with orchestrating a 2016 election disinformation campaign. But the House's focus, they believed, should be on Russia, not Trump; on election security, not impeachment. It was why they had formed a task force to address vulnerabilities in the political system, hoping to draw the public's attention away from breathless speculation about impeachment. Their efforts failed, and when Nadler called for launching proceedings after the Mueller hearings, it had been the final straw.

Schiff nodded sympathetically as the group vented over the course of two hours. He knew each of them well, having helped many of them raise money for their 2018 elections. Schiff also knew how politically toxic the stain of impeachment could be and sympathized with their predicament: Two decades earlier, he had won his congressional seat by campaigning against a Republican incumbent who had voted to impeach Clinton and been a manager in his Senate trial, flipping a district that had been in GOP hands for nearly twenty years.[8]

Yet Schiff was less of an impeachment skeptic than the group of national security freshmen might have known. Like Nadler, Schiff harbored grand designs of bringing down Trump. He too had hired outside investigative staff in preparation for a looming battle with the president, selecting Dan Goldman, a former assistant U.S. attorney from New York with years of experience prosecuting Russian organized crime, to head up his panel's investigations. And even before Democrats flipped the House, Schiff's deputy investigations director, Rheanne Wirkkala, along with his committee counsel, Maher Bitar, were softly preparing the team for a potential Trump impeachment, passing around copies of *How the Good Guys Finally Won*, a book about the effort to oust Nixon.

Schiff mentioned none of that in his meeting that day, however, agreeing with the furious frontliners that the impeachment chatter was unwarranted.

At the end of the meeting, Spanberger, Slotkin, and their colleagues pressed Schiff on one final, critical question: Was Pelosi planning to impeach? Is that where this was all going? If anyone knew, it was him.

"If so, just tell us," one member said. "We don't want any surprises," another agreed.

Nothing was afoot, Schiff assured them. Despite the pressure coming from Nadler and his liberal allies, they could rest assured that Pelosi would be deliberate and thoughtful before diving in, he explained. And as far as the Speaker was concerned, he told them, impeachment just wasn't in the cards right now. On that, he said, they both agreed.

If that changed, Schiff promised them, "I'll be sure to give you a heads-up."

TRUMP FREED

Trump's unabashed victory lap started before Robert Mueller had even left the Capitol campus. The president had been riveted by the televised committee proceedings—despite his claims not to care—and spent the day sneaking glimpses from both the White House residence and a side room off the Oval Office. As the special counsel struggled, the president salivated, barely able to contain his excitement. An hour after Mueller's testimony concluded, he tramped outside to gloat before the cameras.

"We had a very good day today," Trump jovially told reporters. "I think Robert Mueller did a horrible job, both today and with respect to the investigation . . . The Democrats had nothing. And now they have less than nothing, and I think they are going to lose the 2020 election very big."

But Trump's public confidence masked a sense of uneasiness about his upcoming reelection. The next morning, Fox News published a poll that found Trump trailing Joe Biden by 10 points in a potential 2020 matchup.[1] Quinnipiac University also showed the former vice president trouncing him 50 to 42 in the key swing state of Ohio, which Trump had won handily in 2016.[2]

The numbers unnerved the president. Friends and foes had been warning him for a while that Biden was the Democrat most likely to unseat him in a head-to-head matchup. He was popular among the economically displaced white union workers who had helped Trump win several pivotal Rust Belt swing states in 2016. That morning, the president resolved to do something to put his mind at ease.

At nine a.m., Trump knew he was scheduled for a call with the newly elected leader of Ukraine, Volodymyr Zelensky, who was fighting a war with Russian-backed separatists in the eastern part of his country. Trump's aides were advising him to make friends with Zelensky, arguing that such an alliance would quiet critics who said the American president was too chummy with Russian president Vladimir Putin.

But his aides were fighting an uphill battle. For several months, Trump's personal attorney Rudy Giuliani had been spinning him up on conspiracy theories that Ukraine had interfered in the 2016 election to try to help Hillary Clinton win. Giuliani, relying on the word of a handful of corrupt and disgraced Ukrainian prosecutors-general, had also told Trump that Ukraine was sitting on bombshell information about Biden that could expose him as a cheat and a fraud. They just needed to get Ukraine to give up the dirt to prove it.

That morning, an unshackled Trump decided to press Zelensky about the Giuliani-fueled scandals he had come to embrace.[3] Their call, the contents of which would remain hidden for weeks, became the first of a series of unprecedented moves the president would make that summer. As Democrats bickered over how best to hold Trump to account, Trump began to flout norms with a sense of presumed impunity, declaring himself untouchable.

"I have an Article II, where I have the right to do whatever I want as president," Trump announced the same week of Mueller's testimony, a dubious interpretation of the Constitution that no respected legal scholar agreed with.

In the days after Mueller's hearing, Trump started demanding that independently functioning parts of the government bend to his will—and punished senior officials who resisted. When the chairman of the Federal Reserve refused to cut interest rates to juice the economy ahead of the 2020 election, Trump lambasted him on Twitter as an "enemy" of the people. He forced out the director of national intelligence for maintaining that Russia's 2016 election interference campaign was real.[4] And he privately encouraged Homeland Security Department officials to break the law if they ran into legal trouble while constructing his border wall with Mexico, promising them that "I'll pardon you" for running afoul of environmental and eminent domain restrictions.[5]

As Trump's antics became increasingly bizarre, his aides began to refer to those weeks as the summer of "self-sabotage." He mused that he wanted to give himself the Medal of Honor.[6] He accused Jews who voted for Democrats of being "very disloyal to Israel and to the Jewish people," while promoting a conspiracy theorist who likened him to "the King of Israel" and "the second coming of God."[7] He declared himself "the Chosen One" to take on China.[8] At one point, he even floated the idea of buying Greenland from Denmark—and canceled an official state visit to Denmark when the prime minister declined to sell.[9]

In late August, Trump also began growing bolder about funneling government money toward his family businesses. He floated the idea of hosting the massive G7 international economic forum at one of his cash-strapped Florida resorts.[10] In early September, he insisted his vice president fly 181 miles out of his way during an official visit to Dublin, Ireland, so he could stay at a Trump hotel in

Doonbeg, racking up nearly $600,000 in expenses.[11] Trump knew that congressional Democrats, as well as the governments of Maryland and Washington, D.C., were already suing him for trying to profit off the presidency.[12] But it had been over two years and the courts still hadn't issued a verdict in their favor, so what did he have to lose?

There would be no accountability for Trump that summer, as the cards continued to break his way. The Supreme Court ruled that Congress could not stop him from declaring an emergency to direct Pentagon funds toward his border wall, despite lawmakers' resistance to funding the structure.[13] A federal judge in New York announced that the FBI's months-long investigations into his 2016 hush money payment scheme, in which Trump's former lawyer Michael Cohen had named the president as a co-conspirator, had been closed with no additional charges.[14] And the House investigations, Trump noted with glee, were stuck in a rut. His stonewalling and the courts' snail-like pace had ensured that Democrats were no closer to getting his tax returns or forcing Trump administration witnesses to testify than they had been when they flipped the House.

Meanwhile, Trump noted, Pelosi seemed to be handling the dirty work of battling back the pro-impeachment tide all by herself. She was doing it with such dedication, in fact, that Trump was growing more confident by the day that impeachment was never going to happen.

As lawmakers headed back to their districts for the long summer recess, a little-known congressional liaison for the liberal group MoveOn.org visited Pelosi's office to deliver a warning. Reggie Hubbard, a self-described hippie and yoga aficionado who had cut his activist teeth rallying voters against George W. Bush's reelection in the aftermath of the Iraq War, believed Pelosi's anti-impeachment stance was unsustainable. The vocal and increasingly powerful progressive wing of the party simply wouldn't stand for it. It was time, Hubbard had decided, for a frank conversation with Pelosi's outreach director, Reva Price, to warn her about the onslaught that was coming.

For months, Hubbard—who had hosted the reception where Rashida Tlaib yelled "impeach the motherfucker"—had held back his allies in the progressive community from coming after the Speaker. Earlier that summer, several prominent liberal groups had privately discussed publicly shaming Pelosi as a coward. Hubbard had talked them down, persuading them not to start a war. But amid the Speaker's continued opposition to impeachment, they had recently coalesced around another gambit to force her hand: confronting Pelosi with a public op-ed demanding the House take up impeachment.

Hubbard knew that directly challenging Pelosi on impeachment could backfire. He had experienced such blowback earlier that year when he privately raised the issue with her during a phone call. For his efforts, he was iced out by the Speaker's office and months went by before some of her aides would even talk to him again. Before going down that road once more—publicly this time—he decided to give diplomacy one last shot.

"What number do y'all need to see to make calling for an inquiry viable?" Hubbard asked Price, as the two sat in a small conference room in Pelosi's suite reserved for staff meetings. At the time, about ninety House Democrats had declared their support for impeachment. Hubbard wanted to know how many more needed to join the movement before the Speaker changed her mind.

When Price ducked the question, Hubbard pressed more insistently. "What number do y'all need to see? . . . 140? 150?" he asked. "My people are pissed off . . . Help me out here."

Privately, Pelosi had made it clear to her team that she would not bend to pressure. During one July staff meeting, she even told her aides, "I don't care if they're all for it!"—meaning she wouldn't support impeachment even if she was the last holdout in the party.

But Pelosi's team knew that the liberal groups were not used to keeping quiet, and that there were potential consequences for igniting the left's rage. So Price threw out what at the time may have seemed like an impossible number.

"One hundred fifty would be nice," she told him.

It was a tall order. Since Jamie Raskin's public push for impeachment began in late May, supporters had barely scraped together a third of the 235-member Democratic caucus. But Hubbard wasn't disheartened. The progressive groups were getting ready to launch a nationwide campaign that summer to pressure House Democrats in their home districts to back the impeachment inquiry.

Hubbard told Price he could make that work. He would keep liberal groups focused on pressuring House Democrats to get the support of 150 lawmakers instead of attacking Pelosi—but only if the Speaker held up her end of the bargain when they reached that threshold.

"If we get to 150 and you still do nothing, you're gonna have a problem with me, because I'm staking my entire reputation on this," he said.

Thus began "Impeachment August," in which armies of liberal demonstrators descended on undeclared House Democrats, demanding they back an inquiry. They buttonholed their targets at town halls and other meetings in their districts, seeking to turbocharge their campaign. They managed to get over half the Democratic caucus—118 members—on board.[15] Only seven, however, were from Republican-leaning districts, and only one came from a district Trump won in 2016. Leaders of the party's liberal wing knew they would need more of the moderates and frontliners Pelosi cared about—the skeptics like Abigail Spanberger and Elissa Slotkin—in order to stand an honest chance of making impeachment not just a political messaging tool, but a true punishment to mete out to Trump on the House floor.

Democratic leaders, however, hadn't left things to chance. Democratic Congressional Campaign Committee chairwoman Cheri Bustos's office orchestrated a concerted counteroffensive to the liberal groups, reaching out to allies in swing districts to recruit people to show up at the same town halls with an anti-impeachment message. If moderates heard from both pro- and anti-impeachment Democrats, her team reasoned, perhaps they would refrain from joining the movement. Democratic leaders also continued to urge caution directly with their members, telling the frontliners in tough reelections: Don't get emotional and box yourself in.

Still, tensions were rising. By late August, the careful détente Hubbard had tried to arrange started to fray, as some liberal activists took their protests straight to Pelosi's hometown.

"Impeach Trump now!" they demanded, interrupting a ceremony in San Francisco where the Speaker was being honored with a lifetime achievement award. A black banner they carried asked the even more damning question: "Which side are you on, Pelosi?"[16]

THE RUNAWAY CHAIRMAN

AUGUST–EARLY SEPTEMBER 2019

Jerry Nadler was sitting at the bar in the main lodge near his vacation shack in the Catskill Mountains when he picked up his phone to call his committee counsel, Aaron Hiller. The encampment of mountain bungalows about two hours north of Manhattan was a popular getaway for progressive New York Jews like Nadler. The food was kosher, Yiddish was widely spoken, and for years, it had been the Judiciary chairman's regular summer escape from the stress of Washington work and the bustle of New York City life. That day, Nadler had news to share—and it had nothing to do with his vacation.

"Aaron!" he declared into his cell phone. "I have *ten articles of impeachment* in front of me!"

When bored, the House Judiciary chairman had a habit of doodling on any scrap of paper within reach, often listing the names of vice presidents in reverse chronological order, just because he could. That day, while the vacationers around him cavorted on the lake and the golf course, his old habit had kicked in again—only this time, Nadler found himself scribbling articles of impeachment against Trump on the paper napkin under his Diet Coke. And he couldn't stop. Obstruction of justice. Obstruction of Congress. Abuse of power. Abuse of pardon power. Emoluments violations. Collusion with Russia. Campaign finance violations. Usurping Congress's power of the purse. Usurping Congress's power to set tariffs. Failing to protect and defend the Constitution.[1] Impressed with his output, he had called Hiller to share his handiwork.

"*Where* are you right now that you're talking about ten articles of impeachment?" Hiller asked, taken aback since Nadler was supposed to be on vacation. "Are you at the bar?"

Guilty.

"I wrote it down on a napkin!" Nadler declared proudly.

Hiller chuckled. "Okay," he responded. "I don't think we're going to need ten."

Nadler considered Hiller's logic. "Eh," he responded wistfully, "you never know."

Nadler knew that his surprise rallying call to draft impeachment articles after the Mueller hearing had put him in the doghouse with Pelosi that summer. But his patience with the Speaker's careful tiptoeing was wearing thin. Every day, reporters would ask him how close the House was to impeaching Trump, and every day he had to bite his tongue and dodge their questions to avoid stoking more arguments with the Speaker. But in private, Nadler was done playing Pelosi's political games. He believed the Democrats had no choice but to eventually impeach Trump. It was on him, he believed, to push the Speaker toward that inevitability, whether she was ready or not.

That August recess, Nadler instructed his staff to secretly start sketching out potential articles of impeachment against Trump without the Speaker's blessing. They also began mapping out a busy investigative schedule for the fall to showcase Trump's presidential misconduct beyond the confines of the Mueller report. Nadler hoped that by widening the aperture on Trump's misdeeds, it would tip the scales on impeachment and possibly grow enough public support to force Pelosi's hand.

When reports surfaced that month suggesting Trump was having administration officials stay at his resorts on the taxpayer dime, Nadler instructed his staff to schedule a public hearing on whether Trump was violating the Constitution's prohibitions against personally profiting off the Oval Office. He also told them to pull in officials for questioning about allegations Trump was considering an abuse of the pardon power to build his wall. And even though the FBI had closed its investigation into hush money payments to his former alleged mistresses without charging Trump, Nadler was convinced they had done so only because of the Justice Department rule barring sitting presidents from being indicted. His staff even discussed the idea of offering immunity to Trump's business associates in exchange for what the Judiciary chairman hoped would be damning testimony.

Still, Nadler knew that no matter how many minds he might change with his strategy, he still had to contend with Pelosi's intransigence. On a joint call that summer between his and Pelosi's staff, the Speaker's top policy aide, Richard Meltzer, insisted to Nadler's chief, Amy Rutkin, that when it came to impeachment, Pelosi was "*never* going to do it." Indeed, for most of the spring and summer, all of Nadler's attempts to cajole Pelosi into embracing impeachment had barely made her budge. But that summer, the Judiciary chairman believed he had finally found a way to box the Speaker in.

When Nadler had begun contemplating going to court to enforce his panel's subpoenas against Don McGahn and Bill Barr, he decided that the filings would have to declare that the committee was at least considering impeachment. Nadler believed that was the only way to unlock what he called Congress's "zenith" power and incentivize the courts to rule quickly on enforcing their summonses. He knew that in previous presidential impeachments, judges had granted lawmakers uncommon access to grand jury information and upheld subpoenas in record time—but only once lawmakers had explicitly declared themselves to be conducting an impeachment investigation. Nadler feared that without such a declaration, the House's lawsuits would take months or even years to resolve—time they didn't have at their disposal.

When Nadler first asked Pelosi's permission to tell the courts that impeachment was on the table, the Speaker had dismissed his request out of hand. The idea of letting the House cite impeachment, even in legalese, was unthinkable to her. So she designated Meltzer, an attorney by trade, to police the Judiciary Committee's filings, prompting weeks of headbutting as they tried to work out a compromise.

But Meltzer ended up proposing a compromise that would become Nadler's salvation: He suggested they tell the courts the Judiciary panel was "investigating whether to recommend articles of impeachment."[2] The idea, he explained, would give Nadler a chance to test his theory that opening the door to impeachment would speed up court proceedings, without committing the House to following through. In Meltzer's estimation, the careful wording would also leave Pelosi enough wiggle room to insist to her skittish frontline members that the House was not actually in a real, bona fide impeachment—just thinking about one.

At first, Meltzer's wordsmithing infuriated Nadler's lawyers, who pejoratively referred to his contorted proposals as the "Magic Dick Language"—both a reference to Meltzer's nickname and the sore feelings they harbored about the tedious approach the Speaker was

insisting on. From their perspective, Pelosi was disingenuously trying to have it both ways: floating the idea of impeachment to the
courts while at the same time shooting it down in public.

But eventually, Nadler and his team came to view Meltzer's solution as a blessing in disguise. By approving the committee's filings,
they realized, Pelosi could no longer claim that the House wasn't
locked and loaded on impeachment. She had effectively backed
herself into a corner without realizing it. They agreed to the language,
submitted the court filing, and immediately made plans to capitalize on Meltzer's "Magic Dick Language." Nadler would declare
impeachment was underway—and Pelosi would be hard-pressed to
stop him.

"WHAT. THE. FUCK?!" Pelosi's communications director, Ashley
Etienne, screamed into the phone at Nadler's Judiciary Committee
counsel Norm Eisen.

Etienne had been at home monitoring an August recess CNN interview with Nadler—and promptly hit the roof when he suddenly
declared the House was in the middle of "formal impeachment proceedings."[3]

Before the segment, Etienne had warned Nadler's team not to
let the Judiciary chairman go off-script. House Democrats were "investigating to see whether to draft articles," she reminded them, *not*
launching official impeachment proceedings. It was very important
that Nadler stay on message. Nadler's team assured her their boss
had no intention of freelancing. But once on set, when the TV host
pushed Nadler to explain whether Democrats were in a real impeachment inquiry, he declared they were—and that Pelosi agreed
with him.

"This is formal impeachment proceedings," Nadler declared,
claiming Pelosi had been "very cooperative" with his efforts.

In short, Nadler had just told the entire country that the Speaker was behind his full-steam-ahead effort to oust Trump when she most certainly was not. Etienne was aghast.

"You guys have to control your chairman!" Etienne yelled at Eisen. "You have to get the chairman on the same page as the Speaker."

But it was too late. Reporters besieged Etienne, trying to figure out Pelosi's next move: *Were they really in impeachment proceedings right now? Was Nadler correct? And if so, why hadn't the House voted to make it official, like they had been in impeachments past?* That night, a furious Pelosi did the only thing she could think of: She clamped down on Nadler, informing him through Etienne that he was no longer allowed to do television appearances.

By the time lawmakers returned to Washington from their summer recess in early September, the Speaker and her Judiciary Committee chairman had done little to resolve their conflicting stances. Nadler bulled forward, announcing that his panel would take a vote to "formalize" impeachment procedures and framing the move as proof that proceedings to consider Trump's ouster were well underway. Pelosi, meanwhile, dispatched Etienne and her deputy chief Drew Hammill to downplay the vote and convince reporters Nadler was mistaken.

The conflicting messaging created confusion among lawmakers, who didn't know whom to believe. House Majority Leader Steny Hoyer sided with the Speaker, declaring publicly that there was no "impeachment inquiry" underway. But Nadler's staff quickly called his office to get him to walk it back, explaining it could undermine the House's court cases. Pelosi, meanwhile, began to realize—as Nadler had predicted—that she had undercut her own ability to refute Nadler's claims by signing off on the "Magic Dick Language" in court filings. When reporters buttonholed her with questions in the halls, asking her to state definitely what the House was doing, she dodged, knowing she could no longer say that impeachment wasn't happening.

The confusion created a schism in the greater Democratic Party, as progressives like Jamie Raskin and the "musketeers" sided with Nadler while centrist Democrats balked. "The politics of impeachment are debatable. Maybe they are good. Maybe they aren't. No one knows," former Obama advisor turned podcast host Dan Pfeiffer tweeted. "But I do know that the current Democratic strategy of telling the base they are impeaching Trump and telling the moderates the opposite is an absolute disaster."

By mid-month, Nadler and Pelosi staffers were screaming at each other behind closed doors and trashing each other to reporters. Pelosi's team argued that Nadler was overplaying his hand and only talking tough because he was getting slammed by a primary challenger questioning his liberal credentials back in New York. Nadler and his team were equally frustrated with the Speaker for her contorted approach. His staff likened her to Keanu Reeves's character Neo from the movie *The Matrix*, due to her frequent bending and twisting to avoid impeachment questions.

No one, however, was more furious than Pelosi—especially when she realized that Nadler's aides had used the Don McGahn filing to effectively box her in on impeachment. In private meetings, she tried to reassure her panicking frontline members that no matter what Nadler said, only the full House could launch an impeachment inquiry. But Nadler had turned into a runaway chairman and she was unable to reel him in.

That the press was obsessed with the palace intrigue only angered Pelosi further. All her work to spotlight her party's policy and pocketbook issues was being thrown out the window. When she saw a *New York Times* headline that read "Is It an Impeachment Inquiry or Not? Democrats Can't Seem to Agree,"[4] the Speaker flipped. At one point during a closed-door meeting with her rank-and-file members, Pelosi lashed out at Nadler's staff, venting that they were out of control. The House, she said, would not be driven to impeachment by a bunch of Judiciary aides.

"And you can feel free to leak this," Pelosi told the members, hoping they would.[5]

To many House Democrats, the campaign to oust Trump in early September seemed effectively dead with Pelosi and Nadler's relationship on life support. Even impeachment cheerleaders knew they could not move forward when they themselves were so brutally divided. Few realized, however, that in the basement of the House, something explosive was brewing that was about to change the dynamics of impeachment completely.

7

WHISTLEBLOWER

AUGUST–SEPTEMBER 17, 2019

As he drove his family back to the airport on San Juan Island in Washington State, Senator Ron Johnson's phone buzzed with a voicemail. It was the last day of August and the end of a weeklong vacation with his family—a vacation that had turned from a relaxing break into a wrestling match with spotty cell service, thanks to an August 28 article in *Politico* that claimed Trump had frozen hundreds of millions of dollars of congressionally authorized military aid to Ukraine.[1]

The news had hit Johnson like a punch in the gut. The conservative Republican from Wisconsin was a stalwart ally of the president, but also a longtime advocate for supporting Ukraine in its struggle against Russian aggression—advocacy he took seriously as the chair of the Senate Foreign Relations Committee's European subpanel. Johnson had been the sole member of Congress to attend Ukrainian president Volodymyr Zelensky's inauguration in May, and ever since, he had been on a mission to change Trump's mind about Ukraine.

Johnson had learned the depth of Trump's hatred for Ukraine when he returned from that trip and joined the president's advisors for a May 23 meeting at the White House to brief the president about the new regime in Kyiv. He had hoped to persuade Trump to invite Zelensky to the Oval Office—a meeting that would have earned the young Ukrainian leader enormous prestige at home and signaled that the United States backed him fully in his ongoing war with Russia. But Trump was extremely hostile to the idea.

"Ukraine tried to take me down. I'm not fucking interested in helping them," he said. "I have no fucking interest in meeting with him."[2]

Johnson knew Trump was referring to conspiracy theories that his personal lawyer Rudy Giuliani had been peddling for months. Giuliani had convinced the president that Ukraine was hiding a Democratic National Committee server that was hacked in 2016—and that it contained thirty thousand of Hillary Clinton's emails that went "missing" while she was secretary of state. Clinton had come under fire for keeping work emails on a private server, not the DNC's server, but that didn't matter to Trump, who took the scattered theory as gospel.

"I want the fucking DNC server," Trump told them in that May meeting.[3]

Trump also had swallowed wholesale Giuliani's assertions that there was proof in Ukraine that Biden was corrupt. The theory derived from the fact that Biden's son Hunter had held a lucrative position on the board of a Ukrainian energy company called Burisma while the elder Biden was vice president. Many viewed Hunter's $50,000-a-month job, for which he had no relevant experience, as a blatant conflict of interest and a naked attempt by Burisma's owner to curry favor with the Obama administration.[4]

But Giuliani took it a step further: He spun up a tale that Joe Biden had tried to protect his son by demanding the ouster of Ukraine's then-top prosecutor for investigating Burisma. Giuliani ignored the fact that Europe, the International Monetary Fund, and Ukrainians themselves had also wanted that prosecutor, Viktor Shokin, to be canned for corruption, as he eventually was. Equally problematic: Giuliani's source for the theory was Shokin himself, who blamed Biden for his downfall and hated the former vice president.[5]

"They are all corrupt. They are all terrible people," Trump grumbled about the Ukrainians.

Johnson had hoped that Zelensky, as a fellow entertainer turned president who ran for office on a promise to root out corruption, could disabuse Trump of his negative feelings toward Ukraine. To his chagrin, however, Trump seemed to be causing the young president more problems, freezing several hundred million dollars of military assistance that amounted to a sizable chunk of Ukraine's military budget.

The question was: Why?

On August 30, Johnson frantically phoned Gordon Sondland, the U.S. ambassador to the European Union, for some answers. In an unusual arrangement, Trump had tapped Sondland to lead his diplomatic effort to Ukraine with Giuliani, though the nation technically fell outside his portfolio.

"Gordon, what's happening here and what can we do?" Johnson asked Sondland.

Johnson was disturbed by Sondland's response. Trump wanted to see Ukraine do something to demonstrate a serious intention to fight corruption, Sondland said. Specifically, Trump wanted Ukraine to investigate Giuliani's unsubstantiated claims that the country tried to help Clinton in the 2016 U.S. presidential election. Then and only then, Sondland told Johnson, "the hold on military aid would be lifted."

Johnson winced. What Sondland had just described amounted to a quid pro quo—and for the most spurious of reasons. The following day, he took his concerns to National Security Advisor John Bolton, who recommended he speak with both Trump and Vice President Mike Pence directly. Trump called back first—but thanks to Johnson's spotty cell service, he missed the call.

"Ron, it's your favorite president calling," the familiar recorded voice said, as Johnson checked the message from Trump. Immediately he looked for a place to pull over, choosing the nearby parking lot of a small outdoor mall. He shooed his wife and son out of the car and told them to go shopping so he could call Trump back in private. There was no time to waste: In less than a week, Johnson was due to meet Zelensky in Kyiv, and he was certain the Ukrainian president would ask him about the frozen military aid.

"We're schmucks, Ron, we're schmucks," Trump complained, once they connected, repeating his gripe that Ukraine was corrupt and arguing Europe should be footing most of the bill for Kyiv's military aid, not the United States.

Johnson summoned his patience and let Trump whine before pressing him on what he needed to know: *Could he tell Zelensky that the military aid, even if late, would still be delivered?* To his disappointment, Trump said no.

Johnson then tried to confirm if what Sondland had told him was true.

"I'm hearing that if Ukraine does something, that you'll release the aid?" Johnson asked, meekly.

The question prompted a fiery backlash, as Trump unleashed a torrent of expletives at Johnson's suggestion.

"No way. I would never do that. Who told you that?" he demanded—and was palpably annoyed when Johnson told him it had been Sondland. "Who is that guy?" Trump scoffed, dismissing the ambassador he had handpicked to coordinate his Ukraine strategy as a nobody before abruptly ending the conversation.

"Ron, I gotta go . . . but I hear what you're saying," Trump said. "We're reviewing it now, and you'll probably like my final decision."[6]

As the call disconnected, Johnson breathed a sigh of relief. Trump had said *you'll like my decision*—which could only mean he was planning to release the aid. Or so he thought.

Nine days later, on the first night the Senate returned from its monthlong congressional recess, Johnson approached the chamber's No. 2 Democrat, Dick Durbin, on the floor in a panic. He had been to Kyiv and back and Trump had yet to free Ukraine's aid, despite several Republicans' concerted efforts to appeal to the president and his top advisors. Johnson knew there were just three weeks left in the fiscal year, and after that, Ukraine's funds would disappear. So he decided to up the pressure on Trump by making a secret alliance with the people Trump hated most: the Democrats.

After two and a half years of kowtowing to Trump, Hill Republicans had backed themselves into an awkward position: They could not publicly oppose the president without risking devastating consequences with his devoted base, which constituted a sizable fraction of the GOP. Johnson didn't have the stomach to see what kind of fresh hell Trump might rain down on him if he publicly cried foul. So he appealed to Durbin to wage the public battle for him.

"We have a problem," Johnson told Durbin, hoping his political rival would help him out of what was shaping up to become a serious geopolitical jam.

Durbin, the top-ranking Democrat on the Senate's defense appropriations subcommittee and co-chair of the Ukraine caucus, heard Johnson out with a look of concern. In mid-August, Durbin's team had caught wind that Ukraine's accounts had been frozen and, in the weeks since, had also been sniffing around for answers. Top Pentagon officials had told his staff that the decision was being orchestrated from the "top levels" of the Defense Department. A week later, a senior White House budget official gave him even more troubling news: The funds may have been *illegally* frozen.

Durbin and Johnson had already teamed up on a bipartisan letter to Trump, urging him to "direct the Department of Defense to obligate these funds immediately." But Johnson told Durbin he needed to do more. That week, the Appropriations Committee was scheduled to finalize the next year's budget. Without mentioning a word of his conversations with Trump, Sondland, or Bolton—or what he knew of Trump's desires for Ukraine investigations of his political enemies—Johnson asked Durbin to craft an amendment that would keep Ukraine's funds from expiring. They needed to send a message to the president.

Durbin agreed.

That night, as Durbin briefed his senior staff about Johnson's desperation, they threw out a provocative theory. The team had been tracking Giuliani's strange summertime obsession with unearthing scandals about the Bidens in Ukraine. That the Trump administration had been simultaneously working to freeze Kyiv's military aid struck them as awfully suspicious timing.

"Could this have something to do with the Bidens?" Durbin's national security advisor wondered aloud.

But the senator was reluctant to level such a charge.

"That's an unfair question," he said. "I can't expect you to get in the mind of President Trump."

Still, they plowed ahead with Johnson's plan to up the ante— and started looking for Republican muscle to help them. Durbin knew exactly whom to call: Trump's closest ally in the Senate, Lindsey Graham.

Graham feigned shock when Durbin told him about the holdup on Ukraine aid. But the truth was he had known about the freeze for weeks—and what's more, had known why Trump was so hell-bent on putting Ukraine into a financial squeeze. Trump was holding up the Ukraine money because he wanted the country to investigate not only whether its former leaders tried to help Clinton win in 2016, but also the Bidens for corruption—and he knew that to be the case because John Bolton had told him so.

Bolton and Graham had been close for years before Trump tapped the prominent neocon and former George W. Bush official in 2018 to serve in the White House. The two had almost identically hawkish views about the world order and were equally horrified when Trump's actions regularly threatened to throw it out of whack. That August, they had commiserated over what they viewed as Trump's latest disastrous foreign policy declaration: His desire to invite Taliban leaders to Camp David to discuss a peace deal in Afghanistan.[7]

It was on the sidelines of their Afghanistan conversations that Bolton mentioned the reasons for the Ukraine aid holdup, appealing to Graham to use his influence with Trump to avoid a catastrophic mistake.

"If you guys on the Hill want this money to go to Ukraine, you've gotta call the president," Bolton told Graham.

Lindsey Graham's foreign policy views were just about as opposite to Trump's as one could find in the GOP. Where Graham believed in engaging allies and fighting enemies, Trump was an unprincipled relativist with a disturbing affinity for dictators and kleptocratic regimes. In the 2016 election season, the sharp-tongued

Graham had called Trump a "race-baiting, xenophobic, religious bigot" and opined that "my party has gone batshit crazy" for voting for him as the GOP nominee.[8] But after Trump became president, Graham changed his tone, becoming the president's closest confidant in the Senate and criticizing Trump only when he dramatically undermined Graham's personal foreign policy orthodoxy.

Bolton knew that what Trump was doing in Ukraine was highly problematic, if not illegal. His team had tried to argue to the president that helping Ukraine was also good for the U.S., and he himself had privately complained about Giuliani's scheme to top White House lawyers. But it had become clear to Bolton that raw political pressure—especially from Republicans on the Hill—was the only means of getting through to Trump, and the only thing that might convince him to reverse course on Ukraine.

Bolton's words disturbed Graham, and not just because withholding military aid from Ukraine was like delivering a wrapped gift to Russian president Vladimir Putin. He was also queasy about Trump's obsession with Biden. After years of working together in the Senate, Graham counted Biden as a friend. "If you can't admire Joe Biden as a person, you've got a problem and you need to do some self-evaluation, because what's not to like?" Graham had said in an interview in 2015. "He's the nicest person I think I've ever met in politics. He is as good a man as God ever created."[9]

But instead of challenging Trump to abandon his anti-Biden crusade, Graham made only private inquiries about the status of Ukraine's assistance package. That is, until Durbin called him in early September, pleading for help.

It would be disastrous for the world order, Graham believed, if Ukraine didn't get that military assistance. Russia would capitalize on the country's weakened state in a heartbeat. But it might be even more disastrous for the president if Democrats learned the real reason it was being held up, Graham realized. It was time to put a stop to the nonsense.

That week, Republican senators blitzed the administration with pleas to release Ukraine's aid. Senate Majority Leader Mitch Mc-Connell personally reached out to Defense secretary Mark Esper and Secretary of State Mike Pompeo, while Ukraine caucus co-chair Rob Portman of Ohio made appeals directly to Vice President Mike Pence, and eventually spoke to Trump himself to beg him to reconsider. Graham also issued a threat to 1600 Pennsylvania Avenue to unstick the situation before Trump did damage to Ukraine—and himself.

"Tell the White House I'm going to be with Durbin," Graham instructed his staff, referring to amendments the senior Democrat was cooking up to force Trump to deliver Ukraine's military assistance and prevent him from holding it back ever again. "Tell them I think I can bring seven or eight Republican votes along with me too."

On Thursday morning, as members of the Senate Appropriations Committee settled into their seats at conference tables in a dimly lit first-floor room of the Dirksen Office Building, Graham asked to speak—and casually announced that Trump had lifted the freeze on Ukraine's military aid.

"Senator Durbin's amendment to release funding to the Ukraine—I was going to support it, I think the White House today has agreed to release the money," Graham said nonchalantly. Turning to Durbin, he added: "So I want to thank you for pushing that issue."

His flippant words landed like a quiet bomb. Durbin had learned the night before, from Republican committee staffers, that finally Ukraine's aid had been released, but he didn't know why. And

Durbin couldn't understand why the South Carolina senator, who had seemed as alarmed as he was by the White House's behavior, was suddenly acting like his concerns were much ado about nothing.

"The administration asked for the money, was given the money, and then refused to spend the money until last night," Durbin said with suspicion, directing his focus to Graham. "Why the delay?"

"Why was it released? Because of your amendment . . . because I was going to vote for it," Graham replied, simultaneously patting himself on the back and refusing to offer any further explanation.

"I think they got the message," he continued dismissively. "If you're listening in, Ukraine, on C-Span: You're going to get the money."

Durbin begrudgingly backed down—and Graham breathed a sigh of relief, thinking he had protected Trump and saved Ukraine. Little did he realize, however, that across the Capitol campus, the House's Intelligence Committee was about to blow Trump's Ukraine scheme wide open.

In late July, a CIA official who had previously been detailed to the White House approached an old colleague of his, who was working as a lawyer for Adam Schiff on the House Intelligence Committee. Because they were off-campus, their meeting had the air of a social visit, but the CIA official had very serious matters of state on his mind. He was worried that Trump—along with Giuliani—had tried to solicit election interference from the president of Ukraine during a phone call that had taken place just days before. The official had not listened to the call himself but had heard enough alarming details from others to feel compelled to do something. Without sharing those details, he asked Schiff's lawyer for advice on what he should do.

Though the particulars of the CIA official's conversation with Schiff's lawyer have never been disclosed in full, they would become the subject of intense, politically charged scrutiny once their meeting came to light. Republicans would later accuse Schiff of coaching the CIA official with step-by-step instructions for how to file one of the most explosive whistleblower complaints in modern history—presumed coordination they would decry as collusion between Trump's impeachers and "the deep state." Schiff's staff would fervently deny those charges, but also refuse to discuss the specifics of the meeting.

What is known, however, is that the CIA official told Schiff's attorney that the president had done something highly unethical regarding Ukraine—and Schiff's counsel suggested he get a lawyer and speak to the intelligence community's inspector general, whose job it was to field and investigate whistleblower complaints.[10] Schiff's attorney also took what he'd learned back to the Intelligence Committee chairman, who began reviving a high-level investigation into a matter that he had contemplated earlier that year but put on a back burner.

Back in the spring, while the rest of the party was gripped by Mueller fever, a handful of staffers on Schiff's panel and the House Foreign Affairs Committee had begun tracking Giuliani's strange antics in Ukraine—particularly after he told the *New York Times* he planned to fly to Kyiv to dig up dirt on the Bidens. Alarmed, they encouraged their superiors to look further into the matter. But their suggestions went unheeded for weeks. In the days and weeks after the whistleblower reached out to Schiff's panel, however, those two panels joined forces with the House Oversight Committee to set up a Ukraine-related investigation.

By the time Congress returned from its summer break, the three panels had done enough research to learn that Giuliani had pressured Zelensky to take up an "investigation of Ukrainian interference" in the 2016 election and address the "alleged Biden bribery" of Kyiv's previous presidential administration.[11] They also knew Trump had spoken to Zelensky on July 25 and, according to a readout of the call from the Ukrainian government, asked him to "complete [the] investigation of corruption cases, which inhibited the interaction between Ukraine and the USA."[12] It all suggested, as Schiff and Democratic investigators wrote in letters sent to the White House and State Department the morning of September 9, that Trump and Giuliani tried "to coerce the Ukrainian government into pursuing two politically-motivated investigations under the guise of anti-corruption activity . . . in service of President Trump's reelection campaign."[13]

But they needed proof. In early September, as senators were trying to get the Ukraine money released, it walked straight into Schiff's committee chambers.

Andrew Bakaj was known around Washington for representing government employees calling foul on sensitive national security matters. So when he reached out to Schiff's Intelligence panel on Sunday, September 8, asking to discuss something sensitive in person, Schiff's counsels promptly agreed. The following afternoon, panel counsel Maher Bitar escorted Bakaj down three flights of stairs to a conference room in the committee's secure chambers, where Dan Goldman, Schiff's investigations director, and another panel lawyer were waiting.

Bakaj opened up the conversation with a bit of shocking news. He was representing a whistleblower who had filed a rather serious complaint to the intelligence community's inspector general in mid-August—but the matter, he continued, was being illegally kept from

Congress. Bakaj knew the ins and outs of whistleblower law and had submitted the complaint in such a way that it should have been disclosed to Schiff's committee as well as the Senate Intelligence panel within three weeks. The inspector general, a man named Michael Atkinson, had determined that Bakaj's client's report was an "urgent concern," necessitating that it be shared with lawmakers. Yet Trump's acting director of national intelligence, Joseph Maguire, was refusing to send it over.

Bakaj hoped that by appealing to Schiff, he could help shake things loose. He had similarly approached Schiff's Senate counterparts, though they hadn't been interested in taking a meeting. But Bakaj had a bit of a problem: Until the complaint was transmitted to Congress, he was duty-bound to keep from dishing details about his client or his allegations. The most he could do was sprinkle hints like breadcrumbs and hope they followed along.

When Schiff's attorneys pressed him for information, Bakaj played coy. "It involves communications, you know, like maybe it could be a phone call," he said, looking at the staff counsels pointedly, to accentuate his coded answer.

Whose phone call? they demanded.

"Someone senior in the White House," Bakaj said, his voice dripping with suggestion.

How senior? they pressed.

"Pretty damn senior," he said, matter-of-factly.

Like the president? they asked, almost breathless with anticipation. Bakaj very deliberately did not steer them off that scent. It was, he said, "not outside the realm of possibility."

"You're pretty smart. Use your own judgment," Bakaj added. Then he dropped another tidbit.

"It involved another country," he said. "I'll just say the investigation you opened up today was on point."

There was no ambiguity in Bakaj's oblique answer: The Ukraine probe was the only investigation they had announced that day. And there was only one phone call of note regarding Ukraine involving a "pretty damn senior" White House official that they were aware of: Trump's, with Zelensky, on July 25. Could this missing whistleblower's report be the silver bullet they had been chasing all summer?

What was discussed on this call? Schiff's counsels asked, hanging on Bakaj's every word.

Bakaj paused. He was hewing awfully close to the limits of what he could say. He would have to be careful about how he delivered his next answer.

"Domestic politics," Bakaj said, carefully. Possibly even elections, he added.

That was enough for Schiff's lawyers to put the pieces of the puzzle together. Giuliani had spent months publicly trying to bully Ukraine into investigating Biden, based on conspiracy theories. Now a whistleblower was alleging—through his attorney's winks and nods—that Trump had asked Ukraine's leader for something inappropriate regarding domestic politics. The room erupted into expletives.

"You gotta be fucking kidding me! This is wrong," Goldman exclaimed.

"Yeah," Bakaj responded, satisfied that his hints had hit their mark. "No shit."

The lawyers had begun to talk about how the Intelligence Committee might bring the whistleblower in to tell his story when suddenly there was a knock on the door. One of the counsels went to answer—then returned a minute later, his face pale. In his hand he held a letter from Atkinson that had just arrived, alerting them to an "urgent concern" Maguire was withholding from the committee against the law.[14] Even without additional details, they knew in their guts Atkinson and Bakaj were referring to the same complaint. They were onto something explosive.

In a phone call with Schiff that Thursday, Maguire tried to defend withholding the whistleblower's report because of "privilege" concerns. But that was just another dead giveaway that the complaint was about the president, as only Trump's own direct words or deliberations could be considered thusly protected.

"We're not going to wait around for them to do a rope-a-dope," Schiff told his staff after the call.

On Friday, with Pelosi's blessing, Schiff subpoenaed Maguire for the whistleblower's complaint, demanding he deliver it within days. Then that Sunday, on *Face the Nation*, Schiff dropped an unmistakable hint that he was coming for Trump—though he declined to lay out the details his team had already gathered.

"The director [Maguire] has said essentially that he is answering to a higher authority . . . Well there are only a few people above the DNI," Schiff said. "I think it's fair to assume this involves either the president, or people around him, or both."

8

THE MESSENGERS

Congresswoman Elissa Slotkin was working late on Thursday, September 19, when she saw a video clip that made her stop dead in her tracks. It was around 9:30 p.m. when she clicked on a link of Trump's personal lawyer Rudy Giuliani admitting on CNN that he had tried to persuade a foreign government to investigate Trump's top political rival, Joe Biden. Slotkin was horrified.

The Michigan Democrat, one of the most outspoken of the national security freshmen, had been closely tracking the news about the mysterious whistleblower complaint as it percolated through the Washington press. The night before Giuliani's interview, the *Washington Post* reported that the document centered on a "promise" Trump made to a foreign leader.[1] Then, about an hour before Giuliani went on CNN, the *Post* revealed that the complaint pertained to Ukraine—the very country to which Trump had suspiciously frozen military aid.[2]

Those developments, Slotkin thought, were troubling enough. As a former CIA agent, she knew how bad things had to get for an intelligence officer to raise this much of a public outcry. And then came Giuliani's brazen admission that he'd solicited yet another foreign government to interfere in the 2020 election.

"Of course, I did!" Giuliani said exasperatedly in the television clip when asked if he had pressed Ukraine to investigate Biden. As president, Trump "had every right," he insisted, to ask President Zelensky to probe a political rival if he suspected him of corruption.[3]

"No. No. NO!" Slotkin yelled as she watched the segment, shaking her head in utter disbelief. "WHAT?!"

To Slotkin, a centrist who'd been fighting the impeachment push all year, it was as brazen an abuse of power as she had ever witnessed in her government career. She had served three tours in Iraq as an intelligence officer before stepping into a lead role managing international security for Obama's Defense Department. She knew how dependent Ukraine was on U.S. support for its armed conflict against Russian-backed separatists—and how beholden its leaders would be to a president trying to manipulate that military assistance. In her estimation, Trump's actions were a gift to Russia and Putin that had potentially dire implications for national security. And it sickened Slotkin to realize that Trump had been pushing Ukraine to interfere in the 2020 elections before Congress was finished vetting Mueller's findings about Russian election meddling in 2016.

For the first time since she came to Congress earlier that year, Slotkin let herself seriously consider doing what she had long resisted: joining the pro-impeachment movement. Over the summer, she, like Abigail Spanberger, had found herself facing enormous pressure from her Democratic constituents to do so. One woman had sought her out after a town hall in Michigan with the Mueller report tucked into the crook of her arm, arguing that by not im-

peaching the president, Democrats were complicit in "the normal-
ization of his behavior."

Slotkin had nodded her head sympathetically. But she had steeled
herself against such pleas. "Quite honestly, I sometimes worry that
a lot of Democrats I know constantly just focus on the president and
they're not explaining to people how they're going to fight to help
their pocketbooks and their kids," Slotkin replied.[4]

Slotkin's matter-of-fact response, however, belied the precarious balancing act she and other moderates were engaged in that
summer. If they staked an anti-impeachment flag too deeply in the
ground, the Democratic base could turn against them, costing them
precious donations and support needed to win their hotly contested
reelections. But if they endorsed an effort to oust Trump, they could
alienate the conservative-leaning independents whom they also
needed in order to maintain their seats.

Slotkin had always told constituents that the party should let the
2020 election be the final referendum on Trump's conduct. But now
it seemed Trump was trying to compromise the very election she
was depending on to be the fair arbiter of his guilt or innocence.
That was a constitutional infraction Slotkin could sink her teeth
into—and one that could get her out of a political logjam. If there
was proof that Trump tried to sell out the country's national security
interests for the price of a cheap political favor, that was egregious
enough to contemplate impeachment without looking like she was
reneging on her principles. Mueller, Slotkin felt, had never given
Congress such hard-and-fast proof when it came to Trump's dealings with Russia. But Giuliani's admission about Ukraine was pretty
damn close to catching the president red-handed.

Picking up her phone, Slotkin did what she always had done when
facing a difficult decision in Congress: She used her colleagues as a
sounding board.

"Does anyone feel like this is impeachable?" she asked her fellow national security freshmen over Signal, an encrypted messaging app they regularly used to chat as a group.

They were all digesting the same news and asking themselves the same question. It was time, the group decided, for another conversation with Adam Schiff.

The next morning, Schiff listened as Spanberger, Slotkin, and a few others from their clique peppered him with questions in a cloakroom just off the noisy House floor. *What was the story with the whistleblower complaint? Would it be a game-changer for Pelosi on impeachment? Did they need to prepare themselves?*

"Does anyone feel like this is different? This Ukraine storyline is just fundamentally different," Slotkin said, turning to the House Intelligence Committee chairman and pointedly asking: "What do *you* think?"

When he had spoken with them in late July, Schiff had suggested to the group that impeachment was effectively dead. But Slotkin was right. Schiff knew the winds were about to change and the moderates wanted him to confirm it.

There was another reason the group wanted Schiff's read on Pelosi—one they would never admit publicly. As vulnerable Democrats in frontline districts, they were particularly concerned about being viewed as lapdogs of the Speaker. If impeachment was coming, they wanted a chance to get out ahead of it—and specifically, ahead of Pelosi.

That they were consulting with Schiff on impeachment at all was a calculated risk. Schiff, by that point, was the well-established boogeyman of the right, and any publicized link to him could have jeopardized their reelections. But the national security freshmen trusted Schiff. And more importantly, they believed he would know what Pelosi was planning.

As other members snaked in and out of the cavernous House chamber, Schiff acknowledged that he didn't have a precise read on the Speaker's plans. But he told the national security freshmen what he had confided to few others: The latest revelations, he predicted, would likely change the trajectory of impeachment in the House. He agreed with them. Trump had crossed a line that merited his ouster.

Schiff's admission prompted a bevy of additional questions: *When would impeachment start and how long would it take? Would Schiff take the reins? Or would Nadler lead the investigation?* On that last question, they all certainly hoped not.

Schiff studiously avoided specifics—but hinted strongly that he anticipated any investigation would run through his committee.

"Don't worry," he told them. "It will all work out."

As they headed to the airport to fly back to their districts, the national security freshmen began discussing whether it was time to take a public stand. After all, if Schiff was embracing impeachment, it was only a matter of time before Pelosi would too.

Schiff's prediction set off an intense debate among the national security freshmen that weekend, and they were far from unanimous on how to proceed. On the one side of the argument was Congressman Jason Crow, an Iraq and Afghanistan war veteran from the Denver suburbs, and the sole member of the group to have already publicly backed the impeachment effort. He suggested they make a splash by cowriting an opinion piece announcing their collective support for impeachment. On the other side was Congressman Max Rose, an Afghanistan war veteran from pro-Trump Staten Island, who agreed that the revelations about Ukraine were bad, but thought it was folly to move forward on impeachment without more evidence. Rose believed that the harder Democrats went after Trump, the more they were "in danger of losing the trust of the American people," as he had recently written in an anti-impeachment editorial in his hometown paper.

"Op-eds are like bullets," Rose argued to the group. "You can't take them back. Why fire one based on unconfirmed news reports? Why not wait to get the whistleblower complaint before deciding what to do?"

But most of the others feared that there was no time to wait; the news was moving too fast, and it was obvious that the train was leaving the station. Just after they had huddled with Schiff on Friday, the *New York Times* had published a story saying Trump himself had pressed Zelensky to investigate Biden's son in their call the day after the Mueller hearing.[5] That night, the *Washington Post* had reported that the White House's own budget office had inexplicably seized control of Ukraine's military aid from the State and Defense Departments sometime over the summer,[6] making it seem likely that Ukraine's taxpayer-funded assistance was part of Trump's scheme.

Still, it was a big step they were weighing. As centrist Democrats who had each flipped a long-held Republican district blue, they knew that as soon as they spoke up about impeachment, people would listen. As former intelligence officials and military service members, they also had authority to speak on matters of national security that other Democrats did not. Their support for impeachment, they believed, would lend an air of extra credibility to the movement, especially since they had spent so long opposing it—and would likely push the House headfirst into proceedings.

What happened next that Saturday remains a matter of dispute.

The national security freshmen publicly maintain that they did not consult Pelosi or Democratic leaders ahead of time. They say they made a pact not to discuss their plans with anyone in order to preserve their independent voice. But multiple people with firsthand knowledge of their efforts insist that not only did members of the group inform the most senior House Democratic leaders and staff of their intention to publicly back an impeachment inquiry as a bloc, but they also received feedback from Pelosi's team on how to frame their proposed op-ed. At the very least, Pelosi, her top deputies, and even Schiff knew by late Saturday that the national security freshmen planned to back the impeachment probe in a public letter, a step from which there would be no turning back.

Regardless, the members' decision to write an op-ed set off an intense weekend scramble as they pondered how to explain their about-face to a national audience. Scattered across the country in their home districts, they kept in touch constantly via phone, juggling writing with family and constituent obligations. Slotkin stole glimpses of their drafts while judging a Pentagon-sponsored hackathon at the University of Michigan. Another member, Mikie Sherrill of New Jersey, checked in while chauffeuring her daughter to a friend's birthday party, attending a memorial service for a community member, and making an appearance at a Naval Academy event.

Spanberger, the former CIA analyst, was on her way to Senator Mark Warner's annual pig roast extravaganza in rural Virginia that Saturday when the sheer magnitude of what she was about to do settled over her. Endorsing an impeachment inquiry, Spanberger knew, would put her fledgling career on the line, potentially undercutting her reelection chances. It could also mean putting her staff out of a job. So when Spanberger's campaign manager picked her up that Saturday morning, she decided she owed her a heads-up.

"I think I'm planning to call for an impeachment inquiry," Spanberger said as she jumped into the car, bracing for blowback.

Surprisingly, she didn't get it.

"Okay, I'm here if you want to talk about it," her campaign manager responded nonchalantly, as she turned on the car radio.

As they drove past farms and vineyards, Spanberger pulled out her iPad and began listing reasons for her change of heart on impeachment—reasons she knew she'd need to spell out for her constituents.

As the national security freshmen worked, the Ukraine controversy continued to unravel. On Saturday morning, the *Wall Street Journal* reported that Trump repeatedly pressured Zelensky to coordinate with Giuliani on a probe of the Bidens, mentioning his political rival multiple times in his July 25 call with the Ukrainian leader.[7] On Sunday morning, the president openly admitted before a row of television cameras that he had asked the Ukrainian president to investigate allegations that Biden and his son were guilty of "corruption."

That afternoon, Pelosi raised the stakes further. In a "Dear Colleague" letter—her favorite tool to signal her thinking on matters of import—she demanded the administration turn over the whistleblower's report, threatening "a whole new stage of investigation" to probe what she called a "violation" of "our national security."[8] Her wording was strategic: Private polling from the Democrats' campaign arm had shown that an impeachment framed as a "national security" matter resonated better in swing districts than one focused on allegations of "abuse of power."

At ten o'clock Sunday night, after tucking their children into bed across three time zones, the national security frontliners jumped on a conference call to hash out the basic themes of their script. Like Pelosi, they agreed to emphasize the national security implications of the president's actions, arguing that subverting foreign military aid and bullying a dependent foreign ally into doing political favors was a brazen misuse of the Oval Office and compromised U.S. interests abroad.

But there was still dissent in their ranks. Rose continued to implore the group to wait, insisting that "we need more information" before embracing impeachment. When most of the group refused, he and one other member, Jared Golden of Maine, announced that they wouldn't be signing on to the op-ed. The seven remaining members, however, forged ahead, giving themselves a deadline of Monday evening—less than twenty-four hours away—to iron out the final wording and find a place to publish.

That night, Spanberger barely slept. Sitting on the carpeted steps of her husband's little office nook off their bedroom, she inserted the points she'd drafted during her country drive into a Google Doc the group had created to hash out their collective voice. Other members did the same. By Monday morning, the seven lawmakers had a Frankenstein-esque document on their hands.

It took most of that day to whittle down their draft to the six paragraphs they would ultimately publish. Crow and Spanberger bickered about how many times they should use the word "allegedly," with the cautious Virginian inserting the word often and Crow, who hailed from a more Democratic-leaning district, urging a more aggressive approach. Some in the group wanted to make an emotional appeal to readers by adding adverbs. But Slotkin demanded that they stick to a clinical, businesslike style.

Shortly after four p.m. they sent the file to the *Washington Post* opinion editors, who had agreed to take and publish the document that night.

"If these allegations are true, we believe these actions represent an impeachable offense," they wrote. "We have devoted our lives to the service and security of our country . . . Now, we join as a unified group to uphold that oath as we enter uncharted waters and face unprecedented allegations against President Trump."[9]

Nancy Pelosi arrived early to the Brookland Baptist Church in West Columbia, South Carolina, on Sunday afternoon, September 22, secluding herself in a private conference room before an evening memorial service. Emily Clyburn, the longtime wife of House Majority Whip Jim Clyburn, had died three days earlier after a lengthy battle with diabetes. The African American megachurch was already brimming with activity, as its two-hundred-person chorus rehearsed for the service. But Pelosi had a serious work crisis to contend with before paying her final respects.

It was the second memorial service Pelosi had attended that weekend and the second that had been interrupted by the latest Trump scandal. She'd spent much of Saturday at the stately Saint Matthew's Cathedral in downtown Washington, D.C., eulogizing the legendary political journalist Cokie Roberts, who died at seventy-five from complications with breast cancer. The pair had been friends for a long time: Roberts's brother, Tommy, had attended Georgetown with Pelosi's husband. But instead of allowing Pelosi to mourn, fellow Democrats and acquaintances kept accosting her, insisting it was time to oust Trump over the latest Ukraine allegations.

For the previous nine months, Pelosi had been a bulwark against the onslaught of Democrats calling to impeach the president for one primary reason: to protect her frontliners facing difficult reelections. She had predicated her entire leadership strategy on trying to avoid matters that would force the moderates who had helped clinch her majority from taking politically treacherous votes. She had delayed contempt citations. She had forgone resolutions to condemn the president. All to keep those politically vulnerable, often skittish members happy. The fact that she sometimes frustrated her base and her investigative committee chairs made no difference. To her, it was worth taking heat to keep the frontliners from getting fried on the campaign trail.

But that weekend, Pelosi was starting to realize she could no longer hold the line. She had learned over the weekend that an influential subset of those majority-makers—the national security freshmen—was on the precipice of calling for impeachment, a move that would undermine the central reason for her opposition. Pelosi knew that their endorsement would create a jailbreak, as others on the fence followed their lead.

Pelosi had maintained an iron grip on power for thirteen years due to one talent above all others: her ability to count. By that morning, the tally of House Democrats supporting an impeachment probe had almost reached 150[10]—the threshold the Speaker's staff had told liberal activists would be enough to change her mind. Whether she liked it or not, Pelosi faced a choice: She could either lose her grip on her caucus, or lead them in this new, almost inevitable direction.

The headlines that were moving her members that weekend had not come as a surprise to Pelosi. She had already known about the whistleblower complaint before that scandal became public, thanks to Schiff keeping her in the loop. But even those revelations hadn't immediately changed her mind. In fact, on the same day that Schiff was hinting to the national security freshmen that the developing facts around Ukraine might pitch the House into impeachment, the Speaker was still deflecting questions about whether it was time to oust Trump, telling NPR that "we don't have the information" to make that decision.[11]

Pelosi wasn't sure they would ever get the evidence to make it worthwhile, even if they launched a formal inquiry. She figured the president would stonewall a Ukraine investigation just as he had resisted every other ongoing House probe into his affairs. Even if Democrats could somehow produce a smoking gun—like the whistleblower's complaint or a transcript of Trump's July 25 call—they still might not be able to get a single witness to testify against the president. Why start an impeachment fight that she didn't have the confidence they could finish?

But that weekend, a major shift began to occur in the party. Democrats' liberal lions, who had refrained from attacking Pelosi personally over her reluctance to take up impeachment, started to cast the Ukraine revelations not only as an indictment of Trump's presidency but of obstinate House Democratic leaders. On the campaign trail Saturday, during Iowa's Polk County steak fry, presidential candidate and Massachusetts senator Elizabeth Warren blamed the House's failed oversight ventures for enabling Trump's latest misdeeds in Ukraine.

"By failing to act, Congress is complicit in Trump's latest attempt to solicit foreign interference to aid him in U.S. elections," Warren had also written on Twitter, a remark that went viral with the left. "Do your constitutional duty and impeach the president."

Far-left firebrand Representative Alexandria Ocasio-Cortez of New York also joined the public assault that night, accusing the House of failing in its duty to defend democracy. "At this point, the bigger national scandal isn't the president's lawbreaking behavior— it is the Democratic Party's refusal to impeach him for it," Ocasio-Cortez wrote on Twitter. "It is one thing for a sitting president to break the law. It's another to let him."

Behind the scenes, other liberals were also running out of patience with the Speaker. Before they left town that weekend, several Democratic members confronted Jerry Nadler, urging him to buck Pelosi and advance articles of impeachment on his own. Meanwhile, the party's network of liberal groups, led by MoveOn.org's Reggie Hubbard, filed for a permit to stage a protest at the Capitol, calling on Pelosi to endorse impeachment once and for all.

The avalanche of vitriol alarmed the Speaker's closest political advisors and staff, who grappled privately with how to confront their boss. The momentum for impeachment was undeniable, and they knew it was time for her to stop resisting. But Pelosi could be stubborn when under attack and didn't take well to being lectured by aides.

Even members who traditionally deferred to her were beginning to plot their defections—and Pelosi wasn't taking it well. When Congresswoman Katie Hill, a fellow Californian and a frontliner on Pelosi's leadership team, phoned Pelosi directly on Saturday to tell her she intended to call for impeachment publicly, the Speaker snapped.

"Do what you have to," Pelosi replied curtly to Hill, in a tone so sharp that Hill decided not to endorse impeachment that day.

Pelosi could—and often did—turn a deaf ear to most members' opinions, but there was one she couldn't ignore. For the first time that Saturday, Schiff, the Speaker's most trusted chairman, told Pelosi they could no longer avoid the inevitable.

"I think it's time to move forward on impeachment," he told her in a private phone call.

The two discussed the national security freshmen's looming op-ed and agreed it would create a seismic shift, likely bringing Pelosi to a moment of reckoning. Schiff asked Pelosi for her blessing to say on CNN the next morning that the House might have no options left but to impeach the president.

The request was largely a formality. Pelosi almost never denied Schiff the way she habitually did Nadler. The two Californians' brains were similarly wired, having both served as the top Democrat on the House Intelligence Committee and as appropriators of foreign assistance funds. If Schiff thought the latest allegations against Trump were grounds enough to impeach him, Pelosi would be hard-pressed to disagree.

On Sunday morning, Schiff went on CNN's *State of the Union* and stated his case.

"I have been very reluctant to go down the path of impeachment . . . this would be an extraordinary remedy of last resort, not first resort," Schiff said. "But . . . we may have very well crossed the Rubicon here."

That afternoon, in the relative quiet of the Clyburns' church function room, Pelosi was still coming to terms with the inevitable. After Trump's confession that morning that he had asked Zelensky to investigate the Bidens for "corruption," she had issued her "Dear Colleague" letter accusing the Trump administration of "endangering our national security." But she had conspicuously left out the word "impeachment," keeping her members guessing.

Yet even for a president who once joked that he could "stand in the middle of Fifth Avenue and shoot somebody" without consequence, Pelosi knew Trump's actions were a stunning and egregious violation of ethical norms at the very least—and possibly a crime against the Constitution.

She reached for her phone to call the Judiciary Committee chairman, whose impeachment entreaties she had been batting down for months, to let him know she was about to change course. *The national security freshmen are writing a letter backing impeachment*, she told Nadler. *It's time to move.*

At 5:30 Monday evening, the national security freshmen gathered around a large, round table in Slotkin's office to officially notify Pelosi by phone about their forthcoming op-ed—the op-ed she already knew was coming. Unlike her terse response to Katie Hill, Pelosi thanked them for their leadership and for giving her a heads-up.

"Go on TV," she encouraged them, revealing nothing about her own plans. "Go explain your reasoning to the nation."

That night, one member of their clique, Elaine Luria, was scheduled to appear on MSNBC's *The Rachel Maddow Show*, just minutes after their op-ed was due to be published on the *Washington Post*'s website at nine p.m. The rest of the group had agreed to gather at another member's Capitol Hill apartment to watch.

On the way over, Spanberger made a quick detour past a campaign fundraising event in Arlington, Virginia, to chat with donors. Two Virginia Democrats buttonholed her over impeachment.

"This Ukraine stuff is just so terrible," they said, softly berating Spanberger for not supporting an inquiry. "How can you not be in favor of impeachment?"

Spanberger checked her watch: 8:45 p.m.

"I need you to give me another fifteen minutes, okay?" she responded. They looked at her quizzically as she scurried away to a car where her campaign manager was waiting to ferry the congresswoman to the watch party.

"I have a present for you!" Spanberger's staffer said as she swung open the door, handing her a 1.5-liter bottle of her favorite drink, kombucha, a tacit acknowledgment that this was turning into the most stressful day of her career.

When their op-ed went live, the members' phones started lighting up with messages. Some friends and supporters thanked them for their bravery in endorsing impeachment; others took the opposite tack, warning them they'd made a huge mistake. In New York, where Pelosi was attending the opening of that year's United Nations General Assembly, one of her aides printed out a copy, handing it to the Speaker as she boarded a plane back to Washington.

As her plane took off, Pelosi studied the printout. Pulling out a pen, she started scribbling in the margins, sketching out the speech she had never wanted to make, one that would affect not only Trump's legacy, but her own.

"No one is above the law . . ." she wrote, a phrase she had said dozens of times publicly during the months she had resisted an impeachment inquiry.

Now, at long last, the Speaker and her Democrats were about to test that theory.

9

A PERFECT CALL

SEPTEMBER 24, 2019

It was just after eight a.m., and in the cool, gilded chambers of his posh Fifth Avenue penthouse in New York City, Donald Trump was sweating. He needed to talk to Pelosi, stat.

The president had chosen to stay that week in his eponymous tower overlooking Central Park while attending the United Nations General Assembly. Usually, the familiar surroundings brought him joy. Between his official duties, campaigning, and visits to his golf clubs, Trump hardly ever made it back to the glittering centerpiece of his real estate empire.

But that Tuesday, September 24, there was little to be happy about. Even from hundreds of miles away, he could tell that House Democrats in Washington were reaching a breaking point on impeachment—and he was desperate to keep the dam from bursting.

When reports first surfaced claiming Trump tried to pressure Ukraine into investigating the Bidens, the president had gone on the defensive. The allegations of misconduct were "another fake news story" from "the Radical Left Democrats and their Fake News

Media partners," he lied, tweeting to the masses that he had done nothing wrong.

When evidence to the contrary kept surfacing, Trump tried a different strategy: copping to what he had done and trying to convince the nation it was completely justified because Biden was the guilty party.

"That call was a great call. It was a perfect call. A perfect call," Trump told reporters. "It was a warm, friendly conversation. There was no quid pro quo. There was nothing."[1]

By Tuesday morning, Trump had lost the "perfect call" narrative completely. While he was rubbing elbows with the diplomatic glitterati in New York, the *Washington Post* had reported that Trump himself had ordered the freeze of Ukraine's military aid at least a week before his July 25 phone call with Zelensky[2]—a revelation that was like rocket fuel to the people calling for his ouster. The cable news shows were in a meltdown, as pundits and political commentators openly accused him of engaging in a "quid pro quo" and predicted his demise.

But what alarmed the president most were reports that Pelosi was on the cusp of endorsing impeachment. For Trump, who had taken solace in the fact that the Speaker hated the idea of impeachment as much as he did, that was a potentially deadly development. He had been counting on Pelosi to hold the line.

The president's associates had tried to convince him that impeachment would backfire on the Democrats and galvanize the GOP to defend him against such "presidential harassment." Trump, however, wasn't so sure. The president was afraid of how the "impeached" designation would tarnish his legacy. It was an asterisk that would accompany his name in every history book, an unacceptable blight for the president who fancied himself the greatest in American history.

So that Tuesday morning, in a last-ditch attempt to stop the process from moving forward, he picked up his phone to call his archrival in the House.

Trump, often drawn to strongmen and even dictators, had once been a quiet admirer of the Speaker. He regularly told White House associates that Pelosi had an iron grip that was unmatched by her GOP counterparts. And for a while, early in his presidency, the two had enjoyed an uneasy détente. The day after Trump had won the presidency in 2016, when Pelosi had called to congratulate him on his surprise victory, the president-elect had complimented her, saying: "You're somebody that gets things done, better than anybody." He also reminded her that in 2006, when she'd visited him at Trump Tower in Manhattan, he'd handed her a $20,000 check to help her flip the House.

"Don't forget I was a supporter of yours," he told her. "I think you're terrific!"

But by the fall of 2019, Pelosi's sheen had worn off completely in his eyes. He had been affronted by her escalated rhetoric against him that summer and had taken to calling her "Crazy Nancy," even accusing her of losing a step with age. She, meanwhile, declared she'd love to see him in prison and publicly implored his family to get him mental help.

At home in her Georgetown condo, Pelosi was surprised when the voice on the phone told her to hold for the president. She was preparing to head to the Hill to make what was likely to be one of the most spectacular flip-flops of her career. If Trump was calling to beg her not to, he was too late.

The Speaker listened impatiently as the president told her he wanted to discuss stalled gun legislation. *Gun legislation?* Pelosi thought. *As if.* She didn't have to wait long, however, for Trump to divulge his true motivation.

"Are you really going to impeach me?" Trump asked, launching into salesman mode. "You don't really want to do this."[3]

"It was so perfect," he said of his July 25 call with Zelensky, "exactly the opposite of what you've been reading. Literally, you would be *impressed* with our lack of pressure . . . Why would I say something bad? I would never have, by the way. I just want you to know that."

Pelosi snorted. "Perfectly unacceptable," she scoffed. "Mr. President, you have come into my wheelhouse," Pelosi warned, launching into a spiel about how she had helped write the law protecting whistleblowers. She was an expert on these issues, she told Trump, and his refusal to turn over the whistleblower complaint—or a readout of the Zelensky call—was beyond the pale.

"Release the transcript," she demanded. "Tell the DNI to release the transcript."

Trump deflected the question.

"I don't have anything to do with that," he said dismissively.

Pelosi didn't believe that for a second.

"Don't be afraid of it," she dared him.

"I'm not!" the president retorted. And he intended to prove it.

A hush fell over the room as the Speaker stood before her caucus in the basement of the Capitol and laid out the moral imperative facing each of them. It was just before five p.m., and House Democrats had gathered for an emergency meeting where, rumor had it, Pelosi would tell her members she planned to back an impeachment inquiry. Even her inner circle was shocked at the speed of her turnaround.

At the front of the room, Pelosi stood and offered weighty words.

"There is no question: [Trump] has admitted that he brought

up the investigation of the Biden family in his call," Pelosi told the room somberly. "Don't get caught in the trap of, 'Oh, there is no quid pro quo!' . . . He is asking a foreign government to help him in his campaign. That is a betrayal of our national security, and a betrayal of the integrity of our elections."

Pelosi then ceremoniously asked the room for permission to officially launch the impeachment inquiry. Her members responded with a roar of approval.

"Our Founders understood that there could be some abuse of powers; they built guardrails into the Constitution," Pelosi continued, after their cheers died down. "They never suspected that a president could undo the guardrails—nor did we."

Just as Pelosi predicted, the national security freshmen's op-ed had triggered a tsunami of House Democratic holdouts to join the impeachment parade. By the time the Speaker stood before her colleagues that Tuesday afternoon, more than 170 House Democrats were demanding an inquiry, including more than half of the 44 members from swing districts.[4]

Only a small cluster of Pelosi's most centrist members in swing districts remained skittish, fearing that the move was premature—and they had taken their case straight to Pelosi. On Monday afternoon, centrist Josh Gottheimer, who led a bipartisan group of moderates known as the Problem Solvers, had called Pelosi while she was attending the U.N. General Assembly in New York and implored her to tread carefully. As a young staffer in Clinton's White House in the 1990s, the New Jersey Democrat had seen firsthand how a president could twist impeachment to his advantage. He worried Trump would do the same and that it would blow back on Democrats like him in 2020—just as it had crippled Republicans in 1998.

Gottheimer and a host of vulnerable members in frontline districts had heard about the op-ed that the national security freshmen were planning—and they were apoplectic that they had not been given a heads-up. The centrist, who knew Pelosi had long opposed impeachment, wanted to make sure the Speaker hadn't changed her mind. But when he called her to check, he learned she had.

"I don't think I can hold this back anymore," Pelosi told him, explaining that the national security freshmen's op-ed was imminent. "The moderates have gone."

Gottheimer had thanked her for the update, got off the phone, and promptly told the other centrists what the Speaker had conveyed.

"This is moving forward," he told them. "We're fucked."

Pelosi understood Gottheimer's apprehension. She felt it too. She was moving into uncharted territory and was under no illusion that impeachment would be a political winner. Still, she was determined to do everything in her power to make the impeachment process as politically painless as possible for her most vulnerable members.

At 5:04 p.m. Pelosi left her members in the Capitol basement, rode an elevator back to her office, and strode to a lectern that had been set up just off the Rotunda, in front of six American flags. Facing the television cameras, she began to address the nation with a civics lesson. In September 1787, she recounted, a throng of newly independent Americans had swarmed Benjamin Franklin as he exited Independence Hall in downtown Philadelphia, where the Founding Fathers had gathered for the Constitutional Convention. "What have we got, a republic or a monarchy?" they asked him. "A republic, if you can keep it," Franklin famously replied.

"Our responsibility is to keep it," Pelosi said. "The actions taken by the president have seriously violated the Constitution."

Left unsaid were Pelosi's lingering concerns about political blowback—at least temporarily.

"I'm announcing the House of Representatives is moving forward with an official impeachment inquiry," Pelosi concluded. "I am directing our six committees to proceed with their investigations under that umbrella of impeachment inquiry. The president must be held accountable. No one is above the law."

10

IMPEACHMENT
BY ANOTHER NAME

SEPTEMBER 24, 2019

Congressman Jim Jordan and his top advisors flipped on the television in his Capitol Hill office to watch Nancy Pelosi's highly anticipated address. Word was out that the Speaker planned to announce the House would move forward with impeachment, and the conservative Ohio Republican—whom Trump counted as a close ally—needed to hear exactly what she would say in order to adequately respond.

As Pelosi spoke, Jordan, his deputy chief of staff Tyler Grimm, his chief counsel Steve Castor, and a host of other top aides started chuckling. Pelosi "looked like she had been taken hostage," someone cackled. One might think announcing Trump's impeachment would be a triumphant moment for a Democratic Speaker, but she seemed stiff, and despite her attempts to smile, they noted, she looked like she simply did not want to be there.

Jordan couldn't blame her. As much as he disagreed with the San Francisco liberal on, well, pretty much everything, he knew Pelosi wasn't stupid. He knew that *she* knew that endorsing impeachment was a politically reckless step. Yet there she was, doing it anyway.

After months of watching the Democrats' investigations run aground, the September rush toward impeachment had caught House Republicans like Jordan off-guard. Pelosi's chairmen—and federal investigators in general—had fired everything they had at Trump, but Trump had coolly sidestepped the barrage. The president's uncanny ability to survive scandals that would have deep-sixed any other president had ceased to surprise them. Neither the *Access Hollywood* controversy, in which Trump boasted on tape he could "grab" women "by the pussy" anytime he wanted,[1] nor the Mueller investigation, nor being identified as a co-conspirator to a federal campaign finance crime had sunk his political fortunes. Instead, they had only solidified the devotion of his ever-loyal base. By August, Jordan figured that Trump was in the clear regarding impeachment too—and maybe even stronger because of its failure to launch.

But sometime around the end of the August congressional recess, his aides began hearing whispers that a whistleblower had come forward alleging Trump had done something terrible. The mutterings had come not from Democrats but from GOP sources within the administration. *But how bad could it be?* Jordan wondered.

In fact, when Schiff announced an investigation into Trump and Rudy Giuliani's actions in Ukraine, Jordan had instinctively dismissed the brewing scandal over the whistleblower complaint as yet another "Schiff special." In his estimation, the Intelligence panel chairman simply couldn't let go of his obsession with Trump—even though his allegations of "collusion" with Russia had never been validated.

"Mueller failed, and here they go again," Jordan had remarked to his team, who agreed that the Democrats' efforts to drum up successive scandals about the president were just getting embarrassing.

But Jordan could not dismiss Pelosi as swiftly as he could Schiff. Would she really have endorsed impeachment, even under duress, for something flimsy? *Why were they doing this? What did Schiff and Pelosi know that he didn't?*

Whatever it was, the Ohio Republican knew it would soon fall to him to lead the president's defense.

Jordan, a former champion wrestler and coach, had always been captivated by the competitive nature of politics and approached everything he did like a face-off on the mat. He was short and wiry, square-jawed and broad-shouldered. He strutted around the Capitol in his shirtsleeves and only donned his jacket on the House floor to comply with the strict dress code.

Even before Trump's presidency, the Ohio Republican had been considered the GOP's most ferocious oversight pit bull. During the Obama administration, he made a name for himself leading the party's charge against the Internal Revenue Service for withholding tax exempt status from Tea Party groups, holding one official in contempt and even advocating impeachment charges against the IRS commissioner. He later served on the contentious GOP-led Benghazi committee, where he exhibited little patience with more senior Republicans who hesitated to adopt his take-no-prisoners approach. Jordan frequently tangled with the select panel's chairman, Trey Gowdy, for not going hard enough after former secretary of state Clinton during the two-and-a-half-year probe. When the committee produced a final report that Jordan thought pulled punches, he teamed up with then-congressman Mike Pompeo to release alternative findings that accused Clinton of a cover-up, believing it would help the GOP beat her in the upcoming presidential election.

With Trump in the Oval Office, the sharp-tongued Jordan made it his duty to defend the Republican president with as much zeal as he had harangued the previous Democratic one. During the first two years of Trump's presidency, he bullied House GOP leaders and chairmen into probing allegations of bias against the president in the ranks of the FBI, insisting they "investigate the investigators" who had looked into Russian election interference. He even tried to strong-arm then-Speaker Paul Ryan into impeaching Deputy Attorney General Rod Rosenstein, who had overseen Mueller's probe.

At the time, Jordan's tactics unnerved many House GOP lawmakers. They had been uncomfortable with the idea of attacking law enforcement agencies, worried about undermining the public's long-term faith in the rule of law and impartial justice. But Jordan didn't care—and Trump loved it.

"He's a warrior for me!" Trump would exclaim to other Republicans about Jordan, showering him with praise whenever he saw his scrimmages featured on Fox News. Jordan was always gracious. In person, he was far less bombastic than his persona on camera or the dais: even-toned, self-effacing, and loyal to a fault. Trump was smitten.

Politically, though, the Trump-Jordan connection wasn't a natural fit. A hardline conservative who came to Congress the same year Pelosi first became Speaker, Jordan had been one of the earliest architects of the right wing's takeover of the Republican Party. After the Tea Party swept the GOP into the House majority in 2010, Jordan organized the new ultra-conservative renegades into the Freedom Caucus. Under his leadership, the group of three dozen rabble-rousers demanded ideological purity, especially when it came to the national debt and federal spending, and shunned compromise. They perfected the art of sinking GOP legislation they found too accommodating to Democrats, forcing the government into a series of shutdowns and even pushing the nation to the brink of defaulting on its debt. And they drove not one, but two Republican Speakers to quit Congress in frustration, leading some to quietly dub Jordan the "other Speaker of the House" for his ability to pummel party leaders into submission.

Trump lacked Jordan's ideological purity, but Jordan liked his brash style and the way he catered to the base. After Trump clinched the nomination in 2016, Jordan and the Freedom Caucus decided they'd be his allies in Congress and never looked back. When some GOP lawmakers withdrew their endorsements after Trump was caught on tape boasting that he could grab women by their private parts with impunity, Jordan and his fellow Freedom Caucus leader Mark Meadows—as well as their wives, Polly and Debbie—drove around the country stumping for him at political rallies. Immediately after Trump's election, Jordan and Meadows offered to take down then-Speaker Paul Ryan as payback for criticizing the president-elect on the campaign trail. The smoke signal from the White House never came, however, as the president made a truce with Ryan. But Trump never forgot Jordan's gesture and, a few years later, even returned the favor. When Jordan was accused of ignoring allegations of sexual abuse during his pre-congressional career as a wrestling coach at Ohio State—which he denied—Trump leaped to defend him as an "outstanding" friend who had been wrongfully accused.

Their confidence in each other had never wavered—until Pelosi's sudden lurch toward impeachment. The president was insisting that his call with Zelensky had been "perfect." But Jordan and his team had heard from other administration officials that the contents weren't so clear-cut—and might even be quite bad for the president. If Trump had actually held back Ukraine's military aid to prompt investigations into the Bidens, as Democrats were insinuating, that was going to be tricky to defend. But would he have actually made such a blatant request?

As they watched Pelosi speak, Jordan and his staff paid close attention to the words she chose. The Speaker had been careful to say that Democrats were only investigating Trump for impeachable offenses, avoiding any commitment to impeach him at the end of that probe. That was almost laughable, Grimm mused to Jordan.

"Endorsing an impeachment inquiry is the political equivalent of jumping out of an airplane to skydive," Grimm said. "Once you're out of the plane, there's no going back."

Jordan liked the analogy. Pelosi's parachute could open and she could glide smoothly into a cheering stadium or she could crash if her parachute malfunctioned. Either way, she was going to land on impeachment.

"We're going to make this landing as difficult as possible for them," Jordan vowed.

Across the Capitol campus, in a suite just feet from the House floor, House Minority Leader Kevin McCarthy and his senior staff were also confused by Pelosi's performance. They had watched and re-watched Pelosi's six-minute address, waiting for the blockbuster announcement that would send the House into hyperdrive on the fourth impeachment probe of a sitting U.S. president. To their ears, it never came.

McCarthy's team had anticipated the Speaker would announce something formal and definite, such as a House vote to launch impeachment proceedings in the Judiciary Committee, as had been done in the past. But Pelosi had framed the investigation as merely the "continuation" of ongoing probes happening across six different panels "under the umbrella of impeachment." What the hell did that mean? They had no idea. And how was that any different from what the House Democrats had been doing all year?

Did she just announce impeachment proceedings or not? McCarthy asked his senior counsel Machalagh Carr.

Carr, a longtime Hill staffer in her late thirties, had cut her maternity leave short that very week to oversee the GOP's counter-impeachment strategy. She had been preparing for the moment all year by studying the few available precedents and was adamant that any legitimate process needed to be authorized by a vote of the House—not simply the edict of a Speaker. At least, that's how it had been done in impeachments past.

"That is not the legal standard," she said. "Definitely not."

McCarthy's other staff agreed. Another of his aides, press secretary Mark Bednar, joked that they were watching a parade of "more Jerry Nadler–Mickey Mouse bullshit"—Democrats acting like they were in an impeachment inquiry to please the base, but not having the guts to really make it official.

Republicans were onto more than they realized. In the hours before Pelosi's public announcement, House counsel Doug Letter had flagged a "Magic Dick"–sized problem with her drafted speech: Pelosi planned to announce the House was launching an impeachment inquiry—but the House had already told the courts that they were engaged in one to accelerate their Don McGahn lawsuit. If Pelosi stated that impeachment was a new undertaking, it could undermine their pending cases, Letter warned in a meeting with her investigative chairs. House lawyers quickly changed her speech to herald a "continuation" of proceedings that had already begun.

In that same meeting, Pelosi also nixed the idea of holding a formal House vote to bless the impeachment probe. While her moderate members were endorsing an inquiry, they were too skittish to vote on anything resembling one at that moment—and she wasn't about to force them. "Now is not the time," Pelosi had said.

As McCarthy's top-ranking members gathered in his office, the only thing that was clear was that the whole group was frustrated. Doug Collins, a lanky lawyer and Southern Baptist minister who was the top Republican on the House Judiciary Committee, railed that the whole thing was a crock. The Speaker "can't just wave her hands and move the House to impeachment proceedings!" he barked in an agitated Georgia drawl. "It doesn't work like that." Real impeachments were the purview of the Judiciary panel, he argued. If Pelosi was out there saying six panels were going to investigate? That was simply a free for all.

"It's not impeachment unless there is a vote," Collins concluded.

Jordan and the other non-lawyers in the room disagreed. "It doesn't matter whether it's legally right or wrong," the former wrestling coach said. "It's happening. We need to get ready."

McCarthy realized Jordan was right. But he still didn't know which of the six committees would lead the investigation, nor which of the Democrats' myriad probes of Trump's businesses, foreign ties, financial records, and policy pronouncements would become the centerpiece of their inevitable charges. Pelosi appeared to be making things up as she went along, making it impossible to plan a counterattack.

In September 1998, on the eve of launching the Clinton impeachment investigation, GOP leaders spearheading the effort had summoned their Democratic counterparts to discuss the looming inquiry. At the summit, both sides agreed to work together to write rules of the road on a bipartisan basis, just as had been done during the Nixon inquiry. The process would soon unravel, as Democrats accused Republicans of being too unfair and heavy-handed. But the gesture had at least been made, the parameters understood by both sides.[2]

Twenty years later, Pelosi hadn't given the GOP so much as a heads-up about her plans. She assumed that Republican leaders would never step out against Trump, and thus didn't bother looping them in. Still, leaving Republican leaders guessing showed just how deeply Congress had descended into partisan trench warfare even before Trump's impeachment began. It was a troubling harbinger of the contentiousness to come.

Democrats weren't the only ones leaving the GOP in the dark, however. So was Trump. He had claimed his actions were "perfect," but on Capitol Hill, many Republicans had no idea what he had actually done. His allies knew that as a general rule, Trump had no respect for limits or boundaries—though they would never admit to such thoughts publicly.

Suddenly, Jordan's and McCarthy's teams understood how the Democrats must have felt during Clinton's impeachment. Back in the 1990s, Democrats had leaped to the president's defense in party solidarity, not knowing if more interns claiming to have had sexual relations with their party leader would come forward. Now Republicans would be called on to blindly defend their president without knowing the full extent of the allegations against him.

They wouldn't have to wait long to get marching orders. That night, a summons came from the White House: *Be here early tomorrow morning. It's time to go on offense.*

11

"THE DYNAMITE LINE"

SEPTEMBER 25, 2019

At eight-thirty the next morning, Jim Jordan walked into the Roosevelt Room of the White House and braced himself for the worst. Trump's advisors had summoned him, House Minority Leader Kevin McCarthy, and about a dozen of the president's most aggressive defenders in Congress to preview the official record of Trump's July 25 call with Ukrainian president Volodymyr Zelensky. Trump had decided to release the transcript publicly later that morning in hopes that it would head off impeachment. But first, he wanted his congressional mouthpieces to be in lockstep with his talking points.

Seated at the conference table under a large square skylight, just below a portrait of former president Teddy Roosevelt on horseback, Jordan grabbed a copy of the five-page document and began reading.

Trump had opened the July 25 conversation by congratulating Zelensky on his recent victory. Zelensky, who had clearly done his homework on Trump, responded by flattering him and saying he wanted to "drain the swamp here in our country" too. Trump then bragged that the U.S. had been "very, very good to Ukraine," before pivoting to say: "I would like you to do us a favor though."

Trump brought up the conspiracy theory he'd learned about from Giuliani: that Ukraine was hiding a hacked Democratic National Committee server on which he would find Hillary Clinton's missing emails. He also suggested pointedly that Zelensky look into "Biden's son" Hunter, who had held a position on the board of one of Ukraine's largest private energy companies, Burisma.

"A lot of people want to find out about that," Trump had said.[1]

But what was most striking to Jordan was what he *wasn't* reading. There was no explicit mention of leveraging military aid. There were no overt threats to Ukraine. Trump hadn't laid out preconditions for anything to substantiate a quid pro quo. In fact, the whole conversation read to him like a polite, dare he say friendly, exchange.

Where was the bombshell? Jordan thought, as he flipped back through the pages to make sure he hadn't missed anything. The document before him seemed completely innocuous. He should have no problem defending this. In fact, the idea of impeaching anyone over this phone call, to him, was laughable.

Next to him, McCarthy had the same reaction.

"Is this everything?" McCarthy said, looking up from the sheets before him, surprised, if not a wee bit skeptical.

"This is it!" White House legislative affairs director Eric Ueland, who was there to brief members, replied. "This is all there is."

But it wasn't everything. Not by a long shot.

Privately, Trump and his top White House aides were extremely concerned about losing GOP lawmakers' support once they learned the full extent of what Trump had done in Ukraine. So they had devised a plan: His aides would sell their top Hill surrogates on the transcript—but deliberately hold back the more damaging allegations in the whistleblower report, which documented how Trump systematically targeted Ukraine over several months to exact political favors, including possibly leveraging U.S. military assistance. If they could corner lawmakers into publicly defending Trump's call with Zelensky, they believed, then GOP lawmakers would be less likely to break with the White House when the full story came out.

That morning, Ueland, White House counsel Pat Cipollone, and longtime Mike Pence aide Marc Short passed out talking points to the members and stressed how important it was that they fight for Trump against what was shaping up to be the most existential threat yet to his presidency.

"You have to stick with the president on this, and you must step forward and aggressively defend him," Short argued. "Republicans need to speak with a unified voice about the call." Ueland echoed that sentiment as well.

Then they called Trump himself to drive the point home. With his voice booming through the speakerphone, Trump argued that reports of a quid pro quo were wrong and that the transcript had exonerated him.

"See? The call was perfect!" Trump boasted.

The assembled Republicans—unaware that the call was just the tip of the iceberg—agreed. *This will show that Democrats launched an impeachment for nothing*, the members assured Trump, laughing that Pelosi had shot from the hip too soon. Someone joked that the call with Zelensky was actually one of Trump's *better* calls with foreign leaders, well aware that Trump had reportedly berated and hung up on the leaders of Australia and Mexico early in his term.[2]

As they exited the White House, Jordan called his staff counsel to deliver the good news.

"This? They're impeaching over *this*?" he said to Steve Castor, throwing all his previous trepidation to the wind. "There's no quid pro quo here. We can defend this."

Back at the Capitol, Mitch McConnell took one look at the transcript of the call and knew he had a problem. Trump's behavior toward Zelensky was entirely inappropriate. And the Kentucky Republican wanted to know immediately if Trump had committed a crime.

The Senate Majority Leader summoned his top aides to his stately suite, where gold-tasseled curtains framed large windows overlooking the National Mall. His chambers, with their high-vaulted ceilings, were across the Rotunda from Pelosi's and one of the oldest offices in the Capitol. In fact, McConnell's rooms had once housed the Library of Congress's first book collection, which the British used as kindling to burn the Capitol during the War of 1812. Now McConnell needed advice on how to extinguish what he feared would be a different kind of five-alarm fire as his eyes froze on the phrase "do us a favor though."

"This is the dynamite line," McConnell's chief counsel Andrew Ferguson told him, pointing to that very phrase that had disturbed the GOP leader. "Politically, this will force the Democrats to act."

They were sitting on upholstered couches and chairs under a chandelier beaming bright yellow light. McConnell listened as Ferguson, who had clerked for conservative Supreme Court Justice Clarence Thomas before coming to the Hill, gamed out the situation. It was true, Ferguson said, that Trump had not brought up military aid, nor directly articulated terms of a quid pro quo to force Zelensky into a Biden investigation. There also wasn't clear evidence of bribery, extortion, or any crime—at least not according to the record before them, he told McConnell. That was the good news.

But there was no escaping the fact that Trump blatantly asked a foreign government to conduct investigations that would help his odds in 2020. Trump's request for a "favor," after articulating how good the U.S. was to Ukraine, was going to cause a serious political problem, Ferguson predicted.

"These are the lines that are going to be the basis on which they do impeachment," Ferguson concluded. "I don't think Pelosi can hold back her caucus anymore."

McConnell, seventy-seven, was famous for rarely betraying his thoughts or emotions—even to those within his close political circle. His leadership team secretly joked that being elected to serve in the party's upper ranks with him was like flying first class: You got to ride in the front, but McConnell remained sealed off in the cockpit, alone at the controls.

Ferguson waited for McConnell's reaction to his assessment. As the leader raised his eyes from the paper before him, he gave Ferguson a slow nod, his face drawn in its typical droopy-jowled frown.

"Mm-hmm," he said in a deep southern drawl. "This is probably not helpful."

When Trump had called earlier that week to take McConnell's temperature on releasing the transcript, the president did not offer the GOP leader a preview—and McConnell did not ask for one. Instead, Trump gave the leader a rose-colored summary that skipped over the more troubling details already blanketing the newspapers. It was all being perverted in the press, he insisted, promising that when the call record came out, it would be completely banal and prove his innocence.

After nearly three strained years of working with the president, McConnell knew that Trump was hardly the most credible judge of his own actions. He lied on a regular basis and frequently contradicted himself, especially when scrambling to escape public criticism or mollify his base. McConnell had learned to manipulate the tempestuous and impulsive president to his advantage, but he did not trust him. And that day, his staffers were downright terrified about what the forthcoming call record might say.

McConnell knew that Washington leaked like a sieve when a potential scandal was afoot, and reasoned things had risen to such a fever pitch that the transcript would eventually get out anyway. Senate Minority Leader Chuck Schumer of New York was already warning that if McConnell didn't "take action" to get the administration to cough up the whistleblower's complaint, he would force a vote to demand the White House release the document to Congress.[3] McConnell was not inclined to have Republican senators—especially those facing tough reelections the following year—fall on their swords for an unpopular president and invite charges that they were complicit in a "cover-up."

"There is no purpose in obstructing the inevitable," he had told his staff simply.

Part of the reason McConnell hadn't panicked when Trump told him he wanted to release the call transcript was because the president had tapped a convincing interlocutor. Pat Cipollone, whom McConnell's team respected, had personally assured their office that the call record was innocuous and would clear Trump's name. Cipollone might have been more of a true believer in Trump than McConnell, but the Senate leader didn't know him to be a liar.

"If you and your lawyers think it's 'perfect,' then go ahead and release it," McConnell told the president.

Once the transcript was out, McConnell realized "perfect" was a far cry from how he would have described it. For a sitting president to ask another world leader to probe his top political adversary was an alarming misuse of authority. McConnell knew instantly that there were bound to be consequences, possible legal trouble, and maybe even an impeachment, as his counsel predicted.

"Do everything possible to learn as much about impeachment as you can," he told his staff. "This is plausible enough grounds that Pelosi may not have a choice. We need to be ready."

In the dozen years that he and Pelosi had faced off, McConnell had developed a keen understanding of how she operated. Pelosi had won her first speakership in 2007, the same year Senate Republicans selected McConnell to be the Senate GOP conference leader. Both were master tacticians and stubborn negotiators. Above all they were survivors, having maintained unchecked authority over their respective congressional quadrants even as leadership of the Senate Democrats and House Republicans changed hands.

McConnell knew that while Pelosi had long disdained impeachment, once she started the process, she was sure to finish it. The best McConnell could hope for was that if House Democrats did proceed, they'd do so based on flimsy and inconclusive evidence that wouldn't be convincing to voters. That would enable him to discredit their case at trial, allowing him to steer the Senate toward a quick acquittal without requiring his members to take any politically difficult votes.

But the document before him would make that challenging. Trump's request that a foreign government probe Biden, a former Senate colleague whom McConnell and many others deeply respected, had thrown a live grenade into McConnell's Senate. It would be up to him to keep it from exploding.

In the spring of 1973, McConnell was an ambitious thirty-one-year-old attorney and the newly elected chairman of the Republican Party of Kentucky's Jefferson County when Richard Nixon was exposed as a crook and a liar. The young Republican Kentuckian knew back then that his party leader had done something "unconscionable" and said so publicly.[4] Nearly half a century later, McConnell was once again troubled by his president's ethical lapse. But having risen to become the second-most powerful Republican in the country, he had also become a cynical realist. His chief objective was no longer declaring what was moral but preserving his slim Senate majority through the next election.

With only a three-seat advantage, McConnell was already facing an uphill battle in the looming 2020 election. He knew right away that the Ukraine controversy could jeopardize his vulnerable centrist members facing reelection from Maine to Arizona. It was only the rare Republican who could break away from Trump and survive. Most of those who had tried—such as former senators Jeff Flake of Arizona and Bob Corker of Tennessee—ended up incurring so much wrath from the president's base that it drove them to early retirement.

If the House impeached Trump, McConnell knew he would have no choice but to conduct a Senate trial, and it was sure to be as vicious and divisive as anything that had ever transpired in the chamber. Senators would be forced to take a position on the president's guilt or innocence. If they voted to acquit Trump, they risked being pilloried for aiding and abetting the president, but if they turned on him, the base would never forgive them.

As the transcript made its way onto most computer and smartphone screens on the Capitol grounds, McConnell's phone began ringing off the hook, as several of his senators called, appalled by what they had read. *Why had Trump released this?* they wanted to know. *How were they supposed to explain it?* Their shock was a stark contrast to the shrugging reaction that Jordan, McCarthy, and the rest of the House Republicans had that same morning. Some senators even asked McConnell if they should speak out against Trump's misconduct.

"Don't box yourself in until you know all the facts," McConnell cautioned them, suggesting they keep their concerns to themselves. It was how the leader had learned to handle almost every crisis of the Trump presidency. McConnell had had plenty of disagreements with the president, but he kept their arguments private—and encouraged his rank and file to do the same.

Yet in the face of impeachment, the usually stoic leader did not follow his own advice. That night, he publicly dismissed the mounting criticism of Trump's call with Zelensky, saying in a statement that it was "laughable to think this is anywhere close to an impeachable offense."

"If this is the 'launching point' for House Democrats' impeachment process, they've already overplayed their hand," McConnell said. "It's clear there is no quid pro quo that the Democrats were desperately praying for."

He added nothing about his own simmering doubts—or the fact that his office was already bracing for the worst: an attempt to oust Trump.

When Trump called McConnell to ask for his reaction, however, the leader was candid. "This call is not perfect," he told him pointblank. "And you are going to get in deep trouble for it."

Across the Rotunda, Pelosi sat before her leadership team, gesturing to an imposing portrait nailed to the wall beside her. The painting of Abraham Lincoln had become a staple of Pelosi's office years ago. Before pivotal moments in her career, the Speaker would habitually nod to the portrait and lecture the members and staff gathered in the room about the importance of justifying their work to voters. The self-educated sixteenth president, she would remind them, was a visionary not just because he steered the country through the Civil

War, but because of his ability to rally public support behind revolutionary ideas.

"'Public sentiment is everything. With public sentiment, nothing can fail. Without it, nothing can succeed,'" Pelosi said soberly, reciting Lincoln's words from an 1858 presidential debate[5] and concluding: "We have to educate the public."

Ironically, Pelosi was about to lay out a strategy that would do nothing of the sort.

In her rush to embrace impeachment, Pelosi had committed the House to an inquiry with no specific parameters or goals—and Republicans had not been the only ones to notice. During a Democratic conference meeting the night before, a fight had broken out between her members over what exactly their strategy should look like and how broadly or narrowly they should cast their investigative net.

Jerry Nadler, the chairman of the Judiciary Committee, had argued impeachment investigators should pursue allegations of multiple Trump crimes, including the obstruction of justice evidenced in Mueller's report. They should build the strongest case possible, he insisted, leaving no stone unturned in their effort to persuade the public Trump needed ousting.

But frontline Democrat Elissa Slotkin had pushed back before the entire room. Rising from her chair, she argued that moderate Democrats who had put their political careers on the line needed a focused investigative strategy.

"If you are asking us to stay on message, give us a goddamn message to stay on!" she barked.[6]

It was clear to Pelosi that her moderates wanted an impeachment process that would be tightly focused on the one thing that had moved them to embrace impeachment—Ukraine—and not on any of the Mueller allegations that had barely resonated in districts like theirs. And they wanted things to move quickly. They certainly didn't want to be stuck talking about impeachment on the 2020 campaign trail.

Neither did Pelosi. She had talked about impeachment as a constitutional obligation in her televised speech, but privately she was fearful of getting bogged down in it. Pelosi knew that Trump would fight them at every turn of their investigation, as he had in every other probe of his business or personal affairs. And experience had taught her that the longer it took to investigate the president, the more inured the public became to the shocking nature of his actions. Fresher revelations would create more momentum, Pelosi calculated. She had even discussed with her chairmen the idea of bypassing public impeachment hearings entirely to speed things along.

Pelosi's vulnerable members from swing districts had one last demand, however, that wasn't so easy to accommodate: They wanted Nadler out of the picture. To them, the Judiciary Committee's members—not only Nadler but Jamie Raskin and his crew of "musketeers" who had been gunning to start impeaching Trump for months—were too liberal to be the face of their effort. If they were going to stick their necks out, the frontliners wanted the chairman they had come to trust—Adam Schiff—leading the charge.

It was, on its face, an unorthodox request. The Judiciary Committee was the traditional forum in which the House carried out impeachment proceedings. To wrest it out of the panel's hands would be an affront to both Nadler and committee members such as Raskin, who were arguably Congress's most knowledgeable constitutional experts. But Pelosi was sympathetic to the frontliners' push. In fact, she had floated a similar idea herself the previous Sunday, sounding out her investigative chairmen on a "special committee" similar to the Watergate panel Democrats created to investigate Nixon in the 1970s. It would have enabled her to pack the panel with trusted

allies like Adam Schiff and easily sideline Nadler. The Judiciary
Committee chairman, sensing a threat to his turf, had quashed the
idea right away, even whipping up an outside lobbying campaign to
pressure Pelosi to drop it.

But Wednesday morning, Trump's decision to release the transcript had given Pelosi the perfect excuse to buck tradition and put
the House's fledgling impeachment in Schiff's hands, just like she
and her moderate members wanted. The call record clearly fell under the purview of Schiff's Intelligence Committee and within the
parameters of the Ukraine investigation he had already launched.
As long as the House effort stayed focused on Ukraine and didn't
wade into Trump's other alleged misdeeds, Pelosi could easily justify putting Schiff at the helm.

Pelosi called a meeting with her investigative chairs and top
leaders to discuss the idea of focusing impeachment entirely on
Ukraine—and leaving all the other probes by the wayside. Nadler,
unsurprisingly, balked, pointing out that Trump had arguably committed several other impeachable offenses that they couldn't simply
ignore. Majority Leader Steny Hoyer and Oversight chairman Elijah Cummings firmly agreed with Nadler. But House Intelligence
chairman Adam Schiff sided with Pelosi and the frontliners, giving
an articulate defense for a simple, focused message. By the time
they left the room, everyone knew where the impeachment was
headed—and it wasn't moving in the direction Nadler wanted. The
Judiciary chairman looked defeated as his aides pulled him and Foreign Affairs chairman Eliot Engel into a small kitchenette in Pelosi's
suite for a download after the meeting.

"It's *beshert*," Engel said, putting an arm around Nadler's shoulder
and trying to comfort him with a Yiddish expression that translated
to "it's destiny."[7]

It was then that Pelosi sent out an emergency summons to her full leadership team, so she could lay out her new plan. House Democrats, she told them, would pursue an "expeditious," limited impeachment inquiry focused specifically and only on the president's actions with Ukraine. Schiff would lead it, she added, with the purpose of projecting a single, simple narrative that Trump had tried to use Ukraine to cheat in the 2020 election. It was a message that would resonate with voters, Pelosi argued, and armed with the transcript, a clean kill shot. If Democrats moved quickly, they might even be able to wrap everything up by the holidays, freeing up all of 2020 for campaigning on the pocketbook issues voters actually cared about.

"Let's strike while the iron's hot," Pelosi told the room. "Now is the moment."

The leadership team that had spent months bickering over impeachment was unanimously supportive. Even the Judiciary Committee faction of Raskin and his "musketeers" happily agreed to hand the reins over to Schiff. They were getting to impeach Trump at long last; that was all that mattered.

"This is totally consistent with what Trump did before, but it's a much better case because it's happening in real time," Raskin rationalized. "He's basically admitted the crime himself."

"Just don't let this drag out like the Mueller investigation," fellow "musketeer" David Cicilline warned Pelosi.

Pelosi went around the table to poll each of them on her pitch. Person after person nodded their agreement to focus on Ukraine alone. It was done.

Pelosi may not have realized it at that moment, but her two overriding priorities during impeachment—galvanizing public support and protecting her majority—would collide in a matter of days. Fast-tracking impeachment would please frontliners like Slotkin and Spanberger, but it would leave little time for the mass public education campaign Democrats needed to make sure the public understood what they were doing. The story of Trump's attempt to exploit Ukraine was not actually the simple and digestible message House Democrats had convinced themselves it was. Most Americans had trouble finding Ukraine on a map; guiding them through the thicket of Ukraine's history battling Moscow's influence and post-Soviet corruption—and using that to articulate why Trump should no longer be president—was going to be a nightmare, especially on Pelosi's timetable.

PART TWO

12

THE RISE OF SCHIFF

SEPTEMBER 25–27, 2019

When Nancy Pelosi tapped Adam Schiff to lead the House's impeachment probe, she wasn't just asking him to spearhead a once-in-a-generation undertaking. She was asking him to do something that had never been done in the history of Congress—and Schiff knew it. It would be up to him, a fifty-nine-year-old former federal prosecutor who represented Hollywood, to find the facts that could persuade the public—and a majority of Congress—that Trump deserved to be forced out of office. And making matters more complicated, he would be doing it alone.

In both the Nixon and Clinton impeachments, Congress had roadmaps to follow in the form of substantial investigative reports issued by Special Prosecutor Leon Jaworski and Independent Counsel Ken Starr. But no outside prosecutor had ever been tasked to look into Trump's Ukraine gambit, meaning House Democrats would be taking the unprecedented step of conducting an impeachment investigation and producing an evidentiary record from scratch.

That was no simple task considering the man Schiff was investigating. Trump, after all, had successfully stymied every Hill investigation against him to date. In fact, Schiff and Pelosi had privately worked out a contingency plan: If the president grounded their probe to a halt, they would simply impeach him for obstructing a congressional investigation.

So it had come as something of a shock to Schiff when Trump abruptly announced on September 24 that he would release the transcript of his call with Ukrainian president Volodymyr Zelensky. Did that mean the call was innocuous? Were Democrats getting out over their skis? Schiff had no idea. Neither did his staff.

"If the president is going to proactively release this, it has to be because it really isn't that bad," his investigations director, Dan Goldman, warned dourly as he filed into Schiff's office in the basement of the Capitol on the morning of September 25, where they had gathered to wait for the transcript to be released.

"What if it's just gibberish?" his general counsel Maher Bitar wondered aloud.

Moments after the transcript was posted online, Rheanne Wirkkala, Schiff's deputy investigations director, ran into Schiff's office with printouts exclaiming: "I have it!"—and the aides who had gathered began furiously scouring the pages. Schiff was stunned. It was, in his estimation, as damning an account as he could have asked for—and plenty of evidence to make his case.

"Holy shit!" he cried out, his staff echoing the sentiment. "I can't believe they would release this! . . . This is how a mob boss talks!"

By that point in his career, Schiff had established himself as one of the president's chief public foils. He was a regular on cable networks and Sunday talk shows and relished his role as the face of the Democratic opposition to Trump. Since Trump took office, Schiff had been using his airtime not only to blast Trump for his ethical lapses and misdeeds, but also to warn the country that the president was capable and likely guilty of even worse crimes.

As he read the transcript, Schiff felt vindicated. Finally, he thought, he had proof in his hands. He whipped out his laptop, opened his Twitter account, and took what he thought was a clean shot at the subject of his new investigation.

"The transcript of the call reads like a classic mob shakedown," he typed. "Nice country you got there. It would be a shame if something happened to her."

In that moment, it didn't occur to Schiff that as leader of the nascent impeachment probe—which promised to be one of the most contentious investigations in congressional history—he might need to adopt a different tone.

He hit send.

In the 1970s, during the Watergate years, Democratic congressional leaders specifically chose members with bipartisan street cred to lead their probes of Nixon. At that time, there hadn't been an effort to remove a president in over a century. And the one precedent available—the three-day whirlwind indictment of President Andrew Johnson in 1868—wasn't exactly seen as a model to follow. The first impeachment had been an extremely partisan, hasty, and ultimately embarrassing affair for Congress. Lawmakers actually passed the articles of impeachment before they had even been written.[1]

Party leaders of Nixon's time wanted to avoid a repeat of that—particularly because Americans did not support an effort to oust the president when the congressional investigations into the Watergate affair began.[2] In the Senate, which launched its probe first in 1973, Democratic leaders shot down a push by the left to install Senator Ted Kennedy at the helm of the chamber's investigation. They

feared that if the outspoken Nixon and Watergate critic—whom the
party had previously floated to potentially challenge Nixon's 1972
reelection—became the face of the probe, it would fuel the president's charges that the whole investigation was a "witch hunt."[3]
Instead, they tapped Senator Sam Ervin, a Harvard Law School–
educated conservative Democrat from North Carolina, who loved
to refer to himself as a simple "country lawyer" and was admired by
both parties for his straight talk, candor, and wit.[4]

When House Democrats launched their own Watergate impeachment proceedings in 1974, Judiciary Committee chairman Peter
Rodino also immediately recognized the importance of maintaining
that bipartisan aura. One of his first moves was to fire his own staff
counsel, who had a reputation for being too unapologetically liberal.
In his place, Rodino hired a GOP prosecutor and wrote the investigation rules with Republican buy-in. He instructed his committee
to refer to their hunt for evidence as an effort to discover "information" so as not to upset GOP members who still supported Nixon.
And he made a point of pushing back on liberal Democratic panel
members.[5]

The effort paid off. Over the course of several months, Rodino
earned the trust of his GOP colleagues; one even reflected later that
Rodino "bent over backwards to be fair."[6] In the end, many Republicans came to support Nixon's impeachment, a bipartisan showing
that pushed the president to resign before the House could vote to
indict him.

Adam Schiff, however, was no Peter Rodino or Sam Ervin. And
he didn't even try to be.

While Schiff's frequent attacks on Trump over the years made
him the darling of the left, by the time talk of impeachment came
about, he held virtually no credibility with Republicans. In early
2017 he had claimed to have seen—via his access to classified information on the House Intelligence Committee that others were

not privy to—"more than circumstantial evidence" that Trump had colluded with Russia to win the 2016 election.[7] In 2018, he had argued that the special counsel's Russia probe was of "a size and scope probably beyond Watergate."[8] His claims drove Republicans crazy, but with Mueller's investigative work under wraps, hidden from the public, there was little they could do to disprove them.

When Mueller completed his report, finding that the evidence against Trump "was not sufficient to support criminal charges,"[9] Republicans finally had their answer to Schiff—and went into revenge mode. They demanded he resign as Intelligence Committee chairman for having misled the public about what he saw, arguing that "we have no faith in your ability to discharge your duties in a manner consistent with your constitutional responsibility."[10]

To Schiff, the criticism was unfounded. He considered himself bipartisan and reasonable,[11] and thought the GOP was either too intoxicated by Trump to see right from wrong—or too afraid to follow their consciences. Instead of taking a lesson from the episode, Schiff refused to apologize, doubling down and excoriating Republicans for turning a blind eye to the unethical offenses detailed in the Mueller report, including Trump's own son meeting with Russian officials offering dirt on Hillary Clinton.

His lectures, unsurprisingly, fell on deaf ears. The president only further singled Schiff out as a favorite target, dubbing him "pencil-neck Adam Schiff" for his slight frame, one of several insulting nicknames he would invent for the chairman. Trump's base resumed attacking him with fresh vitriol, leading to a steady stream of death threats. And even moderate GOP lawmakers began to view Schiff as blinded by a self-righteous, anti-Trump fervor.

Schiff's obvious shortfalls with Republicans and GOP voters didn't faze the one person who mattered most when Democrats launched their historic impeachment effort: Nancy Pelosi. Despite waxing eloquent about moving public sentiment on impeachment, what Pelosi actually wanted was an impeachment leader she could trust—and Schiff had always been that guy.

Pelosi had personally recruited Schiff to run for Congress in the aftermath of Clinton's impeachment, helping him fundraise in what would become one of the most expensive House races at that time.[12] After becoming leader, she had big ambitions in store for her protégé. Before he came to Congress, Schiff had gained a measure of notoriety by becoming the first prosecutor in the country to nail an FBI agent for selling intelligence to the Soviets. So when the House launched a probe into the CIA for destroying taped inter-rogations of al Qaeda suspects in 2007, the newly minted Speaker asked Schiff to take on a role on the panel.

"I thought about you because of your investigative experience," Pelosi told Schiff, cornering him one day across the hallway from the House chamber. "Why don't you think about whether you'd like to be on the committee?"

"I just did," Schiff replied instantaneously. "The answer is yes."

In the years since, Pelosi had tapped Schiff to shepherd the Dem-ocratic Party through several dicey matters at the intersection of intelligence and politics. In 2014, she appointed him to serve on the GOP panel investigating the 2012 terrorist attack on the U.S. consulate in Benghazi, Libya, which swiftly became a forum for at-tacking Hillary Clinton, the party's likely 2016 presidential nomi-nee. Several months later, she picked him to be the top Democrat on the House Intelligence Committee. When Trump came to town, Pelosi backed Schiff in demanding the Intelligence panel's top Re-publican, Devin Nunes of California, recuse himself from the com-mittee's Russia investigation after he was caught coordinating with the White House to influence the committee's work.[13] And when the once-functional Intelligence panel became partisan scorched earth, Pelosi didn't flinch, defending and deferring to Schiff with even more dedication. The two had become so close, in fact, that fellow Democrats referred to them as the backbone of Congress's "California Mafia."

Throughout 2019, Schiff had made a point of remaining in lock-step with the Speaker on oversight matters, especially when other chairmen privately challenged her. He had taken her side for months as she battled Nadler and the left's insatiable demands for impeachment. When he finally reached his own tipping point on the matter, he had pressed his case to the Speaker privately, taking pains never to cross her in public. The careful strategy, and his years-long ability to read and defer to Pelosi, had given Schiff what the other chairmen lacked: Pelosi's trust. So when the Ukraine scandal began to eclipse all other efforts to investigate Trump, it was not a hard decision for Pelosi: Schiff got the nod to lead the probe.

What Schiff and Pelosi did not appreciate was that while their alliance suited them both, it would handicap the Speaker's hope for a "bipartisan" probe from the get-go. Schiff might have been a hero among Democrats, but he had no sway with the right—he hadn't for years. And his opening moves in the impeachment probe would only remind Republicans how much they hated him.

At 9:12 a.m. on Thursday, September 26, a silence fell over the large committee room in the Rayburn House Office Building as Schiff banged his gavel to open the House Democrats' first Ukraine-related hearing. Facing him from behind a long wooden table was Joseph Maguire, the acting director of national intelligence whom Schiff had been battling for weeks to obtain the whistleblower's report—and who had finally released it to the panel just the night before. The hearing was getting off to a slightly late start in part so Schiff could share a declassified version of the report with the public. Now, from the top-center leatherbound seat on the dais, all eyes were on him as the nation looked to the Intelligence leader to make sense of the strange happenings in Washington.

Before becoming a congressman, Schiff had dabbled at writing screenplays and even made one attempt at a spy novel. While working as an assistant U.S. attorney in Los Angeles, he had written a courtroom drama called "Minotaur," about a young prosecutor who tried a murder case while someone committed an identical crime.[14] When he came to Congress, he indulged his flair for the dramatic in his opening statements. Writing them himself, he would map out his orations like film scripts: in scenes, making sure his audience always got a visual, visceral feeling of what he was describing. The more gripping the story, he believed, the more successfully he could make his case. And few subjects in Schiff's career had lent themselves to storytelling as well as Trump's alleged attempts to solicit foreign interference in successive elections.

The night before the hearing, Schiff had worked on his statement from his office, where a stack of framed posters of James Bond films and *The Hunt for Red October* waited to be hung on the wall. The Ukraine call record, he thought, was the perfect script to make his case—proof that Trump, after shaking off the Mueller probe, immediately resumed his habit of soliciting foreign favors to manipulate American elections. All he needed to do was sell it.

"It reads like a classic organized crime shakedown . . . This is the essence of what the President communicates," Schiff said in his opening statement the next morning, as he began paraphrasing the call with hyperbolic flair. "We've been very good to your country. Very good. No other country has done as much as we have. But you know what? I don't see much reciprocity here. I hear what you want. I have a favor I want from you, though. And I'm going to say this only seven times, so you better listen good: I want you to make up dirt on my political opponent. Understand?"

It was a script fit for Marlon Brando—and, Schiff argued, "in sum and character what the President was trying to communicate with the president of Ukraine."

"It would be funny if it wasn't such a graphic betrayal of the President's oath of office," Schiff continued. "It is instead the most consequential form of tragedy, for it forces us to confront the remedy the Founders provided for such a flagrant abuse of office. Impeachment."

Schiff didn't know it at the moment, but he had just handed Republicans a sharpened knife to wield against him—one they would use for the rest of the impeachment investigation. It didn't matter that Schiff had said explicitly that he was putting his own gloss on the president's call. His opening statement went viral on Twitter as Republicans across Washington seized on Schiff's words and accused him of contorting Trump's call in a naked bid to poison the public's perception of it.

The backlash began right there in the hearing room. Mike Turner, a moderate Republican from Ohio, had come to the hearing planning to condemn Trump—and only Trump—for a phone call he deemed "not okay" and "disappointing to the American public." But after Schiff's comments, Turner turned his ire on the chairman and ended up defending Trump as wrongfully maligned.

"While the chairman was speaking, I actually had someone text me: 'Is he just making this up?'" Turner said, glaring at Schiff and accusing him of trying to mislead the public with his opening statement. "And, yes, he was, because sometimes fiction is better than the actual words."

"Luckily the American public are smart and they have the transcript. They've read the conversation," Turner said. "They know when someone's just making it up."

No one was more pleased with Schiff's flub than Trump himself. The president had spent the morning at a breakfast for the U.S. Mission to the United Nations, railing against the whistleblower as "almost a spy" who was guilty of treason. But when he heard from his congressional allies about Schiff's dramatic rendition, he turned his fire back to his favorite target.

"Rep. Adam Schiff fraudulently read to Congress, with millions of people watching, a version of my conversation with the President of Ukraine that doesn't exist," Trump wrote of "Liddle' Adam Schiff" on Twitter. "HE WAS DESPERATE AND HE GOT CAUGHT. . . . I am calling for him to immediately resign from Congress based on this fraud!"

Schiff didn't apologize for his mob-boss rendition of the call. Instead, he shook off the attacks—even when the president accused him of treason that weekend.[15] In his view, it was just more ginned-up, faux Republican outrage and pearl clutching, a sorry and shameful bid to distract from the serious topic at hand.

"Better he make something out of nothing," Schiff reassured himself.

13

"KEEP YOUR POWDER DRY"

Kevin McCarthy was shoveling down a quick dinner during a layover in the Denver Airport on Friday, September 27, when his phone started buzzing with alarming news. Congressman Mark Amodei, a pragmatic and chatty Nevada Republican, had signaled to reporters that he supported Democrats' impeachment inquiry—and his comments were tearing through the internet.

"What I want to know is: Were rules broken?"[1] Amodei had said to Nevada reporters, suggesting the investigative committees should "get to work" looking into the matter.

"Using government agencies to, if it's proven, to put your finger on the scale of an election, I don't think that's right," Amodei had said, declaring himself a "big fan" of oversight in such situations. "If it turns out that it's something along those lines, then there's a problem."[2]

There certainly was a problem all right, McCarthy thought to himself as he read the story. *Was he crazy? Trump would flip when he saw those comments.* McCarthy knew the president would come after Amodei with guns blazing—and that he might even turn his fire on McCarthy himself. The president had already harangued GOP Senator Mitt Romney for saying publicly that his request that Zelensky "do us a favor" was "deeply troubling"—a sentiment that many Republicans privately agreed with. If Trump saw Amodei's comments as a sign that there were House Republicans sympathetic to the Democrats' impeachment effort, McCarthy knew he'd never hear the end of it.

But Amodei's comments presented another, arguably more pressing problem, McCarthy realized: They could inspire other moderate Republicans to follow his lead and begin chiding the president, dividing the party at a time when Trump's presidency was on the line. So McCarthy picked up his phone to quash the sentiment fast.

Amodei had to pull his four-wheeler off on the side of a mountain trail eight thousand feet above sea level to answer McCarthy's call. Gazing out over the peaks and valleys of the Sierra Nevada, Amodei heard the alarm in McCarthy's voice and quickly sought to explain himself.

"No, I was not trying to endorse impeachment," he protested. "I just support a probe to look into the matter."

Amodei, a fifth-term lawmaker who had come to Congress after a long career in the state legislature, was confused by McCarthy's anger. To him, endorsing an investigation wasn't inconsistent with supporting Trump; the congressman for Nevada's sole remaining Republican district had served as the president's 2016 state campaign chair. But his intentions had clearly gotten lost in translation. National outlets like the *New York Times* had posted stories fingering Amodei as the first Republican to support Trump's ouster.[3] Angry Republicans had taken to Amodei's Facebook page to call him a "traitor." And even the White House was directly pressuring him to recant.

When White House chief of staff Mick Mulvaney had called asking, "What's going on?" Amodei had tried to stand his ground. "Listen, Mick, I stand by what I said: If someone uses their office for that, then I got a problem with that—but they have to prove it." But by the time McCarthy got in touch with Amodei, even the usually confident congressman was beginning to doubt himself.

"Oh, man, I screwed up," Amodei told McCarthy, who assured him he understood what the congressman was trying to say. But the backlash, McCarthy warned, would continue to worsen until he walked the comments back.

"Why don't you put out a statement clarifying your comments," McCarthy suggested. Amodei assured him his team was already on it.

A few hours later, Amodei's team released a statement saying: "In no way, shape, or form, did I indicate support for impeachment."

Years before, it wouldn't have been unusual for a member of a president's own party to endorse congressional scrutiny of his actions. During Clinton's impeachment, many senior Democrats—including then–House Minority Leader Dick Gephardt—initially endorsed congressional efforts to fully investigate the allegations that he had lied under oath to cover up his affair with Monica Lewinsky. Clinton was furious, but his frustration did little to dissuade other Democratic members from publicly rebuking his actions as "immoral" and "disgraceful."[4]

Trump, however, had turned his party into a nativist extension of his PR machine. He demanded nothing less than unwavering loyalty—and pummeled those who fell out of line. Knowing that, McCarthy, who wanted to avoid such confrontations with the president, had decided to do the pummeling for him in Amodei's case.

Amodei's very public backpedaling sent a tacit message to other moderates that they too would be yanked back quickly if they dared express doubts about the president's innocence.

Still, McCarthy worried. If the Ukraine allegations had given pause to Amodei, a Trump supporter, then how much harder would it be to keep all nearly two hundred Republicans—including moderates who had never truly embraced the president—in line?

Of all the paths taken by congressional Republicans who came to thoroughly embrace Trump, McCarthy's was among the most perplexing. The tall, silver-haired son of a firefighter hailed from humble beginnings in Bakersfield, a town known as the "armpit" of California's heavily polluted Central Valley. McCarthy, who had dropped out of community college after winning a $5,000 lottery prize that he used to open a sandwich shop, eventually put himself through business school by selling his small deli. That was when he went to volunteer for California congressman Bill Thomas,[5] a moderate Republican who would eventually inspire McCarthy's own run for public office.[6]

For his whole political career, McCarthy had counted himself a centrist. He privately deplored the rise of the Tea Party movement and frequently butted heads with hardliners in his conference, including Jim Jordan. Some on the right even dubbed him a RINO, "Republican in Name Only," while conservative talk radio hosts lumped him into their regular screeds against GOP leadership.

McCarthy began to reassess his feelings about his party's right flank in 2015, after Speaker John Boehner suddenly retired. McCarthy, then the No. 2 House Republican, saw a perfect opportunity to rise up and claim the gavel. But the conservatives he had spent his career scorning banded together to stop his ascent. Their blocking move was a devastating—and embarrassing—defeat for McCarthy. He realized that in order to become Speaker someday, he'd have to find a way to win the hardliners and the GOP base.

When Trump declared his candidacy for president, McCarthy decided to exploit the moment to ingratiate himself to the GOP's conservative base. Paul Ryan, who had succeeded Boehner as Speaker after McCarthy's stumble, had alienated Trump and infuriated the GOP base by criticizing the nominee's attacks on Latinos, Black people, and women. Sensing an opening, McCarthy decided to befriend the real estate tycoon, who he predicted would prove a powerful political ally—and who could shield him from the anger of the right. He reached out and began offering the surging presidential candidate political advice, filling the void Ryan left open.

McCarthy stayed loyal to Trump, even when the *Access Hollywood* video of Trump boasting that he could "grab" women's privates went viral just days before the election. The GOP leader worked behind the scenes to ensure the party apparatus stuck with Trump: he convinced Ryan and several other GOP leaders to fight their urge to abandon Trump's candidacy, earning the lasting gratitude of the soon-to-be president. By the time he took office, McCarthy and Trump were speaking on the phone several times a day. The president affectionately began referring to him as "my Kevin."

The episode solidified yet another lesson for the new GOP leader: The key to survival was unity. No matter how bad things got, no matter how bad the accusation against Trump, the GOP leader believed his party would prevail if his members weathered the storm together. McCarthy was even more convinced of his own wisdom after the 2018 midterm election, when dozens of moderate Republicans who publicly criticized Trump lost their seats to Democrats after the Republican base abandoned them.

When Ryan retired and McCarthy became House Minority Leader, he turned into something of a backstage enforcer for Trump. He didn't scold, lecture, or yell at his members. But he used his personal connections and friendships with the Republican rank and file to cajole even the most politically vulnerable frontliners to stick with Trump publicly, and voice their concerns only in private. Meanwhile, he carefully ensured he never got on Trump's bad side, even sending him jars of red and pink Starburst—his two favorite colors of the chewy candy—to please him.[7]

The tactics inspired jeers that McCarthy was nothing more than a lapdog for the president, even privately from some of his own members. Several implored McCarthy to take a stand against Trump in the summer of 2019, when the president told four congresswomen of color to "go back" to their countries of origin—though all were citizens and only one was born outside the U.S. Even many of the GOP's most conservative members told McCarthy they could not condone blatant racism. But McCarthy refused, telling one of the troubled Republicans, Paul Mitchell of Michigan, that Trump did not take well to being lectured—so why bother? Mitchell was so disgusted with McCarthy that a few days later, he announced his decision to retire.

By the time impeachment rolled around, McCarthy had a firmly established reputation as a Trump apologist. He embraced that role, firmly believing that it would pay off in the long run when he became Speaker someday.

The GOP leader had initially assumed defending Trump through the Ukraine controversy would be easier than tiptoeing around his past racist comments. He, like Jordan, had believed the White House's claim that the July 25 call record was innocuous. But that reprieve didn't last long. The weekend after the Amodei hubbub, it became clear to McCarthy that he had dramatically underestimated how much of a political challenge impeachment was about to pose for Trump—and how far his party would be dragged down with him.

As he was walking his Australian shepherd Mac back in California that weekend, McCarthy realized he needed to come up with a plan. The initial rollout of the president's defense was proving to be a disaster. Everywhere House Republicans went, reporters were sticking microphones in their faces to ask: *Is it appropriate for a president to ask a foreign government to investigate a political rival?* The obvious answer was no. McCarthy, however, had instructed his members to reject the premise of the question outright and refuse to weigh in until they knew all the facts.

"Keep your powder dry," he told them.

But as leader, McCarthy knew he couldn't keep avoiding the questions forever. During a Thursday press conference with reporters, he had stuck to White House talking points, accusing the whistleblower of having no firsthand evidence of what he was talking about. He had blasted Schiff for freelancing during his opening statement at Maguire's hearing. And he had accused Pelosi of being irresponsible for launching into impeachment "without one bit of evidence" or a formal endorsement from the House.

"Tell me one thing in there that's impeachable," he had challenged the press. "Tell me one thing."

Part of McCarthy's defense involved spinning pure fiction. He tried to argue that "the president did not ask to investigate Joe Biden"—though anyone who read the transcript could see Trump had done exactly that. When a reporter called him out on the discrepancy, McCarthy initially accused him of "misstating" the text in the document, before acknowledging the exchange but claiming it was "totally lawful."

McCarthy similarly put his foot in his mouth during a *60 Minutes* interview that aired that weekend. When host Scott Pelley asked him what he thought of Trump's words to Zelensky, "I would like you to do us a favor though," McCarthy appeared surprised.

"You just added another word," he said accusingly.

"No, it's in the transcript," Pelley responded.

"He said, 'I'd like you to do a favor though'?" McCarthy asked, momentarily confused.

"Yes, it's in the White House transcript," the anchor replied, confused by McCarthy's apparent confusion.

As McCarthy floundered, the political sands of impeachment were shifting. That weekend a poll from NPR, *PBS NewsHour*, and Marist found that 49 percent of Americans supported the impeachment inquiry while 46 percent disapproved—the first time that more Americans had backed impeachment than not.[8] A CBS poll that Sunday was even more worrisome for Republicans, finding 55 percent of Americans supported the inquiry.[9] Moderate Democrats who had run from impeachment were suddenly in a full-fledged embrace of it, gloating that public opinion was on their side. And some Republican politicians outside Washington were starting to join the parade too: two Republican governors—Vermont's governor Phil Scott and Massachusetts's governor Charlie Baker—had publicly backed the impeachment inquiry that Thursday.

McCarthy knew his members saw the winds changing. Moderate Republicans were privately reaching out seeking guidance on how to handle the situation. Conservatives, under pressure from Trump to defend him on television, were equally confused about how to offer a credible defense of the president. McCarthy didn't have a good answer. After a few days of reeling, he had come to realize that Republicans were not going to win the impeachment battle on the merits. And the GOP would lose the political war if they didn't reframe the debate.

"If we stay quiet, people are going to assume what [the Democrats] are saying is true," he said to himself. "We need to lean in . . . otherwise the narrative will set in the other way."

McCarthy had always believed that the greatest defense was to go on offense. He needed to find a way for his party to go on the attack. The question was: *How?*

In 1998, House Democrats successfully turned the nation against the GOP's effort to oust President Bill Clinton through a spin campaign that cast Clinton as the victim of an unfair prosecution. Though Clinton had all but admitted to lying under oath about his affair with Monica Lewinsky—the charge at the basis of his impeachment—Democrats argued that the president's impeachers were depriving him of rights and strong-arming the minority in a zealous bid to take him down. Never mind that Republicans, led by House Judiciary chairman Henry Hyde, had copied the celebrated Peter Rodino Watergate procedures nearly word for word.[10] Democrats made a series of additional demands they knew Republicans would reject in a bid to paint their counterparts as unjust, while mustering faux outrage that Republicans were being unreasonable. They dubbed the procedural straw man strategy "win by losing."[11]

That weekend, McCarthy was feeling similarly inspired. He started listing in his head all the procedural oddities of the probe the House Democrats had just launched. No House vote? No rules laid out for the minority? And what about the rights of the president? In previous impeachments, presidents had been allowed to call witnesses and participate in the proceedings through counsel. Democrats hadn't said anything about whether Trump's team would be afforded the same courtesy—or whether the minority would ever get a chance to subpoena witnesses of their own.

An assault on the process, the leader mused as he walked his dog, might be the GOP's best bet. It would be an uphill battle trying to convince all of his rank and file that Trump was innocent. But it was a relatively simpler task to argue that the president would never get a fair shake in a probe Adam Schiff was leading. Every Republican believed in the concept of a fair trial, McCarthy reasoned. If he could convince them that the Democrats were running an inherently unfair investigation, even his most anti-Trump Republicans could justify opposing it.

The GOP leader called his top counsel and instructed her to start drafting a list of procedural complaints with the Democrats' investigation. He told her to put them in a letter to Pelosi, demanding that she suspend Trump's impeachment investigation "until transparent and equitable rules and procedures are established to govern the inquiry."[12]

McCarthy knew that sending a public letter was risky. If Pelosi called his bluff and held a vote that met his demands, he knew there was a strong chance at least some House Republicans would vote for it. In 1998, thirty-one House Democrats had joined forces with the GOP in a vote to begin proceedings against their own party leader following the release of Ken Starr's salacious report, even though only five ultimately voted to impeach him.[13] In 1974, all but four GOP House lawmakers had voted to authorize the inquiry against Nixon following the Senate's Watergate hearings[14]—though few, at that moment, actually supported the idea of recommending his ouster.

But McCarthy was desperate for something to unify his members. Many Republicans were still struggling to reconcile their personal revulsion at Trump's actions with the ever-present pull from the base to remain loyal to the president. He bet—correctly—that Pelosi would be too afraid of foisting such a vote on vulnerable moderate Democrats to take that bait. That left him an open road to paint the entire impeachment as a sham. And it would give Republicans a script to talk about something other than the merits of what Trump had said and done.

14

SPIN FACTORY

OCTOBER 2-4, 2019

Jim Jordan put on his game face as his office hummed with nervous energy. Surrounding him were some of Trump's most aggressive Hill allies: Jordan's best friend and fellow House Freedom Caucus rabble-rouser Mark Meadows, and Lee Zeldin of New York and Scott Perry of Pennsylvania, two early Trump endorsers in the 2016 campaign. Most of them were petrified.

Jordan's crew had gathered early that morning, Thursday, October 3, to sync up strategy before the very first closed-door interview in the House's new impeachment investigation was set to begin in the basement of the Capitol. Adam Schiff and his staff had summoned Kurt Volker, U.S. special representative for Ukraine negotiations, to testify about the allegations against the president. And Jordan knew he had a fight on his hands.

The night before, Volker's attorney had sent investigators fifty-three pages of her client's WhatsApp messages pertaining to Ukraine. They documented in real time how the president's handpicked intermediaries had tried to dangle the promise of a White House meeting to pressure Ukrainian president Volodymyr Zelensky into launching probes that would be politically advantageous for Trump, including investigations into the 2016 election and his likely 2020 rival, Joe Biden.

"Assuming President Z convinces trump he will investigate / 'get to the bottom of what happened' in 2016, we will nail down date for visit to Washington," one of Volker's mangled messages read. In another, he and Gordon Sondland, the U.S. ambassador to the European Union, discussed how to coach Zelensky into publicly committing to the investigations Trump wanted.

The messages showed that the highest-ranking State Department official serving in Ukraine, chargé d'affaires Bill Taylor, was deeply troubled by the scheme. He knew that U.S. military assistance was not only vital to Ukraine's defenses against Russia, but that Zelensky desperately wanted a White House meeting to bolster the image of his infant presidency. Taylor had blatantly pressed Volker and Sondland to clarify whether the Trump administration's policy was "that security assistance and the WH meeting are conditioned on investigations." He later argued in another text that it would be "crazy to withhold security assistance for help with a political campaign."[1]

Jordan knew the texts were bad. But he relished a good fight, and he had already identified a failsafe in the missives: In one of them, Sondland had flatly refuted Taylor's suggestion that U.S. tax dollars were being used to help Trump's reelection efforts, writing: "the president has been crystal clear no quid pro quo's of any kind." Jordan knew that was the point he and his team would have to hit home over and over to protect the president. That, after all, was exactly how he viewed his job. In fact, his staff that morning was making an emergency plan: to stave off bad headlines from what they predicted would be a disastrous interview, they would leak that "no quid pro quo" text to the media sometime that morning, hoping to put a more favorable spin on the news.

Turning to his fellow Republicans, Jordan warned them to keep quiet during Volker's interview and let his investigative team take the lead so they could find a way to poke holes in the Democrats' narrative.

"Let Castor do the questioning," Jordan instructed the small group, nodding to his forty-six-year-old top investigative counsel, Steve Castor, whom senior Republicans had tapped to lead the GOP's impeachment defense.

A Philly native with fifteen years' worth of experience in congressional investigations, Castor did not share the swagger or confidence of his boss. He had been drafted into the job of leading the GOP defense of Trump—a job he never wanted—just the day before, leaving him only one night to prepare for what he realized would be the most consequential interview of his Hill career. In fact, as he stayed up all night readying for Volker's interview, he kept hoping that the Democrats would call it off, buying him more time to prepare for an interrogation session he was dreading.

Castor had gone over the whistleblower's report with a series of highlighters to track how the CIA official had sourced his information. But while Castor was an experienced investigator, he wasn't a foreign policy guy—and had little familiarity with Ukraine. He found the details of the convoluted scandal to be confusing, and he didn't know the first thing about the series of witnesses Democrats had summoned for questioning. He had tried to get a download from the White House about Volker's history and how he related to everything. But White House counsel Pat Cipollone had given him nothing.

Even before Volker's messages had shown up in his email the night before, Castor had been convinced Volker was about to sandbag the GOP. After all, he had resigned from the administration the day he agreed to appear before the panel,[2] and he had hired a talented former Democratic investigative attorney to represent him.

Castor had tried to pump that lawyer, Margaret Daum, for information about what her client would say before the session. But she would not tip her hand—except to say she planned to send Volker's messages over to the panel.

When he heard that, Castor freaked.

"You can't do this," he pleaded with Daum, arguing that the text messages were not hers to give, but the property of the State Department, which had not yet vetted them. Now, having read them, Castor believed he was right to have worried.

A bullish Jordan, however, was prepared to go in swinging. The weekend before, McCarthy had tapped the scrappy, take-no-prisoners congressman to lead House Republicans' investigative strategy. It was an unlikely alliance between two leading Republicans who had been nemeses for years. In fact, it was Jordan who had led the charge to deny McCarthy his dream job as Speaker in 2015.

But with Trump's presidency on the line, Jordan and McCarthy had buried the hatchet. The weekend before, the two had worked out a game plan: If the facts that witnesses presented were unfavorable, as Volker's seemed destined to be, they'd go for broke pummeling the process of the inquiry as unfair. McCarthy, Jordan knew, would be releasing a public letter that day arguing that Pelosi's entire setup was in "direct contradiction" to all modern impeachment inquiries. Jordan resolved to wage the same battle behind closed doors in the Volker interview.

Shortly before 9:30 a.m., they set off, striding shoulder to shoulder from Jordan's office to the basement SCIF like a street gang headed to a rumble. With Jordan in the lead, they moved as a bloc through the snaking underground tunnels of the Capitol complex, as if the solidarity of their march could build up their confidence. As they rounded the final corner into the belowground atrium stairs that led down to the SCIF, they were immediately met by an explosion of clicking camera shutters and reporters shouting questions. They plowed through the heavy doors of the SCIF, surrendering their cell phones to lockboxes in the hallway and entering the Intelligence Committee's underground conference room.

The windowless chamber had light yellow-tinted walls offset by dark wood paneling under fluorescent lighting. A series of six tables, arranged in a large rectangular loop, stood in the middle, surrounded by leather swivel chairs with microphones placed in front of them, and another row of straight-backed leather chairs behind them. At one end of the setup sat Volker, flanked by his attorney and a clerk who kept the time.

When Schiff opened the session by cautioning members "to be professional" and reminding them the interview would be staff-led, Jordan saw his first opportunity to pounce, launching into a series of procedural objections to try to change the subject.

"Mr. Chairman, I've probably sat in on more transcribed interviews than maybe any other member . . . and I have never seen an effort to prohibit members from asking the witness questions," Jordan launched at Schiff, though he'd just told his own members to let Castor do the talking.

Schiff ignored him and began the session.

It didn't take long before Jordan realized that Republicans needn't have worried. Despite his seemingly damning texts, Volker had no intention of validating the Democrats' view of events. If anything, in fact, the onetime Republican aide turned diplomat seemed to be treating the whole Ukraine affair as a big nothing.

When Schiff's staff asked if Trump had ever withheld a meeting until Zelensky committed to investigate the 2016 election, Volker's answer was simple.

"The answer to the question is no," Volker replied flatly. "There was no linkage like that."

The Democrats' counsel tried again, asking Volker if the investigations he had sought would have been to Trump's political advantage.

"We didn't discuss that," Volker said, unemotionally.[3]

The Democratic staffers in the room exchanged glances—these were not the answers they were looking for. Jordan, meanwhile, could hardly believe his good luck. He eyed Castor and Meadows as if to ask: *Are you hearing what I'm hearing?* They weren't sure if the Democrats were asking bad questions, or if they themselves had utterly misjudged Volker as a witness. They decided to find out.

Castor didn't need to know anything about Ukraine to observe something very important about Volker: He bristled any time Schiff's lawyers suggested he might have taken part in a nefarious scheme. In a game-time decision, Castor decided to exploit Volker's defensiveness by fawning over him.

"We were just amazed by your deep knowledge of the region, your ability to recall specific names, pronounce them," Castor said, adding an obsequious, "I'm not as savvy as you."

Volker visibly relaxed. When Jordan's counsel asked if it was a good thing for Giuliani to have been engaging with Ukrainian officials, Volker—who had criticized the president's lawyer minutes before—agreed that it was good for the president to get "accurate and fresh" information from someone he would listen to.

Volker also shrugged off the idea that freezing Ukraine's military assistance was all that alarming.

"Assistance gets held up for a variety of reasons at various times,"

Volker said. "In my view, this hold on security assistance was not significant."

Around the room, Republican members were trying to keep from grinning. But Castor stayed focused: He needed Volker to take the final step of also absolving Trump of any fault.

Was it really that objectionable, Castor asked, for Trump to have asked Zelensky about Burisma, the company that employed Hunter Biden, and 2016?

"Burisma is known for years to have been a corrupt company accused of money laundering. So when someone says 'investigate Burisma,' that's fine," Volker reasoned confidently. "Saying 'investigating Vice President Biden or his son,' that is not fine. And that was never part of the conversation."

As he listened, Schiff fumed. He and his staff had been positively elated by the Volker messages they had received the night before. They had been expecting a cooperative witness. But Volker's equivocations and rationalizations were bordering on the absurd, in Schiff's estimation. As soon as Castor's turn ended, he decided to personally intervene, whipping out a copy of the president's July 25 call record to press Volker on whether the Ukrainians knew that Trump's references to Burisma meant the Bidens.

Volker would not play ball. "I can't speak to what was in his mind," he said, infuriating Schiff all the more.

"We don't need to be naive here, right?" the chairman said in exasperation. "Can we also agree that no president of the United States should ask a foreign leader to help interfere in a U.S. election? . . . And that would be particularly egregious if it was done with the context of withholding foreign assistance?"

Volker resented the badgering. The Democrats were coming off as awfully self-righteous, he thought, for people who, in his estimation, simply didn't have the goods.

"We're getting now into, you know, a conflation of these things that I didn't think was actually there," Volker calmly replied.

"You asked what conversations did I have about that quid pro quo, et cetera. None because I didn't know that there was a quid pro quo," Volker continued. "There is no linkage here."[4]

Republicans did not wait for Volker's interview to finish before publicly declaring victory. As they exited the SCIF, Meadow whispered that "this could not be going any better," while Jordan headed straight for the cameras and reporters surrounding the entryway, eagerly awaiting news.

"Nothing he has said supports the narrative you've been hearing from Mr. Schiff and the Democrats," Jordan crowed to reporters outside the SCIF during a midday break in the testimony. "Nothing."

While Republicans were far more pleased with Volker's interview than they had anticipated, their insurance policy of releasing Sondland's "no quid pro quo" exchange was already in motion. A group of GOP staffers who had not been in the SCIF had leaked the text messages to reporters from ABC and Fox News while Volker's interview was still going. By midafternoon, both had published articles stating that Sondland had declared Taylor's fears "incorrect," because Trump wanted "no quid pro quo's of any kind."[5]

The leak caught Schiff's team off-guard. Since the texts appeared to be strategically chosen to emphasize the "no quid pro quo" line, they instantly believed it was the Republicans' doing—and that they had to counteract it.

Over the next several hours, Democratic staffers scrambled to parse through all of Volker's messages and curate a subset for public release to illustrate just how damaging they had in fact been to

Trump. Volker might have played coy in the interview, but the public did not yet know that—and Democrats were sure that a fuller survey of his text messages would be damning. Maybe even enough to convince the public that their allegations of a quid pro quo were correct.

Just before 10:45 p.m., Schiff's investigators blasted out a twenty-five-page file featuring about sixty of the choicest messages "to help correct the public record" about what he had provided to the committee. Within minutes, they'd gone viral with the Washington media.

Jordan left the Capitol that night in good spirits. His entire team did. In fact, as soon as they rounded the last corner out of the SCIF, leaving the cameras behind them, the entire clan of Republicans broke out into a jig. "That was awesome!" Meadows declared. "Democrats are going to look so dumb for starting impeachment," his colleagues agreed. As they cheered their good fortune, Jordan and his team rushed to share the good news with GOP leaders: Democrats had fallen on their faces, and Volker had dealt impeachment a fatal blow.

Shortly after midnight, however, Jordan's phone began ringing off the hook. Democrats had released the worst of Volker's text messages, and his staff was calling to warn him that GOP leaders were panicking. One of them, Liz Cheney, the House's No. 3 Republican and the daughter of former vice president Dick Cheney, called Jordan directly to complain.

"You said Volker's testimony was good for us!" she said, demanding an explanation. "What is up with these texts?"

15

"THE ONE-WAY RATCHET"

OCTOBER 4–8, 2019

President Trump grew impatient as he read the words typed on the papers his White House counsel had put in front of him. Boring, boring, and more boring. Reaching for a Sharpie pen, he took it upon himself to spice things up.

For more than a week, Pat Cipollone had been working on a letter to House Democrats, challenging the constitutionality of their impeachment inquiry and outright rejecting the idea of participating in their probe. Cipollone had gone through draft upon draft, drawing on the advice of Justice Department lawyers to make his arguments as airtight as possible. He would likely need them to hold up in court, after all, when the House Democrats invariably tried to circumvent the White House's roadblocks.

But first, Cipollone's letter had to earn Trump's approval. As the president sat behind the Resolute Desk reading the lofty legalese, he sneered. Without warning, he started scribbling all over Cipollone's carefully crafted prose, demanding Cipollone fix it at once.

Trump wanted bolder language—and fonts. He wanted italics. He wanted exclamation points. More drama, more outrage, he instructed his counsel. "Never before in the history of the country has the House treated me so badly!" he dictated to Cipollone, insisting he write down his words. Cipollone, wincing, obeyed—making a few tweaks to make it sound ever so slightly less petulant.

It was Friday, October 4, the day after Kurt Volker's testimony, and Trump had been in a foul mood all day. In the nine months since Pelosi had reclaimed her gavel, he and Cipollone had successfully stymied virtually every investigation the Democrats tried to launch, blocking documents and witnesses and all but grinding House oversight to a halt. But Volker had threatened to reverse that trend by being cooperative. It didn't matter to Trump that his ally Jim Jordan had personally assured him the Ukraine envoy's testimony was positive—the damning headlines about his text messages were leading every newspaper and television broadcast in the country. Trump couldn't understand why Volker had been allowed to testify at all. In his view, cooperating with a congressional probe into his affairs was the height of disloyalty—even if it was fairly standard practice over the last two hundred plus years for administration officials to respect congressional oversight.

"You have to *do* something," the president demanded of Cipollone. What he meant was: *You have to stop the impeachment investigation once and for all.*

As Trump awaited word about Volker's testimony the previous day, he couldn't restrain his anger. When reporters on the South Lawn of the White House peppered him with questions about asking Ukraine's president to investigate the Bidens, he doubled down, insisting that China should do so as well.

"China should start an investigation into the Bidens, because what happened in China is just about as bad as what happened with

Ukraine," he insisted. And if they didn't, Trump warned, there could be billions of dollars' worth of consequences for Beijing in ongoing trade negotiations.

"If they don't do what we want," he said, "we have tremendous power."[1]

The president's public demand that yet another foreign government investigate the Bidens—this time proposed on live national television as if there were nothing wrong with what he had just said—floored Democrats and gobsmacked Republicans. Even under threat of impeachment, his anti-Biden crusade was expanding.

"What is he *doing*?" Trump ally Lindsey Graham asked another Trump confidant, Mark Meadows, whom he had frantically phoned after hearing Trump's comments. Then Graham called Trump directly to delicately ask him to back off.

"Somebody needs to look at Biden but it's not the Chinese government," Graham pleaded with the president. "They're *not* reliable."

By that weekend, however, Trump's China comments were the least of congressional Republicans' concerns. Word of Cipollone's draft letter vowing to stonewall impeachment proceedings had made it to the Capitol, reigniting a heated debate between Hill Republicans and the White House that had been simmering behind the scenes for several days.

While House Republicans wanted to protect Trump, House Minority Leader Kevin McCarthy and his top counsel, Machalagh Carr, had privately balked when they heard that the president and Cipollone were thinking about ignoring impeachment proceedings entirely. They viewed the move as an all-out assault on legislative power that would weaken Congress as an institution in the long run.

Carr began referring to the phenomenon as the "one-way ratchet": If one president could successfully disregard Congress, she'd explain, the next was bound to follow in those footsteps—and likely press the envelope even further. McCarthy had a future majority to think about. And any no-cooperation posture in impeachment would create a precedent for future presidents—including Democrats—to undermine Congress's oversight prerogative even further.

"This is simply how it's done," Carr would stress in their meetings. "If Congress asks somebody to testify, we expect them to show up."

McCarthy agreed with Carr—but never expressed such sentiments publicly for fear of being out of step with Trump. Instead, he and his legal team sought to work behind the scenes to change the White House's mind. They had an ally in Jordan and his staff, particularly his counsel Steve Castor. Together, Jordan's and McCarthy's teams tried to convince the Trump White House to cooperate with the impeachment probe and ditch Cipollone's planned missive. It was one thing to demand that House Democrats vote on a resolution delineating the rights of the minority and the president, they argued. It was another thing entirely to expressly forbid witness testimony. The White House shouldn't do it, they argued. Stonewalling impeachment proceedings was not the same as stonewalling an ordinary probe, they explained; it was the only form of oversight enshrined in the Constitution.

To make their argument go down easier for Trump, Hill Republicans made a political case as well. Boycotting the probe would just play into the Democrats' argument that Trump had something to hide, they said. It would also make the GOP's procedural complaints look petty in comparison. Plus, if Trump had done nothing wrong, they said, then the White House should trust the GOP minority to try to help unearth exonerating evidence through the interrogation process. There was no way they could do that if the administration stonewalled, they pointed out.

Their efforts failed to break through. In early October, after hearing Cipollone was on the cusp of issuing his no-cooperation letter, House Republicans enlisted Mark Meadows, who was closest to Trump, to try to walk him off the edge. Meadows tried to convince the White House to over-accommodate Democrats, burying their fledgling probe in paperwork—or at least make an attempt at partial accommodation.

But after Volker's texts came out, the president was inconsolable. What's more, that weekend, Democrats had started coming for his inner circle. They subpoenaed Trump's acting chief of staff, Mick Mulvaney, for documents and demanded his vice president, Mike Pence, hand over records of his own contacts with Ukrainian officials on Trump's behalf.[2] Trump didn't want any more surprises that could be used against him. It was time to send the letter and shut down the probe.

There was another reason Trump and Cipollone had been so rushed that weekend to block more witnesses from testifying in the House. Democrats had summoned Gordon Sondland, the gladhanding ambassador to the European Union, to be deposed in the impeachment investigation the following Tuesday. While Sondland had awkwardly parroted Trump's "no quid pro quo" line in his text messages to Kurt Volker, Cipollone knew he planned to testify to the opposite. His attorney had privately disclosed as much to the White House, setting off a five-alarm fire in the White House counsel's office that weekend.

Sondland, a gregarious and deep-pocketed hotelier from Oregon, had long dreamed of a glamorous career as an influential jet-setting diplomat—and was willing to go to great lengths to get there. The son of Holocaust survivors didn't even try to hide his ambitions, regularly rubbing elbows with politicians and confiding in friends that

he hoped to be rewarded for his fundraising efforts with plum am-
bassadorships. In 2016, Sondland initially bet that GOP presidential
candidate Jeb Bush would be his ticket into the international political elite. He went all in for Jeb, even denouncing Trump for verbally
attacking the Gold Star parents of a slain Muslim American soldier
during the primary. But when Trump shocked the nation and won
the GOP nomination—and later the election—Sondland switched
horses. He donated $1 million to Trump's inaugural committee and
started lobbying the new administration—and Trump's own daughter Ivanka—for his dream job.

When he was named an ambassador in 2018,[3] Sondland signaled
his eagerness to please. He volunteered to add Ukraine, Georgia,
Venezuela, and Iran policy to his portfolio, in addition to his respon-
sibilities with the European Union. He developed a personal connection with Trump, ingratiating himself to the president through
flattery. And within a few months, he effectively became the
point man for Trump's Ukraine scheme, coordinating with Giuliani
and speaking with the president directly about his desire to have
Ukraine investigate Burisma and the Bidens.

For Trump and Cipollone, Sondland posed a potentially serious
threat. Though Democratic investigators didn't know it yet, Sondland had personally informed Ukraine about the quid pro quo, telling officials they would not receive their congressionally approved
military assistance—or the Ukraine president's much-desired White
House meeting—until Zelensky publicly committed to the probes
Trump wanted.[4] He also was a bit of a gadfly, a chameleon, and a
brown-noser. And the president's team worried that under pressure,
he might flip on Trump, damaging the president's defense and triggering mass Republican defections.

When Democratic investigators had identified Sondland as a witness, Cipollone's team was so worried about his testimony that they
tried to get Sondland to agree to a preliminary White House inter-

view to find out what he planned to say. Sondland's personal lawyer at the time had balked, wary of drawing accusations of impropriety. But a few days later, Sondland hired a new lawyer, prominent D.C. attorney Robert Luskin. Luskin signaled a willingness to engage. During a fifteen-minute phone call that weekend, Luskin informed the White House point-blank about his client's plans to tell the full truth, testimony that would refute Trump's "no quid pro quo" defense as well as Volker's blasé tale.

Trump was determined to keep that from happening, and Cipollone moved quickly to shut Sondland down. That weekend, his deputies in the White House counsel's office called Luskin and told him that Trump might block the ambassador from testifying that Tuesday.

Luskin protested.

"Stopping Gordon's testimony will only make it look like you're trying to hide something," he told the White House lawyers. "Let him testify."

Cipollone's deputies offered their sympathies and said they personally agreed with Luskin. But "the client," they explained—meaning Trump—would not stand for it. *This decision is being made above our paygrade*, they told Luskin.

When Jordan walked into the SCIF with Castor and Meadows on Tuesday, October 8, the morning of Sondland's scheduled testimony, they were shocked to discover that the ambassador wasn't there. Just before seven a.m., Cipollone—on Trump's orders—had instructed State Department officials to stop the interview from going forward. No one, however, had bothered to give Trump's top defenders on Capitol Hill a heads-up. And Jordan and Castor were *not* happy.

Jordan and Castor had been bracing for a hard interview. They knew from their own conversations with Luskin that Sondland planned to testify Trump had engaged in a quid pro quo, and they had come up with a game plan to handle that. Sondland, they predicted, would want to please Democrats to keep himself out of trouble, while also trying to stay in Trump's good graces. But they believed there was no way he could do both simultaneously.

"I'll catch him in a lie," Castor told Jordan. If Sondland perjured himself, Castor argued, it would discredit his entire testimony, giving them a better chance at protecting Trump.

It was a brazen strategy that showed once again how House Republicans were more concerned about coming up with ways to protect their party leader than actually learning the truth of what occurred. But Sondland's no-show had robbed them of a chance to test their new playbook.

As Jordan exited the SCIF, reporters swarmed, demanding to know why the administration had blocked Sondland's testimony. Perturbed as he was, Jordan swallowed his frustration and loyally defended the White House's move as justified. The administration "decided not to have Ambassador Sondland appear today" because of an "unfair and partisan process that Mr. Schiff has been running," Jordan argued. Democrats were just trying to smear Trump thirteen months before his reelection "based on an anonymous whistleblower with no firsthand knowledge who has a bias against the president," he continued. They should release Volker's testimony and acknowledge there had been no quid pro quo.

"Look, we were actually looking forward to hearing from Ambassador Sondland; we thought he was going to reinforce exactly what Ambassador Volker told us last week," Jordan lied. "But . . . we understand why [the White House] made this decision at this moment."

The truth was, he didn't. As soon as the press conference was over, Jordan and his posse raced up the marble spiral staircase, out of the Capitol, and into their waiting cars to speed across town and stage an intervention with Trump. On top of canceling Sondland's testimony, the White House, they had heard through the grapevine, was about to release the dreaded Cipollone letter aimed at shutting the whole probe down—the one GOP lawmakers had been trying to hold back all weekend. Though members usually met Trump in the Oval Office alone, Jordan insisted Castor accompany them, hoping he could convince the president to allow administration witnesses to come forward.

A few minutes later, Trump sat quietly behind the Resolute Desk—his favored and only perch for any and all meetings—and listened as Cipollone and Castor presented their competing positions, his head ping-ponging between them as they pleaded their respective cases.

"Schiff has no authority to conduct this probe because the House hasn't voted for it," Cipollone argued.

"They haven't voted and should, but let's let these witnesses come in and see what they have to say," Castor retorted. "We can handle Sondland and use him to help you."

Castor then made a direct appeal to the president, suggesting that participating in the impeachment investigation was in his interest.

"When you take hard positions like this, people will think you're hiding something," he said carefully. "If you don't stonewall, you're in a better position to fight and argue the facts."

Trump listened and nodded along cordially, his demeanor so pleasant and agreeable that Jordan and Castor left the White House sure they had persuaded the president to allow Sondland's testimony to proceed. Cipollone, however, stayed back—and got the last word. Just before five p.m., the White House blasted out his letter eviscerating the impeachment probe in language that bore the un-mistakable markings of Trump.

"Never before in our history has the House of Representatives—under the control of either political party—taken the American people down the dangerous path you seem determined to pursue," the letter read. "Put simply, you seek to overturn the results of the 2016 election and deprive the American people of the President they have freely chosen.

"Given that your inquiry lacks any legitimate constitutional foundation, any pretense of fairness, or even the most elementary due process protections, the executive branch cannot be expected to participate in it," Cipollone concluded.[5]

16

REVENGE OF THE DIPLOMATS

OCTOBER 11-15, 2019

The SCIF buzzed with anticipation on October 11 as Schiff waited to see whether the woman who could make or break his investigation was going to show up.

For days by that point, his lawyers had been engaged in some tricky diplomacy to convince former U.S. ambassador to Ukraine Marie Yovanovitch to be the first to cross Cipollone's picket line of the impeachment investigation. Schiff knew the anti-corruption crusader had been wronged by Trump and his personal attorney Rudy Giuliani—and that she had a gut-wrenching story to tell. He also knew that the future of his probe likely depended on whether she was willing to tell it.

Yovanovitch, a career diplomat whose parents had fled the Soviet Union, had played no direct role in Trump's pressure campaign against Ukraine. In fact, she had been ousted before it even began—and the reason for her removal at Trump's hands had piqued Schiff's interest. Giuliani's Ukraine allies—and one discredited top

government prosecutor in particular—had been subjects of Yovanovitch's anti-corruption efforts. They wanted revenge against her as
well as former vice president Joe Biden for hastening their downfall. So they convinced Giuliani that Yovanovitch was anti-Trump—
and the president's lawyer was only too eager to orchestrate a smear
campaign that eventually led to her being recalled from her post.

To Schiff, Yovanovitch was the first victim of Trump's Ukraine
scheme. But she was also still on the State Department payroll and
a stickler for the rules. Weeks before the impeachment investigation
had gotten underway, the House Foreign Affairs Committee had
reached out to her for an informal, fact-finding interview. She had
refused to talk without permission from her superiors then. In the
wake of Cipollone's letter, Schiff knew it would be even harder to
convince her to ignore the White House's no-cooperation declaration and come forward.

Schiff realized Yovanovitch was facing an impossible choice between obeying her employer or obeying her conscience. Show up,
as Volker had done, and she would be ignoring an administration
request to stay away. But not showing up would mean flouting a congressional summons, an act with potential consequences of its own.

Schiff's team was struggling too. They knew they could force
the issue by subpoenaing Yovanovitch to testify. But they worried
doing so would escalate the White House's stonewalling. If Cipollone took the matter to court, it could bring their investigation to
a screeching halt if a federal judge took weeks or even months to
rule on the matter, just as was happening with Don McGahn's subpoena.

In the days before Yovanovitch's scheduled appearance, Schiff's
lawyers had proposed an arrangement to her attorney: They would
serve her with a legally binding congressional subpoena at the last
minute. That way, she would have the legal cover to appear, allow-

ing her to argue she had no choice but to speak. It would also deprive the White House and State Department of time needed to file a court case challenging the summons.

That morning, Schiff's team issued the subpoena as promised. But Yovanovitch was late. As the minutes ticked by, members and staffers seated around the conference table repeatedly checked their watches. Their whole investigation depended on Yovanovitch walking through the doors of the SCIF. If she didn't, it would be difficult to get any other witnesses to follow.

When Yovanovitch finally settled into her seat—thirty-eight minutes late—Schiff breathed a quick sigh of relief. The plan had worked.

"Good morning, Ambassador, and welcome to the House Permanent Select Committee on Intelligence," he said. "We thank you for complying with the duly authorized congressional subpoena."

Yovanovitch's appearance broke the witness dam exactly as Schiff had hoped it would. In the days that followed, a string of other government officials, similarly armed with last-minute subpoenas, filed into his SCIF. Each offered a compelling story of Trump's misdeeds, emboldening Democrats and expanding their understanding of the president's self-serving Ukraine gambit. It also didn't take long for Jordan and his investigative team to realize that Kurt Volker's interview would be the high point of the depositions for the GOP.

George Kent, a senior State official overseeing eastern Europe who had previously been Yovanovitch's deputy in Ukraine, sported a bow tie and an encyclopedic recollection of how Trump had sidelined traditional diplomatic channels in favor of putting Ukraine policy in the hands of Giuliani and three political appointees—most of whom had little knowledge of the region. He said those three individuals—Volker, Gordon Sondland, and Energy secretary Rick Perry—had pressed Zelensky to promise Trump he'd investigate matters relating to the Bidens, directly contradicting Volker's blasé "no quid pro quo" testimony. Kent also testified that when he raised concerns about the scheme to superiors, he was told to keep his "head down" and focus on the other countries in his portfolio.

Fiona Hill, who had served as the National Security Council's Russia and Europe director under former national security advisor John Bolton, shocked investigators with her testimony about how her boss had likened the Ukraine scheme to a "drug deal." In a dramatic retelling of a July 2019 meeting, she explained how Bolton had flown off the handle when he learned about Sondland's and Giuliani's efforts to get Ukraine to conduct politically advantageous probes for Trump, directing her to report them to NSC lawyers and make it clear he was not involved. Bolton had even likened the president's lawyer to "a hand grenade that is going to blow everybody up," she said.

Yovanovich had also provided a devastating account. She recounted the personal toll that Giuliani's smear campaign had taken on her decades-long career and mental health. She said she was stunned to see conservative columnists, Fox News, and the president's own son promoting spurious charges that she mishandled millions in anti-corruption funds and had handed Ukrainians a "do not prosecute" list to protect Biden allies.[1] And she explained her disappointment when Secretary of State Mike Pompeo had refused to push back on the false allegations for fear that defending his employee would land him in hot water with Trump.

As Yovanovitch described being told that Trump had "lost confidence in me," and packing her bags and returning to the United States permanently, she even started to cry.

"Do you want to take a minute?" Schiff's investigations director, Dan Goldman, asked.

"Yeah, just a minute," she replied.

As Schiff watched Yovanovitch collect herself, he made a mental note to himself to get her in front of the cameras to tell the same story.

While Democrats were positively giddy at their rush of good fortune, Jordan's team began to fall into despair and self-pity. The walls were closing in on the president quickly, and they desperately needed a strategy to turn things around.

Yovanovitch's tale of being targeted, they realized with woe, had made Giuliani and Trump look like unscrupulous monsters willing to destroy anyone—even a dedicated civil servant—who stood in the way of what they wanted. Hill, speaking in her native north-British accent and with the authority of a world-renowned Kremlinologist, had as good as accused Republicans of being unwitting agents provocateurs for Putin for insisting Giuliani and Trump's suspicions of Ukrainian meddling in the 2016 election were justified. And the bombshells Hill had dropped regarding Bolton were even more worrisome: The longtime neoconservative was the GOP's patron saint of national security, and if he essentially agreed with the Democrats' take on Trump, Republicans knew they—and Trump—were in big trouble.

But the headlines were the worst of all. While Schiff was conducting his entire probe in private, every day, the worst revelations were seeping out of the deposition room and getting plastered over the newspapers and cable networks. Reporters would tail GOP lawmakers through hallways, pecking at them like throngs of birds, demanding to know whether they thought Trump's actions were appropriate. None of them had the audacity to admit they didn't.

Each deposition day, the GOP's core investigative team would gather in Jordan's office at six or seven a.m. to review their game plan before marching over to the SCIF with the Ohio Republican leading the way. But each day, their walk to the interview chamber was weighed down with a renewed sense of dread. "Fuck! What is this person going to say today?" they'd joke to each other bitterly. One Jordan aide likened that stage of the probe to the Blitz of 1940, in which Germany bombed London for a relentless fifty-seven days, killing thousands. Republicans had no idea when the next blast would hit them, but they knew another would strike and that each bomb could be devastating for Trump's presidency.

The depositions had not been a total loss for the Republicans. Both Kent and Hill had testified that Hunter Biden's role on the board of Ukrainian energy company Burisma—particularly while his father was vice president—was a problematic conflict of interest, a claim the GOP investigators held up as justification for Trump's scrutiny of his 2020 rival. But it had done nothing to slow the Democrats' momentum. They needed help, Jordan realized. Help from Trump's advisors—who did not seem interested in lending a hand.

Nearly every night when the depositions ended, Jordan and Meadows dragged themselves to the White House, where the president was waiting impatiently for an update. White House counsel Pat Cipollone also wanted full downloads, pressing them for details, despite rules prohibiting the disclosure of what happened in depositions. Yet after just a week of these sessions, it was becoming abundantly clear that the White House had no plans to reciprocate. Jordan, McCarthy, and their impeachment staffers kept asking Cipollone for total transparency about what happened in Ukraine—or at least more details that could aid in staging Trump's defense. But they were getting nothing.

"You guys aren't giving us enough," they complained.

The president, meanwhile, still expected Hill Republicans, operating blindly, to go out there and defend him. And they did.

The lack of communication was only one source of frustration with the White House. From the very start, Hill GOP leaders had implored Trump to take impeachment seriously. But it appeared Trump was getting the opposite message from some of his advisors. They had heard, for example, that Cipollone was whispering to Trump that there was a good chance he wouldn't be impeached at all. That drove the Hill Republicans crazy. *Were they talking about the same Nancy Pelosi?* they wondered. They had to do something to get through to Trump.

The more House GOP members had to pick up the slack, the angrier they got. McCarthy's and Jordan's aides, who had once warred against each other, found themselves bonding over their mutual frustration and fury. The White House was "fucking absolutely goddamn useless," one Jordan aide complained, while another McCarthy staffer likened the White House's approach to impeachment to a toddler playing peek-a-boo: It was as if they thought that by closing their eyes and refusing to acknowledge impeachment, it would simply go away.

Tensions ultimately boiled over during an October staff meeting in McCarthy's office when a White House TV booker asked which House Republicans were going to defend Trump on that weekend's Sunday news shows. Tyler Grimm, one of Jordan's top aides coordinating impeachment messaging, bristled.

"Jim's going out, but I have to be honest with you—every time I ask my boss to go on a Sunday show, he asks me: Where is the White House? Why aren't they on the Sunday shows?" Grimm said, pointing out that Trump's top surrogates were glaringly absent from program lineups.

"Where *is* the White House?" he demanded. "Why are Mark Meadows and Jim and Lee Zeldin and Scott Perry the only guys going out? Where's Kellyanne? Where's Mick?"

The White House aides were unmoved. It was the House Republicans who were out of line for questioning the White House's methods, they angrily retorted, brandishing a story in which an unnamed

Republican lawmaker had complained that Trump was "pulling it out of his ass as he goes along."[2]

"This is so disrespectful," the Trump aide said, holding up the article as she excoriated the Republican Hill aides in the room. They should be grateful, she added, that the White House staff bothered with the Hill at all.

At that, McCarthy's team lost their patience.

"The people in this room are working around the clock, working their asses off *for you*—and you're not doing shit," bellowed Matt Sparks, McCarthy's communications director. "Where the fuck have *you* been? How dare you come in here and chastise us? Fuck you. You can just leave. Leave!"

Alarmed at the outburst, the White House aides—all women—tried to smooth things over, but it was too late.

"LEAVE," Sparks barked at them again, pointing toward the door. They hurriedly gathered their belongings and walked out.

17

DEFENDING THE INDEFENSIBLE

OCTOBER 16, 2019

Congresswoman Jaime Herrera Beutler approached a microphone in a basement conference room and asked House Minority Whip Steve Scalise a simple, straightforward question.

"Someone give me a good reason why I *shouldn't* support this impeachment inquiry," the Washington State Republican, one of only thirteen women in the 197-member GOP conference, challenged. "It's an investigation, right? Why shouldn't I vote for this?"

The forty-year-old mother of three was tall and pretty, with long dark hair and a striking, intense stare. As a Latina—her father was Mexican American—she stood out in the mostly homogenous GOP, though she rarely spoke out in such large GOP gatherings. She preferred to keep her head down, shunning the national media and staying hyper-focused on the needs of her constituents.

But that afternoon, on Wednesday, October 16, Herrera Beutler had sat through a thirty-plus-minute presentation from GOP leaders about why the impeachment investigation was terrible—and she still wanted better answers.

As one of the few centrist Republicans to survive the bloodbath of the 2018 midterms, Herrera Beutler viewed the Ukraine issue through a different lens than most of her GOP colleagues. She hailed from a competitive swing district that had voted for Barack Obama in 2008 but then Trump in 2016. Her constituents, wedged between liberal Seattle and Portland, were a mixed bag politically, with a hefty number of independents among them. Consequently, she always sought to justify the positions she took in Washington to "the bosses back home," as she called them. That often meant prodding her own leadership to give her better reasons to support or oppose legislation than the "R" next to her name.

Early in her career, Herrera Beutler had learned the value of questioning conventional wisdom—and not just in politics. In 2013, just a few months into her second term in Congress and pregnant, she found out she was carrying a baby with a kidney condition known as Potter syndrome. Doctors told her the child would die and encouraged her to have an abortion. But Herrera Beutler refused. She sought experimental treatment instead, fleetingly becoming a pro-life celebrity and ultimately giving birth to a baby girl who survived—the first child in recorded medical history to breathe without any kidneys. A reminder of her fateful decision still hung on her office wall: framed clips of stories about her daughter Abigail's miraculous birth next to a Bible verse that read: "God is in the midst of her, she shall not be moved; God will help her when morning dawns."[1]

It was one of many life lessons that had taught Herrera Beutler the importance of thinking for herself. She considered herself a reasonable person who didn't care about party identity as much as doing what she thought was right for her district. She had no desire to be a puppet of leadership—or Trump—and spout off talking points. She had made no secret of the fact that she didn't even vote

for Trump in 2016: After the then-candidate bragged about grabbing women by their private parts, she wrote in then-Speaker Paul
Ryan's name on her ballot.[2] In the aftermath, she had made a deal
with her district: She would work with Trump when it served their
interests and oppose him when he caused problems.

While Herrera Beutler couldn't be sure if Trump's latest Ukraine
actions merited impeachment, at first blush they certainly struck
her as something worth investigating. She believed his phone call
was inappropriate and that leveraging military aid for political favors
sounded like a pretty egregious abuse of power. But Herrera Beutler
wasn't convinced that that's what had happened. So far, she hadn't
seen any proof.

In fact, Herrera Beutler was unimpressed with what she had seen
of the Democrats' probe so far. She didn't understand why Pelosi
hadn't held a formal vote to start a bipartisan impeachment process,
giving both parties investigative powers like they did in impeachments past. And she was put off that not a single Democrat had
approached people like her to see if there might be common ground
in investigating Trump. The Speaker and Adam Schiff appeared to
be running things without any GOP input whatsoever—a decision
she predicted to local media would backfire on them.

"This is about our entire institution and how our democracy
functions," she had told a local newspaper the prior week. "Unless
someone's going to be the adults and do it the right way, we're going
to make it worse."[3]

Herrera Beutler had come to that Wednesday's GOP meeting
with those concerns in mind, intending to just hear out her own
party leaders, who she knew were critical of the probe. She was no
expert in complex oversight matters; her pet issues were maternal
health and forestry. So she took notes, as was her habit, and listened
intently to the guest speakers.

In the front of the room, Senator Lindsey Graham, a Trump ally who had served as a trial manager prosecuting Clinton's impeachment, skewered House Democrats' probe as unfair and secretive. There had been no vote to officially launch proceedings, he reminded them, and the Democrats had refused to delegate due process rights to the president. To be legitimate, he argued, Schiff ought to be interviewing witnesses in public, instead of sneaking around behind closed doors.

Herrera Beutler considered those compelling arguments. But impeachment was a complicated enough matter that every argument deserved a little prodding. She decided to play a little devil's advocate.

What if Democrats adopted a more acceptable process? she challenged the speakers, toward the end of the conversation. *In that case, shouldn't they support it?*

"Shouldn't we want answers?" she asked Scalise, who'd been overseeing the session.

Standing at the front of the room, Scalise paused. As House Minority Whip, it was his responsibility to count votes and keep House Republicans in line, and Trump had told him personally that he expected "zero defections" from GOP lawmakers on impeachment. The Louisiana conservative was a loyal foot soldier and would be damned before he let his president down.

Since Pelosi's impeachment announcement on September 24, Scalise had been working in tandem with McCarthy to keep their members in line. The fifty-four-year-old New Orleans native was balding and short, with a broad smile and a folksy, backslapping manner that earned him a larger-than-life presence around the House chamber. After surviving a near-fatal gunshot wound just a few years prior, Scalise was also considered something of a walking miracle. Consequently, when he approached his rank and file, they always stopped what they were doing to listen—fondness Scalise used to try to whip votes.

When impeachment took off, Scalise started checking in with Republican centrists, who he knew harbored no love for Trump, and instructed his staff to monitor what they said in public about the ongoing probe. Whenever a GOP lawmaker said something remotely critical of Trump—or positive about the impeachment inquiry—Scalise would pick up the phone or corner them in the halls of the Capitol for a chat. For example, when Michigan congressman Fred Upton told his local NPR station earlier that month that he was not sold on impeachment, but was open to an "inquiry," Scalise had leaped into action.[4]

"Pelosi is running a sham process," Scalise warned Upton. "Don't box yourself in by saying you support this."

Upton obeyed—even as he privately continued to nurse concerns about Trump's behavior.

McCarthy and Scalise had managed to keep Republicans from publicly breaking ranks. But amid the daily barrage of negative headlines, it was getting harder to maintain that unity. They were constantly in a defensive crouch, always fearing that the next news story would be the one to trigger mass defections. It was due to that fear that Scalise had decided to organize a series of impeachment "listening sessions," private meetings in which Republicans could air their concerns and ask tough questions of their colleagues who were taking part in the depositions. Better to give them a controlled forum for letting off steam, he figured, than risk them popping off on Trump in public.

Scalise had gone into the inaugural session that afternoon with one goal in mind: undermine the Democrats' impeachment by claiming their process fouls rendered it illegitimate. But Herrera Beutler's question had thrown him for a loop. Scalise knew she was well respected in the GOP conference for her no-nonsense attitude and her willingness to cut through the BS of leadership talking points if they didn't ring true. And since she didn't pipe up very often in conference, he knew Republicans would take an interest when she rose to speak.

Herrera Beutler's question wasn't unreasonable. But Scalise didn't have a good answer for it. Instead, he reverted to his talking points, insisting that Schiff's process would always be "tainted" and that he would never treat the GOP and Trump fairly.

In the back of the room, White House aides overseeing Hill outreach had listened to their exchange with alarm.

"That response wasn't good enough," one of them told the GOP leadership staff as members left the room. "Republicans need to know that a vote for Democrats' impeachment inquiry is a vote for impeachment."

Luckily, Scalise and McCarthy had another line of attack burning a hole in their back pockets.

On October 2, the day before Volker's testimony, the *New York Times* had broken a story that quickly became a rallying point for House Republicans. It stated that a Democratic staff member on the Intelligence Committee had been in contact with the whistleblower over the summer and told Schiff about it.[5] The revelation directly contradicted Schiff's insistence in multiple TV and print interviews that his committee had had no contact with the whistleblower. Popular fact-checkers who had been friendly to Schiff in the past declared his no-contact claims had been unquestionably "false."[6]

On its face, there was nothing wrong with the whistleblower coming to Congress with concerns. In fact, when it emerged that the CIA analyst's complaint was being withheld from lawmakers in

September, even McCarthy had argued that if the whistleblower "wanted it to go to Congress, they could have come directly to Congress."[7] But Trump and his allies seized on the *New York Times* story, using it to argue that Schiff was a liar who had conspired with the whistleblower to orchestrate sham charges against Trump. It was proof, they crowed, that the "deep state" Trump had warned about was hard at work against him.

McCarthy, despite his previously stated convictions about whistleblowers, pounced on the article to further rally his troops against impeachment. Schiff had always been their villain—this was further proof that he simply could not be trusted, he'd say. When moderate GOP members expressed concerns about the mounting allegations against Trump, McCarthy simply pointed to Schiff's misleading statements regarding the whistleblower to argue he was lying about the probe across the board. Witness statements leaking? Blame Schiff. Bad headlines? Blame Schiff for cherry-picking from the still-secret deposition transcripts. Never mind that it was the Republicans who had started the selective leaking during Volker's testimony—Schiff was too convenient a target.

"This is Schiff lying to you" became McCarthy's answer to nearly every challenging question. "This is only half the story."

He would then send those members to Jim Jordan and Steve Castor, who had been in the SCIF for every deposition, to reinforce the message. *Kurt Volker said there was no quid pro quo,* they told worried members, citing the former Ukraine envoy's testimony like sacred scripture. *Why would you believe Schiff over him?*

Of course, it wasn't just Schiff who was accusing Trump of wrongdoing. Every witness who had come through the SCIF since Volker had offered scathing testimony about Trump's conduct, creating a damning record of evidence. But conveniently, McCarthy knew that there was no way for his members to fact-check his claim that

Schiff was spinning a web of deceit. Thanks to the Democrats' rules—which were turning out to be a blessing in disguise for the GOP—the transcripts were under lock and key and only the relevant committee members could read them.

On the morning of Fiona Hill's testimony, McCarthy came up with another idea to turn his members against Schiff. Matt Gaetz of Florida, a dedicated Trump supporter, had shown up to the SCIF that morning and tried to muscle his way in to her deposition. He had argued that as a member of the House Judiciary Committee—which historically had jurisdiction over impeachment—he had a right to know what charges Schiff was cooking up against the president behind closed doors.

Schiff, with the help of the House parliamentarian, had kicked him out for one reason only: Gaetz wasn't on one of the three panels conducting the probe. But Gaetz's antics made a lightbulb go off in McCarthy's head: If his rank-and-file members similarly tried to see the evidence Schiff was compiling and were blocked, he reasoned, they would be personally aggrieved. They would also be more likely to question the headlines they were reading and believe Democrats were manipulating the entire impeachment narrative.

That week, after Herrera Beutler interrupted Scalise's listening session, McCarthy started encouraging members who voiced concerns about Trump to go down to the SCIF and try to see the evidence for themselves.

"You're a member of Congress. You have a right to go down to the SCIF and read the transcripts," he told them, banking on the knowledge that they would be rejected at the door.

When Herrera Beutler heard that members were getting turned away from the SCIF, the usually taciturn congresswoman was incensed. The notion that she might have to vote on the parameters of an impeachment inquiry without first seeing the evidence against Trump infuriated her. She represented the same number of constituents—and had the same security clearance—as any other rank-and-file member of Congress. As far as she was concerned, she ought to have the same access.

"That's bullshit!" she exclaimed, in a rare moment of cursing.

While McCarthy was ginning up his members to march on the SCIF, he made no mention that there was plenty of precedent to justify excluding members from probes if they weren't on the investigating committees. Half a decade earlier, former Republican Benghazi panel chairman Trey Gowdy, for example, had booted GOP members who similarly tried to sneak into the SCIF for depositions. When the interlopers argued that the proceedings should be taking place in public, Gowdy told them: "If you want to get on the news, then go rob a bank."

But to Republicans, the precedent regarding impeachment was different. In the cases of both Nixon and Clinton, House members had been privy to evidence compiled by outside prosecutors before they were called on to authorize the probes. It didn't matter to them that the evidence-collecting phase—Schiff's probe—was still underway, albeit in the back rooms of Congress instead of the offices of an outside prosecutor. They wanted to see the evidence against Trump now. Many recalled Nixon's impeachment to buttress the point. Those hearings had been public. *Why couldn't Democrats do the same now? What was Schiff hiding?*

Schiff had every intention of taking his case public—eventually. On the same day that Scalise huddled with the Republicans, in fact, he sent his colleagues a letter outlining his plan to release the closed-door deposition transcripts and hold public hearings "at an appropriate point in the investigation." In the meantime, he explained, things had to stay secret "to ensure that witnesses cannot coordinate their testimony."[8]

But like most Republicans, Herrera Beutler did not appreciate that nuance. On the suggestion of GOP leaders, she had made her way down to the SCIF that day to try to see the transcript of Volker's interview for herself. As McCarthy had predicted, she was promptly turned away—and the experience left a bitter taste in her mouth. The next day she returned to the SCIF with an aide in tow, to record a video message expressing her disgust with the impeachment probe.

"Yesterday, I requested the written transcript of the testimony from the U.S. special envoy to Ukraine, and I was denied," she said in the video, which she posted on Twitter.

"I'm left to rely on media leaks and selective bits of information released by Speaker Pelosi and Chairman Schiff about what actually happened," she continued. "So far this is indeed a secret impeachment inquiry, and that's no way to conduct a real investigation where the truth is the ultimate goal."[9]

That night, the woman who had started out wanting answers about Trump's troubling actions ended up tweeting out an attack against the Democrats' investigation. The video itself didn't get much play—only about two thousand people retweeted or "liked" it. But it caught McCarthy's attention. If they could replicate her message on a larger scale, he thought, Republican leaders could win over not only their moderates, but the entire impeachment public relations war.

18

"GET OVER IT"

OCTOBER 17, 2019

The morning of October 17, unexpected tragedy befell the impeachment probe: Elijah Cummings, the chairman of the Oversight Committee, suddenly died—and with him, so did the last fading glimmer of hope in the House that Trump's first impeachment could ever be bipartisan.

Of all the investigative chairmen hoping to bring Trump's worst conduct to light, Cummings was among the most effective because he commanded respect from both sides of the aisle. The civil rights crusader from Baltimore had a booming baritone that could move a crowd to tears or make witnesses quiver in their seats. He had used it to wage some of the Democratic Party's most impassioned defenses of the Obama administration—and most heated condemnations of the Trump administration—from his chairman's perch on the dais. But despite that, Republicans widely found his methods to be reasonable and fair. Trump's close ally Mark Meadows, in fact, counted Cummings as one of his best friends in Congress.

Cummings's staff was considered the most formidable oversight force on Capitol Hill and was the only Democratic shop that had managed to find a way around Trump's blockade of their probes. Just that year, they had exposed how Trump had overruled his intelligence community to give security clearances to allies and relatives and how Trump officials personally profited from nuclear technology sales to Saudi Arabia.[1] Even the White House counsel took Cummings seriously enough to drive to Baltimore over the summer to discuss possible compromises for the chairman's document requests—while Trump jeered online that the congressman's Baltimore district was a "disgusting, rat- and rodent-infested mess."

There was a time when Republicans thought that Pelosi would put Cummings at the helm of any impeachment investigation—a move that would have intimidated them, and Trump, considerably. But they did not realize how sick he had become, nor did their Democratic counterparts. Cummings had been battling a rare form of cancer, thymic carcinoma, for twenty-five years.[2] It was only in the last few, however, that his ailments started to catch up with him. His legs and feet began to swell, tethering his hulking frame to a red scooter he used to zoom from meeting to meeting around the Capitol. But he waved off his colleagues whenever they suggested he take a break, promising them he was on the brink of getting better.

Part of the reason Cummings refused to slow down was because he believed Congress was headed for an epic showdown with Trump—and he wanted to be there to defend the institution. Democrats had come to realize that Trump's no-cooperation strategy to oversight—buttressed by the support of Hill Republicans—had rendered their ability to enforce their investigative powers almost toothless, threatening to upend Congress's constitutional check on the executive branch. That spring, Cummings's staff—alongside Nadler's and Schiff's—had even discussed reviving Congress's long-dormant "inherent contempt" power, a tool that lawmakers had once used to jail witnesses who refused to obey their subpoenas.[3] The practice hadn't been employed for over a century, but Cummings thought the House might be able to revive it to force obstinate Trump administration witnesses into compliance, possibly through fines. Pelosi, fearing ridicule or the House looking overly aggressive, never took the idea seriously. There were also legal complications with the proposal, including the possibility of more court fights to enforce fines if people refused to pay them.

That summer, Cummings wrestled with his desire to take a more aggressive stance and his deference to party leaders he greatly respected, particularly the Speaker. Earlier that year, during a high-profile committee hearing, he had publicly articulated his own preoccupation with the moral responsibility to act: "When we're dancing with the angels, the question will be asked: In 2019, what did we do to make sure we kept our democracy intact?" Though he never publicly crossed Pelosi, he had confessed to a fellow Oversight Committee member that May that he believed impeachment was an inevitability—and that Democrats might be hamstringing their stated goal of protecting democracy by refusing to proceed.

"Let's assume we get the various documents we've asked for by way of subpoena. And he still would disobey all of our laws and destroy the power of the Congress and the American people," he tapped out in a text message to his colleague during a dialysis treatment session. "I am feeling as if we are failing our constituents."

On the morning of Cummings's passing, the impeachment investigators had been preparing to depose Gordon Sondland, the ambassador to the European Union at the heart of Trump's Ukraine operation who had previously skipped his scheduled interrogation session. But the SCIF had taken on the feel of a wake, and leaders did not know whether they should proceed.

"What would Elijah want us to do?" Pelosi asked Schiff over the phone that morning. Should they cancel Sondland's deposition in honor of their beloved chairman? Or press on?

For Schiff the answer was simple. Cummings had never let his ailments get in the way of his work, despite excruciating pain. Though he was too sick to take part in any of the impeachment proceedings, he had hung on every step of the probe, taking calls from his hospital bed and insisting his staff keep him briefed during his treatments. Plus, Sondland reportedly had a personal relationship with Trump, making him the only firsthand witness they had scheduled to date. He had already canceled on them once in deference to the White House; if Democrats tried to delay his deposition, there was no guarantee he would agree to show up again.

"Elijah would want the work to go on," Schiff declared. Pelosi agreed.

At 9:30 a.m., Republicans and Democrats began Sondland's deposition by sharing remembrances of their lost colleague. Meadows, who had been crying that morning, offered his condolences with reddened eyes. Even Jordan, the attack dog who had been Cummings's chief antagonist on the Oversight panel, said he was going to miss him.

"I'm going to miss just debating with him, arguing with him," said Jordan, who had always respected Cummings as a worthy adversary. "He was special . . . He was a good man. He was a good chairman."

It was—and would remain—the only truly bipartisan moment of the entire impeachment investigation. And it wouldn't last longer than a few minutes. In a way, Cummings's death—once both parties had mourned his passing—marked the end of what little comity remained in the impeachment probe. In the days after his passing, Republican leaders determined to lay waste to the investigation and everyone behind it, even if it meant decimating the House's powers of oversight in their quest to save Trump. And Democrats decided it wasn't worth trying to woo Republicans on the fence to their side.

A few hours later, Jordan and Castor were elated as they walked out of Sondland's deposition for a lunch break. Sondland's attorney had told them point-blank two weeks prior that his client would testify to the essence of Trump's quid pro quo. But that morning, Sondland had done nothing of the sort.

Despite his leading role as one of the point men executing Trump's Ukraine scheme, Sondland had played dumb in his impeachment interview. If Giuliani was pushing the Ukrainians to investigate Biden or his son, he did not realize it, he told investigators. He also claimed not to have had any firsthand knowledge that Ukraine's military assistance had been frozen. All he ever wanted was to secure a White House meeting for Zelensky, he had said—and what was wrong with that? He never realized that asking for probes of "Burisma" was tantamount to demanding Ukraine investigate Trump's 2020 rival, he insisted.

"We were faced with a choice. We could abandon the goal of a White House meeting . . . or we could do as President Trump directed," Sondland had said, reading carefully from a script he prepared for the occasion—and claiming he had no personal responsibility for anything untoward that may have happened.

When investigators had challenged his take, Sondland responded with a parade of "I don't recalls." He downplayed his relationship with Trump and his previous public claims that the president had given him a "special assignment" overseeing Ukraine policy.

"I was spinning a little, to be candid," he said, awkwardly fiddling with his gold-plated pen as he tried to distance himself from the president. "I think I've spoken with President Trump . . . maybe five or six times since I've been an ambassador."

While Democrats had bristled at his casual equivocations, Jordan and Castor thanked their lucky stars. Instead of having to lay a perjury trap for Sondland to smear his credibility, he had turned out to be a helpful witness. And his waffling was actually insurance, they agreed. If he ever grew bolder, and decided to start crying quid pro quo, all they would have to do is brandish the transcript to show Sondland had problems telling the truth. And such an accusation could be quite damning: It was a federal crime to lie to Congress, and Sondland had just testified under oath.

Their euphoria, however, was short-lived. At the lunch break, as the GOP lawmakers spilled out of the deposition room and into the red-carpeted halls to grab their cell phones, they heard a familiar voice squawking from a television on the wall. Across town, their old House colleague Mick Mulvaney, now acting chief of staff to the president, was standing at the podium in the packed White House press room, pontificating about the site selection process for the G7. The annual international confab was set to take place in the United States the following year, and to the GOP's great dismay, Mulvaney was announcing it would take place at one of Trump's Florida golf resorts.

"Doral was, by far and away—far and away—the best physical facility for this meeting," Mulvaney said, blithely confident and utterly oblivious to the backlash his words were about to unleash.

As they watched back at the Capitol, Republicans stiffened. "What is he *doing*?" one of them said, appalled. They were used to Trump throwing out ridiculous ideas. But Mulvaney should have known better. For the president to host an international conference at one of his own facilities, lining his pockets with foreign money and taxpayer funds in the process, was beyond the pale—even for his loyalists. It was bound to fuel even more allegations of illicit corruption and constitutional crimes—justifiable ones that they would be hard-pressed to defend. Above all, it was the last thing they needed to deal with in the midst of an impeachment investigation.

At the White House, Mulvaney wasn't finished. When the questions turned to impeachment, he stepped in it even harder.

"You were directly involved in the decision to withhold funding from Ukraine," an ABC News correspondent said to Mulvaney. "Can you explain to us now, definitely: Why was funding withheld?"

"President Trump is not a big fan of foreign aid. Never has been, still isn't," Mulvaney said, with a hint of pride.

"Did [Trump] also mention to me in passing the corruption related to the DNC server?" Mulvaney continued, referring to a conspiracy theory that there was proof out there that Ukraine had interfered in the 2016 election. "Absolutely, no question about that. But that's it, and that's why we held up the money."

On Capitol Hill, Republicans froze in terror. In the briefing room, reporters wanted to know more.

"To be clear, what you just described is a quid pro quo," the correspondent pointed out.

"We do that all the time with foreign policy," Mulvaney snapped back. "I have news for everybody: Get over it. There's going to be political influence in foreign policy . . . That is going to happen. Elections have consequences."

Mulvaney's words landed like a stun grenade on Capitol Hill, as Jordan and his team—still staring dumbfounded at the TV—realized that he had just eviscerated their whole impeachment defense. Mulvaney hadn't just confirmed the quid pro quo Republicans had been trying to deny, he had doubled down on it—on national television.

"What. The. Fuck?" one of the GOP lawmakers watching said quietly.

"Go get me a copy of that transcript," Meadows barked at an aide, seething.

They hustled out of the SCIF hallway, running up a flight of stairs to a space that had been designated for Republicans to debrief. Once safely inside, Trump's core defense team let loose on their former colleague. They knew Mulvaney had a penchant for sticking his foot in his mouth—in recent months, they had even started referring to the man once dubbed "Mick the Knife" as "Mick the Punchline." But how could he do this to them? All that planning. All their work. Gone in a matter of seconds.

It had to have been a miscommunication, Jordan and Meadows, furious as they were, reasoned. They were at a loss for any better explanation. Mulvaney had to have meant to say something—anything—other than what he had just said.

There were just fifteen minutes left before Sondland's deposition was set to restart, but they needed assurances that Trump's team would fix the mess—before relinquishing their devices to reenter the secure facility. Meadows called the White House and was told that a clean-up operation was already underway. Castor tried to crack jokes to lighten up the dolorous room.

"It's not a big deal . . . it's really nothing," he jested sarcastically. "I mean, the house is burning behind you, but it's not *that* warm."

It would take hours before the White House forced Mulvaney to walk back his comments in a written statement, but by then, it was too late. The video of his press conference spoke for itself and had taken on a life of its own.

In Pelosi's office, aides giddily seized on the exchange as the latest weapon in their impeachment messaging war.

"Clip that video right now and blast it," Pelosi's communications director, Ashley Etienne, directed an underling as the conference wrapped up. "That is gold. That is money!"

Back down in the SCIF, Democrats jeered at Republicans as they reentered the deposition room.

"Have fun cleaning that up," Congressman Eric Swalwell, a Democrat on the Intelligence Committee, snickered at Jordan. Jordan said nothing in response.[4]

A few hours later, Jamie Raskin walked into a conference room in the Capitol like a man on a mission. Pelosi had called the first of a series of impeachment strategy sessions to brainstorm messages she hoped would increase public support for impeachment. She'd invited part of her leadership team, including Raskin—as well as her favorite party messaging gurus—to help her find different ways to sell the Ukraine narrative to voters.

Raskin, however, had shown up with his own objective in mind—and it had nothing to do with Ukraine. Mulvaney's Doral announcement had set him off. And he was adamant that House Democrats couldn't sit idly by while Trump raked in taxpayer dollars and foreign funds by hosting an official diplomatic event at his private property.

Since Democrats had taken the majority earlier that year, the Maryland Democrat had tried to persuade Pelosi to do more to blow the whistle on what he dubbed the "original sin" of Trump's presidency: his refusal to divest from his business interests. The fact that Trump was profiting from special-interest lobbyists and foreign government officials who patronized his hotels was, in Raskin's view, blatant exploitation of the Oval Office as a moneymaking operation. It was something the Founding Fathers had both foreseen and forbidden, which is why they had tucked explicit prohibitions against accepting "emoluments"—or personally profiting from public office—into the Constitution.[5]

"The whole purpose of the foreign and domestic emoluments clauses was to guarantee that the president maintained exclusive fiduciary loyalty to the American people and would be neither ripping off the U.S. government, nor on the take from foreign states and corporations," Raskin would stand up to say in private House Democratic caucus meetings, spewing professorial legalese to anyone who would listen.

A group of House Democrats were already suing Trump for having allegedly engaged in the practice. But Raskin was adamant that the House needed to act more officially. The Constitution stated that the president could only accept emoluments with the consent of Congress—but for three years, the House had remained silent while Trump continued to line his family's pockets. Raskin believed that if the House passed a resolution explicitly barring him from taking such gifts, it would not only bolster their court case, but also send a clear signal to the president and the public that Trump was in violation of the Constitution.

Raskin had explained this to Pelosi multiple times. That spring, he'd crafted a resolution rebuking Trump for taking "illegal payments" and had pleaded with the Speaker to put it to a vote.

"We're gonna get kicked out of court otherwise," Raskin warned.

But Pelosi dismissed his arguments—just as she had when Raskin and his "musketeers" urged her to start impeachment proceedings over the Mueller report. Her moderates viewed Raskin as a pesky progressive with little political know-how—and pleasing them was paramount. "Oh, I'm not a lawyer," Pelosi would tell Raskin, deflecting whenever he tried to appeal to her with high-minded, moral arguments about the law. Her office would sugarcoat it even less: The frontliners in pro-Trump districts simply didn't want any more confrontations with the president, they told Raskin.

In late September, following a smattering of national headlines about Trump making Pence stay at his resorts during official trips abroad, Raskin had taken his case directly to the Speaker's beloved moderates in hopes of changing their minds. During a late-night meeting over pizza in centrist leader Josh Gottheimer's office, he donned his old professor cap and tried to impress on his colleagues the importance of rebuking Trump for violating the Constitution's emoluments clause. The conversation, however, veered off course, as the moderates accused him of just trying to find another on-ramp to impeachment.

"We know the end of this story," Gottheimer said. "What's the point?"

Raskin was exasperated.

"The politics don't matter," Raskin responded matter-of-factly. "The administration is running as a for-profit enterprise. Sometimes, we have to do these things."

By the time Pelosi endorsed impeachment, Raskin had mostly backed off his emoluments crusade, knowing the Speaker wanted a Ukraine-focused probe. But Mulvaney's Doral announcement that day changed his calculus. To Raskin, a myopic focus on Ukraine was unsustainable now that Trump was actively engaged in a bigger, and more blatant, constitutional crime.

As Pelosi convened the inaugural messaging meeting, she laid out reasons for their gathering. The party needed talking points to get on the same page and avoid the charge that "Democrats are divided," she said. And they needed "calm, objective outside validators"— like generals, foreign policy experts, and constitutional scholars—to argue publicly that impeachment was what Trump deserved.

"We may not get the Senate to convict him, but we can make it a tough vote for them," Pelosi vowed.

The Speaker also stressed that Democrats needed to ensure that voters didn't dismiss their efforts as an early 2020 campaign stunt.

"We need to separate the elections from protecting the Constitution," she said.

With that statement, Raskin certainly agreed. And when the conversation turned to Mulvaney's disastrous press conference, he saw an opening to make his pitch.

"This is a gift," he said of the White House chief of staff's blunder. It was the perfect opportunity for House Democrats to demonstrate the full scope of Trump's criminal ambitions, he argued—if they were willing to widen the scope of possible charges against him. Plus, it was such an egregious violation of the Constitution, how could they ignore it?

Raskin braced for Pelosi's pushback, but it never came.

"Mulvaney is a liar and a creep—I don't let him in the office," she deadpanned. And Trump, she continued, was a "very sick man and a freeloader" who was clearly, flagrantly, breaking the rules. Still, Democrats had to pick their battles, she added. Trump had committed all sorts of crimes, and there was "a mountain of grievances" they could investigate, she said.

"We need to pick three," she declared. "No more than three."

For the first time, however, the Speaker allowed that Trump's emoluments violations might be one of the matters she would let Democrats probe. She made Raskin no promises—but much to his delight, she told him to dust off his emoluments resolution and get in touch with her office.

19

THE PRICE OF PRINCIPLE

OCTOBER 18-19, 2019

Congressman Francis Rooney knew he was about to put his political life on the line and he didn't care. As a CNN cameraman affixed a microphone to the lapel of his suit jacket the morning of Friday, October 18, the frosty-haired former CEO took a deep breath and prepared to do what had long been unthinkable in Republican circles: take aim at Trump on his favorite medium—cable television.

The moment had been a long time coming for Rooney, sixty-five, a lifelong conservative with close ties to the Bush family. The representative from Naples, Florida, had run a successful multimillion-dollar investment company and served a turn as U.S. ambassador to the Holy See during the George W. Bush administration. He'd decided to try his hand at politics rather late in life, trading his prestige in corporate America for the relative anonymity of being just one of 435 faces in the House. Though he'd entered Congress the same month as Trump took up residence in the White House, Rooney was never a Trump fan. Still, he forged a working relationship with the president by staying focused on parochial issues like trade and the environment—even getting the president to sign protections for the Sunshine State's waterways into law.[1]

But Rooney's taste for transactional politics had soured as the president's moral compass careened off course. He was a devout Catholic and felt an almost religious compulsion to push back against some of Trump's increasingly self-serving antics. He had twice voted against Trump's emergency declarations to fund his border wall, calling the move to usurp Congress's authority "unconstitutional." And he didn't like how Trump would routinely attack his own intelligence community, many of whose members Rooney knew personally.

When the Ukraine scandal hit, it forever changed the way Rooney looked at Washington. He read the July 25 call transcript between Trump and Zelensky and immediately recognized that the president's behavior was wrong. "Trump is using the power of the United States to influence a foreign government on a personal matter," he said to himself. He knew that Trump's instruction to "do us a favor" would have been intimidating to Ukraine, given its dependence on American assistance to stand up to Russia.

As a GOP member of the Foreign Affairs panel, Rooney had eagerly attended every deposition in the Democrats' impeachment inquiry that he could, hanging on the witnesses' every word. He knew, from his days as an ambassador, that State Department officials worked long hours, and in some cases made serious personal sacrifices to serve their country in faraway lands. The stories they had told about Rudy Giuliani's efforts to undermine official U.S. policy, smear an ambassador, and strong-arm an ally into performing personal political favors revolted him.

"It's painful to me to see this kind of amateur diplomacy riding roughshod over our State Department apparatus," he had told reporters, after listening to the sobering testimony.

That Thursday, Mick Mulvaney's public admission of a quid pro quo had shocked Rooney. He had rewatched the press conference at home that night after Sondland's hearing, slack-jawed. To him, the chief of staff's words were confirmation enough of what he had started to believe days earlier: that Trump had tried to pervert U.S. national security policy to serve his own ends. When the White House tried to walk it back, Rooney deadpanned that "it's not an Etch A Sketch" that could be easily erased.[2]

The administration's ham-handed attempt at a clean-up nagged at Rooney's conscience and fired up his motivation. It was time to speak up, Rooney decided, even if no other Republicans would.

"I'm going to be looking at myself in the mirror—and at my children—for a lot longer than I'll be looking at anyone in this building," he said to himself. "I'm not going to do the wrong thing."

There was just one problem with that plan. Rooney hailed from a Florida district that worshipped the president, backing him over Hillary Clinton by 22 points in 2016. He knew how viscerally his constituents defended Trump, refusing to believe anything negative about their dear leader. The enthusiasm at each rally he'd attended dwarfed any displays of fealty he had ever witnessed for Bush or even Ronald Reagan.

"These Republicans say 'No way—impeachment is wrong!' But they have no idea," Rooney said at the time. "It's just like Watergate. We need the evidence."

As the House's impeachment probe of Trump got underway, Rooney had been thinking a lot about Watergate. He had been a student at Georgetown University and an intern on Capitol Hill when the Senate launched its investigation of Nixon. He had attended the Senate Watergate hearings in person, and he remembered precisely how the GOP of the 1970s spent almost two years defending the president before they began to break rank. The morning after the

Saturday Night Massacre of 1973—when Nixon ordered the firing of the special Watergate prosecutor investigating him, prompting the attorney general and his deputy to resign in protest—Rooney had attended Catholic Mass with his father, a Nixon fanatic. When the priest offered up a prayer for those men and the country, Rooney's dad got up and walked out.

"They're just beating up on Nixon," his dad said angrily.

Several months later, however, when the extent of Nixon's crimes crystallized for the public following months of open hearings with all the president's top men, even his father could no longer stomach the betrayal. His—and the larger GOP's—ultimate rejection of Nixon had been a lesson to Rooney: that evidence could emerge, and minds could change.

That's why, unlike most of his GOP colleagues, Rooney vowed he wasn't going to offer a knee-jerk defense of the president. He was determined to keep an open mind as the facts were examined— even if it meant leaving open the possibility of impeaching a man Republicans didn't dare cross. Republican leaders had been putting on a full-court press that week to herd freethinking members like Rooney back into line. Most of his colleagues were capitulating to their talking points—like Jaime Herrera Beutler, who had gone in a matter of hours from questioning GOP strategy to recording a video message attacking the impeachment probe. But Rooney was determined to take a principled stand.

"I'm not going to say a bunch of things that would make me look stupid later or that I would regret," he said to himself. "I want to get the facts."

Rooney knew that there would likely be consequences. Republicans who had stood up to Trump in the past never managed to stick around Washington for very long afterward. Usually, they either lost their next primary to a Trump acolyte or retired early to avoid that sort of blow. The proof was in the numbers: By the time impeachment began in the fall of 2019, more than 40 percent of the House GOP lawmakers who had been present in Washington for Trump's 2017 inauguration were either already gone or on their way out.

But Rooney had already weighed the stakes and made his decision. Just steps from the House floor, with tourists circling the Rotunda behind him, he went on television and accused Trump of "us[ing] government power and prestige for political gain," becoming the first congressional Republican to declaratively state he was open to impeaching Trump.

"I don't think you can rule anything out until you know all the facts," he told CNN. "I'm very mindful of the fact that back during Watergate everybody said, 'Oh, it's a witch hunt to get Nixon.' Turns out it wasn't a witch hunt. It was absolutely correct."[3]

The next day, Jaime Herrera Beutler watched as a trio of moderate Republicans charged the president's chief of staff like a pack of wolves in the middle of woodsy, rural Maryland. She had been invited to Camp David alongside Ann Wagner of Missouri, Peter King of New York, Fred Upton of Michigan, and several other House Republicans, part of a new White House campaign to woo GOP lawmakers to Trump's impeachment defense. But while the members were ecstatic to visit the exclusive, rustic retreat for presidents, the group was still smarting about their former colleague Mick Mulvaney's unfortunate press conference.

"Hell of a week. Can we try a little harder here?" Wagner sneered at Mulvaney as they lounged around a crackling fire before dinner, a cocktail in her hand. "Like *really*, Mick?"

That morning, Hill Republicans had watched in shock as their colleague Francis Rooney had been all but forced out of his seat for suggesting on television that he might support impeachment. His constituents had been so furious that they demanded he resign on the spot. About twenty-four hours after his turn in the spotlight, Rooney announced that this would be his last term serving in Congress.[4]

He was not the only Republican to have been punished for speaking his mind about Trump since impeachment began. Earlier that month, the president had taken Mitt Romney to task on Twitter for criticizing his Zelensky call as "deeply troubling," deriding the Utah senator as a "pompous 'ass'" and a "fool who is playing right into the hands of the Do Nothing Democrats!" Conservative groups took the hint and, right around the time Rooney had his turn on CNN, started running ads in Utah that accused Romney of "colluding" with Democrats "to take down President Trump with impeachment."[5]

The episodes served as a cautionary tale to lawmakers on the fence, like Herrera Beutler. Getting trolled by the president on Twitter was one of the worst possible punishments for an elected Republican. But Rooney's situation was worse: Speaking his conscience against Trump had ended his fledgling political career. He was walking proof that there was little room for breaking with their party leader. Trump didn't even have to go after Rooney; his own GOP constituents—who put Rooney in office in the first place—did the work for him.

Though Rooney's political demise would make Republicans think twice about publicly voicing frustrations, the moderates at Camp David that day still had a beef with Trump that they were determined to raise with Mulvaney—albeit, in the privacy of the forest retreat. "Your performance was kinda abysmal," one told their former colleague bluntly of his press conference that week. And the pitch to host the G7 at Doral, another added, was "a stupid idea."

"You need to make clear to the president that we can't defend him on this," Wagner told Mulvaney. "This is an unacceptable, unforced error. We won't defend it."

As they argued, Herrera Beutler watched, mostly in silence. She was flattered to have been invited to Camp David at all, but she was more eager to talk policy than the scandal du jour. The White House had conspicuously sidestepped disclosing the actual reason for the impromptu confab—impeachment—and instead told her that the weekend would be an opportunity to bend the president's ear about her legislative ideas. And who wouldn't want that? Herrera Beutler had dropped everything and decided to go.

As the moderates criticized him, Mulvaney was silent too. The members' complaints weren't the first he had received since his presser—nor would they be the last. Since almost the moment he left the podium Thursday, Republican members had been blowing up White House officials' phones, demanding Trump retract the announcement about Doral. The move was nothing short of pouring salt in the wound for centrists already squeamish about defending Trump on Ukraine. The Constitution specifically stated that presidents were barred from taking money from foreign governments—yet there was Trump, preparing to do exactly that with impunity.

Indeed, Mulvaney's remarks had unleashed weeks of pent-up GOP frustration. The Doral bombshell came barely a week after Trump announced he would pull U.S. troops out of Syria, where they were helping to fight the terrorist group ISIS—a move that crossed a red line for almost the entire GOP.[6] Coming on top of impeachment, there was a growing sense among Republicans that Trump was taking advantage of their loyalty. He was, in the words of one GOP lawmaker, forcing Hill Republicans to "defend the indefensible," pressuring them to go on television to fight for him while he did whatever he wanted.

Some of them were losing their patience.

"You have to go out and try to defend him. Well, I don't know if I can do that!" a frustrated Congressman Mike Simpson of Idaho fumed just off the House floor that Friday. "I have no doubt that Doral is a really good place—I've been there, I know. But it is politically insensitive. They should have known what the kickback is going to be on this, that politically he's doing it for his own benefit."[7]

The backlash, Mulvaney realized, was going to jeopardize the tenuous GOP coalition that they needed to keep intact in order to defend Trump from the impeachment inquiry. He knew that if Trump kept acting out, some members would find it impossible to keep resisting the pressure to support at least the framework of an investigation. Within days, House Democrats would be holding a vote on the rules of the road for their ongoing probe. When that happened, Trump needed the GOP to be unified in their opposition, not still simmering over Doral.

Mulvaney wasn't the only one trying to get Trump to step it up with the congressional GOP. House Minority Leader Kevin McCarthy was also nudging the president to try a charm offensive to head off the relentless impeachment assault. Rank-and-file members who might be inclined to criticize Trump in a vacuum would absolutely swoon if he made a personal appeal to them, McCarthy argued. "Woo them," he told Trump, "as only you can."

With that in mind, Mulvaney had pitched Trump that week on an unorthodox idea: *What if we win over House Republicans by inviting them to Camp David?*

While previous presidents had used the rustic mountain retreat about ninety minutes outside Washington for private family getaways, Trump had always preferred the gold-and-marble elegance of his own resorts like Mar-a-Lago. He hadn't much cared for the historic appeal of the grounds, where presidents had charmed foreign leaders and negotiated pivotal peace accords.

Since the place was empty, Mulvaney proposed they use it to wine and dine key Republican members who were either on the fence about impeachment or who had influence in the GOP conference.[8]

At first, Trump was confused.

"Who would want to go there?" he had asked in surprise, not understanding the rustic appeal of a place he considered to be a run-down shithole.

Mulvaney laughed. As a former lawmaker himself, he knew members fawned over presidential nods—a visit to the Oval Office, or a call from the president, could send their hungry egos soaring. Inviting the members to stay in a place where so few Americans—let alone lawmakers—had set foot could help Trump win over even the most moderate of Republicans, Mulvaney explained. If they felt like valued members of the White House family, they would be more likely to stick with the president when the big impeachment moment came.

That Saturday, however, things were getting off to a rocky start. While the members were over the moon at their surroundings, they were impatient with Mulvaney. It was imperative that he tell Trump to cancel his Doral plans, they insisted. Mulvaney passed the message up the chain to the boss.

Following dinner, lawmakers dispersed to various corners of the complex to ooh and aah at the marvels of Camp David. Upton was with his wife in the basement bowling alley. Others were nursing beverages while playing billiards at the arcade. Despite her blunt confrontation with Mulvaney, Wagner had turned positively giddy at the historic surroundings and was spending thousands of dollars in the gift shop on "Camp David"–emblazoned merchandise.

Hoodies. Throws. T-shirts. Golf balls. Decanters. Cuff links. Baby bibs. So much that her husband got an alert asking if their credit card had been stolen.

Suddenly, a White House press aide interrupted their recreation, summoning the four moderates to a small huddle in the hallway. "The president wants to talk to everybody," the staffer said, holding up his cell phone, which was on speaker. Trump's voice blared from the other end, challenging them on Doral.

"Why don't you think it's a good idea?" he asked the group, prattling on about the spacious accommodations and existing security protocols at his Florida resort. "It's a great venue! Everyone will love it!"

The members looked at each other, wondering if Trump truly was as naive as he sounded. Herrera Beutler was shocked by something else: that Trump was actually seeking their input.

King, who had known Trump from their shared years in New York, started off gently, explaining that holding an international summit at his own resort looked self-serving, and like something he stood to benefit from financially. Wagner chimed in, suggesting he have the event at Camp David.

"This place is awesome; why don't you have it here?" she said. "Or *anywhere* else."

Above all, they stressed, holding the G7 conference at Doral would be an unforced error. Don't give the Democrats ammunition, they told Trump, especially in the middle of impeachment.

"We don't want to have to defend you on this," Wagner said. "We're already defending you on a lot of other stuff."

Back at the White House, it was taking Trump a while to get the picture. He didn't understand what all the fuss was about. He had expected blowback from Democrats, who hated everything he did. But he hadn't predicted he would also be contending with Republican outrage—or that even his closest allies would be scolding him.

"This is *not* worth the fight," Senator Lindsey Graham had told
Trump privately when the president tried to argue he was going to
save taxpayers money by giving world leaders a discount for staying
at the resort—and Uncle Sam for hosting it. The price tag wasn't the
point, Graham said. "Stay focused on the task at hand."

Mark Meadows had also weighed in on the unfolding drama, phoning Trump to tell him that he had better not take any cash from the
summit. Republicans could not risk giving Democrats additional
ammunition to use against them on impeachment, he warned, suggesting that Trump donate the conference proceeds to charity—or
host the event for free.

Begrudgingly, Trump listened to his advisor. Even his cheerleaders at Fox News had been giving him flack—and he knew what he
had to do.[9]

Sitting in the residence that night, Trump began to draft an announcement calling off his plans. A half hour later, he called back
the aide at Camp David and instructed him to once again put the
members on speakerphone.

"Okay! I thought about what you said," Trump said, trying to
sound jovial. "I hear you. All right. I'm going to tweet something
like this out. How does this tweet sound?"

Trump proceeded to read the group a draft tweet walking back
his Doral plans. That's great, they agreed. Minutes after they hung
up, Trump blasted out the message on Twitter.

"I thought I was doing something very good for our country by using Trump National Doral, in Miami, for hosting the G-7 leaders . . .
But, as usual, the Hostile Media & their Democrat Partners went
CRAZY!" he wrote, going on to praise his hotel's amenities before
announcing he was pulling the plug.

Trump's reversal constituted one of the few times he recognized a limiting factor to his own power: the rest of the Republican
party. The experience also proved to be an unpublicized win for

the president. His accommodation of the moderates' demands made him look reasonable and accessible to his rank and file. He gave them a false sense of empowerment and fellowship that would make defending him—and turning a blind eye to the conduct that had been rankling them—more palatable.

That small but important turnaround also came just in time—before the most devastating witness yet walked through the doors of Adam Schiff's SCIF.

20

GET TOUGHER

The president's meeting with members of the House Freedom Caucus had been on the books for a while, and for Trump, fortuitously so. The group's forty-something far-right Republicans were the president's most devoted henchmen on the Hill—and on that Tuesday, October 22, Trump felt he needed them more than ever.

All of Washington had been in a tizzy that afternoon over the latest damning testimony unfolding in the SCIF. Bill Taylor—the seasoned ambassador who had deemed Trump's Ukraine scheme "crazy" in texts with Kurt Volker—had testified that Trump dangled not only the promise of a White House meeting, but Ukraine's military assistance, to compel President Zelensky to investigate the Bidens. Multiple administration officials, including U.S. Ambassador to the European Union Gordan Sondland, had told him so—and Taylor had taken notes of their conversations.

"President Trump wanted President Zelensky in a box by making a public statement about ordering such investigations," Taylor recalled Sondland telling him, a quote that promptly leaked and was now plastered all over every news website in the country, dominating cable news. Sondland had rationalized the scheme by arguing Trump was a "businessman." "When a businessman is about to sign a check to someone who owes him something, the businessman asks that person to pay up before signing the check," Taylor said, continuing to quote what Sondland had said to him.

It was the first time that a witness had connected the dots between Ukraine's money and Trump's probes, and the explosive revelation had leaked to reporters within just an hour of Taylor delivering it.

Trump had taken it all in from the White House, seething. In the deposition room, his ally Jim Jordan was already working furiously to undermine Taylor's testimony by claiming he wasn't a credible witness. None of his information came firsthand from Trump, Jordan and his compatriots argued. But Trump wanted more than nuance to sink his teeth into. The irascible president didn't want to quibble over what counted as hearsay—he wanted to hit back.

For days, Trump had been trying to get congressional Republicans to fight harder for him. He had heaped praise on those who had stepped forward to offer him public support to let them know he was listening and was grateful. He couldn't understand why every Republican wasn't blanketing the airwaves to come to his defense. Democrats, he told reporters, "fight dirty." He wanted his party to do the same.

"Democrats are lousy politicians with lousy policy . . . but two things they have: They're vicious and they stick together," Trump complained. "You never see them break off."[1]

Sensing his disquiet, even some of Trump's own family members had begun to pressure Republicans to beat back harder against the Democrats' impeachment inquiry. That Monday, after GOP leaders launched an effort to censure—or publicly rebuke—Adam Schiff on the House floor, Donald Trump Jr. retweeted a list of the twenty-three more moderate-minded Republicans who hadn't signed on to the resolution, a list that included Jaime Herrera Beutler and Francis Rooney. It was a page ripped right from his father's playbook, and it worked: Angry constituents read the list and called those GOP lawmakers' offices, and at the vote, not a single Republican defected.[2]

But to Trump, the procedural slap on the wrist—which failed in the Democratic-led House—was wholly unsatisfying. He wanted a more dramatic gesture, a show of force to turn heads and seize the impeachment limelight away from the Democrats' witnesses.

By the time two dozen Freedom Caucus hardliners settled around the glossy conference table in the Cabinet room of the White House for their visit that evening, the White House had gone into full damage-control mode, dismissing Taylor's revelations as "a coordinated smear campaign from far-left lawmakers and radical unelected bureaucrats."[3] But Trump still wanted Hill Republicans to get tougher.

"I need you to take the gloves off," he told them.

There was no debate: All of them agreed.

As it happened, GOP Whip Steve Scalise had already been cooking up a plan with Congressman Matt Gaetz, the die-hard Trumper from Florida who had already tried and failed to muscle his way into an impeachment interview. The pair had floated the idea of a mass protest outside the SCIF, an image they hoped would help punctuate their complaints about the Democrats' secrecy and unwillingness to conduct their probe in public. They had meant to stage the show the previous week but postponed it out of respect when Cummings died.

On the day of Taylor's deposition, the idea found new life in the White House among Trump and his staunchest supporters. If they gathered outside the SCIF, and were denied entry en masse, the videos of GOP members being turned away were sure to go viral, they agreed. And if they just so happened to push through the doors and get in, what a spectacle that would be.

Trump loved the idea. As the members filed out, they agreed to execute the plan the next morning.

At about 9:45 a.m., a swarm of GOP lawmakers descended the spiral staircase leading down to the SCIF and stood grouped before the cameras outside the secure facility, filling the marble-floored space. Overnight, Scalise and Gaetz had whipped together a coalition of Freedom Caucus hardliners and more traditional establishment Republicans to take the fight straight to Adam Schiff, just as Trump wanted. A podium with microphones had been carted in and placed outside the secure facility ahead of their arrival, just a few yards from the heavy, wooden doors.

"What is Adam Schiff trying to hide?" Scalise cried out, pointing toward the SCIF, where behind the closed door, Democrats were waiting to begin the day's deposition. "Over there, Adam Schiff is trying to impeach a president of the United States behind closed doors . . . Maybe in the Soviet Union this kind of thing is commonplace. This shouldn't be happening in the United States of America!"

The group nodding their heads emphatically behind Scalise and Gaetz were a visually homogeneous bunch of mostly white men. Still, the fact that so many had turned out on short notice—and that leaders were in lockstep with the ultra-conservative right flank they'd been warring with for years—highlighted how the GOP was unifying around an impeachment counter message.

"Show your face!" howled Mo Brooks, an Alabama conservative

so rabid and erratic that GOP leaders hardly ever agreed to appear alongside him in public. Here, his feral passion was welcome. "We demand open proceedings! The American people deserve nothing less!"

After about twenty minutes of such displays, Gaetz announced: "We're gonna go and see if we can get inside." And just like that, the Republicans all turned and shuffled away from the cameras and toward the SCIF doors, pushing past bright red "Restricted Area" signs affixed to the entrance. Once inside, they filed toward the back of the red-carpeted lobby, where a young, bewildered-looking security guard was blocking the entrance to the impeachment room. She told them she could only allow members of the three panels running the probe to enter—but the Republicans weren't taking no for an answer.

Scalise began pounding on the security officer's desk, yelling, "Let us in! Let us in!" In a bold violation of rules prohibiting electronic devices in the secure space, some had their phones out, filming as they took up Scalise's battle cry. When the security officer opened the door to let a single authorized member enter the conference room, the group lunged forward and poured inside, surprising the investigators assembled around the interview table—including Steve Castor, the Republicans' top questioner, who frowned with concern.

With their invasion complete, GOP members whooped in victory and started tweeting out videos of their hostile takeover. Texas congressman Louie Gohmert, a fervent Trump surrogate with a penchant for making spectacles of himself, screamed about "injustices" against Trump. Congressman Bradley Byrne, then running in a packed Alabama Senate primary, got in Schiff's face and started shouting. Schiff stared back, cold and stone-faced, as other Democrats in the room objected to the dramatic interruption.

"There are no cameras here, so it won't help your Senate campaign," Congressman Gerry Connolly, a Virginia Democrat, snarked at Byrne from across the room.

"Do these morons know they're not allowed to have electronic devices in here?" an annoyed Eric Swalwell asked of no one in particular.[4]

Mike Quigley, an Illinois Democrat on the Intelligence panel, had brought a bag of candy with him to the proceedings. In an effort to defuse the tension in the room, he turned to the Republican interlopers and offered them a candy bar. "You're not acting like yourself right now. Here, have a Snickers," he joked, mimicking a well-known Snickers television commercial.

Schiff, however, was too furious to crack a smile. He warned the invading Republicans that they were violating House rules, disturbing the deposition, and compromising national security by bringing their phones inside the SCIF. But his admonitions only seemed to egg them on. Seeing the potential danger, senior Intelligence panel Republican Mike Conaway started walking around with a bucket, asking the intruders to at least surrender their phones while they were in the SCIF. But he did not try to kick them out.

Aggravated, Schiff recessed the proceedings and retreated to his office with some of his staff in tow to figure out what to do. If they had the House Sergeant at Arms escort the invading Republicans out in restraints, Schiff knew the right-wing media would have a field day. It would only help the Republicans make the case that they were being forcibly kept from the impeachment probe. No, they'd have to wait out the intrusive filibuster until the interlopers got bored or decided to leave of their own volition, Schiff decided.

To speed things along, Maher Bitar, Schiff's general counsel, organized a call between impeachment leaders and the House parliamentarian. Summoning Jim Jordan and a handful of Republican members to join him, they huddled around the speakerphone in a small room off the conference area as Bitar explained to the House's official referee what had just transpired. The parliamentarian was unequivocal: The raiding Republicans were breaking the rules. If members were not on the three panels investigating the matter, they needed to leave.

But Schiff was appealing to an arbiter who no longer held sway in such a toxic environment. The Republicans simply ignored the parliamentarian's ruling, continuing to breach norms governing the security of classified information that had long been respected by both parties without a second thought. It was a decision with potentially staggering implications: If the parliamentarian's rulings could be flouted without consequence, there could be no guarantee of maintaining order in the halls of the Capitol at all.

The GOP members, however, were having too much fun to think about that. Settling in for a stay, they ordered pizza, offering some to both Democrats and the press. "There is no quid pro quo. You can eat it!" Meadows called out to reporters, who declined due to ethical obligations. Inside the SCIF, Dan Goldman, Schiff's investigations director, relented and took a slice. "It's not as good as pizza from New York," he quipped.

Unexpectedly, the sit-in had turned into a bonding opportunity between the Republicans who had been in the trenches of the impeachment depositions for weeks and those who were defending Trump from outside the bunker. Congressman Chip Roy of Texas, who had taken part in the depositions as a member of the Oversight Committee, kept turning to Castor and imploring him to regale the masses with the story of how Volker had testified there was no quid pro quo.

"Steve, tell it again!" he'd say.

For the first time since the impeachment probe had started,

Republican lawmakers felt as if defending Trump was fun, not just their duty. Even usually dour Castor was now smiling, seeming to have shed concerns about impropriety that plagued him when the SCIF stormers had entered the room.

Democrats, meanwhile, were livid. "You should be ashamed of yourselves," Val Demings, a Florida Democrat on the Intelligence Committee, scolded Republicans—not just for breaching the SCIF but for standing by the president. She began quoting the Gospel of Mark: "For what shall it profit a man if he shall gain the whole world and lose his own soul?"

An hour later, having made no progress whatsoever to resolve the standoff, both sides crammed into Schiff's small office. Meadows, Jordan, and several Republican members squished into one side of the room, while Schiff, his staff, and several Democratic members stood shoulder to shoulder on the other. In the middle, sitting at his desk by the north wall, Schiff excoriated Jordan, telling him to get the invading Republicans out.

"Call off your members," Schiff demanded angrily.

Jordan refused. He had not been part of the SCIF storming planning and hadn't even known about it. But he was not about to tell other members how to act. When Schiff and his staff grilled Jordan further, Meadows leaped in to defend him.

"Look, Adam, we don't control our members," Meadows said. "We told them this isn't productive. But, you know, they refuse to leave, and there's nothing that we can do about it."

Meadows tried to explain to Schiff that GOP members were upset because they were learning about the depositions via leaks in the news media—and had no way of verifying what they were hearing.

"You want them to stop? Release the transcripts so they know how to respond to questions about these leaks," he said, giving Schiff a pointed look.

Standing next to his boss, Bitar went rigid at Meadows's insinuation. He knew that the charge that Schiff was "a leaker" had taken hold in GOP circles, and it infuriated him to no end. Schiff personally was not the source of any escaping information and had repeatedly instructed staff and Democratic members in the room not to say a word to the press. When his members broke those rules, he had even admonished them in private.

Like most investigators involved in the probe—including most Republicans—Bitar suspected the witnesses' attorneys were actually the source of the daily headlines, leaking their clients' testimony to steer the narrative as best as they could. But Bitar also knew the GOP had selectively leaked at least once: when they put out Volker's first text messages.

"We are *also* keeping close track of all the leaks that appear to be occurring from the minority side," Bitar snapped at Meadows.

"Thanks a lot, smart-ass," Meadows shot back.

The room blew up. "That is so inappropriate!" Schiff said. "We don't talk to staff like that," another Democrat chimed in.

The meeting soured any hope of resolving the standoff. Democrats departed the room aghast at Meadows's behavior and incensed that he and Jordan wouldn't call off their dogs. Republicans left infuriated over Schiff and Bitar's insinuation that Jordan had orchestrated the GOP's invasion of the SCIF.

They were saved from coming to worse blows only by the sound of a bell. Five hours after a Republican horde had plowed into the SCIF, a loud buzzer sounded through the Capitol to alert members that it was time to take votes on the floor. At the blaring sound, the Republicans shuffled out of the room, leaving behind empty pizza boxes and the faint smell of pepperoni.

The "storming of SCIF"—as it became known—changed everything for House Republicans. After weeks spent scrambling to save themselves from free fall, they had found their footing and learned a valuable lesson: They too could seize the impeachment headlines by perfecting the art of distraction. The president had ordered them to fight, and their punches landed on the front page of every national newspaper in America.

21

"MORE LIKE NIXON"

Jerry Nadler squared his shoulders as he faced off with his Democratic colleague and perennial rival Adam Schiff, the man who'd become the overnight star of the impeachment he'd been pushing for all year—and who, Nadler worried, was about to make a grave mistake.

After weeks of hand-wringing, Democrats were finally preparing to take a step they had long delayed: holding a full House vote on a resolution laying out a structure for the rest of the impeachment proceedings. The GOP's insistence that the impeachment investigation would be a sham until the House approved some ground rules was starting to resonate with some voters—and the moderate Democrats Pelosi had been trying to protect wanted to kill that GOP talking point once and for all. Plus, with ten interviews and depositions completed, and the year's end looming, it was time to start thinking about next steps, such as drafting the articles of impeachment.

But when Nadler leafed through the final wording of the resolution on Tuesday, October 29, alarm bells started going off in his
head. Schiff, he worried, had convinced Speaker Nancy Pelosi that
Trump didn't deserve a guarantee of due process rights, a proposition Nadler found absolutely ludicrous. So that afternoon, he
marched to the SCIF to demand Schiff amend the document before
they inadvertently armed Republicans with further ammunition.

"It's unfair, and it's unprecedented, and it's *unconstitutional*," Nadler told Schiff sternly.

"I don't appreciate your tone," Schiff responded curtly, accusing
Nadler of being unhelpful. "I worry you're putting us in a box for
our investigation."

Since Pelosi had handed the impeachment baton to Schiff in late
September, Nadler and his staff had been largely sidelined. Even as
of mid-October, they had no idea whether they would play a role in
impeachment at all. They had assumed when Schiff was done with
his investigation, the Judiciary panel would get its turn in the spotlight to have public hearings before writing articles, as was its traditional role. But the more time went by without getting the nod, the
more they fretted. They worried Pelosi would ultimately ice them
out to punish Nadler for his months-long effort to push her into impeachment against her will.

That month, as Washington's eyes were fixed on the heavy doors
of Schiff's SCIF, Nadler made an intentional effort to get back into
Pelosi's good graces. His aides sucked up to her staff relentlessly,
as Nadler set about trying to prove to the Speaker that his panel
was ready and up to the task of taking the wheel at a moment's
notice. He knew they wouldn't get two years to do their work, or a
budget to hire a massive investigative staff like Watergate chairman
Peter Rodino had. But Nadler scrambled together the resources to
hire more legal power in anticipation of having at least a bite at the

apple, bringing in Joshua Matz, a young constitutional lawyer who was already one of the country's foremost authorities on impeachment, having written a book on the subject.[1] Judiciary aides also raided the congressional libraries, hauling in hundreds of books and papers from previous impeachments, and studying them until they knew the precedent by heart. They checked out the entire record of the Andrew Johnson and Richard Nixon impeachments from the National Archives, documents that cluttered every surface of the already stuffy Judiciary office.

The combined effort worked. By late October, Pelosi and Schiff had signaled they were ready to bring the Judiciary panel back into the fold. But much to Nadler's dismay, they had their own ideas about how he should run his committee process—and in his view, they departed from precedent in some disturbing ways.

Pelosi, still smarting from Nadler going rogue on impeachment that summer, was adamant that public hearings with fact witnesses should occur only in Schiff's committee—not Nadler's. In fact, she didn't want the Judiciary panel to interview witnesses at all. Pelosi simply didn't trust the panel—which was stacked with liberal crusaders and hotheaded conservatives—to handle the rollout of the complex Ukraine narrative with the careful, compelling treatment it required. She couldn't afford another Nadler screwup. The Judiciary chairman could focus on the legal business of crafting the articles of impeachment and have academics testify, she allowed. But that was it.

Nadler and his team, however, immediately realized a problem with her edict that had nothing to do with their bruised egos. In impeachments past, they knew from their studies, presidents were given a chance to defend themselves before the House Judiciary Committee. Their lawyers had been allowed to attend hearings and cross-examine witnesses who testified, or call their own. They had been given the chance to challenge or present evidence, give statements and make presentations.

To Schiff, that didn't matter. By his logic, he was running the equivalent of a grand jury probe and therefore was under no obligation to let Trump's lawyers take part in the private or public proceedings that fell under his purview. But that raised the stakes dramatically for Nadler. If Pelosi was going to keep the Judiciary panel from conducting its own witness interviews, Trump would never get to face his accusers before he was impeached—or call his own witnesses to counter their story.

That, to Nadler, was unacceptable. It was the equivalent of destroying a defendant's right to due process and a break with precedent that would backfire, he argued to Pelosi and Schiff. Even someone who disdained legal norms as much as Trump deserved a chance to challenge his accusers, Nadler stressed.

"If we're going to impeach, we need to show the country that we gave the president ample opportunity to defend himself," Nadler told them.

His staff had tried to reinforce the point through a series of leadership meetings, carting in heavy binders of impeachment literature and emphatically pointing out passages about precedent to make their case. Trump's impeachment, they argued, needed to look "more like Nixon." Schiff's lawyers didn't take their lectures well. "Fuck Donald Trump," they'd respond.

To Nadler, giving Trump his due process rights was also smart politics. He knew from experience how powerful arguments about fairness could be. As a vocal Clinton defender in 1998, he had mercilessly attacked the GOP for running an unfair impeachment process—even though then–Judiciary chairman Henry Hyde had adopted virtually the same procedural rules as Rodino's bipartisan probe of Nixon.[2] If Democrats had successfully used that argument to swing public sentiment against Clinton's accusers, imagine what Trump's GOP would be able to do if Pelosi and Schiff didn't tread wisely. In fact, Trump ally Lindsey Graham was already out there wailing that the president's lawyers weren't allowed in depositions, while House Republicans had stormed the SCIF crying foul on secrecy. Democrats had to avoid playing into the script that Trump was being treated unfairly.

"Stick close to the Nixon and Clinton cases," Nadler said. "You have to arm yourself against these process complaints."

Pelosi and Schiff, however, weren't worried about adhering to the confines of precedent and didn't think the GOP's process arguments would resonate with voters. Technically, they could run impeachment however they wanted, they'd tell Nadler. The Constitution laid out no specific procedures when it gave the House the power to indict a president for "treason, bribery or other high crimes and misdemeanors." What's more, after years of dealing with Trump's stonewalling, Pelosi and Schiff were not inclined to let Nadler re-interview witnesses just to extend to Trump what they viewed as extra privileges. Trump was a bad-faith actor, they argued, who would use any platform they gave him for grandstanding, misdirection, and mucking up Democratic messaging. His lawyers would probably just take the opportunity to amplify their spurious allegations against the Biden family, they warned, sullying their party's best shot at ousting Trump in 2020.

There was also the calendar to consider. Allowing Nadler to re-interview witnesses would only bog down the probe, and Pelosi was on a strict timetable. That month, the Speaker's top policy staffer, Dick Meltzer, had summoned Nadler's aides to the Speaker's office and told them the Judiciary Committee would have approximately three weeks to complete its impeachment work. Nadler's staff flipped. In past presidential impeachments, the committee had been given months to conduct their investigations. There was no way, Judiciary counsel Aaron Hiller argued, that they would be able to complete their work in such a short timeframe.

"Jerry Nadler will insist on these hearings," he said, laying out his boss's demands for the umpteenth time.

"Jerry Nadler?" Schiff's counsel Dan Goldman, also in the room, scoffed. "With him, *everything* is negotiable."

Hiller, affronted, started yelling in frustration.

The meeting triggered yet another tug-of-war between Schiff and Pelosi on one side, and Nadler on the other. Their teams bickered over how many of the waning weeks each committee would control before December 19, the last day Pelosi wanted the House to be in session—and by that self-imposed calendar, the last possible date they could impeach Trump. Privately, Nadler's staff griped that they were being screwed because Schiff, whom they called a "control freak," wanted to steer the process for as long as possible.

The tensions boiled over that Tuesday when Schiff sent Nadler his latest draft of the resolution laying out the rules for impeachment—a draft reflecting none of Nadler's due process concerns. The Intelligence Committee leader had proposed making Trump's rights in the Judiciary panel contingent on his cooperation with Schiff's panel beforehand. In other words, if Trump wanted his say, he would first have to cough up all the outstanding evidence and witnesses Schiff wanted.

Nadler's staff flipped. "These lawless HPSCI bastards!" one Judiciary aide said, decrying the House Permanent Select Commitee on Intelligence—Schiff's panel—by its acronym. "It's dumb. It's illegal!" another said.

Nadler also hit the roof. Summoning his posse of fed-up lawyers around one p.m., they marched over to Schiff's basement chambers for a confrontation.

As they jumped aboard an underground congressional subway car, Nadler had his new impeachment guru Matz phone an influential ally to help make his case. Matz had co-authored his impeachment book with Laurence Tribe, a prominent Harvard Law School scholar who also happened to have taught and mentored Schiff. "If a resolution were presented as follows, what would you think?" Matz asked, reading the resolution out loud. Tribe's answer left little wiggle room. "I think it's unconstitutional," he said.

"Can you repeat for the group what you just told me?" Matz asked, putting Tribe on speakerphone so Nadler could hear Tribe's verdict as the subway car sped across the Hill campus.

When Nadler and his entourage arrived, an annoyed Schiff excused himself from Democrats' latest impeachment deposition to meet with them. Just hours earlier, he'd huddled with Pelosi and Nadler to talk through the final language of the resolution—and as far as Schiff was concerned, he thought Nadler had been in agreement. He didn't understand the need for the emergency meeting. What's more, National Security Council European Affairs director Lieutenant Colonel Alexander Vindman, who listened in on Trump's July 25 call with Zelensky, had been testifying down the hall that Trump's requests for a Biden investigation were so alarming that he reported the call to the NSC's top counsel. But Vindman's story would have to wait.

The room was tense as Schiff and Nadler got down to business.

"You can't do this," Nadler said, arguing that conditioning Trump's due process rights on anything—including impeachable levels of obstruction—would not only play into the GOP's hands, it would be "unconstitutional."

"They're going to argue we don't have due process for Trump. Why make that argument real?" he asked. Plus, he added, Schiff had no business trying to boss the Judiciary Committee around.

"I write the rules of my committee, not you," Nadler said. "I resent you telling me how to run my committee."

"I don't really care about your resentment," Schiff, clearly irritated, snapped. "Neither the Speaker nor I agree."

Nadler's aides, miffed that Schiff had pulled what they had dubbed "the Speaker card," immediately jumped in to defend their boss.

"We're giving up the high ground if we do it your way," Barry Berke, the salty-mouthed New York attorney, chimed in.

"No, we're unilaterally surrendering to Trump in the face of his obstruction and bad behavior," Schiff shot back, unmoved.

To bolster their argument, one of Nadler's hired guns, Norm Eisen, tried to tell Schiff about the conversation they had just had with Tribe. He too had studied with Schiff's former professor and was so animated that his already high-pitched voice was especially squeaky as he described how their common friend and mentor believed Schiff's draft proposal trampled on Trump's constitutional rights.

"Larry Tribe will tweet bad things about us!" Norm squawked, hoping the threat of a public hit from a liberal ally might move him.

His appeal didn't work.

"I'm sure it was neutrally presented by you, Norm," Schiff retorted sarcastically.

In fact, Schiff wasn't budging at all. Calling Nadler's demands a "mistake," he doubled down on Pelosi's verdict that there would be no fact witnesses in Judiciary—then boned up his defense by again name-checking their party leader. "This was a Speaker call," he said sternly. With no solution in sight, Schiff returned to the Vindman deposition, leaving the matter in the hands of his general counsel, Maher Bitar.

The two sides knew they didn't have much time to argue: Pelosi, committed to her end-of-year schedule, was demanding the resolution be introduced that very day to set up a vote before the end of the month. They needed to find a workable compromise quickly.

Bitar suggested a middle ground: What if they wrote rules giving Trump and his attorneys the right to participate, but Nadler the right to revoke that if they continued to obstruct the probe? The idea would leave the final decision about Trump's due process rights to Nadler, but give Democrats the option to hit back if Trump kept stonewalling.

Nadler considered the proposal—and his options. If he stood his ground and insisted on sticking with precedent, Pelosi might try to sideline his panel even further. But as a practical matter, he noted, accepting Bitar's compromise still left him ample room to maneuver around Pelosi. While the Speaker had forbidden Judiciary from calling fact witnesses, the resolution left all decisions about Trump's defense to Nadler. If the president wanted to present witnesses, Nadler could allow it—and in that situation there was no way Pelosi would prevent him from responding with a fuller investigation, he calculated.

Nadler's own staff would later debate whether the compromise was still unconstitutional. But in that moment, the chairman was under the gun. He took the deal, viewing it as the lesser evil.

Their handshake agreement set off a mad dash to meet Pelosi's end-of-day deadline. With the clock ticking, Bitar ran to his office to quickly type up the proposal—then ran back to show Judiciary aides what he had written.

"Should the President unlawfully refuse to make witnesses available for testimony . . . or to produce documents requested by, the investigative committees . . . the chair shall have the discretion to impose appropriate remedies, including by denying specific requests by the President or his counsel under these procedures to call or question witnesses," Bitar had typed out.[3]

As they worked, the House buzzer rang for evening votes. Bitar and Eisen scrambled to print out copies of the resolution, running up the basement stairs and jumping into an elevator that took them to the second floor of the Capitol, where they made a beeline for the House chamber to find Schiff and Nadler and get their final approval. From opposite sides of the chamber, Bitar and Eisen motioned to each other that they were good to go, prompting one last race up a flight of stairs to the House Rules Committee. They filed the document just minutes before Pelosi's deadline.

But as they left that chamber that night, some of Nadler's aides had a queasy feeling. The entire situation was so slapdash and hastily thrown together that they began questioning what they had just agreed to. Was it even constitutional? Would the compromise even blunt the GOP's procedural attacks?

It wouldn't. In fact, the language they had just negotiated was about to become the cudgel House Minority Leader Kevin McCarthy would use to beat his final GOP holdouts into line against the impeachment inquiry.

That evening, Pelosi gathered her impeachment messaging team for another brainstorming session—this time to contend with a more urgent problem. She'd been watching the polls and the numbers were unequivocal: The public by and large was not coming along with the Democrats on impeachment.

"We need to make the case more strongly that this is a national security issue," Pelosi told her team. "Eighty percent plus say it's not okay for the president to ask for foreign assistance [in an election]— despite Trump asserting that he can do it. I just think we need to make this case to rural voters, evangelicals, and Republicans."

It was not the first time the group had shared their private concerns that to date, their impeachment efforts had proceeded with no discernible Republican support. The prior week, Pelosi's longtime ally and friend in the group, Congresswoman Zoe Lofgren of California, had delivered a long lecture about how they needed to find better ways to reach Trump supporters. Asking Trump voters to embrace impeachment was basically like asking them to admit they made a mistake electing him, she said. Democrats would need to be gentle about how they approached those voters, "not to push people away," Lofgren said.

Pelosi said she agreed entirely. "It's like telling someone that their art is fake and their wife is ugly," she quipped.

Since then, the Speaker had been obsessed with finding "third party validators" who could pitch impeachment to Republicans on their behalf. She had opened that night's meeting playing a clip of Fox News commentator Judge Andrew Napolitano, a conservative who argued that Trump had not only broken the law but committed high crimes worthy of removal.[4]

"We need to play up Napolitano saying he committed impeachable offenses," Pelosi declared. "The public awareness on the details of this is very low . . . So we need clarity and repetition over and over again. 'National security threat.' 'Abuse of power.' 'No one is above the law.'"

Despite her zeal to strike the right message with GOP voters, Pelosi stubbornly refused to consider that the sales pitch those voters were getting from Republicans might also be compelling. "Due process" and "fairness" were just as pithy as "national security threat" or "abuse of power"—and as concepts, they were a whole lot less esoteric to explain.

But Pelosi had dismissed the Republicans' arguments out of hand. She had lumped them in with the GOP's stunts, like the storming of the SCIF, as childish antics to distract from the probe.

"Let's not give them any attention," she told her strike team when GOP process arguments came up. They were a non-issue that would never resonate with voters, she said.

Pelosi informed her team that in a matter of days, the House would be voting on a resolution to establish formal rules and procedures for the impeachment inquiry that would put any GOP process arguments to rest.

"Democrats are giving Trump more rights than the Democrats had under the Clinton impeachment," she said confidently, instructing her team to make that argument part of their talking points.

It wasn't true, and Pelosi knew that Nadler had been viscerally arguing the contrary. But Nadler wasn't there, and Pelosi made no mention of his concerns. She presumed she could out-message the GOP by simply declaring the Democrats' resolution was fair. As it turned out, ignoring the Republican counterarguments was a gross miscalculation.

Late that evening, at the Trump International Hotel across town, McCarthy grabbed Fred Upton by the arm to drag him to the president's private restaurant booth. House Republicans were wrapping up their annual "Take Back the House" fundraiser, and hundreds of GOP donors were still flitting about the hotel's glitzy ballroom. Attendees had paid at least $35,000 a plate to hear Trump speak, banking McCarthy and his leadership team more than $13 million— and likely netting Trump's business a handsome profit as well.[5]

Trump had been scheduled to return to the White House right after the event. But at the last minute, he turned to McCarthy and demanded: "Have dinner with me." For the first time in a long time, McCarthy noticed the president was in a bright mood—and the leader wanted to capitalize on that energy.

McCarthy knew that in a few days, his party would face its first test of unity when Democrats put their impeachment rules resolution to a vote. If he could ensure all his members voted against it, he knew it would be much easier to hold the party line against the final vote to impeach a few weeks later. Once Republicans had declared the whole process was flawed, he figured, there would be no logical way they could support charges stemming from such a mangled setup.

In the month since the impeachment probe had started, McCarthy had already rallied most of his members to Trump's side. Pelosi's decision not to hold an early vote on the impeachment rules had bought him time to cajole and whip his rank and file, a task that played well to his strengths as leader. While McCarthy was no genius or policy wonk, what he lacked in smarts he made up for in people skills. He made a point of memorizing the names of his members' spouses and dogs, and where their kids went to college. He was affable and chatty, and most GOP lawmakers genuinely liked him.

Still, McCarthy knew he had some work to do with his centrist members. And that night, he figured a little presidential face time wouldn't hurt his whipping effort against the upcoming vote on the impeachment rules.

McCarthy scanned the crowd to find Upton, one of the moderate lawmakers whose vote he worried might be at risk. Snaking through the masses, he grabbed Upton's arm.

"Come with me," McCarthy said, pulling him into an elevator as they made their way to where Trump was waiting.

McCarthy had known Upton, an even-keeled and friendly Michigander, for years. The former leader of the powerful Energy and Commerce Committee was a trusted member of the GOP leader's inner circle—even though he wasn't particularly fond of the president. Early on in Trump's tenure, Upton had gotten into an expletive-laced shouting match with the president over his plan to replace the Affordable Care Act with one that lacked protections for people with preexisting conditions, a proposal Upton had vowed to oppose. Then in July 2019, Upton became one of only four House Republicans to join Democrats in formally denouncing Trump's comment that four liberal congresswomen of color ought to "go back" to their countries of origin.[6]

McCarthy had been working on Upton ever since he told a local radio station in early October that questions "need to be raised" about Trump's actions in Ukraine. It was why McCarthy and his Whip Steve Scalise had recommended that the White House include Upton as well as the elusive Jaime Herrera Beutler in the first of their Camp David bonding trips. The leaders had also been bombarding both offices with information to convince them the inquiry was unfair—so much so that Upton had told McCarthy to bug off.

"I have everything I need," Upton insisted.

With the impeachment resolution vote around the corner, however, McCarthy wasn't leaving anything to chance.

The president had been in rare form that night. Ever since the storming of the SCIF, in fact, he had a new pep in his step, confident that Republicans were starting to get the hang of countering the Democrats. He was riding extra high that week too, having just ordered a raid that took out the leader of the terrorist group known as ISIS. Feeling untouchable, that night he turned on the charm, regaling the crowd with lighthearted and endearing roasts of House Republicans. Congressman Patrick McHenry had the most patriotic-sounding name in the history of history. "If I had that name, I would have been president 10 years ago!" he quipped. When Scalise almost died from his gunshot wound a few years back, his wife had "cried her eyes out"—but "not many wives would react that way to tragedy—I know mine wouldn't!" Trump joked. He teased Congressman Greg Pence, the vice president's older brother, for not donating enough money to his campaign. "How did you get that good of a seat in here, ya cheap-o!?" he ribbed.[7]

McCarthy hoped that Trump would be just as winsome one-on-one with Upton. The moment they walked into the dining room, he put the centrist lawmaker on the spot.

"Mr. President," McCarthy said, half-jokingly, "Upton wants to talk to us about this vote."

Trump grinned and didn't flinch. As he munched on a jumbo shrimp cocktail, the president chatted up the congressman, with nary a mention of his previous disloyalty. When McCarthy mentioned that Upton was thinking about retiring, the president made a personal pitch for him to stay in office, arguing that the party needed Republicans like him.

The flattery was sure to seal the deal on Upton's vote, McCarthy thought. But he wanted insurance. Before the party broke up, he asked a waiter to snap a picture of the table—and much to Upton's dismay, tweeted it out with the caption: "Great night with the president. Republicans are united!" Just in case.

At the Capitol the next day, McCarthy's top counsel, Machalagh Carr, set out to find Herrera Beutler on the House floor. She and McCarthy had been keeping tabs on the Washington Republican for weeks, fearing she might break ranks and vote with Democrats on the impeachment rules resolution. That morning, though, Carr was confident she could convince her to oppose it.

"This is an easy, easy 'no,'" Carr told Herrera Beutler, clutching a copy of the resolution and pointing to it emphatically as lawmakers milled about the cavernous House chamber.

House GOP leaders, who had hung their entire protest of impeachment on process complaints, had been on tenterhooks for days waiting for the Democrats' proposal. They knew that if it fully heeded the GOP's calls for transparency and due process, it could upend the arguments they had been using to convince moderates like Herrera Beutler to stick with the team. In that case, they had no Plan B to fall back on.

But when they read the resolution the night before, they breathed a collective sigh of relief. The Democrats' proposal barely even acknowledged a role for Trump and gave the Judiciary chairman unchecked power to deny him any participation. Their rules flew in the face of both the Clinton and Nixon precedents with reckless abandon, McCarthy's team decided. It was a political misstep and a messaging gift from the Democrats that had fallen in their lap at the perfect moment.

Carr set to work immediately, instructing her staff to blitz members with copies of the resolution and a twenty-point list contrasting it with the Nixon and Clinton impeachments. They reminded their members that the GOP had had no say in writing the proposal and would be given no chance to amend it. Scalise likened the process to a "Soviet style" inquisition, while McCarthy started arguing to moderates that the very integrity of Congress depended on them opposing the resolution.

As she spoke to Herrera Beutler and other members on the fence that day, Carr pointed to the exact wording of Schiff and Nadler's last-minute compromise—"the chair shall have the discretion"—to argue the rules were unfair. Sure, Trump could have counsel attend the Judiciary portion of the proceedings, but "the chair shall have the discretion" to strip that away. Sure, the president's lawyers could try to call witnesses and evidence, but "the chair shall have the discretion" to rule them out of order and deny them the chance to cross-examine anyone else.

"This will forever change impeachment," Carr argued. "Presidents could be ousted without any process to defend themselves. You may not think Trump is innocent, but we need to protect the institution from this assault."

For Herrera Beutler, Carr's process arguments reinforced her gut instinct to oppose the inquiry. Despite her initial concern about Trump's behavior with Ukraine, she would vote no and had no misgivings about the decision.

By the day of the vote, on October 31, the only lawmaker whom GOP leaders truly worried about losing was Francis Rooney. He was what McCarthy and Scalise liked to call a "delicate whip": Pressure him too hard to go one way, he'd more than likely run in the opposite direction. The CNN interview in which he had criticized Trump was proof of his gumption—and now that he had announced his retirement, McCarthy knew there was nothing to keep him from voting his conscience and speaking his mind. He had nothing to lose.

To McCarthy, Rooney's turn before the camera had not come as a total surprise. The Florida Republican had always been a bit of a Boy Scout, and he had privately been suggesting to fellow Republicans that the fact pattern emerging in the SCIF was becoming more troubling. Trump, however, had been infuriated by the public castigation. "Who the hell is this Rooney guy?" he fumed to his Hill allies, prompting a personal plea from McCarthy not to attack him.[8]

"Leave him alone," McCarthy warned Trump of Rooney. "Let me do my job and at the end of the day we'll be fine."

After his TV comments, McCarthy had sought Rooney out on the House floor to get a download on his thinking. Rooney had acted almost defensively, arguing he needed to learn more information before making a decision on impeaching Trump.

"You can't fault somebody for wanting to get all the facts," Rooney had protested to McCarthy. "I just don't want to rush to judgment."

Though Rooney had publicly stated his openness to impeaching the president, McCarthy knew he had a critical grievance against the mechanics of the probe. He thought the Democrats were rushing and were doing too much behind closed doors. He seemed particularly annoyed that the Democrats' inquiry to date had looked nothing like what happened during Nixon's impeachment proceedings. He wanted to see evidence fleshed out in public.

For McCarthy's team, that provided an opening. While the resolution and its accompanying report directed Schiff to hold "one or more" public hearings, that was hardly the Watergate-style display that Rooney wanted. The rules made no promise that all individuals who had testified behind closed doors would get their time in the spotlight. McCarthy also stressed to Rooney that the rules gave Democrats the right to limit testimony in the Judiciary Committee—meaning the president might never get a chance to challenge his accusers.

On the day of the vote, the mood across Washington was jubilant. Late the night before, the city's Major League Baseball team, the Washington Nationals, had clinched their first-ever World Series title in a nail-biting Game 7 finish. But in the Capitol, the business of impeachment wasn't skipping a beat. Bleary-eyed investigators had scheduled a deposition at eight a.m. sharp—their earliest session yet—to ensure that Tim Morrison, one of the witnesses from the National Security Council, could finish in time to go trick-or-treating with his kids. In McCarthy's office, the Minority Leader and Carr held one last debrief with Rooney and his chief of staff. At the White House, Trump tweeted a deluge of angry warnings to any Republicans thinking about changing their minds: "Now is the time for Republicans to stand together and defend the leader of their party against these smears," he wrote, adding an hour later: "READ THE TRANSCRIPT!"

Whether it was from fear of Trump, McCarthy's whipping effort, apprehensions about the Democrats' process, or perhaps a little of all three, every last House Republican opposed the impeachment resolution that day—even Rooney. For the first time in modern history, the vote to begin impeaching a president passed without the support of a single member of the minority party. What's more, two moderate Democrats—Collin Peterson of Minnesota and Jeff Van Drew of New Jersey—joined Republicans in voting no.[9] Their act of rebellion gave the GOP its newest talking point: Pelosi had once said there needed to be bipartisan support in order to impeach the president. Now, there was documented bipartisan opposition against it.

22

PLANNING AHEAD

LATE OCTOBER 2019

As House Republicans closed ranks, Senate Republicans watched the dramatic narrative forming across the Capitol with growing concern. Kevin McCarthy's and Jim Jordan's teams had been regularly briefing aides to Senate Majority Leader Mitch McConnell on what was happening in the SCIF, vowing that the headlines they were reading weren't the full story. Mark Meadows, who boasted the closest relationship with Trump of any of them, also worked the phones with his colleagues in the upper chamber, telling them the impeachment probe had uncovered no proof the president had tried to strong-arm Ukraine for political favors.

But the appeals missed their mark. Most Senate Republicans had followed the reports emerging from the SCIF and were convinced Trump had almost certainly tried to bait Ukraine into a quid pro quo. The pertinent question, in the senators' minds, was not whether Trump had done what he was being accused of—but whether it was impeachable.

McConnell had answered that question for himself right away: It wasn't. And he knew most Republicans agreed with him, making Trump's eventual acquittal all but a certainty. "We all know how this is going to end," McConnell had told Senate Republicans during a mid-October lunch.

But there was still the question of at what political cost. While Trump was the one who would soon be on trial, McConnell knew that his Senate majority would also hang in the balance of what transpired. *How could Republicans—particularly vulnerable Republicans—justify siding with a president who had clearly engaged in unethical behavior?*

With that question in mind, McConnell and his team had begun engaging with the White House immediately after Nancy Pelosi formally launched impeachment proceedings, eager to guide the unpredictable Trump from making decisions that would blow back on his members. McConnell was disturbed by what he regarded as the West Wing's unrepentantly cavalier attitude toward the entire effort to oust him. Trump and White House counsel Pat Cipollone seemed to think they could defeat the effort in the House—or that it was so obvious Trump did nothing wrong that they didn't need to go through the trouble of concocting a persuasive defense.

McConnell and his top legal counsel, Andrew Ferguson, sought to disabuse them of that notion right away. Claiming the call was "perfect" might work with a bunch of House Republicans from deep-red districts, they argued, but it simply wouldn't cut it for a swath of more moderately minded senators representing large blocs of independent voters who didn't trust the president. The White House needed to offer additional, loftier, and more constitutionally oriented defenses tailored to the needs of the more politically nuanced Senate, even if Trump resisted it.

At one point, McConnell cornered Trump's son-in-law Jared Kushner to reinforce the point. Pulling Kushner aside after a meeting in his office to discuss immigration, he urged him to convince Trump to build a comprehensive defense operation, just as Bill Clinton had done during his impeachment.

"Take this impeachment seriously," McConnell told Kushner. "Pelosi would not have done this if she didn't think she could end it, so you should be preparing as though you're going to lose in the House."

McConnell also implored Cipollone to start building a legal shop with experienced outside litigators, pointing again to the example of Clinton, who had hired prominent, hard-charging attorneys in anticipation of his Senate trial. He even floated names like Paul Clement and Ted Olson, two well-known conservative attorneys who had argued dozens of cases before the Supreme Court, including the GOP's case against Obamacare, and had far more trial experience than Cipollone. "Whomever you pick, the person needs to have constitutional gravitas," McConnell said. "That's the only way to convince moderate GOP senators that these acts are not impeachable."

McConnell suspected that Cipollone was considering running Trump's defense on his own, and the idea worried him. McConnell believed that the White House counsel could not possibly split his attention between his regular duties and impeachment and do either job well.

"You're the president's lawyer—you have a day job," McConnell told Cipollone. "You guys should be assembling a team."

McConnell's advice also extended to the president, whom he forcibly encouraged to stop attacking senators who weren't publicly defending him. Siccing his fiery base against GOP senators wouldn't benefit anybody, McConnell argued to Trump—and might just cost him Republicans' support in the long run. "In order to let us win in the end," he told the president, he had to restrain himself.

That McConnell was taking such an active role in organizing the president's defense might have struck some as unethical. The Constitution designated the Senate to act as jury during impeachment trials, and Senate procedures called on each juror to swear an oath to do "impartial justice" in casting their verdict.[1] But the idea of shelving politics for the duration of an impeachment had become something of a joke. During Clinton's impeachment, Democrats coordinated their defense with the White House. Nobody truly thought things would work any differently in the Trump era.

McConnell thought the notion of a politics-free trial was naive—and positively ludicrous. He encouraged his moderate senators to play up their roles as "impartial jurors" when there was an obvious political benefit to doing so—such as for Senator Susan Collins, who was facing a difficult reelection in blue Maine. But otherwise, he believed it would be foolish to pretend impeachment was apolitical—and possibly politically risky.

The fact that Trump, the shoot-from-the-hip president, was even hearing out McConnell's advice was a testament to how much control the Senate GOP leader had learned to assert over the impetuous party leader. They were polar opposites: Trump, a former Democrat, often overshared on social media and rode a populist wave to Washington. McConnell, a lifelong conservative, was notoriously taciturn and calculating and a Beltway insider who wielded a deep-pocketed corporate fundraising machine.

McConnell did not like Trump and found him uncontrolled, unadvised, unpracticed—and absolutely infuriating to work with. During the 2016 campaign, he figured Trump was a walking dead man—only to be shocked, and impressed, when the nominee won. McConnell, who had once been booed at the GOP's national convention, admired Trump's savoir faire with the GOP base, raw power that he believed could be transformed into policy wins.

During their first meeting at the Capitol after Trump's shocking election victory, McConnell sought to convince Trump to channel his influence into fulfilling his own career-long goal: reshaping the ideological bent of the judicial branch completely by appointing a record number of conservatives to the bench. If they could pull it off, it could change the course of American jurisprudence for at least a generation and cement his legacy. But McConnell made sure to tell Trump that he would get all the credit for the turnaround. The pitch worked, the first in what would become a transactional relationship between Washington's two top Republican powerbrokers.

And so it was that the Drain the Swamp president and Washington's ultimate Swamp Thing struck up a tentative partnership. Trump appointed McConnell's wife, Elaine Chao, who had previously served in George W. Bush's Cabinet, as his Transportation secretary. McConnell went on to help Trump pass major legislative wins and confirm more than two hundred of Trump's judicial nominees, including three conservatives to the Supreme Court.

Trump found McConnell to be dry and boring, and he didn't like that he rarely laughed at his jokes.[2] But he appreciated that McConnell was willing to go to bat for him when the chips were down and came to view McConnell as an asset. During the 2018 battle over Supreme Court nominee Brett Kavanaugh, who had been accused of sexual assault, the Senate leader had calmed Trump's nerves by assuring him he was "stronger than mule piss" about the nominee and would force the bid through one way or another.[3] Trump later commented to others that while McConnell was certainly stubborn, his counsel was also usually more trustworthy than that of GOP leaders like Kevin McCarthy, who always told him what he wanted to hear.

Trump also had learned through experience that when he ignored McConnell, there were usually consequences. A year before his impeachment, McConnell had warned Trump against shutting the federal government down to try to procure money for his border-wall project. Republicans had been there and done that, he cautioned, and it never worked—only hurt them in the polls. "There is no education in the second kick of a mule," McConnell told Trump. The president ignored him, shuttering Washington for thirty-five days—and making nary a dime of wall money for it. The nation also blamed him for the chaos. Trump never did it again.

But despite his working relationship with the president, McConnell knew he would have a serious challenge on his hands that winter. Controlling Trump through impeachment—the most direct threat yet to his presidency—would prove a tall order, he knew. But to save his majority, McConnell would have to find a way.

23

MISSED OPPORTUNITIES

EARLY NOVEMBER 2019

Adam Schiff was facing down perhaps the most pivotal legal decision of the entire impeachment inquiry as he and a team of rival lawyers gathered in Pelosi's conference room for a critical meeting at the beginning of November. Just over a week prior, impeachment investigators had summoned former national security advisor John Bolton's right-hand man for testimony. But Bolton's deputy had thrown a monkey wrench into Schiff's investigative strategy, requesting a subpoena late on a Friday days before his scheduled deposition—and then surprising House investigators by taking it straight to a federal judge. His lawyer, prominent conservative attorney Charles Cooper, had asked the courts to decide which should win out: a congressional summons for testimony, or a White House order to ignore it?

The court challenge stung all the more for coming just as Schiff thought he was finally about to net a witness from the president's inner circle. Cooper also represented Bolton and warned impeachment investigators that if the former national security advisor were subpoenaed, he would join his deputy and appeal to the courts for a similar ruling. That meant Schiff had a serious decision to make: *Should he fight for Bolton's testimony in the courts? Or impeach Trump without it?*

"If we're going to go with Bolton, we've got to go—the sooner the better," Schiff told the top counsels from the Intelligence and Judiciary Committees, who had put down their swords that day to make a plan.

Schiff knew that sympathetic testimony from Bolton, a lifelong Republican who had worked for five GOP presidential administrations, could be a game-changer. Even before he spent eighteen months as Trump's national security advisor, the mustachioed, bespectacled strategist was one of the nation's most iconic neoconservatives and most celebrated of Fox News's experts. Though he had resigned from the White House in early September—Trump declared he'd been fired—he could still speak to the president's thinking firsthand. If Bolton stood on the witness stand and testified that Trump had engaged in a quid pro quo, people—and especially Republicans—would listen.

But entering litigation for Bolton's testimony opened up a host of political complications. And Schiff wasn't sure the potential prize was worth the struggle.

On the Friday night that Cooper had filed the surprise lawsuit, Nadler's attorneys had joined forces with House counsel Doug Letter to implore their Intelligence panel counterparts to let Bolton go. Schiff's top investigator, former federal prosecutor Dan Goldman, was initially inclined to chase his testimony. But doing so could upend their plans, Nadler's team warned in a phone call. Suing for Bolton's testimony would take at least three to five months, they estimated, blowing well past the Democrats' end-of-the-year deadline for impeachment. And if they tried to impeach Trump while the court's decision was pending, Republicans and even skittish Democrats might argue that the question of whether the president was guilty of obstructing Congress simply wasn't settled yet.

"If you do this, then the judge controls the timeframe and it's going to be really awkward to impeach," Nadler's impeachment expert Joshua Matz had warned on the call. Letter agreed. Democrats would look like jerks if they rushed ahead to impeach mid-litigation, he concurred. It was either go for Bolton or impeach by Christmas in accordance with Pelosi's timeline. They couldn't do both.

There had been signs that Bolton was sympathetic to the impeachment cause. After all, his deputy Fiona Hill had told investigators that he likened the Ukraine gambit to a "drug deal." House Democrats also had other, then-unpublicized reasons to think Bolton might help them: Two weeks after departing the White House, Bolton had called House Foreign Affairs Committee chairman Eliot Engel and told him that Democrats should be investigating Ambassador Marie Yovanovitch's abrupt firing, hinting something improper had occurred. He had also cryptically warned the New York Democrat that his party should broaden their probe beyond Ukraine if they wanted hard evidence of Trump's misdeeds.

Yet Democrats weren't sure they could—or even wanted to—trust him. They reviled Bolton for his legacy as one of the Iraq War's chief architects who helped craft the spurious predicate that Saddam Hussein was harboring weapons of mass destruction. *If they called him in, how could they guarantee he would even tell the truth?* the Judiciary and Intelligence panel lawyers asked each other during the late-Friday call. Matz and Norm Eisen began referring to Bolton as "the Joker," likening him to the Batman villain. They predicted that he was dangerous for Democrats and might do their case more harm than good by failing to link Ukraine's military aid to the Biden investigation.

"You never know if he's going to shoot you or shoot the other guy," one of the attorneys involved said.

Nadler's staff and House counsel Letter also worried that the court might not rule in their favor. They agreed they couldn't trust the judge who had been assigned to the case: Richard Leon, a George W. Bush appointee who had helped Hill Republicans push back against the Iran-Contra affair and investigate Bill Clinton's Whitewater scandal before joining the federal bench. Leon actually had a track record of siding with Congress on high-profile matters: In 2013, he ruled that the NSA's bulk data collection of Americans' phone records was unconstitutional, and in early 2018, he ordered a firm behind allegations that Trump had colluded with Russia to cough up subpoenaed records to the House Intelligence panel. But Nadler's aides and Letter argued to their colleagues that Leon often employed erratic reasoning and was a "loose cannon" who could not be trusted. If they subpoenaed Bolton and Leon shot it down, they warned, it would decimate their argument that Trump was obstructing Congress—and neuter that impeachment article completely.

The fact that Nadler's staff was so eager to sidestep the courts with Bolton was a striking about-face. For months, his team had advanced the theory that judges would litigate questions related to impeachment quickly. In 1974, it had taken only about two months for the Supreme Court to rule on whether then-president Richard Nixon had to comply with subpoenas issued by Congress and a special prosecutor for tapes of his conversations in the West Wing. Congress, Nadler's team had always said to Pelosi, should enjoy the same deference and prioritization. Yet when it came time to test that theory fully, they balked.

Part of that was because they'd become jaded by their own experience suing to force former White House counsel Don McGahn to comply with their Mueller-related subpoenas. They had told the courts that August that the information they sought could be relevant to an impeachment inquiry, hoping to light a fire under the federal bench and get the judges to move faster. But three months later, they were still waiting on a verdict.

"Let the McGahn case be the test for Bolton," Eisen implored his Intelligence Committee counterparts during their call on the Friday night Bolton's deputy took his subpoena to the courts. "It's the exact same situation: both are former senior White House officials challenging a House subpoena. And McGahn's case, slow as it's going, is further along." Plus, he added, McGahn's case had a "great judge" who would likely rule in their favor.

The truth was Bolton's and McGahn's cases weren't identical, despite the Nadler team's efforts to present them as such. The House's invocation of impeachment in the McGahn lawsuit had ignored the political reality of the moment in which it was filed: Pelosi had never seriously considered, much less formally blessed, the idea of impeaching Trump over the Mueller findings. By the time House Democrats were wrestling with the Bolton question, however, there was no ambiguity about where the House stood: Not only had Pelosi endorsed the impeachment proceedings, but the House also had passed a resolution declaring the process to be fully underway.

Amid their panic about waiting on the courts, the impeachment investigators had also lost sight of their original mission: unearthing the facts to create a full record of Trump's misdeeds that could convince the public to back his ouster. In the 1970s, it had taken more than two years—and a months-long court fight—for Democrats to build a compelling case against Nixon, who had been even more popular with voters than Trump before his downfall. But House Democrats were so worried about dragging impeachment into the 2020 election cycle that they never considered the damage they might do to their own case by rushing ahead without securing key, firsthand witnesses to the alleged crime.

By the time Judiciary and Intelligence lawyers gathered to debate all those matters in Pelosi's office in early November, House Democrats had already secured an accelerated schedule from the judge hearing the Bolton case. Leon, despite Nadler's team's warnings about him, had promised to hear opening arguments on December 10, a breakneck pace for courts that often took months to move.[1] He had also indicated to both Bolton's legal team and House attorneys privately that he intended to fast-track the case due to its sensitivity and urgency. But by that point, impeachment investigators were coming to the consensus that Bolton wasn't worth the fight.

"Bolton won't show up without a court order," Eisen told the room, a prediction they all knew was true.

"He won't show up regardless," Schiff said dolefully, adding that Bolton "should do his patriotic duty" and testify.

The group relitigated all the same ups and downs of calling Bolton that they'd been discussing for days by that point. By the end of the meeting, everyone knew where things were headed.

"So it's decided then," Schiff said. "We're not going to go to court over Bolton."

There was, however, still the question of how to back out gracefully. Democrats had a pending subpoena for Bolton's deputy—and the court case he had launched questioning it—to contend with. And as they'd discussed that week, they couldn't let that case hang out there if they were going to charge Trump with obstructing Congress.

"How do we justify withdrawing the subpoena?" Schiff asked the assembled attorneys.

Soon after, on Monday, November 4, Judge Leon announced he would further expedite his decision, demanding final arguments about the subpoena for Bolton's deputy on December 10, instead of just an initial hearing. But Schiff and his investigators were already moving on. That Wednesday, the House voided their subpoena for Bolton's No. 2 and asked Leon to drop the case. In an effort to dissuade them, Bolton's attorney Cooper even sent the House a letter claiming his clients had information about "many relevant meetings and conversations" involving Bolton "that have not yet been discussed."[2] Cooper actually wanted the fast-tracked ruling to give his clients protection to testify since the White House indicated it would assert privilege over Bolton's story. But House Democrats never looked back.

Ultimately, Democrats would publicly defend their decision to avoid the courts—and forgo high-profile, firsthand witnesses from Trump's inner circle like Bolton—by arguing that they couldn't afford to wait. Trump was trying to cheat in the looming 2020 election and had to be stopped—impeached—right away, they'd insist, saying nothing of the political fears that had motivated their retreat.

But their decision to sidestep key evidence in favor of an artificial deadline would cripple their bid to try to persuade the public. It would haunt every move they made in the Senate trial and alienate the few open-minded GOP lawmakers—not to mention contribute to their failure to convince virtually anyone beyond their loyal base that Trump needed to be removed.

Congress, meanwhile, would start to get a reputation for doubting the strength of its own subpoenas as time after time, lawmakers opted against enforcing them. In some ways, Trump had conditioned them to do his dirty work. By avoiding confrontations in the courts and choosing not to fully test the limits of their impeachment power, they, as much as he, were contributing to the erosion of congressional oversight.

Publicly, almost every House Democrat maintained a unified front behind Pelosi, as she and Schiff whittled the case against Trump into what they hoped would be a digestible narrative, singularly focused on Ukraine. But privately, some Democrats began complaining late that fall that they were pulling punches unnecessarily, weakening their arguments against Trump in the process.

One of those most troubled was Jamie Raskin, the House Democrats' in-house constitutional expert and most gung-ho impeachment supporter.

Raskin, like the rest of Pelosi's leadership team, had nodded his assent to the Ukraine-only impeachment strategy when the Speaker pitched it on September 25; he had simply been elated that she had finally agreed to impeach at all. But in that moment, Raskin hadn't realized what he was agreeing to. It hadn't occurred to him that the strategy would mean effectively sidelining nearly all other scrutiny of Trump's personal misconduct—much of which Raskin believed was more dangerous to the republic and would be more compelling to the public.

When Raskin realized that, he got a sinking feeling. He understood why party leaders wanted to focus only on Ukraine: They wanted to present Trump's pressure on Zelensky as so egregious that it rose above everything else he'd done—and thus had forced their hand on impeachment. But by doing that, House Democrats had made Ukraine look like a unique circumstance when it was actually part of a pattern. Trump had—and was still—running a host of other schemes out of the Oval Office aimed at benefiting himself, financially or politically. By highlighting all of them, Raskin believed, Democrats might actually stand a better chance of moving the public.

Raskin had also begun to fear that the Ukraine narrative was proving to be hopelessly esoteric. Despite the powerful testimony Democrats had collected, it was difficult to follow the storyline, which wove through arcane politics, financial problems, and the energy sector of an unfamiliar post-Soviet nation before landing back in the Oval Office. There was no way it was going to resonate with Americans, he thought.

Raskin began to pitch Pelosi and her leadership team to change course. Broadening their probe to include things like Trump's emoluments violations, Raskin argued, could let Democrats weave a narrative that centered on corruption and self-enrichment. It would be simple and easy for voters to follow. And once everyday Americans understood how Trump was fleecing taxpayers for his own benefit and wooing anyone who wanted to curry favor with him to spend money at his hotels, Raskin argued, it would be easier to digest the notion that Trump had also used congressionally authorized military assistance to get a foreign government to help sabotage his most formidable 2020 rival.

"Ukraine is complicated . . . we need something people can understand," he would say at Pelosi's leadership meetings. "And Donald Trump is a one-man crime wave producing constitutional crimes on a daily basis."

Raskin wasn't the only one questioning Pelosi's decision to sideline other investigations to keep public attention focused on Ukraine. Throughout that fall, other senior Democrats privately argued that they were shirking their constitutional duty to pursue non-Ukraine leads with equal vigor.[3] Some wanted to continue scrutinizing Trump's alleged obstruction of Mueller's probe, hush money payments to women, and campaign finance violations. Others pushed for House investigators to expand their Ukraine probe geographically—especially after Trump publicly invited China to "start an investigation into the Bidens" in early October.

The China thread in particular seemed an obvious one to pull. As Bolton would later write in his memoir released in the spring of 2020, Trump had not just made the alarming quip about Beijing—he had also tried to leverage trade negotiations to force China into helping his 2020 reelection efforts.[4] But the Speaker didn't yet know that—and swiftly dismissed her members' entreaties, just as she had Raskin's.

Pelosi's unwillingness to budge made some Democrats wonder if she was intentionally muzzling all investigations under the Judiciary Committee's purview as a way of keeping Nadler at arm's length from the impeachment probe. Others speculated that Schiff was simply being territorial and didn't want to share the impeachment limelight and turf.

For a fleeting moment in mid-October, Raskin thought he had achieved a breakthrough. Pelosi had responded to Mick Mulvaney's Doral announcement by finally teeing up Raskin's emoluments resolution for a vote on the House floor. But when Trump canceled his plans to hold the G7 at Doral, Pelosi scrapped the vote. Raskin was crestfallen.

"But it's *not* over!" he tried to protest. "Trump is *still* engaging in other emolument violations!"

It did him little good. The House never took that vote. And Trump continued spending more than a third of his time at his own properties, racking up enormous bills for his security detail that went straight to his companies on the taxpayer dime[5]—and continued profiting off U.S. or foreign officials looking to get the attention of Trump World by staying at his properties. Just as Raskin predicted, the D.C. circuit court would eventually throw out the Democrats' lawsuit because it never had been reinforced by a vote of the lower chamber—only two days after Trump's acquittal, no less.[6]

After his resolution got shelved, Raskin continued to prod his colleagues to reevaluate their approach. He worried that even within their Ukraine-focused inquiry, investigators were failing to expose a much larger corruption scheme. He believed Trump's pressure campaign against Zelensky was just the tip of the iceberg, and he couldn't understand why investigators weren't redoubling their efforts to uncover the fuller story.

"We should be following the money," Raskin told Schiff and Dan Goldman, Schiff's lead investigator, as he challenged them to dig deeper in their probe. "Those guys were not over there to get a press release about Hunter Biden. They were over there to reestablish channels of corruption that go all the way to Vladimir Putin . . . We shouldn't ignore the money operation."

Raskin had good reason for his suspicions: There were reports circulating that a Ukrainian oligarch with links to the Kremlin had agreed to help Rudy Giuliani try to find dirt on Biden—if the president's lawyer took care of his own legal problems in the United States. The oligarch was facing extradition on bribery and racketeering charges and was curiously being represented by two lawyers with close Trump ties.[7] House investigators had a strong hunch that the oligarch had also bankrolled Giuliani's two Soviet-born cronies in their hunt for anti-Biden material. But their efforts to interview those two individuals—Lev Parnas and Igor Fruman—had been stymied just a few weeks before, when U.S. prosecutors charged them with campaign finance violations. The night before Parnas was scheduled to testify in the House's impeachment probe, the FBI had picked them up at Dulles airport with one-way tickets to Frankfurt, Germany, in their pockets.[8] And they had disappeared since into the black hole of the federal prosecution system.

Schiff and Goldman told Raskin that they agreed there was an economic motivation to the Ukraine story but that they didn't have the resources and the time to investigate it—especially when they could not be sure the money trail would lead back to Trump. They were also loath to move mountains to talk to Giuliani. He had a penchant for lying, and there was a serious risk that he could turn their otherwise serious inquiry into a spectacle. "He changes his story every day—it would be a waste of time to bring him in and have him just lie to us," the chairman's staff explained, whenever anyone raised objections. As with Bolton's deputy, investigators ended up dropping their subpoena against Giuliani, fearful he would only slow them down.

By early November, the practice of letting the president's top advisors flout congressional subpoenas with impunity had become a pattern. White House chief of staff Mick Mulvaney and his top advisor, Robert Blair, ignored compulsory summonses to appear, with Mulvaney claiming "absolute immunity"[9]—the same catchall that Trump had issued for blocking ex–White House counsel Don McGahn from testifying to Congress. Office of Management and Budget director Russell Vought and his underlings Michael Duffey and Brian McCormack also refused to testify,[10] despite having been issued subpoenas to discuss their roles in withholding Ukraine's security assistance. At the White House, the National Security Council attorneys who had fielded internal complaints about Trump's July 25 call, John Eisenberg and Michael Ellis, also skipped their own subpoenaed depositions.[11] And key actors like Secretary of State Mike Pompeo, Defense secretary Mark Esper, and Energy secretary Rick Perry resisted turning over required documents to investigators.[12]

The situation infuriated Democrats on the Intelligence Committee, some of whom privately prodded Schiff to do more to enforce their subpoenas. Before and after depositions, Congressmen Jim Himes of Connecticut, Joaquin Castro of Texas, and Mike Quigley of Illinois would try to rile up their colleagues into calling for action. *Officials can't just run roughshod over Congress and get away with it,* they would argue. *There have to be consequences for people who ignore our oversight power or lie to us.* When Bill Taylor's testimony made it clear that Gordon Sondland had, at best, withheld vital information from them in his deposition—and may have even been dishonest with them—the group wanted to refer him to the Justice Department for lying to Congress.[13] When the news broke on November 9 that Bolton had just signed a multimillion-dollar book deal,[14] right after he eschewed an invitation to testify in the impeachment probe, it only infuriated them more.

Yet still, House Democrats did nothing.

"This will only further add to the body of evidence on a potential obstruction of Congress charge against the president," Schiff said amid the mounting pile of no-shows.

Letting go of Bolton's testimony was perhaps the most bitter pill for rank-and-file Democrats to swallow. But as Schiff forged ahead, they muzzled their private objections and fell in line. By the start of November, Schiff was confident that Democrats had what they needed to make their case against Trump, even without witnesses from his inner circle. It was time to see if the public agreed.

24

SHOWTIME

NOVEMBER 5-21, 2019

In the early 1970s, few Americans had paid attention to the Watergate scandal before the Senate Watergate Committee started holding high-profile hearings on the matter—and those didn't commence until almost an entire year after the infamous break-in. While the cloak-and-dagger story of five burglars who got caught bugging the Democratic headquarters had been plastered across the pages of the *Washington Post* and the *New York Times* throughout the summer of 1972, it hadn't registered with the public. According to a Gallup Poll that fall, about 48 percent of respondents had never heard the word "Watergate" at all.[1] Nixon, running for a second term, went on to win 520 Electoral College votes and carry forty-nine of fifty states that fall, one of the most decisive victories in U.S. history.

Nixon was popular, and part of the public's initial skepticism was because he denied all wrongdoing and passionately accused the media of bias against him—just as Trump would nearly five decades later. The idea that a president who was signing nuclear arms control treaties with the Soviets, negotiating an end to the Vietnam War, and charting new diplomatic ground with Communist China would stoop to petty burglary of his political rivals was just too fanciful for many voters to believe. It barely registered that the walkie-talkies used in the break-in had been reportedly traced to the Republican National Committee, or that one of the burglars had deposited a $25,000 cashier's check meant for Nixon's reelection committee in his bank account.[2] Even when the *Washington Post* reported that the FBI was probing Nixon's campaign for attempted political sabotage,[3] the revelations bounced off Nixon like a Ping-Pong ball.

But in 1973, all of that started to change. Five of the men involved in the Watergate burglary pleaded guilty to charges of conspiracy, burglary, and bugging Democrats' campaign headquarters while two others were convicted of the same crimes.[4] And lawmakers still intent on accountability from the White House created the special committee to conduct what its chairman called "the most important investigation ever entrusted to the Congress."[5]

Over three months that spring and summer, the Senate's Special Committee on Presidential Campaign Activities paraded the convicted Watergate burglars and Nixon's closest aides before the public in a steady stream of hearings that brought the scandal to life in the living rooms of almost every American.[6] The hearings also presented new and shocking evidence: One White House aide revealed that Nixon had made tapes of his conversations in the Oval Office— tapes that would prove Nixon's personal involvement a year later, once the House and the special prosecutor jointly procured them in a two-month-long court battle.[7] James McCord, a former CIA operative caught bugging the DNC, testified that he had routinely been ordered to tap Democrats' phones and faced "political pressure" to plead guilty when he was caught to avoid unwanted questions about the president's involvement.[8] Former attorney general John Mitchell spoke about how one Nixon confidant even proposed drugging liberal activists and hiding them in Mexican safehouses to stop them from causing problems for the president during the next Republican National Convention.[9]

The hearings became must-watch TV and turned Americans into "Watergate junkies." Some took breaks at work to gather around television screens in their office and watch them live, while others would catch them at home, where they were replayed nightly on PBS in prime time.[10] Lawmakers became celebrities: Watergate panel chairman Sam Ervin was plastered across the cover of *Time*, and Ervin fan clubs cropped up nationwide celebrating his folksy-yet-stern style of questioning and his controlled displays of righteous indignation.[11] His GOP counterpart, Howard Baker of Tennessee, meanwhile, gained fame for his regular query: "What did the president know, and when did he know it?"

While Nixon still maintained the loyalty of most of his party, the hearings began to swing public sentiment against him. Just a month after they started, polls found that 97 percent of Americans recognized the significance of the Watergate affair and 67 percent thought Nixon had engaged in a cover-up.[12] By the end of the summer, more than 70 percent of Americans had told pollsters they watched at least some of the hearings.[13] By the time they concluded, the panel had logged fifty-one days of public hearings amounting to 250 hours of testimony[14]—a staggering amount of evidence that compelled a bipartisan House majority to declare they were ready to begin impeachment proceedings.

In 2019, Nancy Pelosi gave her investigators just two weeks to pull off the same feat.

By mid-November, Adam Schiff's team had amassed a mountain of evidence against Trump that was only growing. Even some witnesses who had been initially cagey about what they knew were starting to bend under the pressure. On November 4, Ambassador to the European Union Gordon Sondland—who had equivocated his way through his deposition—felt compelled to correct the record, submitting a three-page "supplemental declaration" saying that the reports emanating from more recent witness depositions had "refreshed" his memory. He now recalled having "presumed" that the freeze on Ukraine's military assistance was linked to Trump's desire that the Bidens be investigated—and to having relayed that message to Ukrainian president Zelensky's top aide, just as Bill Taylor had testified.[15]

But the evidence at Schiff's disposal didn't solve the main problem before House Democrats: how to translate the severity of Trump's crimes to the public and tell the complicated Ukraine story so that everyday Americans understood it. The public hearings were their best chance to do that. The cameras would be rolling, and they would fleetingly have the attention of a distracted public that they knew didn't have the patience or time to sift through the thousands of pages of deposition transcripts they had just started releasing.

The stakes were incredibly high. Since Pelosi had endorsed the impeachment inquiry in late September, nationwide support for Trump's ouster had grown somewhat, from an average 39 percent supporting and 48 percent opposed, to about an even 46 percent split, according to a *Washington Post* analysis of major polls that summer and fall. But by early November, that momentum had started to plateau. Making matters worse, new polling out of key swing states was starting to show voters growing skeptical of Democrats' case.[16]

For Schiff's team, that meant there was no room for error. On the night of November 5, they locked themselves in the SCIF with a whiteboard to sketch out how to weave all their information into a single Ukraine narrative, a task that would require cramming twelve witnesses into seven hearings in five days. Since time was short, everything had to be planned with precision. The case against Trump was far more complicated than Watergate, which was in essence a robbery and a cover-up. To accept Trump's guilt, the public would need to develop a working knowledge of foreign assistance, diplomatic leverage, and the arcane history of a former Soviet Socialist Republic's attempted pivot away from Moscow.

As if that wasn't enough of a challenge, Schiff's team was also swimming against a current that had never affected Nixon's prosecutors: shock fatigue. By late 2019, Trump had already broken so many institutional norms and upset so many American customs that the idea of him trying to pressure the leader of a dependent nation into doing a personal political favor hardly seemed out of character. Indeed, attitudes about Trump were fixed in ways they had never been with Nixon. Trump's support had a ceiling, but it also had a floor.

To rouse such a jaded public to call for Trump's ouster, Democrats needed to put on a truly mind-blowing show, filled with explosive testimony and incontrovertible evidence. It would prove to be an impossible task.

The second day of the public impeachment hearings was barely an hour underway on Friday, November 15, when the tweet popped up on the device of Schiff's communications chief, Patrick Boland. A few feet away from him, bright lights beamed onto an imposing two-tiered wooden dais, where twenty-two members of the Intelligence Committee had arranged themselves before a backdrop of columns and dark blue velvet curtains. In front of them, a redheaded witness sat primly before a microphone, as reporters behind her typed furiously and photographers jockeyed for a position to snap the best possible picture.

Boland had been sitting backstage, in a cramped, dark antechamber off the hearing room floor that had become the Democrats' control center. What the space lacked in comfort, it had in proximity to the dais—precisely for emergency situations like this.

"Everywhere Marie Yovanovitch went turned bad," read the president's tweet as it flashed up on Boland's phone. "She started off in Somalia, how did that go?"

Boland knew their team had selected Yovanovitch as one of only two impeachment witnesses to appear solo at a hearing for one key reason: They wanted the ousted ambassador's story to capture the viewing audience's hearts—and to remind them that Trump had unfairly targeted her, and the Ukrainian government to boot, to serve his own personal political ends. At that exact moment, in fact, Schiff's lead counsel, Dan Goldman, was asking former ambassador to Ukraine Marie Yovanovitch about the Rudy Giuliani–led smear campaign that had led to her ouster. Now, the president was doing it again in real time, Boland realized as he read Trump's tweet. It was the perfect opportunity to illustrate just how much of a bully the president really was.

"Holy shit! Did you see this?" Boland texted his colleagues Maher Bitar and Rheanne Wirkkala, who were seated just behind the lawmakers on the dais, alerting them to the tweet and offering to bring printouts to Schiff's and Yovanovitch's counsel. They readily agreed. Boland also flagged the missive to the committee's audiovisual staff so they could display the offending tweet on the television screens when Schiff was ready to reference it.

In a small but stately library in the back of the hearing room, Trump's tweet was also sending Republicans into a panic in their own control center. Their plan for the day had been to handle Yovanovitch with kid gloves. They would express sympathy for her plight while arguing it was irrelevant to the impeachment case against Trump and that the president had every right to choose his own ambassadors.

But in a couple dozen characters, Trump had upended that strategy, attacking Yovanovitch at the very moment she was explaining to the nation what it felt like to be intimidated by Trump's army of henchmen. Jim Jordan's and Kevin McCarthy's aides groaned in exasperation. Mark Meadows, who rarely cursed or lost composure, was irate.

"What the hell?! What is he *doing*?" a red-faced Meadows exclaimed.

"This is so dumb and distracting—*why*?" bemoaned Machalagh Carr, Kevin McCarthy's general counsel, throwing up her hands in defeat.

The president's attack was exactly what McCarthy had warned Hill Republicans *not* to do. The White House had been pressuring panel Republicans to go after the witnesses personally to discredit their testimony. But over a series of practice sessions, McCarthy had specifically told House Intelligence Committee Republicans to ignore that advice—even if it came from Trump himself.

Trump's Hill allies instantly realized that the president's tweet would arm Democrats with new talking points—and possibly new allegations of witness intimidation. Someone had to take Trump's phone away or have a serious talk with him, they all agreed. At that, Meadows stormed into a small room inside the antechamber, slamming the door to make a phone call to the president.

Back on the dais, when Schiff received the printout of Trump's tweet, his eyes widened. On its face, Trump's charge was ridiculous: Yovanovitch had been a low-level diplomat in her mid-twenties when she had been stationed in Somalia during the late 1980s; she bore no responsibility for the decades of humanitarian tragedy that had befallen the war-torn country in the wake of the Cold War. About twenty minutes after the tweet went online, Schiff interrupted Goldman's questioning and invited Yovanovitch to respond to it in real time.

"Ambassador Yovanovitch, as we sit here testifying, the president is attacking you on Twitter," Schiff interjected, reading the tweet aloud. As he read, Yovanovitch winced, her face momentarily pained. But a moment later, her expression broke into a half-smile—a sign that she too found the whole charge ridiculous.

"Well, I—I mean I don't—I don't think I have such powers," Yovanovitch said, stammering slightly.

Schiff, however, had a point to make and was determined not to let Yovanovitch shrug off Trump's attack.

"The president in real time is attacking you. What effect do you think that has on other witnesses' willingness to come forward and expose wrongdoing?" he pried.

Yovanovitch blinked several times and glanced down before looking up and offering, "Well," she said, pausing, "it's very intimidating."

A few minutes later, Schiff called a break in the hearing. He wanted the public—and all the pundits anchoring the wall-to-wall coverage of the hearings—to ruminate on what had just happened.

As the room broke into a commotion, Republicans on the dais slipped into the library where Meadows, Carr, and other staffers were trying to do damage control. In a way, the break had been a godsend: They needed a minute to figure out how to spin away what Trump had said. Their best option, they agreed, was to try to distract people from it by giving them redder meat to chew on. And since Yovanovitch herself was off-limits, that left only one other target: their go-to punching bag, Adam Schiff. The only question was: Who would take the swing?

Before the public hearings began, McCarthy had come under intense pressure from the White House and Trump confidants to pack the House Intelligence Committee with allies of the president, such as Meadows and Matt Gaetz. They were worried that the panel's few centrist Republicans would refuse to defend Trump ardently enough when the chips were down. But McCarthy actually viewed the centrists as an asset. A passionate defense of Trump from a die-hard loyalist might satisfy the president's followers and conservative news pundits, but it was far less likely to appeal to skeptical independents whom they wanted to win over to their side. So McCarthy went with his gut, refusing to replace his moderates on the committee. Now, as House Republicans searched for an escape hatch from Trump's Yovanovitch catastrophe, everyone was glad he had.

A few days earlier, during the inaugural public hearing, one of those moderates, Elise Stefanik of New York, had been mocked by an ABC News pundit for challenging Schiff on the rules of the hearing. Stefanik, he said, was "a perfect example of why just electing someone because they are a woman or a millennial doesn't necessarily get you the leaders we need," a sexist remark that sent conservative media into an indignant rage.[17] The right raced to defend Stefanik—a thirty-five-year-old former acolyte of Paul Ryan who had never been a darling of MAGA World—as a maligned, wronged woman.

After Trump's attack on Yovanovitch, the GOP realized that it was awfully convenient to have a female victim of their own to showcase. If they could make it look like Schiff was trying to shut Stefanik up, they calculated, it could give the GOP a way to argue that what Trump had done to Yovanovitch was no worse than what Schiff was doing.

Stefanik had never been a particularly strong Trump supporter.

In fact, she had a history of openly criticizing the president over everything from his Muslim ban and border wall to his plans to make deep cuts at the Environmental Protection Agency.[18] But she was willing and eager to step into the limelight—and, in fact, had offered to personally challenge Schiff during the GOP's practice sessions days before.

When the panel regrouped to continue questioning Yovanovitch, Republicans put their plan into action. Under the hearing rules, only the top panel Democrat and Republican, or their counsels, were entitled to ask questions during the first ninety minutes. But McCarthy and Jordan were willing to bet the public didn't know that. They made sure that when the GOP's turn came up, they put Stefanik center stage.

"Ambassador Yovanovitch, thank you for being here—" she started, before Schiff leaped in to object, repeatedly banging his gavel to silence her. It was exactly what they had hoped for.

"What is the interruption for this time? It is our time!" Stefanik said in faux outrage, leaning into her microphone to make sure her protestations were heard loud and clear, as others accused Schiff of "gagging the young lady from New York."

"The gentlewoman will suspend," Schiff said, still banging his gavel, as he pointed out that Stefanik was not yet entitled to speak.

"This is the fifth time you have interrupted members of Congress, duly elected members of Congress," Stefanik protested, prompting Schiff to start beating his gavel again.

Their argument lasted only a minute, but it succeeded in making Stefanik a celebrity in Trump circles and giving the GOP the momentary distraction they craved. The next week, after her office posted the clip of the exchange, she raised $250,000 in fifteen minutes for her reelection campaign,[19] further proof of how toxic impeachment had become. The exchange did little, however, to change the course of the hearing. At the end, the audience rose to its feet applauding Yovanovitch for her service and bravery.

In the White House, meanwhile, Vice President Mike Pence, White House counsel Pat Cipollone, and Trump's son-in-law Jared Kushner cornered Trump in the Oval Office to make sure he knew that he couldn't attack witnesses mid-proceedings.[20] Publicly, Trump was defiant about his tweet, telling reporters that "I have the right to speak." But in the safety of his office, sitting behind the Resolute Desk, Trump, in a rare moment of contrition, agreed. He wouldn't do that anymore.

Trump's tweet during the Yovanovitch hearing was just one of several moments in the impeachment hearings that left the GOP scrambling—and Democrats gloating. From the very first session, the witnesses delivered blow after blow against the president, often making the Republicans look craven for defending him.

Ambassador Bill Taylor, the chargé d'affaires in Ukraine, revealed the existence of new evidence: One of his top aides, he said on live television, had overheard Gordon Sondland and Trump discussing the Ukraine scheme on his cell phone just one day after the president's July 25 Zelensky call. The disclosure directly refuted Sondland's suggestion that he barely knew the president and rarely spoke to him, an assertion Trump was also making around that time in a bid to distance himself from the State official who knew too much.

Just hours after the fiasco of Trump's Yovanovitch tweet, Democrats summoned that aide, David Holmes, to the SCIF to tell his story—in more colorful language. Holmes recounted how he had heard Sondland tell Trump over the phone that Zelensky would do the investigation—or "anything you ask him" to—because he "loves your ass." Sondland also told Holmes that Trump "doesn't give a shit about Ukraine"—except when it came to "big stuff," like investigating the Bidens.

The juiciest bits, of course, promptly leaked to the media and went viral on television and Twitter, producing more bad headlines for Republicans and the president.

Back in the public hearing room, the GOP was likewise getting ceremonially walloped on substance. The witnesses offered authoritative stories delivered with professional gravitas that cut straight through the president's attempts to spin the proceedings as a farce. On several occasions, they took pains to stress that they were nonpartisan government servants who had served both Republican and Democratic presidents and were there to state the facts, not take a side. Still, Trump kept taking swings at them on Twitter, deriding them as "NEVER TRUMPERS!"—and urging the GOP to hit back. After Yovanovitch's hearing and Holmes's deposition, Intelligence panel Republicans heeded the call, ignoring McCarthy's plea not to attack the witnesses.

One of their top targets was Alexander Vindman, an Army lieutenant colonel and National Security Council detailee who had been assigned to listen in on Trump's July 25 call. The round-faced, bespectacled immigrant from the former Soviet Union had been so alarmed by what he had heard during the presidents' exchange that he reported it to the NSC lawyers. But that wasn't the main thing that bothered the GOP. Vindman had also admitted to having discussed Trump's call with a member of the intelligence community—yet categorically refused to name him. To Republicans, that was as good as admitting he had been the whistleblower's informant, setting the entire impeachment inquiry in motion.

It didn't matter to Republicans that Vindman had earned a Purple Heart fighting for the U.S. Army in Iraq. It angered them, in fact, that he had shown up to testify in uniform and asked to be addressed by his rank. They sought to undermine him, arguing that his former superior at the National Security Council Tim Morrison had testified he had concerns about Vindman's work. Meanwhile on Fox News, a pundit suggested Vindman was guilty of "espionage" because he had conducted his work in fluent Russian and Ukrainian in accordance with his duties.[21]

Their assaults only ended up making Vindman look more sympathetic. His hands shook when he read his opening statement, which included a line assuring his father that while dissidents in Russia might be killed for pushing back against their own government, "I will be fine for telling the truth." And when asked why he decided to come forward, despite the attacks, Vindman answered calmly: "because this is America . . . and here, right matters."

Republicans did manage to land a few punches in the public hearings, most of them tied to the charge that the bulk of the testimony was hearsay. Jordan got Bill Taylor to confirm that he never spoke to the president, chief of staff, or anyone close to Trump's inner circle about whether Sondland's allegations were true.

"And you're their star witness!" Jordan exclaimed, feigning shock.

But in general, the GOP simply took blow after blow.

The worst came when Kurt Volker took the stand. For weeks, Volker had been their go-to witness, the one whose testimony they would turn to any time someone began bellyaching about a "quid pro quo." Volker, they reminded their colleagues like a broken record, had repeatedly refuted the idea during his closed-door interview. But in public, on the hot seat, Volker recanted.

"In hindsight, I now understand that others saw the idea of investigating possible corruption involving the Ukrainian company, 'Burisma,' as equivalent to investigating former vice president Biden," he admitted. "I saw them as very different, the former being

appropriate and unremarkable, the latter being unacceptable. In ret-
rospect, I should have seen that connection differently—and had I
done so, I would have raised my own objections."

By the end of the first week of hearings, Democrats were riding
high, drunk off the glowing praise from TV pundits, their peers,
and the media. But there was still the question of whether their
hearings were resonating beyond the Beltway to make a difference.
As it turned out, they weren't.

Each of the impeachment hearings drew between approximately
11 million and 13 million viewers on broadcast television.[22] Those
numbers were a far cry from the over 80 percent of Americans who
had watched the Watergate hearings,[23] and even a marked decline
in viewership from more recent high-profile congressional events.
Nearly 20 million Americans had tuned in when newly fired FBI
director James Comey testified in June 2017 about Trump asking
him for a loyalty pledge. A similar number watched Christine Blasey
Ford testify in September 2018 that then–Supreme Court nominee
Brett Kavanaugh had sexually assaulted her when they were in high
school. Even former special counsel Robert Mueller's shaky testimony earlier that year had drawn a bigger audience than most of the
impeachment hearings.[24]

Part of that was because Democrats had moved forward without marquee names from Trump's inner circle. Additionally, almost
none of their witnesses could speak firsthand to Trump's own intentions. Even the man who arguably could—Gordon Sondland—
would only raise more questions than answers.

The morning that Sondland showed up for his public hearing,
Democrats were giddy, anticipating that the ambassador to the
European Union would finally turn on Trump. In his opening
statement—which Sondland sent to the panel shortly before walk-

ing into the hearing room—he was planning to admit that Trump had indeed tried to orchestrate a quid pro quo in Ukraine and that "everyone was in the loop."

"I know that members of this committee frequently frame these complicated issues in the form of a simple question: Was there a quid pro quo?" Sondland had written in his prepared remarks. "The answer is yes . . . It was no secret."

"Did you see this?" an excited Schiff asked his fellow Intelligence panel Democrats, waving to a copy of the opening statement as they awaited the start of the hearing.

Except in the flesh, Sondland was not the savior Democrats had hoped he would be. He delivered his opening statement in full. But he couldn't—or wouldn't—account for a single time he heard Trump say that Ukraine's military assistance depended on the investigations of Trump's adversaries. Instead, Sondland said he received his directions from Giuliani and just "presumed" they came from the president, because "two plus two equals four."

Making matters worse, the ambassador said Giuliani had never mentioned Ukraine's military assistance was contingent on the investigations at all.

"President Trump never told me directly that the aid was conditioned on the meetings," Sondland said under questioning from Goldman. "The only thing we got directly from Giuliani was that the Burisma and 2016 elections were conditioned on the White House meeting. The aid was my own personal, you know, guess."

If Democrats were disappointed, they didn't show it. Schiff called a break and walked straight up to a bank of TV cameras to proclaim that Sondland had offered "the most significant evidence to date" showing "potential high crimes or misdemeanors."

But Schiff's declaration of victory didn't make it so. And Republicans spent the rest of the hearing highlighting the gaping holes in Sondland's testimony. "This is the trifecta of unreliability!" Steve

Castor exclaimed at one point. "A lot of it's speculation, a lot of it is
your 'guess'—and we're talking about an impeachment of the President of the United States, so the evidence here ought to be pretty
darn good."

Despite the discrepancies, many in the national media seized
on Sondland's quip that "everyone was in the loop," painting the
ambassador as a winning witness for the Democrats. Some even
likened him to John Dean, the White House counsel who had publicly turned on Nixon and implicated him in a cover-up during
a blockbuster Senate Watergate hearing in June 1973. In reality,
the comparison wasn't even close: In a 245-page opening statement
that took him an entire day to read on national television, Dean
had spoken of his direct conversations with Nixon about creating an
"enemies list" and paying off the Watergate burglars with $1 million
to keep quiet.[25] Sondland, by contrast, couldn't recall a single White
House official who had told him his "personal presumption" about
the quid pro quo was correct.

"So no one told you. Not just the President—Giuliani didn't tell
you, Mulvaney didn't tell you. Nobody. Pompeo didn't tell you. Nobody else on this planet told you that Donald Trump was tying aid
to these investigations," moderate GOP congressman Mike Turner
asked him during the hearing. "You really have no testimony today
that ties President Trump to a scheme to withhold aid from Ukraine
in exchange for these investigations."

"Other than my own presumption," Sondland answered.

As polls would later show, Sondland's words failed to move the
needle on how the public viewed impeachment. But in the moment,
they also prompted more nonpartisan criticism of the Democrats'
fast-moving strategy. That day, in a break from liberal-leaning cable
TV networks, the *New York Times* editorial board encouraged Schiff
to keep trying to produce more compelling witnesses who could fill

in the gaps of Sondland's testimony. "You know what would help clarify some of these issues? Sworn testimony from the many key players in this scheme who have yet to appear before Congress," they wrote.

Schiff's team, the editorial continued, had already found "abundant evidence" that Trump had abused his power to go after his political rival, subverted national security interests, and tried to obstruct Congress. But while "Americans shouldn't be distracted by Republican smoke bombs . . . they should also not be satisfied with a truncated inquiry," the *Times* wrote. People like John Bolton, Mick Mulvaney, and Giuliani all needed to testify.

"Right now, the House Intelligence Committee has not scheduled testimony from any witnesses after Thursday. That is a mistake," the editorial continued. "No matter is more urgent, but it should not be rushed—for the protection of the nation's security, and for the integrity of the presidency, and for the future of the Republic."[26]

At the beginning of the impeachment inquiry, Pelosi had spoken about the need to bring the public along on Trump's impeachment investigation, quoting Lincoln for effect. But in many ways, she never gave her team the chance. Her insistence that Trump's impeachment be wrapped up before Christmas forced investigators to concede fights for better witnesses prematurely and rush through public hearings at a dizzying pace that overwhelmed viewers, left little time for the details to sink in, and was difficult for even seasoned Washington reporters to keep up with.

By the time the *New York Times* came out with its editorial urging further investigation, the impeachment train had already left the station—without the American public fully aboard.

By the final public hearing, Republicans had also decided they— and Trump—were in the clear. As John Bolton's former deputy

Fiona Hill used the final public hearing to lambast the GOP for being Kremlin shills by even considering Trump's conspiracy theories about Ukraine, McCarthy's and Jordan's staffers watched from the back room, casually fawning over how impressively she was roasting them. They knew they were getting grilled on the facts— and smoked on substance—but it simply didn't matter. The nation wasn't watching.

"BUILD A BETTER CASE"

NOVEMBER 19, 2019

Francis Rooney scanned the buzzing floor of the House of Representatives in search of the one person he desperately needed to speak with. Lawmakers flowed past the Florida Republican, crossing the threshold of a pair of ornate double doors flanked by security officers behind him, and into the high-ceilinged, walnut-paneled chamber to vote. Hundreds of members were milling around the long rows of brown leather armchairs arranged in a semicircle on tiered platforms, gossiping about the latest churn in the high-profile impeachment hearings. Rooney, however, was eager to get something serious off his chest—something that had been bothering him for a while.

Rooney's eyes darted around the assembly room in desperation as he peered above heads and around shifting throngs to find the petite figure with whom he so urgently needed an audience. Finally, he spotted his target, surrounded by her ever-present posse of staffers near the large wooden rostrum at the front: House Speaker Nancy

Pelosi. He had to warn her Democrats were about to make a fatal error in their case.

Ever since Rooney had gone on CNN and dared to say he was open to impeaching his president, he had become a pariah in his own party. Republican leaders called his office, complaining to his staff. And his Trump-loving constituents in the Sunshine State—including longtime allies Rooney had known for years—lit up his phone demanding he resign.

"You have betrayed the Republican Party and the president . . . We can't have you representing this district if you feel this way," one local Republican whom Rooney considered a friend had told him over the phone. Another local leader who had helped Rooney get elected sent him a text insisting he had to step down immediately and offering to be next to him for moral support when he made the announcement.

Rooney, stunned by the force of the backlash, had bowed to the pressure and announced his retirement. He'd been souring on Washington for a while and decided that even he, a lifelong conservative, couldn't represent a district like his in the Trump era.

Still, Rooney believed he had unfinished business in Washington, particularly when it came to impeachment. Retirement hadn't made the question of how to vote on the effort to oust Trump any easier for him. Unlike the majority of his GOP colleagues who had willingly stuck their heads in the sand, he was open to considering voting to impeach his party leader—if the evidence demanded it.

From his perch on the House Foreign Affairs Committee, Rooney had immersed himself in the impeachment investigation with purpose. He had attended most of the private depositions in the secure facility and taken notes on each witness who came in to testify. He kept a diary of his internal thoughts and hungrily followed news coverage of the successive revelations, eager to connect the dots.

Though he had a law degree, Rooney also solicited input from GOP attorneys he believed were smarter than he. He frequently prodded former White House counsels for Presidents George W. Bush and Ronald Reagan about whether Trump's offenses, if proven, were impeachable.

All his research had still left Rooney unsatisfied and craving one thing in particular: Before he took the plunge and voted to impeach, he wanted to hear from a credible, primary source who could put the quid pro quo in Trump's mouth. It wasn't that he didn't believe the State officials who had testified in the depositions—and were now being featured in public hearings he'd been watching from his office. Each one had an extremely believable story to tell. But no one had yet delivered the knockout punch Rooney desired. No one had said they heard directly from Trump's lips that he was leveraging Ukraine's military aid on a promise to investigate the Bidens. Someone like John Dean, who had delivered Nixon a devastating blow when he testified that Nixon told him personally to pay off the Watergate burglars to keep them silent. The kind of witness who could prove Trump was dead-to-rights guilty.

As far as Rooney was concerned, Democrats had had several opportunities to produce such a witness but had shied away from all of them. National Security Advisor John Bolton, Trump's chief of staff Mick Mulvaney, and his personal attorney Rudy Giuliani had all been named as participants in or witnesses to Trump's Ukraine scheme. Rooney could not understand why Democrats hadn't already subpoenaed the lot of them. He couldn't understand their strategy at all.

Rooney had spent hours researching the impeachment proceedings of Nixon and Clinton and couldn't comprehend why Pelosi was trying to jam what was typically a months-long, if not years-long, process into just a few weeks. Trump's impeachment was advancing at a breakneck pace compared to the slow grilling of Nixon's aides and co-conspirators he had watched transpire over the course of more than a year as a college student and Capitol Hill intern. It had taken that long for the Senate Watergate Committee, and then the House Judiciary Committee, to drive closer and closer to the thirty-seventh president until they penetrated his inner circle—and only then persuaded Republicans who initially defended Nixon to turn away from their president, prompting him to resign in shame.

Yet Democrats, Rooney noted with regret, appeared to have no interest in that kind of slow, methodical work. Rumor had it that after the public hearings they were preparing to charge forward to vote on the articles of impeachment, eviscerating any chance to hear from high-level witnesses the probe was lacking. In his estimation, the process was being short-circuited. And for that, he blamed Pelosi.

In Rooney's estimation, Democrats might actually be able to pull off a bipartisan impeachment if they just took enough time to pull on every investigative thread they had in their hands. If Democrats were serious about finding the truth, he believed they needed to go to the courts to fight for blockbuster witnesses—and he resolved to tell Pelosi as much that very day.

Rooney wasn't typically in the business of cornering the most powerful woman in the nation. Despite his recent foray into the spotlight, he was still considered a backbencher on the Hill. But Rooney shared a little-known, personal connection with Pelosi. He'd gotten to know her and her husband, Paul Pelosi, decades ago through alumni circles of Georgetown University. They both had deep Catholic roots, similarities Rooney thought might assist in getting Pelosi to take him seriously.

With his eyes locked on Pelosi, Rooney crossed the chamber, passing the elevated rostrum adorned with a large American flag on his right as he walked to where she stood, near a massive portrait of George Washington, on the Democrats' side. Rooney drew a quick breath before offering a greeting of "Madam Speaker!"

"Why don't you slow down and fight Bolton's privilege claim in court so you can get all the evidence—like Peter Rodino and Sam Ervin did in Watergate?" he asked Pelosi.

In the 1970s, he reminded Pelosi, lawmakers successfully fought in court to get secret tapes of Nixon's conversations, evidence that, once procured, instantly turned the public—even the crooked president's most ardent defenders—against him. The real jury, Rooney continued, "is the American people." And if Democrats took the time to get firsthand evidence from the former national security advisor, the chief of staff, and other top witnesses, they'd have a real shot at convincing the public and changing GOP minds in turn—just like in Watergate.

"Take your time and build a better case," Rooney implored her.

Pelosi smiled wanly at Rooney. She wasn't used to being challenged directly about strategy from individual rank-and-file members. But this was no ordinary appeal. Pelosi knew that Rooney had been one of the few Republicans brave enough to say publicly that Trump's Ukraine gambit was unethical. His comments had allowed Democrats to hope for the first time that maybe—just maybe—some Republicans would have the courage to break with Trump, no matter how much the Republican base worshipped him.

"I appreciate that, but we can't change gears now," Pelosi told Rooney. Going to the courts to secure the testimony of top Trump officials, she argued, would trigger court battles that could take months they didn't have to spare.

Rooney was unsatisfied by her answer. During past impeachments, the House Judiciary Committee had sued for records and testimony, unearthing key evidence in the process. There was no reason, he argued, that Democrats shouldn't do the same with Trump.

"I think time is going to be your ally," Rooney pressed. "The longer this drags out, the more allegations are going to come out."

Plus, even if it took extra time, wouldn't an admission of Trump's guilt from Giuliani, Bolton, or Mulvaney be worth it, he asked Pelosi—especially if it persuaded moderate Republicans like him to back the charges?

"If there is enough evidence to justify impeachment, I will vote for it," Rooney said. "But there's not enough evidence right now. It looks like more of a political process—and I can't vote for that."

Pelosi rarely changed her mind. Throughout her decade and a half in leadership, her stubborn streak had become well known to her colleagues and staff, and she had even once declared that she had "no regrets" whatsoever in life or in politics. Once she plotted a course forward, it took an earthquake to move her. And though Rooney's appeal rang clear with sincerity, he was one man—not necessarily a sign of a groundswell in the greater GOP.

Democrats, she told Rooney, "have a process—and we're going to follow it." And that was that.

As Rooney walked away, he woefully concluded that Democrats were as bad as the Republicans. The magnitude of Trump's conduct called for a thorough and nonpolitical process, but Democrats cared more about scoring political points than getting to the truth, he thought sourly.

"I don't need to be a political pawn for either party," he said to himself, his decision on impeachment made final. He would join the Republicans in voting no.

Pelosi was in a spicy mood as she gathered with her impeachment messaging team later that day, lobbing all sorts of insults at the president. Trump, she said, was losing his mind over the public hearings—and good. He was a "freeloader in chief." Or maybe the "parasite in chief." Actually, his whole family was, she added, correcting herself: "The Trumps are *all* parasites."

"This guy is a thug—and he still ropes in 40 percent of the country," she fumed. "The Statue of Liberty is crying."

Back in September, when Pelosi had first gathered her leadership team for the emergency session in her office after announcing an inquiry, she had told them that they had a duty to bring the public along with them as they laid out the extent of Trump's alleged crimes. By mid-November, however, the Speaker had come to the conclusion that Trump's impeachment investigation was never going to elicit a Watergate-style breakthrough. She had essentially given up on the idea of winning over swaths of Republicans—a significant admission of defeat from a Speaker who had once insisted that it was imperative impeachment be bipartisan.

Even before Democrats took their case public in the hearings being aired that week, Pelosi had been tempering expectations, warning her leadership team that the sessions wouldn't likely change the public's perception of the Democrats' case. During an impeachment messaging session just after State officials Bill Taylor and George Kent testified, she had brandished a chart demonstrating how partisan the nation had become since Nixon's ouster. In the decades since, one of the top indicators for whether a person supported their president was simply party affiliation. In that sense, there were parts of the nation Democrats would never be able to reach, she told the room.

That didn't mean her team had surrendered on the messaging war. After all, there were still independents they could try to reach. In fact, they'd spent their entire messaging meeting the week before trying to come up with responses to the latest GOP criticisms being lobbed at their public hearings—a brainstorming exercise that quickly turned into a venting session.

David Cicilline, who led the discussion, complained that Republicans were arguing that what Trump did was "not a crime"—huffing in frustration that "YES, IT IS!" As for the GOP's suggestion that the evidence against Trump was "secondhand" or "hearsay," he offered another pithy, heated retort: "NO, IT'S NOT!"

Jamie Raskin, getting into the spirit, had also jumped into the fray. The GOP's defense of the president effectively boiled down to "no harm, no foul," he scoffed. "Just because you get caught before committing a crime doesn't make it okay," he said. Ukraine's military assistance, he added, "was only released because he got caught."

Zoe Lofgren, a Pelosi ally and senior member of the Judiciary Committee, argued that Democrats "need to make the point that holding up this aid cost people their lives in Ukraine." Hakeem Jeffries, the No. 4 House Democrat, suggested they emphasize the point that "it's clearly all about Biden and the 2020 campaign." Others thought the Democrats should lean into arguments about "broad corruption."

"If we don't compete with Trump on the anti-corruption angle, we cede that ground to him," another member of Pelosi's leadership team, Maryland congressman John Sarbanes, said.

Pelosi had listened to the ideas and offered her own take. "What Trump did makes Nixon look like small potatoes," she quipped.

That day, as all eyes were on the opening impeachment hearings, Pelosi had done a little rhetorical escalation of her own to try to appeal to voters: She accused Trump of committing bribery.

It wasn't an off-the-cuff remark: The House Democrats' campaign arm had previously tested the word in focus groups and found it resonated in swing districts.[1] Progressive groups were also pressing Democratic leaders to use the word, eager to employ more aggressive language.

But while the left applauded Pelosi's embrace of "bribery," Nadler's team had instantly flown into a panic. The impeachment lawyers had briefly considered a bribery charge early on—and summarily dismissed the idea because there were too many discrepancies between the constitutional and statutory definitions of the crime, making it too tough to prove. There was no sense in giving the GOP an easy out, they had determined, thinking they'd closed the door on the word once and for all.

Until November 14, when Pelosi used it in a press conference.

"What the fuck?" one of Nadler's lawyers exclaimed, as the panel's attorneys scrambled to hash out a game plan to get her to walk it back. Nadler's impeachment expert Joshua Matz even drafted a series of secret memos on the pitfalls of the word—memos that Nadler's staff sent to Schiff's team in hopes that Pelosi's "favorite son" could pull the Speaker back from the brink.

When Pelosi gathered her messaging team again on November 19, the clean-up operation was still underway.

"They're using the bribery line against us," Raskin argued.

Pelosi, luckily, was starting to get the message.

"Yes, 'abuse of power' is a better framing. Bribery only satisfies the exuberant left," Pelosi said—as if her quip hadn't been what had sparked the dustup. "The criticism I get is we aren't tough enough. The perception on the left is Trump is getting away with everything and we aren't doing anything about it."

Pelosi confided in the room that she had another concern that day: She was worried that the GOP's charge that the Democrats' impeachment process had been unfair was starting to resonate. Cicilline suggested they double down on simply disputing the argument.

"We've given them more minority rights than under Clinton and Nixon," he said, reminding the room of what Pelosi had said a few weeks prior.

Ted Lieu, meanwhile, said they shouldn't even bother responding to the GOP's talking points at all.

"If the GOP is complaining about process, they're losing," Lieu,
a fellow "musketeer" of Cicilline and Raskin, said. "People don't
care."

Pelosi tended to agree, but she knew members like Rooney did
not. It wasn't rocket science to figure out that if he had a problem
with the way the investigation was being run, then every other
House Republican did too. But Pelosi never mentioned her encounter with Rooney to her team. The Speaker was already moving
on: It was time to start drafting the articles and getting the entire
impeachment exercise over with.

26

THE CLIENT

NOVEMBER 21–DECEMBER 2, 2019

As all eyes in Washington—though not the nation—were trained on the House's last day of impeachment hearings on Thursday, November 21, Senator Ted Cruz was at the White House, losing his patience with Trump's defense team. The two-term senator and onetime presidential candidate was arguing with Pat Cipollone that it was time to change tactics: Now that the Senate trial was just around the corner, it was well past time for Trump's team to do more than just repeat the president's "no quid pro quo" line. That might have worked as counter-messaging in the House, Cruz said, but it would be a losing argument with more independently minded Senate Republicans.

"Why defend that plot of land?" Cruz asked Cipollone, visibly annoyed. "It doesn't give you the victory at the end—and it's a much weaker position to defend."

Before winning his Texas Senate seat in 2012, Cruz had made a name for himself as a conservative firebrand and one of the most brilliant attorneys in the GOP. He had graduated magna cum laude from Harvard Law, clerked for Supreme Court Chief Justice William Rehnquist, and litigated George W. Bush's dispute with Al Gore over the 2000 election results in Florida. He later argued nine cases before the Supreme Court, most as Texas's solicitor general, becoming a high-profile warrior for conservative causes on everything from guns to religion in schools.[1]

Nothing revved up Cruz like a good legal fight. He reveled in trouncing his opponents, believing himself to be the smartest person in any room. He approached constitutional arguments with both the obsessive geekery of a law student and the shrewd tactical planning of a military strategist. His critics, however, considered him to be arrogant, amoral, and a political opportunist. Even most of Cruz's Senate GOP colleagues hated his guts, rolling their eyes whenever he spoke. "If you killed Ted Cruz on the floor of the Senate, and the trial was in the Senate, nobody could convict you," Senator Lindsey Graham quipped of Cruz in early 2016.[2]

As Democrats and Republicans bickered over whether Trump had engaged in a quid pro quo that fall, all Cruz could think was: *Who the hell cares?* The only thing that mattered was whether Trump's actions were justified—and as far as Cruz was concerned, they were. Trump had every right to use his influence to finagle investigations of Biden, in his opinion—especially given Hunter Biden's lucrative association with a questionable Ukrainian businessman while his father was vice president. Cruz had been making that case to his GOP colleagues, arguing that quid pro quos happen all the time in foreign policy and are "not inherently illegal."

"Don't fall into the trap of 'Oh, if there's a quid pro quo then Trump is screwed!'" he told them during one late-October lunch, deriding his colleagues for getting hung up about a phrase that was "just Latin" for an exchange. "It's all about intent."

None of his fellow Republican senators had pushed back. But at the White House, convincing Cipollone was proving more difficult.

"If you're defending this regime by quibbling about 'was there a quid pro quo,' you'll be much more likely to lose," Cruz tried to tell Trump's White House counsel during their late-November meeting. All it would take to eviscerate that defense was one convincing witness with firsthand information to show Trump had tried to leverage Ukraine's military assistance, he pointed out. Instead, Cruz argued, the narrative should be: *Does the president have the constitutional authority to investigate corruption?*

"If that's the narrative, you win. It's game over," he told the White House lawyers confidently. "Because the obvious answer to that question is yes."

Cipollone, however, refused to budge. Trump, he explained, would never allow his lawyers to say there was any truth to the quid pro quo allegations against him—not even if it would get him off the hook.

"You're not the client," Cipollone said dryly to Cruz, as the rest of the White House group nodded in agreement.

That Cruz was present for the meeting at all was something of a miracle. He and Trump had had a frosty relationship since they'd run against each other during the 2016 presidential campaign. On the trail, Trump had dubbed Cruz "Lyin' Ted," suggested his wife was ugly, and even falsely accused Cruz's father of collaborating with President John F. Kennedy's assassin. Cruz dished it right back, calling Trump a "pathological liar" and a "sniveling coward."[3] He had even refused to endorse Trump on the floor of the GOP convention, snubbing the nominee by telling Republicans to "vote your conscience" instead.

But Cruz hadn't come to the White House that day to please Trump. He had come at the behest of Mitch McConnell.

That fall, McConnell had watched with concern as a pair of trial ideas floating around MAGA World and Fox News began to permeate his own GOP conference. During an October lunch, Senator Rand Paul, a hard-core libertarian ophthalmologist from McConnell's home state, had suggested his colleagues consider calling Joe Biden as a trial witness in order to grill him about his son Hunter's cushy job in Ukraine—or just vote to dismiss the charges without even having a trial at all.

"What is the earliest possible moment you could dismiss?" he asked the room.

Senator Mike Lee of Utah, a former prosecutor whose conservative libertarian bona fides rivaled Paul's, had pushed back. Democrats hadn't given Trump a chance to defend himself in the House. So logically, he countered, the president should seize the chance to defend himself in the Senate.

"Six days is better than six minutes," Lee declared, chiding Paul.

"Six minutes is better than six weeks!" Paul shot back.

To McConnell, both of Paul's ideas were politically problematic. Dismissing the articles of impeachment to avoid a trial would expose GOP senators facing reelection to criticism they were aiding in a cover-up. And drawing out proceedings in order to pillory Biden was potentially just as bad. It risked turning the Senate into a political circus and making vulnerable senators look like complicit clowns. McConnell was certain, though, that Lee and Paul's spat wouldn't be the end of the debate: Trump had caught wind of the ideas and liked them, advocating for both on Twitter.

It wasn't the only way that McConnell thought the White House was undermining its own trial defense. Trump and Cipollone were still refusing to back off the claim that Trump's call with Zelensky was "perfect"—despite McConnell's frequent warnings that his more moderate members from swing states would not be able to use such a flimsy argument to justify an acquittal vote. McConnell had even dispatched his staff, including his top attorney, Andrew

Ferguson, to press Cipollone's team to embrace more compelling legal arguments "about our institution, about why proceeding on impeachment articles like this is bad for the Senate, about why it's bad for the presidency."

"Our goal here is to win," McConnell told them. "We need to make the arguments necessary to win."

But each time, McConnell's entreaties were ignored.

"I hear what you're saying, but we have a client," Cipollone would retort, referring to Trump, a sentiment his deputies also echoed. And "the client" liked the simple, albeit clearly erroneous, "perfect call" defense.

Cipollone was also dragging his heels on rounding out Trump's defense team, despite McConnell's earlier warnings. Each person he interviewed had been driven away by the Byzantine politics of the White House or shot down for one reason or another. It was clear to McConnell and his team that Cipollone wasn't interested in sharing the spotlight with GOP lawyers whose expertise might eclipse his own. He wanted to be in full control.

While Trump World talked that fall of subpoenaing the president's adversaries as part of a trial, McConnell had sketched out a plan for a short, two-week process—one that would enable senators to address the charges with legitimate legal arguments, then move quickly to dismiss them without calling witnesses. But McConnell knew he would need help selling that strategy. For all the power he wielded in the Senate, the Majority Leader had never managed to connect with the GOP base. He'd need powerful, credible allies in his corner if he was going to convince the White House and conservatives nationwide to go with his more monotonous process.

McConnell began recruiting an in-house brain trust of well-known, legally accomplished senators to serve as his interlocutors. Each had the respect of GOP voters and the trust of the White House

due to their backgrounds and close relationships with Trump—and
each could help McConnell ensure the Senate trial didn't go off the
rails. Or so he thought.

The group, which McConnell dubbed his "legal eagles," included Cruz, Mike Lee, Lindsey Graham, and McConnell's former
right-hand man John Cornyn. They were not natural allies. Cruz
had been a frequent thorn in McConnell's side, preferring to lob
attacks cheered by the far right rather than oversee the tricky business of actual governing. He'd even once accused McConnell on
the Senate floor of lying to his own members, likening him to Je-
sus's disciple Peter, who denied having known him just before the
crucifixion.[4] But Cruz still wanted to be president someday, and to
do that, he needed to rebuild his credibility with Trump's populist
base. Being center stage, defending Trump through his impeachment, would leave him well positioned to someday inherit the president's supporters—and so he agreed to tag-team with McConnell
and try to corral the White House.

By the time Cruz and the other legal eagles headed to the White
House on November 21, the Senate trial was just a few weeks away,
but the disputes between McConnell and the White House remained unresolved. McConnell's legal eagles sought to attack them
one at a time, as they pushed Cipollone to reorient his arguments.

They urged him to hire a real defense team. Cipollone seemed
unmoved.

"We got this," he replied nonchalantly, surrounded by a White
House posse that included Trump's son-in-law Jared Kushner, White
House chief of staff Mick Mulvaney, and two recent hires they'd
brought in for messaging assistance.

The senators pitched the White House on McConnell's plan
for a two-week Senate trial, framing the idea as good for the president. Why not use the forum to make their case to the public, they

argued, especially since House Democrats never gave them the chance?

To their great relief, Cipollone agreed. Two weeks sounded sufficient, he said[5]—so long as "the client" would go for it.

Nancy Pelosi was holed up in a Madrid hotel room when her staff dialed her into a call with concerned moderate Democrats half a globe away. Over Thanksgiving weekend, the Speaker had led a delegation of more than a dozen House Democrats to Spain for an international climate summit. It was a bid to remind the world that despite the impeachment drama playing out on television screens, America still cared about clean energy and reversing carbon emissions. And for a Speaker who never wanted to impeach, it was also a much-needed reprieve focused on policy issues she cared about.

But on the Monday afternoon of December 2, Pelosi's attention was yanked back to the troubles of Washington. There, a new internal Democratic fight over impeachment simmered, awaiting her attention.

On the other end of the line, from thousands of miles away in her Michigan district, Elissa Slotkin was sounding off over a rumor she'd heard that there were going to be multiple articles of impeachment. She and the other national security freshmen, who had tipped the scales with their September op-ed, were expecting an abuse of power charge about Ukraine—and perhaps a second dinging Trump for obstructing Congress's probe. But word on the street was that Jerry Nadler was building support for a third: obstruction of justice, based on evidence from the Mueller report. Slotkin's group was wholly opposed and wanted Pelosi to put a stop to it.

"We want the articles to be the smallest number we can credibly get away with," Slotkin said, explaining that her group calling in from their respective districts feared looking overzealous. "We brought the country along on Ukraine. It's better to sell at home."

Collectively, Slotkin and her fellow centrist members had little experience in constitutional law or congressional investigations. Aside from their op-ed that had all but pushed Pelosi into supporting impeachment, they had played virtually no role in the impeachment investigation whatsoever.

But to them, that didn't matter. Back home in their Republican-leaning districts, they were getting grilled for having endorsed impeachment at all—and that took precedence over any arguments about what was morally right.

In Abigail Spanberger's case, the op-ed had prompted multiple eager Republican politicians to declare they were interested in challenging her for her congressional seat.[6] Mikie Sherrill's New Jersey constituents had been so angry that during one town hall, a Boy Scout who had helped lead the Pledge of Allegiance begged attendees to stop fighting.[7] In Slotkin's Michigan district, which supported the president by 7 points in 2016, Trump supporters had interrupted her town halls with shouting, some toting signs that read "impeach Slotkin, keep Trump."[8] Constituents were so fired up that they would line up for blocks just to give Slotkin a piece of their mind, and the congresswoman found herself scheduling additional public events to explain her reasoning.

Slotkin, like the other six members who crafted the fateful *Washington Post* op-ed, had been stunned by the vitriol coming from the right. She'd grown up in a household where her mother was Democrat, her father was Republican, and they could disagree on politics civilly. But Republicans in her area had bought Trump's line that he hadn't done anything wrong and that Democrats were moving hastily and unfairly.

"Not true!" Slotkin's constituents would shout at her when she tried to articulate why what Trump did was impeachable. "Fake news!" they'd boo in reply. Some constituents pressed Slotkin to explain why she wasn't concerned about whether Hunter Biden's work in Ukraine was a conflict of interest. Others argued that she as well as the FBI and CIA were engaged in some kind of "coup."

The latter allegation set her blood pressure rising. *How could they say that about her?* she thought. She had served in the CIA and the Pentagon, including three tours in Iraq; she was married to a thirty-year Army veteran and had a stepdaughter in the military. The Democratic message on impeachment, she realized, was failing.[9]

Meanwhile, deep-pocketed outside groups, including American Action Network, were spending millions of dollars running TV ads in their districts, knocking the vulnerable Democratic lawmakers for supporting a "politically motivated charade."[10] The House Republicans' campaign arm was ginning up Trump supporters in an effort to win back their seats. "All Elissa Slotkin cares about is impeaching President Trump and keeping her radical socialist base happy," read one GOP pamphlet jeering her and inviting residents to attend her town hall.[11]

Slotkin and her moderate colleagues knew their constituents were having a hard enough time understanding the Democrats' allegations on Ukraine. Returning to the failed script of the Mueller report with an extra impeachment article would only make things more complicated and hurt them more politically, they believed. It was why they had decided to personally appeal to Pelosi for an intervention.

By the time Pelosi took the phone call from Slotkin's group, she was already leaning toward a short roster of charges. She knew that Trump had obstructed Mueller's probe—six months earlier in the SCIF, she had seen with her own eyes the evidence suggesting the special counsel thought Trump had lied to them. But the Speaker was sympathetic to the frontliners' concerns that resurrecting Mueller's narrative risked muddying the Ukraine narrative and repelling more swing voters. She wasn't about to waste that kind of political capital—or time.

Pelosi also had another problem on her hands: Some of her members were beginning to lose their nerve. In a mid-November meeting, her ally Zoe Lofgren had suggested an off-ramp to impeachment. "If he apologizes, we may not have to impeach him," she had proposed during one of Pelosi's impeachment messaging meetings.

The suggestion had made the entire room stop short and stare at Lofgren, dumbfounded.

"The offense is serious enough that even if he apologized, impeachment is still warranted," Pelosi had responded gently.

"It's not like he hit his brother in the playroom," whispered one top aide on the side of the room, aghast. "He tried to shake down a foreign country. You don't just get to apologize!"

Lofgren had quickly backtracked, but Pelosi knew she was not alone. That week, one of her liberal rank-and-file members from Michigan told a local podcaster that the House should censure Trump instead of impeaching him[12]—a softer form of public rebuke. If a progressive member was expressing reservations, what would this mean for Democrats in Trump-carried districts?

As she sat in her hotel room, listening to the pleas of her "majority makers," Pelosi tried to dispel their fears. As soon as everyone was back in town, she promised, she'd meet with her chairmen and get them to settle on "a small number of articles so we don't lose impact."

"We have to recognize our purpose," she told them broadly.

In other words, Jerry Nadler was in for yet another rude awakening.

NADLER'S LAST STAND

DECEMBER 5, 2019

Jerry Nadler spoke to the entire room—but really, he was addressing only one person. Standing before Nancy Pelosi's leadership team
on Thursday, December 5, the Judiciary chairman made an impassioned speech about how House Democrats had a duty to charge
Trump with obstruction of justice among their articles of impeachment. Special Counsel Robert Mueller, he said, had articulated at
least five instances in his report where an average American would
likely be indicted—if not imprisoned—for trying to screw with a
federal investigation. Trump shouldn't get a pass just because he
was president, he argued—and they, as leaders, had a duty to make
sure of it.

"Mueller intended for us to pick this up," Nadler said.

The Judiciary chairman had been prepping for this moment for a
while, knowing it would be his last chance to broaden House Democrats' case against Trump. Before the meeting, he'd met one-on-one
with most of the members in attendance in search of allies, huddling

with Majority Leader Steny Hoyer and Majority Whip Jim Clyburn, hoping to enlist them in his cause. But Nadler knew this decision boiled down to a single individual: Pelosi herself. And as usual, his lofty appeals about justice and the Constitution were about to clash headfirst into Pelosi's political buzzsaw.

That week, when Nadler's panel had finally received the impeachment baton they'd so long desired, the Judiciary chairman had watched all of the most dire predictions he had made to Pelosi and Schiff come back to haunt his committee. During a seven-hour public hearing with four constitutional law experts, the GOP had relentlessly lambasted the Democrats' process as unconstitutional, just as Nadler had privately warned they would.

"What a *disgrace* to this committee—to have the committee of impeachment simply take from other entities and rubber-stamp it!" ranking Republican Doug Collins had said in his thick Georgia drawl with the speed of an auctioneer and the intensity of a revivalist preacher. "Put witnesses in here that can be fact witnesses who can be actually cross-examined . . . *That's* fairness, and every attorney on this panel knows that. This is a sham!"

Making matters worse for Nadler, the GOP's single legal expert had done more to highlight the absurdities of the Democrats' impeachment process than the Democrats' three did to support their case. Jonathan Turley, a law professor from George Washington University—whom Nadler regarded as a partisan hack-for-hire— kept asking Democrats why they were trying to "set the record for the fastest impeachment" and encouraging them to go to court to fight for better witnesses.

"This is not how you impeach an American president," said Turley, who noted that he was no Trump shill and did not vote for Trump in 2016. "Fast is not good for impeachment . . . This isn't an impulse buy item."

Historically, the Judiciary Committee had always had a bigger footprint in impeachment proceedings. Forty-five years earlier, the gripping three-month debate in then-chairman Peter Rodino's Judiciary Committee convinced several House Republicans to turn on President Nixon. Rodino had staged a sequel to the Senate Watergate hearings, calling stars like John Dean and John Mitchell back to the witness table to retell the gory details of their interactions with Nixon. Even during the committee's relatively slapdash Clinton impeachment in which none of Ken Starr's witnesses took the stand,[1] Judiciary members still spent more than a month holding hearings.[2] That included a marathon session with the independent counsel on his findings and thirty hours for Clinton's lawyers, who called fourteen of their own witnesses to try to bolster the president's image.[3]

Nadler, much to his chagrin, was not conducting an impeachment investigation—not really. Though the Judiciary panel had once been regarded as the most formidable and prestigious oversight forum in the House, it had deteriorated into a box-checking formality. Due to Pelosi's year-end deadline, Nadler was allowed only two hearings: an overview of Schiff's case, and something resembling a crash course in constitutional law. Even staging those would prove to be a challenge. The forty-one-member panel had devolved into a sandbox of each party's ideologues: Not a single Republican was open to ousting Trump, and not a single Democrat was willing to fathom he might be innocent.

Nadler had tried to give the process more legitimacy. Over the Thanksgiving recess, his outside guns, Norm Eisen and Barry Berke, had called the White House to implore Pat Cipollone's deputies to stage a full defense of the president during their hearings.[4] They dropped heavy hints that if Cipollone wanted to cross-examine Schiff's witnesses, Nadler would allow it—despite Pelosi and Schiff's private opposition. But their entreaties fell on deaf ears. Trump's team that week sent a letter declining to participate, complaining of "countless procedural deficiencies" and an "unfair process."[5]

Nadler and his crew were still adamant that they would make the best of the situation. The chairman had privately told his members and top aides that while this process was less than ideal, impeaching Trump was still the right thing to do.

"There is a record that proves our allegations," Nadler told them. "We have a solemn obligation, and we need to make our case as best as we can."

Everyone on his staff agreed.

While Nadler had given up on changing Pelosi's and Schiff's minds about the way to conduct impeachment hearings, there was one traditional Judiciary role he was desperate to protect: writing articles of impeachment. Nadler firmly believed that he and his team of attorneys had the firmest grasp on how the constitutional indictment should be carried out—more than Schiff and certainly more than Pelosi. It was why his staff had worked through Thanksgiving, in fact, drafting language and committee reports justifying three charges: abuse of power, obstruction of Congress, and obstruction of justice.

Still, Nadler knew he had a fight on his hands if he wanted to keep control of the process. In November, the Speaker had tasked his and Schiff's lawyers to work together on articles—and unsurprisingly, they often found themselves in conflict. While Nadler pushed to have obstruction of justice represented among the impeachment charges, Schiff sided with moderates like Elissa Slotkin who believed expanding their aperture beyond Ukraine would only confuse the public. The Intel chief was also working behind the scenes with other groups of frontliners, encouraging them to voice their pushback with Pelosi in a bid to head off Nadler.

The Judiciary chairman had also learned that frontline Democrats were getting skittish about charging Trump with obstructing Congress, despite Trump's relentless stonewalling. That was bonkers to the Judiciary Committee chairman. He couldn't understand why they had endorsed the impeachment inquiry all those weeks ago, only to run scared when it came time to follow through on what he believed was Trump's most unabashed offense against a co-equal branch of government. The only plausible explanation was that they were too young and new to Congress to realize that Trump had done lasting damage to lawmakers' ability to conduct oversight, Nadler thought. Either way, he resolved to fight them and win.

In early December, much to Nadler's dismay, Pelosi had initially deputized House counsel Doug Letter to write a first draft of the articles of impeachment. Working through reams of submissions from academics across the country, Letter had created a long, Frankenstein-esque document that quietly horrified Nadler and his staff. When Pelosi vetoed the draft for having "too many words" and lacking clarity, the chairman saw an opening and volunteered to take the pen. Pelosi, surprisingly, actually agreed, giving Nadler's team less than twenty-four hours to complete the task.

On the morning of December 5, well before dawn, Joshua Matz, Nadler's impeachment guru, arrived at the Capitol and locked himself in his closet-sized, windowless office to fine-tune the draft articles they'd been working on into frameworks that could earn Pelosi's approval. He hung a "moratorium" sign on the doorknob— Judiciary panel code for "do not disturb." On his desk lay the House Intelligence Committee's final report and copies of the articles from every past impeachment. Over the course of several hours, Matz refined three separate charges, militantly keeping each to no more than one page. Keep it simple, he had told himself, remembering Pelosi liked things pithy and punchy—and personally aiming to make the articles as reader friendly to average Americans as possible. Trump had subverted U.S. national security for his political benefit. He had issued a blanket order to defy legitimate congressional investigations. And he had tried to obstruct a federal investigation. Those were grounds enough to indict.

When it came time to pitch the articles to Pelosi later that day, Nadler was ready. His quiet lobbying campaign had paid off: All of Pelosi's most senior deputies agreed with him that an article on obstruction of justice was vital. "Don't lose sight of Trump's other offenses," Hoyer had advised the Speaker. "Ukraine is actually all about Russia," Clyburn had chimed in.

But Pelosi had also come prepared—and the Speaker's allies, whom she had lined up to speak in advance, promptly sprang into action to shut them down. Democratic Congressional Campaign Committee chair Cheri Bustos said the caucus had a duty to protect vulnerable members who could face political blowback for backing an obstruction of justice charge. Pelosi's close friend Congresswoman Rosa DeLauro (D-Conn.) grew animated as she advised the room to stay focused on Ukraine.

"This is what we need to do!" she barked.

Sitting at the head of the table, Pelosi said little. She had already made up her mind days before, when the moderates had called her in Spain.

Pelosi had had it with the impeachment questions and wanted to change the subject. For the first thirty minutes of a prime-time CNN television town hall later that same evening, she dutifully— albeit at times curtly—answered the barrage of queries about the status of Democrats' effort to oust Trump. *Why couldn't Democrats wait until the election to send Trump packing? Would she have regrets about proceeding if Trump got reelected? Had she failed to meet her own bipartisan standard to oust a president?*

By 9:30 p.m., Pelosi had had it.

"Can we not have any more questions about impeachment?" she asked the host and audience with exasperation, trying to steer the subject to her recent climate policy trip. "Let me tell you about Spain!"

Pelosi had reluctantly embraced the effort to oust Trump. But by early December, impeachment was the last thing she wanted to talk about. Her moderates who had stuck their necks out to back the effort were getting crucified for it at home, and the more the nation focused on their investigation, the harder she knew it would be for those vulnerable members to win reelection.

Pelosi's frontliners reminded her of that every chance they got. "We need to change the narrative," Congressman Anthony Brindisi, a New York Democrat from a Trump district, had told her in one meeting that fall. "We need a trade deal!" Congresswoman Haley Stevens of Michigan piped up in another, demanding Pelosi prioritize those negotiations with Trump over the endless barrage of impeachment messaging.

Pelosi sought to assuage them. "We'll have USMCA by Christmas," she promised, referring to the forming trade agreement, the U.S.-Mexico-Canada Agreement, by its acronym. "A prescription drug bill as well."

The truth was Pelosi was just as desperate as her moderates were to push back against the suggestion that Democrats were solely focused on impeachment. She had been throwing the weight of her gavel behind a series of easy-sell bills on feel-good subjects like helping veterans and improving voting rights. She also started calling out Senate Republicans for refusing to take them up. Twice that fall, she had even marched over to Mitch McConnell's office to protest his lack of action on gun control and immigration legislation,[6] a dramatic gesture that at any other time would have garnered major headlines. Against the backdrop of the final throes of impeachment, however, it barely made the media blink.

That week, Pelosi's rank and file had begun to sense her frustration. Those who traveled with her to Madrid had noticed she was a different person abroad. There, she had been cheerful and bubbly, eager to talk climate policy and act as the statesman to America's top allies around the world. But on her flight home, that happy Pelosi disappeared. The Speaker was almost doleful as she implored her leadership team for help messaging the party through the last throes of their campaign to oust Trump. *Impeachment headlines will dominate the next few weeks*, she warned them at the beginning of December, *but we need to focus on our legislative achievements*. They knew she was serious.

Republicans, meanwhile, were starting to smell blood in the water. In a closed-door meeting in the Capitol basement that week, Vice President Mike Pence had encouraged the GOP rank and file to "turn up the heat" on House Democrats and accuse them of obsessing over impeachment instead of solving the nation's problems.[7] Republicans heeded the advice: By the morning of Pelosi's CNN town hall, McConnell and Trump were both accusing her of engaging in "performance art for coastal elites" rather than addressing the "things the American people actually need us to address."

"Working Americans and their families are not well-served by Democrats' political performance art," McConnell said on the Senate floor. "What they really need are results. The only path to results is bipartisan legislation."

The accusation infuriated Pelosi—particularly coming from McConnell. The Senate leader was sitting on roughly four hundred bills the House had passed, nearly three hundred of which were bipartisan.[8] The Speaker, who had always had a frosty relationship with McConnell, had even dubbed him "Graveyard Mitch" and "the Grim Reaper" for killing legislation. Now *he* dared attack *her* for intransigence?

That morning, Pelosi's impatience with the all-encompassing impeachment intrigue was palpable. In a brief televised address to the nation, she announced that Democrats would officially proceed with drafting articles—as if that was ever really in question. But from her frayed demeanor, it was clear that the Speaker was merely going through the motions and taking no joy in her words. That same morning, she intentionally upstaged her own historic announcement by rolling out legislation to control the cost of prescription drugs, just as she promised her skittish moderates.

A couple hours later, at her weekly press conference, Pelosi acted as if impeachment were nonexistent. She gave a long speech about the Democrats' work on insider trading, gender pay equity, violence against women, a minimum-wage hike—anything other than the topic du jour—before finally agreeing to take questions about impeachment. As a worn-down Pelosi turned to exit the room, a conservative journalist yelled out a question that set her off.

"Do you hate the president, Madam Speaker?" the reporter asked.

Pelosi stopped in her tracks, whirled around, and marched straight over to where he was sitting in the front row, wagging her pointer finger as if at a misbehaving child.

"I don't 'hate' anybody," Pelosi sneered, her voice quivering in fury. "I was raised in a Catholic house! We don't hate *anybody*, not *anybody* in the world!"

She stomped back to the podium.

"This is about the Constitution of the United States and the facts that lead to the president's violation of his oath of office!" she huffed, glancing about the room before turning her deadly glare back on the offending reporter. "And as a Catholic, I *resent* your using the word 'hate' in a sentence that addresses me. I don't hate anyone . . . So don't mess with me when it comes to words like that!"

Then she stormed off.

For Pelosi, the question underscored everything that was going wrong with impeachment. Republicans were accusing her of being on a crusade to oust the president because she was blinded by her hatred of him. The exact opposite was true. Impeachment was an albatross around Pelosi's neck and always had been. She had never wanted to be in this position.

By the time the CNN town hall began that evening, it was clear that the pressure was getting to Pelosi. Her smile was forced, if she smiled at all. Her fuse was short. Her body was tense. And she had developed a cold and a cough, which was so pronounced during the town hall that twice the host offered her some water.

Sitting with her knees bent to one side in a white leather chair, dressed in a black pantsuit with navy blue trim, Pelosi tried again and again to change the subject, brushing off impeachment questions and struggling to redirect the conversation to her policy agenda. Asked about whether 2020 would be a referendum on Trump's guilt, Pelosi argued that voters cared most about health care. Pressed about Trump's personal attorney Rudy Giuliani's travels to Ukraine that week to try to continue stirring up dirt on Biden, she shrugged.

"I'm a busy person . . . I don't have time to keep track of Rudy Giuliani," she said.

At one point, a woman asked a question that crystallized Pelosi's worst, but still unacknowledged, nightmare: that an impeached Trump might nonetheless be reelected and continue his corrupt behavior with abandon.

"What recourse will the House have, since the impeachment

process will already have taken place?" she asked. "What will the checks be on this President if he is reelected?"

"Let's not even contemplate that," Pelosi said stiffly, not missing a beat. It was a possibility she could not—and would not—wrap her brain around. Perhaps because the honest answer was too awful to consider. The answer, Democrats were finding, was very little.

28

COLD FEET AND A DEFECTION

Nine days before the impeachment vote, a group of about ten Democrats hailing from mostly Trump-carried districts huddled for an emergency meeting in a first-floor conference room at the Capitol. Josh Gottheimer, who had tried to warn Pelosi off embracing impeachment in late September, was among those gathering to consider an alternative to the party's campaign to oust Trump. He and each of the moderates present had only begrudgingly backed the effort to impeach, hoping that the investigation's momentum would pick up at least some bipartisan support to give them political cover. It hadn't. The looming vote to oust Trump was promising to be just as politically treacherous as it had been when they started—maybe more so.

Censure, the group reasoned, was a possible way out of their jam.[1] Such congressional rebukes were rare, but as a far lesser form of punishment, they could possibly attract bipartisan support. No Democrat would dare vote against it, they reasoned, and it was an easier sell for Republicans looking for a way to condemn Trump without kicking him out of office.[2]

Twenty years earlier, when Gottheimer was working as a White House aide during Clinton's impeachment, House Democrats, then in the minority, had approached Republican leaders with a similar offer to avoid indicting the president while still rebuking him for what he'd done. Censure, Democrats reasoned then, would satisfy moderate Republicans as an unequivocal, bipartisan condemnation of Clinton's efforts to cover up his affair with Monica Lewinsky, while saving the president—and by extension, themselves—from having to shower off the political stink of an impeachment. With the White House's blessing, several Clinton intermediaries and eventually his legal team secretly approached Henry Hyde, the Republican chairman of the House Judiciary Committee, to see whether a censure deal could be struck. It ultimately failed.[3]

Remarkably, during Trump's impeachment, Republicans never even contemplated making a similar gesture—an indication of how deeply partisan congressional oversight had become during his presidency and how politically secure the GOP felt in their opposition to Democrats' probe. Even moderate Republicans disquieted by the president's actions knew their base was too loyal to Trump, and his wrath too fierce, to risk calling for something like censure and openly stating that Trump did something wrong. Plus, polling showed Democrats were losing most swing voters on the issue, so why bother?

That Democrats were the ones floating a censure vote for Trump reflected how the politics of impeachment had turned against them. But as the moderates vocalized their fears in the conference room that day, they realized there was no easy answer to their conundrum. If they voted for impeachment, conservatives in their districts were sure to punish them; if they backed off and called for censure, the

Democratic base would crucify them. Plus, they acknowledged, the chances were slim to none that Pelosi would actually go for it.

Gottheimer and his group decided to stress test their idea anyway. They agreed to start quietly broaching the notion with some Republican colleagues while simultaneously pitching Pelosi directly. She had listened and catered to the moderates' demands for virtually the entire impeachment effort, after all. And they figured she had to be spooked too by how well the Republicans were holding rank.

But their hopes were quickly dashed. Even moderate Republicans scoffed at their censure proposal, saying it was "too late." Pelosi too was uninterested in relenting at the eleventh hour.

"Thank you very much for your suggestion," she snipped shortly. "That's NOT going to be happening."

While moderates looked for an off-ramp, some progressives in the lower chamber also started to get cold feet—albeit for a very different reason. Concerns started bubbling in liberal circles that if the House transmitted articles of impeachment to the Senate that month, the Democratic Party would be relinquishing their best opportunity to take down the president. McConnell appeared to be preparing for an abridged trial that would include no witnesses, ensuring a quick acquittal for Trump that could possibly make him stronger. Democrats had to use their only remaining leverage, the thinking went, to build a stronger case—and give investigators more time to persuade the public.

It was in that vein that a low-profile liberal Democratic congressman approached the Speaker on the House floor offering some free impeachment advice. Earl Blumenauer of Oregon, who was best known for his bright-colored bow ties and a lapel bicycle pin he sported on a daily basis, had not played any role in impeachment. His fiefdom was taxes, energy, and climate issues. That day, however, he was among several dozen House Democrats taken with an odd proposal: that the House should impeach Trump, refuse to send the articles to the Senate, and continue to investigate the president in the new year to ensure they left no stone unturned.

"There's no advantage to rushing those articles across the Capitol," Blumenauer told Pelosi emphatically, pitching her on his proposal.

The idea of impeaching but not trying Trump had first been floated in a June *Washington Post* op-ed written by investigators' perennial legal guru, Harvard professor Laurence Tribe.[4] At the time, Tribe—who was advocating to impeach based on the Mueller report—sought to alleviate Democratic leaders' concerns that it might be politically costly to do so if the GOP-led Senate simply turned around and exonerated Trump. The idea largely flew under the radar. But in early December, Tribe began personally pitching Judiciary Committee members, Schiff, and Pelosi on the notion.

Few senior lawmakers and top investigative aides took the idea of holding back impeachment articles seriously. Jerry Nadler, who saw the transmission of impeachment articles to the Senate as self-executing and not optional, wrote off the idea as ridiculous, as did many of his panel members and staffers—including Joshua Matz, the resident impeachment scholar. Pelosi's staff had also snickered at it. The move, they argued, would look like political gamesmanship, only causing them more of a headache in the end.

Yet the notion found its followers. In the days before the final impeachment vote, Blumenauer buttonholed about fifty of his colleagues, arguing that House Democrats should check every possible investigative box against Trump to show the public they had been "thorough." He even made rare TV appearances to stump for the strategy, telling viewers that he hoped Democratic leaders would be deliberate in the timing of sending the articles.

Blumenauer had been around long enough to know that Pelosi called the shots—and that she recoiled at grassroots efforts to force her hand, jealously guarding her authority. So as he recruited converts, he also approached her directly on the House floor to ask her, peer to peer, to consider the unorthodox strategy.

"I hope we're not in any hurry to move that across the Capitol," he said, referring to the charges against Trump. "I hope that we can allow it to ripen."

Pelosi put on her poker face.

"I'm thinking about it" was all she offered.

"You're a brave man," Trump said, turning on the charm with Congressman Jeff Van Drew, the backbench freshman Democrat to whom he had granted a rare one-on-one White House meeting.

It was Friday, December 13, and with the vote to impeach him just days away, Trump was eager to win a prize he knew would infuriate Pelosi. As one of just two Democrats who had voted against the House impeachment rules on October 31, the vulnerable New Jersey lawmaker had been the target of a GOP guerrilla operation to persuade him to become a Republican. Picking off one of the Speaker's prized "majority makers" would be an unprecedented public relations win on the eve of impeachment—the ultimate condemnation of what they considered her partisan, anti-Trump venture. Now the president was coming in to seal the deal.

"I'd really like to have you on my team," Trump said.

It was an unorthodox and audacious request. It had been fifteen years since a sitting Democratic congressman had switched parties. But Trump and his advisors had been watching the sixty-six-year-old veteran of Garden State politics for a while, smelling an opportunity. Van Drew was an odd duck. He strutted around the Capitol in loud pinstripe suits, offset with a pocket square and an American flag pin in the shape of a tooth—a nod to his decades-long career in dentistry. He had won his heavily Republican district, they believed, only because his GOP opponent had been labeled a racist.[5] Knowing his longer-term political fate depended on maintaining good relations with Trump's GOP, the new congressman immediately took steps to protect his right flank. He quickly became a staple on Fox News, where he would freely blast the left as he delivered platitudes about wanting to work with the president.

Voicing his opposition to impeachment had been a natural extension of Van Drew's practice of political survival. But it also endeared him to Trump. When Van Drew told the hosts of *Fox & Friends* in late September that he'd seen no evidence of high crimes and misdemeanors, it came as music to the ears of a president eager for Democratic allies.

"Let the people impeach," Van Drew had said. "We are going to have an election very shortly."

It was around that time that Trump and his team began plotting. Two of his political advisors who hailed from New Jersey—Bill Stepien, the former political hand to Governor Chris Christie, and Kellyanne Conway, who grew up in Van Drew's district—set to work courting Van Drew. Conway invited him to have Thanksgiving with her family, while Stepien, who had run GOP opponents against him in years past, had his old boss Christie phone Van Drew personally to egg him on.

House Minority Leader Kevin McCarthy, meanwhile, played bad cop. Seeking him out on the House floor, McCarthy told Van Drew that he would be a top target for Republicans next election—unless he wanted to change jerseys and run as a Republican himself.[6]

Trump wants you to do it, he said. *And if you don't, we'll take you out next fall,* he promised, only half-joking.

Van Drew, who kept a portrait of GOP president Ronald Reagan hanging in his office, found their outreach intriguing. Since he had come to Congress, he had grown increasingly frustrated with his own party's demand for ideological purity. When he occasionally voted with Republicans, progressives like Alexandria Ocasio-Cortez started threatening to recruit other Democratic candidates to run against him in the next primary. Local officials also threatened to screw with him on the ballot if he didn't back impeachment.

"You're going to have to vote for this," one Atlantic County party chairman had told Van Drew at a well-worn diner just inland from the city's bustling staple boardwalk. "Or I'll make sure that you're not running in this county at all."

The political threats infuriated Van Drew—and only made him consider Trump's proposition more seriously. But before he made the jump, he wanted assurances: GOP candidates were already lining up to challenge him. And if he switched parties, Van Drew knew he'd be labeled a flip-flopper. To ensure his party switch wouldn't be in vain, he wanted Trump's endorsement to clear the field.

Van Drew didn't know the president well. He had crossed paths with Trump a few times because of his Atlantic City casinos, which were in the congressman's district. When he walked into the Oval Office, however, he was impressed at how well the president seemed to know him. The two talked for more than ninety minutes about their views on life and politics. The notoriously demanding president reassured Van Drew that it would be okay if he wasn't in lockstep with him on everything as a new Republican. Trump also agreed to endorse Van Drew over his Republican challengers and even offered to unveil Van Drew's party conversion at a Rose Garden ceremony, standing shoulder to shoulder with him to announce the big news.

Van Drew needed no further convincing.

"Mr. President, I'm going to do this," he told Trump.

"Let's do it now!" Trump responded, excitedly.

As aides and advisors filed into the room to congratulate them both, they encouraged the pair to be patient. Van Drew shouldn't switch parties until after he voted against impeachment as a Democrat, they counseled. That way, Pelosi would suffer the maximum number of party defections possible—and Van Drew's announcement the day after would be the final "fuck you" to her party.

"Plus," Van Drew sought to assure the president, "I've got to go home and tell my wife and kids."

Trump left the meeting elated. In less than a week's time, he would be impeached—that was inevitable. But at least opposition to impeachment would be bipartisan.

Within twenty-four hours, the news leaked out about Van Drew's plans and his meeting with Trump, sending Democrats reeling.[7]

"Wow, that would be big," Trump wrote, as if it were news to him. "Always heard Jeff is very smart!"

29

IMPEACHED

DECEMBER 18, 2019

On the morning of the impeachment vote, Nancy Pelosi took a moment to pray. It was something she did every day: prayed for the country, for her party—and even for her nemesis in the White House, whom she planned to impeach that evening. The man might be unhinged, but he did hold the nation's fate in his hands.

Across town, in his own way, Trump also began the day with an appeal for divine intervention.

"Can you believe that I will be impeached today by the Radical Left, Do Nothing Democrats, AND I DID NOTHING WRONG!" he tweeted from the White House. "This should never happen to another President again. Say a PRAYER!"

As Pelosi dressed for the day in her Georgetown apartment, she picked out a black sheath dress—the color of mourning—to convey the gravity of the occasion. She had warned her colleagues in a private meeting that week that they needed to maintain an air of sobriety when they passed the articles. There was to be no cheering on the House floor. No celebratory smiles.

Pelosi also donned a gleaming gold brooch in the shape of a mace topped by an eagle. It was a symbol of the House and its legislative power dating back to the late eighteenth century. She would wield that power that day to impeach a president for only the third time in American history.

By that morning, all the political hand-to-hand combat in the three months leading up to Trump's impeachment had given way to a sense of anticlimactic inevitability. Despite most Democrats' refusal to admit it publicly, the case for impeachment had been made to the public—and had clearly fallen flat. Polling by Gallup released that morning showed that national support for impeaching the president had actually dropped by six points since the House Democrats launched their Ukraine-focused probe. Trump's approval numbers, meanwhile, had risen by the same margin.[1]

The Speaker had done everything in her power to limit the scope of the impeachment probe to shield her moderate members from political blowback. She had held the panels to a strict schedule to ensure that her majority makers would have time to pivot back to less partisan talking points on the 2020 campaign trail. She had heeded their demands and kept the investigation focused only on Trump's actions with Ukraine, forgoing pursuit of his other misdeeds.

Yet as the vote neared, Pelosi remained troubled. Impeachment was going to end as it began: as a Democratic project against a Republican president. Exactly the political stain Pelosi had wanted to avoid. The night before the vote, in a rare moment of vulnerability with her leadership team, Pelosi expressed her exhaustion.

"If we can just get through tomorrow, I think we'll come out in okay shape," she told her team.

Congressman Eric Swalwell of California sought to reassure her.

"'Okay shape'?" he said. "You're downplaying how you've handled this. I think history will judge us for how well we've done this, start to finish. Speaker, we're going to come out more than okay."

Pelosi said nothing in reply.[2]

Most days, Pelosi kept her distance from the House chamber, swooping in only to vote or deliver a few minutes of commentary during pivotal debates. But this was no ordinary day. Pelosi wanted to be in the chamber for the entirety of the historic debate to indict Trump. She arrived at the Capitol early and walked onto the floor just as the deliberations began.

At 12:08 p.m., Pelosi strode to the lectern to offer her remarks about the task before them. Trump, she argued, had "violated the Constitution" and "gave us no choice" but to impeach him. Lawmakers would be "derelict in our duty" if they did not take this step to protect the integrity of America's democracy and its elections, she said. She quoted the Pledge of Allegiance and the Founding Fathers for maximum effect—and recalled haunting words from her late friend Elijah Cummings. The former House Oversight chairman— "Our North Star," as Pelosi called him—had said early that year that "when we're dancing with the angels," each of them would be asked what they had done "to make sure we kept our democracy intact."

"When the history books are written about this tumultuous era, I want them to show that I was among those in the House of Representatives who stood up to lawlessness and tyranny," she said, quoting the statement in which Cummings later declared his support for impeachment.

On the Democratic side of the chamber, Judiciary panel members—including the original "musketeers"—had also shown up early to watch every moment of the process they had helped to set in motion seven months before. Ted Lieu sat in the back by himself, taking in the surroundings. In the front of the room, Joe Neguse bent heads with David Cicilline.

Next to them was Jamie Raskin, who had spent the prior few weeks trying to convince anyone who would listen that they should add Trump's emoluments violations to their impeachment effort. He had used his Thanksgiving break, in fact, to write a thirty-five-page treatise on the matter and pressed Pelosi's office to attach it to the impeachment charges as an addendum. But his enthusiastic lobbying wasn't received well: Pelosi rejected the idea. And Raskin was warned by staff that if he didn't stop pushing his cause, the Speaker would bypass him for the impeachment managers team, the select crew charged with presenting the House's case in the Senate trial. It was a position he had desperately wanted.

While the House chamber, unlike the Senate, had no assigned seats, an observer could have painted a bright yellow line down the center of the cavernous, dimly lit room that day. Democrats stayed to the left of the chamber while Republicans clung to the right. On either side, warring podiums faced the rostrum, one for Democrats to make their case, the other for the GOP to rebut it.

At one point, Jeff Van Drew, dressed in a bright blue plaid suit, entered the room looking lost, not knowing which side to sit on. Though he was still technically a Democrat—and would be for twenty-four more hours—he eventually found his way to the GOP side of the chamber. Party leaders Kevin McCarthy and Steve Scalise came up and shook his hand, having caught word of his looming party switch. Meanwhile, Justin Amash, the ex-Republican who had left the GOP that summer in protest over Trump's actions in the Mueller report, sat by himself in the middle of the chamber, aware that he too had no home. That is, until some of the national security freshman Democrats whose op-ed had triggered impeachment—including Elissa Slotkin and Abigail Spanberger—approached the independent congressman with nods of respect, taking seats by him.

Above their heads, activists, tourists, history buffs, and other spectators from around the country trickled in to watch the debate from the House's public galleries. They all took in the back and forth, as each party quoted the Framers of the nation's Constitution to argue that they were on the right side of history.

As House members orated, debated, and stated their final thoughts, Pelosi slipped quietly around the chamber, engaging rank-and-file members as well as her senior lieutenants who had shepherded the impeachment from its inception. She chatted with Cicilline, one of the "musketeers" with whom she had clashed in the spring over their early push to impeach Trump. And she bent heads in private consultation with Adam Schiff, her impeachment architect and guide, who sat in the front of the chamber, exchanging whispers about what was transpiring on the floor.

As a display of unity and equanimity, Pelosi had deputized Jerry Nadler to take the first turn presiding over the impeachment debate. Nadler stood at the Democrats' podium, flanked by his aides, as top Judiciary Republican Doug Collins railed against the impeachment probe from the opposite side. As Nadler listened to the back and forth, he scribbled down notes; after all, there was a trial to prepare for.

Nadler, like Pelosi, was dragging himself through impeachment's final throes. Four nights before the vote, he had taken his wife of forty-three years, Joyce, to an urgent care center because she felt sick. Within a few hours, they were sitting in NYU Langone hospital being told that she had pancreatic cancer. He had missed all the procedural impeachment events earlier in the week, deputizing Raskin to take his place so he could be by his wife's side. But Joyce, who ran a public policy consulting outfit and once taught political science at Columbia University, had insisted he return to Washington to preside over the momentous vote. That night, Nadler would tell his staff that he didn't know if he felt like former Judiciary chairman Peter Rodino, who cried in his office after his panel passed their articles of impeachment against Nixon—or General Winfield

Scott, who declared, "Thank God the republic is saved!" after the Battle of Gettysburg, as depicted in an old 1940s film.[3]

For the most part, Nadler let Republicans lob their due process complaints and procedural charades without acknowledging them. But when he heard Trump ally Louie Gohmert of Texas repeat the Trump-backed conspiracy theory that Ukraine had "interfered" in the 2016 election, Nadler angrily objected.

"Madam Speaker, I am deeply concerned that any member would spout Russian propaganda on the floor of the House," Nadler said in protest.

Gohmert, who had turned to leave the chamber after speaking, whirled around and lurched back into the room, angrily shaking his finger as he stormed toward the Judiciary chairman.

"He calls me guilty of Russian propaganda!" he yelled, demanding that Nadler recant. "You called me a Russian agent!" he huffed. "You called me a Russian stooge! You take that back!"[4]

Nadler's staffers stepped in front of Gohmert to block the altercation. Nadler, uncowed, ignored him and just kept looking forward.

The temperature of the debate continued to rise into the night as the vote neared. Both sides cheered at the mention of the Constitution to justify their positions, vowing that they were actually the ones engaged in righteous combat while the other side was blinded by politics. At one point, Scalise angrily tore up a copy of the House rules regarding rights of the minority to hold hearings for effect. At another, when Majority Leader Steny Hoyer commended Justin Amash for leaving the Republican Party to say he supported Trump's impeachment, Republicans in the room jeered.

As his soldiers waged war, McCarthy stood on and watched. Like Pelosi, the Republican leader had risen that day with a sense of fatigue. The last few months had been an adrenaline rush, as he led the impeachment countercharge. But fanning the flames of the political dumpster fire engulfing Washington had been exhausting work. How many weeks had they spent on this in the Intelligence Committee? How much political capital had they burned?

Not that McCarthy had any regrets. His members were more united behind Trump than they had ever been, and for that, Trump was more grateful to "my Kevin" than he had ever been. McCarthy knew that approval would endear him more to the GOP base—and, sometime in the future, finally help him clinch the Speaker's gavel he so desperately wanted.

When it was McCarthy's turn to address the chamber, the GOP leader turned his ire on Pelosi.

"She said impeachment is so divisive that the evidence must be overwhelming, compelling, and bipartisan. *Not one* of those criteria have been met today," he said, looking across the chamber at the Speaker as he criticized her. "What we've seen is a rigged process that has led to the most partisan and least credible impeachment in American history . . . That is your legacy!"

Pelosi, sitting with her legs crossed in the back of the chamber, paid McCarthy no notice. She smiled as she leaned in to talk to the staffer next to her, refusing to give the GOP leader the satisfaction of listening to his spiel.

Pelosi never took the chance to retort on the floor. She had trusted Schiff to begin the House's impeachment, and she would leave it to him to finish it by delivering the party's closing argument right before the House voted on the articles.

Schiff had prepared mightily for the occasion and reveled in the moment with righteous indignation.

"We used to care about democracy. We used to care about our allies. We used to stand up to Putin and Russia," he said, admonishing the GOP for putting loyalty to Trump over their oaths of office. "I know the party of Ronald Reagan used to!"

Republicans booed. Democrats cheered.

"If you say the president may refuse to comply, may refuse lawful process, may coerce an ally, may cheat in an election because he is the president of our party, you do not uphold our Constitution. You do not uphold your oath of office," Schiff continued, his voice rising. "Well, I will tell you this: I will uphold mine. I will vote to impeach Donald Trump!"

At that very moment, Trump stepped up to a podium in Battle Creek, Michigan, to deliver a campaign speech at an outdoor rally for more than six thousand supporters. Die-hard attendees had camped out all night to claim a place at the festivities, enduring below-freezing temperatures just to get a glimpse of their president. Onstage, a Christmas tree sparkled with a "Make America Great Again" hat where a star or angel would usually go. The crowd welcomed their idol with chants of "USA! USA!" as Trump basked in the reception, waving at his followers.

With the exception of the rally, the president had kept his schedule clear that day and spent hours watching the House impeachment proceedings from the White House. He tweeted out screeds trashing Democrats, praising Fox News's fawning coverage, and proclaiming the inadequacy of the impeachment charges against him. "The evidence has to be overwhelming, and it is not. It's not even close," he wrote, quoting Ken Starr, the independent counsel from Clinton's impeachment whom Trump was eyeing for his own legal team. "This is all about convicting a President based on innuendo, not on the facts. Even the Ukrainian President said there was no pressure!" he typed, parroting his friend and confidant Mark Meadows, whom he would soon tap as White House chief of staff.

The previous day, reporters had asked Trump if he took any

responsibility for his own impeachment. The president, totally un-chastened, gave a firm "no."

"I don't take any. Zero, to put it mildly," he said, calling his corre-spondence with Ukraine's president a "perfect phone call."

Despite his lack of remorse, the president had been agitated by the impending vote. He had worked for more than a week on a let-ter that he sent Pelosi the night before, rejecting Pat Cipollone's input and even shutting the White House counsel out of his suite to ensure he could not water down what he wanted to say. The let-ter, which Trump personally dictated to aides, read like one of his Twitter diatribes, riddled with words in capital letters and dozens of exclamation points.

"You have cheapened the importance of the very ugly word, im-peachment!" Trump wrote. "By proceeding with your invalid im-peachment, you are violating your oaths of office, you are breaking your allegiance to the Constitution, and you are declaring open war on American Democracy . . . You have found NOTHING!"[5]

Predicting that Trump would be in a foul mood, his team had intentionally scheduled a campaign rally for impeachment night, knowing the president always looked forward to such events with his fans. They even selected a smaller venue than usual to ensure it would be filled to capacity, as the president seemed happiest feed-ing off an oversized, adoring crowd. That evening, as Trump disem-barked Air Force One in southwestern Michigan, he stiffly told the reporters gathered on the tarmac that he was "doing good." When he arrived at the rally and saw the sea of supporters who had gath-ered to hear him, he brightened.

"It doesn't really feel like we're being impeached," Trump quipped as the crowd cheered. "The country is doing better than ever before. We did nothing wrong!"

At that exact moment, back in Washington, the House began

voting on the first article of impeachment. In honor of the historic nature of the occasion, House leaders decided that members would vote the old-fashioned way: Instead of pressing buttons in an electronic roll call, they would hold up colored cards—red for no, green for yes—to indicate their positions. Hundreds of lawmakers crushed toward the front of the chamber, waving their cards in the air to be seen and counted. Scalise, wobbly on his feet without his cane, pushed to the front of the room holding aloft a flicker of red, while the national security freshmen strode up to the front desk together, holding up green cards to cast their vote.

After several minutes, Pelosi stepped up to the Speaker's podium, interrupting the hum of bodies and voices to declare the first article, abuse of power, had passed.

"On this vote, the yeas are 230, the nays are 197, present is one," she declared, looking quizzically at the slip of paper in front of her. The "present" vote—essentially not taking a side—belonged to Tulsi Gabbard, a Democratic representative from Hawaii running a long-shot presidential campaign.

"Article One is adopted," Pelosi said, regaining her poise and banging her gavel on the desk for flourish. As Democrats began to cheer, Pelosi bit her lip and raised her eyebrows disapprovingly, silencing their celebration with a stern look and a slicing motion with her left hand.

Back in Michigan, Trump was doing the opposite, egging his base on.

"These are truly dishonest people," Trump bellowed. "After three years of sinister witch hunts, hoaxes, scams, tonight the House Democrats are trying to nullify the ballots of tens of millions of patriotic Americans capped off with one of the greatest election evenings in history!"

As the vote on the second article of impeachment—obstruction of Congress—got underway back in Washington, GOP lawmakers were determined to bring the spirit of the Trump rally into the room. They began chanting: "Four more years! Four more years!" In the back, on the Republican side of the chamber, Jim Jordan and Mark Meadows eased into adjacent leather chairs, drinking it all in. A few paces over, Jaime Herrera Beutler—still convinced that Pelosi wanted a partisan, unserious process—voted no without regrets.

On the Democratic side, meanwhile, Maxine Waters, the chairwoman of the House Financial Services Committee and the first of Pelosi's investigative chairs to embrace impeachment, hugged Rashida Tlaib, who was finally proudly making good on her promise to "impeach the motherfucker."

As they milled about, some made a point of bridging the partisan divide. Ann Wagner, who had been wooed to Trump's cause over a weekend at Camp David, crossed the room to mingle with her Democratic friends. "What the hell, let's all have dinner together!" she squealed. Meanwhile, Doug Collins, who had been going round for round in debate with Nadler all day, approached the Judiciary chairman to inquire after his sick wife and say that he was praying for her.

Francis Rooney, the Florida Republican who had once contemplated voting to impeach, also crossed over to the Democratic side of the chamber to have a word with the chairman of the House Rules Committee. Earlier that week, Rooney had tried to get the panel to consider a proposal to hold off on the impeachment vote until Trump's inner circle testified to the charges. Democratic leaders had ignored him, blocking his amendment from receiving any consideration.

Out of avenues, Rooney had taken to his journal to record his frustrations. "All Democrats have is the phone call and the overheard cell call with Sondland," he jotted down that week. And to impeach over obstruction of Congress, he'd scribbled, was prema-ture. "I agree [the stonewalling] is improper and unsettling but not illegal since they have the executive privilege claim of right," he wrote to himself. Democrats needed to go to court, he concluded, "to fight that down." Following the impeachment votes that night, he would write in his journal that he voted no "reluctantly, because of the lack of evidence and the rushed process, which makes it po-litical and partisan."

Forty-two minutes after the impeachment votes had begun, it was over. By a vote of 229 to 198, Trump had been charged with ob-structing Congress as well—this time with an additional Democrat, Jared Golden of Maine, joining the naysayers.

It took several minutes for the news to reach Trump, still mid-speech in Michigan. Kayleigh McEnany, his spokeswoman, had positioned herself at the front of the crowd to get his attention, hold-ing up a large white poster board with the vote total written on it in block numbers.

"Oh, I think we have a vote coming in," Trump said, interrupting himself. "So, we got every single Republican . . . Whoa!" he said triumphantly as the crowd cheered. "And three Democrats voted for us!"

"The Republican Party has never been so affronted," Trump continued, "but they've never been so united as they are right there, ever."

As the president raved, Pelosi and her six investigative committee chairmen exited the chamber and headed to a high-ceilinged cere-monial room off the House floor for a press conference. It was sup-posed to be a moment to reflect on all that had transpired and a chance to applaud her chairmen for their work. But as Pelosi stepped before a bank of American flags and a microphone, she quickly lost her footing.

Earlier that day, the Speaker had privately warned her leadership team to focus on the impeachment vote while talking to the press. There should be no musing about next steps, who would prosecute Trump as impeachment managers during a Senate trial, or when the articles would be transmitted to the Senate to begin the trial. But the message never trickled down to the rank and file. Midway through impeachment day, Earl Blumenauer went straight to the *Washington Post* and told them the Speaker was considering holding on to the articles of impeachment in the House rather than sending them to the Senate immediately.[6] The story set off a scramble among reporters, who prodded Pelosi at her post-impeachment press conference to detail her plans.

As she looked out over the sea of reporters crammed shoulder to shoulder, Pelosi gave a knee-jerk answer. House Democrats would not transmit the articles "until we see the process on the Senate side," she said simply, hoping it would be the end of those inquiries.

A murmur spread through the room as the intensity of the questions from confused reporters picked up. *How long was she planning to wait? Could she hold on to them for weeks?* Pelosi would not say. "We'll make a decision as a group," she demurred, trying to change the subject.

"Right now," Pelosi said, banging on her podium for emphasis, "the president is impeached!"

But the questions kept coming. "Is it possible you would *never* send the articles over?" one reporter shouted out above the din.

Pelosi bristled and wiped a loose hair from her eyes.

"We're not having that discussion," she said coldly.

On either side of the Speaker, the committee chairs stood stone-faced—and let Pelosi keep talking. They hadn't seen this coming. Neither had the staffers who had been managing the impeachment process. Norm Eisen, Nadler's counsel, shot a horrified glance at Ashley Etienne, Pelosi's communications director. "What?" he mouthed. Etienne, with a look of equal bewilderment, pointed at the card of talking points she held in her hand. "It's not on the card!" she mouthed back, silently.

Pelosi's freelancing was running off the rails—but that only made her dig in deeper.

"Can you guarantee that impeachment articles will at some point be sent to the Senate," another reporter said, fishing for a definitive answer.

A simple "yes," with no time certain, would have sufficed to correct course. But Pelosi was never one for mea culpas.

"That would have been our intention, but we will see what happens over there," she said dismissively, leaving open the possibility she would never send the articles over. Glancing from side to side, she looked to her chairmen to bail her out. "Do my colleagues want to say anything about this?" she asked. None of them did. Even the reliably overeager Nadler pointedly shook his head no; he wasn't about to get muddied in this mess.

Pelosi's aides called an abrupt end to the press conference and reporters flew out of the room, eager to file their latest stories on the dramatic turn of events. The Speaker, meanwhile, herded her chairmen into her office to digest what the hell had just happened. As they filed into the Speaker's suite, everyone was shell-shocked. They had poured three months into the impeachment investigation, carefully orchestrating and planning each turn of the probe to demonstrate that they were mounting a serious prosecution of the president's purported crimes, free from political gamesmanship. Now, during what was supposed to be their victory lap, Pelosi herself had undercut their efforts.

The chairs left the meeting at an impasse.[7] They couldn't agree whether the Speaker should try to walk her comments back or embrace her stumble as a strategy. Some Democrats suggested that maybe she could hold the articles over Senate GOP leader Mitch McConnell's head as a way to try to leverage more advantageous trial proceedings. Pelosi promised to discuss the matter with the Senate's top Democrat, Chuck Schumer, and come up with a plan.

Across the Capitol, Pelosi's stumble had also caught the attention of the Republican leader of the Senate—and not in a good way.

As members flew home for the holidays, McConnell called Steny Hoyer, whom he liked better than Pelosi, to deliver a message: If the Speaker was trying to strong-arm him into running the trial the way she wanted, she could forget it.

"I don't tell you how to run your chamber, don't tell me how to run mine," he said.

PART THREE

"MUTUALLY ASSURED DESTRUCTION"

Senate Minority Leader Chuck Schumer knew a political storm was headed his way and was eager to take advantage of it. On Sunday, December 15, just days before the House voted to impeach Trump, the brash New York Democrat penned a letter to his GOP counterpart and chamber nemesis, Mitch McConnell, demanding the chamber call witnesses as part of the president's looming trial.[1] The position, Schumer knew, was politically popular. What kind of trial, after all, didn't include witnesses? And best of all, he knew McConnell was against the idea—opposition Schumer thought he could use to wallop Republicans on the campaign trail.

As guilty as Schumer believed Trump was, he had already come to the conclusion that the president's acquittal was inevitable. A conviction required two-thirds approval, or sixty-seven senators—a threshold that had never been met in American history. With the

Senate in the GOP's hands, there was little expectation that Trump's impeachment would break that mold.

Knowing that, Schumer decided to focus his efforts where he believed he could actually win: in the court of public opinion. That night, he had his team leak his letter to the national media before bothering to send it to McConnell—then booked an interview for the next morning on CNN to stump for including witnesses at trial.

"I don't know what they'll say, maybe they'll say something ex-culpatory about President Trump," Schumer said, feigning inno-cence as he promoted his letter. "We're trying to get to the bottom of what actually happened."[2]

The move was classic Schumer. After two decades in the Senate, and three years as leader of the chamber's Democrats, Schumer's habit of exploiting legislative fights to leverage a political advan-tage was notorious. The sixty-nine-year-old Brooklyn native was eager to beat McConnell. And more importantly, Schumer wanted his job: He was desperate to flip the Senate and become Majority Leader.

Schumer had learned long before Trump that politically ugly im-peachment brawls could pay hefty dividends to the lawmaker who most shrewdly spun the case. In fact, he owed his Senate seat par-tially to the bungled GOP effort to oust Bill Clinton in 1998. That year, Schumer—then an ambitious nine-term House member—challenged Republican senator Alfonse D'Amato, a dogged Clinton critic who had led the investigation into the Whitewater real estate dealings of the former Arkansas governor and his wife, Hillary. The eighteen-year incumbent had even quipped that he wanted "ev-ery child in America to know how to spell 'subpoena.'" But polls showed the effort to oust Clinton was unpopular, and Schumer ran against D'Amato on a promise to acquit the president if elected.[3] He went on to crush D'Amato by 10 points, despite being massively outspent throughout the campaign.[4]

By then, Schumer was already known for his brass knuckles and ambition. At twenty-three, the son of an exterminator who had graduated from Harvard Law School ignored his mother's advice to enter private practice, and ran for public office instead.[5] He became one of the youngest members of the New York Assembly before turning his sights on Washington and running for a House seat six years later. Once in Congress, he quickly became known for always viewing decisions through a political lens—and always craving the spotlight. Senator Bob Dole, the onetime Republican presidential nominee, once joked that "the most dangerous place in Washington is between Chuck Schumer and a camera."[6] The reputation stuck.

When Trump's impeachment rolled around, Schumer saw an opportunity to merge his constitutional duties and his political ambitions: Impeachment, he mused, might be the perfect way to secure that longed-for promotion to become Majority Leader. McConnell's fifty-three Senate Republicans outnumbered his forty-seven Democrats, and Schumer figured the GOP would stick with Trump to the end. But like his House counterpart, Nancy Pelosi, Schumer reasoned he could make the process as politically painful for Republicans as possible—and hope some of them paid for their trial votes with their Senate seats in the next election.

In early December, Schumer had taken note as McConnell advocated for a short two-week trial that avoided calling new witnesses. While the GOP leader appeared to be arguing to his members that witness testimony would create a "partisan circus," it was obvious to Schumer that the Majority Leader feared something greater: that hearing from Trump's inner circle would make voting to acquit even more politically toxic for his members. So Schumer, naturally, formulated a counterstrategy: Instead of campaigning to remove Trump from office, which he figured was a lost cause, he would turn the entire trial into a fight over witnesses—and argue the proceedings could not be "fair" without them.

The move, Schumer reasoned, would be a win-win by putting moderate Republicans facing difficult reelections in 2020 in an impossible situation: If they voted *against* hearing from witnesses, he could accuse them of engaging in a "cover-up" and trying to hide the truth from the public, pummeling them with those charges on the campaign trail. If they voted *for* witnesses, Democrats could unearth possibly more damaging information on Trump, making the president's eventual acquittal an even more powerful cudgel to be wielded against the GOP.

The strategy hearkened back to the "win by losing" philosophy Democrats honed during Clinton's impeachment and trial, which the Republicans of Trump's era had already loosely replicated in the House. Schumer was essentially ripping off that same playbook: By accusing McConnell of orchestrating a "sham trial," he would turn the proceedings into a referendum on fairness—just like Trump's acolytes had done to Pelosi.

To execute his plan, Schumer had identified four witnesses he would hammer Republicans to call for testimony: former national security advisor John Bolton; acting White House chief of staff Mick Mulvaney; top White House budget advisor and Mulvaney confidant Robert Blair; and Michael Duffey, who had signed the letters freezing Ukraine's military assistance. All four were sure to have firsthand information about Trump's Ukraine scheme. And all four had been on the House Democrats' shortlist of people they initially wanted to interrogate before they decided to move on.

Schumer's trial strategy directly contradicted the House Democrats' contention that they had fully proved their case. But to the

Democratic leader, that didn't matter. He was prepared to argue the exact opposite in the Senate: that additional witnesses *had* to be called to uphold the integrity of the impeachment trial and learn the full truth. Despite the obvious discrepancy, Nancy Pelosi and Adam Schiff quietly signed off on Schumer's plan, hoping few would pick up on the contradiction. Nadler's lawyers—still awaiting a court ruling on their Don McGahn subpoena—also quietly blessed the idea, figuring the courts might move faster to uphold subpoenas issued mid-trial if Trump challenged them.

In his letter to McConnell, Schumer argued those witnesses' testimonies were imperative to determine Trump's guilt or innocence—and that calling them would also adhere to precedent. He was right on the latter: Of the fifteen impeachment trials the Senate had ever conducted for presidents, judges, and other high-level officials over its 230-year history, witnesses had been part of every single one.[7] In President Andrew Johnson's, in fact, senators had called forty-one witnesses, dragging the trial out for several months. In Clinton's, senators subpoenaed three fact witnesses for private depositions,[8] including Monica Lewinsky, and played video excerpts of them on the Senate floor.

Schumer's arguments would do little to move McConnell. In fact, the Democratic leader's publicity stunt would only make McConnell dig in deeper.

The day after the House impeached Trump, McConnell sat across from Schumer in a narrow hall just off the Senate floor, scowling at the man who'd become his main rival. Above their heads, a chandelier sparkled, reflecting light on the elegant marble patterns that adorned the ceiling and the floor of the senators-only space known as the Marble Room. How many times had senators used the private recluse to strike deals with their adversaries? That day, however, a deal was not in the cards.

For days, McConnell's office had repeatedly tried to coordinate a time for the Majority Leader to speak with his Democratic counterpart about the rules of the road for the inevitable impeachment trial. But his repeated entreaties had gone unanswered. Then Schumer's letter blindsided him. An annoyed McConnell griped to his staff that the Minority Leader was clearly more interested in running a media blitz about witnesses than actually negotiating a trial strategy. He also bet that Schumer was behind Pelosi's surprise announcement that she wouldn't be sending over the impeachment articles anytime soon.

That afternoon, the chamber was brimming with excitement, as senators, eager to leave town for the holidays, took the final votes of the year. But McConnell had one last, unpleasant task to complete: He had to talk trial rules with Schumer, no matter how ticked off he was at him.

Despite serving together for more than two decades, McConnell and Schumer had never had a good relationship. In 2008, as the leaders of the Senate scrambled to respond to a spiraling subprime mortgage crisis, they promised each other not to use an unpopular, pricey compromise they passed to shore up the economy as a cudgel against each other on the campaign trail. But the Senate Democrats' campaign arm, which Schumer was leading, broke that pact. They ran ads accusing McConnell of triggering the financial meltdown by refusing to regulate Wall Street—then bailing out the fat cats who caused the crisis. McConnell was furious and refused to speak to Schumer for some time.[9]

When Schumer became Minority Leader in 2017, the two attempted a fresh start. But their reset didn't last long. In one of his first moves, Schumer voted against confirming McConnell's wife, Elaine

Chao, as Transportation secretary. Only five other Democrats—all of them unabashed liberals—dared to join Schumer in that gesture. "If they were looking for 10 different ways to get off to a bad start, this would be 11," GOP senator Lamar Alexander, a McConnell ally, told the *Washington Post* of Schumer's snub.[10]

Their relationship further soured over Trump's Supreme Court nominees. When Schumer filibustered Trump's first high court pick, Neil Gorsuch, McConnell changed Senate rules to lower the vote threshold for confirmation and jam him through. Later, when Schumer and Democrats seized on allegations that Trump's second nominee, Brett Kavanaugh, had sexually assaulted a young woman while both were in high school, McConnell responded by plowing him through to confirmation regardless.

Their personalities clashed almost as badly as their politics. Where McConnell was steely and stone-faced, Schumer was an unabashed extrovert and dedicated schmoozer. He alternated between the menacing mien of a CEO in a boardroom—especially when power-walking through the halls of Congress yelling into a flip phone he refused to upgrade—and almost grandmotherly gabbing, particularly when regaling colleagues with anecdotes about his grandson.

Between the two of them, Schumer had the thinner skin. McConnell was content to play the villain, chuckling at the creative insults Democrats lobbed his way—even framing and hanging newspaper comics that jeered him on his walls. Schumer, however, cared deeply about what others thought of him. McConnell was never one to socialize unnecessarily, especially with his political rivals. But Schumer would show up at the senators-only gym at seven a.m. just to try to befriend Republicans. He'd jump on a stationary bike and start slowly pedaling—then loudly start gossiping about the day's news to whoever was in the room, more interested in making new friends than burning calories.[11]

It wasn't that they couldn't work together. They had frequently held their noses to hammer out budget and debt-ceiling deals. In early 2018, Schumer even appeared alongside McConnell at his alma mater, the University of Louisville, for a forum on immigration and border security. There, McConnell offered perhaps the most glowing review of their relationship that he could muster.

"We don't *dis*like each other," McConnell said. "We have to work together."[12]

As the impeachment trial approached, McConnell knew he and Schumer were headed for their latest collision, this time on witnesses. Even before Schumer sent over his demands, McConnell had firmly made up his mind: He simply would never allow witnesses to be part of Trump's trial. There was no point in re-hashing what the public had already heard during the House's hearings, McConnell reasoned. And calling new witnesses risked unearthing new, damaging information about Trump that would make justifying an acquittal vote all the more complicated—especially for moderates already under pressure to break with the president.

In a mid-December Senate GOP lunch, McConnell began to drive home the notion that witnesses were dangerous to his rank and file. He likened their inclusion at trial to "mutually assured destruction," the doctrine that opponents with nuclear weapons would destroy each other before either could claim victory.[13] If the Senate called Bolton, his testimony stood the chance of damaging Trump's defense significantly. It would also incentivize Trump's lawyers to seek to haul in Hunter Biden in order to create a bigger, competing scandal for the former vice president on the cusp of the Democratic presidential primaries. It was a Pandora's box McConnell did not want to open. Better to avoid new witnesses altogether, McConnell argued to Senate Republicans. Plus, he said, it wasn't the Senate's responsibility to call witnesses the House hadn't bothered to call themselves.

"The Senate Democratic leader would apparently like our chamber to do House Democrats' homework for them," McConnell said in his first public retort to Schumer's witness demand. "He wants to volunteer the Senate's time and energy on a fishing expedition."

When they met in the Marble Room on December 19, McConnell and Schumer made a half-hearted attempt to haggle out a deal. McConnell argued that the Senate shouldn't try to fix what wasn't broken: During Clinton's 1999 impeachment trial, senators had voted 100 to 0 to settle the question of whether to call witnesses *after* hearing opening arguments from either side.[14] McConnell wanted the same "Clinton model" for Trump, arguing "if that was good enough for Clinton's trial then, why shouldn't it be good enough for Trump's trial now?"

Schumer balked. He had listened to McConnell talk disparagingly about having witnesses and guessed that all the "Clinton model" quibbling was nothing more than a distraction. In his estimation, McConnell was putting off the witness question to buy time to whip his members to vote against them.

"No deal until you agree to witnesses," Schumer told him.

The two leaders parted without coming to an agreement. But with fifty-three Republican senators at his disposal, McConnell was confident he could muster the votes needed to pass the trial rules he wanted. He had already been laying the groundwork with four critical moderate Republicans he knew held all the cards: Maine's Susan Collins, who was facing a tough 2020 reelection; Alaska's Lisa Murkowski, who had an independent streak; Utah's Mitt Romney, who had fully embraced his role as a Republican iconoclast and occasional foil to Trump; and Lamar Alexander, the retiring pragmatist from Tennessee who also happened to be a close friend to the GOP leader.

But while McConnell was sure he could convince those four swing votes to follow his lead on the trial process, he was less sure he could convince them to eschew the idea of witnesses altogether. On that front, he knew he had his work cut out for him.

31

THE MODERATES

DECEMBER 24-25, 2019

Lisa Murkowski was wrapping Christmas presents in a cabin outside her hometown of snowy, mountainous Anchorage when her son interrupted her peaceful holiday ritual.

"What did you *do* today, Mom?" he asked accusingly, breathlessly. "You're trending right now."

It was near midnight and the family had just returned home from attending Mass. Murkowski, like she did most Christmases, had holed up for the holiday with her family outside a ski resort in the foothills of Alaska's Alyeska mountain. She had hoped to steal a few quiet days before the circus of the impeachment trial that was set to begin in January.

Murkowski paused her wrapping, confused. The centrist Alaska senator, sixty-two, knew what "trending" meant—that the whole nation was talking about her all of a sudden on social media. But, *why?*

"I'm *trending?*" she asked her son for clarification. "Trending on what?" she demanded.

Whipping out his smartphone, her son showed her the screen, where, sure enough, her name was scrawled all over Twitter and going viral on the internet. "You must have said something controversial today," he said with a smirk.

Earlier that day, during an on-camera interview with a local media outlet, a reporter had asked Murkowski her thoughts about a recent interview Mitch McConnell gave to Fox News. In it, the Senate GOP leader had vowed to work in "total coordination" with Trump's defense team and "take my cues from the president's lawyers."

"There will be no difference between the president's position and our position," McConnell had declared.

The remarks had prompted outrage among Democrats accusing McConnell of trying to skew the trial in Trump's favor. In Alaska, Murkowski was also displeased. When asked about it by a local reporter, she did what she had always done when talking to journalists: She answered the question honestly.

"When I heard that I was disturbed," she had told the reporter, lifting her chin slightly as she insisted that fair trials require separation between the defense and the jury. Donned in jeans, a blue knit sweater, and a rainbow scarf, she argued it was vital for senators to maintain impartiality. "We have to take that step back from being hand in glove with the defense . . . I heard what Leader McConnell had said. I happen to think that that has further confused the process."[1]

In her eighteen years in the Senate, Murkowski had developed a reputation for having a strong, if not stubborn, independent streak. She was known for speaking her mind—at times to the chagrin of her communications shop—and for being an unabashed pragmatist. She shunned the stilted, talking-points-driven rhetoric of Washington politicians. And above all, she hated the notion of putting party loyalty over doing what was right—something her GOP colleagues did far too often, in her view.

As a third-generation Alaskan and the first senator born in America's Last Frontier, Murkowski had always been sure of her own convictions. She had grown up the daughter of a rising conservative politician, spending her free time hiking glaciers, duck hunting, and fishing king salmon. She graduated from Georgetown University in 1980, the same year her father won his first Senate election. Eighteen years later, following stints as a district attorney and in private practice, Murkowski, then forty-one, decided to try her own hand at politics—and quickly signaled she was no carbon copy of her father. In the state legislature, she pushed GOP leaders far senior to her to address a $1 billion budget shortfall by raising taxes—an idea her dad was actively campaigning against in his 2002 bid for governor. Still, when Frank won the gubernatorial race, he appointed his daughter to fill the remainder of his Senate term, sending Lisa back to Washington to take his place.

Once in Congress, Murkowski forged a path distinct from her father's staunchly conservative legacy. She backed abortion rights. While fighting for Alaska's right to drill in the Arctic, she also signaled a willingness to hear out environmentalists. But in Washington, her independence came at a cost. In 2010, amid the Tea Party uprising, Alaska governor Sarah Palin—who had ousted the elder Murkowski after just one term—endorsed a primary opponent against Murkowski. When that Tea Party challenger beat her in the primary, Murkowski launched a rare write-in campaign. In a shock to the political world, she actually won.[2]

Murkowski's politics didn't change a bit after the near-defeat—if anything, she seemed to feel even less beholden to toeing the party line. As Washington grew more partisan, she moved closer to the political center. She immediately backed the Democrats' repeal of

"Don't Ask, Don't Tell," the military policy banning openly gay people from serving.[3] A few years later, she endorsed gay marriage and voted to limit the reach of the Patriot Act that allowed intelligence officers to survey Americans' phone data.[4]

Trump's arrival in Washington didn't change Murkowski much either, even as he tightened his grip on nearly all her colleagues. She had refused to endorse him on the campaign trail and called for him to step aside when he was caught on video bragging about groping women.[5] A year later, she helped sink Trump's promised Obamacare repeal effort, arguing that it would upend the health care of millions of Americans and protections for people with pre-existing conditions.[6] She was also the only Senate Republican who refused to back Brett Kavanaugh for the Supreme Court.[7]

Trump knew Murkowski didn't like him. And instead of heeding McConnell's advice to woo her impeachment vote with parochial perks for Alaska, he shot jabs in her direction. During a private fundraiser for a McConnell-backed super PAC in early November, the president asked if Murkowski was in the audience. When he was certain she wasn't, he deadpanned: "She hates me. I kind of like her but she really doesn't like me. We do so much for Alaska you'd think we'd get her vote for something one of these days."[8]

In the context of impeachment, even with Trump's presidency on the line, Murkowski hadn't softened her critical stance. When Trump's "do us a favor" transcript surfaced, she didn't hesitate to tell reporters the president's conduct was "highly improper"[9]— despite McConnell asking his members not to weigh in. As someone who had borne the brunt of Trump's bullying before, she knew his demands were not easy to dismiss—especially for a nation as dependent on U.S. support as Ukraine.

But to her increasing dismay, almost no other Republicans would even chide Trump for conduct that to her seemed so obviously wrong. When she raised her concerns with them, they brushed off the president's words with a shrug. "There goes Trump again!" they would say, as if his actions were no big deal.

It wasn't until that fall that Murkowski grasped just how much her peers had fallen under the president's spell. They'd become so accustomed to Trump's rudeness, so numbed to his breaking norms—or his "unconventional ways," as she tried to put it diplomatically—that they just yawned at the latest scandal, no matter how bad. When Trump announced he would hold the G7 international economic conference at his struggling resort in Florida, she was again slack-jawed to find that she was one of just a few Republicans willing to excoriate the move as wildly inappropriate. "Doesn't surprise me," one of her GOP colleagues said to her, as if using the presidency to pad his wallet was just the latest crazy thing Trump did. "That's how he rolls."

To Murkowski, the party had transformed into a mindless herd of Arctic musk ox: eight-hundred-pound beasts that form a protective circle around their young, with their horns turned outward and their rears tucked inside. Republican leaders, much to her frustration, were constantly telling their rank and file: "You gotta circle. You gotta circle together to protect one another here"—which meant, of course, circling to protect Trump. Just like musk ox, Murkowski thought.

As the House probed the Ukraine matter that fall, Murkowski had instructed her staff to tuck stories on all the major impeachment developments into her daily package of must-read news clippings. But the twists and turns of the saga were so arcane that she quickly found herself overwhelmed, especially while trying to juggle her duties as a senator primarily focused on energy and budget issues. As a result, as the trial approached, she decided she'd keep an open mind. She would not determine if Trump was innocent or guilty until hearing the arguments on both sides.

Much to her annoyance, almost none of her GOP colleagues did the same. It quickly became clear that most had already decided to acquit him, the latest indication that the entire exercise was going to be a partisan charade. Still, she was determined to follow her own conscience. When her colleague Lindsey Graham circulated a resolution condemning the House process in late October, Murkowski was one of just three GOP senators who refused to sign on.[10] Senators, she reasoned, hated it when House members complained about their chamber rules. To her, the Senate had no more right to tell the House how to do its job.

When McConnell went on Fox News and declared himself to be "in total coordination" with Trump's defense team, it didn't surprise Murkowski. She had heard him say something similar in private GOP lunches. The Majority Leader, who thought the idea of "impartial jurors" was quaint to the point of ridiculous, had argued that during Clinton's impeachment, Senate Democrats went so far as to flash the president's lawyers hand signals on the floor to coach their arguments. Everybody does it, McConnell had said casually. Murkowski looked around at her colleagues with her eyes widening, as if to say, "Is he *really* saying this?" But to her disappointment, no one else seemed to have a problem with the GOP leader's unapologetic embrace of such partisan tactics.

When she criticized McConnell's words to the Alaska reporter on Christmas Eve, Murkowski didn't give a second thought to her rebuke. It was an honest answer to an honest question, she thought to herself. Besides, she had knocked Democrats in the interview too: She had blasted Pelosi for conducting a rushed impeachment by skipping over key firsthand witnesses and leaving it to the Senate to finish their probe.

Still, Murkowski should have realized how much of a stir her comments would cause when her phone buzzed earlier that evening with a text from Mitt Romney, the first she'd ever received from the Utah Republican. Murkowski and Romney were not particularly close. He was relatively new to Washington, yet somehow he had found her number—and couldn't wait until morning to punch out a note.

Good statement today, he told her. *Know that I feel much the same.*

Huh, Murkowski thought to herself. *How did Mitt Romney hear what I said all the way up here?* She brushed it aside and hustled out the door in her Christmas best, not realizing until her son approached her around midnight that she had, essentially, broken the internet.

As she lay in bed that night, unable to sleep, Murkowski still didn't understand why it was such a big deal for a Republican to say what she viewed was extremely obvious. *There should be separation between the White House and the Senate*, she thought. *Wasn't that the point of a trial?*

Of course, it wasn't so simple. The next morning, on Christmas Day, Murkowski awoke to find a snarky email from McConnell in her inbox—a missive that would zap all the holiday cheer out of her for two days. The leader was not happy with her comments. And he wanted to talk to her.

Murkowski wasn't happy either. She had always had a good relationship with McConnell, but he had to bug her on Christmas about this? Nonetheless, she phoned him—and was relieved when he didn't answer. This was her time with family—politics could wait. She would call the leader back in a few days.

A thousand miles away in Utah, Romney, the longtime Trump antagonist, was grappling with a similar predicament and looking for allies. More than any of the four possible Senate Republican swing votes, Romney, the former Massachusetts governor and onetime

GOP presidential nominee, knew he was Trump's favorite punching bag. They were, in many ways, the ultimate rivals for a GOP
grappling with impeachment. Trump the populist, with his win-
at-any-cost bullying tactics, was tightening his clutch on the party
more with every passing day, while Romney appealed to his party's
deeper morality and conscience—attributes that, in his estimation,
had gone dormant since Trump's takeover of Washington.

Their feud had started in earnest during the 2016 presidential
campaign, when Romney criticized Trump for calling Mexican immigrants "rapists" and "killers" and questioning whether Senator
John McCain, a former prisoner of war, was really a hero. Trump,
who had supported Romney's bid for president in 2012, responded
by asking why anybody would listen to him. "He lost an election that
should have easily been won against Obama," Trump said. When
Romney suggested Trump was refusing to release his tax returns
to hide a "bombshell," Trump called him a "dope" and "one of the
dumbest" GOP candidates in history.[11] Shortly after, when Romney
implored voters not to support a "phony" and a "fraud" like Trump,
the future president retorted that Romney "choked like a dog" in
the 2012 election.[12]

When Trump became president, the two men had tried to
smooth things over—or at least that's what Romney thought they
were doing. After he congratulated Trump on his victory, the
president-elect had actually floated Romney for secretary of state.
But the whole thing had been a setup. Trump confidants tipped
off the media about where the two men planned to meet so they
could snap a photo. The president later used it to claim Romney
had groveled and begged for the job—a clear attempt to embarrass
the former governor while denying him the position. Several months
later, Romney was back to openly criticizing Trump, this time for
expressing sympathies for white supremacists who had rallied in
Charlottesville, Virginia, in August 2017.

In early 2018, after Orrin Hatch of Utah announced he would retire his Senate seat, Romney and Trump tried once again to bury the hatchet. Trump endorsed Romney for Hatch's replacement, calling him a "worthy successor." Romney then praised Trump for his accomplishments as president—sort of. "The things he's actually done have been better than I expected," Romney said.[13] But their détente didn't last. Later that year, when Trump refused to criticize Russian president Vladimir Putin for interfering in the U.S. election—effectively siding with him over the U.S. intelligence community—Romney called Trump's actions "disgraceful and detrimental to our democratic principles." He later said he was "sickened" by the level of deceit Special Counsel Robert Mueller's probe had revealed in Trump World.

For Romney, the impeachment charges eclipsed all of Trump's previous offenses. On the day the transcript went public, he told *The Atlantic* in a live interview that the president's request to Zelensky was "deeply troubling." Behind the scenes, things were more frantic. A small cadre of Romney advisors had implored him to challenge Trump for the party nomination in 2020. The president was newly vulnerable, they argued, and Romney should primary him and free the GOP from his grip.

But Romney balked at the idea. He thought he was the wrong man at the wrong time, and with the GOP squarely in Trump's corner, he knew it would be a suicide mission. Hopes flared in Never-Trump World nonetheless that perhaps Romney could organize a GOP resistance in the Senate—maybe even enough to oust the president during the impeachment trial.[14]

On October 4, a day after Trump implored China to also investigate the Bidens, Romney took a direct shot at the president on Twitter. "When the only American citizen President Trump singles out for China's investigation is his political opponent in the midst of the Democratic nomination process, it strains credulity to suggest that it is anything other than politically motivated," he wrote that Friday. "By all appearances, the President's brazen and unprecedented appeal to China and to Ukraine to investigate Joe Biden is wrong and appalling." Trump volleyed back the next morning, unsurprisingly, with his famed name-calling. "Mitt Romney never knew how to win," he wrote. "He is a pompous 'ass' who has been fighting me from the beginning, except when he begged me for my endorsement for his Senate run (I gave it to him), and when he begged me to be Secretary of State (I didn't give it to him). He is so bad for R's!"

Romney had been visiting a pumpkin patch with his wife, Ann, and two granddaughters when Trump sent his public missive. He responded by ignoring the remark completely, tweeting out a picture of his family searching for the perfect pumpkin instead.[15]

But within days, the attacks became more personal. Club for Growth, a conservative group that had once criticized Trump but now acted as his muscle, placed a TV ad in Utah labeling Romney a "Democrat secret asset" conspiring to "take down President Trump." "Now his cover's blown," it said. "Tell Romney, quit colluding with Democrats on impeachment."[16]

It wasn't that Romney liked criticizing Trump. Each time he did, it made his political life more difficult. But as a devout Mormon, Romney felt a duty to be a voice of reason and conscience when his party refused to stand up against the president's misdeeds. Impeachment, however, was posing a special challenge. When Pelosi announced the inquiry, Romney's heart sank. Though he had committed himself to standing up to Trump when necessary, he had not guessed that would mean weighing an impeachment vote less than a year into his Senate tenure.

As revelations continued to pour forth from Adam Schiff's SCIF that fall, Romney worried about finding himself on an island, rejected by the GOP for speaking his mind. So the principled Utahn

started to reach out to possible Republican allies discreetly, looking for cracks in the party's bulwark of support for Trump. In mid-
October, Romney phoned Congressman Francis Rooney to praise
him for declaring on CNN that he was open to impeaching Trump.
Rooney had been a financial backer for Romney in his 2012 presidential campaign and had spent time at Romney's lake house in
New Hampshire. The two agreed to continue to speak out from
their respective chambers.

As the trial drew nearer, the stress of Romney's unique situation
weighed on him. He didn't know if he was ready to convict Trump,
but he certainly knew he was open to it. He prayed about the situation. He consulted his wife, Ann, about each development. And
often, he found himself thinking about his father, the late George
Romney, a former Michigan governor and onetime Republican presidential contender who had suffered politically for breaking with his
party to take principled stands.

Romney's team sensed his burden and decided that winter to try
to cheer him up. During the office holiday party, a dinner at the
Cosmos Club in downtown Washington, they had just finished eat-
ing and exchanging gifts when a man dressed as Santa Claus showed
up and started ho-ho-hoing at the group while passing out Twinkies,
Romney's favorite snack. As staffers gathered for an office photo,
Santa inserted himself into the middle of the entire group, sitting
right next to Romney and his wife, Ann. Then, with a flourish, he
pulled down his fake beard. It was Paul Ryan inside the fluffy red
suit, the former House Speaker and Romney's 2012 presidential
running mate, who had become a dear friend.

The room lit up in laughter as the two men embraced each
other. They were both cut from the same fabric: deeply religious,
driven by not just ideological but moral convictions—and extremely
concerned about Trump's leadership. Ryan had spent his entire

speakership walking on eggshells, trying to find a delicate balance between accomplishing his favored policy goals and steering a politically unwieldy GOP conference around an unpredictable president. The task ended up being too much for him, and Ryan—who, at forty-eight, was once considered one of the most promising stars in the GOP—retired in frustration at Trumpism after barely more than two years as Speaker.

Romney, then a spritely seventy-two, wasn't ready to call it quits on his career. As one of Washington's newest senators, he, unlike Ryan, would have to find a way to balance his conscience and his political ambitions.

It was in that mindset that Romney read on Christmas Eve about how Murkowski had called foul on McConnell's plan to be in "total coordination" with Trump's impeachment defense. To Romney, Murkowski's willingness to speak up and criticize not just Trump, but also the GOP leader for pledging loyalty to him, was heartening. Romney knew he wasn't alone.

TRUMP WHISPERER

Lindsey Graham had flown down to Palm Beach for Christmas for one reason, and one reason alone: to try to save Donald Trump from himself. Since Nancy Pelosi had announced her decision to hold the articles of impeachment in the House—possibly denying the president an acquittal in the Senate—Trump had flown into a distracted rage. Cocooned in his happy place—his favorite lavish resort, Mar-a-Lago, nicknamed the "Winter White House" for how much time he spent there basking in the Florida sunshine during the colder months—he whined to confidants that the Speaker was being completely unfair to him. He wanted Senate Republicans to vote to dismiss the charges immediately and skip the business of a trial. Or, if they had to go through with one, to use the proceedings to subpoena his political enemies, like Joe Biden and Adam Schiff.

Graham knew both options were non-starters with his longtime ally and friend Mitch McConnell—and frankly, he agreed with the Senate GOP leader. Such displays might please the president, but the two agreed they risked turning the Senate into a shitshow—and either would hurt the GOP moderates up for reelection.

Graham was aware that McConnell had tried to impress his concerns upon Trump himself. Two days before Christmas, the president had called the Majority Leader to try to convince him to adopt one of his preferred trial strategies. McConnell had told Trump what he never liked to hear: No.

"You are getting a lot of advice," McConnell had said. "I know the Senate better than any of those people you're talking to . . . Let me take control here."

Trump had relented in the moment, but both McConnell and Graham knew the mercurial president was likely to revert to his gut instincts—especially when surrounded by the MAGA sycophants who frequented Mar-a-Lago. They feared his surrender wouldn't last long, and so Graham flew south for the holiday to stage an intervention.

Three years into Trump's presidency, Graham could have written a dissertation on how to cut through the noise of MAGA groupthink to bend Trump's ear. The South Carolina Republican had become a master of sucking up to the president to earn his trust, racking up chits he calculated he could cash in with Trump to sway him when it was most necessary. In fact, he and McConnell had adopted a "good cop, bad cop" approach: Graham buttered up Trump while McConnell delivered the tough love, with both senators always working toward the same goal.

The two had employed the strategy when it came to impeachment, but for Graham, being Trump's Senate whisperer wasn't always easy. All fall, he had studiously tiptoed around a pressure campaign from Trump, Rudy Giuliani, and even members of the president's family to use his position in the Senate to run a counter-investigation of the Democrats' impeachment effort. As chair of the Senate Judiciary Committee, Graham wielded a gavel, a megaphone, and subpoena power. Trump wanted Graham to use all of those tools to go after Adam Schiff and the whistleblower. He also dispatched Giuliani to harass Graham to investigate information about the Bidens he had procured from shady Ukrainian sources—some of whom had Kremlin ties.

Graham had been wary of Trump's and Giuliani's attempts to pillory the Bidens. That fall, the GOP chairman of the Senate Intelligence Committee had warned his colleagues that going after the Bidens would bolster a Russian-orchestrated disinformation campaign aimed at sowing discord in the U.S. before the 2020 election. Graham believed it. Graham also recoiled at the idea of subpoenaing the chairman of another committee, even if that chairman was Schiff.

"If you've found evidence of misconduct, take it to the FBI," Graham had told Giuliani, trying to shrug off his heavy-handed tactics.

But the pressure from Trump World only intensified. Trump's son started going on television and Twitter to demand Graham do more to fight back. The far right struck up the hashtag "#WheresLindsey"—suggesting he was missing in action in the push to protect the president. And some Trump campaign aides started threatening that if Graham didn't meet Trump's demands, the president might not endorse him in his 2020 reelection race.

Graham, eager to stay in Trump's good graces, had teetered around on what to do. He went so far as to begrudgingly announce on Twitter that Giuliani had raised "disturbing allegations" that were worth investigating regarding Ukraine and promised to invite him to testify before his panel—though he had no intention of actually following through. Graham also began proactively campaigning against the House's impeachment probe. In mid-October, he suggested to his Senate GOP colleagues that they write a letter to Nancy Pelosi, pledging to vote against any articles of impeachment the House produced, no matter what they said. Most Republicans had already decided Trump wasn't guilty anyway, Graham argued—and if thirty-four were willing to sign such a declaration, they could preemptively deny Democrats the two-thirds Senate majority they needed for a conviction.

But when he presented the idea to fellow senators in a private lunch that fall, his colleagues balked at his proposal. "Bad idea," McConnell ally Roy Blunt of Missouri had responded, arguing there was no way that centrist Republicans would endorse such a stunt while the probe was still in its fact-finding stages. Romney, who was already getting grilled for voicing his own concerns about Trump's conduct toward Ukraine, said Graham's idea would put a target on the backs of people who wouldn't sign it, like him. Even Senator Tom Cotton, a fiercely conservative hawk from deep-red Arkansas, was opposed to it, arguing that Graham probably couldn't even get thirty-four people to sign such a letter.

Graham, knowing he was on thin ice with the president's inner circle, was determined to make some sort of public demonstration of loyalty to get the president's henchmen off his back. It wasn't his style to pick up a pitchfork and throw himself at the doors of a SCIF like his House GOP counterparts. But Graham had experience with impeachment that he knew others did not. In 1999, Graham had served as one of the managers in Clinton's impeachment trial—a notch on his political résumé that gave him more authority to cry foul against the Democrats' process than anyone else in the Senate. With his back against the wall, he decided to use that expertise to push a new plan: a resolution condemning the House inquiry for having failed to inaugurate the impeachment probe with a House vote or give Trump and the Republican minority iron-clad guarantees of certain rights.[1]

Mercifully, McConnell liked it. And with his blessing, Graham had urged his colleagues to sign on, winning over all but three of them. Graham had hoped his gesture would satisfy the president and Giuliani. It didn't.

That Christmas, Mar-a-Lago was teeming with influential members of Trump Nation and had become a veritable echo chamber for Trump's rage and desires. Rush Limbaugh, the conservative talk radio personality, made an appearance, while Sean Hannity, the president's favorite Fox News host, hobnobbed with the family during an event nearby. Giuliani flew down to gab—and beg for a spot on Trump's trial defense team that would argue against impeachment charges in the Senate. Trump's allies in the House were also visiting and gunning for starring roles, vowing to give Schiff hell on the floor, if only he gave them the chance.

The circus, Graham noticed, fed Trump's worst instincts. He couldn't attend a meal without crossing through throngs of well-heeled club members eager to rub elbows and snap photos with him—and praise his idea of calling the Bidens to testify as genius. Others would tell him he was the best president since Ronald Reagan, fueling his expanding ego.[2]

Graham realized glumly that none of them seemed to appreciate the political danger Trump was still in—or just how counterproductive it was to egg Trump on. If the president's combative antics alienated the moderates in the Senate, Graham feared they might revolt by siding with Democrats to subpoena witnesses at trial. And if that happened, the acquittal that all the Mar-a-Lago revelers were

so sure of—the one most of Washington was predicting no less—
might slip from the GOP's grip.

"Impeachment is about three or four people in the Senate," Graham told Trump, referring to the moderates who were not naturally
inclined to be loyal to him. The Senate was not a rally crowd or Fox
News's prime-time audience, Graham reminded the president as
they moved between the dining room and the links. Trump would
have to resist his instinct to play to the base—and he would need
to trust McConnell. That meant no vote to dismiss the articles of
impeachment, no calling in the Bidens, and no appointing lightning
rods for ridicule like Giuliani—or any of his House GOP attack
dogs—to his defense team in the Senate.

"Listen to Mitch; Mitch knows what he's doing," Graham told
Trump, promising that if the president didn't rock the boat, his acquittal was assured. "Mitch doesn't want a long trial, I don't want a
long trial," Graham continued. "You're winning . . . Get the damn
thing started, and then get it over with as soon as possible."

Over a week's worth of stolen breakfasts, dinners, and golf games,
Graham dragged the president into an accord: Trump capitulated
and agreed to a two-week, witness-free trial, just like McConnell
wanted. But just as both good cop and bad cop had feared, he
wouldn't yield to them for long.

PRE-TRIAL POSITIONING

JANUARY 8-21, 2020

Mitch McConnell listened as one of the moderate Republicans he'd been bending over backwards to protect lectured him in his own office, essentially accusing him of hypocrisy. It was Wednesday, January 8, and Senator Susan Collins of Maine had usurped a meeting of about half a dozen Republican committee chairs to go on a tear about McConnell's proposed "Clinton model" rules for an impeachment trial.

Collins, who had been a first-term senator during Bill Clinton's trial, knew her history—and knew that McConnell, despite his claims about adhering to precedent, was actually breaking from it. The Clinton trial rules had allowed for an initial vote to dismiss the charges entirely, she reminded McConnell.[1] McConnell's proposed rules for Trump's trial, however, bypassed such a vote completely.

It was just the latest incoming for McConnell, who had been taking it from all sides that week. Former national security advisor John Bolton had sent Washington into a tizzy a few days earlier by publicly volunteering to testify in the trial if subpoenaed. Trump had reacted by going rogue again on the trial process. That very morning, the president had given McConnell an earful in the Oval Office for refusing to do exactly what Collins was suggesting: hold an early vote throwing out the trial charges. And to top it all off, Speaker Nancy Pelosi was still refusing to transmit the articles of impeachment to the Senate, further delaying the proceedings that McConnell so desperately wanted to put behind him.

It had been three weeks since the House impeached Trump, and the GOP leader thought his chamber would have been halfway through opening arguments of the impeachment trial by then. Instead, he was utterly clueless about when it would even start.

Publicly, McConnell had maintained a nonchalant, even blasé attitude toward Pelosi's noncommittal stance on transmitting the articles, which he dubbed her "one-woman blockade." He had even dared Pelosi to hang on to the charges forever, insisting that it didn't matter to him what she did. Yet privately, McConnell feared he was starting to lose control of the situation. Despite Graham's "good cop" efforts over the holiday break, Trump was antsy and had started organizing a mutiny of rank-and-file Senate Republicans to forcibly dismiss the charges against him. Usually, McConnell could maintain control of his members. But the more time elapsed, the more unwieldy his caucus was becoming. The longer Pelosi held out, McConnell knew, the more pressure he would face from the GOP base to throw out the trial altogether—a politically toxic proposition that would blow back on his fragile majority.

So that week, as he gathered his top lieutenants in his Capitol office for their regular meeting, McConnell pressed them to reach across the aisle for help. The GOP leader had heard through the grapevine that more than just a few Senate Democrats were equally annoyed with Pelosi's hold-the-articles stunt. Perhaps they could assist in unsticking the situation.

"If you are close with any of the more reasonable Democrats, suggest to them that it's time to send the articles over," McConnell said.

It wasn't just Trump's efforts to whip his allies that was causing McConnell problems. Bolton's offer to testify was also increasing the already considerable pressure on his moderate members to vote in favor of allowing witnesses in a trial. In fact, Chuck Schumer and Senate Democrats had already leaped into action, taking to the Senate floor and TV airwaves to hold up Bolton's words as proof that he had vital testimony to offer against the president.

McConnell had moved quickly to calm the uproar. He gathered his four swing votes—Collins, Lisa Murkowski, Mitt Romney, and Lamar Alexander—and doubled down on his pitch for the "Clinton model," in which the Senate voted on whether to call witnesses only *after* the opening arguments were finished. It would buy him precious time to convince them—hopefully with the help of Trump's lawyers—that witnesses were not necessary, though McConnell kept that ulterior motive to himself. Luckily, all four agreed with him.

McConnell hadn't expected that his "Clinton model" plan would come back to bite him. Yet that's exactly what happened when Collins marched into his office that Wednesday with a copy of the Clinton trial rules from 1999, pointing out McConnell's inconsistencies.

It wasn't that Collins wanted to dismiss the trial. She planned to vote against any such motion—and then trumpet that stance on the campaign trail in blue Maine as proof of her independent spirit. But if the Senate was going to profess to follow the "Clinton model," she argued to her colleagues, they couldn't cherry-pick from it. They had to embrace the entire precedent.

"Just change the name 'Clinton' to 'Trump,' and the year '1999' to '2020,'" Collins insisted, referring to the old resolution.

Earlier that day, when Trump had been haranguing McConnell to dismiss the trial, the leader had given him a pithy reason for why he couldn't: They didn't have the votes to pass it. McConnell knew Collins would never support such a vote, and believed that his other three GOP swing votes wouldn't either. Kicking off the trial with a failed vote would embarrass the president and divide the GOP at a critical time, he told Trump.

"It's better to be united than divided," McConnell had said.

But privately, the leader was less concerned about what such a fissure would mean for Trump than for his members. McConnell knew that he could not protect his Senate majority in 2020—and his own job—without protecting the Republicans up for reelection in swing states. People like Senator Cory Gardner, who was facing difficult odds in increasingly blue Colorado, and Martha McSally, taking heat in Arizona. A vote to dismiss would put them in a bad position no matter how they handled it, McConnell feared: If the vulnerable Republicans voted against dismissing the charges, as Collins was ready to do, Trump and the base would pillory them for disloyalty and turn their backs on their reelection effort. But if they voted to dismiss, they'd look like they were engaged in a cover-up, hurting them with independent voters they also needed to maintain their seats—and McConnell's Senate majority.

"I view the motion to dismiss as a really tough vote and so I don't want to write that in," McConnell admitted to Collins.

"Schumer knows what he's doing. He's trying to set up a situation to inflict maximum harm . . . so he can take back the majority," McConnell continued, listing the GOP senators up for reelection in 2020, including her. "We know how this is going to end up, so let's do what we can to keep the majority."

As McConnell planned and plotted, Democrats on the Hill were also privately getting unnerved by Pelosi's refusal to transmit the articles to the Senate. Even her fellow leaders didn't know what she was doing or why—and certainly didn't see an endgame in her strategy. After the Speaker's impeachment day press conference went off the rails, Schumer had suggested Pelosi embrace her accidental outburst as a planned move to force McConnell into writing fairer trial rules—or at least draw more public attention to his refusal to entertain new testimony. Pelosi agreed, saying she would hold the articles through the holidays.

But as lawmakers returned to Washington the first week of January, many Democrats worried that Pelosi's unorthodox stance was backfiring. The party had defended the House's speedy impeachment probe by arguing that they had no choice but to rush because Trump posed a risk to the integrity of the upcoming election. Now Republicans were pointing out the fundamental hypocrisy in Pelosi's move: If impeachment was so pressing, why was Pelosi taking her sweet time delivering the charges to the upper chamber?

Meanwhile, Trump's defenders that week started arguing that Pelosi was playing games by trying to deny the president his inevitable acquittal. One of the more liberal-leaning legal scholars who had advocated for Trump's impeachment before the House Judiciary Committee just weeks prior chided the Speaker for deviating from precedent and even suggested that Trump technically might not be impeached until the articles had been transferred.[2] And a group of Democratic Judiciary aides upset with the move even discussed resigning from their posts to protest their work being upended by what they regarded as a stunt.

In the Senate, Schumer was also growing concerned. He had thought Pelosi would release the articles as soon as Congress returned after the New Year. When a week later she still had not, he took it upon himself to give her a gentle nudge in a press conference. "The Speaker has said all along that she wanted to see the

arena in which she was playing . . . so she could appoint impeachment managers," he told reporters that Tuesday. "Now it's becoming clear that Mitch McConnell wants to do everything he can to
avoid a fair trial."

Pelosi, however, never liked to be strong-armed—and the pressure from her own kind only made her dig in deeper. She bristled
when reporters asked how long she would wait, snapping back that
she wasn't telling. At a gathering with her members in the basement
of the Capitol just hours after Schumer's comment, Pelosi doubled
down, insisting she would hold out until she saw what kind of trial
terms Republicans would propose.

By Wednesday, January 8, Schumer's staff, thoroughly confused,
was calling other leadership offices across the Hill campus, frantically trying to find out what Pelosi was up to. They too had no
idea. "I stopped predicting Pelosi a long time ago," one top aide to
Majority Leader Steny Hoyer said to another in the basement of
the Capitol that morning. "We'll see how she gets out of this clus-
terfuck she put herself in."

As Pelosi doubled down on holding the articles, speculation
started to spread—even privately among Democrats—that the
Speaker was trying to help former vice president Joe Biden win the
Democratic nomination to run for president. The Iowa caucuses—
the opening act of the Democratic primary season—were slated for
early February. And the longer the trial ran, the more likely senators
also running for the nomination would find themselves stuck on the
Senate floor serving as trial jurors, unable to campaign. Senators,
after all, were required to attend every hour of debate. The later the
trial got going, the more encumbered presidential candidates like
Senator Bernie Sanders, then the frontrunner, and Senator Elizabeth Warren would be.

The Speaker had not endorsed in the crowded primary to challenge Trump. But it was no secret that Biden, the more centrist former veep, was more closely aligned than his challengers to the Speaker's own philosophy of governing by consensus and protecting the moderate middle. In fact, earlier that fall, Pelosi had issued a stern warning to the Democratic field, admonishing them that liberal ideas such as Medicare for All and free college—ideas espoused by Sanders—would not sit well with the American electorate. Biden was one of the few Democratic candidates who happened to agree with her.

By the end of the first week of January, Democrats began to take their frustrations with Pelosi public. On Thursday, January 9, House Armed Services Committee chairman Adam Smith of Washington State went on CNN to declare "it is time" for Pelosi to transmit the articles. But Pelosi's staffers pressured him to retract the statement a few hours later. "I misspoke this morning," he wrote on Twitter.

Behind closed doors, Congresswoman Debbie Dingell—whom Pelosi had dispatched to stamp out Rashida Tlaib's "impeach the motherfucker!" cry a year before—tried to gently encourage Pelosi to transmit articles before the Martin Luther King Day recess. Politically vulnerable frontliners, Dingell said, might otherwise face heat from their constituents for backing an impeachment the party didn't have the guts to see through.

Pelosi said nothing. But she was too shrewd a politician to keep swimming against the tide, especially if it was disquieting her "majority makers." On Friday, January 10, she issued a "Dear Colleague" letter to the House Democrats, announcing that she would transmit the articles "next week."[3]

Despite their private freak-out, Democrats would go on to publicly defend Pelosi's unorthodox move as inadvertent genius. They'd claim it bought time for important developments in the case against Trump, pointing to Bolton coming forward and volunteering to testify, and the revelation of a tranche of newly unredacted emails outlining a "clear direction from POTUS" to freeze Ukraine's military assistance, published by the website Just Security.[4] But that was mostly a cover story designed to make Pelosi look good.

In fact, Democrats would do very little with the information that came to light during Pelosi's orchestrated pause. Even when a witness came forward bearing notes, text messages, and other receipts indicating multiple Trump lawyers and even a senior aide to the House Intelligence Committee's top-ranking Republican were involved in the president's Ukraine scheme.

Rudy Giuliani's operative Lev Parnas had fallen off the impeachment investigators' radar screen since the FBI nabbed him while trying to flee the country the night before he had been called to testify in the House. But in early January, the judge in his case had given him permission to share his texts, emails, and other records with Congress.[5] On Sunday, January 12, his lawyer drove the files from New York to Capitol Hill to hand-deliver them to impeachment investigators and implore Trump's impeachers to call his client as a trial witness.

Schiff's team knew immediately that Parnas had provided them a potential gold mine. But Pelosi wanted the impeachment articles delivered to the Senate that week, and Schiff was wary of asking for more time. The Soviet-born Parnas had struck lawmakers as a sketchy character even before he was facing federal conspiracy charges. What if nobody believed what he had to say? Schiff's team agreed not to call him, publicly releasing his documents instead for reporters to scrutinize.

That Wednesday, January 15, Parnas booked an hour-long interview on MSNBC's flagship prime-time show to make his case to the public—and in hopes of changing Schiff's team's mind.

"President Trump knew exactly what was going on. He was

aware of all my movements," he told host Rachel Maddow. "That's the secret that they were trying to keep: I was on the ground doing their work."

But Parnas's public gambit failed; impeachment investigators continued to ignore him. That evening, Pelosi had formally signed the articles of impeachment, dispatching the House managers to deliver them to the Senate in solemn procession. In a sign of the discord that was to follow, McConnell refused to accept them, informing the managers that they should come back the next day.

With just hours to go before trial arguments began on Tuesday, January 21, Chuck Schumer found himself quelling a private Democratic uprising of his own. The previous week, Senator Ted Cruz had started pitching senators on the idea of a one-for-one witness trade, whereby each side would get to call their own people in what he dubbed "witness reciprocity." And some of Schumer's members wanted him to accept such a deal.

Most Democrats didn't know it, but the notion was actually a failsafe that had been floated and blessed by McConnell and his "legal eagles." The idea of giving each side an equal number of witnesses had absolutely no foundation in courtroom jurisprudence. But it had the gloss of fairness—and the utility of a scare tactic. McConnell believed that the idea of calling someone like Hunter Biden alongside John Bolton or Mick Mulvaney might repulse not only Democrats, but more importantly, his own moderate Republicans. Many of them, after all, had served alongside the elder Biden in the Senate and would be loath to go down that rabbit hole—and thus be convinced to support his campaign against witnesses.

The small band of Senate Democrats gathered in Schumer's office the morning of the trial saw something else in the "witness reciprocity" notion: a chance to call the Republicans' bluff. A witness trade, they argued to the Democratic leader, might not be ideal, but it could possibly allow them to secure firsthand testimony of people like John Bolton, who could solidify the case against Trump. And if the price of getting Bolton was the Bidens—well, Biden was an experienced statesman who had logged thirty-six years in the Senate, they reasoned. If Trump's lawyers dared put him on the stand, he would make mincemeat out of their case, the assembled Democrats argued to Schumer that afternoon.

"What have we got to lose?" prodded Oregon senator Jeff Merkley, a liberal Democrat who showed up to the meeting with a draft amendment to work the arrangement into the trial rules.

Schumer's answer was an unequivocal no. To him, witness reciprocity reeked of naïveté. This was about winning—not striking some nonexistent middle ground that might or might not lead to a conviction of Trump. Plus, witness reciprocity would also be an inconvenient distraction from a different plan he had brewing for the trial that afternoon.

Like McConnell, Schumer's endgame was not what was about to transpire on the Senate floor, but how that would affect the 2020 election. He knew that every impeachment-related vote Republican senators took from that point on could be used against them during the campaign season. And he wanted to exploit that.

Schumer intended to force a series of votes that afternoon to subpoena new testimony and evidence from Bolton, Mulvaney, and practically the whole Trump government. He knew that the votes would fail. The motions flew in the face of the Clinton impeachment model that the GOP had embraced, which dictated that any witness-related questions be dealt with after opening arguments—not before. But that actually played to Schumer's advantage. Polls were showing that more than 70 percent of Americans wanted a trial to include witnesses[6]—and Schumer bet most voters wouldn't give a lick about arcane precedents regarding timing if they saw their senator voting no.

The GOP senator most squarely in Schumer's political crosshairs was Susan Collins, who was running neck and neck with a Democratic challenger in Maine. Collins, one of the most vulnerable senators on the ballot that cycle, had already stated publicly that she would likely vote for witnesses at the appropriate time in the trial. But Schumer didn't care about her intentions. Nor did he bother to have a conversation with her about them, or about striking a possible bipartisan deal to secure more testimony. All he saw was a chance to flip Collins's seat—and trapping her in an early "no" vote, he believed, would help him do it.

Schumer already had the Democratic machine fully locked and loaded on Collins. That day, the Democratic Senatorial Campaign Committee launched a new campaign targeted directly at her, digging up comments from 1999 in which she had insisted that witnesses were necessary during the Clinton trial. The campaign committee also launched a website, whatchangedsusan.com, to accuse her of hypocrisy, while a billboard truck parked outside the Capitol grounds levied the same charge, playing videos of Collins making the case for Clinton trial witnesses.[7] Meanwhile, the outside advocacy group Demand Justice, run by a former longtime Schumer aide, joined the fray by announcing it would spend hundreds of thousands of dollars on ads to sink Collins's 2020 reelection bid.[8] That was on top of the $700,000 in negative advertising that a political action committee aligned with Schumer had pledged earlier that month to spend campaigning against her in Maine.[9]

Schumer didn't feel at all badly about his overtly political tactics. But he also didn't lay out his political motivations to Merkley and the others when they made a last-minute plea for witness reciprocity in his office that Tuesday. Instead, he argued that the GOP's proposal was simply a bad-faith power grab that defied proper legal procedure: No court in the world would impose a one-for-one witness trade. Either people had testimony that was relevant to the case or they didn't. And Biden was not relevant to Trump's case, he argued.

Schumer had another motivation for being so forceful: He knew that Biden wanted no part of the trial, and he told the Democratic senators in his office that day that the campaign was concerned Biden might be dragged in against his will. The candidate, sensitive to attacks on his family, had made clear to his advisors that he did not want his son, a recovering drug addict, to be called as a witness. Biden aides also worried that forcing Hunter to testify would elevate allegations of wrongdoing Trump had been levying against their boss at a critical time during the campaign—or that Hunter would simply put his foot in his mouth and say something that would get his dad in trouble while being deposed. At the very least, highlighting Hunter Biden's questionable employment in Ukraine would create a major headache for Biden at a time when the former vice president was lagging far behind more progressive candidates in the Democratic primary matchup. They couldn't take the risk of allowing the trial to further handicap his chance at the nomination.

That afternoon, Biden—and Schumer—got what they wanted. The group of senators who had petitioned Schumer in his office reluctantly gave up their push for witness reciprocity. Merkley agreed to shelve his resolution and did not speak of it again.

Down the hall in McConnell's office, Collins—realizing she was under attack by Schumer—was once again angrily gesturing to a copy of the procedural rules for Clinton's impeachment. Over the weekend, in response to pressure from White House counsel Pat Cipollone,

McConnell had made two glaring changes to the proposed rules for Trump's trial, both of which wavered from the original Clinton precedent. The first dealt with evidence: Instead of accepting the House impeachment investigation's findings, McConnell wanted the Senate to vote on whether they should be included in the trial record. The second had to do with pace: Each side was going to get twenty-four hours to present its case. But while the Clinton trial had stretched those arguments over three days, McConnell wanted to squeeze them into just two, in the hopes that senators sick of being stuck in their seats for twelve hours a day would lose their patience and vote against witnesses, just to get the affair over with.

Collins demanded he change them back.

"You said you were going to follow the Clinton model," she said, forcefully pointing to the pages in her hand. "*This* is the Clinton model."

At a lunch with the full Senate GOP just before the trial was set to begin, McConnell was chagrined to find even more of his conference—including die-hard Trump supporters like Ron Johnson—agreed with Collins. Facing a mutiny at the eleventh hour, he had no choice but to relent. Grabbing a pen, his staff quickly edited the resolution to reflect Collins's demands. There was no time to run the resolution down to the printing office before the trial was set to begin.[10]

34

SCHIFF'S LECTURE HALL

JANUARY 21-25, 2020

Jerry Nadler sat quietly fuming, trying to contain his rage. He had been watching silently for eleven straight hours on Tuesday, January 21, as the House managers and Trump's lawyers presented their opening arguments. One by one, the other six managers had risen from the curved wooden table wedged between the elegant front rostrum and the senators seated at their tiered desks, walked to the center lectern, and defended the integrity of their case.

Nadler had been in a sour mood before the presentations had even begun. Officially, he was a co-leader of the impeachment team—but once again, the Judiciary chairman had found himself playing second fiddle to Nancy Pelosi's golden boy, Adam Schiff, who everyone knew was the one running the show. Schiff—who had long been considered the party's best orator—had allotted himself more than 40 percent of all their argument time. That was nearly three times as much as any other member and, to Nadler's frustration, over five times more than his.[1]

But as he listened to the presentations, the relative lack of spotlight wasn't what made Nadler's blood boil. It was the blatant lies being spewed by Trump's defense team—and the infuriating lack of attention that Senate Republicans were paying to the proceedings.

Several seats down from Nadler, Schiff had been proudly watching as all the other managers dutifully delivered carefully scripted presentations that he and the Speaker had pre-approved. Schiff had run his team through practice round after practice round and instructed his staff to work closely with each presenter to ensure their words landed just right. But Nadler could see their arguments were missing their target. Several Senate Republicans were fidgeting in their seats, checking their watches, or reading books to pass the time, he noted with disgust. Some, including Rand Paul of Kentucky, were even doodling pictures in their notebooks.

The GOP's flippant attitude was like a slap in the face to Nadler, who in that moment was shouldering a considerable personal sacrifice to be present for the trial. His wife, Joyce, was still in a recovery ward at NYU Langone hospital, where she had undergone emergency surgery to remove a tumor from her pancreas. Nadler had celebrated Hanukkah from her hospital room and prepared for the trial from her bedside. In his mind, if he could leave his wife's side for Trump's trial, Senate Republicans could sure as hell pay a little more attention.

But from the very start, Trump's team had been inviting the GOP side of the aisle to view the House's case with derision. White House counsel Pat Cipollone had begun by delivering a less than three-minute statement about how Trump had done "nothing wrong." Then he had the nerve to argue that Nadler had denied the president due process rights in his committee—a sore subject given how fiercely Nadler had advocated for Trump to have his day during the House's investigation.

"Adam, we have to do something," he hissed to Schiff, leaning over at the managers' table to whisper. "These are blatant lies."

When Schiff stayed the course, Nadler decided he would have to take matters into his own hands. Just after midnight, when he finally got his turn to approach the podium, the Judiciary chairman and longtime Trump nemesis let it rip.

"I am struck by what we have heard from the President's counsel so far tonight. They complain about process, but they do not seriously contest any of the allegations against the President," he began. "They insist that the President has done nothing wrong, but . . . they will not permit the American people to hear from the witnesses, and they lie and lie and lie and lie."

Then Nadler took aim at the senators themselves.

"I am sad to say, I see a lot of senators voting for a cover-up," he said, looking at Republican senators as he chided them for their position on witnesses. "An absolutely indefensible vote, obviously a treacherous vote, a vote against an honest consideration of the evidence against the President, a vote against an honest trial, a vote against the United States."

In his seat, Schiff froze, as one hundred drowsy senators snapped to attention. It was an interruption he didn't need. After three years of tangling with Trump, the Intelligence Committee chief knew that the GOP would pounce on the tiniest slip-up or miscalculation as proof that Democrats were on a witch hunt to overturn the 2016 election. With the question of witnesses on the line, and votes like Lisa Murkowski's and Susan Collins's still in play, Schiff knew he didn't have any room for error: A perfect presentation was his only option. And Nadler's outburst had ripped a hole in Schiff's carefully woven tapestry.

At their adjacent desks near the center on the floor, Murkowski turned to Collins with a look of shock, and the two bent their heads together to whisper. Looking up, Collins grabbed a pencil and a scrap of paper to dash off a note to Supreme Court Chief Justice John Roberts, who was sitting on the rostrum at the front of the chamber, presiding over the trial. Nadler, she wrote, had likely just violated the Senate rules, which prohibit directly impugning another lawmaker.[2]

Cipollone sought to exploit Nadler's screwup. Approaching the microphone for a rebuttal, he told GOP senators that Nadler just "accused you of a cover-up" and demanded the House Judiciary chairman apologize.

At the front of the room, Roberts had been behaving like a wallflower for most of the trial, intentionally taking as unobtrusive a role as possible given the politically hyper-charged nature of the proceedings. The most senior justice on the highest court in the land had long been sensitive to public perceptions of the judiciary's credibility, and he hated the idea of being dragged into anything political. But when it came to a presidential impeachment trial, he had no choice: The Constitution stipulated he had to preside. And at that moment, it fell to him to restore decorum on the floor before the tit for tat spiraled out of control.

"Those addressing the Senate should remember where they are," Roberts said in response to Collins's note, directing his scolding at both Nadler and Cipollone for "using language that is not conducive to civil discourse."

Roberts's warning stayed the fight temporarily. But Nadler's unforced error had already repelled the very moderate members to whom the Democrats were trying to direct their appeals. "As one who is listening attentively and working hard to get to a fair process, I was offended," Murkowski told reporters later that night.[3] Collins was equally irate.

When the trial finally broke for the night at almost two a.m., multiple Democratic senators requested that the House managers change tone going forward. Schumer sent the message to Pelosi, who later shared it with her managers before the trial resumed.

A little softer around the edges, she told the impeachment managers in a private meeting before the trial resumed. Though she did not specifically mention Nadler, her meaning came through loud and clear.

"Get out!" bellowed Jay Sekulow, Trump's longtime personal attorney and one of his two lead impeachment defenders, as he rushed into the team's makeshift green room off the Senate floor mid-trial. "The client is on the line!"

The president was calling from Air Force One on his way home from the annual World Economic Forum in Davos, Switzerland, where he had bragged about the U.S. stock market, ridiculed climate change activists, and assured every foreign dignitary within earshot that the impeachment charges were "a total hoax."[4] But on Wednesday, January 22, the president was also learning that the consensus in Washington was that his lawyers had botched their opening presentations in the Senate trial. And he was pissed.

Trump had been stewing over the trial since Christmas, struggling to focus despite his staff's greatest efforts to divert his attention. During one January event touting White House support for prayer in schools, Trump fumed to the assembled young children about impeachment sucking up the headlines. He grilled campaign aides for updates about how he was doing in the polls.[5] And despite Republicans vowing to stick with him at trial—guaranteeing his acquittal and likely giving him a campaign bounce—Trump continued to complain that he was a victim of Democratic vitriol and bias.

"Why are they doing this to me?" he had asked one confidant at Mar-a-Lago the previous weekend.

The prior week, Trump had added some heavy hitters to his defense squad in hopes of creating shock and awe around his legal team. He had tapped Ken Starr, the former independent counsel who had recommended Clinton's impeachment, and Alan Dershowitz, the prominent former Harvard professor and ex–O. J. Simpson trial lawyer who had become a regular at Mar-a-Lago. Both had beguiled Trump with their ardent defenses of him on Fox News. But neither had yet made appearances in the trial, frustrating Trump, who was obsessed with putting on a good show.

The unflattering comparisons between the impeachment managers and Trump's legal team had gotten under the president's skin. Senate Republicans had been calling him from across the pond to complain that his team was lousy. According to the news reports and the op-ed writers, "Pencil Neck" Adam Schiff's impeachment managers—save for Nadler's hiccup—had come out of the gate with a bang. The opening statements of Trump's lawyers, on the other hand, were being summarized in a single word: Lies.

Trump didn't mind the lying so much as the losing. So from tens of thousands of feet in the air, he phoned the anteroom outside the Senate chamber, where he knew at least some of his legal team would be waiting. He demanded to speak to Sekulow, who was quickly summoned off the Senate floor for the call.

Over the course of the next few minutes, Sekulow listened as Trump demanded he do something drastic. Sekulow tried to explain that he couldn't. The House Democratic managers had three full days under the Senate rules to make their case without interruption, he told Trump. Under the rules, Sekulow couldn't rebut a single word until it was the defense's turn to present.

But the president didn't care about the rules. He wanted Sekulow to storm into the chamber and hijack the proceedings by rising to object—or make some sort of commotion—just like the House GOP had done in the SCIF that fall. When Sekulow explained again that his hands were tied, Trump insisted he find a camera right away and defend him on TV.

The president's phone call lit a fire under Sekulow, and Trump's defense team sent out a command to all Trump allies: Get on TV now. During the next break in the trial, they blitzed the airwaves, hoping Trump would take note of their full-court press to refute the impeachment charges. Sekulow made a beeline for TV cameras just off the Senate floor. Lindsey Graham, Jim Jordan, Mark Meadows, and a host of Trump's House defenders made their way to the cameras in the basement.

"There's a lot of things I'd like to rebut, and we will rebut," Sekulow announced, trying to muster a bored bravado as he argued that Schiff and his team had presented no evidence of the quid pro quos they accused Trump of orchestrating. "That's because they didn't exist."

When a reporter asked him to describe the president's mood, he noticeably sidestepped.

"I don't do that, I don't discuss conversations with the president," Sekulow said, laughing nervously and coughing, as he claimed to have "no idea" where Trump even was.

The truth was Trump's tirade wasn't the only thing that had his legal team on edge. They knew that Schiff had outperformed them—even Senate Republicans were telling them so. And since the facts of the case were also against them, they had only one thing to fall back on: attacking Schiff himself.

Sekulow and Cipollone knew that pillorying Schiff would not be enough of a defense to carry them through the whole trial. Republican senators wanted to see them argue a real defense of

Trump, complete with constitutional and institutional arguments aimed at moderates. But their irascible client didn't care if they argued about facts; he just wanted them to argue—the louder the better.

Later that day, Trump would try to soothe his wounded ego by retweeting others' defenses of his actions in Ukraine, resulting in his most prolific day on Twitter since the start of his presidency.[6] The 142 tweets seemed an unsubtle hint to his lawyers that the internet was doing a better job of defending him than they were.

Schiff was losing his audience—but he barely seemed to notice. When Trump became president, he had gone almost overnight from being a respected committee ranking member toiling in relative congressional obscurity to a breakout superstar. When he spoke, Democrats practically swooned. When the GOP attacked him, Democrats sang his praises louder. Loved or loathed, for three years, he had never failed to command the attention of an audience.

But by Friday—the last day of the managers' opening arguments— the Senate Republicans were fidgeting like a group of high school students itching to get out of a history lecture. They yawned at his slides. And they stared blankly at his lofty appeals to their sense of constitutional duty.

Schiff had been the only House manager with previous experience trying an impeachment before the Senate. In 2010, he had led the trial team that successfully ousted Judge G. Thomas Porteous for taking kickbacks from lawyers arguing in his courtroom.[7] As such, Schiff thought he knew best how to try the case. He ran a tight ship, insisting his team tell a gripping story, replete with slides, plenty of video evidence, and constant reminders that the senators had a duty to uphold their oath, even when political sense told them not to.

"I want this to be like a Ken Burns–style documentary," he had told his staff as they began their preparations for the trial.

After Nadler's hiccup on the first day, Schiff had thought he had righted the ship. For three days, his team had argued well into the night that Trump was the living image of the "unprincipled" and "despotic" president for whom Congress's impeachment clause had been designed. He appealed to senators' memories of the Cold War to punctuate how Trump had undermined a democratic ally in the struggle against Russia—all for the cheap prize of a Biden investigation. And he argued that if the Senate gave Trump a pass for his stonewalling, it would eviscerate congressional oversight and "permanently alter the balance of power among the branches of government."

"If this conduct is not impeachable, then nothing is," Schiff said.

Democratic senators were downright giddy about his performance. As Schiff held forth, Schumer gazed at him fondly from the front row, smiling like a proud papa. Even some Republican senators said they found Schiff to be surprisingly compelling—at least initially. Graham, who spent the first day of the managers' opening arguments railing that they were "on a crusade to destroy" Trump, nonetheless approached Schiff to shake his hand as he left the building that night.

"Good job," Graham told Schiff, lawyer to lawyer, as they stood by the elevators. "Very well-spoken."[8]

But it didn't take long for the sheen to fade for GOP senators—if it had been there at all. After two marathon days, the managers' speeches were getting repetitive—and starting to sound like lectures. Republican senators started to declare themselves "bored" and liken Schiff's voice to "nails on a chalkboard" as they made fun of him in their private daily lunches. Even Graham, despite his early praise for Schiff, was yawning through his arguments.

"It became mind-numbing after a while," Graham told reporters that week. "I got the general point you're trying to make the fourth time you told me."

Schiff, however, either didn't get the memo or consciously ignored it. In his zeal to beat down the GOP's counterarguments—and in his self-assurance that he was right—he began to lecture senators even more.

"He is guilty. You know, is there really any doubt about this?" he asked at one point. "If you find him guilty, you must find that he should be removed, because right matters . . . and the truth matters. Otherwise, we are lost."

In the managers' prep room that final night of their three-day presentation, Democrats were all but popping champagne bottles in appreciation of Schiff's appeal to conscience. "All you needed to do was drop the mic at the end!" exclaimed Val Demings, one of the impeachment managers.[9] Judiciary attorney Norm Eisen started crying, he was so moved. A moment later Senator Tom Carper of Delaware walked into the room and gave Schiff a hug, and then turned around and departed.

But where Democrats saw brilliance, most Republicans saw arrogance. Where Democrats praised Schiff for his moral conviction, most Republicans saw a self-righteous snob. And where Democrats revered Schiff's expertise and intelligence, most Republicans saw a cunning snake, whose prime motivation was denying Trump the legitimacy of his presidency.

And Republicans weren't the only ones turning a deaf ear to the House Intelligence chairman. Viewership was tanking, dropping from a high of 11 million on the first day of the trial to only 6.7 million as Democrats wrapped up their arguments—less than half the

peak audience for the House's impeachment hearings.[10] Impeachment was falling flat in the Senate—even flatter than it had in the
House.

During his final speech, Schiff laid the guilt on thick. He cited
Thomas Paine, a writer whose works had helped inspire the American Revolution—slightly misquoting his seminal work "The American Crisis" as he argued that prioritizing the Constitution over the
siren song of politics was hard, but necessary. He invoked the GOP's
Republican forebears who broke with Nixon to back his impeachment, holding up former Illinois Republican congressman Thomas
Railsback, who had died that week, as an example of how an ethical
Republican would act.

But as he delivered his big finish, Schiff stuck his foot in his
mouth with even greater flourish than Nadler.

"CBS News reported last night that a Trump confidant said that
GOP Senators were warned: 'Vote against the President, and your
head will be on a pike,'" Schiff said.

Gasps and murmurs echoed through the room. "Not true!"
shouted an angry Collins, who rarely lost her composure.

Schiff scanned the room in an unfamiliar panic, his eyes widening as he scrambled to respond to the sounds of repudiation.

"I don't know if that is true: 'Vote against the President, and your
head will be on a pike,'" Schiff said, seemingly unable to stop utter-
ing the offending phrase. "I hope it is not true . . . that whoever that
was would use the terminology of a penalty that was imposed by a
monarch—'head on a pike.'"

"That's where he lost me," Murkowski told reporters as she left
the Senate chamber that night.[11]

Schiff had succeeded in waking up the Senate Republicans. But
his screwup overshadowed his closing argument and the dire, pre-
scient warning it contained.

"Whether you like the president, or dislike the president, is immaterial . . . What matters is whether he is a danger to the country," Schiff said that night, recapping Trump's efforts to tip the scales of the election and warning of consequences if they let it slide. "Because he will do it again. And none of us can have confidence, based on his record, that he will not do it again because he is telling us every day that he will."

35

BOLTON'S BOMBSHELL

JANUARY 26-27, 2020

Adam Schiff and the House Democratic managers were huddled in Pelosi's suite early in the evening of Sunday, January 26, when the *New York Times* breaking news alert flashed up on their phones, instantly scrambling their quiet practice session. The newspaper had unearthed eye-popping details contained in former national security advisor John Bolton's forthcoming book. Bolton had written that Trump told him in August that he was leveraging Ukraine aid for a probe on Biden, the story said.

"Trump Tied Ukraine Aid to Inquiries He Sought, Bolton Book Says," the headline read.[1] Stunned, everyone in the room dropped their notebooks and pencils and pulled up their phones to read the story.

"Holy shit!" more than one person said aloud as the stunned lawmakers scrolled through the article.

Weeks before, and unbeknownst to much of Washington, Bolton and his attorney Charles Cooper had submitted a transcript of his tell-all about serving in Trump's White House to lawyers at the National Security Council to scrub for any classified information. Bolton was confident there was nothing sensitive in his book. To his chagrin, however, the review had still languished—a delay he viewed as an attempt to smother the work entirely and hide it from public view. The White House would later try to sue to stop the book's publication entirely.

Ironically, when he started to write the book, Bolton hadn't even envisioned a chapter about the Ukraine saga. To him, Trump had done far worse things in his presidency—and some of his actions toward other foreign leaders were arguably better fodder for impeachment. But given the heightened interest in Ukraine, due to the House's probe, Bolton had divulged what he knew—and despite the White House's best efforts to muzzle him, his recounting of the Ukraine saga was now rocketing across Washington.

That Sunday, Adam Schiff, ever the meticulous planner, had summoned the managers to Capitol Hill to prepare for the next phase of the trial: the senators' question-and-answer session, which he predicted could become unruly. Strewn across the tables were massive binders in which Schiff and the impeachment staff had sketched out every possible question they could imagine fielding from senators, from the facts of the case to the legal arguments supporting impeachment. Jason Crow, the military veteran, would take the queries about the significance of Ukraine's military aid. Nadler, ironically, would defend the House process he had fought against privately for months. There was to be no freelancing. If the staff told a manager to answer with what was on tab 33, they were to turn straight to tab 33 and make that point.

Squirreled away in Pelosi's offices, the team had barely taken note of major national news that morning: legendary Los Angeles Lakers basketball player Kobe Bryant, forty-one, died suddenly in a helicopter crash along with his thirteen-year-old daughter. But the Bolton news snapped them out of their studious reverie.

The story was everything Schiff had been searching for: an ex-Trump official with firsthand knowledge of Trump's intentions. Gone were the private concerns that had haunted his impeachment investigators that fall, when they fretted about whether Bolton was "trustworthy" and likened him to Batman nemesis the Joker. Bolton's testimony, Schiff and the room all agreed, would eviscerate Trump's defense that the quid pro quo never occurred—and be a nail in the coffin for the GOP's argument that the impeachment charges were based on mere "hearsay."

Just as he had done after first reading Trump's July 25 call with Ukrainian president Zelensky, Schiff jumped up and pulled out his iPad. With staff huddling over his shoulder, he typed out a statement to blast out to the media, arguing that the revelations only further underscored the need to hear from Bolton.

"There can be no doubt now that Mr. Bolton directly contradicts the heart of the President's defense and therefore must be called as a witness at the impeachment trial of President Trump," he wrote, saying nothing of his own fateful decision to forgo fighting for Bolton's testimony in the House months before. "Senators should insist that Mr. Bolton be called as a witness, and provide his notes and other relevant documents. The Senate trial must seek the full truth and Mr. Bolton has vital information to provide."

Excitement swept over the room. They would surely win the witness fight now, the assembled Democrats buzzed. The Senate would have no choice but to call Bolton to testify. Staff began reworking their scripts for the question-and-answer session. They'd have to play up the need to hear from Bolton even more. Others began speculating—and questioning: *Did Trump's lawyers know about this? Had they lied on the Senate floor by saying no one had firsthand*

*information about a quid pro quo when they knew about Bolton's book
allegations? And if so, shouldn't there be consequences?*

Across town, Mitch McConnell was furious and asking the same
question: *What did Trump and Pat Cipollone know and when did they
know it?* The leader had been blindsided by the Bolton story and
immediately called the White House counsel to demand answers.
*Why was he not given a heads-up about this? How could he not have been
told that this bombshell was sitting in some office in the executive building, waiting to go off?* Someone had to have known about it—and
McConnell was determined to find out who.

Much to his dismay, Trump's defense team was scattered about
Washington that night, enjoying a night off instead of preparing for
the next day's arguments. It was a pure dereliction of duty in Mc-
Connell's eyes, and yet just the latest proof that Trump's lawyers
had no idea what they were doing.

To McConnell, the entire quagmire was entirely predictable. He
had always seen Bolton as the biggest threat to Trump's acquittal.
It was why, after Bolton offered to testify in early January, he had
repeatedly prodded the White House for more information and a
plan. McConnell had wanted to know exactly what Bolton knew of
the Ukraine scandal—and what the White House would do if he
stepped into the spotlight. Each time, the White House had been
dismissive, scoffing at the notion that the former national security
advisor would have anything damaging to say.

"It's under control," White House counsel would tell the GOP
leader. "Don't worry."

When the *New York Times* story emerged, proving McConnell's
fears were well founded, the GOP leader was livid. Bolton's claims
wouldn't change his vote. But he knew they would drastically increase

the pressure on his GOP rank and file to vote in favor of calling witnesses. In that sense, Trump hadn't only screwed himself—he might have just screwed McConnell's majority by giving Republicans a reason to buck his carefully scripted process.

Fear of Bolton's testimony was exactly why McConnell had implored Cipollone and Trump's team for months to stop denying the quid pro quo and argue simply that Trump's actions weren't impeachable. Yet Trump's team had continued to ignore his advice. The prior day, in their opening arguments before the Senate, they had had the audacity to argue that "not a single witness testified that the president himself said that there was any connection between any investigations and security assistance, a presidential meeting, or anything else." McConnell had sat there watching, his arms folded in his lap, his back stiff, and said nothing. Trump's lawyers were practically daring someone to come forward and contradict them. Twenty-four hours later, the Bolton bombshell was proof that Trump's line of defense was bogus.

Within a few hours of the story breaking, McConnell learned that at least one of Trump's attorneys had been briefed on the contents of Bolton's draft memoir. He suspected that Cipollone in particular, who as the president's counsel had the right to attend National Security Council meetings, might know more than he was letting on. But there was no use dwelling on the past. He had to patch the Bolton-sized hole in the GOP's ship before it sank.

That night, McConnell's senators were in full-fledged panic mode. Conservative and moderate Republicans alike were calling him. *What the fuck is this?* they wanted to know. *Did you know about this? How do we not call Bolton now?* Even Lindsey Graham, the ardent Trump defender and interlocutor, was aghast.

"The game has changed here," Graham told McConnell on the phone that night. "You have to find some outlet for this. Some of the members are going to be rattled."

To each member who phoned, McConnell offered the same advice. "Keep your powder dry," he told them. "Don't lose your cool." The report, he argued, was not necessarily dispositive. He also asked them to refrain from weighing in publicly about Bolton until the GOP senators could discuss the article as a group.

"Let things play out," he advised. "If you go out and take a position on it right now, then you're stuck . . . Don't let the press talk you into taking a position."

But McConnell's advice wasn't calming his troops. His counsel Andrew Ferguson heard from swing vote Lamar Alexander's staff that their boss was suddenly unhappy and "in a bad spot" on the witness vote. *What was the best argument for not calling Bolton?* they wanted to know.

McConnell's entire office understood that if they lost Alexander, a close ally of the GOP leader, they were sure to lose all the moderates on the witness vote—and potentially then some. So the leader's team flew into hyperdrive to keep him in line. Ferguson stayed up into the wee hours of the morning writing a legal memo for Alexander, outlining the same legal arguments that he and the leader had been trying to get the White House to make since October. Bolton is irrelevant, Ferguson scribbled. Even if one stipulates that everything that the Democrats have alleged is true—and even if Bolton testifies to those events—those actions are not impeachable, he argued. They might have constituted heavy-handed diplomacy, but they were hardly constitutional crimes. Thus, Ferguson concluded, Bolton's testimony was unnecessary. The memo also hit on a point Alexander had raised in the media in recent weeks: The nation was only ten months out from a presidential election. It was better to acquit now and let the voters decide Trump's fate.

Ferguson also cracked down on the White House. That night, around one in the morning, he called Trump's defense team to ask them for the umpteenth time to pivot from solely denying any quid pro quo to incorporating arguments about why calling witnesses was unnecessary. Especially now that the Bolton news was out, it was imperative they make the argument skittish senators needed to hear, he argued.

"Our goal here is to win," Ferguson said.

Cipollone's team tried to negotiate. Alan Dershowitz, they said, could argue the next day that in order to be impeached, a president needed to have committed a statutory crime, and that because Trump had not committed a statutory crime, his Ukraine conduct was not impeachable. Dershowitz had actually argued the exact opposite during Clinton's impeachment—but Cipollone's team hoped it would be an olive branch.

Yet Ferguson was still dissatisfied. He didn't buy that argument, and neither would most experts on constitutional law or the media, he warned.

"Republican senators are going to react badly to his argument if their staff and the press are telling them, 'Hey, Dershowitz is the only person on the planet who believes that this is correct,'" Ferguson retorted, again repeating what he wanted Trump's defenders to say. "You can't put all of your stock in this one statutory crime argument because politically it's going to come across as a dud."

Before they hung up, Trump's team finally allowed that they would make the arguments that McConnell had been pushing for months. They were about to find out if it would be too little, too late.

As Senate Republicans reconvened for the trial on Monday, the sheer breadth of the damage the Bolton story had caused began to dawn on McConnell and his team. A group of Trump loyalists in the Senate had been scheduled to give a press conference that morning defending Trump. All of them—from Graham to die-hard conservatives Josh Hawley and Mike Lee—suddenly canceled. The White House's top impeachment communications specialist, Tony Sayegh, raced over to Capitol Hill to beg someone—anyone—to step into the void. "Trump needs you now more than ever," he told senators as he pleaded for their help. Only two of the fifty-three Senate Republicans agreed to go talk to reporters.

McConnell, meanwhile, had summoned his leadership team to an emergency meeting around eleven a.m. to stanch the bleeding. Graham, deeply anxious, resurrected the idea of a witness trade—Bolton for Hunter Biden—and raised the notion of demanding the White House allow senators to read Bolton's unpublished manuscript in a classified setting. McConnell's staff looked at him with alarm. If Graham was suddenly taking seriously the idea of witness reciprocity—something that was never intended to be more than a scare tactic to keep Republicans in line—they were in trouble.

As Republicans convened for a private lunch that afternoon, only one GOP senator found himself in a markedly better mood than before. Senator Mitt Romney had phoned his senior staff the night before to discuss Bolton's revelations and how they might impact the witness vote. This decision to him now was a no-brainer. Romney was a committed "yes" on witnesses. And in the face of this news, others would have to support witnesses too—or so Romney thought.

Inside the GOP's lunchroom, the invigorated Utah senator made an emotional appeal to his colleagues to call witnesses, saying they had a duty to hear all the relevant evidence—otherwise they would look like they were trying to hide something. If Trump sought to block Bolton's testimony and drew the Senate into a court battle over his subpoena, Romney insisted they could just appeal to the Supreme Court for a quick ruling. After all, he told his colleagues, the high court had done something similar in 2000, when the results of the Bush-versus-Gore presidential election were thrown into question during the Florida recount.

McConnell observed Romney, unmoved. He had never doubted that Romney was going to vote for witnesses. But he had not anticipated that the unapologetically earnest Utahn would try to lead a rebellion. Suddenly, other senators were sounding sympathetic to Romney's argument—senators whom McConnell had considered firmly in the "no" column on witnesses. Bill Cassidy, the normally quiet doctor from conservative Louisiana, seemed legitimately disturbed by the prospect of ignoring Bolton. Pat Toomey, a pragmatist from Pennsylvania, said he liked Graham's idea about a one-for-one witness trade. Rob Portman, the Ukraine advocate who had privately lambasted witnesses as a "trap" a month earlier, was suddenly skittish. So too was Senate Intelligence Committee chairman Richard Burr. Even eighty-three-year-old conservative senator Pat Roberts, who had had his nose buried in a copy of *Gone with the Wind* when the news broke Sunday, said he couldn't understand the logic of not calling Bolton.

Susan Collins warned her colleagues that Bolton's book would eventually be published no matter what anyone did—and the GOP would be accused of covering up whatever it said if they didn't call him to testify. But mercifully for McConnell, one key GOP swing vote said nothing: Alexander, who had digested Ferguson's legal memo that morning, was content to simply listen. McConnell was grateful for his silence.

Standing before the room, the leader realized for the first time that he might actually lose the witness vote. Still, he urged calm. You'll get to vote on witnesses eventually, he told the members, but in the meantime, let the defense finish their presentations.

"Take a deep breath," McConnell continued, trying to project composure. "Let this play out."

But as he exited the room with his aides, some thought he looked even paler than usual.

As GOP senators argued over lunch, Trump's allies were already springing into action. Senator Kelly Loeffler, who had just been appointed to fill a vacant Georgia seat and was looking to score points with Trump, tweeted an attack on Romney, accusing him of wanting to "appease the left by calling witnesses who will slander" the president. On TV, Trump acolytes lit up the airwaves attacking Bolton.

Meanwhile, McConnell dispatched Ferguson to reiterate to Trump's defense team that they needed them to argue Bolton's revelations were irrelevant, once and for all. "You will lose the GOP on Bolton if you don't make this case," Ferguson told them.

That day, the defense team responded to the Senate leader's wishes. As they wound down their opening arguments, Dershowitz stood and made the point Republicans had longed to hear.

"Quid pro quo alone is not a basis for abuse of power. It is part of the way foreign policy has been operated by Presidents since the beginning of time," Dershowitz said. "Nothing in the Bolton revelations, even if true, would rise to the level of an abuse of power."

Sitting in the back, Romney was nonplussed. During a break in the presentation, he had retreated to the cloakroom to try to sell his colleagues on subpoenaing Bolton for testimony. As jurors, they had an obligation to hear the former national security advisor's testimony, Romney argued. But Senator Kevin Cramer, a North Dakota Republican, was having none of it.

"We are jurors, but we still serve our constituents," Cramer retorted. "We also have an obligation not to divorce politics from our decision. I need to represent my state interests in all my votes."

"That's a partisan way of looking at it," Romney shot back as other senators gathered around to hear the impromptu debate. Most sided with Cramer.

By the end of the day, Dershowitz's performance had given a life raft to Republicans looking for an excuse to give Trump a pass. But McConnell knew a sizable faction of his rank and file were not there yet. It was time to take matters into his own hands.

36

MITCH'S PRESSURE COOKER

JANUARY 28, 2020

"We can be smart . . . or we can be stupid," McConnell said gravely, standing before a room full of his GOP senators before the trial was set to resume. "The choice will be up to us."

It was Tuesday, January 28, and with the vote on whether to call witnesses just three days away, McConnell had no time to waste getting his ranks in line. The prior day, Trump had taken to his favorite social media platform to decry Bolton as a liar who was just trying to sell books. In the Senate, however, it was the president whom no one believed.

McConnell had always known that ultimately it would likely fall to him to steer his conference away from witnesses. The Trump attorneys had proved to be of little help—they were too worried about blowback from the president to make legal arguments that might have gotten the job done. Plus, the GOP leader knew better than anyone how to reach each of his rank and file to achieve his desired outcome.

In the days before the trial, McConnell and his team had discussed what might happen if pressure to call ex-Trump officials as witnesses reached a boiling point—and more importantly, what their best argument would be to ensure the chamber didn't succumb. McConnell's counsel Andrew Ferguson had proposed that the most compelling case for resisting would be highlighting how long interbranch court fights usually lasted. Trump, he warned, would almost certainly try to invoke executive privilege to block his deputies from testifying, kicking the matter to court and leaving the Senate in a never-ending impeachment trial. Ferguson said he didn't know if Trump would actually win those court battles. But that didn't matter. It would still take time to adjudicate such disputes in court, he explained, keeping the Senate from doing anything as they awaited rulings.

After Cipollone's team privately confirmed to McConnell's in early January that the White House would indeed seek an injunction to stop Bolton from complying with a Senate subpoena, McConnell and his staff had begun to make that very argument to the GOP conference—just in case. They circulated a legal memo laying out the dangers of a protracted legal battle and spoke about it in private meetings. McConnell and his "legal eagles" also began to frame the question of witnesses around protecting the Senate as an institution.

Some of the moderates still pushed back. In one January Senate lunch, Susan Collins stood up and told the room that she had been doing her own research into the matter and had heard from a nonpartisan government analyst at the Congressional Research Service that the courts might actually move quickly mid-trial; they might even get a ruling in a few weeks, she told them, leading some senators to begin questioning whether they ought to fight in the courts for Bolton after all.

McConnell's staff, however, disagreed and flew into containment mode. In a series of calls with Collins's and other GOP senators' offices, Ferguson argued that the only time the high court had litigated that fast during impeachment proceedings was for Nixon. There was simply no guarantee it would do the same now. And with Chief Justice John Roberts presiding over the trial, he might have to recuse himself from a final decision, complicating the situation even more, he added.

To help put the counterarguments to bed, McConnell had invited George W. Bush's onetime attorney general Michael Mukasey to reinforce his message to his members. Over lunch during the first week of the trial, Mukasey had told Senate Republicans just what McConnell had hoped he would: that it would take months to resolve any mid-trial subpoena fight in court. McConnell had also sought to use the Democrats' own words to bolster his point. When impeachment manager Zoe Lofgren defended the House's decision to eschew witness court battles because they would take months or years to resolve, he made sure to highlight her speech to his rank and file.

"Make sure that Mitt, Lisa, Susan, and Lamar see it," he whispered on the floor to Ferguson, who had staff print fifty-three copies of the presentation, one for each Senate Republican.

The Bolton news had thrown a monkey wrench into McConnell's efforts. But by Tuesday, he was ready to whip the last holdouts into line. As senators dined on halibut and chicken, he warned them that the longer the Senate bickered about witnesses, the longer all non-impeachment business would grind to a halt. That, McConnell said flatly, would be disastrous for the institution.

The leader then called on a group of vulnerable 2020 incumbents to speak. One by one, they appealed to their colleagues to end the trial without witnesses—for the sake of their reelections, if nothing else. *Allowing the trial to linger plays right into Schumer's hand and is going to crush me politically,* Senator Cory Gardner of Colorado, who was staring down a potential upset, pleaded. Martha McSally of Arizona and Joni Ernst of Iowa, in similarly tight spots, echoed him. Only Collins voiced an alternate view. But McConnell already considered Collins a special case. *Do what you need to do to win Maine,* Collins's colleagues told her. The rest of the party would have her back—but everyone else had an obligation to fall in line.

The successive, impassioned pleas of frontline senators were effective. No senator wanted to be in the minority, and each personally understood the pressures of campaigning. But McConnell wasn't done. It was time to bring the trial to an end.

Around three p.m., just after the defense rested its abbreviated case, McConnell summoned his members to a little-used room off the side of the grand Capitol Rotunda. He employed the small, stuffy chamber only in extreme circumstances, and the assembled senators knew they were in for a stern talking-to as they squeezed into the couches and chairs.

When full, the ornate room had the feeling of a pressure cooker. A large, gilded mirror atop a white marble fireplace dominated the room. A bronze bust of the late senator Strom Thurmond, the pro-segregationist southerner for whom the room had been named in 1991, rested in the corner. On the walls, ornate canvas landscapes and decorative wall murals depicted scenes of iconic American pursuits and values: Justice. Prudence. Fortitude. Peace. War. Intellect. And Courage.

On that day, there was little of that final quality on display.

In preparation for McConnell's final pitch, his staff had carted in a projector loaded with PowerPoint slides. The displays showcased the comparative lengths of past impeachment proceedings in a bid to emphasize that the House's investigation was rushed—and that without restrictions, the Senate trial could wear on for weeks. But when McConnell walked in, he ignored the projector completely. Instead, the leader who rarely betrayed emotion began making an impassioned appeal, speaking off-the-cuff as he sought to rally his troops for what he believed was a make-or-break moment for Trump's presidency—and his majority.

"This is not about this president. It's not about anything he's been accused of doing," McConnell said, indignantly. "For the other side, this is about November 3, 2020. It has always been about November 3, 2020. It's about flipping the Senate."

"The longer you let this linger," he added, glancing around the room to his members, "the more likely it is that that will happen."

McConnell tore into the Democrats, accusing them of short-changing the House's impeachment process and looking to senators to do their dirty work. *They should have called Bolton in the House if they wanted him. But they didn't,* he said. *Schumer doesn't care about witnesses. He doesn't care about Ukraine. He cares about one thing: becoming Majority Leader.*

"So we can be smart and we can call him on his own game, and refuse to play it and say we are ending this now and we are getting back to the people's business," McConnell said. "Or we can be stupid, and we can let him drag the Senate into the mire for six months and then use this to try to win the election."

It was the stern voice of fatherly wisdom that most of the panicking senators had needed to set them straight. The leader rarely hammered his rank and file. Whenever possible, he liked to give vulnerable senators the freedom to vote in a way that suited their parochial interests. But this day was an exception. For the second time that day, McConnell was making his expectations of his members crystal clear.

Holding up a whip card that had each senator's position on the vote, McConnell informed the room that as of that moment, they weren't yet in a position to shut Schumer's witness gambit down.

"We don't have the votes right now to end this thing," he said, his eyes wandering over each member. "We're not there yet. But we're going to get there."

McConnell's final pitch featured no discussion of whether Trump had used his office to try to undercut a political enemy. There was no deliberation of the facts or evidence that had been presented, or of their congressional duty to check a president most of them knew had done something wrong. In the end, the GOP leader's closing argument was exclusively about maintaining power.

After he finished speaking, McConnell once again deferred to the vulnerable senators up for reelection in 2020 to stand and speak. And once again, each implored their colleagues to end the trial for the sake of their reelections.

As senators made their presentations, Senate Majority Whip John Thune worked the room, rechecking the whip count. Thune informed McConnell and his staff that their argument had worked. They were back in the same place they were before the Bolton news: forty-nine against witnesses, including several who had seemed shaky just the day before. Even better, swing vote Lamar Alexander indicated he likely would be a no, leaving only Collins, Mitt Romney, and Lisa Murkowski in doubt. That meant the roll call would be a split fifty/fifty—just enough to deny Democrats the fifty-one votes they needed to call witnesses. McConnell had not only stanched the bleeding; they were now on the cusp of victory.

For McConnell, however, that wasn't enough. A fifty/fifty vote was still a tie, and McConnell simply couldn't allow that. It was time to put the screws to a certain Alaska senator.

37

THE MUSK OX CAUCUS

JANUARY 29–31, 2020

Lisa Murkowski sat across from Mitch McConnell and thought of her Catholic mother. McConnell never threatened. He never bullied. And though he often left her space to follow her own intuition, he was an expert at laying the guilt on thick and backing her into a corner. On the morning of Wednesday, January 29, it was all too obvious what he expected her to do. He wanted her to help save the judicial branch by going against her conscience. He wanted her to vote against witnesses.

"The most consequential vote during this impeachment is not about whether to convict or acquit," McConnell said carefully. "It's about how to vote on witnesses—and what position that will put the courts in."

Despite their ideological differences, the moderate Murkowski and conservative McConnell had always gotten along just fine. The Christmas episode had been a blip in an otherwise healthy relationship, and since his angry email to her over the holiday break, the pair had made amends. The first day back from the recess, McConnell had summoned Murkowski over to him on the Senate floor, beckoning with his finger. "You and I are on the same page," he told her, recalling how the Alaska senator had criticized Nancy Pelosi for rushing impeachment in the very same interview[1] as she had chided McConnell for coordinating with the White House. He also tried to justify to her his "total coordination" comment, noting Democrats had done the same thing with Clinton.

"Well don't advertise it!" she had snapped back.

Over the previous week, as the impeachment lawyers made their trial presentations, Murkowski had filled multiple notebooks with tortured musings, privately wrestling with how to vote. She hadn't taken notes like this for decades—since she was practicing law, she thought. But she was determined to make a choice she could defend—not only to her constituents but to herself.

Murkowski had been disgusted with Trump's behavior long before he began trying to bully Ukraine. But as she watched Adam Schiff and his team, she kept coming back to the same questions: *Why on earth had House Democrats dropped the subpoena for Bolton's deputy? And why didn't they ever issue a summons for Bolton himself?* These were giant, pluggable holes in their otherwise solid case. But instead, it seemed to Murkowski that they had prioritized a Christmas deadline over making the strongest case possible. Bolton was like a dead cat on Pelosi's doorstep, she thought to herself. The Speaker had wanted to get rid of it—so she laid it at the Senate's feet.

Murkowski found Schiff's exhortations to the Senate to fight for Bolton's testimony in court to be inherently hypocritical. He made it sound so simple—like all they had to do was wave a magic wand and call Bolton in and they'd get answers in a week. But Schiff was selling them a rotten bill of goods and he knew it, she thought.

"What wand do we have procedurally here in the Senate, that we can remove Trump's assertion of executive privilege?" she'd huff, as if speaking to Schiff. "What makes you think that we can do it any more quickly than you could have?"

Worse, Murkowski worried Democrats were setting a terrible precedent for future impeachments, creating a standard where the House could charge a president quickly—then demand the Senate fill the holes of their investigation. "We are opening ourselves up to the possibility of the House doing this to us over and over for all time—and we need to be cautious about that," she had complained to her GOP colleagues during a mid-January lunch.

When Murkowski had privately pressed other Senate Democrats to explain why the House had not done its homework, all of them agreed—in confidence—that it was a glaring flaw. Still, they refused to criticize Schiff publicly. And they asked her a difficult question in return: *Why should the Senate forgo an opportunity to hear from Bolton just because the House screwed up?*

Murkowski was not sure how to answer. She and her close friend Susan Collins had spent hours discussing their shared agony at the looming decision on witnesses, bending heads during trial breaks at their adjacent desks to whisper about what they should do. Murkowski knew Collins was inclined to vote to hear more evidence. She was leaning that way too. But now McConnell was imploring her to go against her gut and telling her the fate of the constitutional order was at stake.

As he sat across from Murkowski in their one-on-one meeting, McConnell had one goal: to keep her from becoming the fiftieth senator to vote in favor of witnesses. If the Senate ended up in a fifty/fifty tie, McConnell knew many in the country would look to Chief Justice Roberts to break it. There was no way for him to do so—or refuse—without being flagellated by political activists on either side of the aisle for his choice.

If Roberts ruled in favor of witnesses, he was sure to incur the wrath of Trump and his supporters. But if he refused to weigh in, the Democratic machine would come after him. Either way, Roberts, and the entire court system by extension, would be dragged into the same political dumpster fire consuming Congress and the executive branch—the last thing McConnell wanted.

Roberts, McConnell knew, had tried to stay above politics his entire life—and ensure the courts did the same. Since former president George W. Bush nominated him to the bench in 2005, the former Reagan White House lawyer had worked hard to maintain the reputation of a principled conservative willing to side with the liberal justices when he felt it necessary, such as when he voted to uphold Barack Obama's Affordable Care Act in 2012.[2] He almost never commented on politics, breaking with that policy only momentarily in November 2018 to defend a member of the federal bench whom Trump had derided as an "Obama judge."[3]

As the trial loomed, Roberts had made clear to lawmakers that he intended to adhere to the standard his predecessor, Chief Justice William Rehnquist, had set during Clinton's impeachment: He would only act as an umpire, not take an active role in the trial.[4] McConnell reasoned that meant Roberts would likely reject the idea of casting a tie-breaking vote—logic the Majority Leader considered sound. As hell-bent as he was on winning—and on stacking the federal bench with conservative judges—McConnell viscerally understood that the judicial branch of government still had to maintain the appearance of staying above the political fray. But he knew the left saw things differently.

In fact, from the very start of the trial, McConnell had observed Democrats ramping up a pressure campaign against the chief justice in a bid to force his hand on witnesses. On the first day of arguments, Senate Democrats had all voted to empower Roberts to issue witness subpoenas by fiat, though the effort failed along party lines. Schiff had argued that the Senate should "have a neutral arbiter decide—much as he may loathe the task—whether a witness is relevant or a witness is not." That arbiter, he explained, was the chief justice.

Outside the chamber, liberal groups were also sharpening their knives for Roberts, demanding that he approve the managers' witnesses and not be such "a potted plant." The leader of Demand Justice, an outside group run by a former Schumer staffer, had taken to Twitter that Monday to argue that "Roberts shouldn't get a free pass as he goes along with McConnell's sham trial."[5] The group had even launched a call-in campaign, telling supporters to call the Supreme Court's main switchboard and "Tell John Roberts: Do Your Job."[6]

McConnell was adamant that the left not have any more excuses to pillory Roberts. But he was also unwilling to sacrifice his own objectives in order to protect the leader of the courts. Had McConnell been less of a political animal, he could have chosen a different course. He could have encouraged more Republicans to support the moderates' call for witnesses and left Trump to his fate. But McConnell wanted a specific outcome—a speedy Trump acquittal—and was not wavering. That left him only one person to lean on: Murkowski.

McConnell knew that his Alaskan colleague disapproved of Trump's behavior toward Ukraine, was interested in hearing from witnesses like Bolton, and would not shy away from crossing the party line. She hated the GOP's blind loyalty to Trump, and McConnell knew that meant she would scorn politically motivated appeals to reject witnesses in order to save the president—or her own colleagues' reelection campaigns.

But Murkowski was also one of Washington's rare remaining institutionalists. She admired the way Roberts ran his court. And

McConnell believed that if he could appeal to a higher purpose, he might be able to get her to change her mind.

During their meeting, he laid it on thick. It was up to her, McConnell explained, to preserve the integrity of the judicial branch and keep impeachment from doing long-term damage to the federal bench.

"If you don't want to do this for the presidency, if you don't want to do it for the Senate, if you don't want to do this for 2020 colleagues, do it to save the courts," McConnell told Murkowski.

She told him she would think about it.

Lindsey Graham came flying into the coatroom off the Senate floor that Thursday afternoon, cursing Trump's legal team. "We are FUCKED. We are FUCKED!" he fumed, throwing his hands up in dramatic fashion.

Moments before, Trump's legal team had delivered an argument Graham was sure would alienate basically the only moderate Republican still on the fence about witnesses. In response to a question from Murkowksi about why they shouldn't call Bolton, Trump attorney Patrick Philbin had responded simply that it was too late. Democrats should have called him in the House, he argued.

Graham was furious. He knew McConnell's entire trial strategy boiled down to winning over his Alaskan colleague—and arguing that the timing was simply too inconvenient to bother calling witnesses wouldn't be enough to sway her. She needed to hear what McConnell had been trying to get them to say: that Bolton's testimony was "irrelevant."

"This is going to lose us Murkowski," Graham said angrily, turning to McConnell's counsel Andrew Ferguson, sitting in the cloakroom.

It wasn't the Trump defense team's first screwup during the Q&A

portion of the trial. The previous day, just hours into the back and forth, Alan Dershowitz had set off a firestorm by arguing that the president could do whatever he wanted to secure his own reelection if he thought it would be in the public interest. "If a president does something which he believes will help him get elected, in the public interest, that cannot be the kind of quid pro quo that results in impeachment," he said.

A murmur of reproach had echoed through the chamber, as senators realized how Dershowitz had essentially equated presidential powers to those of a king. During a break, one of McConnell's top allies, Senator Roy Blunt, walked up to Cipollone to tell him to fire Dershowitz on the spot. Dershowitz didn't show the next day.

As Graham bent heads with Ferguson in the cloakroom on Thursday, other GOP senators streamed in, looking equally worried.

"What are we going to do?" Senator Ted Cruz asked.

"Let's just ask a quick clean-up question," Ferguson offered, suggesting they prompt the Trump team to clean up their answers. Everyone agreed.

The group gathered around a laptop to weigh in as Ferguson typed. "Assuming for argument's sake that John Bolton were to testify in the light most favorable to the allegations . . . isn't it true that the allegations still would not rise to the level of an impeachable offense?" they agreed to ask. "And that therefore . . . his testimony would add nothing to this case?"

But the senators were worried. Trump's lawyers had already proven themselves unreliable, even when lobbed the easiest softball questions.

"Is Trump's team going to answer this the right way?" Graham asked.

"I will go down there and tell them to answer it the right way," Ferguson vowed.

Just after nine p.m., Ferguson approached McConnell's other

senior staff as the volley of questions and answers continued. They needed a five-minute break to prepare for a critical question coming up; the defense needed to be briefed on how to answer it.

McConnell's top aide shook her head. The senators were exhausted, and the leader just wanted to push through to the end so they could go home. But Ferguson was adamant.

"I'm just telling you, it needs to be answered in the right way and I need to go down there and tell them how to answer it," Ferguson said emphatically.

At 9:13 p.m., McConnell asked for a short break, and Ferguson wasted no time. As senators rose from their desks to stretch their legs, he made his way to the Trump team's green room to explain the question that was coming and how they needed to respond. But just as they had before, Trump's team sputtered about whether they would answer it the way the GOP senators wanted them.

"That's asking us to concede that what Trump did was wrong," one of the lawyers objected.

"No, it's not," Ferguson said, exasperated. "Come on, guys. Be lawyers . . . You are saying we do not believe the president committed the act he's accused of committing. But even if you assume that he did, you, the jury, still must acquit because everything that they accused him of is not a high crime and misdemeanor."

The president's attorneys were still uneasy.

"We need to talk to the client," Cipollone grumbled.

Seconds later, Graham flew through the doors to reinforce Ferguson's point.

"This is the pivotal question," Graham insisted. "There's only one way you can answer it."

Ferguson and Graham left the room without a commitment from Trump's legal team that they would heed the senators' advice. Cruz, sensing the uncertainty, decided to follow up with a reality check.

Personally, Cruz—an experienced litigator—felt Trump had outfitted his legal team with a battery of paper-pushing blockheads who didn't know the first thing about winning trials. Now, late on Thursday night, Cruz had hit the limits of his patience with their incompetent deference to Trump.

"Let me just tell you: Out of one hundred senators, you have zero who believe you that there was no quid pro quo," Cruz said sternly. "None. There's not a single one."

Make the right arguments, Cruz demanded, almost threateningly, and left.

A few minutes later, when Roberts read the senators' Bolton question, Cruz eyed Philbin warily as he stood to speak.

"Let me start by just making very clear that there was no quid pro quo," Philbin started in. "And there is no evidence to show that."

Not again, Cruz thought. It took all of his willpower not to walk over and punch Philbin in the face.

"But let me answer the question directly," Philbin continued, referencing the *New York Times* report about Bolton's book. "Even if that happened, even if he gave that testimony, the Articles of Impeachment still wouldn't rise to an impeachable offense."

In that moment, the tension escaped the Republican side of the Senate chamber. Cruz smiled. Graham ran back into the cloakroom for a victory dance, clicking his heels and giving Ferguson a high-five.

Murkowski, meanwhile, listened at her desk, unaware that the answer to her question had been entirely concocted by her own colleagues, not the president's lawyers.

But in the end, all of the GOP's hand-wringing about the Bolton question wouldn't be what influenced Murkowski's decision about witnesses. As she reflected on the trial later that night, it was a

question from one of the most liberal senators in the chamber that
proved to be most pivotal.

McConnell could scarcely believe his ears—or his luck—when Elizabeth Warren challenged Chief Justice John Roberts in front of the
entire chamber that same day. The liberal Massachusetts senator,
then running for the Democratic presidential nomination, asked
point-blank if the fact that Roberts was presiding over a witness-
less trial would "contribute to the loss of legitimacy of the chief
justice, the Supreme Court and the Constitution." That Roberts
had had to awkwardly read the question aloud to the chamber made
things even worse. He looked stone cold as he did so. Senators in
the chamber murmured their discomfort.

It was exactly the sort of politicization of the judicial branch that
McConnell had warned Murkowski about—and it was happening
on the Senate floor in real time. Warren's question had clearly been
drafted to score points with the party base at a time when her poll
numbers were flagging in a crowded Democratic presidential primary. It was a desperate plea for attention that Murkowski would
disapprove of.

Grabbing a piece of paper, the leader scribbled a note to Murkowski, seated just a few feet behind him. He wanted her to pay
attention: They were attacking Roberts before her eyes.

Liberal groups had been leaning in particularly hard on Roberts
that day, accusing him of siding with the Republicans by not just
ruling from the bench that witnesses should be part of the trial. A
group run by Schumer allies had even circulated a doctored video of
the chief justice presiding over the trial wearing a MAGA hat.[7] When
Ferguson saw it pop up on Twitter, he immediately darted out of the
cloakroom to share it with McConnell, sitting in the front row.

"Get that to Lisa right now," McConnell had whispered to him. It would only reinforce the fallout of Warren's question.

When the trial wrapped up late that night, just before eleven p.m., Murkowksi knew her work for the evening was far from finished. During a dinner break, Lamar Alexander had pulled her aside to tell her he would vote no on witnesses. Mitt Romney and Susan Collins had come out the opposite way, announcing they'd vote to hear more evidence and testimony.

Murkowski knew that meant McConnell's prediction was coming true. She would either be the fiftieth vote for witnesses—throwing a tie to Roberts—or be the deciding vote against them. It was a position she never wanted to be in. And she wouldn't have much time to decide: the final vote was the next day.

As she made her way through the basement of the Capitol back to her office for what was sure to be the most stressful deliberation of her career, Murkowksi didn't even try to run from the throng of congressional reporters who assailed her with questions. *Would she vote for witnesses? Would she vote to convict? What was she thinking? How was she feeling?* She had been hearing the same queries for weeks. But that night, she actually had to come up with an answer.

Yet all she knew at the moment was that she was tired.

"I am one pooped puppy," she told the journalists. "I'm going to go home. Maybe have a glass of wine. Maybe even take a bath!"

Murkowski did neither. When she returned to her office, she spent another several hours debating with her staff about the right course of action. She dimmed the lights in the office, as she was prone to do while in deep thought. She made lists of pros and cons, spitballing each out loud. When the tension grew to be too much, she challenged one of her staffers to a game of Ping-Pong to lighten the mood. *After all, why have a Ping-Pong table in your office if not for moments like these?*

McConnell had been right that Warren's question had enraged Murkowski, and the Twitter attacks on Roberts had raised her anger to a rolling boil. She wanted to hear from Bolton, who clearly had more information on what happened between Trump and Ukraine. But she could, for the first time, feel the urgency of McConnell's warning. Roberts was already being dragged into the conflagration. And with Alexander, Romney, and Collins now publicly committed to their votes, she knew she was the only one who could keep the whole court from being assailed by the left and permanently tarnished.

Murkowski departed her office that night without having made a final decision. She slept fitfully, replaying arguments for and against witnesses over and over again in her head. The Democrats' attacks on Roberts were absolutely out of bounds in her view, and she could not get over the House process being half-baked. Democrats, she mused to herself, knew the only possible way impeachment would be successful would be if it were bipartisan. Pelosi had said so herself for the first nine months of last year. Yet in the end they hadn't even tried.

The entire exercise wasn't about checking a rogue president. McConnell was right. It was about political expediency. And it made Murkowski want to vomit. Trump had done something terrible that required serious and sincere oversight. *Why had the House not handled this with more care and concern?* To Murkowski, it seemed both sides were playing politics. Republicans were too afraid to actually check this president, and Democrats didn't really care about putting him away—just about getting impeachment over with and using it to do maximum damage to the GOP in the 2020 election.

Because of that, she thought sourly, Trump would get away with everything. And she had no choice but to be complicit.

In the wee hours of morning, in the pitch black of her bedroom,

Murkowski realized what she had to do. Fumbling for a pencil and pad of paper, she didn't bother switching on the lights before she started scribbling.

"There will be no fair trial in the Senate," she wrote, the first draft of a statement she would release the next morning. "It is sad for me to admit that, as an institution, the Congress has failed."

McConnell hadn't been the only senator making a play for Murkowski's conscience during the trial. Her close friend on the Democratic side, Hawaiian senator Brian Schatz, had also been working on her. He appreciated—and tacitly agreed with—Murkowski's dissatisfaction about the incompleteness of the case House managers had made. He also recognized that the most pivotal question in the trial rested on her vote—and that she was being put in an impossible position on witnesses.

Schatz and Murkowski had struck up a friendship as senators representing states outside the Lower 48, often finding common cause despite their drastically different party politics and home climates. They'd have dinner together to talk policy; Murkowski had even cooked him her favorite meal, Alaskan salmon. Those friendly soirees had been suspended, though, during the weeks leading up to the impeachment trial. Murkowski even stopped taking Schatz's phone calls.

Schatz was worried. He knew his friend put principle before politics and that, in a vacuum, she would want more information from the witnesses who had not been called. He also guessed that she was coming under tremendous pressure to vote against witnesses anyway. He wanted to cast her a lifeline.

So one afternoon during the trial, Schatz made a point of waiting for Murkowski by the elevators outside the Senate chamber to pitch

her on the idea of asking a joint question for the impeachment managers and defense. It would be a good thing, he suggested, if in a
moment as partisan as this, they could manage a bipartisan question
as part of the Q&A session. She agreed, and the two began passing notes back and forth on the Senate floor, fine-tuning what they
would ask.

"Where is the line between permissible political actions and impeachable political actions?" they asked together that Thursday,
as Graham and a phalanx of Republicans plotted in the cloakroom
about how to orchestrate the defense lawyers' answers to appeal to
Murkowski. Would the lawyers agree "that almost any action a
president takes . . . is to one degree or another, inherently political?"

It was as far as Murkowski would let him push her. After that, she
went dark on him again.

By Friday, the day of the witness vote, Murkowski's disgust had
turned to outright rage. Everyone was guilty. Trump. The GOP.
The Democrats. The entire process was rotten to its core. The
impeachment exercise had only empowered Trump at the very moment when he needed curbing. Meanwhile, Democrats, either too
clueless or too proud to acknowledge that fact, had gone back into
their corners, claiming a self-righteous victory of conscience—when
they too had put politics ahead of the country.

Murkowski instructed her staff to send out her statement condemning everyone that she'd started writing overnight.

"It has also become clear some of my colleagues intend to further
politicize this process and drag the Supreme Court into the fray . . .
I will not stand for nor support that effort," she continued. "We have
already degraded our institution for partisan political benefit, and I
will not enable those who wish to pull down another."

On her way to the trial, Murkowski's frustration was palpable. A
longtime congressional reporter she knew well stopped her in the

hall, asking if she was all right. In a moment of candor, Murkowski admitted she was not.

"This is the saddest day that I've seen in the Senate," she said. "I'm really disgusted with everybody, just really—the House, the Senate, the Republicans, the Democrats. It's just a sad day."[8]

On the Senate floor a few minutes later, the clerk in the chamber alphabetically read out the names of senators, who stood at their desks to announce their votes on the question of witnesses. As expected, Alexander voted against witnesses. Collins voted for them.

"Murkowski," the clerk called out, about two and a half minutes later. She looked neither McConnell nor Schatz in the eyes, facing forward to call back her response: no on witnesses. The trial would conclude without hearing from Bolton.

When the vote was over, Schatz left his seat and made his way to Murkowski's desk. She rose to meet her friend, bracing herself for what he would say.

"I'm not having this conversation with any other Republicans, because they didn't disappoint me," Schatz said, a pained look on his face. "I didn't have them as capable of doing the right thing. But I'm bummed. I am bummed and disappointed about the decision you made."

Murkowski wasn't defensive. She nodded in agreement.

"I'm more disappointed than anyone," she said.

38

AUTOPILOT

After the witness vote failed that Friday, the trial might as well have been put on autopilot. Not a single senator or aide in the Capitol thought a conviction was possible. Neither did any reporter in town. After nearly two weeks, nationwide public support for removing Trump remained the same as it was on the day arguments had begun, hovering right around 48 percent. And in Washington, both sides were ready to be done.

During Clinton's trial in 1999, senators had deliberated over the evidence and the president's actions for hours in closed-door session before returning to the chamber to take the final impeachment vote.[1] Many would later say that the private debate was among the most fulfilling and substantial in their lives, leading to the bipartisan vote acquitting Clinton. But twenty years later, McConnell and Schumer didn't see the need for such niceties. Neither even suggested it.

Still, as they huddled in a back room just off the Senate floor following the vote, Mitch McConnell and Chuck Schumer bickered about how to bring the trial to a close. Their disagreement was a perfect microcosm of all the problems that had plagued the trial and impeachment overall: There could be no agreement on anything between the two parties—even on how to wrap the process up after the conclusion was foregone. McConnell and Senate Republicans wanted to get the final vote over with that very day. They feared that if they waited, Bolton might break his silence and go on the Sunday news shows to state that the *New York Times* story about his book was true, upending the trial. Schumer had his own motives for arguing that they delay until the following Wednesday: Trump was slated to deliver his annual State of the Union address that Tuesday. And Democrats were damned if they would allow a newly acquitted president to use the forum for a victory lap.

With their top aides surrounding them, Schumer laid down a threat: If McConnell didn't agree to postpone the final vote until after Trump's address, he would pull enough procedural stunts to force already exhausted senators to sit in the trial all weekend. McConnell knew Schumer meant it and caved. And a few hours later, senators flew home for the weekend and a long-awaited reprieve.

Schumer had another problem on his hands that weekend: Two moderate Democrats—Joe Manchin of West Virginia and Kyrsten Sinema of Arizona—were still undecided on whether to convict or acquit. Their noncommittal stances had garnered fewer headlines than those of the moderate Republicans, but Schumer knew that the political fallout would be terrible if Democrats could not maintain a united front to repudiate Trump as a bloc vote in the final vote.

In the final days of the trial, Manchin had circulated a pair of resolutions to censure Trump, a move he hoped would result in a bipartisan repudiation of the president's actions.[2] But Schumer worried the effort would give moderate Republicans and even Democrats like Manchin an excuse to vote to acquit. Once again, Schumer's political instincts kicked into high gear as he sought to squelch Manchin's venture.

Ultimately, it was the GOP that helped Schumer do the job: Not a single Republican—even GOP moderates—agreed to put their name on the document. Manchin eventually just gave up, though he continued to be noncommittal about his final vote.

As Schumer focused on his rank and file, Adam Schiff was also dealing with some unfinished business. Over the weekend, he directed his staff to make one last run at John Bolton to see if they could pry his lips loose. That Saturday, they implored Charles Cooper, Bolton's attorney, to have his client sign an affidavit stating that what had been reported in the *New York Times* was true. Maybe it would be enough to shore up wary Democrats and flip a wavering Republican or two.

Democrats didn't know it, but Bolton had actually grown increasingly concerned about going down in history as the person who had withheld blockbuster information while Trump's trial went sideways. It was part of what had motivated his offer to testify in the GOP-led Senate, which he and his lawyer considered a more acceptable arbiter than the Democrat-led House. But without a subpoena for cover, or a court order, Cooper did not want his client coming forward. They rejected Schiff's offer the next day—a refusal Democrats chalked up to a desire on his part to sell books. Pre-sales for Bolton's unpublished manuscript were, after all, already topping the Amazon charts.[3]

To some Democrats, Schiff's attempt to secure Bolton's testimony felt half-hearted. In the House, Jerry Nadler and his staff privately discussed whether the House should serve Bolton a last-minute subpoena that very weekend. If the Senate wasn't going to do its duty to call him, they privately reasoned, why shouldn't they? He had, after all, volunteered to talk. But no sooner had the idea crystallized than they dismissed it. Pelosi "would cut out our vocal cords if she overheard such a conversation," Judiciary aides joked—and they knew Schiff would never go for it. Sure enough, the Speaker and the Intelligence panel chief rebuffed the idea when some members floated it publicly. Everyone was ready to move on.

Nancy Pelosi could not hide her revulsion—and the television network cameras were capturing her every scowl. As the president pontificated to a House chamber packed to the brim with members of Congress, the Speaker pursed her lips and glowered at the back of Trump's head. The verdict in his impeachment trial was just hours away, and with his acquittal all but guaranteed, the president was positively glowing, vindication dripping from every word of his State of the Union address. He didn't even have to mention the word "impeachment"—his tone alone made Pelosi boil with rage.

Pelosi had donned white, the color of suffragettes, for the occasion, and wore the same gold mace brooch she had sported on the day her chamber voted to impeach Trump. But this time, the emblem of congressional power had been tarnished: The House had failed to bring Trump to heel—and by the next day, his victory would be official.

The Speaker, like almost everyone on Capitol Hill, had been anticipating the president to be unhinged that night. After all, Trump was obsessed with the House Democrats' "hoax" impeachment. Why wouldn't he use the occasion to lambast his impeachers? But almost forty minutes into his address, Trump was staying on message. Instead of ranting about the effort to oust him, he had turned the annual policy address into a stump-speech-cum-reality-TV-show extravaganza.

Trump's performance took on the feel of an Oprah Winfrey show rather than a wonky oration. He lavished praise on one of the final living Tuskegee airmen, a former Black fighter pilot who had just turned one hundred and sat in the audience. Touting school choice, he announced a scholarship for a young Black girl to attend a private school of her choosing, as her single mother, sitting in the gallery, cried with joy. He honored an Army wife sitting in the balcony with her two children, beaming as her husband, who had been deployed to Afghanistan, burst through the chamber doors to surprise them. And then, just because he could, he awarded a Presidential Medal of Freedom to Rush Limbaugh, a conservative shock jock who spent his popular radio broadcasts spewing vitriol at Democrats.

Pelosi—and the rest of her caucus—were slack-jawed at the boldness of Trump's pandering. He had used the annual address meant to report on matters of state to Congress, in keeping with the Constitution, to instead score reelection points with appeals to minorities, suburban moms, and his unrepentant base. As far as Pelosi was concerned, he was disrespecting her and her chamber. And yet how could Democrats argue against giving a high-achieving minority student scholarship money, or reuniting a military family? All Pelosi could do was choke down her disgust.

The showmanship, however, was not what infuriated Pelosi most. Rather, it was Trump's attempt that night to claim credit for policies she and her party had championed for years—and that he, more often than not, had tried to kill. He was vowing to protect Americans with preexisting conditions at the same time as his Justice Department was trying to gut the Affordable Care Act in the courts. He claimed he wanted to fortify Medicare and Social Security when in fact he had moved to dismantle benefits for the disabled. He was suddenly endorsing paid family leave and lower prices for prescription drugs, two Pelosi priorities she'd tried to get him to compromise on all year.

The president's speech, Pelosi thought to herself, was nothing more than a dressed-up pack of lies. Trump was a snake oil salesman duping the American people. And yet this bells-and-whistles act, on the eve of his acquittal, would undoubtedly resonate with some voters, making Democrats look like the bad guys.

As Trump continued to speak, three House Democrats in the audience—including Rashida "Impeach the Motherfucker" Tlaib—stormed out of the chamber.[4] Pelosi, simmering, decided to stage her own protest as well. Grabbing the printout of Trump's address before her, she began making little tears in the document as she followed along. Each time she saw a lie, she ripped the top part of the sheet. *Claiming to care about the poor and people on food stamps?* Bullshit—tear. *Acting like he gave a damn about Black Americans, even invoking Martin Luther King?* Fat chance—tear. And so it went. Lie. Tear. Lie. Tear.

In many ways, Trump's speech was the manifestation of everything Pelosi had feared about impeachment. The Democrats had impeached Trump, yes, but now his stock was soaring. That morning, a Gallup Poll showed Trump had the highest approval rating he'd ever had: 49 percent. Over the course of the trial, his numbers with Republicans had all but topped out, reaching 94 percent approval. Even independents had a more favorable rating of Trump, rising 5 percent since early January.[5] Meanwhile, Pelosi's moderate members were getting raked over the coals back home for ever having voted to impeach the president at all. Swing voters, simply put, were sick of all these investigations—or simply weren't convinced Trump was all that bad.

Pelosi too had had it with the endless oversight and was already plotting a dramatic change of course. Though she often said publicly that House Democrats could walk and chew gum at the same time, the reality was that the Trump probes were overshadowing all their policy work, and she couldn't allow that in a campaign season. As soon as the trial was over, she was planning to bring her investigative chairmen to heel. No more high-profile investigations of the president.

Lie. Tear. Lie. Tear.

Adding to Pelosi's frustration was the fact that the entire Democratic Party was in a meltdown that day over problems that had arisen during the Iowa caucuses the night before. The contest still hadn't determined a winner. In a humiliating turn of events, the smartphone app that precinct captains were meant to use to report their vote tallies had failed to register all the results, prompting demands for recounts.[6] Worse: Biden—the candidate most aligned to Pelosi's own thinking on how to govern and win, and the candidate considered the most likely to actually defeat Trump in a head-to-head matchup—had finished fourth. Fourth!

Lie. Tear. Lie. Tear.

As Trump's speech wound to a close, he began to opine on American exceptionalism, with a MAGA twist.

"Ladies and gentlemen, our ancestors built the most exceptional republic ever to exist in all of human history," Trump said triumphantly. "And we are making it greater than ever before."

Republicans applauded and beamed. Pelosi grimaced.

By the time Trump's speech ended, the Speaker knew how she would register her protest. As Pence rose to give his president a standing ovation, Pelosi rose too, with a copy of Trump's speech in her hand. As the vice president clapped, the Speaker ripped the pages in half with a flourish before the entire chamber and all the cameras. Her point, she was sure, would not be lost on anyone watching.

"POLITICS WILL
BREAK YOUR HEART"

EARLY FEBRUARY 2020

Romney unfolded the note he had just been handed on the Senate floor and took in the words scrawled across the paper. The missive had been handed to him by a Senate page, one of over a hundred such messages flying across the Senate floor as senators used an army of high schoolers as carrier pigeons to communicate during the trial. He kept his face frozen as he read, though the message from the Democratic side of the chamber struck a chord deep within him.

"With John McCain gone, it has gotta be you," it said.

For two weeks, Romney had fielded a steady stream of notes from Republicans and Democrats alike, each bearing arguments for why he should vote for or against witnesses. Each time a young page would come racing across the chamber to him, Romney would open the note they handed him and swiftly tuck it away, refocusing his eyes on the podium and redoubling his efforts to listen to the speaker at hand.

But of all the senators sending him notes, there was one in particular who kept bugging him. One who seemed undaunted that
his missives were going unanswered—and determined to convince
Romney to not just vote for witnesses, but to convict.

Romney had worked with Brian Schatz on legislation before, but
he and the Hawaiian progressive weren't exactly close. In fact, Romney, still new to the Senate, wasn't particularly close with any of his
colleagues. Still, in Schatz's estimation, the Utah Republican had
already shown a willingness to buck his party when it came to supporting a subpoena for John Bolton. Maybe if Romney had the right
nudge, Schatz thought, he would be open to breaking with the GOP
again and vote to convict the president.

Schatz had another reason for being so insistent: He thought it
was vitally important to get just one Republican to back Democrats'
impeachment effort. It would imbue the charges with credibility
and save this bid to oust Trump from being remembered as an entirely partisan exercise. Romney, to Schatz, was their best hope—
particularly now that his friend Murkowski had failed them.

So Schatz kept writing. He laid his appeals to Romney on thick,
with blatant attempts to tug on the former Republican presidential
nominee's heartstrings and his conscience. By the end of the trial, he
had scribbled notes to Romney almost twenty times. *Please, save the
Republican Party from itself,* he wrote in one. *Save the republic. Remind
the voters that there is a light at the end of this tunnel,* he said in another.

On the eve of the final vote, Romney was still in shock at how
many of his fellow Republicans had rejected calling trial witnesses.
He thought for sure the revelations about Bolton's book would move
his colleagues, reminding them of how much they still did not know.
But Romney's attempts to reason with them had fallen flat in the
face of McConnell's practiced whipping effort—and only made the
target on his back larger.

National conservative groups were already buying up ads in Utah, attacking him for wanting witnesses. "There's Mitt Romney threatening to vote with Democrats again to trot out spotlight-seeking blowhards who will trash President Trump on the witness stand," the narrator said in one television spot paid for by Club for Growth. "If Mitt wants the truth, what about the Bidens?"[1] Another conservative group, FreedomWorks, bought an ad in the *Salt Lake Tribune*, imploring him in all caps: "DON'T DESTROY THE INTEGRITY OF OUR INSTITUTIONS . . . VOTE FOR NO NEW WITNESSES!"[2] In the Utah state legislature, Republicans were even touting new legislation giving themselves the right to remove a duly elected senator. The effort was purely unconstitutional, but that wasn't the point. The point was to troll Romney.[3] Even some Republicans whom he considered friends were joining in the fray, dumping on Romney to curry favor with the president. Senator Kelly Loeffler's assault had burned in particular, as she had once welcomed him into her home and donated generously to his presidential campaign.

The day before the witness vote, Romney's frustration with the pressure had boiled over. During yet another private GOP-only lunch before the trial, when McConnell was once again arguing that calling witnesses would be bad for the GOP, Romney had snapped.

"If this is meant to persuade me, it's not working," he had said heatedly, feeling ganged up on. "You can come talk to me one-on-one, if you have a problem . . . Don't pressure me in a room full of people."

"We don't have you in the undecided column, Mitt," McConnell had retorted dryly, acknowledging to the room that he fully expected Romney to vote yes on witnesses. "This is not directed at you."

For Romney, the witness vote had never posed a dilemma. Rather, it was the final verdict that tormented him most. It was one thing to vote to hear more evidence in the trial—it was another matter entirely to vote to convict the leader of your own party. Not a single Republican had dared vote to impeach Trump in the House. And Romney was fairly certain none would be so bold as to do it in the Senate. In fact, no senator in history had ever voted to convict a president of his own party. If he took the plunge, he would be making history—and signing up for an onslaught of revenge.

Romney had learned at a young age that refusing to toe the party line could cost even the most promising politician his career. He was just seventeen when his father, then–Michigan governor George Romney, rebuked the Republican Party's embrace of Barry Goldwater's fearmongering at the 1964 GOP convention. Romney had been in the crowd as his father tried to appeal to the party's better angels and heard the deafening boos he received in reply.

Four years later, George Romney again fashioned himself as the guardian of the establishment GOP, running in the 1968 primary against Nixon. He argued that there was a "credibility crisis" in Washington. He recanted his previous support for the Vietnam War, saying military leaders were "brainwashing" the nation. He broke with the Mormon Church to take a principled stand in favor of civil rights, marching with Black demonstrators in Detroit. For his campaign of conscience, and his unflinching honesty, he was rewarded with political backlash, as his allies in politics, the press, and the church turned against him. Romney withdrew from the 1968 primaries to avoid an embarrassing defeat.

"Politics," the elder Romney told a good friend soon after, "will break your heart."[4]

Now his words were ringing true for the next generation, as his son found himself in a similar position.

While Romney wanted to believe his career in public service was an extension of his dad's legacy, others saw him as a different political animal entirely. During his unsuccessful 2012 presidential bid, it was not lost on Romney that many political pundits remarked that while George had unwavering principles, his son often tried to have things both ways. He'd try to appeal to the base but also the center and sustained ample criticism in the process for being wishy-washy.

A decade later, there was no room for waffling. The most pivotal decision of Mitt Romney's career came down to a binary choice: convict or acquit. His father would have known the right thing to do and would have summoned the courage to do it. But did Romney have the same conviction? Was he, once the standard-bearer of the Republican Party, now willing to buck it and embrace the role his dad played against Goldwater? Was he willing to adopt the role of spurned centrist, the role of the anti-Trump?

In the days before the final vote, the weight of what he was about to do hit him. Lamar Alexander announced he would vote to acquit, arguing the managers had "proven" their case but the offenses did not meet the "high bar" of impeachment. Lisa Murkowski announced that she "cannot vote to convict" because the House sent the Senate a half-baked case—while blasting Trump's behavior as "shameful and wrong." Susan Collins sided with them as well. She would vote to acquit, rationalizing it by surmising that Trump had already learned "a pretty big lesson."[5]

"I believe that he will be much more cautious in the future," she predicted.

Romney wished he could join them—and in fact had tried to find a way out. After the *New York Times*'s Bolton story, he had even reached out to the White House through a colleague, asking them to let officials like Bolton and White House chief of staff Mick Mulvaney provide the Senate with affidavits about whether the story was true. They refused. Romney also sought more information from the trial lawyers directly. During one break, he buttonholed House manager Jason Crow in the hall, pressing him for details about when Ukrainian leaders became aware their funds had been frozen. During another, he approached Ken Starr, who had just delivered a long monologue about how partisan impeachments were bound to fail.

"Haven't things changed so much that a bipartisan impeachment might no longer be possible?" Romney challenged Starr.[6]

As Romney struggled, several GOP colleagues tried to talk him out of his tortured grappling, urging him to just acquit. *The election is only nine months away—let the voters decide*, they implored him. *Let the election decide.* It was an intriguing appeal. But ultimately, Romney couldn't stomach it. There had been times in his political career when Romney chose expediency over conscience—and he always regretted it. Impeaching a president was too serious a matter to take the easy way out.

After spending hours poring over the Federalist Papers, Romney knew what he had to do. The Trump defense didn't stack up. The president had used his office to try to force another nation—an ally dependent on U.S. support—to go after a political adversary. Romney had heard Adam Schiff's argument—if this wasn't impeachable, nothing was—and he agreed. He decided he would vote to convict.

After coming to that conclusion, however, Romney didn't rest easy. Each night in the days before the final vote, he'd lie awake in bed worrying about the backlash, which was already raging. Republican voters had accosted him on a flight from Salt Lake City to Washington, D.C., calling him a "traitor" for voting to call witnesses. Another had found him in a grocery store and sneered that he needed to "stick with the team." The Conservative Political Action Conference, an annual gathering of Republicans in Washington, formally banned him from their event.

Even some former advisors called Romney to implore him to

acquit. And these were not Trump supporters; they were friends who worried about his career and the inevitable consequences that would come from voting his conscience. The pain he'd endure—that his family would endure—shouldn't be discounted. *Think about your career*, they told him. *Think about your family.*

But Romney *was* thinking about his family. What kind of man would he be if he did the politically expedient thing when he knew it was wrong? What example would that set for his sons, for his grandchildren? In the final days before the vote, he talked over his decision with his wife, Ann. She was—and always had been—his closest and most trusted advisor. She told him to do what he believed was right.

Romney gulped back tears and tried to steady his voice. "I swore an oath before God to exercise impartial justice," he said, pausing to compose himself. "My faith is at the heart of who I am. I take an oath before God as enormously consequential."

It was just after two p.m. on Wednesday, February 5, and an emotional Romney was standing at his desk in the Senate chamber, announcing his decision to convict Trump on one of the two charges against him—abuse of power—before a relatively empty Senate chamber. Gone was the man who rarely betrayed his feelings. Rather, Romney seemed pained as he delivered his address.

In just two more hours, the Senate would vote to acquit Trump of both impeachment charges against him. But even at that late hour, no one saw Romney's announcement coming. He had declined to even give McConnell a heads-up. Instead, he had penned a letter explaining himself to his Republican colleagues, dispatching an aide to tuck a copy into each GOP senator's personal mailbox in the cloakroom as he headed to the Senate floor.

Over the course of eight minutes, Romney laid waste to every defense Trump's attorneys had used. Their contention that impeachment ought to be used just for statutory crimes flew so boldly in the
face of the Founders' stated intent that it "defies reason," he said.
Some breaches of public trust, while not statutory crimes, could be
so egregious that they would merit removal, he argued. Trump's attorneys' suggestion that the Bidens' activities in Ukraine justified
Trump's actions was also nonsensical, he added, despite Hunter's
"unsavory" attempts to capitalize on his last name.

"There's no question in my mind that were their names not Biden,
the president would never have done what he did," Romney said.

And the idea that the voters should decide Trump's fate? "While
that logic is appealing to our democratic instincts, it is inconsistent
with the Constitution's requirement that the Senate, not the voters,
try the president," Romney said declaratively. He had wrestled
with this point the most, but ultimately determined the president
had tried to compromise the very election to which his supporters
now wanted to defer. There could be no integrity in that.

Romney wanted his fellow senators and the whole nation to understand that his vote was a matter of conscience. "Were I to ignore
the evidence that has been presented . . . it would, I fear, expose my
character to history's rebuke," he said. "Corrupting an election to
keep oneself in office is perhaps the most abusive and destructive
violation of one's oath of office that I can imagine."

"With my vote, I will tell my children and their children that I
did my duty to the best of my ability believing that my country expected it of me," he concluded.

Across the room, Schatz, who had cleared his schedule so he
could be on the Senate floor when Romney spoke, openly wept
as a flood of relief coursed over him. Finally, one Republican had
demonstrated the courage to withstand the pressures of Trumpism.

As Romney finished and ducked into a Senate lobby to avoid the press, Schatz darted to catch up with him.

"Thank you," Schatz called out to Romney as he was leaving. "You've given me hope for the country."

Romney whirled around to face him and paused.

"Thank you," he answered. "I've been getting your notes."

Down the hall, in the Majority Leader's suite, McConnell sat watching Romney's speech on Fox News, which aired it in a split screen with a one-on-one interview he had given in advance to longtime network host Chris Wallace. Sure, McConnell had known all along that Romney would vote to allow witnesses to testify against Trump. But he had not seen this final twist coming.

Just minutes before Romney's speech, an aide had come running into the Majority Leader's suite holding the letter the Utah Republican had left in McConnell's cloakroom cubby. The aide handed it to counsel Andrew Ferguson, who immediately barged into McConnell's office to warn him what Romney was about to do.

As they flipped on the television to watch, McConnell's staff fumed. Romney was going to screw Collins's reelection campaign, depriving the Maine senator of needed political cover for her planned "not guilty" vote, they predicted.

But McConnell stayed calm, and as he watched, the corners of his mouth started to turn up. He hadn't expected this—but losing one Republican wasn't about to quell his sense of victory that day. Regardless of Romney's antics, the president was about to be acquitted and emerge stronger than ever.

McConnell had gone through the whole trial without ever publicly vocalizing what he privately felt about the president's conduct. Despite finding Trump's Ukraine pressure campaign repugnant, he had never once openly rebuked Trump for those actions. McConnell had simply loaded his quiver with procedural arrows, taking shots at the way the Democrats had presented their case to avoid having to weigh in on the merits of what Trump had done.

Some Democrats would always paint McConnell as a politically driven, self-serving operator for having helped Trump. But as far as the GOP leader was concerned, he had just saved the judicial branch, saved a Republican presidency, and, best of all, saved his Senate majority—or so he thought in that moment. He had turned the threat of Trump's ouster into a uniting, rally-around-the-flag moment for the vast bulk of the GOP. Against that backdrop, who cared about Mitt Romney's vote?

Trump World certainly did. Donald Trump Jr. was already taking to Twitter to insist Romney be "expelled" from the GOP for becoming "a member of the resistance." Romney's own niece, Ronna McDaniel, the chairwoman of the Republican National Committee, also tweeted against her uncle—and approved a mass email accusing him of turning his back on Utah.

"This is not the first time I have disagreed with Mitt, and I imagine it will not be the last," she wrote. "I, along with the @GOP, stand with President Trump."

McConnell's staff warned him that the onslaught against Romney was just starting.

"There are going to be calls from some of our members and from the right and probably from the president to do something very drastic to take revenge on Romney—like kick him out of the conference," Ferguson said.

But McConnell shook his head at the suggestion. "Oh, come on," he said, scoffing. "That's not how this place works." Impeachment was about to be put behind them, and he had other political battles to worry about.

"We need Romney for the other important stuff we need to do in the future," McConnell said. "On to the next thing."

Across the Capitol, Schiff was stealing a rare quiet moment alone when Romney started to speak. He had tucked himself into a cloakroom off the House floor to take stock of the trial. His work was done, and there was nothing to do but wait for the verdict, just a few hours away. In the meantime, Schiff had turned a television on to a livestream of the Senate floor. The managers were sure to lose, but how badly? Would they secure every last Democratic vote? Was there any hope of turning a single Republican?

Every GOP senator but Romney already had announced his or her intention to acquit. So when the Utah senator rose to speak, Schiff turned up the volume and braced for the worst.

As Romney condemned Trump, Schiff felt a weight lift off his shoulders. He had been intermittently watching the senators' speeches that day, and nearly each one had referenced him. Some Democrats had nice things to say about his presentations. Most Republicans had blasted him for bringing them an incomplete case.

Schiff was too steeled by partisan politics to be personally hurt by the attacks. He fervently believed he had had no choice but to bring these charges against Trump, and no option but to work around the courts, leaving determinations about witnesses ultimately in the Senate's hands. But had his efforts always been doomed to fail? If they ended up with nothing more than a party-line vote on impeachment, would it have been worth it?

The answer, Schiff thought to himself, was yes—and in his mind, Romney had proved it. His vote to convict—even on just one charge—was vindication, in Schiff's estimation, for his case and, most importantly, for impeachment.

Schiff rose from his chair. It was time to meet up with the other managers and make their way into the Senate to watch the final vote. As he exited the cloakroom, he smiled to himself. American democracy, he thought, was going to be okay.

He was wrong.

40

"THE IMPEACHMENT
THAT WASN'T"

FEBRUARY 6, 2020–JANUARY 6, 2021

Trump proudly held up a copy of the *Washington Post* and gestured at the words emblazoned in big bold letters across the front page: "Trump acquitted."[1] All around him, his supporters were cheering. They had filled the East Room of the White House that morning of February 6 to celebrate the end of the impeachment trial and the redemption of the leader they had all risked their reputations to defend. Pat Cipollone and Trump's defense team received a standing ovation when they entered the room. Jim Jordan and Mark Meadows clapped and hooted in celebration. Kevin McCarthy smiled ear to ear with his deputy Steve Scalise grinning next to him. Even the edge of Mitch McConnell's frown turned up momentarily into a contented smile, as he stood next to McCarthy, taking in the scene.

Minutes before, Trump had stridden through a pair of wooden double doors and down a plush red carpet to a triumphant recording of trumpets blaring "Hail to the Chief." Traditionally, such choreography and staging were used only for the most serious announcements related to American national security or moments of public mourning. Years earlier, President Barack Obama had walked through those doors with solemnity to announce the killing of 9/11 mastermind Osama bin Laden. But on that day, Trump had organized this party to celebrate himself.

The atmosphere in the East Room was as close as one could get to a Trump rally within the White House walls. For more than an hour, the president tore into his perceived enemies, lashing out at anyone who had been involved in investigating him and calling them "evil." He derided Special Counsel Robert Mueller's Russia probe as "bullshit," railing against the FBI as "leakers and liars." Nancy Pelosi was a "horrible person." Adam Schiff was "vicious." Former FBI director James Comey was a "sleazebag." And Mitt Romney, who naturally had not been invited to the celebration, "ran one of the worst campaigns in the history of the presidency."

"We went through hell unfairly!" the president crowed. "Did nothing wrong. Nothing wrong!"

As an epilogue to impeachment, Trump's self-celebration in the East Room broke the mold. In 1999, Bill Clinton had offered an apology following his acquittal, stating he was "profoundly sorry" for his actions and imploring the nation to come together after a divisive trial.[2] But where Clinton had urged reconciliation, an unapologetic Trump promised retribution. Everyone—from the "dirty cops" and "bad people" at the FBI, to the Democrats who had "made up facts" and engaged in "tremendous corruption"—was on his list for payback.

"We went through hell . . . but I'm sure they'll try and cook up other things," Trump said, predicting the House would try to impeach him again. "In my opinion, it's almost like they want to destroy our country. We can't let it happen."

The Republicans gathered in the room nodded approvingly. For months, they had shelved their private concerns about the propriety of the president's conduct in the name of party unity, hoping their gamble on Trump would pay off. In return, he had come through the fire of his trial stronger than ever—and he had the poll numbers to prove it. A Pew Research poll taken in the weeks after Trump's acquittal showed that only about 46 percent of voters believed Trump "did something wrong regarding Ukraine and that it was enough to justify his removal from office," compared with 53 percent who said the opposite.[3] And from a public relations perspective, impeachment had flopped: Only 24 percent of respondents said they had followed the trial "very closely" and only 28 percent of people said they had understood the facts and evidence against him.[4] In fact, had the 2020 elections taken place that afternoon, Trump likely would have sailed smoothly to a second term.

But the rest of the year would throw a series of curveballs that would test not only the Republican Party, but the country. The president who could not win gracefully had not yet plumbed the depths of his own capacity for institutional destruction in the face of possible defeat. In subjugating their principles in deference to Trump, the GOP had unleashed a monster—and he was only beginning his rampage.

Heads started rolling the next day, as the unbound president claimed his first victims: key witnesses who had testified against him in the House's impeachment investigation. GOP lawmakers had spent months trying to convince Trump not to exact that kind of revenge[5]—but on the far side of his acquittal, Trump no longer heeded their advice. He knew they would be loyal no matter what he did.

Alexander Vindman, whose "right matters" statement had so rankled Trump's supporters, was the first to get the boot, alongside his twin brother, another NSC staffer. Gordon Sondland, the affable ambassador who ultimately told Congress that "everyone was in the loop" about his side operation to leverage Ukraine into investigating the Bidens, was canned the same day.[6] Then it was the government watchdogs' turn. Trump pushed out acting director of national intelligence Joseph Maguire after one of his staffers told lawmakers Russia was once again trying to interfere in the 2020 election to help Trump win.[7] A few weeks later, he axed Michael Atkinson, the inspector general of the intelligence community, who had flagged the whistleblower's complaint to the Hill and deemed it an "urgent concern." By April, Trump had expelled five inspectors general, unshackling some of his administration's largest departments from the internal checking mechanisms meant to keep their operations aboveboard.[8] The purge of nonpartisan watchdogs—whose sole duties were to ensure ethical standards in government—was unprecedented.

It was around this time that Trump also began overtly putting his thumb on the scale of ongoing Justice Department probes, making good on his repeated threats to bring prosecutors to heel. He blasted federal prosecutors for recommending a seven- to nine-year prison sentence for his friend Roger Stone, who had been convicted of lying to Congress and witness tampering. When senior officials in Bill Barr's Justice Department subsequently ordered the sentencing request to be reduced, four of the prosecutors on the case quit in protest. Trump would later commute Stone's sentence and ultimately pardon him, alongside other allies charged as part of the Russia probe.

Trump also doubled down on his political crusade for dirt on the Bidens. Only this time, instead of crossing an ocean to pressure a foreign ally, he went straight to his supporters in the U.S. Senate, getting Ron Johnson, the Republican senator who had once urged him to release Ukraine's military assistance, to take up the mantle of a probe.

It was against this backdrop that a deadly virus from the hinterlands of China reached the United States, the beginning of the most fatal pandemic in a hundred years. Prior to his acquittal, Trump had already been briefed twice that the so-called coronavirus would spread globally.[9] But the president saw the dire warnings as a threat to his reelection. He downplayed the severity of the virus, shrugging it off as no worse than the flu. He scoffed at scientists and health officials, accusing anyone and everyone who sounded an alarm of fearmongering in order to make him look bad—or trying to cripple the strong economy that had become the centerpiece of his pitch for a second term as president. He made fun of people who wore masks to prevent transmission of the disease. He mused that Americans ought to inject themselves with bleach to combat the virus.

As the U.S. death toll skyrocketed, Democrats struggled to hold the White House's feet to the fire. Pelosi, under public pressure, impaneled a special committee to investigate the administration's bungled response to the pandemic. But when Trump ignored their inquiries as usual, they did little to try to force compliance.

After Trump's acquittal, Pelosi had clamped down on congressional oversight. In a series of mid-February meetings, the Speaker, who had soured on the impeachment experience, insisted that Democrats stop focusing on Trump's misdeeds and pivot all of their attention to policy before the election. No more high-profile Trump hearings, no more never-ending investigations.

"No more freelancing, no more emoluments," she said sternly during a February 11 meeting. "Get back to jobs and health care."

Jerry Nadler, Jamie Raskin, and their allies had tried to object, insisting they could legislate and investigate simultaneously. But Pelosi had allies on her side, including Schiff, and her word was final.

For months, as Trump went on his retribution binge, House Democrats issued no new subpoenas for Trump administration officials' testimony, eager to keep the focus on issues that resonated with voters before Election Day. They sidestepped multiple opportunities to ask Trump officials their unanswered questions about the Ukraine saga at congressional hearings.[10] Even when Bolton's memoir finally hit bookshelves in June, Democrats averted their gaze.

Bolton's first-person account showed that Trump had done exactly what Democrats had accused him of in Ukraine and even alleged Trump sought political favors from China. The president, Bolton recounted, had offered to bless China's worst human rights violations, including the construction of concentration camps, in order to secure more favorable conditions from Beijing during trade negotiations that he could parlay to farmers, a key constituency of his base.[11] It was a stark reminder of how much Democrats had left on the cutting-room floor during impeachment by electing not to run down Bolton's testimony.

But instead of calling Bolton in to testify, Pelosi's Democratic caucus found themselves exactly where they were in early 2019: torn between a cautious Speaker who viewed oversight as a distraction from an otherwise winning campaign message and members who felt they had a duty to make sure Congress's authority was respected. It was only when Trump ousted a U.S. attorney for the Southern District of New York who had been investigating his associates that some House Democrats began demanding action. The liberal rank and file once again insisted that Pelosi launch an investigation into the politicization of the Justice Department and subpoena Bolton's testimony. By midsummer, Barr appeared for a public hearing, but Bolton would never be called.

Meanwhile, all the House's lingering investigations of Trump—from his taxes to emoluments and Mueller-related issues—were hopelessly stuck in the courts. By the time the 2020 election kicked into high gear in the early summer of 2020, talk of impeachment and Trump probes writ large had essentially vanished amid the pandemic and its ensuing chaos. Impeachment didn't even merit a mention at the Republican or Democratic Party's national convention.

"It was the impeachment that wasn't," Raskin lamented at one point. "It's like it never happened."

Ultimately, the thing that ended Trump's presidency had little to do with impeachment; what tanked him was his fumbled response to the pandemic. By Election Day, more than 200,000 people had died from coronavirus infections and those numbers were only growing.[12] Though Trump won more than 74 million votes—more than any other presidential candidate in any previous presidential election—Joe Biden beat him with more than 81 million, posting about 51.3 percent to Trump's 46.8 percent.[13]

Trump, however, would never accept the loss. Instead, the man who had spent the last four years accusing Democrats of trying to overturn the results of the 2016 election that won him the presidency, was about to lead a campaign to do just that in 2020.

"Just go declare victory right now."

That was the advice Rudy Giuliani gave Trump on Election Night,[14] just minutes after Fox News shocked the nation and called Arizona for Joe Biden. That declaration, from the network that the president had always counted in his corner, rang out like a death knell: It meant Trump's time in the White House was all but over. But the president who mocked losers, and couldn't stand to be considered one himself, would not admit defeat. Instead, he took Giuliani's advice—and refused to concede.

"As far as I'm concerned, we already have won," Trump said that night as returns showed Biden undeniably ahead.

Such began the final chapter of Trump's presidency and his most blatant attempt yet to bend democracy to his will. Over the course of the next several weeks, Trump promulgated the false claim that the election was stolen from him and tried to strong-arm the Republican Party into subverting the results to keep him in power. He had gotten away with so much over the years, what was one more desperate act—even if it went against all the country had stood for since the dawn of the republic?

Trump had set the stage to discredit the election early. Over the summer, he'd claimed that mail-in ballots—which millions had relied on to vote amid the pandemic and which usually swung Democratic—were "fraudulent" attempts by liberal operators and foreign instigators to boot him out of office. He openly vowed to financially hamstring the U.S. Postal Service so it couldn't process the expected deluge, threatening to keep millions of legitimate votes he thought would benefit Biden from being counted.

After he lost, Trump's antics grew more desperate. Giuliani and a group of far-right collaborators spun the president up on a series of conspiracy theories about ballots being dumped into rivers and state officials cooking the books against him. They even alleged that Venezuela, Cuba, China, and operators of Italian satellites had fixed voting machines to help Biden, encouraging Trump to try to seize those machines and launch a massive investigation.

As swing state after swing state declared Biden the victor, Trump and his lawyers filed more than sixty court cases seeking to invalidate legitimate votes—all but one of which ultimately failed.[15] By early December, a total of eighty-six judges—nearly half of them appointed by Republicans—had rejected their appeals as frivolous, lacking standing, or devoid of substantial evidence of fraud.[16] One of those was an appeal by seventeen GOP state attorneys general to the Supreme Court asking the judges to invalidate the results of four key swing states that went for Biden. Trump had pressured his allies to take up the charge, believing the conservative-leaning high court would do him a favor. Instead, they ruled the states had no authority to question the election processes in other states.

Having failed in the courts, Trump sought other avenues to overturn the election results. In an early-December meeting, the president tried to squeeze his attorney general, Bill Barr, to start a Justice Department investigation into the election. But even the ever-loyal Barr balked, likening Giuliani and his team of radical lawyers to a "clown show" peddling "bullshit."[17] By that point, Barr had already publicly declared that the department had looked into the issue and found no evidence of fraud widespread enough to change the results.[18] He tried to explain to Trump that the Justice Department couldn't be used to take sides in an election. But Trump kept pressuring him, prompting Barr to propose he quit.[19] Before Christmas, he had resigned as attorney general.

When Barr refused to act, Trump began putting the screws to Republican state and local officials to take up his claims of foul play. He personally lobbied GOP legislators from Michigan and Pennsylvania, imploring them over a series of Oval Office meetings and phone calls not to certify Biden's victory. In Georgia—where Trump had demanded a recount but then refused to accept the results confirming Biden's win—he took a more bullying posture: He began labeling Republican election officials who wouldn't toss votes the "enemy of the people," spinning up such a fervor that one of them warned "someone's going to get hurt, someone's going to get shot, someone's going to get killed."[20] Trump—joined by his new chief of staff Mark Meadows, who had defended him through the House impeachment investigation—would go on to pressure Georgia's GOP secretary of state on a private call to "find 11,780 votes," one more than his exact deficit to Biden.[21]

When his judicial and legislative pressure gambits fell through, Trump turned his sights on Congress to make a final stand. On January 6, 2021, the House and Senate were slated to count the Electoral College votes, in what was typically a pro forma affair to certify the results. Trump, however, saw it as a choke point to deny Biden his victory and began leaning on his allies in the House and Senate to object to the results of the swing states he had lost.

Trump had gotten away with lying for more than four years, buttressed by a Republican Party that catered to his whims and rarely rebuked him. So when he began spouting lies that winter about the election being stolen, he had every expectation that the GOP would echo his charges once again. But Barr was far from the only Republican to balk. For the first time in four years, party leaders were gripped by panic about what might happen if they let Trump have his way and refused to blindly follow him.

In the West Wing, Vice President Mike Pence paid public homage to Trump's claim to have won, even tweeting a few days after the election that "it ain't over til it's over . . . and this AIN'T OVER!" But privately, his staff complained about what they called "crazy town" Trump ideas. They tried to keep their boss as far away from the president as possible, planning day trips away from Washington so they would not have to appear in public together. Cipollone, meanwhile, found himself on the outs with the president for privately telling him that he couldn't just seize voting machines via executive order.[22] Others got iced out for simply saying the election was over. Slowly, a mass exodus began to take place, as Republicans who worked for Trump scrambled to salvage their reputations by putting distance between themselves and the president's antics.

Elsewhere around town, Trump's top Cabinet officials and military leaders feared the president was becoming unhinged—so much so that General Mark Milley, the chairman of the Joint Chiefs of Staff, worried the president might try to use the Insurrection Act to enlist the military to keep himself in power. He also privately likened Trump's rhetoric to Adolf Hitler's.[23] Former Republican secretaries of defense began blasting public and private warnings that the Pentagon should never be used to disrupt the election—no matter what Trump wanted.

On Capitol Hill, Mitch McConnell's concerns also skyrocketed. Even before the president's loss, the GOP leader had been alarmed by the groundwork Trump appeared to be laying to discredit the election, including his attacks on mail-in voting. He defended Trump's right to file the lawsuits alleging election fraud, but didn't believe a word of his claims. In a bid to keep the GOP unified, however, he didn't publicly push back—at least not right away. Control of the Senate chamber had been left up for grabs after a pair of critical Georgia races went to a runoff scheduled for January 5. McConnell decided he couldn't antagonize Trump while he needed his help turning out Georgia's Republican base to the polls.

Privately, however, McConnell was more vocal with his concerns. He phoned Pence to ask what on earth Trump's endgame was. He pushed Barr to unequivocally refute Trump's election conspiracy theories. "You are really the only one who can do it," McConnell told Barr, explaining that the unfinished Senate battles had tied his own hands.[24]

McConnell's group of so-called legal eagles from impeachment were equally perplexed, even as some of them—like Lindsey Graham—paid homage to Trump publicly. Graham spent much of November and December trying to privately talk Trump into accepting the results of the election, encouraging him to think of the future and a possible 2024 run for the White House. Graham prodded Giuliani for proof—any proof whatsoever—of his allegations of fraud. But each batch of "evidence" Giuliani sent was riddled with inaccuracies and fanciful ideas, leaving Graham frustrated.

Yet as some of Trump's leading allies backed away from him, others were all too willing to fill the void. In mid-December, a few stalwart loyalists—led by Jim Jordan in the House and Josh Hawley in the Senate—stepped up to meet the president's call to arms, declaring that they would object to the results from the states Trump had tried to contest in court. Most privately acknowledged that the effort wouldn't make a difference—so if it made Trump and the base happy, their thinking went, what did they have to lose?

One of those who jumped on the bandwagon was Senator Ted Cruz. The skilled but cocky Republican had initially scoffed at the idea of objecting to the Electoral College count when Trump's House allies privately pitched him on the plan. But when Hawley volunteered, Cruz recalculated. A band of longtime Cruz advisors—including Charles Cooper, John Bolton's prominent attorney from impeachment—attempted an intervention, warning the Texas senator against joining Trump's crusade and predicting it could result in violence. But Cruz had already made up his mind—and his decision led almost a dozen more to follow.

Trump, meanwhile, began to whip up his base for the upcoming showdown, arguing that their voices and votes were being ignored by Washington. His most fervent allies blanketed conservative channels, carrying his grievances to the nation via Fox News, One

America News Network, and Newsmax—and promising January 6 would be the day they'd right the wrongs.

"Big protest in D.C. on January 6th," Trump tweeted on December 19, one of several missives promoting a rally to overturn the election results. "Be there, will be wild!"

PART FOUR

SHATTERING THE GUARDRAILS

JANUARY 6, 2021

Sitting in the Oval Office, just hours before Congress was set to certify Joe Biden as the next president, an angry and agitated President Trump called Mike Pence and demanded he do something no other vice president had done in the history of the nation. He wanted him to overturn the results of an election.

Trump had been browbeating his No. 2 since mid-December to exploit his role presiding over that day's joint session of Congress to reject the Electoral College results. His longtime advisors and allies, from White House counsel Pat Cipollone to Senator Lindsey Graham, had been telling him for weeks that Pence had no authority to do so. Indeed, almost every constitutional scholar thought the idea was completely ludicrous—not to mention antithetical to the fundamental principles of election by the people. But Trump wasn't listening. Having failed to maintain power through other means, he viewed Pence as his last hope—and he was getting desperate.

By that morning, the idea that January 6 would be his last stand had become something of an obsession for Trump. Throughout

December, when he turned on *Fox & Friends* in the White House residence, one particular commercial would repeatedly taunt him: "The end is coming, Donald," said the ominous voice on the ad. "On January 6, Mike Pence will put the nail in your political coffin when he presides over the Senate vote to prove Joe Biden won. It's over."[1] The commercial, sponsored by a group of so-called Never-Trump Republicans, enraged the president so much that he ordered Pence to send them a cease-and-desist letter.[2]

As far as Trump was concerned, Pence owed him. In his mind, he had made the former congressman turned Indiana governor's career by choosing him as a running mate and elevating him to the second-highest office in the land. Yet by January 6, Pence was still resisting Trump's demands.

"I have no authority as vice president to do that," Pence had told Trump two days prior during an Oval Office meeting, explaining that his role presiding over the congressional session was wholly ceremonial.

Trump tried again on January 5—and grew angry when he received the same answer. "You don't understand, Mike," Trump said, yelling. "You CAN do this. I don't want to be your friend anymore if you don't do this."[3]

By the morning of January 6, Trump's desperation was reaching a boiling point. The supporters he had invited to Washington were already amassing on the Ellipse outside to protest the Electoral College results. Despite the near-freezing temperature, Trump had opened the door off the Oval Office to hear the sounds of his followers, whom he would address later at a rally they were dubbing "Stop the Steal."

But the cheers weren't enough to soothe the president. He grabbed his phone and made one last attempt to change Pence's mind.

"All Mike Pence has to do is send them back to the States, AND WE WIN," he wrote on Twitter, shortly after eight a.m. "Do it Mike, this is a time for extreme courage!"

Then he dialed Pence.

The vice president was at his residence in the Naval Observatory that morning, putting the finishing touches on a public statement he'd been meticulously working on—and dreading—for days. The conservative Republican had been fiercely loyal to Trump for four years, bending over backwards to ensure he never found himself crosswise with the man whose personal conduct regularly flew in the face of his own Christian values. But the president's latest demands were too much for Pence's conscience. He had sought advice from all corners of the conservative world on how to handle the situation, even phoning former GOP vice president Dan Quayle to triple-check that he could not do what Trump was demanding.[4] Everyone, universally, told him no—that what Trump wanted was not only absurd but illegal. That morning, Pence was preparing to release a statement explaining why he was defying a president he had fawned over for years.

The president, of course, wouldn't hear of it.

"You can either go down in history as a patriot," Trump told Pence on the phone, "or you can go down in history as a pussy."[5]

Pence recoiled at Trump's words. But he kept his cool, and for the first time ever, he told the president no. Minutes later, as his motorcade sped toward the U.S. Capitol, where he would preside over Biden being declared the forty-sixth president, Pence's staff released his statement reminding voters that four years ago he swore an oath to defend the Constitution.

"Today, I want to assure the American people that I will keep the oath I made," the statement read. "So help me God."[6]

McConnell froze in shock when a Capitol Police officer rushed into the Senate chamber carrying a massive semiautomatic weapon. The Majority Leader had been so engrossed in the Electoral College debate happening before him that he hadn't even realized anything was amiss—until pandemonium engulfed the chamber.

Mere moments before, Pence's Secret Service detail had entered the chamber and beckoned the vice president away from the dais where he was overseeing proceedings, a rarity for the agents, who usually loitered just outside the doors. A hum spread through the chamber as staff shut down the debate, whispering to senators that "protesters are in the building." The senator who had stepped in to cover for Pence on the dais was quickly replaced by a security officer making an ominous announcement.

"This is a security situation," he said into the microphone. "We're asking that everyone remain in the chamber. It's the safest place."

Suddenly, armed guards raced to McConnell, pulling him from his chair and hurriedly escorting him out of the room with as much speed as a man handicapped by childhood polio could muster.

With no access to a cell phone or television—neither was allowed in the chamber—McConnell had no idea what was happening. But he certainly had a guess. During a brief break in the proceedings, he had caught a few televised snippets of Trump's speech at the Ellipse. The president was spinning up his supporters, encouraging the thousands who had come to Washington to take their protest to the Capitol.

"They rigged an election! They rigged it like they've never rigged an election before!" Trump had told the crowd. "You'll never take back our country with weakness . . . And if you don't fight like hell, you're not going to have a country anymore."

McConnell had expected trouble of some sort that day. He had spent the previous week trying to convince his GOP members not to object to the peaceful transfer of power that had been the bedrock of the country for over 230 years. Their oaths of office took precedence over any political fealty to Trump, he argued.

"This is the most important vote I will cast in my thirty-six years of the Senate," McConnell had told his colleagues on a December 31 GOP conference call. "It goes right to the heart of our democracy. There is no ambiguity about it. Once the Electoral College makes the decision, that's it."

But McConnell knew his arguments were falling on deaf ears. Just under a dozen of his most Trumpian members had publicly vowed to their constituents to carry out the president's orders. It was one of the reasons McConnell had insisted that Pence meet with the Senate parliamentarian before the certification began, so the chamber rule-keeper could reinforce that the vice president had one job and one job only: to count votes.

It was rare that McConnell ever took his disagreements with fellow Republicans public. He had spent four years, in fact, desperately trying to project a united front through political crises and an impeachment—even, for a time, while Trump spouted falsehoods about the 2020 election. But by that morning, even McConnell had reached his limit. The night before, Democrats had all but declared victory in a pair of special runoff elections in Georgia, making it a near certainty that the GOP would lose the Senate majority—and McConnell would lose control of the chamber. For that, he blamed Trump and Trump alone. The president's unrepentant lies about the election had depressed GOP voter turnout and invigorated Democrats, McConnell believed. But McConnell knew Trump didn't care about the party; only about himself. And as far as the Senate Republican leader was concerned, his rank and file needed to understand it was time to move on.

At 1:30 p.m., as the Senate began debating Arizona's election results—the first to be challenged—McConnell once again implored his GOP colleagues to stand down. From a podium in the Senate chamber, he noted that there was no proof of fraud on the level Trump was alleging. And he argued that "if this election were overturned by mere allegations from the losing side, our democracy would enter a death spiral."

"We cannot simply declare ourselves a national board of elections on steroids. The voters, the courts, and the states have all spoken," McConnell continued. "If we overrule them, it would damage our republic forever."

At almost that exact moment, unbeknownst to McConnell, about ten thousand Trump supporters were besieging the Capitol. Agitators had broken through a series of flimsy bike racks marking the Capitol's outer perimeter and climbed over a stage and bleachers that had been erected for Biden's forthcoming inauguration. They had scaled the sides of the Capitol building while chanting, "We want Trump! We want Trump!"

Capitol Police tried to push them back with riot shields, dispensing tear gas into the crowd. But they were quickly overwhelmed by the swelling mob. Trump supporters began beating up the cops as they pushed toward the entrances, calling the officers "traitors" as they dragged one down a set of stairs and kicked another lying on the ground trying to shield his head. They picked up metal bike racks to use as weapons to mow down police officers. They turned their flagpoles—carrying a mix of Confederate, American, Trump, and "Don't Tread on Me" banners—into makeshift lances and spears, felling law enforcement officers who blocked their path to the Capitol.

"We will not stop!" they chanted. "We will not stop!"

Inside the Senate chamber, McConnell was still unaware of the encroaching mob when assailants in Trump gear and tactical body armor used a wooden beam to shatter a first-floor window one floor below him. As the president's supporters began spilling into the halls, a band of the nearly all-white, all-male horde carrying metal baseball bats and riot shields they'd wrested from police officers began hunting for lawmakers. They bore down on a lone Black police officer, backing him up a set of stairs that led to a hallway just outside the Senate chamber, as he beat his billy club on the walls to warn of the encroaching danger.[7]

Four minutes later, an internal blast text from the Capitol Police flashed across the phones of every lawmaker and staffer on campus: "Due to security threat inside, immediately move inside your office, take emergency equipment, lock the doors, take shelter."[8] But because Senate floor rules prohibited the use of cell phones, McConnell missed the message.

After security officers finally pulled him from the chamber, McConnell's detail whisked him down to the Capitol basement and through the snake-like tunnels that weaved through the complex. As his staff updated him on the unraveling situation, officers led him to a Senate office building to escape the chaos, then hurried him away to an underground parking garage and shoved him in a car to get him off the property. Once safely on the road, McConnell's aides pulled up pictures and videos on their phones to show their boss the chaos outside. McConnell was dumbfounded. For the first time in over two centuries, the Capitol was under attack.

As McConnell's SUV pulled away from the Capitol grounds, the D.C. police officers who had rushed to help campus security were begging for backup and trying vainly to hold back the rioters. A mayday appeal for help had gone out to every sworn officer in the city, and a plea for armed backup had been issued from the D.C. mayor to the National Guard.[9] But it was too late to turn back the tide. The officers were overwhelmed and outnumbered, and the frenzied, violent crowds were still coming. At 2:28 p.m., seventeen minutes after the first rioters broke into the Capitol, a commanding officer from the D.C. police declared there was nothing left to do but retreat.

"We've lost the line," he declared over the radio, his voice breaking in exhausted defeat.[10]

In a small private room off the side of the Senate chamber, Mike Pence was refusing to evacuate. Despite the security situation and the rioters coursing through the hallways outside, the vice president was damned if he was going to give Trump's backers the satisfaction of seeing him turn tail and run. So when his Secret Service detail told him it was time to go, he said no.

"I am not leaving the Capitol," he said firmly, as his wife, daughter, and brother Greg, a GOP congressman, huddled in the room with him.[11]

A few minutes later, his Secret Service tried again. And once again, Pence refused.

"The last thing I want is for these people to see a motorcade fleeing the scene," he said. "That is not an image we want. I'm not leaving."

Earlier that afternoon, Pence had barely picked up the gavel to launch Congress's election certification proceedings when Trump excoriated him in front of his supporters at the other end of the National Mall. "Mike Pence, I hope you're going to stand up for the good of our Constitution and for the good of our country," he told the crowds at the "Stop the Steal" rally. "And if you're not, I'm going to be very disappointed in you!" Now, as Pence hid from the mob, those same MAGA fanatics had erected gallows in front of the Capitol building, the rope noose ready for his neck. Down the hall, mere feet from where Pence and his family hid, they searched for him to a chilling chant: "Hang Mike Pence! Hang Mike Pence!"

As Pence resisted his evacuation, Trump continued to taunt him on Twitter. "Mike Pence didn't have the courage to do what should

have been done to protect our Country and our Constitution, giving
States a chance to certify a corrected set of facts, not the fraudulent
or inaccurate ones which they were asked to previously certify," he
wrote, as Pence hid from the mob. "USA demands the truth!"

Two minutes later, Pence's Secret Service agents stopped giving
him a say in the matter. Pointing to the glass panels on the chamber
door, they told the vice president they could not protect him or his
family there.

"We need to *go*!" a Secret Service agent said.

The officers managed to get Pence as far as the basement garage
of the Capitol before the vice president began protesting his evacuation again. His security detail implored him to at least sit inside
the armed limousine they had standing by. Again, Pence adamantly
refused.

"I know what you're going to do," Pence told his detail, suggesting that the second the car door closed, his guards would peel rub-
ber out of the complex. "I am not sitting in that car."

Standing stubbornly in the parking garage, Pence turned to his
chief of staff, Marc Short, to devise a plan. Trump, by design or by
circumstance, wasn't responding to the chaos unfolding above their
heads inside the Capitol. Someone needed to act presidential and
end this madness.

"Get Kevin McCarthy on the phone," Pence instructed. Short
pulled up his cell and pressed the call button.

McCarthy screamed into the receiver at the president as his detail
whisked him away from the Capitol, where protesters had overrun
his office. Bombs had been discovered at the RNC and DNC, the
House Minority Leader told Trump. Someone had been shot.

"You've got to tell these people to stop," he said, demanding the president intervene—or at least release a statement renouncing the mob's violence. "I've never seen anything like this . . . Get them out of here. NOW!"[12]

Trump wasn't interested.

"Well, Kevin, I guess these people are more upset about the election than you are," he replied blithely.[13]

Minutes before Trump's followers broke into the building, McCarthy had been in his second-floor suite, fine-tuning a floor speech justifying the GOP's objections to the Electoral College results. His heart wasn't in it—he had struggled for weeks over whether to follow through on Trump's demand. But McCarthy wanted to be Speaker someday—and that meant staying in the president's good graces.

As McCarthy had prepared to head to the floor to address the chamber, one of his members, Bruce Westerman, rushed into his office to ask if Trump was headed to the Capitol. The Arkansas Republican described how he just heard the president encourage his followers at the "Stop the Steal" rally to head to the Capitol building and even suggested he might follow. McCarthy was perplexed. There was no way Trump would come to the Hill. Or was there?

A few minutes later, McCarthy's chief security officer had poked his head into McCarthy's office. "We may need to relocate you," the officer told him. McCarthy waved him off—but the interruptions prompted him to pay closer attention to the rioting crowds outside his window. He dashed out a tweet calling on protesters to remain peaceful, but it did little good. Within minutes, the sound of pounding on the doors below started reverberating through his entire office. Then suddenly, his detail was back, instructing McCarthy that it was time to go.

Initially, McCarthy refused. He wasn't leaving his staff behind, he told the guard. If he was in danger, then so were they; either they all left or they all stayed, he said. The officer looked around the room. At a loss for how to get McCarthy out otherwise, he agreed to the leader's terms.

"FOLLOW!" the guard bellowed through the room.

"I guess I'm not going to the floor," McCarthy said dryly as he ran out the door, his aides close on his heels.

As McCarthy's crew raced down the steps to the Capitol basement, they could hear protesters yelling down the hall. In the underground hallways, they came across a group of cafeteria workers cleaning up after the lunch rush as if nothing were amiss.

"You gotta get out of here!" someone yelled toward them. "Run!"

Once they reached the underground parking garage, McCarthy jumped in an SUV manned by Capitol Police officers ready to whisk him to safety. As they sped him away, he took out his phone and dialed Trump. The president, he believed, was the only person who could stop this.

When Trump told McCarthy the rioters must "like Trump more than you do," the GOP leader hit the roof. How many times had he bent over backward to protect the president? How many times had he turned a blind eye when he knew the president's actions were wrong? Trump owed him—and all House Republicans—an intervention to stop the attack. Their lives were on the line. Yet here was Trump, acting like a put-out child.

"Who the fuck do you think you're talking to?" McCarthy yelled.

Trump told McCarthy that Antifa—a violent, left-wing anti-racism group—was actually behind the violence, not his own supporters. McCarthy was aghast. *Did Trump actually think that he, who had been in the Capitol and watched the attack unfold with his own eyes, was so stupid as to fall for this drivel?*

"They're *your* people," McCarthy said, noting that Trump supporters were at that very moment climbing through his office window. "Call them off!"

As the car sped away from the besieged Capitol, McCarthy frantically tried to come up with a plan. He called the president's son-in-law Jared Kushner, begging him to get to the White House and make Trump put an end to the violence.[14] But Kushner wasn't even in town. McCarthy began to think about trying to reach Trump via television. Maybe, if he took to the networks, he could break through by calling the president out publicly.

Before McCarthy could do anything, his phone rang. It was Pence. He told the vice president what Trump had just said to him. They would be on their own.

At the other end of Pennsylvania Avenue, Trump sat in a dining room abutting the Oval Office and marveled at the television coverage of his devotees storming the Capitol. Multiple aides were rushing in and out, begging him to make a public statement calling for peace. "This is out of control," Pence's national security advisor Keith Kellogg told him, imploring Trump to send a white flag via Twitter. His daughter Ivanka also kept running in and out of the room, imploring her father to call off the riot. "Let it go," she pleaded with her dad, speaking of the election.[15]

Even Trump's son Donald Jr., who had urged Trump's followers to "fight" at the rally that morning, had been alarmed by the chaotic scene at the Capitol. From the airport, before he departed town, he had tweeted: "This is wrong and not who we are. Be peaceful." He also texted White House chief of staff Mark Meadows, imploring him to get his dad to stop the violence.

"He's got to condemn this shit ASAP," he texted. "We need an

Oval address. He has to lead now. It has gone too far and gotten out of hand."[16]

Don Jr. wasn't the only one appealing to Meadows. As Trump continued to bask in the televised images of his followers fighting for him, Fox News personalities from Laura Ingraham to Sean Hannity begged the White House chief of staff to get the president to call off the crowds. Down the hall, Meadows's staff warned him that Trump's supporters "are going to kill people."

But Trump was unruffled. His ego was too tickled at the sight of his followers doing just what he had asked: waging war in his name.

Shortly after 2:30 p.m., Trump had begrudgingly issued a tweet calling on his supporters to "please support our Capitol Police and Law Enforcement." But that was as much as he was willing to do. As far as Trump was concerned, the riot was Congress's problem, he told his aides. It was their job to defend the Capitol, he said, not his.

Perversely, the riot had actually buoyed Trump's hopes that he might be able to strong-arm his way to overturning the election. When the situation started to unravel, he began calling his GOP allies in Congress—not to check on their well-being but to make sure they didn't lose their nerve about objecting to the election.

On the second floor of the abandoned Rayburn House Office Building, David Cicilline began scribbling down a makeshift article of impeachment on a piece of scratch paper. The Rhode Island liberal and close friend of Jamie Raskin hadn't been in the chamber when the riot began. Due to pandemic-era social distancing rules, he had remained back in his office, awaiting his turn to vote during the Electoral College roll call.

Since Trump supporters started arriving at the Capitol that morning, Cicilline had been concerned that the unruly demonstration could turn violent and spiral out of control. Still, he was startled when a little box with two antennas in his office—which he had never even realized was there—began blaring a warning: "Shelter in place!" Cicilline had never heard anything like it in his few years on the Hill.

Minutes later, his chief of staff came rushing into the room reading aloud from an emergency email telling all offices to lock their doors, draw the window shades, and keep quiet.

It was around that time that Cicilline's staff received a call from a top aide to Congressman Ted Lieu, a fellow so-called "musketeer" who had made an early push for Trump's impeachment in the spring of 2019. Due to his office's close proximity to the newly discovered bombs at RNC and DNC headquarters, the California congressman had been forced to evacuate his office and had nowhere to hide. Cicilline invited Lieu to hole up with him.

In Cicilline's office, the two men and their chiefs of staff gaped at the images on the television screen before them. Protesters were inside the Capitol, thrashing around the Rotunda and climbing on the grand sculptures in Statuary Hall. In the House chamber, where some of their colleagues had been trapped trying to evacuate, Capitol Police were engaged in an armed standoff, pointing their guns at protesters trying to break down the doors of the chamber.

On Twitter and in text chains, the reports were even more ominous. Their colleagues in the chamber were being told to put on gas masks and duck for cover. There was even talk that someone had poured gasoline inside the Rotunda and was ready to set the place afire. As they tried to sort the rumors from the facts, Raskin's chief of staff began texting them in a panic from the second floor of the Capitol, where she was stranded alongside Raskin's daughter and son-and-law. The rioters were on the scaffolding, she said. Then in the Capitol. Then outside the door.

What do we do? she asked, her terror growing.

It was the sort of nightmare narration one might expect to hear from a hostage in an active shooter situation. At his desk watching the coverage, Cicilline's expression devolved from shock to rage. This was nothing short of sedition, he said.

"There is no way we can just allow this sort of behavior to pass," Cicilline argued aloud. "We are going to have to impeach Trump again."

Lieu needed no convincing. He had been following news about Trump's attempt to pressure Georgia election officials to "find" votes for him and was already convinced that those actions alone were enough to merit a second impeachment. Plus, who knew what Trump would do next? It was time to fight back against this hooligan president, he said.

Grabbing his phone, Lieu began punching out a tweet, reading it aloud to Cicilline as he wrote.

"This assault on our nation's Capitol is a coup attempt and all those involved should be prosecuted as such," he said. "Also, for those Dems saying we shouldn't impeach @realDonaldTrump again? You are wrong."

The two men began texting fellow House Judiciary Democrats and their staff to get them on board. Their panel, Lieu wrote to them, "should start drafting articles of impeachment now, regardless of what leadership says."[17]

"We have seen the consequences of being weak against Trump and not holding him accountable these last couple months," he added.

To their surprise, the response was mixed. Some told Cicilline and Lieu to calm down, noting that they were in the midst of a potentially deadly crisis. Others mentioned that Trump had only two weeks left in office. *What was the point?*

But pragmatism had never been the strong suit of the idealistic "musketeers." Trump had to go now, Cicilline said. Tonight. The two men agreed: *Let's do this.*

"This is outrageous, and the president caused it," Cicilline tweeted. "We should impeach and convict him tomorrow."

With that, he grabbed a notebook and began drafting the charges.

Across the Capitol campus, in a large Senate conference room guarded by armed cops, tensions were reaching a boiling point. The typically even-keeled Mitt Romney was ferociously lambasting Josh Hawley, blaming him for triggering the riot by endorsing Trump's outlandish election objections. Lindsey Graham, Trump's closest ally in the chamber, flew into a fit of rage at the "yahoos" who had invaded the Hill and screamed at the Senate sergeant at arms, who was hiding in the safe room with them.

"What the hell are you doing here? Go take back the Senate!" Graham barked at the chamber's top security official. "You've got guns . . . USE THEM!"

Graham only grew angrier upon hearing a rumor that started circulating among Trump allies in the room: that the president was refusing to send in troops to help secure the Capitol. From their lockdown, he tried to call Trump to get clarity. When the president didn't answer, he phoned his daughter Ivanka, pressing her on whether her dad was intentionally keeping the National Guard from responding to the crisis. He couldn't see any other reason it was taking so long for reinforcements to arrive.

Ivanka assured Graham that wasn't the case, but Graham was still furious at Trump's nonchalant response to hundreds of his followers laying waste to the Capitol. He pressed Ivanka to do more to get her dad to call off his dogs. He then called Cipollone and threatened that Republicans would forcibly remove Trump from office using the Twenty-Fifth Amendment if the president continued to do nothing.[18]

Lisa Murkowski was equally shaken as she waited out the violence. The Alaska Republican had been in her private hideaway office in the Senate basement when the riot had begun. All of a sudden, she had heard someone stumbling into the bathroom next to her office and heaving into the toilet. Peeking outside, she saw a bathroom door open and a police officer washing his face in the sink.

"Can I help you?" she asked, surprised. "Are you okay?"

The officer had paused and looked up at her, his eyes red and swollen shut from what appeared to be tear gas.

"No, I'm okay," he said almost frantically, racing out of the bathroom. "No, I got to get out there. They need my help."

As they waited out the violence, hoping the marauders wouldn't find them, Murkowski could still hear the police officer's retching, playing like a track on repeat, over and over in her head.[19]

A couple of miles away, at a military installation along the Anacostia River, Nancy Pelosi and Chuck Schumer were trying to figure out what the hell was going on with the National Guard. The Speaker and Minority Leader had been evacuated to Fort McNair alongside the other most senior lawmakers in Congress from both parties. Since the moment they'd arrived, they'd turned their holding room into a command center, trying frantically to figure out how to save the Capitol.

Sitting around a large break room with a leather couch so worn that it was held together with red duct tape, Pelosi and Schumer tried to make sense of the unfolding situation. Pelosi had been spirited away so quickly—and was caught so off-guard by the invasion— that she'd left her cell phone on the House chamber dais. Schumer had his antiquated flip phone out and was calling his members and aides, asking for updates. Every few minutes, their Capitol security details hovering in the hall would race into the room with a bit of news. Lawmakers in both chambers had been led to secret holding rooms in the congressional office buildings, though there was no telling if the mob would follow and find them. There were reports that some of the rioters were armed. And a group of Pelosi's aides had barricaded themselves in a conference room, hiding under a table as rioters yelled "Where's Nancy" and tried to kick down the doors. One of Steny Hoyer's top aides was calling him frantically, insisting the leaders clear the Capitol.

"You've got to get these fucking people out of here," she insisted from a locked holding room in the building.

But how?

On the wall across from a framed picture of George Washington on horseback, a large five-by-seven-foot projection screen had been lowered and tuned to CNN. The leaders gaped as, for the first time, they took in the full scene outside the Capitol. It looked like a war zone—with Congress on the losing side. Outnumbered cops clashed with protesters. Anarchists were breaking down doors and shattering windows. Police were getting sprayed with tear gas.

"This is all Trump's fault!" Hoyer cried out helplessly, to no one in particular. "This is all Trump's fault!"

Pelosi agreed. The man who started all of this, she reminded them grimly, still had control of the nation's nuclear codes.

"I can't believe this," she said indignantly. "Have you ever seen *anything* like this?

Elsewhere in D.C., the head of the National Guard had put armed troops on buses as soon as the Capitol Police chief alerted him to the unfolding riot. But he had still not received required orders from the Pentagon to deploy them. Troops in Virginia and Maryland were also ready to move, the Democratic leaders were hearing—yet they too had not received the green light.

At 3:19 p.m., just over an hour after the Capitol was breached, the Democratic leaders connected via phone with top Pentagon brass and demanded answers. Army secretary Ryan McCarthy insisted that his superior, acting Defense secretary Christopher Miller, had already approved mobilization of armed National Guard units. But seven minutes later, the besieged House sergeant at arms told them the opposite: He was still hearing from D.C. Guard leaders that no such order had been given.

Hoyer was getting a similar message from Larry Hogan, the governor of Maryland, who had a thousand National Guard troops on standby, ready to move. In a frantic phone call, Hoyer tried to explain to Hogan that the Pentagon had given those troops permission to mobilize—the top Army brass had just told Schumer so. But Hogan protested.

"Steny, I'm telling you, I don't care what Chuck says," the governor said. "I've been told by the Department of Defense that we don't have authorization."[20]

The Democratic leaders looked at each other, alarmed. What the hell was really going on? They asked each other the unthinkable: Could the problem be Trump? Was it possible that the president of the United States was telling the military to stand down—or worse, helping to orchestrate the attack?

Down the hall, Kevin McCarthy was working other channels—and also running into brick walls. Pacing the nondescript conference room where GOP leaders were sequestered at Fort McNair, he screamed at Dan Scavino, a top White House aide who often handled Trump's Twitter account. The tweet Trump had put out around 2:30 p.m. calling for calm was not good enough, McCarthy insisted. They had to do more to stop the violence.

"Trump has got to say: 'This has to stop,'" McCarthy growled into the phone. "He's the *only* one who can do it!"

Republican leaders had been escorted to a separate holdover room from the Democrats—peculiar silos given the ongoing crisis. In the GOP room, McConnell, his No. 2 John Thune, House Minority Whip Steve Scalise, and other GOP lawmakers were also working the phones trying to figure out what was going on. It was clear that McCarthy's appeals to Trump were falling flat. They would need to find a way to work around the president—the man they had collectively defended for four years—if they wanted to get the National Guard to the Capitol.

The GOP leaders, however, could not figure out who was in charge. They kept returning to basic questions: Who had the authority to order in the troops? Was it the Army secretary? Was it the acting Defense secretary? Did they need Trump's approval?

Since he had arrived at Fort McNair, McCarthy had ordered his aides to get him on as many television networks as possible. He kept darting in and out of the room to take their calls, hoping that Trump would be watching one of the channels where he was speaking.

"This is so un-American," McCarthy said in a Fox News appearance at 3:05 p.m., hoping to shame Trump into acting. "I could not be sadder or more disappointed with the way our country looks at this very moment."

At one point between television hits, McCarthy announced to the room that he had finally won a concession from the White House: Trump, after much begging, had begrudgingly agreed to record a video calling for calm. The news, however, was not particularly reassuring to the Republicans in the room. The president was entirely unpredictable. *Would such a video even help—or make it worse?* they asked each other. *And what of the Guard?*

Off in the corner, Scalise was scrolling through Twitter on his iPad, looking at images of the melee at the Capitol. One photo in particular made him stop short: a rioter rappelling down the wall of the Senate chamber and onto the rostrum where Mike Pence had been presiding. Scalise held his device out so McConnell could see.

"Look, they're in the Senate chamber," he said.

McConnell's face paled.

Since the evacuation, McConnell had been torn between feelings of utter disbelief and irrepressible anger toward Trump for fomenting the assault. The Capitol had been his home for decades. The members and the staff who worked there might as well have been his family. Yet the president had put them all in mortal danger. McConnell's aides had been texting his chief of staff, who accompanied him to Fort McNair, about the situation at the Capitol as it grew more precarious. Rioters were banging on their office doors, claiming to be Capitol Police officers to try to gain entry. Others were scaling the scaffolding outside their windows, trying to peer inside. In the hallway outside their barricaded doors, staffers could hear a woman praying loudly that "the evil of Congress be brought to an end." All the while, the "stop the steal" chanting continued as the crowds coursed through the Capitol.

McConnell knew his aides had been coordinating with Schumer's office from their lockdown, working their Rolodexes to summon help from the federal agencies. They had been calling and sending cell phone pictures of the chaos to anyone and everyone they knew at the Pentagon and Justice Department. They even roused former attorney general Bill Barr and his chief of staff to work internal channels.

"We are so overrun we are locked in the leader's suite," McConnell's counsel Andrew Ferguson had whispered desperately to Barr's former chief from his hiding place, keeping his voice down so as not to be heard by rioters. "We need help. If you don't start sending men, people might die."[21]

Having worked with the president for four years, McConnell knew that appealing to Trump directly would be a waste of time. He hadn't spoken to the president since December 15, the day McConnell publicly congratulated Biden for winning the election. Trump had called him after in a steaming rage, hurling insults and expletives his way for stating the inevitable.

"The problem you have is the Electoral College is the final word," McConnell had told him calmly. "It's over."

McConnell didn't bother calling Trump again. Even on the morning of January 6, he purposefully ignored a phone call from the president,[22] believing he could no longer be reasoned with. So when the Capitol came under attack, McConnell focused on getting in touch with military leaders, leaving it to his chief of staff to communicate with White House chief of staff Mark Meadows in order to enlist the White House's help to quell the riot—if they would help at all.

An FBI SWAT team had arrived on campus just as the leaders of Congress were being escorted into Fort McNair. But McConnell knew they would need more manpower to put the rampage down. It was why he called the chairman of the Joint Chiefs of Staff Mark Milley to implore him to help dispatch the Guard. But as far as he could tell, the Guard still wasn't moving.

As the duty officers at Fort McNair tried in vain to hook up a television so Republicans could watch the latest scenes of destruction at the Capitol, McConnell huddled with his staff around a telephone, desperately trying to reach the Pentagon. "I have the Majority Leader on the line," McConnell's aide announced, trying to connect her boss with acting Defense secretary Miller. They were promptly put on hold, infuriating GOP lawmakers in the room who couldn't understand why the Pentagon was dodging their inquiries.

Around 3:40 p.m., an hour and a half after the breach occurred, McConnell's patience gave out. He stormed out of the room and crossed the hall to find Pelosi, Schumer, and Hoyer—party affiliation be damned. *What are you hearing?* McConnell asked his Democratic counterparts as the other GOP leaders followed him into the room. *Do you know what the holdup is with the Guard?*

They didn't know anything more than he did. At a loss, Pelosi and Schumer had just signed off on a joint statement demanding Trump call for an end to the violence. Everyone knew it was little more than a gesture; the president wouldn't save them. It was time to bring the combined weight of all four congressional leaders to bear on the administration.

"Get Miller on the phone," someone barked, sending staff scrambling once again to respond.

As aides worked to set up the call, the Republican leaders and aides who had just entered the room stared, mouths agape, at the CNN footage on the large projector screen. It was the first time they saw the enormity of the scenes at the Capitol on anything larger than their phone or tablet screens. The footage rolling in was shocking: Rioters, having ransacked the building, were now taking selfies and cheering. They were stealing historic artifacts as keepsakes; one even carried away the Speaker's podium, waving with glee at the camera. On one end of the Capitol, protesters were storming the Senate chamber and rummaging through senators' desks. On the other, insurrectionists were doing the same in Pelosi's office.

"That's my desk!" one Pelosi aide present blurted out when an image of a man sitting in her chair with his feet propped up by her computer flashed on the screen. "They're going through my desk!"

Hoyer, still furious, started lecturing Scalise that the riot was the GOP's fault for enabling Trump.

"This isn't the time for that," Scalise shot back. "Right now, we need to get the chamber back, secured and open."

As they awaited news, Pelosi went around the room, checking on everyone's welfare. She comforted Ilhan Omar, a refugee from Somalia and one of Congress's first two Muslim congresswomen. Omar received death threats so regularly that she had her own security detail, who evacuated her to Fort McNair alongside the leaders. As the Speaker and the congresswoman bent heads, one of Omar's staffers sat in the corner, feverishly typing on a laptop she had brought with her. She, like Cicilline back in his office, was crafting articles of impeachment against Trump.

McConnell, Schumer, and the other lawmakers, meanwhile, eagerly stood by awaiting the call. Amid the chaos of the afternoon, two special elections in Georgia had been officially called for the Democratic candidates.[23] That meant Schumer's party would be taking control of all of Washington—and he would soon be taking McConnell's job. McConnell had already congratulated Schumer on his forthcoming promotion.

A few minutes later, staff finally got the Pentagon chief on the line. Huddled around a cell phone, the leaders jointly excoriated the acting secretary Miller for his snail-like response to what had all the markings of a coup at the Capitol. It was perhaps the first time since Trump took office that the congressional leaders had presented such a united front. *Why hadn't they sent troops already?* they demanded to know. *Where was the National Guard?*

"Tell POTUS to tweet everyone should leave," Schumer insisted, yelling into the device over speakerphone.

"Get help in ASAP," McConnell said firmly. "We want the Capitol back."

Miller stammered that Pentagon leaders needed to formulate a "plan" before they moved troops.

"Look, we're trying," Miller said. "We're looking at how to do this."

His vague answer did not suffice. There was no time to waste, the leaders insisted, as they pressed him to say how soon armed troops would arrive. After demurring several times, Miller finally gave them a partial answer: It could take four hours to get the National Guard to the Capitol, and up until midnight until the building could be cleared.

At that, Schumer lost it.

"If the Pentagon were under attack, it wouldn't take you *FOUR HOURS* to formulate a plan!" he roared. "We need help now!"

Scalise pressed Miller to tell them how many troops they could expect to arrive. When again the secretary declined to answer, Pelosi exploded.

"Mr. Secretary, Steve Scalise just asked you a question and you're not answering it," she demanded. "What's the answer to that question?"

But Miller simply dodged again, murmuring that they were trying their best.

That the most powerful nation in the world didn't have a plan in place to protect its own Capitol from attack was unthinkable to the leaders. And the fact that Miller was refusing to give clear answers appalled them. There was only one more person in Washington who might have more sway than they did. Hanging up on Miller, the leaders reached out to their last hope: It was time to call Mike Pence.

In the parking garage in the basement of the Capitol, Pence listened as the congressional leaders beseeched him to help dispatch troops to the Capitol. As vice president, he had no authority to assume Trump's powers as commander in chief and give orders to the secretary of Defense. But he couldn't understand why the Guard wasn't already on its way. Something had to be done—and he reckoned that the military brass wouldn't dare refuse a call from the vice president in a moment of crisis.

"I'm going to get off this call and call them, then call you right back," Pence told congressional leaders, hanging up the phone to dial Miller and Milley.

Beside him, Pence's brother Greg and longtime chief of staff Marc Short were still seething at how cavalierly Trump had abandoned them. They had read the president's most recent Twitter attack against Pence on their phones in the Senate basement, fuming that in the heat of the riot the president had chosen to stir up more vitriol about the vice president instead of calling to check on him. Trump's conspiratorial advisors were also emailing Pence's team, telling them the entire riot was their fault for not helping overturn the election. It was outrageous.

The vice president, however, didn't have time to dwell on the slights. When they'd first arrived in the garage, he had phoned McCarthy and McConnell, then Schumer and Pelosi, to make sure they all were safe. He didn't bother dialing Trump. Short, however, angrily called Meadows to tell the White House they were okay. And in case they were wondering, Short added snidely, "we are all planning to go back to the Capitol to certify the election tonight."

Meadows didn't object.

"That's probably best," he had replied.

At the White House, aides were gradually giving up hope that the president would do anything useful to restore order at the Capitol, though by midafternoon, the pressure on Trump to act was all-consuming. Republican lawmakers, longtime Trump allies from

Barr to former chief of staff Mick Mulvaney, and conservative influencers such as Ann Coulter excoriated him publicly.[24] Even former president George W. Bush had issued a reprimand.[25] Trump ignored all of them.

As they worked the phones, Pence's staff had heard that a high-level meeting had been convened at the White House to discuss the chain of command and how to get the National Guard moving. The fact that the administration could not figure out who was in charge as the Capitol was overrun was beyond alarming—though, in their estimation, Trump at any point could have picked up the phone and forced the Pentagon to move faster. That he hadn't, they all agreed, spoke volumes. And because of that—and the Hill leaders' desperation—Pence knew it was time for him to step up.

At 4:08 p.m., Pence called the acting Defense secretary and the chairman of the Joint Chiefs of Staff. Mustering his most commanding tone, he gave an order that technically was not his to issue.

"Clear the Capitol," he said. "Get troops here. Get them here now."[26]

Back in lockdown at Fort McNair, McConnell was issuing orders of his own.

"We are going back *tonight*," he insisted to Pence and Pentagon officials on a 4:45 p.m. phone call with Hill leaders. "The thugs won't win."

The vice president's order to the military seemed to have finally snapped things into place. Pence had let congressional leaders know that armed Guard troops were on the way. It would take another half hour for them to arrive, but the nightmare was almost over.[27]

McConnell, however, was still livid. He had spent decades trying to move Americans to the right of center, enticing average Joes to believe that the GOP was the defender of the highest American values: liberty, self-reliance, and exceptionalism. But in just one day, Trump had made a mockery of his life's work. The party, McConnell knew, would now be tarnished with the president's attempted coup, and stained by the conspiracy theories that led his supporters to carry out the assault.

McConnell had always delighted in good political combat. But when the votes were in, he believed in accepting outcomes with dignity. There was no dignity in what had happened that day—only embarrassment for the Republican Party. And McConnell was just that: embarrassed. Trump didn't even have the decency to be sorry. That afternoon, as congressional leaders joined forces across party lines to get reinforcements to the Capitol, the president had been egging on his supporters.

"These are the things and events that happen when a sacred landslide election victory is so unceremoniously & viciously stripped away from great patriots who have been badly & unfairly treated for so long," Trump wrote falsely on Twitter. "Remember this day forever!"

Even in the video he released calling for "peace," Trump praised his followers for revolting against a "fraudulent election," calling them "very special" and adding, "We love you."

It was too much for McConnell to stomach. After four years of trying to accommodate the president's demands, Trump had threatened *his* Capitol, and McConnell was finally done with him. They had to certify Biden as the next president, and they had to do it that night, in prime time, he insisted. The whole country had to know that Trump's time was up.

There was one major impediment to McConnell's plan. Capitol Police were saying the building would not be secure enough to welcome lawmakers back that night. They had to sweep the entire chamber for bombs and ensure there were no straggling rioters hiding in a bathroom—and there was no way to do that quickly. Defense officials had even suggested bussing lawmakers to Fort McNair to certify the election that night from the military base.

To McConnell, waiting until morning was entirely out of the question. He was not about to let Congress capitulate to lawlessness and intimidation. In fact, getting the Capitol back up and running had been his driving motivation all afternoon. Even before he had marched down the hall to meet with Schumer and Pelosi, he had dispatched a member of his staff to deliver a message to them. "Go tell the leaders that we are going back tonight," he had instructed. Two hours later, when he joined forces with the Democratic leaders and Pence to take on the Pentagon, he was equally determined.

McConnell knew the vice president and the other leaders had his back. They were just as adamant as he that Trump's flunkies would not push Congress out of its own Capitol. Pence had even offered the Capitol Police his own K-9 unit to help sweep the building faster.

Given the sensitivity of the discussion, the congressional leaders had gathered in a smaller space down the hall, away from the probing eyes and ears of aides and other lawmakers who had joined them at Fort McNair after their arrival. Within minutes, Pelosi lit into the military brass, accusing them of sitting on their hands and ignoring the blaring warning signs of coming violence in the days before the attack.

"Were you without knowledge of the susceptibility of our national security here?" Pelosi demanded of Miller, her patience growing short.

"We assessed it would be a rough day," Miller said. "No idea it would be like this."

When the Pentagon leaders echoed the warnings of the Capitol Police, suggesting Congress wait a day before returning, McConnell flatly refused. Lawmakers had to be back in place by prime time that night, he said, so that the country—and the president—could see that the attempted coup had failed, that democracy had prevailed, and Trump's reign was over. He was damned if he would allow the president's mob to have the last word at the Capitol that day.

"We're going back into the Capitol and we're finishing this tonight," McConnell said again, as Pelosi and Schumer indicated their agreement. The military brass, outnumbered, had to relent.

Congressman Jamie Raskin was holed up with his traumatized daughter, Tabitha, and son-in-law, Hank, in the House-side lockdown when his phone buzzed with a text.

"Ted and I are working on a resolution of impeachment . . . and we'd love for you to join us," Cicilline had written to their quartet of friends, including fellow "musketeers" Lieu and Joe Neguse on the chain.

Raskin was intrigued—but he was also distracted. He was one of only four House Democrats whom the Speaker had tapped to put down the GOP's objections to the Electoral College that day. It was just after seven p.m., and congressional leaders had let it be known that Congress would go back into session within the next hour to finish the work they had started—and stay until they could declare Biden was the next president. Raskin needed to get his thoughts in order. After Trump's riot, his job of rebutting Republican objections would be even more important to execute flawlessly.

The horrors of that afternoon were also weighing on Raskin. It had taken almost an hour after Trump's supporters broke into the Capitol to be reunited with Tabitha and Hank, who had been hiding in a side office near the House floor during the attack. Being separated from them, just days after his son and their brother, Tommy, had committed suicide, had been among the most harrowing situations he'd ever experienced.

More than three hours had elapsed between when the assailants breached the building and the first unit of 155 National Guard members arrived to begin clearing the Capitol. Hundreds more followed in riot gear, pushing the Trump crowds outside the security perimeter and restoring order with makeshift fencing and patrols. Their presence gave the Capitol grounds the distinct feeling of a military base.

As Raskin watched the coverage, he couldn't help but wonder if the riot had been the start of another civil war. The nation's last one had been triggered, after all, by South Carolina's refusal to abide by and honor the election of Abraham Lincoln. *Is that where we're headed?* he wondered. In a day, Trump supporters had almost laid waste to the Capitol. There was no telling what they might attempt in the next two weeks before Biden's inauguration, he reasoned.

Despite his sense of foreboding, Raskin had his doubts about his friends' idea to attempt another impeachment. Impeachment had never been a very fast undertaking, and Trump's rioters were calling for revolution.

As a constitutional law expert, Raskin knew the Twenty-Fifth Amendment to the Constitution contained a safety hatch allowing the vice president to take over if the president was deemed physically or mentally unfit to serve. The provision had never been used, and there was a high bar to invoking it: The vice president and a majority of either the Cabinet or another congressionally created body had to make the call. But Raskin believed that if anyone deserved to be the inaugural target, it was Trump.

"Go for the Twenty-Fifth Amendment first," Raskin suggested to his friends. "It will be quicker." But if that didn't work, he agreed, "he must be impeached."

In Cicilline's office, he and Lieu had already spent the afternoon crafting a letter encouraging Pence to invoke the Twenty-Fifth Amendment. But they were more fixated on impeachment, looping in Jerry Nadler's House Judiciary Committee counsel Aaron Hiller to help them fine-tune a draft article. With Cicilline at his desk and Lieu at a conference table in the room, they had sketched out the language in a spiral-bound notebook, reading sentences aloud to each other as they worked.

Hiller, who lived just blocks from the Capitol, had watched from his front yard that day as National Guard units assembled and prepared to force the rioters out. By that evening, he was busy sorting through calls for accountability flying from all corners of the Democratic conference, as lawmakers insisted they expel or censure Republicans who objected to the Electoral College. But the moment he saw Cicilline and Lieu's proposal, Hiller knew their idea—a second impeachment of Trump for inciting the violence—was the right approach. He called his boss, Nadler's longtime chief of staff, Amy Rutkin, with a warning.

"I'm about to do something that's completely unauthorized by leadership," he admitted. "Should I tell you, or not?"

Throughout 2019, Rutkin had played the part of intercessor between Nadler and Pelosi, maintaining a posture of deference to the Speaker's office even as she quietly encouraged Raskin's crew to work around official channels and rally their colleagues on impeachment. She knew from experience that Pelosi didn't like to be caught off-guard or forced out of her comfort zone. And she knew a second impeachment would be controversial.

But this time, Rutkin didn't care. Nadler had almost had to squeeze himself into a tiny heating closet in the Judiciary Committee suite to hide from the rioters that day. Pelosi could not possibly put his panel in a more uncomfortable situation than that. There was no time for quibbling.

"Do it," she said.

Hiller, who knew all too well how skittish Pelosi's leadership team could be about impeachment, hung up the phone and immediately called Cicilline.

"Go find two hundred co-sponsors *right now* to get it done," he demanded. "Don't wait for a blessing from leadership."

42

IMPEACHMENT 2.0

JANUARY 9-13, 2021

Nancy Pelosi couldn't believe she was considering impeachment again. A year had elapsed since she had put the first, politically harrowing experience behind her. Yet late on the night of Saturday, January 9, the Speaker was meeting with her top deputies to discuss ousting Trump again. This time, due to the ongoing coronavirus pandemic, they huddled via video conference. But just as before, they were divided.

Adam Schiff, Pelosi's closest ally and the leader of Trump's first impeachment, argued against attempting a second. At the Speaker's personal request, he'd been making the case privately to fellow Democrats all week: if they went after the president in his waning days in office, it would look like they were just trying to keep him from running again. President-elect Biden was also clearly worried that if Congress got bogged down in another impeachment trial, it would upend his chances of accomplishing anything during his first months in office. Democrats, Schiff had told colleagues privately that week, "should be on the same page as the new president."[1]

On the video call that night, Schiff again ticked through the reasons not to impeach—though he had declared his public support for the effort just the day before. A second impeachment would likely end exactly as the first had, Schiff told the others on the call, with Democrats on one side and Republicans on another. What was the point, he asked, when acquittal was likely a foregone conclusion?

"We need to be looking forward," Schiff said.

But Jerry Nadler had been through this fight before—and this time he'd come prepared. The Judiciary chairman who'd been sidelined through the bulk of Trump's first impeachment argued that they had no choice: Trump's actions were so severe that they necessitated taking articles straight to the floor. Forget an investigation, Nadler continued. Forget a Judiciary Committee markup. Lawmakers had watched a crime unfold right before their eyes, he pointed out. They didn't need to gather evidence and hold hearings.

"Impeach him now," Nadler argued. "They can give him due process in the Senate trial."

It was a sharp departure from the principled stand the New York Democrat had taken during the first impeachment—and yet another sign that the ground beneath the Speaker was shifting rapidly. Nadler had always been a stickler for doing impeachment the "right" way—not to mention fiercely territorial about protecting his committee's jurisdiction and giving the president due process rights in the House. Pelosi knew that if Nadler was willing to skip an investigation and throw the impeachment rule book out the window due to the gravity of what had happened, others would follow.

The pressure to act had been building for three days by that point, ever since the rioters had been cleared from the Capitol. As Congress returned to finish certifying the Electoral College that night, Congressman David Cicilline had cornered Pelosi's deputy Steny Hoyer on the House floor and implored him to allow an immediate vote on an impeachment resolution he'd drafted from lockdown.

"This is something we should do at the conclusion of the Electoral College," the Rhode Island Democrat had said, thrusting the papers into his hands. "We should vote on this now in immediate response."

Hoyer had passed the message on to Pelosi. But with the smell of tear gas still in the hallways, the pair needed time to cool down and think. They tried to buy time by arguing that chamber rules would not permit such a move during a joint session. Pelosi's senior staff also sent Cicilline a more blunt message behind the scenes that night: A second impeachment was a non-starter and he would do well to focus his attention elsewhere.

But Cicilline was far from alone. On the far-left end of the party, Congresswoman Ilhan Omar had also gone public with her own push to impeach Trump. And by the next day, dozens of Democrats—including some from competitive districts—had approached party leaders to say they needed to do something to rebuke Trump now.

Pelosi couldn't blame her members. Days after the insurrection, she was still utterly infuriated at the damage Trump's supporters had wrought upon the Capitol and everyone in it. Evidence of the assault was still visible everywhere: splintered furniture, smashed windows, doors riddled with bullets. Bloodstains remained on the floor outside the chamber, where police shot and killed a Trump supporter trying to enter their sanctum. Her staff, who had barricaded themselves inside a conference room in her office, were still traumatized. Videos taken by the mob—some of whom carried zip ties to manacle lawmakers—captured marauders chanting about killing lawmakers, yelling "Heads on pikes!" "String 'em up!" and "They need to pay the ultimate price!" Five people had died, including a Capitol Police officer who suffered two strokes the day after rioters sprayed him with chemicals.[2] About 140 cops were injured, including one crushed by the mob in a door and another who had his eye gouged by Trump supporters.[3]

The realization of how close lawmakers had come to a massacre unsettled Pelosi's rank and file and fueled demands for accountability. But while the attack was unprecedented, so was the idea of impeaching a president less than two weeks before leaving office. It would cast a pall over the opening days of the Biden presidency, Pelosi knew, just as Democrats like her were desperate to turn the page on the nightmare of the past four years. And yet, the other side of the argument was equally powerful: How could there be no punishment for a crime as egregious as inciting a coup against Congress?

The morning after the riot, incoming Senate Majority Leader Chuck Schumer had poured gasoline on the impeachment fire by endorsing the effort.[4] The typically centrist Schumer was facing re-election in 2022 and fretting about a potential primary challenge from the left. But while backing the campaign pleased liberal Democrats, it also boxed Pelosi in. With him in favor of impeachment, how could she be against it?

Yet the Speaker who'd been a one-woman blockade against the first impeachment still wasn't ready to give in. She'd been hearing that Vice President Mike Pence and Majority Leader Mitch McConnell were worried about Trump's stability and what additional havoc he might wreak in the balance of his presidency. That presented a potential off-ramp: If the Twenty-Fifth Amendment were invoked against Trump, she presumed, he could be removed from office without the messy business of impeachment, allowing Pence to serve out the remaining few days of his term.

Pelosi knew the idea was a long shot. To remove the president, Pence himself would need to be on board, and that would be nothing short of mutiny. But knowing that Trump supporters had chanted

"Hang Mike Pence" and erected gallows in front of the Capitol, Pelosi figured it was worth a try. The day after the riot, she and Schumer jointly called Pence to ask him to consider the move—but they were put on hold while Pence's team fretted about the optics of him even taking the call.[5] After a considerable pause, they realized Pence wasn't going to speak with them and hung up. The idea, it seemed, was going nowhere.

As she scrambled to figure out next steps, Pelosi turned to a lawmaker whose impeachment advice she had previously discounted, but whose counsel she had come to rely on increasingly in recent months. In the year since Trump's first acquittal, Congressman Jamie Raskin had been privately warning the Speaker that the president would likely try to hold on to power any way he could. While Pelosi had previously ignored Raskin's direst warnings, she had been alarmed enough by his prescience about Trump's election antics to ask him to explain the threat to her leadership team. So when Trump began challenging the integrity of the 2020 results, Pelosi turned to Raskin to help come up with a strategy to defend the election results.

The day after the riot, Pelosi prodded Raskin on how he thought they should proceed. Raskin agreed that Democrats should try to use the Twenty-Fifth Amendment to boot Trump from office immediately. But if that didn't work they would have no choice but to impeach, he told her. Pelosi listened but expressed skepticism: *Couldn't Trump defend himself by hiding behind the First Amendment and claiming freedom of speech?*

Raskin scoffed.

"Just because a president uses words to commit his constitutional crimes does not strip Congress of the power to impeach and convict him for betraying his oath," he said, an argument the Speaker agreed with.[6]

Pelosi was acutely aware that there were other potential dangers to be taken into account as well. News reports suggested that some of the president's more conspiratorial confidants were trying to get him to impose martial law.[7] Trump had refused to save the Capitol, but what if he went even further in his final days in office, starting a war or trying to use the military to stop the Biden inauguration? The Speaker was worried enough that on Friday, January 8, two days after the riot, she called Trump's chairman of the Joint Chiefs of Staff, Mark Milley, to press him to restrain the president from using the country's nuclear codes to create a global crisis—and to remind Milley of the military's duties to the nation as well as to the commander in chief.

"If they couldn't even stop him from an assault on the Capitol, who even knows what else he may do?" she railed.

Milley had assured Pelosi that there were safeguards protecting the nation's nuclear stockpile and the peaceful transfer of power.[8] But his words didn't quell her fears. Pelosi began to see that her members were right: A second impeachment might be the only way to keep Trump in line.

Of the four previous times in U.S. history that Congress had tried to impeach a president, only one had transpired without a full investigation and debate: the impeachment of Andrew Johnson. In 1868, lawmakers impeached Johnson in a fit of rage over a weekend when he sacked the secretary of war and replaced him with a political crony. Only after that vote did the House draft articles, listing their various grievances against him.[9] It was so shoddily done that most impeachment experts rarely spoke of it, holding up Congress's painstaking investigation of Nixon a century later as the gold standard. In fact, many influential scholars would come to view the entire exercise as congressional misuse of power, assessing that the charges fell far short of "high crimes and misdemeanors."

To the risk-averse Speaker, reverting back to impeachment by snap vote was a risky proposition. Could they really do this without a full impeachment process? Could they move forward without a committee report and evidentiary record?

Those were the central questions gripping Pelosi as her team beamed in from around the country for their Saturday-night video call, just eleven days before Biden's inauguration. After Schiff and Nadler spoke their piece, Congressman and "musketeer" Joe Neguse argued that the Johnson impeachment provided "strong legal footing" for indicting Trump quickly. "If Johnson could be hastily impeached for replacing a Cabinet secretary, we can charge Trump for inciting an armed rebellion against Congress," he said, turning what scholars considered the signature flaw of Johnson's impeachment—its speed—into a virtue. When Steny Hoyer pushed back, saying Republicans would hammer them for having no hearings and process, Raskin was emphatic in his retort.

"If you want a long, drawn-out investigation of your case, don't storm the police station and prosecutor's office," he argued pointedly. "This incitement case can be made on the public record."

By that day, David Cicilline's yet-to-be-introduced resolution impeaching Trump for "inciting an insurrection" had more than 180 co-signers, representing 80 percent of Pelosi's caucus. Even impeachment skeptic Josh Gottheimer, whose centrist Problem Solvers Caucus had briefly discussed imploring Biden to call for peace to head off a second impeachment, had joined the bandwagon. Most of the remaining holdouts—Schiff, Zoe Lofgren, and Pelosi's top leadership deputies—were on that video call debating.

Despite the differences of opinion, the group collectively shared one key concern about a snap impeachment: If they indicted Trump in the waning days of his presidency, what would become of the

Biden agenda? A Senate trial could not possibly take place before his inauguration. And if it dragged on, it would be a damper on Biden's opening weeks in office.

Clyburn, a close Biden ally who had almost single-handedly helped him win the Democratic nomination, made an unorthodox proposal: The House should impeach, he said, but then hold back the articles for the first hundred days of Biden's term to give the Senate time to confirm his Cabinet nominees. But the group unanimously slapped down that idea. Democrats had taken enough of a beating when they sat on Trump's first articles of impeachment for a few weeks. They couldn't conceivably claim a second impeachment was necessary, then sit on their hands for months.

"The Senate will do what the Senate will do," Pelosi said firmly. "That's not our concern."

Toward the end of the call, Schiff, who had been jotting down notes, began to realize that calculated skepticism no longer had any place in the conversation. Picking up on the sentiments being expressed, he began to articulate his own alternative pitch for what the charges against Trump should say.

"Here's what I'm thinking about an article of impeachment," Schiff began, turning to the paper in front of him.

Pelosi studied Schiff. He had always been her most trusted advisor and had single-handedly carried the House's first impeachment of Trump. The Speaker had repeatedly deferred to his expertise and his political instincts, prioritizing his counsel over every other member of her leadership circle—particularly during the first impeachment. She valued his continued loyalty. But Schiff's time had come and gone. If they were to impeach Trump again, she'd need to pick someone else to shepherd the effort.

"Well, Adam, David already has a resolution with nearly two hundred members," she told him, shocking meeting participants with her gentle dismissal of her golden boy. "I don't think we need to start from scratch."

Kevin McCarthy was trying to thread a needle between his ambition and his conscience when the text from Jaime Herrera Beutler popped up on his phone. It was Monday, January 11, and with Trump's second impeachment vote just two days away, the GOP leader knew the moderate Washington Republican desperately wanted a private word. She was trying to figure out how to vote.

Since January 6, Herrera Beutler had been digging for details about Trump's involvement in the horrors of that day, determined to discern his level of culpability. Her office had been calling around town trying to figure out if Trump had spoken to Pentagon leaders or ignored pleas to send in the National Guard. She wanted to know what the Secret Service observed in the president's behavior. And she'd written a letter to McCarthy asking for a vivid recounting of his own interactions with the president.

"I need to know this information," she told McCarthy that night. "Can we talk?"

There was a time when McCarthy would not have thought twice about whipping his moderates to fall in line behind their party leader, despite their—or even his own—private concerns about Trump's behavior. During Trump's first impeachment, in fact, he and his team had single-handedly helped steer Herrera Beutler to side with the president, pumping her full of procedural arguments against the Democrats' case to overwhelm her discomfort with what the president had done. This time around, her office was signaling to McCarthy's that she was likely a yes on impeachment. Here was his chance to change her mind.

But when Herrera Beutler reached out, the typically chipper

GOP leader was in a dark place. He had fallen deep into despair as he wrestled over how to respond to the president's actions on January 6. He knew viscerally that Trump had done something horrible and needed to be rebuked for it. Yet at the same time, breaking with the president he'd catered to for so long would be like cutting off his own arm—and, he worried, it would have devastating consequences for his political future.

McCarthy's crisis of conscience had started in November, as the president began ranting about a "stolen election." The Minority Leader knew Trump had lost and that embracing his denials could trigger national turmoil. It was why he had hesitated when Trump pressured him to sign on to a December amicus brief asking the Supreme Court to throw out the results in swing states Biden had won.

But Trump had put him in a bind. He began going around McCarthy to demand other conservative House Republicans sign on to the court objections—conservatives McCarthy had worked hard to win over to buoy his rise to the top of the GOP. They began mercilessly pressuring McCarthy to join them in parroting Trump's election falsehoods.

Torn between Trump and what he knew was right, McCarthy had turned for advice to Liz Cheney. The most senior Republican woman in the House and daughter of former vice president Dick Cheney had taken to openly excoriating Trump for his refusal to accept the election results. She told McCarthy the lawsuit was unconstitutional and undemocratic, and would be destructive to the country. McCarthy tended to agree. And in mid-December, just before a GOP press conference, he pulled Cheney aside to confide as much to her.

"I'm not signing the amicus brief," he said, laying out his plans to hold the line against Trump's pressure campaign. "It would give the federal government too much power over elections."

McCarthy's burst of courage, however, was short-lived. When the list of House Republican signatories to the effort went public, Trump and his allies erupted upon learning that McCarthy's name was missing. Within a few hours, the GOP leader who had told his staff to ignore what he deemed a "rank and file" effort, caved. He pledged his support to keep the peace with Trump and insisted to the media that a "technical glitch" was the only reason his name wasn't on the list in the first place.[10]

When Trump subsequently began pressuring McCarthy's members to object to the Electoral College results on January 6—and insisting the California Republican lead the effort—McCarthy once again faced the same dilemma. He knew objecting was wrong—and might even cause political problems for some Republicans in swing districts that Biden had won. But with the president and Trump's allies in the House breathing down his neck, he couldn't bring himself to push back. Unlike McConnell, who had argued to his rank and file that refusing to certify Biden as victor on January 6 was antithetical to democracy, McCarthy dodged questions from members seeking guidance on how to handle the situation. For a while, he wouldn't even tell them how he personally planned to vote, frozen between his fealty to Trump and his own ethical compass.[11]

Just as before, McCarthy's political ambitions won out. He not only announced on January 3 that he would support the effort to overturn the Electoral College results, but also allowed aides to Trump ally Jim Jordan to set up a recruiting station in the GOP's cloakroom off the House floor to round up members to join their campaign. The move troubled some of his own staff, as well as moderate Republicans who warned that the effort was futile and might cause violence. McCarthy dismissed their concerns out of hand, arguing that they were overblown.

Even on the night of the riot, after Trump's supporters sacked the

Capitol, a torn McCarthy again found himself doing the president's bidding against his better judgment. He had consulted Cheney from his lockdown at Fort McNair about whether to insist House Republicans abandon their efforts to challenge the Electoral College results. Cheney told him unequivocally that it was time to put an end to the dangerous farce, and again McCarthy promised her that he'd do the "right thing." But Trump's enforcers in the House, including Jordan, wouldn't hear of it. They argued that if the GOP backed down now, it would look like they never truly believed in their electoral objections.

At a loss over what to do, McCarthy had convened a meeting with his senior staff when he returned to the Capitol that night to discuss whether they should recant their mass protest of Biden's victory. He knew the day's violence had changed everything—and that Trump and Trump alone was to blame. Yet McCarthy couldn't muster the courage to change course. He caved again. That night, as workers swept up broken glass and scrubbed bloodstains from the halls of the Capitol, McCarthy led nearly 140 of his members in continued opposition to the election results, knowing full well that those very lies had triggered what was essentially a terrorist attack on the Capitol.

In the days after January 6, McCarthy's internal struggle over how to act toward Trump only intensified. The blowback for his actions that day had been intense: Corporate donors vowed to keep their money from the GOP campaign coffers,[12] accusing the Republican leader of being an accomplice to Trump's antics. The media was all over him. Dozens of McCarthy's rank and file griped that his cowardly bending to Trump's will deprived them of the political protection they needed to decry the president's actions.

Meanwhile, Trump was in trouble, as the riot triggered a momentary schism in the GOP's governing class in Washington. Cabinet members denounced their own president. Conservative editorial boards, including the *Wall Street Journal*'s, called on Trump to resign. Even McCarthy's counterpart across the Capitol, Mitch McConnell, privately let it be known that he believed Trump had committed impeachable offenses.

McCarthy knew they were right. Privately, he vented to his allies that Trump had crossed a line. He even asked trusted colleagues if he should call on the president to step down, and briefly consulted his leadership team about whether the Twenty-Fifth Amendment was a viable option for removing the president.

"I've had it with this guy," he privately told the group. "What he did is unacceptable. Nobody can defend that, and nobody should defend it."[13]

But for McCarthy, publicly breaking with Trump wasn't that easy. A large chunk of the GOP base—not to mention his own rank and file—had fervently embraced the president's election lies. If he turned on the president, they would never forgive him—meaning he could kiss his dreams of being Speaker goodbye.

In McCarthy's estimation, his long-term strategy of appeasing Trump had worked from a political standpoint. The president might have lost in 2020, but after two years of catering to Trump, McCarthy's Republicans had posted huge gains, nearly flipping the House.[14] Now, with a Democrat in the White House to campaign against, the chances of a GOP takeover in 2022 were incredibly high, putting McCarthy within striking distance of the speakership. Still, the GOP leader's lust for power had come at a heavy price: In refusing to push back on the president, McCarthy had helped turn the GOP into a party that promoted conspiracy theories and lies. Now those lies had led to violence and an insurrection. And much as he loathed to admit it, McCarthy was ashamed.

As Democrats moved to impeach the president, McCarthy only

grew more flummoxed about what to do. He urged Trump to make peace and call Biden to congratulate him on the election. But the president stubbornly refused. In fact, Trump showed no remorse whatsoever, continuing to insist that he won the election while blaming his critics—not his supporters—for storming the Capitol. McCarthy couldn't believe what he was hearing.

"It's not Antifa, it's MAGA . . . I know. I was there!" a livid McCarthy told Trump. "Stop it. It's over. The election is over."[15]

"I don't know what happened to you in the last two months," he yelled at Trump. "You're not the same as you were for the last four years."[16]

Meanwhile, rank-and-file Republicans were coming to him, seeking answers on whether they should vote to impeach the president. McCarthy didn't know what to tell them. *How could he turn on Trump when he needed him to land his dream job someday—yet how could he corral his rank and file into opposing impeachment when he knew Trump was guilty?*

McCarthy was in that mindset when Herrera Beutler reached out to talk.

"Kevin, you talked to the president," she pressed him. "What was his frame of mind?"

McCarthy and Herrera Beutler had built a good relationship over the decade they had served in the House together, becoming friends as well as colleagues. Since she was juggling her congressional duties with the demands of being a busy mother of three, McCarthy had stepped up over the years to personally help her raise reelection funds. When she almost lost her firstborn child, spending weeks upon weeks in doctors' offices undergoing experimental treatment, McCarthy had been a support system.

But instead of taking advantage of that bond to whip her in line, McCarthy decided to tell Herrera Beutler the ugly truth. When she called, the words poured out of him like a therapy session. He told her that Trump had jeered him for his panic and praised the rioters. He recounted how Trump had refused to act. He acknowledged the president's lack of remorse and refusal to take responsibility. McCarthy knew it would cost Trump a vote, but for once, he didn't care.

The GOP leader went on to recount the same story to multiple Republicans on the fence. He also made them a promise, a vow he'd never even considered during the first impeachment: If they voted to indict Trump, he wouldn't punish them. They were free to do what they thought was right[17]—even if McCarthy believed he personally was not.

Two days later, on Wednesday, January 13, a wary McCarthy stood before the House chamber and offered the strongest public rebuke of Trump he felt he could muster.

"The President bears responsibility for Wednesday's attack on Congress by mob rioters," McCarthy said, proposing that lawmakers censure the former president and start "a fact-finding commission" to investigate what happened. Trump, he added, "should have immediately denounced the mob when he saw what was unfolding."

Outside, the Capitol had turned into a fortress. A non-scalable eight-foot-tall fence had been erected around the entire campus. National Guard troops in camouflage with assault rifles stood along the perimeter and at each door and entryway, scrutinizing every person on and around the grounds. In total, about fifteen thousand troops had been mobilized to protect the Capitol[18]—more than were deployed to Iraq and Afghanistan combined at the time.

But even with reminders of Trump's riot everywhere, McCarthy stopped short of the full condemnation he knew Trump deserved. Instead, he called for national unity and blamed Democrats for forestalling reconciliation by impeaching Trump again.

"A vote to impeach would further divide this nation," he said in a tone that rang hollow. "A vote to impeach will further fan the flames of partisan division."

McCarthy knew it was a dodge and that he was trying to have it both ways. When the Speaker called the vote, he didn't linger in the chamber or gab with members. McCarthy pressed the button—no on impeachment—then swiftly left the chamber in shame.

43

SPEAK REPUBLICAN

LATE JANUARY 2021

"I'm thinking about adding a Republican to my team," Jamie Raskin told Liz Cheney, letting the suggestion hang in the air.

It was late January, and Raskin, Pelosi's newly appointed lead impeachment manager, was considering throwing a curveball into his trial strategy: He wanted a Republican to help him present the case against Trump to the Senate—and he had a particular Republican in mind.

The liberal lawmaker had grown close to the classically conservative daughter of former vice president Dick Cheney, a politician whom Raskin had long despised for masterminding George W. Bush's presidency and pushing the United States into the Iraq War. Liz Cheney was the total opposite of Raskin on nearly every policy matter imaginable: a defense hawk where he was a dove; a small-government federalist where he advocated a version of the welfare state.

The two of them had arrived in Congress in 2017—the same year

Trump came to Washington—and bumped into each other one day when Cheney was giving her daughter a tour of the Capitol.

"This is Congressman Raskin. He's the one who wrote the book on why your grandfather should never have been vice president," Cheney said to her daughter, smirking.

Raskin was shocked. In the early 2000s, he had indeed written a book entitled *Overruling Democracy*, on why he believed the Supreme Court's ruling in *Bush v. Gore* was faulty. That Cheney knew who he was—and had even read his book—impressed him.

The two struck up a friendship, as they both ascended quickly to leadership positions in their respective parties. They ribbed each other about being a stereotypical Republican and Democrat: To her, he was an out-of-control liberal who had no concept of how national debt would ruin the nation; to him, she was a heartless conservative who liked guns, Wall Street, and war. Yet the two had something important in common: their mutual love of all things pertaining to the Constitution—and their shared disdain for Trump. They had bonded over it in secret for most of his presidency.

After January 6, their talks took a more serious turn. During the riot, while Raskin was comforting his daughter and son-in-law, Cheney had been trying to convince fellow Republicans to drop their objections to the Electoral College as members hid in the Ways and Means Committee room. When McCarthy told her he would give a "unifying speech" on the House floor, she had assumed he would be calling for an end to the GOP's protest. She had taken a seat near the front of the chamber that night to support him. When the GOP leader did the exact opposite, doubling down on his objections to the vote count, Cheney stood up and walked straight out of the chamber.

That night, Cheney had been stunned at the number of SWAT teams and National Guard units swarming around the Capitol. As she went to inspect the damage to the Rotunda and Statuary Hall and thank the troops for their service, she ran into Congressman Greg Pence. He was still smarting at what Trump had done to his brother, the vice president.

"The pressure on him has been unbelievable," he fumed. Cheney had hugged him—and later sought the vice president himself out to thank him for being the final man standing between the continuation and the end of democracy.

When Democrats had started talking about impeachment, Cheney knew right away she would be all in. Dozens of rank-and-file Republicans on the fence sought her counsel as they struggled to decide whether to follow their conscience and join her, or toe the party line. She laid out her own thinking—country over party—and facilitated conversations with high-ranking Trump officials so lawmakers could ask about what they had witnessed that day. But in the end, many who wanted to join her said they were too afraid to do so. They said they were worried about their families amid ongoing death threats from an angry, Trump-loving base that blamed Republicans for not doing enough to keep the president in power.

On January 13, Cheney became one of only ten House Republicans to vote to impeach the president, taking a principled stand despite enormous pressure from the vengeful head of her party. But Raskin hoped she might be willing to do even more. Adding the voice of the third-highest-ranking GOP member in the House to his impeachment team would go a long way in securing Trump's conviction in the upper chamber, he believed.

Cheney was already secretly advising House Democrats on how to improve their chances. Even before Raskin was named lead manager, she was giving him pointers on how to build a team of prosecutors that could appeal to the GOP. She had pulled him aside on the House floor to warn him that veterans of the first impeachment—

particularly Adam Schiff and Jerry Nadler—couldn't play any part in the trial if Democrats wanted to win a conviction.

Raskin wanted to make their off-the-record conversations official. He needed someone who could speak Republican fluently—and who was gutsy enough to stand up to the GOP. He needed Cheney.

When Pelosi asked Raskin to take the lead in the trial, the Marylander had been flattered—and surprised. Raskin knew Pelosi respected him—she had made that clear when she tapped him to co-lead the House Democrats' defense of the Electoral College on January 6. But Raskin had learned through experience that the Speaker had a penchant for plucking her closest allies for the highest-profile starring roles. He had simply never been one of them.

Still, there had been signs that the move was coming. Since his son's death, Pelosi's maternal instincts had kicked into high gear. She'd been checking in on Raskin almost daily, sending flowers and inquiring after his wife and daughters. She began seeking his advice with more frequency than usual, sounding him out about impeachment and feasible alternatives—like his resolution calling for Pence to invoke the Twenty-Fifth Amendment.

Raskin had welcomed the Speaker's sudden interest. He considered her tasks a respite from the all-consuming misery and grief of having lost his son to a tragic suicide. But his wife and daughters felt differently. Since January 6, Raskin had been receiving death threats, prompting his family to beg him to retreat from the limelight.

Yet when Pelosi approached him to become lead manager, Raskin didn't hesitate. He viewed prosecuting Trump as his duty and a way to honor his son—and to ensure nothing like January 6 ever happened again. Raskin had just one condition: If he was to spearhead the second impeachment trial of a president for the first time in history, he had to have his people.

For nearly two years, Raskin and his "musketeers"—Joe Neguse, David Cicilline, Ted Lieu, and the other Judiciary Committee Democrats—had been thorns in Pelosi's side. From their perch on her leadership team, they had organized a near-mutiny, pushing the bulk of the House Democrats to endorse an impeachment inquiry that Pelosi had resisted for months and forcing her to act. For their efforts, they had been iced out of Trump's first impeachment, and the Judiciary staffers who had worked with them were treated as second-class aides to the impeachment managers' team.

But now Raskin would be in charge and entrusted with succeeding where the first impeachment had failed. He could not live up to the task without the help of his band of like-minded lawyer friends, he told the Speaker. Much to Raskin's surprise, Pelosi consented.

During the impeachment managers' first team meeting on January 15, Raskin declared that this trial would be different from the last. This was not a messaging operation aimed at making the other side look bad, he said, or a bid to pummel Republicans at the ballot box for a vote against witnesses. Rather, this would be an effort to get sixty-seven votes—meaning at least seventeen Senate Republicans—to put Trump away for good.

To do that, Raskin told the group of blue-hearted progressives, they would bend over backwards to try to win over the GOP senators. They would learn to think like Republicans and speak like Republicans. They would sympathize with their position. They would appeal to their better angels.

"We need to convict," Raskin told the team. "We need to tell a spellbinding story that Republicans will understand, hear, and agree with."

Amy Rutkin, Nadler's chief of staff, began discreetly contacting sympathetic House Republicans and conservatives on the outside for messaging advice, including prominent Trump critics Steve Schmidt and Bill Kristol. They made spreadsheets of every seemingly gettable Senate Republican and began pulling together data on each one's background, mentors, and passions—anything that could be useful for appealing to them to convict. They took note of language and images that GOP advisors said would resonate with Republican voters and senators.

Republicans often gave the managers the same advice: Don't be like former impeachment trial leader Adam Schiff. Don't condescend. No self-righteous sermons or flourishes about "constitutional duty." No high-minded political science lectures. Just facts. Ironically, Raskin had received the same advice from Chuck Schumer. Much as the Senate Democratic leader had personally admired Schiff's presentations, he knew moderate Democratic senators Kyrsten Sinema and Joe Manchin had resented the Intelligence chairman's patronizing tone. He had called Raskin to warn him against alienating them this time around as well.

Raskin did not disagree with their assessment. He had followed every word of the first impeachment and noticed how Republicans bristled at the lectures about "oath" and "duty"—even as Democrats oohed and aahed at Schiff's rhetorical flourishes. As far as Raskin was concerned, Schiff's approach hadn't gotten the job done. Still, he took Schiff out to lunch in mid-January to ask for his insights and solicit his advice, despite knowing that he would take a far more bipartisan approach. His managers, all of them liberal House Democrats, would have to fight their political instincts to meet the challenge.

At Raskin's instruction, his team resisted the urge to scold Republicans for refusing to remove Trump a year before when they had a chance. While writing scripts for the trial, lawyer Barry Berke—one of Nadler's hired guns from the first impeachment whom Raskin brought back for the second—suggested they include a reference to Susan Collins's attempt to justify her acquittal vote by naively suggesting Trump had "learned his lesson." Raskin and other staff quickly nixed it. They steered so methodically clear of the first impeachment, in fact, that Joshua Matz, Nadler's impeachment guru who also returned to serve in Raskin's stable of attorneys, joked that Impeachment One had come to be known as "the Great Forgetting."

At times, the strategy caused internal friction. Every member of Raskin's team believed Republicans had enabled Trump's assault against the election, either by promoting his steps to flout the democratic process or by willfully ignoring them. But in order not to lose votes, they had to find a way of letting Republicans indict Trump without indicting themselves. The House managers had no choice but to find a way to treat Republicans as fellow victims of the president, not accomplices, keeping in mind that Trump's followers had attacked the Republicans in Congress as surely as the Democrats when they stormed the Capitol.

There was no better example of how Trump had turned on his allies than the case of Mike Pence, who had fled the rampaging mob calling for his head. Republicans advised Raskin to highlight Pence's story as much as possible. The knowledge that Pence's life was endangered during the attack—and that Trump did nothing to protect or even check on him—appalled the GOP. If Trump had abandoned his loyal second in command, there was no one he wouldn't sacrifice to serve his own ends.

Raskin wanted to do more than just talk about Pence, however. He wanted senators to hear his story firsthand—if not from the vice president, then from those who were at his side that day. Quietly, his team began reaching out to Pence World through a host of intermediaries and receiving signals back that the vice president might allow his staff to testify if subpoenaed at trial.

One of those came through an extremely unlikely ally: Charles Cooper, the conservative lawyer who had represented John Bolton during the first impeachment, frustrating Democrats' case by threatening to take his subpoena to court. This time around, however, he was on their side. Cooper was apoplectic about how Trump had tried to overturn the election—and about the pressure he had been putting on the vice president, which Cooper had heard about through his longtime friend, Pence attorney Richard Cullen. Cooper had been so angry that he took it upon himself to help Trump's impeachers, reaching out to Norm Eisen, an attorney from Trump's first impeachment who stayed in close touch with the staff for his second. Cooper told Eisen that Pence World was so upset with Trump that it wasn't out of the realm of possibility they might be willing to allow a top staffer to testify against Trump at the trial. And if the impeachment managers wanted to get in touch with Pence and his team—or wanted to discuss the possibility of testifying—he was happy to act as an interlocutor. Eisen passed the word to the managers, who took Cooper up on that offer.

Raskin made some cold calls of his own. He knew that during Pence's years in Congress, he had been particularly close friends with former senator Jeff Flake. The two men had worked at conservative think tanks during the 1990s before winning election to the House in 2000. As newly minted members, they had watched together as Al Gore gracefully conceded the 2000 election, despite winning the popular vote. Pence and Flake had nicknamed each other "Butch" and "Sundance," likening themselves to the iconic western outlaws of film for the way they took on big government spending.[1] During a 2017 shooting at a GOP congressional baseball practice, when GOP Whip Steve Scalise had almost died, Pence had been the first person to call and check on Flake, then frantically trying to save his colleague's life on the practice field.

When Raskin called Flake for help, the former senator explained that he and Pence weren't as close as they had once been. Flake had resigned in frustration over Trump's grip on the party, while Pence had maintained his status as Trump's loyal right-hand man. But Flake promised to reach out to Pence personally and try to convince him to let his team testify about what had happened. He also gave Raskin some advice on trying to move his old GOP colleagues.

"They need to be constantly reminded that at some point they won't have the Senate pin on their lapel anymore," Flake told Raskin. "Sooner or later, they'll be left with just their conscience and their grandkids—and conscience will forever ask, and their grandkids will always remember: 'Did I do what I could when I had a vote to protect our democracy?'"

It was a powerful message, Raskin thought. And it would be even more powerful if senators could hear it as he just had: from a Republican.

While Pelosi had been very hands-on during the first impeachment, by and large she allowed Raskin to run things his own way during the second. The Judiciary staff who had worked on both impeachment efforts noticed the difference immediately. But the team knew their newfound liberty was not unlimited. Pelosi hated the idea of having a Republican impeachment manager on board; she had made that abundantly clear to Raskin when he floated the notion to her in late January.

Knowing that, Raskin decided it would be better to ask for forgiveness than permission. Discreetly and carefully, he approached Republicans behind Pelosi's back, dropping heavy hints that he wanted them to join his squad without directly asking for their assistance.

The first Republican Raskin tapped was John Katko, a moderate from upstate New York whom he had befriended while working on a congressional ethics investigation. In Raskin's estimation, Katko was a talented and principled lawyer. More importantly, he had voted to impeach Trump. But in a sign of how politically difficult the proposal was, Katko physically recoiled when Raskin inquired: "What if someone were to make you an offer to join our impeachment team?"

No way, Katko said. He couldn't do it.

In the end, it wasn't Pelosi who shattered Raskin's dreams of a bipartisan impeachment team. Raskin decided himself that he was asking the impossible. It was one thing to vote to impeach, but entirely another for a Republican to join Democrats in prosecuting the leader of the Republican Party. Many of the ten House Republicans who voted to impeach were getting death threats. Some had even taken to wearing bulletproof vests.

Cheney in particular had become a top target. In the days after the House's impeachment vote, Trump's allies had come after her with a vengeance as the president vowed to oust her from Congress by backing a primary challenger. In the midst of that, Jim Jordan— the pugnacious Trump loyalist who had masterminded Trump's defense in the House—launched a campaign to boot Cheney from the ranks of GOP leadership. All because she refused to stop calling Trump out for his continued election lies.

Raskin had hoped that having a Republican like Cheney serve as an impeachment manager would force GOP senators to take their arguments seriously. But he couldn't risk putting his friend in an even worse position—politically but also in terms of her personal safety. In fact, he was so worried about putting Cheney in danger that he even offered to scale back the number of references he was planning to make to her rebukes of Trump during the trial.

"Don't be shy," Cheney replied with a wry smile. "You can quote me."

Raskin never mustered the courage to ask his friend outright to join his team. It would be too much for her, he reasoned to himself. What he didn't realize then was that Cheney was so determined to end the era of Trumpism that if he just asked for her help convicting him, she would have jumped at the chance. He would come to realize that only when she told him so, weeks after the trial was over.

44

PEER PRESSURE

Mitch McConnell sat in his office on Tuesday, January 26, agonizing over how to cast what he knew would be one of the most pivotal votes of his career. Since the harrowing events of January 6, the Senate GOP leader—recently demoted to the minority—had been all but certain that his party was finally going to shun Trump, a development he'd welcomed with a sense of relief. The former president, he was sure, had committed impeachable acts and posed a toxic danger to democracy.

But while McConnell was ready to be done with Trump, his party, it seemed, was not. To his chagrin, a large chunk of his members were once again coalescing around the former president. And they were about to put him in a bind.

That afternoon, Senator Rand Paul, McConnell's younger and far more pro-MAGA Kentucky delegation mate, was forcing all senators to go on record and declare whether a post-presidential conviction of Trump was constitutional. It was a question McConnell had been grappling with for the two weeks since the House had impeached him—and he was still far from being ready to answer it.

The vote, McConnell knew, would be seen as a test for the looming impeachment trial, making the stakes of his choice incredibly high. If GOP senators, under his leadership, were willing to endorse the constitutionality of the proceedings, it would signal that a Trump conviction was a real possibility. But if they voted the opposite way, condemning the entire trial, it would foreshadow that Republicans would likely help the former president escape accountability—something McConnell was loath to do.

McConnell knew many of his rank and file were torn over how to handle the situation—and that in their uncertainty, they would look to him for guidance. If he declared the trial to be constitutional, breaking with Trump in the process, he could set the stage for a party mutiny, helping the GOP turn the page on Trump for good. It was an appealing prospect: conviction could enable the Senate to bar Trump from holding office again—and McConnell didn't ever want Trump in office again.

But in all his years as GOP leader, McConnell had never led such a rebellion. And that day, he wasn't sure he was up to the task.

Mounted on the office wall above McConnell's head was a framed portrait of his mentor, the late Kentucky senator John Sherman Cooper, for whom he had interned in the summer of 1964. Cooper, a Republican, had helped pass the Civil Rights Act despite a flood of angry pro-segregationist letters he'd received from his constituents. The twenty-something McConnell had once asked Cooper how he squared his vote with what his constituents wanted.

"There are times you follow, and times when you lead," Cooper had told him, an adage that stuck with McConnell decades later.[1]

Was this McConnell's own moment to lead? And if he did, would enough Republicans follow him to make it worthwhile?

McConnell was still shaken by the siege of the Capitol. The night of the riot, when he returned to the building from Fort McNair, he had seen the splintered wood in the door to his Capitol suite left by marauders who had tried to break into his office and attack his staff. He had watched, stunned, as his aides moved furniture they had used to barricade the entrance out of the way to make room for his return. Overcome with emotion at the trauma they'd experienced, McConnell had made a vow to his aides.

"We've all known that Trump is crazy," he had said. "I'm done with him. I will *never* speak to him again."

For a while, it looked like McConnell's confidence was well placed. In the immediate aftermath of January 6, Republicans across the political spectrum had turned on Trump, calling on him to resign. The day after the riot, McConnell's wife, Elaine Chao, re-signed her position as secretary of Transportation,[2] prompting other Cabinet members to follow. The exodus was so great, in fact, that McConnell began fearing that Trump, left unfettered, might start to act upon his worst instincts. He personally urged top Trump offi-cials like White House counsel Pat Cipollone and National Security Advisor Robert O'Brien to serve out their terms, looking to them to restrain the president who had already proved himself a threat to the nation.

McConnell was stunned at the speed with which that powerful anti-Trump sentiment had faded by the time the House voted to impeach, an indictment supported by just ten Republicans. It was clear that many of his members still feared that the outgoing pres-ident and his loyal base would come after them if they broke with Trump. In the days after the riot, as anger at Trump gave way to panic that blaming him could cost lawmakers their jobs, a large crop of rank-and-file Senate Republicans also began frantically search-ing for an escape hatch—a way to vote against impeachment with-out defending what Trump had done.[3]

Those senators had found salvation in a January 12 *Washington*

Post op-ed written by well-known conservative attorney J. Michael Luttig, who had served as a U.S. Court of Appeals judge for fifteen years. In it, Luttig argued it was unconstitutional to impeach a former president—or for the Senate to conduct a trial against an ex-president who had been impeached while in office.[4] The next morning, as the House prepared to impeach Trump again, Arkansas senator Tom Cotton sent the piece around to his colleagues. Soon, Trump's most hard-core defenders became obsessed with the idea, pressing other senators to embrace the argument as a reason to oppose removal.

McConnell himself wasn't convinced by Luttig's logic—and he knew some of his GOP colleagues weren't either. The argument seemed to him a "procedural off-ramp." And McConnell was not yet sure he wanted one.

In a series of meetings, McConnell and a host of skeptical GOP senators debated the merits of a similar argument with his trusted legal advisor from the first impeachment, Andrew Ferguson. Ferguson, who had barely escaped the rioters as they tore into the Capitol on January 6, had wrestled with the subject for days and concluded that the Founders conceived of impeachment only as a means of removing people still in office. He pointed out that Benjamin Franklin once argued that impeachment was a necessary constitutional escape hatch for removing a tyrant because the only other recourse was assassination[5]—and no one wanted that. Since there was simply no way the Senate could convene and speed through a trial in the days remaining before Biden's inauguration, Trump could not be subject to conviction, Ferguson advised his boss and the members.

McConnell, still skeptical, challenged his counsel: *Why would the Founders have given Congress the absolute power of impeachment in the Constitution if it was limited?* he wanted to know. *Why would the Founders include a provision in the Constitution to bar someone from running for office ever again—only to limit a conviction to current office holders?*

Ferguson acknowledged it was a tough question. But if McConnell's endgame was to keep Trump from running for office again, Ferguson warned, a Senate conviction was no guarantee of that goal. Some scholars believed that the Constitution did not actually permit an impeached president to be disqualified from holding office again, as it did judges and other public officials, he explained to McConnell and other GOP members considering conviction. It was a minority view that few constitutional experts agreed with, Ferguson acknowledged, noting he personally didn't accept it either. But it didn't matter: Trump could try to run again in 2024 and sue any state that kept him off the ballot, he said. It would turn into an explosive legal battle that would catapult the ex-president back into the headlines, possibly resurrecting his efforts to stage a political comeback, right when the party was trying to heal.

"Barring him from office wouldn't be a slam dunk," Ferguson warned.

As McConnell pondered what to do, he entertained other arguments for and against conviction from various corners of the GOP. Liz Cheney made a personal appeal to McConnell to use his leadership position to step out against the president to give his rank-and-file Republicans political cover to do the same. She pressed him in a series of phone calls to bring the Senate back from a congressional recess before the Biden inauguration and quickly convict Trump before he left office. Republicans would follow his lead, she insisted to McConnell. And besides, Trump still posed an ongoing threat to the country.

McConnell told Cheney he did not disagree on her last point, though he was adamant that logistically the Senate could not convict Trump in a week. In his view, Trump deserved the right to find counsel and prepare a defense no matter how guilty he was. But McConnell also acknowledged another fear to Cheney that had started to creep into his psyche: that conviction might make Trump a martyr in the eyes of his followers, empowering him in the long run. That might pose even more of a threat to the Republican Party, he feared.

"We don't disagree on the substance; we just disagree on the tactics," McConnell told Cheney as they conferred about how to free the GOP from Trump's iron grip. "Let's just ignore him."

Meanwhile Lindsey Graham, the longtime ally whom he had leaned on for legal advice during the first impeachment, was trying mightily to get McConnell right with Trump. He popped into the leader's office at least twice that month to argue that conviction was out of the question. The GOP would be legitimizing a snap impeachment with no due process for the president. And besides, he said, Trump was not guilty of incitement.

"What he said—it's political speech! The MOST protected form of speech," Graham firmly told McConnell. "If you're going to start holding politicians accountable based on the actions of others—from a speech? That's a dangerous place to go."

McConnell, still considering his options, said nothing in response.

The way Graham had rationalized Trump's actions since January 6 had been particularly craven—and a perfect example of how McConnell was quickly losing his members to Trump. The night of the riot, Graham had declared in an emotional speech that he and the president were through.

"Trump and I, we had a hell of a journey," he had said on the Senate floor, his voice catching. "I hate it being this way. Oh my god I hate it . . . but today all I can say is count me out. Enough is enough."

Two days later, Trump supporters had harassed Graham as he

walked through Reagan National Airport, calling him a "traitor."[6] Graham's resolve crumbled almost immediately. By the time the House was voting to impeach the following week, he had resumed his position as captain of the president's cheering squad. He even found Trump an impeachment trial lawyer when no one else would step forward to defend him.

In some ways, McConnell's passivity had enabled such whiplash. Like Graham, many Senate Republicans who experienced a flash of conscience and self-reflection in the wake of the riot had it quickly beaten out of them by Trump's base. Many of those senators were looking to McConnell for a smoke signal on what they should do, but the Senate GOP leader kept his cards close to the chest.

McConnell did drop occasional hints of his fury with the president, hoping to give others the courage to take the principled stand he still wasn't sure he wanted to make himself. In private conversations, he made clear he thought Trump had committed impeachable offenses. The day after Luttig's argument made a splash with his members, McConnell penned a letter to his colleagues saying he was open to voting to convict—an enormous turnaround for a leader who had declared during Trump's first impeachment that he was "in total coordination" with the president's defense team.[7] And when it came to the facts of what had happened on January 6, McConnell didn't mince words; he put the blame squarely on the ex-president's shoulders.

"The mob was fed lies," McConnell said on the Senate floor on January 19. "They were provoked by the president."

But McConnell stopped short of perhaps the one thing that may have made a difference: He never actually encouraged his colleagues to convict. Instead, he told them the verdict would be a "vote of conscience." And while some senior Senate Republicans privately predicted in mid-January that double digits of their ranks would be

willing to convict Trump—if not the full seventeen that would have
been necessary to bar him from serving in office again—McConnell
never did a whip check.

Instead, as the trial neared, Trump's defenders quickly filled the
void—in part by trying to pressure McConnell back in line with
Trump. A week after the impeachment vote, on the day of Biden's
inauguration, a group of them told CNN that if McConnell voted to
convict Trump, he could no longer be leader—a very public warning that the Kentuckian needed to check himself.[8] Even Graham
argued the party needed Trump to win back the Senate—despite
evidence that Trump had just cost the party two Senate seats in
Georgia.

On a conference call with the GOP senators that week, McConnell listened as a group of Trump allies pressed him to find a way
to avoid a second impeachment trial—and to do more to defend the
ex-president. *Couldn't he get the Supreme Court to throw out the charges,*
they asked. *After all, Trump was not president anymore. Why go through
this at all?*

A year before, McConnell had used his position to secure the most
advantageous conditions possible for the president at trial, assuring
his acquittal almost single-handedly. But this time, he refused to
intervene. Even when Senator Kevin Cramer warned McConnell
on the call that some of the GOP's biggest-name donors wanted to
see a more robust effort to exonerate the ex-president, McConnell
remained unmoved. He had defended Trump for too long. Others
could do as they wanted, but as far as he was concerned, this time
the former president was on his own.

If you have ideas about defending Trump, talk to Graham, he told the
senators during the call.

Over the next few days, as an increasing number of GOP senators coalesced around the argument that a post-presidential impeachment was unconstitutional, McConnell made one last attempt

to change their minds. He asked his leadership team to invite well-respected Republican legal experts to advocate both for and against the constitutionality argument so his members could hear both sides. Roy Blunt of Missouri, who oversaw the GOP Senate lunches, agreed. To kick things off, he invited Jonathan Turley—the constitutional lawyer Jerry Nadler's attorneys had mocked as a "rent-a-quote" machine during the first impeachment—to lay out the anti-impeachment position at a January 26 luncheon. They'd settle on a pro-impeachment GOP scholar later.

But the night before Turley's session, Rand Paul cornered McConnell's staff in the cloakroom and demanded an immediate vote on the constitutionality of the looming trial. If McConnell didn't schedule such a vote himself, Paul insisted he would force the issue. And he would do it the next day, right after the luncheon.

McConnell knew the vote was sure to fail, but that wasn't the problem. The issue was that it would compel every senator to pre-emptively declare on the record whether they thought convicting Trump was constitutional or not—including McConnell, who was still at war with himself over that very question. Much to McConnell's chagrin, it also would require his members to take a position without having heard any prominent GOP scholar argue why it might, in fact, be constitutional to convict an ex-president, as he had originally wanted.

As lawmakers left the Turley lunch the next day and headed to the chamber for the snap vote Paul had demanded, McConnell retreated to his office for a private moment. On the floor, several GOP senators who had just sat through arguments about why they must acquit Trump still weren't sure if they agreed and started button-holing McConnell's staff.

"How's he voting?" they asked over and over, eager for guidance—and to know if they'd have political cover to vote that the trial was constitutional. "How's he voting?"

McConnell's aides confessed to the senators that they had no idea what their boss would do.

In his memoir, McConnell had written that a "true leader is one who doesn't take a poll on every issue."[9] Cooper, his mentor, had been a shining example of leading with conviction where there was a clear right and wrong. But that day, McConnell decided to neither lead nor follow, leaving his members without the guidance and protection they needed to take a very politically risky position. He walked to the floor and voted with the bulk of the GOP to declare the trial was unconstitutional, an argument he wasn't even sure he agreed with. If McConnell was going to break with Trump on impeachment, it would have to happen another day.

A thousand miles away, at the Florida resort the former president had decided to make his full-time home, Congress's other Republican leader was making a pilgrimage to kiss the ring. Trump had not taken Kevin McCarthy's call to censure him well. In fact, he had been apoplectic, refusing to speak with him and telling everyone who would listen that the man who had once been "my Kevin" was in fact the biggest "pussy" in Washington.[10]

For McCarthy, Trump's irate reaction had been devastating. After the madness of the Capitol attack, McCarthy figured calling for censure was a modest rebuke, but clearly the former president didn't agree. He had taken inordinate umbrage and was trying to turn the entire MAGA apparatus against McCarthy as revenge—political support McCarthy knew he needed to flip the House in 2022 and fulfill his dream of becoming Speaker.

Had Republicans continued to shun Trump as they had in the immediate aftermath of the Capitol siege, McCarthy knew he could have weathered the storm. But that month, something extraordinary happened. After Facebook and Twitter shut down the president's social media accounts for spreading lies about the election, Republicans of all stripes began rallying around their party leader once again. Their shared sense of victimhood at the hands of what the president's supporters decried as "cancel culture" only intensified after Democrats impeached Trump. And it made the House GOP leader who had publicly rebuked Trump second-guess himself for ever having criticized the president.

If McCarthy had been brave enough to stand firm, there were some Republicans willing to stand with him. During a private meeting with his congressional deputies that month, Steve Womack, a conservative congressman from Arkansas, urged McCarthy not to cave to Trump but instead to punish the rank-and-file members who had appeared onstage with him at the January 6 "Stop the Steal" rally. Womack played a reel of Congressman Mo Brooks, a staunch Trump ally from Alabama, asking Trump supporters if they were ready to "fight" with their blood, sweat, tears, and lives—and encouraging them to march on the Capitol to "start taking down names and kicking ass."

"Kick Mo Brooks off his committees," Womack recommended. "We have to send a signal that this sort of action is unacceptable."

Multiple GOP lawmakers in the room backed Womack, including some of McCarthy's closest allies. McCarthy didn't disagree with them. In fact, he had mused privately to other GOP leaders that they needed to rein in lawmakers like Brooks who were stirring up vitriol against their own colleagues, including Liz Cheney—and that he hoped Twitter would take away their accounts too.[11]

But McCarthy knew taking such bold action against a member of Trump's inner cabal would only anger the former president more. After two weeks thinking about it, he changed course completely, opting to protect the very Trump allies whose actions had sparked

such concern. Shortly thereafter, Womack resigned from one of Mc-
Carthy's top advisory teams, writing a private letter to the leader
explaining that he couldn't serve under someone so cowardly who
refused to do the right thing.

By then, McCarthy had already begun publicly walking back his
previous rebukes of Trump. The day after Biden's January 20 inauguration, he told reporters, "I don't believe he provoked [the riot] if
you listen to what he said at the rally." It directly refuted his own
floor speech from the impeachment vote just a week before, when
he said that "the president bears responsibility for Wednesday's attack on Congress by mob rioters." Now McCarthy wanted people to
believe his speech had been misinterpreted.

"Everybody across this country has some responsibility," he said
during a television interview with Greta Van Susteren a few nights
later.[12]

McCarthy also began reneging on his promise to members that
they were free to vote their conscience on impeachment without
fear of reprisal. When Jim Jordan and Trump's allies went after Liz
Cheney, McCarthy did not defend her, stating in that same Van
Susteren interview that his No. 3 "has a lot of questions she has to
answer."

The flip-flop was spectacular. McCarthy instantly became the
butt of jokes in Washington, as even friendly journalists pointed out
how weak and desperate he looked. It got so bad that McCarthy had
to beg the party's public messaging minds to defend him.[13]

McCarthy knew his about-face had put some of his members in
an uncomfortable position, so he was ready when moderate Republicans came to him privately expressing alarm. Trump's star would
fade in a few months, he told them. In the meantime, it was better
not to rock the boat and risk alienating the 74 million voters who
backed him in the election. McCarthy also reminded them that

Trump was already promising revenge on the ten House Republicans who voted to impeach him. He said he would go to Mar-a-Lago to make peace with the ex-president to ensure he didn't.

Convinced that compromising his convictions would be worth it in the end, McCarthy made a beeline to Florida to wriggle back into Trump's good graces. He was not above groveling.

As the Senate trial loomed, Raskin's impeachment lawyers privately found themselves facing off with an unexpected adversary: the heads of their own party. Chuck Schumer, newly in charge of the Senate, had been the first Democratic leader to endorse a second impeachment the day after the riot. But in the days leading up to the trial, the New Yorker began pressuring the managers to cut corners. Schumer wasn't alone: Raskin's team was shocked when the incoming Biden White House also snubbed their requests for help in trying to secure new evidence they thought could help end Trump politically, and keep him out of government for good.

In Trump's first impeachment, the lack of high-profile witnesses had been a key catalyst in the Democrats' failure to remove him from office. In the House, investigators had lost at least some GOP support by sidestepping a chance to fight for Trump's inner circle in court. In the Senate, Republicans' refusal to call former national security advisor John Bolton had all but ensured the president's smooth acquittal. This time around, Raskin was determined not to repeat those mistakes. He wanted to find someone who could take the stand in the trial and shock Republicans into a conviction. He wanted a Republican witness who could speak to Trump's actions firsthand and catch the attention of the GOP writ large—what he began referring to as the "Holy Grail."

Following the impeachment vote in the House, Raskin's team

spent hours engaged in a top secret—and sensitive—extensive search for witnesses who could do just that. The team had assembled a wish list, filling it with former aides to Vice President Pence who had been with him in lockdown during the riot, and White House advisors who interacted with Trump that day and might be sympathetic to their cause. They also had their eye on top Pentagon brass who might be able to illustrate for the Senate jury how Trump sat back and watched as the Capitol burned—and whether he intentionally kept the National Guard from responding.

It didn't take long, however, for Raskin's team to encounter resistance. Schumer, who had never been Majority Leader before, was panicking about the start of the Biden presidency and wanted to start confirming Biden nominees right out of the gate. With the Senate now evenly divided between fifty Democrats and fifty Republicans, Schumer knew he had no margin for error—and thus wanted to move quickly. There was also an understanding in his office that every day spent on the trial was a day that they couldn't use to try to help Biden kickstart his Democratic administration and agenda. Plus, after four years of watching Senate Republicans cater to Trump, Schumer had little faith that any witness would truly change their minds on a conviction.

The new Majority Leader had plenty of company when it came to that sentiment. Many of Schumer's Democrats felt it was futile to chase the Republican votes needed to convict—particularly after forty-five GOP senators voted against recognizing the constitutionality of a trial, including McConnell. That set off a scramble, as with the first impeachment, for alternatives to avoid considering the impeachment charges altogether. Virginia senator Tim Kaine, who had once been Hillary Clinton's running mate, began pressing colleagues to think about invoking Section 3 of the Fourteenth Amendment, which prohibits anyone who "engaged in insurrection or rebellion" against the country from holding federal or state office. Legal experts believed that all it would take was a simple majority vote in Congress to establish that Trump fell under that prohibition for his actions fomenting the January 6 riot—a roll call that could occur without lengthy proceedings or a single GOP vote.

The move failed to gain momentum, however, as Democrats fretted that it would look overtly partisan and blow back on the party. Several legal scholars also warned that Trump might challenge any disqualification on running for office again in court and potentially win. Still, the pressure to move quickly continued—impatience that the new Majority Leader capitalized on to try to clear the decks as soon as possible.

In late January, Schumer began to publicly argue for a swift trial—and downplay the need for witnesses.[14] He and his staff were even more relentless behind the scenes. While Schumer's office signaled that the leader would support calling witnesses if Raskin decided to go down that road, they made it clear that the leader thought their testimony was utterly unnecessary. Lawmakers had witnessed the violence of January 6 themselves, the Democratic leader reasoned. Therefore, the trial should focus on questions of constitutionality, not relitigating facts.

Raskin and his team knew that Biden and Pelosi agreed with the Democratic leader. The new president was eager to show the country there was a new sheriff in town, and Pelosi wanted to deliver on the Democratic agenda after four years of Trump. She had privately told fellow leaders she thought the trial could be done in three or four days. But Raskin refused to succumb to the pressure to rush. Secure in the knowledge that Pelosi had deferred to his judgment thus far, he decided to go about trying to secure witnesses anyway.

One of the first ideas Raskin and his team toyed with was calling

Trump's Secret Service detail. The agency charged with guarding the president could be a treasure trove of information detailing not only Trump's actions that day, but all communications that had taken place between Pence and Trump or their teams. Their recollections could reveal what Trump had known about the riot and when he knew it, key information for securing GOP votes.

There was precedent for the move. In 1998, following a court order, special White House agents assigned to protect Clinton were deposed under subpoena as part of Ken Starr's investigation.[15] The agency and the president had both protested the summons, arguing the agents' insights were privileged. But when a judge upheld the subpoena, they went along with the ruling.[16] Their testimony ended up helping to confirm Clinton's affair with Monica Lewinsky at a time when the president was still denying it had happened.

Yet when Raskin's team reached out to the Biden White House to inquire about deposing Secret Service officials in a similar fashion, they were rebuffed. It would set a terrible precedent if they came after the Secret Service, incoming Biden aides told them, and the Biden administration would fight it. The new president's team also put the kibosh on the idea of deposing a group of long-term, nonpartisan White House stewards. The managers had received word that the servers who witnessed Trump's behavior on January 6 might be willing to share what they knew. But the new Biden White House wanted nothing to do with the idea.

Biden's reluctance to use his newfound power to help the impeachment team extended to the executive agencies as well. His new Justice Department leaders denied the managers' request for proof of a rumored FBI memo warning about a looming threat to the Capitol that had been shared with Trump's White House in the days before the riot. The document would have helped Raskin's team make the case that the president knew of the threat of violence before he urged his supporters to march on the Capitol. But Justice officials told him that disclosing it would complicate upcoming prosecutions of rioters.

They ran into a similar predicament with the Pentagon. Impeachment investigators had heard through various intermediaries that there had been serious issues regarding the chain of military command on January 6. There were reports that Trump had rebuffed pleas to send in the National Guard, leaving it to Pence to step in, a seeming dereliction of duty that the managers wanted to highlight. But again, Raskin's team found that Biden was no help, making no effort to furnish senior Defense Department witnesses for the impeachment managers.

A year before, Raskin wouldn't have thought twice about fighting for such materials, no matter how long the odds or who he had to face down. He and his fellow "musketeers"—now his fellow impeachment managers—had always advocated subpoenaing recalcitrant witnesses and going to the mattresses to get them to show up. But it was one thing to fight Trump in court; it was another thing entirely to start a fight with Biden in his first days as president.

Raskin and his team believed they were in a strong position to enforce any subpoenas the Senate issued mid-trial. Since Trump was no longer president, claims of blanket immunity and executive privilege would be Biden's to make alone—and surely, he would not invoke them to help protect the former president. But when they reached out for assurances that their assumptions were correct, the White House aides balked. They did not even want the question to be posed to Biden for fear it might sully him by association with Trump's trial.

The new administration's skittishness also extended to incoming vice president Kamala Harris, who as president of an evenly divided Senate could have played a critical role for the managers.

Raskin's team wanted to keep Harris in reserve to cast tie-breaking votes, especially if all fifty Republicans tried to block their efforts to call witnesses. But Schumer's counsel Mark Patterson told the team that she wanted nothing to do with the trial.

"She will not like it, and we will not like it," he said, urging the managers to avoid anything that wasn't supported on a bipartisan basis.

In a series of late-night phone calls in late January, Patterson became Schumer's hammer as the new Majority Leader tried to corral Raskin's team into a quick, witness-free trial. He fervently pushed back on the managers' push to change trial rules in order to call witnesses at the start of proceedings. Despite Schumer's earlier insistence on a similar strategy during the first impeachment, the Senate leader was unsympathetic to the argument that it might help them secure the needed votes to land new evidence. The managers should simply accept the same procedures McConnell had laid out the last time, Patterson argued.

"You mean the rules that McConnell intentionally drafted to screw over the House's case and fuck us left, right, and center last time?" impeachment attorney Barry Berke asked furiously.

Schumer's office and Patterson would later argue that their efforts to push back on the managers' plans were to ensure the trial looked as bipartisan as possible. Schumer, they would say, wanted a strong bipartisan vote on trial rules so that Trump couldn't allege the proceedings had been rigged by the Democrats against him. They would also argue that their resistance to using Harris as a tie-breaker was due to concerns that it would look overtly partisan and risk repelling GOP senators otherwise open to a conviction.

But in the moment, Raskin's team felt like they were being bullied—and found Schumer's heavy-handedness insulting. While the Senate's new Majority Leader may have viewed the entire trial as a nuisance and distraction, the managers viewed their task as sacred. Prosecuting Trump for inciting an insurrection against Congress— hands down the most egregious abuse of office they could think of in American history—was the most serious undertaking of their professional lives. This, they believed, was Congress's last chance to reassert itself and reclaim the power of oversight Trump had spent four years usurping.

That Schumer was the one throwing a monkey wrench into the managers' witness strategy was particularly grating. During Trump's first impeachment, he had urged the chief justice to break potential tie votes on witnesses, rousing the whole Democratic Party apparatus to lean on him. It was hypocritical and obnoxious, Raskin's team seethed, that Schumer was now trying to quash their similar efforts to secure testimony after Trump had done something even more damaging to the country.

After each session with Patterson, Raskin's top legal minds would regroup in a phone call, spewing expletives about Schumer behind his back. They couldn't believe he wasn't willing to use his new majority to go full bore after Trump, and they complained that he was tying their case into knots. Schumer didn't give a damn about the trial or securing Trump's conviction, they agreed. His initial embrace of impeachment had been a ploy to stave off a 2022 primary challenge, they spat: He showed the left side of his face in New York and the right side of his face in Washington.

But a sense of paranoia had started to settle in. Was the new White House trying to send them a message?

"Is this coming from Schumer—or from Biden?" they'd frantically asked each other. "*Who* doesn't want us to try our case?"

Realizing the sensitivity of the internal Democratic fight, Raskin and the staff had decided to keep their witness search close to the chest, lest someone blab to the media. They even kept the other managers largely out of the loop on their plans. But the lack of clarity surrounding their strategy had become an issue with the other eight lawmakers who had been tapped to present new evidence at trial. *When are we going to talk about witnesses?* they would ask at each meeting, so frequently that one of them called it the perpetual "giant elephant in the room."

The team's video conference on February 3, less than one week before the trial, was no different. Raskin's managers pushed him for a decision, arguing that while they may not win a Senate conviction, they had to tell the American public the whole story. Even Joe Neguse and David Cicilline, Raskin's closest friends in Congress, sided with the rest of the group, noting that they had a duty as prosecutors to follow the evidence where it leads.

"Jamie, I do think at some point we need to talk about witnesses," Cicilline said gently on the February 3 call. "The public expects us to call witnesses. There are witnesses who could be helpful, so we should talk about that."

On a private call afterward, Raskin assured Neguse and Cicilline he was working as hard as he could, confiding to them about the pressure he was under from Schumer's office.

"We're trying," he promised. "We're seeing what we can do."

Raskin and his impeachment staff made a decision that day that they hoped would get Schumer off their backs. To signal that they were willing to do their own thing, Raskin and his team decided to send a letter to Trump asking him to testify—but to do it without consulting Schumer.

They had no expectation that Trump would take the bait. But the move would kill two birds with one stone, they reasoned. It would show their fellow managers—and the Democratic Party at large—that they were willing to fight. And it would defang any accusations from Trump's team that they hadn't given him a chance to weigh in on the charges against him.

Raskin released the letter the next day, intentionally giving Schumer just a five-minute heads-up.[17]

His power play, however, wouldn't settle the battle of wills between Raskin and the Senate Majority Leader. Within hours of his sending his letter, Senate Democrats panned the idea of calling Trump as a witness.[18] As Raskin's team had suspected, if they wanted to find a way to take down Trump, they would get no help from Senate Democrats or the White House. They would have to do it themselves.

45

TRIAL TAKE TWO

FEBRUARY 7–12, 2021

It was the eve of the trial and Raskin had a serious problem: He could not get through his opening speech without crying.

Huddled with his team in an otherwise empty House committee room late on Monday, February 8, Raskin's voice cracked as he recounted his own personal tragedy on January 6—a story he was slated to tell the entire nation in less than twenty-four hours. Clutching the paper in front of him, he spoke of burying his son the day before the attack, only to be gripped by terror that he might also lose his youngest daughter, Tabitha, who had joined him at the Capitol that day. How they had been separated amid the riot and how she had cowered under a desk in Hoyer's office to hide from Trump's mob, thinking she would die.

But each time he neared the close of his remarks, Raskin stumbled. He was supposed to finish by reciting the words Tabitha spoke when they had finally reunited: that she never wanted to set foot in the Capitol ever again. Raskin had tried in ten separate rehearsals to say those words—and each time, he broke down. That Trump's insurrection had made his own daughter too afraid to ever return to the building he considered the citadel of democracy struck him like a knife through his heart.

"I'm sorry, I'm sorry," Raskin said to the skeleton crew that had stayed late to rehearse their presentations for the opening day of the trial. "Let me try that again."

Raskin wasn't the only manager struggling. Unlike the first team of impeachment managers, each person on his squad had a personal connection to the underlying charges. They had all lived through the events of January 6, and they had each suffered some form of their own trauma. A few, like Raskin, had been evacuated off the House floor. Others, like Madeleine Dean of Pennsylvania and Diana DeGette of Colorado, had been trapped in the House balcony, where they flattened themselves between rows of chairs as rioters repeatedly tried to ram their way into the chamber and shots were fired below. Joe Neguse and Eric Swalwell had texted their wives that they loved them in case the worst happened and they failed to escape.

Team members who hadn't been in the Capitol that day made a point of learning the stories of those who had. Before the trial began, Judiciary counsel Aaron Hiller walked Barry Berke over to Pelosi's office and pressed his hand against the splinters of a doorframe that had been kicked down by marauders trying to enter a conference room where Pelosi's staff hid. Joshua Matz frequently found himself sobbing at his laptop as he read the words the managers would say—and saw their raw emotional reactions in meetings.

In Raskin's view, there was a silver lining to their shared trauma. If the House managers were still reeling, then odds were senators were too. Not only had the Senate chamber been breached by the mob, but the senators' near-brush with death had been much closer than any of them realized. The case the managers planned to make was both more powerful and more emotional than Trump's first impeachment, a prosecution that hinged on a private phone call with the leader of a nation most Americans could not find on a map. This time the crime was right there for everyone to see: Trump had revved up his followers, pointed them straight at the Capitol, and unleashed them to wreak havoc on Congress. To secure a conviction, Raskin thought, all they should have to do is remind the senators that they themselves were witnesses.

Still, Raskin knew from years of standing in front of a classroom that even the most compelling subject matter could fall flat if a presenter couldn't engage his audience. A year before, he had watched from the sidelines as Adam Schiff and his team had repelled Republican senators by effectively lecturing them that it was their constitutional duty to convict the president. Now that it was his turn, Raskin was determined not to lose the crowd.

To do that, Raskin believed his team needed to speak from the heart and make their appeals with empathy. The video evidence they planned to feature would help the senators relive January 6—and show them how closely they had missed falling victim to Trump's mob. But the managers shouldn't hide their emotions while making their presentations, Raskin said. And they needed to share the spotlight. Raskin didn't want to dominate the show the way Schiff had. He wanted each of them to have a turn to tell their own story.

By the weekend before the trial was set to begin, Raskin and his team had reluctantly decided to forgo calling for new testimony at trial. Their search for witnesses had come up empty. No Republicans had been willing to step forward. That, combined with pressure from Democratic leaders to move quickly, had led the team to determine that a quick trial was in order. Plus Raskin, ever the op-

timist, convinced himself that the presentations they'd prepared—
especially the new, powerful video footage of the attack they'd
procured—would be enough to move even the staunchest Trump
acolytes. Despite the heated fights with Schumer's office, the managers agreed to go with the Senate Democratic leader's advice for
trial rules, a vote that would receive strong bipartisan support.

Of all the managers grappling emotionally with the case, none
struggled as much as Raskin. Because of his son's death, everyone
on the team felt a degree of protectiveness toward him. The managers and the staff were in collective awe that he was still standing. In
fact, most of them viewed Raskin as nothing short of a superhero for
coping with so much loss as he led one of the most important battles
in congressional history—with more grit than any of them.

But Raskin's gusto for the trial preparations also worried his fellow
managers. They suspected he was dedicating the trial to his son—a
risky connection given that an acquittal might cause him to shatter.
What's more, Raskin was clearly treating Trump's impeachment not
only as a constitutional calling but also as a personal distraction. The
more hours he dedicated to ousting Trump, the fewer he spent lost
in the dark corners of his unfinished mourning. What would happen
to him once the trial was over?

The morning before the trial, as managers nervously made their
way to the Senate floor for their pre-trial walk-through and microphone check, all were worried about how Raskin would handle the
moment. When they arrived, he stepped up to the podium, cleared
his throat, and stunned them into reverent silence.

"These are the times that try men's souls," he said, deliberately
and calmly, in words the managers immediately recognized.

Raskin was reciting from memory "The American Crisis," by
Thomas Paine, a mainstay on the syllabus of every budding lawyer
and student of American history. But the managers knew the greater

significance of the selection: Raskin had named his now-deceased son after Paine. In that moment, in his first turn on the Senate floor, they could see what he was doing: He was talking to Tommy.

The sound levels were fine. But Raskin kept going.

"The summer soldier and the sunshine patriot will, in this crisis, shrink from the service of his country; but he that stands by it now, deserves the love and thanks of man and woman," Raskin said, his words flowing out like muscle memory. "Tyranny, like hell, is not easily conquered; yet we have this consolation with us, that the harder the conflict, the more glorious the triumph."[1]

As Raskin spoke, the cleaning staff tidying the chamber for the next day's trial stopped to listen. The officers of the Senate parliamentarian, who had been shuffling papers on the dais at the front of the chamber, ceased their fussing to focus on Raskin. Even the Capitol Police, who moments before had tried to hustle the managers along so they could complete their security sweep, stopped, folded their arms, and listened.

As they watched him, the managers hoped this would be the Raskin who opened the trial the next day. His poise was assured, his voice was sincere, and despite his slight presence, he was filling the room. There was no way the senators would be able to hear him, they thought, and vote to acquit.

But that night, as he huddled with Neguse and Cicilline for a final rehearsal, Raskin was weeping again. Neguse and Cicilline looked at each other. There was still endless work to do, but if Raskin couldn't make it through his speech, none of it would matter. He needed a break.

"Go home, Jamie," Neguse told him. "We've got this," Cicilline agreed.

On Tuesday, the opening day of the trial, a calmer and more composed Raskin arrived at the Rayburn Room on the House side of the Capitol. He had dressed in a black suit, with a black mask to match—though with an academic's indifference to style, he still had his regular brown shoes on. The managers greeted him warmly, and he smiled in return.

"I'm proud of you," he told them.

Neguse, Cicilline, and the staffers who had been with Raskin the night before breathed a quiet sigh of relief. Collectively, the managers straightened themselves, got into formation, and began their formal procession across the Capitol.

But just outside the Senate chamber, Raskin began to breathe quickly, and turned to the impeachment staffer closest to him.

"My mouth is very dry," he said, his eyes widening with panic. "Somebody needs to call a doctor."

Hiller met Raskin's panicked stare. After working on both House impeachments of Trump, he understood how much pressure was on the managers—and Raskin in particular—to carry this case over the finish line. He also realized that Raskin especially was shouldering a heavier burden than any of them—and in that moment, likely nearing his breaking point.

"We have to talk about something that's not impeachment," Raskin said pleadingly, his voice growing breathy and hoarse.

Hiller thought back to the day before. Inspired by Raskin's extemporaneous delivery of Paine's treatise, he had stuffed his own worn law-school copy of the writer's pamphlet *Common Sense* into his bag of notebooks and materials that he wanted to keep close during the trial. He quickly fished it out and handed it to Raskin, who opened it hungrily. As Raskin read, his breathing slowed, and the color came back to his face. Moments later, he handed the book back to Hiller, thanked him, and walked onto the Senate floor.

Raskin, Neguse, Berke, and Matz raced out of the Senate chamber the moment the gavel fell at the end of the first trial day. The chamber had just taken an opening vote on the key question of whether the Constitution permitted the Senate to hold an impeachment trial for a former president—the GOP's central argument against holding Trump to account. And they couldn't believe it, but a Republican had just flipped.

Raskin and his team had known that it would be an uphill climb to change the minds of the forty-five GOP senators who had sided with Rand Paul on that very question two weeks before. But Raskin refused to count any of those votes as immutable.

"If we can move just one Republican, then we can do this," Raskin had told the other managers.

During his presentation, Raskin had tried to give Senate Republicans a simple explanation for why refusing to convict Trump simply because he had already left office was unacceptable. It would create "a January exception," he argued, that would allow a president to act with impunity in his final weeks in office and get off scot-free.

"Everyone can see immediately why this is so dangerous," Raskin continued. "It's an invitation to the president to take his best shot at anything he may want to do on his way out the door . . . the 'January exception' is an invitation to our Founders' worst nightmare."

The parliamentarian was only a few names into the roll call when Senator Bill Cassidy, a conservative from Louisiana who had previously voted that the trial was unconstitutional, surprised everyone by voting "aye." At the managers' table, Raskin's head whipped around. The others tried to maintain their game faces but were giddy at Cassidy's unexpected turnaround.

As soon as the vote closed, Raskin and his team ran back to their ornate anteroom off the Senate floor to cheer their mini-victory and watch the recap on television. Cassidy was on the screen, explaining his vote. The managers "made a compelling argument," Cassidy told reporters. Trump's lawyers, he continued, had appeared "embarrassed of their arguments."

"Now if I'm an impartial juror, and one side's doing a great job, and the other side is doing a terrible job . . . I'm going to vote for the side that did the good job," Cassidy added.

Raskin was almost beside himself at the validation.

"See, we *can* persuade them!" Raskin exclaimed, pointing at the television joyfully.

Neguse grabbed Raskin squarely by the shoulders in a sportsman's celebration.

"One down, 44 to go," Raskin declared.[2]

Indeed, the first day had gone off with a bang. Raskin, Neguse, and Cicilline had both Democratic and Republican senators hanging on every word of their presentations. But it was the visuals that truly moved the room.

The impeachment staff had prepared a professionally edited thirteen-minute montage of the riot, showing protesters swarming the Capitol, pushing their way past lines of police and into the building, and laying waste to its innermost sanctums, including the Senate chamber. No one except the first day's presenters and the staff—not even the other managers—had seen it before Raskin showed it on the floor. They had bet that it would be so powerful, in fact, that they had rewritten Raskin's entire opening statement the night before the trial to make sure the video would be the first thing to grab senators' attention.

And grab their attention it did. Even senators who had publicly committed to exonerate Trump watched in horror, their expressions freezing as they took it all in. They paled as they saw rioters spit menacingly in the faces of Capitol Police and an officer get crushed and pinned trying to hold them back—and how Trump egged on his followers as the Capitol came under attack, refusing to call back the crowd.

"Fuck the blue! Fuck the blue!" the rioters on the screen yelled as they broke through the Capitol doors, streaming into the building, where they confronted more cops. "You're outnumbered, there's a fucking million of us out here—and we are listening to Trump, your boss!"

A handful of Republicans studiously stared at their laps and desks as the scenes played out. Rand Paul intently doodled images of the Capitol dome on his white legal pad with a blue ballpoint pen. But apart from them, every eye in the chamber was glued to the screens at the front of the room. For many senators, it was the first time they had watched a holistic presentation of what had occurred on January 6—and as the film came to a close, most were visibly shaken.

"You ask what a high crime and misdemeanor is under our Constitution? That's a high crime and misdemeanor," Raskin said, as he brought the presentation away from the screen and back into the room. "If that's not an impeachable offense, then there is no such thing."

Much to the relief of his entire team, Raskin made it through the part of his opening statement about his own personal trauma, faltering only once. The flash of raw emotion he showed when describing his daughter Tabitha's reticence to reenter the Capitol—the line that always caught in his throat—made his grief real.

"Senators, this cannot be our future," Raskin said, collecting himself. The senators—even the Republicans—couldn't help but feel for him.

By contrast, Trump's lawyers bumbled their way through their opening remarks. Lead attorney Bruce Castor—a cousin of Jim Jordan's chief counsel, Steve Castor—perplexed both Republican and Democratic senators with his meandering presentation. He began by offering platitudes about the special nature of being a senator, marveling at how patriotic senators were as a species. He recommended they read the Federalist Papers without explaining why or connecting it to the case. He talked about manslaughter, murder, and his childhood in the Philadelphia suburbs, but said barely anything about the substance of the impeachment charges. At the end of his nearly hour-long presentation, he admitted why.

"I will be quite frank with you: We changed what we were going to do on account that we thought that the House managers' presentation was well done," Castor said. "I wanted you to know that we have responses to those things."

By the time the other Trump counsels tried to offer those responses, the defense had already lost the room—and the respect of the senators in it. Even the Republicans publicly ripped the Trump lawyers for shoddy work, while complimenting Raskin and his team for their skill and professionalism.[3]

On the Democratic side of the aisle, Schumer was pleasantly surprised by the managers' reception. Despite his fears the liberal band of House managers would repel his moderates, they were doing the opposite, and winning over conservative Republicans—Cassidy's vote proved it. Schumer's entire posture toward the team changed, and he congratulated Raskin on a job well done.

The momentum only built from there. Over two days of presentations, Neguse took senators through Trump's efforts to undermine the 2020 election, which had come to be known as the "Big Lie," laying bare his motivations for igniting the storming of the Capitol on January 6. Delegate Stacey Plaskett of the Virgin Islands, a former student of Raskin's at American University's Washington College of Law, had senators squirming in their chairs as she showed them newly released footage from the Capitol building's security cameras depicting their own evacuation. She coupled it with interactive maps to illustrate just how close senators had come to being intercepted by Trump's mob as they evacuated.

Senators were moved by a video showing how one heroic officer, Eugene Goodman, had bought them time to escape by diverting advancing rioters away from unlocked Senate doors, right after hurrying an unwitting Mitt Romney back into the chamber for safety. As he watched the chamber take it all in, Raskin could see that nearly every senator was riveted. They flinched as they saw Vice President Mike Pence scurry down a flight of stairs and away from the rioters, who were at that very moment calling for his head. They recoiled at images of protesters yelling "Where the fuck are they?" as they romped through the chamber only minutes after their escape. They grimaced at rioters rifling through the very desks where the senators now sat, listening to the trial arguments.

By the time Congressman Eric Swalwell stood to present previously unveiled footage of rioters beating officers with a crutch, a hockey stick, a bullhorn, and a Trump flag, the senators were visibly shaken. In one clip, rioters pummeled an officer lying on his back, in an attack caught by his own body camera. As he struggled to break free, an American flag flying over the Capitol slipped out of his view.

Oklahoma senator James Lankford was so distraught that he leaned his head down on his desk. As one of the Republicans who had initially joined Trump's campaign to challenge the 2020 results, Lankford had abandoned his protest with a mea culpa following the riot. Now, he was trying to hold it together while the senator next to him put a hand on his arm.

As they presented their case, there was one senator whom Raskin—and his entire team—watched closely. Mitch McConnell, they believed, was the key to unlocking the seventeen GOP votes necessary to convict. If he went there, others would follow. At times, his stoic presence in the front row unnerved them. He sat motionless, his poker face fixated on every utterance of the trial. But there were moments when Raskin swore he saw tears in his eyes. McConnell, he believed, was with them—despite his votes saying the trial was unconstitutional. There was no one who could have convinced Raskin otherwise.

Outside the chamber, Republicans were expressing clear sympathies for the managers' case. Some of President Trump's most ardent supporters, including Ted Cruz and Lindsey Graham, approached Neguse to compliment his presentation. Senator Richard Burr found DeGette in the hall and gave her a hug as he praised their work. Senator Rob Portman approached Ted Lieu in the bathroom and told him that of all the arguments in the trial, his presentation of what might happen if Trump ran for office and lost again was the one he'd remember most. The comment struck the managers as promising: Plaskett, who had worked as a counsel to Portman in the House two decades prior, told her fellow managers that her ex-boss had indicated to her privately that week that he might vote to convict if he was sure that seventeen Republicans—enough to secure the outcome—were on board.

At another point, another Republican senator complimented a manager on their team dynamic.

"It helps that you guys actually like each other," the Republican had said, recalling the palpable tensions between Nadler and Schiff during Trump's first trial. "Last time, you know, the whole Jerry-Adam thing . . . Man, it was just so obvious that nobody liked each other."

The feedback started to go to the managers' heads. They felt more certain than ever that they were in striking distance of a conviction. Plus, a mid-trial revelation from one of Trump's staunchest Senate supporters buoyed their confidence even more.

At the end of the second day, Tommy Tuberville of Alabama, a well-known college football coach who had been a senator for all of three days on January 6, told reporters that he had informed Trump mid-riot that Pence was being evacuated. The fact that Tuberville

and Trump had spoken by phone during the evacuation wasn't a secret; the managers had mentioned that fact in their arguments that
day. But that Tuberville had informed Trump directly that Pence
was in danger was an illuminating—and potentially damning—
revelation.[4]

It had been clear to both the managers and the defense that highlighting Trump's indifference to Pence's welfare would be pivotal
in winning over the persuadable Republicans. Trump's team had
argued the former president had acted to address the violence, par-
tially out of concern for the vice president. But the call with Tuberville, which would have occurred right around the time Trump
tweeted that Pence "didn't have the courage" to object to the election results, showed that the president knew his vice president was
caught in the crosshairs of the riot. Still, he did little to quell the
violence.

None of those revelations made Trump's guilt an open-and-shut
case, however. While the managers had succeeded in shocking, up-
setting, and depressing the senators, their arguments did not seem
to be resulting in more Republican pledges to convict. Many of
the same Republican senators telling the press that they found the
managers' case compelling would, in the next breath, say that they
couldn't condemn a former president. The Senate had voted 56 to
44 that Trump's second impeachment trial was constitutional. But
Republicans refused to let the argument go, clinging to it as a procedural life raft to let them avoid convicting Trump based on the
facts of the case.[5]

On the third day of the trial, Raskin received a heads-up about
something he thought might break through the partisan bulwark
surrounding the president. During a break in the trial, a reporter
called him to say they were about to post a bombshell story about
a phone call between McCarthy and Trump—and wanted to know

if he would comment. On January 6, the forthcoming story would claim, the president ignored the Minority Leader's pleas for help, praising the insurrectionists instead. More importantly: A House Republican, the person said, had come forward with proof of it.

Standing at a window looking out over the National Mall, Raskin could hardly believe what he was hearing. He called his Republican friend Liz Cheney, who had previously warned him that a reporter would be reaching out about something big—though she hadn't offered many more details. Still, Raskin knew Cheney wouldn't have involved herself in such a story, or alerted him to it, for nothing. He told his staff to watch the next day's headlines closely.

"Something major is coming," he told them.

THE *OTHER* JAIME

FEBRUARY 12-13, 2021

Jamie Raskin's eyes bulged as he skimmed the CNN story on his phone. Huddled in the managers' holding room with his team after proceedings finished on Friday evening, the Maryland Democrat was stunned at the revelations: a moderate House Republican Raskin had never met was claiming to have firsthand evidence that Trump had sided with the mob on January 6.

Congresswoman Jaime Herrera Beutler of Washington wasn't mincing words. McCarthy, she told CNN, had confided in her about a conversation he had had with the president during the insurrection. She said Trump had flatly refused McCarthy's plea for help, despite knowing how chaotic and horrific the Capitol break-in had been. In her notes, she had scribbled down one particularly damning utterance from the former president. "Well, Kevin," McCarthy had recounted Trump as saying, "I guess these people are more upset about the election than you are."[1]

Raskin gaped at the quote. He had been waiting for the story to drop all day, stranded on the Senate floor without his phone. It was even better than he had imagined.

"How can anybody hear this news and not convict him?!" he exclaimed.

The story's revelations only got more staggering. Other unnamed Republicans also confirmed hearing about the McCarthy-Trump exchange. One even told CNN that Trump was "not a blameless observer. He was rooting for them."

But Herrera Beutler had stuck her neck out furthest of all, going on the record to describe Trump's selfish nonchalance that day.

"That line right there demonstrates to me that either he didn't care, which is impeachable, because you cannot allow an attack on your soil, or he wanted it to happen and was OK with it, which makes me so angry," she told CNN. "We should never stand for that, for any reason, under any party flag."

Who was this woman? Raskin wanted to know. She had been among the ten Republicans who voted to impeach Trump. But his familiarity with her began and ended there. Whatever her story, Raskin knew one thing: This other Jaime was about to become his best friend.

As Raskin read the CNN piece, he realized that the revelations had been hiding in plain sight for weeks. In a bid to justify her vote to impeach Trump to her GOP constituents, Herrera Beutler had actually disclosed the contents of the McCarthy-Trump call to a local newspaper reporter in January and to constituents in an early-February town hall. But in Washington, D.C., nobody had noticed.

The delay didn't matter to Raskin. The story was dynamite, he thought, and could blow up the last of the Trump team's slipshod defense. Just a few hours earlier, the president's counsel Michael van der Veen had argued—weakly—that Trump tried to protect his vice president from the hordes of rioters calling for his head. "I'm sure Mr. Trump very much is concerned and was concerned for the safety and well-being of Mr. Pence and everybody else that was over here," he had said. It was a flimsy conjecture that everyone knew was a lie—and here was the proof.

"We should try to reach out to this Jaime Herrera Beutler and get her notes," Raskin told the managers in their prep room.

Brimming with excitement, everyone agreed.

"I know Jaime really well," Diana DeGette of Colorado piped up, offering to be the go-between.

Raskin nodded in agreement. "Try her and see if other House Republicans know about this call too," he instructed.

Herrera Beutler's revelations complicated an already frenzied Friday night. The managers had been caught flat-footed by how quickly the trial was moving to the finish line: Trump's lawyers had rested their case after just a couple of hours, setting up closing arguments for Saturday morning. The managers hadn't expected to give their closing statements until Sunday or Monday at the earliest and hadn't yet written a word of them. Even before the CNN story landed, they were staring down another all-nighter in a week where they had barely slept.

Raskin instructed anyone who wasn't responsible for delivering final arguments to go home and get some rest. But as the managers started collecting their belongings, one of them, Eric Swalwell, posed a question to the room.

"Hasn't this CNN story changed things?" the California Democrat asked, pointing out that in much of that afternoon's Q&A session, GOP senators had been asking questions about what Trump knew and didn't know about the violence happening at the Capitol on January 6. The report, he argued, was an opportunity to give them answers in real time.

"Shouldn't we be calling for witnesses now?" Swalwell asked.

Raskin paused. Swalwell had a point. But it was too massive a change in strategy to contemplate on a dime.

"We aren't going to talk about witnesses now," he said. "I'll be in touch."

For weeks, Raskin had searched for a firsthand witness from the president's inner circle who could add something valuable to the narrative. When none volunteered, he had shrugged it off, projecting confidence that witnesses weren't necessary to win. But Herrera Beutler's account was making him rethink his decision. *How could they refuse to have her explain her bombshell story?*

About an hour later, DeGette poked her head back in the room with a double whammy of bad news. Herrera Beutler's cell had gone straight to voicemail. DeGette had sent a text asking to talk, but the Washington Republican still hadn't responded. And DeGette's efforts to find other Republicans aware of the McCarthy-Trump conversation had also come up short. Fred Upton of Michigan, one of the ten GOP impeachers, told her that only Herrera Beutler had heard McCarthy's tale. That limited the number of people who could confirm the report to one, she conveyed to the team.

At 9:30 p.m., just as Raskin and the rest of the managers were about to head home, signs of life from Herrera Beutler gave them new hope. She texted DeGette that she was on the West Coast with her children but would be in touch soon, inquiring about the managers' timeline. DeGette told her they would resume the trial at ten a.m. the next morning and to call her ASAP, indicating that they'd be interested in seeing her notes about McCarthy's call.

About fifteen minutes later, Herrera Beutler's office released a statement reconfirming the details in the CNN story. *Maybe she'll cooperate after all*, Raskin thought as he departed the Capitol.

As his security detail drove him home that night, Raskin began thinking seriously about calling witnesses again. It would be a bold move, but they had a duty to put on the strongest case they possibly could to showcase Trump's guilt. If Herrera Beutler's testimony could help secure enough GOP votes to take out Trump for good, they had no choice but to ask the Senate to call witnesses and extend the trial.

Raskin was up late that night, waiting for smoke signals from Herrera Beutler, when team attorney Barry Berke called with more encouraging news. Swalwell had texted Congressman Greg Pence that night to inquire if his brother, the former vice president, would be willing to sit for a deposition. Pence had responded by texting back a shrug emoji—which as Swalwell read it, wasn't saying no. Swalwell had then reached out to Congressman Adam Kinzinger, another of the ten Republicans who voted to impeach Trump, who had also been in close contact with Pence World throughout the trial and whose wife was a former Pence staffer. Kinzinger told him that the vice president's team was furious at Trump's lawyers for suggesting the president had cared about Pence's safety on January 6 when he hadn't checked on him once during the riot. He suggested the vice president might actually allow his team to testify to set the record straight and advised Swalwell to contact Pence's former chief of staff, Marc Short, who had been with him through the riot. Kinzinger gave Swalwell Short's cell phone number, and Swalwell fired off a text.

"We would like to receive your testimony about January 6 in any manner you were comfortable," Swalwell wrote, after introducing himself to Short. The managers, he continued, would be willing to conduct a deposition behind closed doors, eschew cameras, and even stick to subjects Short was comfortable with. Anything to get his cooperation.

"We are also able to provide a subpoena if that makes it easier to do so," Swalwell offered. "Anything you can add would be helpful . . .

We have to know soon as this may wrap tomorrow if we don't have a witness."

While he awaited a reply, he called Berke with an update.

As Berke recounted Swalwell's efforts to Raskin, he added that he had also enlisted the managers' new ally Charles Cooper to help. Right before the trial, the prominent conservative attorney had done them an unexpected favor, penning an op-ed in the *Wall Street Journal* stating the impeachment trial was entirely constitutional—directly contradicting the GOP's favorite talking point.[2] Berke thought maybe Cooper would assist them in convincing Short to testify. Cooper said he'd reach out to his Pence contacts and report back.

As he hung up the phone, Raskin could hardly believe their developing good fortune: The former vice president's inner circle might be willing to refute Trump's case! But what about Herrera Beutler?

He looked at the clock. It was after eleven p.m.—eight p.m. on the West Coast—and his team still hadn't heard back from the Washington Republican. He picked up the phone to try her himself, but she didn't answer and her mailbox was full. Desperate, Raskin left a message on her office's general line, even though it was well after hours on Friday. He crossed his fingers that some staffer would get the message by morning and call him back.

In his frustration, Raskin dialed Liz Cheney to vent.

"We're trying our hardest to get in touch with Jaime Herrera Beutler, and we can't," he said.

Cheney's answer was less than encouraging.

"Yeah, she seems to have gone into hiding," Cheney replied.

"I'm trying to get in touch with her," Raskin said again.

"I think she knows that," Cheney said dryly.

A few hours later, when Raskin phoned Herrera Beutler again, she had cleared out her crowded voice mailbox. He tried to make himself sound as friendly and welcoming as possible.

"We haven't met yet, but I am a fellow Jamie and I'm eager to talk to you about impeachment," he said. "Sorry these are arduous circumstances. Please call me back when you can."

The Signal chain on Raskin's phone started exploding around 7:40 the next morning. His managers were unequivocal: They wanted witnesses.

Congressman Joaquin Castro sent a link to a New York *Daily News* story headlined: "Schumer says Senate will call witnesses for Trump's trial—if impeachment managers want them."[3] *Schumer is clearly putting this decision solely on us,* Castro wrote. *If we don't call witnesses, we're going to get massacred for pulling punches if we fail to convict.*

Swalwell chimed in to agree. Without tipping his hand about his late-night effort to woo Marc Short, which went unanswered, Swalwell suggested they subpoena the former vice president, his former chief, and even the Secret Service agents who had been with Trump on January 6. If those witnesses challenged their summons in court, Swalwell wrote, "we can ultimately say that we've tried."

"We can't rest without asking for witnesses," Swalwell continued.

The rest of the managers piled on.

"Can someone explain to me the rationale for not trying to call witnesses?" manager Ted Lieu asked in clear frustration. Stacey Plaskett joined in, writing that while it may be "uncomfortable for the Senate" to extend the trial, the managers had a duty to take this case all the way.

A senior staffer from the impeachment team pushed back and began highlighting all the complications with such a last-minute call.

The people Swalwell recommended—including Short and Pence—"are likely to be hostile to us," the staffer wrote. Plus, if they objected and took the matter to court, the legal battle could drag out for weeks or even months, the aide said, echoing—ironically—the same argument Adam Schiff had made to justify sidestepping court fights for witnesses during Trump's first impeachment, and which McConnell later adopted during the trial.

As Raskin's security detail drove him the seven miles of North Capitol Street from his house to Capitol Hill, he quietly digested the frenzied messages dancing across his phone. Herrera Beutler still hadn't called him back, and in less than two hours, he was expected to launch into his closing arguments.

But Raskin knew his team was right. The managers had put only one night of effort into securing testimony that could seal the former president's fate, hardly enough to warrant giving up. Didn't they have a duty to present the fullest story possible about what Trump had done—if not to secure a conviction, then at least for the history books?

When Raskin walked into the managers' trial anteroom, Neguse was staring out the window, whispering the last lines of his closing speech to himself in careful rehearsal. Cicilline was also practicing for what was supposed to be the final moments of the trial. In the center of the room, Raskin's staff was fighting over what to do. He joined them, knowing the final call would be his to make.

The pro-witness camp, led by Berke, argued witnesses could be a powerful tool in convincing the nation—particularly Republican voters—of Trump's misdeeds. The right witnesses might even change the minds of some GOP senators, he said, earning them enough votes for a conviction. Berke reminded them that Pence's team had indicated through intermediaries that they might comply with a Senate subpoena. And they had two well-connected

Republicans running interference: Cooper was reaching out to Pence's team as they spoke, and Senator Jeff Flake had also promised the night before to make a personal appeal to the former vice president and his team, particularly Short.

"Let's start with Herrera Beutler and then see if others like Marc Short feel compelled to testify as well," Berke proposed. "We have to try. If we don't, the American people will never forgive us."

But team attorneys Joshua Matz and Aaron Hiller thought upending the trial with a witness Hail Mary was insane. "Once you open the door to witnesses, you destroy the momentum we've built—and we've already done a bang-up job," Hiller argued. Plus, it was common knowledge that Pence wanted to run for president in 2024. *What if he uses the opportunity to grandstand and curry favor with the base*, the two lawyers posited as the conversation grew heated. *What if he surprised them by saying the president did nothing wrong?*

"You want to call witnesses? Which witnesses? We don't know!" Matz vented, laying out the possible dangers of going down that path. "Are they coming? We don't know. What will they say? We also don't know! How long will it take to get their testimony? Also unclear."

As Raskin's legal hands bickered, rank-and-file managers still on their way to the Capitol continued to press for calling witnesses on their Signal chain, flagging tweets from Democratic senators indicating they would back a motion to depose people at trial. Sheldon Whitehouse of Rhode Island, a Democrat who had been a federal prosecutor before joining the Senate, pointed out on social media that the revelations in the CNN story directly refuted Trump's defense. He wanted the team to call the relevant lawmakers and Secret Service officials to testify at trial to set the record straight.

"One way to clear it up? Suspend trial to depose McCarthy . . . under oath and get facts," Whitehouse wrote in a Twitter post that was shared across the managers' text chain. "What did Trump know, and when did he know it?"

By Saturday morning, the idea had caught on. It was becoming clear that if the managers made a play for witnesses, they would have the votes.

Raskin nervously checked the time. In less than an hour, everyone—Pelosi, Schumer, Biden, and the entire watching nation—was expecting him to walk onto the floor and argue that the managers had proven their case beyond a reasonable doubt and then end the trial. But there was nothing stopping him from calling for witnesses instead. The move, Raskin knew, was high risk, but potentially even higher reward: Republican senators had been signaling their keen interest in learning more of what Trump had said and done during those critical hours when the Capitol was under siege. Here was an opportunity to find out.

And who knows, Raskin thought. *One witness could entice others to come out of the woodwork to tell their stories.*

Raskin knew that Democratic Party leaders wouldn't be happy. They were eager to put impeachment behind them and move on to confirming Biden's nominees. But Raskin had always eschewed the political calculations that habitually guided those in leadership. For him, this wasn't about political messaging, or the next election, or even how the trial would impact Biden's planned policy agenda. This was about building the strongest case possible and convincing most Americans that Trump should never hold office again—especially in that moment, when Trump was the weakest, politically, that he'd ever been.

The lawyer in Raskin cringed at the idea of suddenly jumping into the unknown. If they overplayed their hand and things backfired, he knew he would be blamed for having led the managers' case astray. But the idealist in him, the one who had pleaded so hard with his party superiors to chase every investigative lead that presented itself to hold Trump accountable, could feel the lure of going all in.

He just needed one more gut check.

Raskin picked up his phone and dialed Liz Cheney, peppering her with one final volley of queries for any insight she could offer. *Would Herrera Beutler be a reliable witness? Were there others who might follow her lead? What did she think about calling witnesses in general?*

Cheney agreed with the move. Herrera Beutler, she assured Raskin, was an honorable woman who would tell the truth under oath. She would not lie. She would not grandstand. And better yet, she would make a compelling witness.

That was all Raskin needed to hear: If Cheney trusted her, then he would as well.

Just before 9:40 a.m., with the start of the trial twenty minutes away and still no word from Herrera Beutler, Raskin called the bustling anteroom to attention. Managers and staff dutifully gathered around a coffee table in the center of the room, filling an embroidered couch and chairs set up in a big circle. Once the room quieted, Raskin turned to his lead attorney, who he knew was the most pro-witness of the bunch.

"Barry, what do you think we should do?" he asked.

"We don't have a choice," Berke responded. "We have to call witnesses."

"Yes, you're right," Raskin declared.

A ripple of excitement spread through the team as managers seconded the decision with sighs of relief and cheers of *Absolutely!* and *Yes!* Immediately the room descended into chaos, as everyone jumped up to recalibrate their plans. In one corner, Matz, Berke, and Hiller began frantically rewriting Raskin's opening statement for the day. *How would Trump's attorneys react? And how will we respond to that response?* No one knew.

"Just write something fast!" one attorney shouted as they began scribbling a makeshift script.

The other managers, meanwhile, began to plan their next steps. DeGette volunteered to try again to get ahold of Herrera Beutler, whom she'd been trying to reach all morning. Others began plotting when and how they could depose her if she agreed to testify. *Would she come back to town today? If not, was a video interview possible?*

As a staffer informed Schumer's team of their last-minute change in plans, Raskin made the most important phone call of all. In a dramatic departure from the first impeachment, Pelosi had let Raskin make the day-to-day decisions for the trial, as she promised she would. But this was a big enough shift that the Speaker deserved a heads-up, Raskin reasoned. He gave her a chance to object, but he did not ask her permission.

"We've got to go for this," he told her. "We've got an opening."

Pelosi listened.

"I trust your judgment," she told Raskin. "It's up to you."

At ten a.m., a Senate aide appeared at the door, interrupting the pandemonium to announce it was time to start. As Raskin headed to the floor, he made a quick call to his Republican friend John Katko for the first of what would become a series of last-minute sales pitches to unearth possible witnesses. As one of the ten who had voted to impeach, Raskin figured Katko knew about this McCarthy tale that Herrera Beutler and the CNN story had exposed.

"Are you willing to testify?" Raskin asked Katko as he walked into the chamber.

Katko said no. While he had heard personally from McCarthy about his January 6 call with Trump, the New York Republican didn't mention that and played dumb.

"I don't have any relevant information," he lied. "You need Jaime. She's all you need."

Jaime Herrera Beutler's cell phone started ringing off the hook again just after seven a.m. Pacific time. On the other line, calling from Washington, D.C., one of her aides was in a panic. Raskin had just marched to the Senate floor and shocked the nation by making a pitch to call witnesses as part of a trial—including her. The motion had actually passed, 55 to 45, with almost no debate.

"Oh my gosh, you're being talked about in the middle of this!" the aide told her.

Herrera Beutler was dumbfounded. She knew the managers had been trying to get in touch overnight. But neither Raskin nor De-Gette had bothered to tell her that they planned to call her as a witness the next morning. A little heads-up would have been nice. Herrera Beutler was with her family that Presidents' Day weekend, hoping to get some time off the grid after the chaos of the day before. She had not even been watching the trial.

As soon as she received the news, however, she flipped the television on. And sure enough, there, in the well of the Senate, Raskin was standing at the podium and citing the statement she had instructed her staff to release the previous evening as reason to call witnesses. The Senate had no choice but to hear straight from her about "the president's willful dereliction of duty," he had told senators.

"Awesome," she said sarcastically.

Just a year before, Herrera Beutler had voted against Trump's first impeachment, citing Democrats' process fouls she felt could not be overlooked. She had even voted to reelect Trump in 2020 after refusing to back him in 2016. But Herrera Beutler had been deeply disturbed by what happened on January 6. After evacuating in an astronaut-like escape hood from the balcony of the House chamber, where lawmakers had been trapped longest, she barricaded herself in the office of a fellow female Republican. When Trump went on television to praise his followers as "very special" people, she had lost her usual cool.

She was so upset, in fact, that she had decided to record a video in her office around nine o'clock that night. In it she implored the nation to come together and reject fear, albeit without naming Trump specifically. Americans, she argued, had died for this democracy, and those rioters were making a sham of those sacrifices.

"I had never thought I'd see this day. I felt like we were under siege!" she said. "Every American should be heartbroken. That's how I felt."[4]

While Herrera Beutler believed Trump had engaged in an impeachable dereliction of duty, she instructed her team to learn exactly what happened at the White House on January 6 before deciding to condemn him. She carefully studied the article Cicilline circulated among members and scoured legal texts to understand the meaning of an "incitement" charge. And she pumped her own contacts for info, particularly one well-connected friend: Kevin McCarthy.

The details McCarthy disclosed about his January 6 call with Trump had been the deciding factor in Herrera Beutler's vote. It was clear to her that Trump was not only responsible for the violence but had reveled in it. If that didn't rise to the level of impeachment, she believed, nothing did.

Herrera Beutler had known that her vote would jeopardize her standing with Trump supporters in her GOP district. It was why she made a point of being up front with constituents and explaining her thinking in interviews with local reporters and in town halls, including the details of her talk with McCarthy. So it came as a bit of a surprise when Liz Cheney called her a few days into the impeachment trial with an unusual request: A CNN reporter had heard about McCarthy's call with Trump and was trying to confirm it, Cheney told her. She asked Herrera Beutler if she'd be comfortable talking to the reporter.

Herrera Beutler rarely engaged with the national press, preferring to keep her head down. But due to the gravity of the situation, she agreed to be interviewed. She had already shared the details of McCarthy's Trump call with her constituents, after all,[5] and they might prove critical to establishing Trump's thoughts and motivations at the trial.

When the story had posted, Herrera Beutler realized she had poked the hornet's nest. She braced for a call from McCarthy—but by late Friday night, she still hadn't heard a peep from him. Instead, it was the Democrats who were leaving her frantic messages.

Herrera Beutler had a pretty good idea of what they wanted. What good investigator wouldn't want more information on the McCarthy-Trump phone call? But she felt it was not her story to tell; it was McCarthy's. What's more, she knew that there were others who could tell a similar tale. Halfway through the trial, before the CNN story shot Herrera Beutler into the spotlight, she had texted the other GOP impeachers to ask if McCarthy had ever shared the story of his Trump call with any of them. Multiple members on the chain—a support group of sorts they had dubbed "the band of brothers"— responded that he had.

After the story broke, Herrera Beutler had instructed her team to issue a press release detailing the McCarthy-Trump call. They closed it with a line encouraging anyone who knew anything to step forward, hoping McCarthy especially would get the message.

"To the patriots who were standing next to the former president as these conversations were happening, or even to the former vice president: if you have something to add here, now would be the time," it read, in Herrera Beutler's words.

She then turned her attention back to her family.

But on Saturday morning, thanks to Raskin's surprise move on the Senate floor, her hopes of having a calm weekend flew out the window. She needed to come up with a plan.

Herrera Beutler considered her options. She could decline to testify and take the easy way out—or she could do the brave thing and agree to tell her story. It was a choice that would come with consequences either way, she thought. But she had come this far already. After bucking her own party with a vote to impeach, what more was a deposition in the Senate?

Find me a lawyer, she told her team. She needed to get professional advice before she took the plunge.

Back in Washington, D.C., as soon as the motion to call witnesses had passed, Schumer had called for an emergency recess and Raskin and his team retreated to their holding room. They were awash with adrenaline, but also struck with terror. They had succeeded in upending the trial completely—and they had no idea what to do next.

Huddled in a corner with Berke and Matz, Raskin began furiously calling sympathetic Republicans to see if any would volunteer to come forward. He dialed Herrera Beutler again. Still no answer. He left a message. Then he tried Katko again. That too went to voicemail.

Steve Womack, however, did pick up the phone. *Did he know about the Herrera Beutler story? Did he know anything else that could help them?* Raskin asked. *Or did he know anyone who did know something— anything?* Womack said he did not. Ditto with Peter Meijer, another

House Republican who had voted to impeach and sounded physically pained when Raskin introduced himself and asked for assistance.

"You should talk to Pence's people," Meijer told Raskin, sighing
loudly.

Upton, the friendly Michigander who had indicated that other
moderates would not be able to corroborate Herrera Beutler's story,
wasn't much help either. When asked if he would be willing to be
deposed, Upton declined apologetically and simply wished them
luck. He, like Katko, still said nothing about how other moderates
had heard the same story from McCarthy.

Outside, Washington was in an ecstatic fervor over Raskin's surprise move. The city had expected Trump's second impeachment
trial to end that afternoon—but now, it seemed, there was a chance
the Senate would be in it for the long haul, and possibly hearing
firsthand evidence about Trump's actions on January 6. Progressive Democrats cheered the managers on, encouraging them not
to leave a single stone unturned. Trump supporters panicked, decrying Raskin's move as a sneak attack and threatening revenge.
Cable networks that had covered the minute-by-minute trial developments salivated over the prospect of more blockbuster ratings, as
the public tuned in to their wall-to-wall coverage of the proceedings.
Meanwhile, reporters frantically worked their sources to figure out
what witnesses the managers were about to produce.

Inside the managers' room, Raskin's team had no idea.

As Swalwell tried to call Greg Pence, Berke phoned Cooper to see
if he'd had any luck finagling permission for Marc Short to testify.
Raskin, standing next to him, watched on tenterhooks—and saw
his counsel's face sink. Berke then passed the phone over so Raskin
could hear the bad news for himself. Cooper had spoken to Pence's
attorney Richard Cullen: They were not going to cooperate volun-

tarily. In fact, Pence's team planned to fight the subpoenas if they were summoned, Cooper said, and had refused to give a preview of what Short might say if called. That meant the managers would have little indication of whether his story was even worth pursuing.

"Don't fuck this up by calling witnesses you might not get," Cooper told Raskin candidly. "You have a good case right now . . . If I were you, I don't think I'd want to risk the record you have . . . How does it get better? It sure as hell can get worse."

Cooper's words gave Raskin pause. The influential conservative lawyer was a partisan, but in that moment, he was also their ally—and to date, he had been straight with them. If he thought they should drop this effort, maybe they should listen.

"Well, that came up . . . Short," Raskin joked awkwardly, making the obvious pun with the elusive witness's surname.

A few minutes later, Swalwell came back relaying his own dead-end: Greg Pence hadn't even answered his phone.

In the midst of the commotion, Senator Chris Coons walked through the door. The stocky lawyer from Delaware with a purposeful demeanor was a committed Democratic moderate with a penchant for trying to forge cross-party coalitions. He had developed a habit over the years of inserting himself into high-profile situations to broker compromises. Most importantly, he was known around the building as Biden's closest ally in the Senate. Biden's late son, Beau, who had died from a brain tumor, had even personally asked Coons to run for his father's Senate seat after the elder Biden became vice president. Consequently, everyone looked up when Coons entered, unannounced.

As soon as Schumer had called for a break following the witness vote, Coons had flown into something of a tizzy. He couldn't understand the logic of the managers' witness gambit. And he was worried about the trial dragging out and hurting the new president. In fact, Trump's defense lawyers, furious and blindsided by Raskin's witness move, had vowed just before the vote that if Raskin called even *one* witness, they would seek to depose at least one hundred of their own, including Speaker Nancy Pelosi and Vice President Kamala Harris. That meant possibly hours upon hours of floor debate about which witnesses were relevant—and possibly days or weeks of testimony that could hamper Biden's presidency until late February or March.

It was a threat that met its mark, as senators on the floor fretted about having to endure elongated proceedings, including other Democrats who had just backed Raskin's witness ploy. What's more, several Republicans had indicated to Coons that they were ready to convict the president—but if the trial spun out of control, there was no telling what might happen.

With those frustrations in mind, Coons had marched into Schumer's office and demanded to know what the hell was going on. Schumer, also befuddled by Raskin's move, had told Coons he didn't know. His counsel Mark Patterson, in fact, had gone to find Raskin's team to ask what their game plan was, who they intended to call, and how long the entire thing could take—and they didn't yet have answers. The Democratic leader was skeptical the ploy would work. If running for their lives on January 6 wasn't enough to persuade Republicans to convict Trump, then it was hard to believe any other witness would, Schumer reasoned.

Coons, who held a similar mindset, offered to go talk to Raskin's team himself to shut the entire thing down. When Schumer gave him the nod, the senator headed to find the managers.[6]

"I know when a jury is ready to vote, and this jury is ready to vote," Coons declared when he entered the frenzy of the managers' room.

As the team gathered around him with curiosity, Coons argued that Republicans had already made up their minds and that calling witnesses was a waste of time—though he, along with the rest of the Democrats and more than a few Republicans, had just voted in favor of doing so. Democrats, he argued, had bigger fish to fry: Biden still needed the Senate to confirm most of his Cabinet, and he had a legislative agenda to get onto the floor.

"Dragging this out will not be good for the American project or for the American people. We're trying to do a lot," he said, choosing terms that sounded to the managers like they came straight from the White House.

Coons floated a possible compromise: Have Herrera Beutler make a written affidavit detailing her story, Coons instructed. Then let the defense get one from McCarthy and be done with it.

Raskin and his team balked. McCarthy, they all agreed, would just obfuscate and undercut Herrera Beutler's statement, finding a way to squirm out of a confirmation.

"I'm not taking that deal," Raskin said flatly, stunned that Coons, as a fellow lawyer, would expect any prosecutor to entertain such unsavory terms. "No way are we allowing McCarthy to deny Herrera Beutler's story without cross-examining him."

But Coons was adamant. "You're going to lose Republican votes," he warned them. "Everyone here wants to go home. They have flights for Valentine's Day. Some of them are already missing their flights."

Berke jumped in, telling Coons the managers hoped to depose Herrera Beutler and McCarthy by video conference that very day.

"Listen, Senator, we hear you on the delay," he said. "But I have to tell you this is going to go quickly . . . And we can do closing arguments tomorrow."

Coons, however, was incredulous at Berke's naïveté. "That's nuts!" he shot back. McCarthy would never agree to testify before retaining counsel, he retorted. If they were lucky—and that was a big if—it would take days to depose the GOP leader, not hours.

"I encourage you all to just do affidavits," Coons said sternly. "Do it today and reach a swift resolution."

As he turned to leave, Coons added one more thing. "And just to be clear," he quipped over his shoulder, "I'm here speaking only for myself."

When the door closed behind him, the room broke into collective outrage.

"Are you fucking kidding me?" Cicilline said, turning to Neguse. "We are impeaching a president of the United States for inciting a violent insurrection against the government, and these motherfuckers want to go home for Valentine's Day? Really?"

He wasn't the only one who felt that way. The managers viewed their jobs as one of the most serious things they would ever do in their lives. And yet their own party was pressuring them so they could go enjoy the long weekend. How shortsighted. How repugnant. And how disrespectful.

But for Raskin, Coons's warnings began to revive the doubts that had plagued him earlier that morning. They had succeeded in getting the Senate to agree to witnesses in concept—but the truth was they still didn't have any witnesses in hand. Moreover, everyone in the room agreed that Coons wasn't actually speaking for himself. He might deny it, but his words were as good as a warning from Biden, they speculated. *Was the White House sending them a message?*

Despite the uneasiness caused by Coons's words, the managers continued to forge ahead trying to come up with a witness plan. Berke, Plaskett, and Swalwell began working on questions for a potential cross-examination of McCarthy about his Trump call. Others, including Raskin, debated whether McCarthy would be willing to commit perjury under oath to protect Trump—or if he'd deny the Herrera Beutler story altogether, pitching the trial into an unresolvable he-said-she-said spat that would give Republicans another excuse to acquit.

Raskin called Cheney again to get her take.

"If we call McCarthy, will he be honest?" Raskin asked her.

On the other end of the line, Cheney thought about all the times McCarthy had flip-flopped, vowing to do one thing—then doing the exact opposite.

"I don't know," she admitted.

It was a deflating turn of events for the managers, who still weren't ready to throw in the towel. They started brainstorming backup plans. "Maybe we give up on McCarthy and Short, and just subpoena Herrera Beutler," one of them suggested. "Or we could subpoena just her notes to buy some time," another offered.

"We should delay the final vote at all costs so we can get the votes to convict," Lieu declared. "And buy time to see if we can get in touch with anyone willing to tell their story."

Berke, seizing on the managers' energy, offered an even more aggressive suggestion: So what if no one was offering to testify? *Let's call their bluff and ask the Senate to subpoena these witnesses anyway,* he proposed. If acquittal was the alternative, what did they have to lose?

But Raskin wasn't so sure he agreed. During Trump's first impeachment trial, impeachment attorneys had argued that the courts would settle any disputes over Trump's claims to privilege or immunity within a matter of weeks due to the serious nature of a Senate trial. The fact that Trump was no longer in the Oval Office—and could no longer make such claims—should have made their subpoenas even less vulnerable to lengthy court challenges. Yet in the heat of the moment, those same impeachment lawyers on Raskin's team started losing their earlier confidence about the speed of judicial review. They began to ask themselves: What if these impeachment subpoenas turned out to be no different from their fight over former White House counsel Don McGahn, which was still crawling at a snail's pace through the courts almost two years later?

Further complicating that calculus was the Trump team's vow to call a hundred witnesses. Technically, the threat was hollow. The Senate—not Trump's lawyers, and not the managers—had the ultimate authority to approve which subpoenas to issue by a simple majority vote. That meant Trump's team could try to summon Pelosi or Harris or whomever they wanted. But as long as Senate Democrats stuck together, their efforts would fail.

Nonetheless, the House managers began to worry. The time it would take to hold such partisan witness votes might undercut the impact of their presentations, some argued. The entire thing could unravel into a partisan circus, others agreed, spinning out of control and undermining their arguments. Matz and Hiller were growing more certain by the minute that they'd made a mistake in even making a motion for witnesses at all.

"This isn't working," Matz pushed back on Berke. "We *do* have something to lose: time, momentum, credibility, and persuasion."

As they deliberated, Schumer's counsel Mark Patterson arrived with another possible deal to end the trial without witnesses. He'd been trying to negotiate a way out with the Trump team through McConnell's counsel Andrew Ferguson, who also wanted to bring the trial to a swift end. They had all come to an agreement that "we are prepared to accept," Patterson told Berke: the Trump team would allow Herrera Beutler's statement to be entered into the record without any sort of retort from McCarthy—so long as the managers promised not to call a single witness.

Patterson indicated that he thought the managers should take the deal.

Raskin was still wrestling with the decision when Coons appeared a second time at the doorway to hammer home his end-the-trial message. Republican senators were organizing to hamstring the managers' witness plans, he declared. Two dozen of them had already decided that they were in lockstep with Trump's lawyers' threat: If the managers called even one witness, they would force votes to call Pelosi, Harris, and dozens more.

"Everybody wants to go home," the Delaware senator said impatiently. "Everybody is pissed, and this trial will unzip if even a single vote on a witness occurs."

The managers recoiled at Coons's accusing tone.

"We *also* answer to the American people, Senator!" Stacey Plaskett exploded.

Coons took a deep breath.

"Look, you have somewhere between fifty-four to fifty-six votes to convict, but you are losing a vote per hour," Coons said, his annoyance escalating. "You have to make a decision. You've got to do it within the hour. Nobody's mind is really open at this point."

With that, Coons disappeared again, and a pall fell over the room. The president's unofficial interlocutor might as well have just clipped their wings—and the managers were plummeting back to reality. The Delaware senator's warning that they might be losing the room to jury fatigue—just like Schiff's team had during Trump's first impeachment—petrified them. They'd been adamant that they would do their utmost to secure as many Republican votes as they could; now the suggestion that they could be undermining their own efforts by simply trying to unearth the truth was shocking, and crushing.

The managers couldn't believe they had found themselves in such a position. They had been chosen by the Speaker of the House to bring charges against a president who had incited an attack against a co-equal branch of government that had resulted in death and destruction and could have cost lawmakers' lives. The calling of witnesses to prosecute that outrage should have transcended any partisan roadblocks or practical inconveniences. It hadn't. Even Senate Democrats—the people who were supposed to be their allies—were putting intense pressure on them to wrap up so they could move on to other things. *Could they not appreciate that this was Congress's last chance to oust Trump from American politics for good?*

For two years, Raskin and his friends on the managers' team had rejected political expediency as the easy way out of difficult constitutional duties. They had pushed their party leadership to hold Trump accountable at a time when few were even willing to consider impeachment. They had pressed their colleagues to unearth every last shred of evidence to be had against Trump during his first impeachment—and mourned what might have been if Democrats had just been a little more thorough or taken a little more time.

But back then, they had been the outsiders. Now they were in charge and facing an impossible decision. New presidents, even in the best of circumstances, had only a few months of a honeymoon period with Congress before the pull of midterm elections eroded cross-party goodwill. If they forged down the uncertain path of witnesses, they would stay true to their ideals. But they might end up dragging the whole Biden presidency down under the weight of the impeachment trial. And if Coons was correct, they might even lose votes to convict the former president in the process.

Raskin knew his decision went beyond the tribulations of one political party. Trump was already on the rebound, with polls showing Republican voters once again rallying around him and GOP lawmakers growing more comfortable with re-embracing him. If there were ever a moment to stop that trend, or reverse it, the moment was now. Raskin had one shot at a captive audience in the Senate, as well as the millions of potential voters watching across the nation.

Raskin might have been willing to risk all the political complexities of plowing forward—including the wrath of his own party—but for one glaring problem: In the two hours since the Senate vote, not a single witness had stepped forward. He had no idea that Herrera Beutler's staffers, at that exact moment, were frantically reaching out to lawyers, hoping to consult one before she agreed to testify. She had even sought assistance from Pelosi's House counsel Doug Letter, though Letter said he could not help her because he was working with the managers. He never conveyed her interest to Raskin.

As the managers looked to him to make a decision, Raskin felt his hands were tied. He had always known it would be a long shot to get a Republican to testify against Trump. Still, he had hoped the gravity of the moment would compel at least one of them to step into the spotlight and put the good of the republic before the pull of their party. It came as a gut punch to realize that when he needed it most, there was no help to be found. Even after a president had tried to lay waste to the fundamental tenets of representative democracy, politics—not principle—was still king of the Hill.

Not ten minutes after Coons left, Raskin caved.

"Let's take the deal," he said.

FALLING SHORT

FEBRUARY 13, 2021

As senators cast their votes that afternoon, Jamie Raskin fixed his gaze dead ahead, on the one man he knew could single-handedly finish Trump: Mitch McConnell. Raskin knew that the GOP leader's vote, more than that of any other Republican, would dictate whether Trump once again would get away with impeachable crimes. But McConnell, ever the stoic, betrayed no hint of his thoughts. He didn't even flinch when another Republican announced a vote that quietly rocked the room.

"Mr. Burr," the parliamentarian called, as the North Carolina conservative rose from his seat.

"Votes guilty," Senator Richard Burr said, and sat back down.

Raskin, who had been keeping track of the roll call tally and scribbling down senators' votes in pencil on a legal pad, was too nervous to glance at his colleagues. Neguse and Berke, seated at the House managers' table next to him, exchanged a surprised look. Like Cassidy's vote to let the trial proceed five days earlier, Burr's was another unexpected vote in their column. Coming early in the alphabetical roll call, it buoyed their hopes that others might follow suit.

But Raskin knew that the road to sixty-seven votes to convict went through McConnell and McConnell alone. If the leader voted to convict, more GOP senators whose surnames came next would no doubt follow his lead. Without McConnell, however, Trump was sure to get off.

That morning, just prior to the witness vote, McConnell had released a statement announcing he planned to vote for the former president's acquittal. But Raskin and his entire team had refused to accept that as a final determination. Neguse had crafted his closing speech to specifically target the Minority Leader. Knowing the stakes, he had immersed himself in McConnell's personal and professional history, taking care to invoke one of McConnell's personal heroes, Kentucky senator Henry Clay, and his most revered mentor, John Sherman Cooper.

"The history of this country has been defined right here on this floor," Neguse said, recalling how Cooper bucked the state GOP to champion the Civil Rights Act in 1964. He then likened Cooper's principled stand to a vote McConnell took in 1986, overriding Ronald Reagan's veto of sanctions on apartheid South Africa. Neguse said the move resonated with him personally because his parents were African immigrants.

"That vote was not about gaining political favor," Neguse continued. "In fact, it was made despite potentially losing political favor. I have to imagine that that vote was cast, like the decisions before it, because there are moments that transcend party politics and that require us to put country above our party because the consequences of not doing so are just too great."

"Senators, this is one of those moments," Neguse concluded.

In his seat at the front of the chamber, McConnell had cracked a slight smile as he listened to Neguse speak. The young congressman from Colorado had done his homework. But would it make a difference?

As the clerk continued to read out senators' last names, Raskin wondered if Neguse's words had landed—and dared to hope a conviction was coming. Bill Cassidy, another Republican guilty vote. He jotted it down. Susan Collins, also guilty. He noted that too.

When the clerk reached the surnames beginning with *M*, Raskin's hand froze over his legal pad as he waited to hear McConnell's name.

Manchin . . . guilty. Markey . . . guilty. Marshall . . . not guilty. No surprises.

Anticipating his place in the order, the Republican leader stood before the clerk read out his name. Raskin looked up from his tally.

"Mr. McConnell," the clerk read out. The Republican leader answered almost inaudibly, and the clerk repeated his verdict. "Mr. McConnell, not guilty."

That's it, Raskin thought, as he wrote the vote down on his notepad. *It's over.*

Minutes later, the clerk announced the total: 57 to 43. Ten shy of the sixty-seven needed to put Trump away for good. Seven Republicans had voted to convict, including Senators Lisa Murkowski and Mitt Romney. But while seven was better than the first impeachment, it still wasn't enough. The former president had been acquitted. Again.

The room became a blur as Raskin shuffled his papers together. In a daze, he accepted the congratulations of senators who approached him. *Congratulations?* he thought. *For what?* When he and Neguse finally walked off the floor, his younger friend pulled him aside in the hallway and hugged him.

"We did the best we could," Neguse said softly.

It wasn't until Raskin walked into the managers' anteroom that the loss hit him. As he entered, his team showered him with a round of spontaneous, grateful applause. Raskin wasn't sure he deserved it.

Glancing from side to side, Raskin bashfully hushed his team and began offering them words of praise. "All of you are amazing," he told them before calling out each of the counsels and managers by name, running through their contributions to the trial.

But as he offered his accolades, his voice started to crack. Soon he was crying, overwhelmed by the realization that Trump had escaped justice.

"I thought they'd convict him. I can't believe they didn't," Raskin said quietly, as he wiped away tears. "It just makes me so sad."

"Was it us?" he asked. "Was there a way we could have done this differently where we could have made them see?"

The other managers exchanged quizzical glances. Raskin had brought this impeachment team closer to a conviction than party leaders had thought possible. He had led them, a ragtag bunch of relatively unknown lawyer-lawmakers, from congressional obscurity to overnight national celebrities. They knew Raskin was humble. But was he really blaming himself for not dealing a fatal blow to Trumpism in just one month?

The other managers tried to comfort him, but Raskin could not be consoled. He had really thought they could win. A teacher at heart, he believed that people could always be persuaded to do the right thing, if one only used the right words in the right way. But it hadn't worked. And for Raskin, discovering that his best efforts to bring Trump to justice had fallen short was as crushing as knowing that loving his son with all his might couldn't save him from his fatal depression.

"I'm sorry if we didn't do it right," he blurted out. "I don't know if there's something more we could have done, if we should have tried harder."

Dumbfounded, the other managers shook their heads.

"No," they replied. "You tried a hell of a case."

Raskin kept crying.

McConnell stepped to the microphone to unleash the blistering rebuke he'd been holding back all week. Standing in a nearly empty Senate chamber minutes after Trump's second acquittal, he let loose on the man he believed had tarnished the party he loved. The violence. The conspiracy theories. The blatant attempts to upend the democratic order. It was all spurred by Trump's selfish whims, McConnell declared. He was "an outgoing president who seemed determined to either overturn the voters' decision, or else torch our institutions on the way out."

"There is no question—none—that President Trump is practically and morally responsible for provoking the events of the day," McConnell said forcefully. "The people who stormed this building believed they were acting on the wishes and instructions of their president."

But then came the words McConnell had never wanted to say: the argument he had initially scoffed at, but now was swallowing wholesale to justify his acquittal vote.

"If President Trump were still in office, I would have carefully considered whether the House managers proved their specific charge," McConnell said. "But in this case, the question is moot because former President Trump is constitutionally not eligible for conviction."

Even as the trial began, McConnell had still not made up his mind on how to vote. After Rand Paul forced the roll call on the constitutionality question in late January, McConnell had told his members that it was still possible to change their minds and vote to convict. After all, a majority of the Senate had voted that the proceedings were constitutional, which should have freed them to cast a verdict based on the merits of the case. McConnell had spent hours and hours thinking about doing that himself, going through the upsides and downsides with his legal advisor Andrew Ferguson. The leader's staff had even talked through arguments for two versions of McConnell's final speech: one justifying a vote to convict, another explaining a vote to acquit.

McConnell had been moved by the impeachment managers' presentations. In his estimation, they couldn't have tried the case better. They were persuasive and struck the right notes, and he had been tremendously impressed—and flattered—by Neguse's appeal to him in their closing arguments. The leader knew as well as any Democrat who inhabited that chamber that Trump deserved removal. On January 6, he had lobbed a live grenade at the Capitol and then sat back and watched it burn. Whatever the former president claimed publicly, whatever his lawyers tried to argue, Trump had seen the same chaotic scenes they all had experienced that day—the mob carrying his banners, chanting their allegiance to him, pummeling police officers, and hunting for lawmakers—and chose to do nothing. For that, McConnell believed he was guilty of breaching his oath.

But despite a strong desire to convict Trump, in the end, McConnell couldn't—or wouldn't—make the leap. To do so would have been political suicide for the Republican leader. And McConnell was far from ready to retire.

"I didn't get to be leader by voting with five people in the conference," a pair of *New York Times* journalists later reported McConnell told a friend.[1]

McConnell had always viewed himself first and foremost as the leader of a GOP conference. To step out and break from the majority of his members on such a politically charged issue would do more damage to them in the long-term, he had come to believe. There was no way the Senate GOP could split any further on the question of Trump's guilt without splintering the Republican Party itself.

So despite his private reservations about the constitutional "off-ramp," and despite his private belief that Trump was guilty, he voted to acquit. In doing so, McConnell was taking a gamble: that after the trial, Trump would fade from the headlines and he could finally lead the party out of the Trump-sized hole they had dug for themselves. It was a stunningly naive calculation for a leader with so much political acumen and experience. And his central bet—that Trumpism could be ignored out of existence—would be proven dead wrong.

Pelosi had had enough. To her ears, McConnell's speech, which she had watched from her office, had been designed to make him—and the GOP by extension—sound reasonable. He was trying to have things both ways by condemning Trump without having the guts to convict him. And what was worse, her own House managers, at that moment, were praising him for it.

"Senator Mitch McConnell just went to the floor essentially to say that we made our case on the facts, that he believed Donald Trump was practically and morally responsible for inciting the events of January 6," Raskin told the media assembled in the Capitol basement, just over an hour after the trial verdict. "The bottom line is that we convinced a big majority in the Senate of our case."

For the politically minded Pelosi, Raskin was missing the point: McConnell was *not* validating the managers' case. In Pelosi's estimation, he was just being a hypocrite, trying to avoid responsibility for having created the monster that had inspired the assault on the Capitol—and hoping to evade notice that he was still protecting him. He had cast himself as a guardian of the Constitution, but when McConnell had a real opportunity to stand up for Congress's oversight authority in a meaningful way, he had reached for a politically convenient escape hatch. Someone needed to call him out.

Pelosi had not planned on speaking publicly that day. But as she watched the press conference in her office, she decided she had no choice. She flagged her security detail and made a beeline for the elevators. When she strode into the press conference room, Raskin ushered her to the podium, where she let loose.

"What we saw in that Senate today was a cowardly group of Republicans," Pelosi said of GOP lawmakers who were too "afraid," she said, to "respect the institution in which they serve."

"What is so important about any one of us?" she continued. "What is so important about the political survival of any one of us, that is more important than our Constitution, that we take an oath to protect and defend?"

Given her history of prioritizing political expediency, the Speaker was perhaps not the purest vessel for the message she delivered that day. She had spent the run-up to Trump's first impeachment downplaying evidence of his wrongdoing to protect the moderates who had helped make her majority. She then straitjacketed the House Democrats' impeachment investigation to keep it from encroaching on the 2020 primaries. After Trump's first trial was over, and throughout the 2020 election season, she had kept the House from conducting meaningful oversight of Trump's continued antics, fearing blowback at the polls. Even after Congress was physically attacked on January 6, she had initially balked at the idea of impeaching Trump a second time. And as hands-off as her approach to

Raskin's team had been, she had still championed speed over com-
pleteness, lest the trial draw too much attention away from Biden's
nascent presidency.

But in that moment, Pelosi was not thinking about the nuanced
contradictions of her own record. She was angry at McConnell. She
was angry at every last GOP senator who believed Trump was guilty
but had voted to acquit him.

Pelosi had just turned to leave the room when a reporter asked
if the House Democrats planned to follow Trump's acquittal by
censuring him instead as some Republicans were suggesting. The
Speaker marched right back to the podium.

"Oh, these cowardly senators—who couldn't face up to what
the president did, and what was at stake for our country—are now
going to have a chance to give a little slap on the wrist?" Pelosi said
incredulously, smacking the podium for effect. "We censure people for using stationery for the wrong purpose. We don't censure
people for inciting insurrection that kills people in the Capitol!"

For two years, Pelosi had held her caucus back as they struggled
to flex the full power of Congress's muscle to check a president who
seemed hell-bent on shattering the guardrails of the American democratic system. Trump had fulfilled the direst of warnings voiced
by her most vigilant Democrats, bringing the country to the brink
of catastrophe—and still it hadn't been enough to mold public sentiment decisively against Trump. Even the election that Pelosi had
put so much of her faith in had failed to strike a fatal blow to Trump's
power. He might not be president anymore, but he still posed a danger to political order, Pelosi realized. More had to be done.

So the Speaker did the only thing she could think of. She promised an oversight investigation.

"We will be going forward to make sure that this never happens
again," she said, vowing "to investigate and evaluate what caused"

the January 6 riot and ensure the Capitol was never vulnerable to attack again.

It was a promise she would have a hell of a time delivering.

In the wake of the January 6 attack on the Capitol, there had been a moment—however fleeting—for Congress to unify the nation against Trump. But both parties failed to do what it would have taken to seize it, leaving the president room for a comeback—and themselves more riven by political strife than ever.

On the Republican side of the aisle, Kevin McCarthy, who initially condemned Trump from the House floor as responsible for the Capitol riot, proved too focused on his political ambitions to maintain his defiance. Many Republicans would come to believe that McCarthy's late-January pilgrimage to Mar-a-Lago single-handedly revived Trump's fortunes, decisively reestablishing the ex-president who might have been a pariah as the GOP's kingmaker.

Though McConnell refused to kiss the ring like McCarthy and maintained his distance from Trump, his decision to acquit Trump did just as much damage. Though he almost certainly could have finagled the seventeen Republicans needed to bar Trump from political office, his dodge enabled the ex-president to begin contemplating another presidential run. Within a few weeks of impeachment, he would buckle even further, telling Fox News he would "absolutely" support Trump if he became the nominee in 2024.[2] It was a shocking about-face from a man considering conviction a few weeks prior.

The toxic combination of political ambition and fear of Trump even afflicted those who had taken decisive steps to reject his attempts to steal the election. Former vice president Mike Pence, who had defied orders to disrupt the Electoral College and became a prime target of the rioters, helped block for Trump by refusing to allow his top aides to testify in the impeachment trial. Though Pence would eventually become bolder in pushing back against Trump a year later, even allowing his staff to cooperate with a congressional probe into the events of January 6, his team worried that turning on his former boss mid–impeachment trial would cost Pence any chance at the Republican nomination in 2024. Meanwhile, most of the ten House Republicans who had voted to impeach Trump in mid-January also lost their nerve by the time the trial got underway. When the managers approached them in their hour of need, they simply pleaded ignorance, refusing to testify to what they knew about McCarthy's January 6 call with Trump.

Democrats, however, also bear some blame for undercutting their own best opportunity to excommunicate Trump from public life. While Raskin's work resulted in the most bipartisan vote of any Senate presidential impeachment trial in history, and Beltway pundits lauded his team for delivering a fatal blow to Trump's fortunes, the truth was that their message barely made a dent with most GOP voters. Raskin had warned early on that the only way to appeal to Republicans was to have one of their own testify against Trump. But in the heat of the political moment, with his party leaders pressuring him to free Biden's fledgling presidency from the cloud of Trump's trial and Republicans threatening to muddy the process, Raskin had compromised his convictions. He gave up the fight mere hours after Jaime Herrera Beutler emerged as a possible witness.

In the end, Raskin, despite vowing to do things differently, repeated the mistakes of the past: The second impeachment trial, just as the first, suffered for the lack of an eyewitness close to Trump delivering an incriminating account. The result was that the second effort to convict and bar Trump from office—arguably Congress's most pivotal prosecution of a president—became the most rushed in history.

Few realize how close lawmakers came to permanently removing Trump from political life. Raskin would learn only a few weeks after the trial ended that Herrera Beutler had been open to testifying had they not reversed course and wrapped up their case so quickly. And it would remain a secret until this book that she reached out to Pelosi's House counsel Doug Letter to ask how to proceed—and that Letter failed to pass on the message to Raskin and his team.

Still, it is difficult to predict what might have happened had the prosecutors been less rushed. Would Herrera Beutler's testimony have set off a domino effect, perhaps even prompting Pence officials to testify? Would Pence's staff really have ignored a mid-trial Senate subpoena, or taken the stand? Would the courts have moved quickly to litigate any Trump claims of privilege should the managers have subpoenaed his top White House officials? And would that testimony have convinced enough GOP senators to convict Trump? It is impossible to know.

What we do know, however, is that Democrats and Republicans never fully committed to the impeachment that most of them believed Trump deserved. They prioritized their fear of political consequences over flexing Congress's constitutional muscle and doing what most, in the moment, believed was right. Trump, meanwhile, emerged from his second impeachment wounded, but not crippled, and would soon enjoy a popular resurrection. Once he started gaining political momentum, it would become harder than ever to stop him.

EPILOGUE

Two weeks after Trump's second acquittal, Kevin McCarthy summoned Jaime Herrera Beutler to his office for a stern dressing down. In the weeks following the ex-president's second acquittal, the California Republican had been bending over backwards to try to get back into Trump's good graces. He had dodged questions about Herrera Beutler's account of their January 6 headbutting, and he continued to walk back his criticism of Trump's actions on the day of the Capitol siege. But Trump was still furious with him—and for a man with his eyes on the Speaker's gavel, that posed a problem.

McCarthy had hoped to put the uncomfortable business of impeachment behind him and was frustrated with Trump's endless demands for payback against those who voted to impeach him. But he was politically astute enough to realize he couldn't yell at the ex-president to get off his back. Neither could he take out his anger on the press. So instead, he called a meeting with Herrera Beutler and directed his rage toward the one woman he figured he could excoriate without consequence, ripping her in his office for telling the world about his January 6 call with Trump.

"After all the work I have done for the Republican Party, the money I have raised! After all the work I have done for *you*!" McCarthy snarled at the Washington Republican. "I alone am taking all the heat to protect people from Trump! I alone am holding the party together! I have been working with Trump to keep him from going after Republicans like you and blowing up the party and destroying all our work!"

Never mind that the two had once been friends, not to mention political allies—or that McCarthy had told his rank and file after January 6 that they could vote their gut on impeachment without fear of retribution.

"You should have come to me!" he growled. "Why did you go to the press? This is no way to thank me!"

Standing across the room, Herrera Beutler was so startled that she started to cry. Struggling to regain her composure, Herrera Beutler apologized for having failed to give McCarthy a heads-up that the CNN story was coming. But when it came to the merits of what she had said, she stood her ground.

"What did you want me to do? Lie?" she challenged McCarthy. "I did what I thought was right!"

McCarthy's tirade against Herrera Beutler was just the start of what would become a GOP-wide campaign to whitewash the details of what happened on January 6 in the aftermath of the second impeachment. Over the next several months, most Hill Republicans would bend over backwards to muzzle their concerns about what transpired behind the scenes that day in an effort to sanitize Trump's legacy—and by extension, preserve their own political necks.

The first significant casualty of their efforts was Nancy Pelosi's proposal to have an independent commission investigate the events of January 6. The idea was to take the investigation out of the political boxing ring and place it in the hands of well-respected nongovernmental leaders and experts. A similar framework had been used to study the September 11, 2001, terrorist attacks, producing an exhaustive report based on over 2.5 million pages of documents and interviews with more than twelve hundred people in ten countries—including President George W. Bush himself.[1]

The idea had been widely popular in GOP circles in the immediate aftermath of the Capitol riot, including with McCarthy and Senate Minority Leader Mitch McConnell. But soon after, Republicans began to realize such a probe might come back to bite them. There would be no discrediting a nonpartisan investigation if it found fault with the GOP for January 6. And thus they made a complete turnaround, killing the commission before it could get off the ground.

In the House, McCarthy had allowed Congressman John Katko to negotiate the terms of a potential commission on his behalf, despite his pro-impeachment vote. McCarthy laid out a list of demands, many of which he believed Pelosi would never agree to. But when Katko secured virtually all of them, the GOP leader reneged on the agreement. He realized that such a commission, if it ever came to fruition, would likely call him to testify about his explosive January 6 phone call with Trump—and he was loath to allow himself to be put in such a predicament. So McCarthy turned on his longtime ally Katko, urging his members to oppose the bipartisan commission—though it eventually passed the House with nearly three dozen GOP votes.

In the Senate, McConnell ferociously whipped his rank and file against the proposal, ensuring he had the numbers to filibuster the commission.[2] Publicly, McConnell justified his opposition by arguing that such a panel would be "slanted and unbalanced," and duplicative of law enforcement efforts to round up and arrest the rioters who had stormed the Capitol. In a private meeting with his members, however, he was more blunt: The findings of the commission might surface in the middle of the 2022 campaign season, he warned, undercutting the GOP in their effort to seize back the Senate. McConnell's squeeze play was successful: All but six Republicans voted against the commission, quashing it once and for all.

The death of the January 6 commission was only the beginning of the GOP's effort to muzzle anti-Trump voices and enforce party

discipline on rank-and-file members. Three months after the trial,
McCarthy blessed a campaign to oust Liz Cheney from her No. 3
spot in House GOP leadership because she refused to stop criticizing Trump for lying about the 2020 election. McCarthy backed an
effort to replace Cheney with Elise Stefanik, the erstwhile moderate from the Intelligence Committee who had reinvented herself
during Trump's first impeachment, becoming one of his loudest
cheerleaders.

Meanwhile, McConnell—who had vainly hoped that Trump
would fade from relevance once he left office—did little to check
the former president's resurging influence. While Trump continued to peddle his lies about the election and express sympathies
for those who stormed the Capitol on January 6, McConnell kept
his frustrations to himself. He viewed public pushback as a political
loser—and besides, criticizing Trump would distract from his efforts to attack the new Democratic president, Joe Biden.

Trump's base ensured the rest of the party fell in line. In the
months after his acquittal, most Republicans who voted to impeach
or convict were eventually either censured or denounced as traitors
by their local or state parties.[3] All of those up for reelection in 2022
drew pro-Trump primary challengers, prompting several, including
Katko, to announce their early retirements.[4]

Meanwhile, an increasing number of Republicans began embracing Trump's Big Lie and emulating it closer to home. GOP-
controlled state houses across the country began passing laws to
restrict voting and allow partisan politicians to certify, reject, or even
overturn election results in place of nonpartisan administrative officials. In 2021 alone, at least nineteen states adopted just under three
dozen such statutes.[5] At the same time, election officials who had
refused to bend to Trump's demands to throw out legitimate votes
found themselves replaced with people who subscribed to the ex-
president's conspiracy theories.

The all-out ideological cleansing continued from there. Members of Trump's base began recasting the violent assault on the Capitol as nothing more than a "normal tourist visit."[6] While federal prosecutors charged hundreds of participants on everything from assaulting police officers to seditious conspiracy, the ex-president's followers defended them as "political prisoners."[7] By late summer, polls indicated that nearly 80 percent of Republicans believed Trump was the rightful victor in 2020.[8] And embracing the Big Lie became somewhat of a litmus test for Republicans running for—or seeking to stay in—office.

By the end of 2021, Trump's grip on the party was almost as strong as it had been while he was president. He continued to fundraise, pulling in more money than most other Republican leaders combined.[9] His endorsements were more sought after than ever. The former president, meanwhile, continued to rebuild and cast his eye toward 2024. Two-thirds to three-quarters of Republicans said in October of that year that they wanted Trump to be the GOP's next presidential nominee.[10] And as late as the spring of 2022, polls showed that in a prospective head-to-head matchup with Biden, he would win.[11]

The GOP's rejection of Biden's 2020 win hung like a shadow over everything Congress attempted to do after Trump left office—particularly when it came to a full reckoning over January 6. After Republicans blocked the creation of an outside commission, Pelosi turned to a Plan B to investigate the insurrection, creating a select House panel to try to dig deeper. Impeachment leaders Adam Schiff and Jamie Raskin were given two of the eight committee seats designated for Democrats. To give the probe the air of bipartisanship—and by extension, credibility—Pelosi also named Republican Liz Cheney as one of her picks, following the advice of Raskin, who had wanted to do the same during the second impeachment.

The effort, however, hit a stumbling block right away when Pelosi rejected two of the five Republicans McCarthy nominated for GOP positions on the select committee, including longtime pro-Trump attack dog Jim Jordan. The unprecedented move prompted McCarthy to declare a boycott of the panel, yanking all his Republicans off in protest. In an attempt to right the panel's political balance—and smooth over an obvious optics problem—Pelosi added Adam Kinzinger, the only other House Republican who hadn't opposed its creation. But the gesture fell short. Republicans had already begun campaigning against the committee as lopsided and biased, giving GOP voters an excuse to dismiss the committee's work as tainted.

Despite the rocky start, the select committee pursued an aggressive and exhaustive probe, running a fact-finding mission that stood in stark contrast to Democrats' comparatively tepid approach and limited scope during the two Trump impeachments. Panel members subpoenaed dozens of people from the former president's inner circle, calling on his family, his campaign advisors, senior administration officials, and even fellow lawmakers like Jordan to speak to what transpired during the Capitol siege. They interviewed hundreds of witnesses and planned weeks' worth of hearings for the spring of 2022 to educate the public. They demanded thousands of January 6–related documents from the White House and publicly leaned on the reluctant Biden administration to waive executive privilege.

Most notably, the select committee did not shy away from court battles—nor back down when Trump allies threatened lawsuits to block their compulsory summons. They even held several top Trump allies in criminal contempt for flouting subpoenas, enlisting the Justice Department to arrest at least one of them as a signal that the panel would not recoil from muscling recalcitrant witnesses into compliance.

The committee's leave-no-stone-unturned ethos hearkened back to the days of Watergate. And the strategy actually worked: The committee unearthed text messages showing just how concerned Trump's inner circle was on January 6,[12] even though his allies sought in the aftermath to paper over his alleged crimes. Investigators won in court over and over again, as even the conservative-leaning Supreme Court slapped down Trump's frivolous claims of privilege.[13] And their aggressive tactics prompted other witnesses to come forward without a fight, including members of former vice president Mike Pence's team whom the impeachment managers had chickened out of calling.

But by then, it was arguably too late. After years of Trump investigations, compound crises, and escalating declarations that the sky was falling, the nation was exhausted—and the select committee's work failed to break through. People had moved on—and despite the continued fixation of the national media, Washington's quest for Capitol riot accountability became an afterthought to the other crises: an ongoing pandemic that claimed over a million American lives, a chaotic evacuation from Afghanistan and the end to the U.S.'s longest-ever war, a punishing Russian invasion of Ukraine that triggered talk of a potential World War III, and an inflation crisis that left everyday Americans struggling financially.

While the select committee's track record was formidable, their successes also could not entirely fix a problem that Trump's two impeachments had exposed: weakened congressional oversight in the face of an obstinate administration. Even if they did not intend to, the Democrats' efforts to oust Trump created a paradigm for hostile presidents to ignore subpoenas and buck Hill oversight without a fight—a track record that still threatens to render congressional subpoenas all but toothless. In fact, while the January 6 select committee convinced many witnesses to cooperate, many Trump allies flat-out refused to comply, some with no legitimate excuse at all. When the January 6 panel did secure resistant witnesses, the successes were often aided by the Democratic Biden White House's willingness to help. But such wins won't necessarily dictate what may happen when an out-of-control executive branch needs checking by Congress.

Part of the protracted uncertainty stems from Democrats' refusal during Trump's impeachments to launch the court battles that might have affirmed the authority of congressional subpoenas over a resistant administration's protestations. Not once during either impeachment did House Democrats sue for documents or testimony, leaving what Jerry Nadler had once dubbed Congress's "zenith power" untapped and untested. What's more, Democrats actually folded on the one pre-impeachment case they had believed would affirm their oversight power: After waiting two years for a ruling on the Don McGahn case, House investigators relented to pressure from the Biden White House to settle the matter without a final verdict from the Supreme Court.[14] The Biden administration, fearing a GOP takeover in Congress, saw the case as too great a threat to executive authority and autonomy. And congressional Democrats begrudgingly deferred to Biden, putting party over branch in a betrayal of their entire objective in bringing the case in the first place.

The story of how Trump overcame two impeachments is, at its core, a story of how Congress, repeatedly, missed opportunities to check him. Republicans capitulated to political pressures and failed to act on their private revulsion with the president's conduct, emboldening Trump and fueling the cult of personality around him at junctures when he might otherwise have been restrained. Despite myriad opportunities to change course, they doubled and tripled down on their fealty to Trump, protecting him when they could have sidelined him and thereby inuring a shock-fatigued public to the outrageousness of his increasingly dangerous behavior.

But Democrats, when presented with the opportunity to flex the full muscle of the Constitution against Trump, also hesitated, prioritizing their political security over the long, time-consuming course of bringing a rogue president to justice. The corners they cut for political expediency created a playbook for future administrations to slow-walk and deny Congress vital witnesses and documents—and possibly expect to get away without a fight.

House Democrats, to their credit, recognized those loopholes and endeavored to close them on the sidelines of their impeachment effort. In fact, before the ink had even dried on the first set of articles against Trump, they had started drafting a set of "post-Trump reforms" inspired by the series of laws that Congress passed after Watergate. The list, spearheaded by Adam Schiff, included requirements that courts rule quickly on interbranch disputes regarding oversight matters, thus limiting exploitation of the slow-moving judicial branch that Trump had so ably perfected. But while the package eventually passed the House, it stalled in the Senate, leaving the strategy of stonewalling ripe for future abuse.

Historians and political scientists will likely study the two failed impeachments of Trump—which now constitute half of all the completed presidential impeachments in U.S. history—for decades to come and try to take lessons from them for the future. Our reporting revealed two key takeaways. First, that Pelosi's initial gut instincts on impeachment were correct: Impeachment must be bipartisan to work. And second: Impeachment now appears destined to become a political weapon instead of a failsafe instrument to bring a president abusing office to justice.

Regarding the first lesson: Partisan impeachment exercises,

regardless of their merit, are too easy to be dismissed as witch hunts—and when they do not expand their base of support, risk strengthening the hand of the person in the White House. Watergate, which took years of painstaking, time-consuming work, illustrated this: Nixon, seeing his party turn on him, fled office before he could be ousted. During Trump's impeachments, Democrats, mostly acting alone, came nowhere near posing such a formidable political challenge to the president. The breakneck pace they pursued and the corners they cut guaranteed that an impeachment process that was politically divisive at its inception only became more so by its completion.

On the second: Most Democrats have defended their impeachment efforts as successful, blaming the GOP for Congress's ultimate failure to convict Trump and bar him from seeking future office. They argued that they did what they had to do, pointing to the fact that almost every Democrat in Congress agreed—twice—that Trump had to go. But party unanimity was not the standard to which impeachment was designed to appeal. The writers of the Constitution intended for impeachment to be a tool to remove a self-aggrandizing despot or would-be dictator from power.

To be sure, the Framers didn't make it easy. By setting a two-thirds requirement for conviction, they essentially dictated that any impeachable infraction would have to be egregious on its face—or exposed as such through scrupulous and persuasive investigation. The power of impeachment, properly wielded, was thus envisioned as a daunting check on the executive, but also a heavy responsibility for the would-be congressional accusers—which explains why, in the history of the country, it has been so seldom exploited.

But neither party was willing to assume that responsibility. Republicans made an early and fateful decision to help cripple Congress's impeachment power when they endorsed the Trump administration's stonewalling tactics—despite recognizing the long-term dangers of doing so. Democrats also contributed to the long-term damage when they declined to fight back with every mechanism at their disposal. When they encountered Republican resistance, they prioritized acting swiftly over fully, ignoring specific appeals for evidence if it proved too cumbersome to obtain.

These decisions created a new, unfortunate standard for future impeachments that can easily be exploited in the future. There is now clear precedent for giving short shrift to the fact-finding process and for sidestepping key witnesses to an alleged constitutional crime. There is now clear precedent for presidents to assume that impeachment subpoenas will not be enforced; Trump's two impeachments were the first ever in which no investigator or prosecutor appealed to a judge to enforce their demands for evidence or witnesses. There is arguably also clear precedent now for plowing ahead without buy-in from members of the president's party, and for bypassing the custom of due process that says an accused president can cross-examine the witnesses against them. And there is clear precedent for dismissing impeachments that come too close to the end of a presidency to do all the above.

The result of the Democrats' two impeachments of Trump is that the Constitution's ultimate check on a president is now in critical danger of being reduced to a mere political messaging tool. The threshold for impeachment has been lowered, and the once-extraordinary process is at risk of becoming an everyday vehicle to express the heights of partisan rage instead of a failsafe to protect the American democratic order.

By the time this book was published, the transition was already underway. During Biden's first year in office, as Republicans eyed a congressional takeover in 2023, GOP lawmakers who had accused Democrats of pursuing half-baked vendettas filed a record-shattering six resolutions of impeachment against Biden—five more than Democrats had filed at the same point in Trump's presidency. Some cited the haphazard and chaotic withdrawal from Afghanistan in August. Others fixated on policy disputes, expressing animus against Biden for things like stopping construction on Trump's border wall or extending an eviction moratorium during the COVID-19 pandemic— hardly the "high crimes and misdemeanors" standard articulated by the Founders.

There is a potentially worse consequence of the debasement of impeachment that shouldn't be overlooked: that a party with congressional supermajorities may one day oust a president based on no evidence at all. In other words, the most dangerous legacy of Trump's impeachments is not that impeachment will become a broken, partisan battle cry that never works again. But that someday in the future, and for the first time in American history, it just might— for all the wrong reasons.

ACKNOWLEDGMENTS

We want to, first and foremost, acknowledge the scores upon scores of sources who took the time—sometimes what amounted to several days' worth of time—to share their notes and careful recollections for this book. Telling this tale would have been impossible without their candor, generosity, and sometimes bravery, in telling us what they witnessed, participated in, and knew to be the true series of events and decisions that went on behind the scenes of Donald Trump's two impeachments and acquittals. They are in every corner of Washington, D.C., and in the furthest reaches of each party, and while we cannot name them, they know who they are and we thank them.

We also want to thank our agent, Keith Urbahn, and the whole team at Javelin, who decided to take a chance on a pitch from two first-time book writers at a time when much bigger names and institutions in the publishing industry were clamoring for a piece of the impeachment space. Keith believed from the start that as the two *Washington Post* reporters closest to the action, we would have a story to tell that others would not, and remained our cheerleader and advocate as one impeachment became two and a story of backroom intrigue became a lesson of warning for the durability of congressional oversight in America. We also want to thank our editor Mauro DiPreta—and Vedika Khanna, and the whole team at the William Morrow imprint of HarperCollins—for enthusiastically seizing upon our proposal just days after Trump's first impeachment, extending our deadlines so we could incorporate the second, and challenging us to write not just as newspaper reporters, but as storytellers. Our book is better because of it.

We would also be remiss if we did not devote enormous thanks to our outside editor Bill Duryea, whose expert pen and calm counsel were invaluable for turning a mountain of reporting and endless pages of copy into a manuscript. When we first met to discuss bringing him on to the project, both of us were blown away by how voraciously he'd been devouring books on impeachments past and present—and how confident he was that our book could stand apart. It was Bill who encouraged us to put the impeachments of Trump in the context of former presidents Nixon and Clinton, and not to shy away from saying what we knew to be true: These historic events did lasting damage to congressional oversight and both parties shared the blame. He, more than anyone, was our sounding board, our guide, and our ally in the trenches—and always believed that we would write a book that would not just sell but would matter.

We also benefited tremendously from the help of our fact-checker, Hilary McClellan, whose tireless work ethic was an inspiration as we pushed toward the finish line, whose questions made us think, and whose eagle eyes saved us from the embarrassment of more than a few boneheaded errors we will now never have to admit to.

We owe the *Washington Post* a debt of gratitude for trusting us to cover this story as it unfolded, and later giving us time away from the grueling demands of our jobs to begin to make sense of all the unpublished observations and unanswered questions we had scrawled in our notebooks. We want to thank the editors who stayed up late with us and worked through weekends to catch the constant flow of articles and updates we filed as the impeachment investigations and trials took shape, especially Matea Gold, Peter Finn, Andrew deGrandpre, Donna Cassata, Dave Clarke, Dan Eggen, Tiffany Harness, Cathy Decker, Naftali Bendavid, Desikan Thirunarayana-puram, Peter Wallsten, Lori Montgomery, Steven Ginsberg, Cameron Barr, and Marty Baron. And countless others who jumped in to offer insights, grab updates, or man the live blogs along the way.

An even bigger debt of gratitude goes out to our reporting colleagues at the *Post*, who shared in so many parts of the impeachment slog with us. We would have been lost without the partnership, support, and constant therapeutic counsel of the rest of Team Congress: Mike DeBonis, Paul Kane, Erica Werner, and Seung Min Kim. And so much of our coverage depended on teaming up with the ace reporting of our colleagues on the *Post*'s politics, national security, investigative, and breaking news teams, particularly Devlin Barrett, Bob Costa, Alice Crites, Aaron Davis, Josh Dawsey, Karen DeYoung, David Fahrenthold, Anne Gearan, Tom Hamburger, Shane Harris, Rosalind Helderman, Peter Hermann, Spencer Hsu, John Hudson, Colby Itkowitz, Greg Jaffe, Michael Kranish, Carol Leonnig, Greg Miller, Carol Morello, Ellen Nakashima, Toluse Olorunnipa, Ashley Parker, Beth Reinhard, Phil Rucker, Felicia Sonmez, Paul Sonne, Julie Tate, Elise Viebeck, John Wagner, and Matt Zapotosky.

We would also like to thank CNN for bringing both of us on as official political analysts during the Trump presidency, giving us a platform to feature our reporting and a medium to become familiar faces to many of our eventual sources for this book. And we want to acknowledge how much we benefited from the tireless reporting of our colleagues at rival news publications, many of whom we are proud to call friends. Thank you for challenging us, for informing us, and for the work that you do to shine a light on the inner workings of Washington every day.

Rachael would like to independently thank her husband, Alex Bishop, who brought her countless coffees and meals, insisted she took time to sleep, and provided constant encouragement and mental support while she balanced full-time work and this massive project. It is an understatement to say writing a book is difficult. The reality is that the all-consuming process sucks up not just standard work hours but evenings, weekends, and virtually all vacation and free time. In that, it impacts not just the writer, but the writer's family. Yet Alex never complained, and for that, Rachael will forever be grateful.

Rachael would also like to thank her biggest fans: her late grand-father Richard Bade, whom we tragically lost six months into this project, and her grandmother Wilma Bade. It takes true love for a pair of Fox News fanatics to watch and cheer their granddaughter opining on CNN, even as she calls out a president they both ad-mired. Their openness to hearing another side is what makes her job as a reporter so fulfilling. Rachael would also like to thank her mom, Laura; her dad, Mark; her brothers, Jonathan and Daniel; as well as her mother-in-law, Joanne, and sister-in-law, Emma, for put-ting up with her endless whining about deadlines and the fact that Rachael turned into a hermit for two years. She should have more time for visits now. And of course, her two cats, Princess Leia and Jay Jay, for keeping her lap warm while she wrote and made phone calls late into the night.

Lastly, Rachael would also like to thank the big bosses at *Politico*, who not only allowed her to take over *Politico Playbook* while she still had a massive book project on her plate, but who gave her the space to finish the work. A special thanks to Mike Zapler, her editor and boss, who gave feedback and let her take time when needed to meet deadlines. And to her *Playbook* co-authors, especially Ryan Lizza, who picked up the slack in her place when book duty called. She'd also be remiss if she didn't give a shout to her TV agent at CAA, Rachel Adler, who's been a great advocate and connector, en-couraging Rachael to think long-term about her journalism career and goals.

Karoun would like to begin her acknowledgments by thanking

the crew of stakeout reporters that became her second family over four years of covering successive Russia investigations and impeachments on Capitol Hill. Jeremy Herb, Katie Bo Williams (now Lillis), and Nick Fandos especially made the drudgerous hours fly by, lifting her spirits and keeping her going by always being there with everything from words of encouragement or commiseration, as appropriate, to cell phone chargers, which she never could seem to remember to keep on her. Here's to the friendships forged in the SCIF stairwell that have blossomed aboveground.

Professionally, Karoun would additionally like to thank the *Washington Post*'s foreign editor Douglas Jehl and its former Moscow bureau chief Michael Birnbaum for taking a chance and bringing her into the newspaper when she emailed them out of the blue, armed with a fellowship to Russia and asking for a job—and *Post* editor Rachel Van Dongen for later giving her the position that brought her back to Washington, D.C., Capitol Hill, and the eventual heart of the impeachment story. Even more thanks is due to her former editors and perpetual mentors Michael Tackett and Gordon Witkin, not only for giving her her first reporting jobs in Washington, D.C., and later talking her up to the *Post*, but also for urging her to bet on herself and get on that plane to Moscow when more arguably practical options presented themselves. It was impossible to know then that covering a war in Ukraine and the international fallout with the Kremlin would have such direct relevance to domestic news during the Trump era, but the experience gave her an invaluable background for the Russia story that followed her home. Karoun would additionally like to thank Michael Glennon, her former professor from the Fletcher School at Tufts University, whose classes almost—*almost*—made her pursue law over journalism and whom she fortuitously met up with for lunch right around the time she and Rachael were writing the proposal for this book. Don't just write about political intrigue, he advised her. Write a book that says something about government and the Constitution.

Now Karoun would like to stop talking in the third person in order to appropriately thank the incredible women in her life who were her rock through all the personal and professional ups and downs of the two years it took to bring this book from an idea to fruition. A lot of life happened over the course of this project, and Heather Horn, Sophia Macris, Julia Harte, Karly Domb Sadof, Abby Hauslohner, Emma Burrows, Kelsey Snell, and Molly O'Toole—you made me laugh, mopped up my tears, took me on daily pandemic marches around the neighborhood, got me to train for a half-marathon, organized two surprise birthday parties, helped keep the literal roof from falling in over my head (extra hat tip to Molly's partner, Tim Bowden, there), and cheered me on like a rock star every time I felt like I was failing. Even at a distance—thank you, COVID-19—you helped me figure my way through every pickle and made sure I never felt alone.

Finally, I want to thank the people without whom I wouldn't be anywhere. My kid brother, Aram Demirjian—who is not a kid anymore but an accomplished orchestral conductor—has been my most constant source of consolation and inspiration in adulthood. I have always emulated his grit and dedication, which it takes a lot more of to succeed in music than it does in journalism, and benefited endlessly from the generosity and love that he and his wife, Caraline, extended to me, no matter how busy or complicated things got. My life would have crumbled during the course of writing this book if not for my partner, David Salvo, who cleaned, chauffeured, and took care of our two cats so that I could write—and edit, and write some more—without interruption. He was endlessly patient as nights, weekends, and vacations became swallowed by the book, and his gentle reminders to sleep, exercise, and occasionally shower—and his uncanny ability to make me laugh in my darkest moments—are the reason I didn't implode from stress during this process. I must also thank our two cats, April and Reuben, for staying up with me when I had to work late, purring and nuzzling me through many a round of writer's block, and being very careful not to step on the computer keyboard, almost always. Finally, I want to thank my parents, Karen Aykanian Demirjian and Ara Demirjian. To call them my biggest cheerleaders would be an understatement; to say they have always had my back seems trite. They have always been unconditional in their love, fierce in their support, unfailingly present no matter what I needed or when, and guilty of thinking their kids can do or learn to do basically anything. I dedicated this book to them, in part, because projects like this are daunting, but confidence like theirs is infectious—and oftentimes, it's everything.

NOTES

PROLOGUE

1. Jamie Raskin, *Unthinkable: Trauma, Truth, and the Trials of American Democracy* (New York: HarperCollins, 2022), 9.
2. Benjamin Segel and Allison Pecorin, "Rep. Liz Cheney criticizes 'disgraceful' GOP attempts to 'whitewash' Capitol attack," ABC News, May 16, 2021, https://abcnews.go.com/Politics/rep-liz-cheney-criticizes-disgraceful-gop-attempts-whitewash/story?id=77695739.
3. Raskin, *Unthinkable*, 29.
4. Alex Daugherty and David Smiley, "Gas masks, a prayer and guns drawn. Inside the riot at the U.S. Capitol Building," *Miami Herald*, January 6, 2021, https://www.miamiherald.com/news/politics-government/article248317480.html.
5. Raskin, *Unthinkable*, 153.

CHAPTER 1: "IMPEACH THE MOTHERFUCKER"

1. Mike DeBonis, "'It's like a manhood thing for him': Pelosi's power play with Trump serves as message to opponents," *Washington Post*, December 11, 2018, https://www.washingtonpost.com/powerpost/pelosi-questions-trumps-manhood-after-confrontational-white-house-meeting/2018/12/11/2b2111be-fd79-11e8-862a-b6a6f3ce8199_story.html.
2. Gallup, "Presidential Approval Ratings—Bill Clinton," accessed December 10, 2021, https://news.gallup.com/poll/116584/presidential-approval-ratings-bill-clinton.aspx.
3. "Why Pelosi thinks these midterms are about 'honoring the vision of our founders,'" *PBS NewsHour*, Transcript, November 6, 2018, https://www.pbs.org/newshour/show/why-pelosi-thinks-these-midterms-are-about-honoring-the-vision-of-our-founders.
4. Marisa Lagos, "Protesters continue vigil outside Pelosi's S.F. home," *San Francisco Chronicle*, March 23, 2007, https://www.sfgate.com/bayarea/article/Protesters-continue-vigil-outside-Pelosi-s-S-F-2607468.php.
5. Patient Protection and Affordable Care Act, Pub. L. No. 111-148 (2010).
6. U.S. Congress, House of Representatives, *Impeaching Donald John Trump, President of the United States, of high misdemeanors*, H.Res. 646, 115th Congress, 1st sess., introduced House on December 6, 2017.
7. U.S. Congress, House of Representatives, Office of the Clerk, Roll Call 658, H.Res. 646, December 6, 2017, 2:09 p.m., https://clerk.house.gov/Votes/201765.

CHAPTER 2: "ALL THE SUBPOENAS"

1. Robert S. Mueller III, *Report on the Investigation into Russian Interference in the 2016 Presidential Election*, Volume II (Washington, D.C.: U.S. Department of Justice, March 2019), 78, https://www.justice.gov/storage/report_volume2.pdf.

2. Robert Khuzami, Acting U.S. Attorney for the Southern District of New York, "The government's sentencing memorandum," in *United States v. Michael Cohen*, 18 Cr. 602 (WHP), December 7, 2018, https://s3.documentcloud .org/documents/5453395/USDOJ-Cohen-20181207.pdf; Michael Rothfeld and Joe Palazzolo, "Trump lawyer arranged $130,000 payment for adult film star's silence," *Wall Street Journal*, January 18, 2018, https://www.wsj .com/articles/trump-lawyer-arranged-130-000-payment-for-adult-film-stars -silence-1515787678; and Ronan Farrow, "Donald Trump, a Playboy model, and a system for concealing infidelity," *New Yorker*, February 16, 2018, https:// www.newyorker.com/news/news-desk/donald-trump-a-playboy-model-and -a-system-for-concealing-infidelity-national-enquirer-karen-mcdougal.

3. U.S. Department of Justice, "Michael Cohen pleads guilty in Manhattan federal court to eight counts, including criminal tax evasion and campaign finance violations," News release, August 21, 2018, https://www.justice.gov /usao-sdny/pr/michael-cohen-pleads-guilty-manhattan-federal-court-eight -counts-including-criminal-tax.

4. Erica Werner, Damian Paletta, and Mike DeBonis, "Trump says he won't sign Senate deal to avert shutdown, demands funds for border security," *Washington Post*, December 21, 2018, https://www.washingtonpost.com/business /economy/trump-continues-retreat-on-government-shutdown-threat-pledges -to-renew-border-control-battle-in-2019/2018/12/20/3143a752-0457-11e9-b6a9 -0aa5c2fcc9e4_story.html.

5. Linda Qiu and Mike Tackett, "The shutdown according to Trump," *New York Times*, January 4, 2019, https://www.nytimes.com/2019/01/04/us/politics/fact -check-trump-shutdown.html.

6. John Santucci, Tara Palmieri, and Katherine Faulders, "President Trump in a 'great mood' as Washington waits for Attorney General William Barr to act on special counsel report: Sources," ABC News, March 24, 2019, https://abcnews .go.com/Politics/president-trump-great-mood-washington-waits-attorney -general/story?id=61892356.

7. Ewan Palmer, "Kid Rock and 'down to earth' Donald Trump enjoy Florida golf resort trip that probably cost taxpayers millions," *Newsweek*, March 24, 2019, https://www.newsweek.com/donald-trump-kid-rock-golf-mueller-report -taxpayer-mar-lago-florida-1373251.

8. Michael Burke, "Trump golfs with Graham, Gowdy and Mulvaney as White House awaits Mueller findings," TheHill.com, March 24, 2019, https://thehill .com/homenews/administration/435519-trump-golfs-with-graham-gowdy-and -mulvaney-as-white-house-awaits.

9. William Barr, Attorney General, Letter to House and Senate Judiciary Committees, Washington, D.C., March 24, 2019, https://judiciary.house.gov

/sites/democrats.judiciary.house.gov/files/documents/ag%20march%2024%20
2019%20letter%20to%20house%20and%20senate%20judiciary%20committees
.pdf.

10. Isabel Vincent, "How Trump's Television City started a decades-long feud
between Trump and Nadler," *New York Post*, July 27, 2019, https://nypost
.com/2019/07/27/how-trumps-television-city-started-a-decades-long-feud
-between-trump-and-nadler/.

11. Rachael Bade and Josh Dawsey, "Trump's feud with Jerry Nadler rooted in
decades-old New York real estate project," *Washington Post*, April 8, 2019,
https://www.washingtonpost.com/politics/ive-been-battling-nadler-for-years
-feud-between-trump-democrat-rooted-in-decades-old-new-york-real-estate
-project/2019/04/08/1c848f7e-57af-11e9-a047-748657a0a9d1_story.html.

12. Richard Neal, House Ways and Means Committee Chairman, Letter to Internal Revenue Service Commissioner Charles Retting requesting six years
of President Donald Trump's federal income tax returns and associated records, Washington, D.C., April 3, 2019, https://waysandmeans.house.gov/sites
/democrats.waysandmeans.house.gov/files/documents/Neal%20Letter%20
to%20Rettig%20%28signed%29%20-%202019.04.03.pdf.

13. Karoun Demirjian, "House Democrats subpoena Deutsche Bank, other financial institutions tied to Trump," *Washington Post*, April 15, 2019, https://www
.washingtonpost.com/world/national-security/house-democrats-subpoena
-deutsche-bank-other-financial-institutions-tied-to-trump/2019/04/15/00d0042e
-5fee-11e9-9ff2-abc984dc9eec_story.html.

14. Elijah Cummings, House Committee on Oversight and Reform Chairman,
"Cummings sends 51 letters to White House and others insisting on full
compliance with previous GOP document requests," News release, December 19, 2018, https://oversight.house.gov/news/press-releases/cummings
-sends-51-letters-to-white-house-and-others-insisting-on-full-compliance.

15. Carol D. Leonnig and Rosaline S. Helderman, "Trump has chosen Washington lawyer Pat Cipollone as next White House counsel, people familiar
with decision say," *Washington Post*, October 13, 2018, https://www.washington
post.com/politics/washington-lawyer-pat-cipollone-emerging-as-trumps-pick
-for-white-house-counsel-person-familiar-with-decision-says/2018/10/13
/f3d54d3a-cf18-11e8-a360-85875bac0b1f_story.html.

16. Michael Kranish and Robert O'Harrow Jr., "Inside the government's racial
bias case against Donald Trump's company, and how he fought it," *Washington
Post*, January 23, 2016, https://www.washingtonpost.com/politics/inside-the
-governments-racial-bias-case-against-donald-trumps-company-and-how-he
-fought-it/2016/01/23/fb90163e-bfbe-11e5-bcda-62a36b394160_story.html.

17. Charles V. Bagli, "Trump sues Asian partners over sale of West Side site,"
New York Times, July 12, 2005, https://www.nytimes.com/2005/07/12/nyregion
/trump-sues-asian-partners-over-sale-of-west-side-site.html; Hillel Italie,
"Ivana Trump writing memoir about her children with Donald," Associated
Press, March 15, 2017, https://apnews.com/article/2dc345709a5b4d80820dd6af
c402ca8e; Jessica Graham, "Court tells Trump to pay Marla on time," *New*

York Post, October 20, 1999, https://nypost.com/1999/10/20/court-tells-trump
-to-pay-marla-on-time/; Ed Payne, "Trump sues Maher for $5 million for orang-
utan sex joke," CNN, February 6, 2013, https://www.cnn.com/2013/02/06
/showbiz/trump-bill-maher-suit/index.html; Al Delugach, "Trump files suit
against Merv Griffin: Rival bidder for resorts casino to countersue," *Los Angeles
Times,* March 19, 1988, https://www.latimes.com/archives/la-xpm-1988-03-19
-fi-1208-story.html; Nick Penzenstadler and Susan Page, "Exclusive: Trump's
3,500 lawsuits unprecedented for a presidential nominee," *USA Today,* June 1,
2016, https://www.usatoday.com/story/news/politics/elections/2016/06/01/donald
-trump-lawsuits-legal-battles/84995854/; and *Trump International Golf Club
Scotland Limited and another (Appellants) v. The Scottish Ministers (Respondents)
(Scotland),* UKSC 74 (2015), January 23, 2022, https://www.supremecourt.uk
/cases/uksc-2015-0160.html.

18. Nick Penzenstadler, "New *USA Today* interactive database shows Trump
lawsuits surpass 4,000," *USA Today,* July 7, 2016, https://www.usatoday
.com/story/news/politics/onpolitics/2016/07/07/new-usa-today-interactive
-database-shows-trump-lawsuits-surpass-4000/86809010/.

19. Josh Gerstein, "Subpoena fight over Operation Fast and Furious documents
finally settled," *Politico,* May 9, 2019, https://www.politico.com/story/2019/05
/09/fast-and-furious-documents-holder-1313120.

20. Mark Hosenball, "White House fights and loses battle to withhold Benghazi records," Reuters, May 17, 2013, https://www.reuters.com/article/us-usa
-benghazi-legal/white-house-fights-and-loses-battle-to-withhold-benghazi
-records-idUSBRE94G0VZ20130517.

21. Eric Lipton, "White House declines to provide storm papers," *New York Times,*
January 25, 2006, https://www.nytimes.com/2006/01/25/politics/white-house
-declines-to-provide-storm-papers.html; "Bush withholds CIA leak records,"
Associated Press, via CBS News, July 17, 2008, https://www.cbsnews.com
/news/bush-withholds-cia-leak-records/; and Nina Totenberg, "Miers Told
to Defy House Judiciary Subpoena," NPR, *Morning Edition,* July 12, 2007,
https://www.npr.org/templates/story/story.php?storyId=11903777.

22. Rachael Bade and Josh Dawsey, "White House ignores House panels' requests
for documents, Democrats say," *Washington Post,* March 19, 2019, https://
www.washingtonpost.com/powerpost/white-house-intent-on-challenging
-democrats-request-for-documents-in-probe-of-trump/2019/03/19/7286a74c
-4a83-11e9-b79a-961983b7e0cd_story.html.

23. Jeremy Diamond and Allie Malloy, "Trump at war with Democrats: 'We're
fighting all the subpoenas,'" CNN, April 24, 2019, https://www.cnn.com
/2019/04/24/politics/donald-trump-fight-subpoenas-don-mcgahn-ridiculous
/index.html.

CHAPTER 3: PRESSURE POINTS

1. Nicholas Fandos, "In fight for Judiciary slot, Democrats broach the 'i' word:
Impeachment," *New York Times,* December 18, 2017, https://www.nytimes

.com/2017/12/18/us/politics/judiciary-committee-democrats-impeach-trump
.html.

2. Barry H. Berke, Noah Bookbinder, and Norman L. Eisen, *Presidential Obstruction of Justice: The Case of Donald J. Trump*, 2nd ed. (Washington, D.C.: Brookings Institution, August 22, 2018), https://www.brookings.edu/wp-content /uploads/2018/08/GS_82218_Obstruction_2nd-edition.pdf.

3. Norman Eisen, *A Case for the American People: The United States v. Donald J. Trump* (New York: Crown Publishing Group, 2020), 46.

4. Justin Amash, "Opinion: Justin Amash: Our politics is in a partisan death spiral. That's why I'm leaving the GOP," *Washington Post*, July 4, 2019, https://www .washingtonpost.com/opinions/justin-amash-our-politics-is-in-a-partisan -death-spiral-thats-why-im-leaving-the-gop/2019/07/04/afbe0480-9e3d-11e9 -b27f-ed2942f73d70_story.html; and Justin Amash, Twitter post, May 18, 2019, 3:30 p.m., https://twitter.com/justinamash/status/1129831622868635649.

5. Lois Romano, "Passed over by Pelosi, Harman doesn't get even. She gets mad," *Washington Post*, January 4, 2007, https://www.washingtonpost.com /archive/politics/2007/01/04/passed-over-by-pelosi-harman-doesnt-get-even -she-gets-mad/09c3ee55-1271-4b8a-a964-2cfd066d0933/.

6. John M. Broder and Carl Hulse, "Behind House struggle, long and tangled roots," *New York Times*, November 22, 2008, https://www.nytimes.com /2008/11/23/us/politics/23waxman.html.

7. Heather Caygle, Rachael Bade, and John Bresnahan, "Pelosi gets revenge against one of the Dem rebels," *Politico*, January 15, 2019, https://www.politico .com/story/2019/01/15/pelosi-rice-judiciary-committee-1102772.

8. Sarah Ferris and Andrew Desiderio, "Pelosi's hard line on impeachment splits House Dems," *Politico*, March 11, 2019, https://www.politico.com/story /2019/03/11/pelosi-democrats-impeachment-1216738.

9. Rachael Bade and Mike DeBonis, "Some in Pelosi's leadership team rebel on impeachment, press her to begin an inquiry," *Washington Post*, May 20, 2021, https://www.washingtonpost.com/politics/pelosis-leadership-team-rebels-on -impeachment-presses-her-to-begin-an-inquiry/2019/05/20/263c11de-7b5b-11 e9-a66c-d36e482aa873_story.html.

10. Devlin Barrett, Spencer S. Hsu, Rachael Bade, and Josh Dawsey, "Judge rules against Trump in fight over president's financial records," *Washington Post*, May 20, 2019, https://www.washingtonpost.com/local/legal-issues/us -judge-denies-trump-bid-to-quash-house-subpoena-for-years-of-financial -records/2019/05/20/74e45880-7b21-11e9-8bb7-0fc796cf2ec0_story.html.

11. Pat Cipollone, White House Counsel, Letter to House Judiciary Committee Chairman Jerrold Nadler, rejecting demand for information, Washington, D.C., May 15, 2019, https://www.washingtonpost.com/context/white -house-rejects-house-demand-for-information-in-abuse-of-power-inquiry /c5d3656a-1065-425d-bffb-f5a653fef9b8/?utm_term=.3062b9b3fe91&itid =lk_interstitial_manual_15.

12. Donna Borak and Lauren Fox, "Mnuchin refuses to turn over Trump taxes to House Democrats," CNN, May 6, 2019, https://www.cnn.com/2019/05/06

/politics/tax-returns-trump-congress-showdown/index.html; David H. Carpenter, Todd Garvey, and Edward C. Liu, "Congressional access to the president's federal tax returns," *Congressional Research Service Legal Sidebar*, March 15, 2019, updated on May 7, 2019, https://sgp.fas.org/crs/secrecy/LSB10275.pdf.

13. David A. Fahrenthold, Rachael Bade, and John Wagner, "Trump sues in bid to block congressional subpoena of financial records," *Washington Post*, April 22, 2019, https://www.washingtonpost.com/politics/trump-sues-in-bid-to-block-congressional-subpoena-of-financial-records/2019/04/22/a98de3d0-6500-11e9-82ba-fcfeff232e8f_story.html.

14. Rachael Bade and John Wagner, "Pelosi tells colleagues she wants to see Trump 'in prison,' not impeached," *Washington Post*, June 6, 2019, https://www.washingtonpost.com/powerpost/pelosi-tells-colleagues-she-wants-to-see-trump-in-prison-not-impeached/2019/06/06/afaf004a-8856-11e9-a491-25df61c78dc4_story.html.

15. Chris Cillizza, "Nancy Pelosi is winning the impeachment fight," CNN, June 4, 2019, https://www.cnn.com/2019/06/04/politics/nancy-pelosi-impeachment-trump/index.html.

CHAPTER 4: RELEASE VALVES

1. Jennifer Agiesta, "CNN poll: Democratic support for impeachment rises, Trump approval steady," CNN, June 2, 2019, https://edition.cnn.com/2019/06/02/politics/trump-impeachment-mueller-testify-cnn-poll/index.html.

2. Mary Clare Jalonick and Lisa Mascaro, "Pelosi says Democrats 'not even close' to starting impeachment," Associated Press, via *Denver Post*, June 11, 2019, https://www.denverpost.com/2019/06/11/pelosi-impeachment-turmp-subpoena/.

3. Quinta Jurecic, "What's new in the unredacted Mueller report?," *Lawfare*, July 2, 2020, https://www.lawfareblog.com/whats-new-unredacted-mueller-report.

4. Todd S. Purdum, "Robert Mueller and the tyranny of 'optics,'" *The Atlantic*, July 25, 2019, https://www.theatlantic.com/politics/archive/2019/07/mueller-testimony-congress-optics/594676/.

5. David Axelrod, Twitter post, July 24, 2019, 9:17 a.m., https://twitter.com/davidaxelrod/status/1154017858168508416.

6. Carl Hulse, "Lack of electricity in Mueller testimony short-circuits impeachment," *New York Times*, July 26, 2019, https://www.nytimes.com/2019/07/25/us/politics/mueller-impeachment.html.

7. Jenna Portnoy, "Spanberger turns to tough reelection bid in Trump district," *Washington Post*, December 14, 2019, https://www.washingtonpost.com/local/virginia-politics/spanberger-turns-to-tough-reelection-bid-in-trump-district/2019/12/14/f727124a-1858-11ea-8406-df3c54b3253e_story.html.

8. Scott Shafer, "Clinton's impeachment ended this man's congressional career, and started Adam Schiff's," KQED Los Angeles, January 15, 2020, https://

www.kqed.org/news/11796234/clintons-impeachment-ended-this-mans
-congressional-career-and-started-adam-schiffs.

CHAPTER 5: TRUMP FREED

1. Dana Blanton, "Fox News poll: Biden holds commanding lead for Democratic
nomination," Fox News, July 25, 2019, https://www.foxnews.com/politics/fox
-news-poll-biden-holds-commanding-lead-for-democratic-nomination.

2. Quinnipiac University Poll, "Biden is only leading Dem to top Trump in
Ohio, Quinnipiac University poll finds; former V.P. has big lead in Demo-
cratic Party," News release, July 25, 2019, https://poll.qu.edu/Poll-Release
-Legacy?releaseid=3633.

3. White House, Memorandum of Telephone Conversation between President
Donald Trump and President Zelenskyy of Ukraine, July 25, 2019, 9:03–
9:33 a.m., Declassified by order of the President, September 24, 2019, https://
www.washingtonpost.com/context/official-readout-president-trump-s-july
-25-phone-call-with-ukraine-s-volodymyr-zelensky/4b228f51-17e7-45bc-b16c
-3b2643f3fbe0/.

4. Maggie Haberman, Julian E. Barnes, and Peter Baker, "Dan Coats to step
down as intelligence chief; Trump picks loyalist for the job," *New York
Times*, July 28, 2019, https://www.nytimes.com/2019/07/28/us/politics/dan-coats
-intelligence-chief-out.html.

5. Nick Miroff and Josh Dawsey, "'Take the land': President Trump wants a
border wall. He wants it black. And he wants it by Election Day," *Washington
Post*, August 27, 2019, https://www.washingtonpost.com/immigration/take-the
-land-president-trump-wants-a-border-wall-he-wants-it-black-and-he-wants
-it-by-election-day/2019/08/27/37b80018-c821-11e9-a4f3-c081a126de70_story
.html.

6. Quint Forgey, "Trump says he wanted to give himself Medal of Honor,"
Politico, August 21, 2019, https://www.politico.com/story/2019/08/21/donald
-trump-give-himself-medal-of-honor-1470950.

7. Felicia Sonmez, "Trump says that Jewish people who vote for Democrats
are 'very disloyal to Israel,' denies his remarks are anti-Semitic," *Washington Post*, August 21, 2019, https://www.washingtonpost.com/politics
/trump-says-that-jewish-people-who-vote-for-democrats-are-very-disloyal-to
-israel-denies-his-remarks-are-anti-semitic/2019/08/21/055e53bc-c42d-11e9
-b5e4-54aa56d5b7ce_story.html; and Bess Levin, "Trump declares himself
'King of Israel,' the 'second coming of God,'" *Vanity Fair*, August 21, 2019,
https://www.vanityfair.com/news/2019/08/donald-trump-king-of-israel.

8. Kevin Brueninger, "'I am the Chosen One,' Trump proclaims as he de-
fends trade war with China," CNBC, August 21, 2019, https://www.cnbc
.com/2019/08/21/i-am-the-chosen-one-trump-proclaims-as-he-defends-china
-trade-war.html.

9. "Trump cancels Denmark visit amid spat over sale of Greenland," BBC News,
August 21, 2019, https://www.bbc.com/news/world-us-canada-49416740.

10. Patricia Mazzei, Michael D. Shear, and Eric Lipton, "Trump has just the place for the next G7 meeting: His own golf resort," *New York Times*, August 26, 2019, https://www.nytimes.com/2019/08/26/world/europe/trump-doral-g7.html.

11. Allan Smith, "Pence's Doonbeg detour cost nearly $600K in ground transportation fees," NBC News, September 11, 2019, https://www.nbcnews.com/politics/donald-trump/pence-s-doonbeg-detour-cost-nearly-600k-ground-transportation-fees-n1052401.

12. *Blumenthal, et al. v. Trump*, Case 1:17-cv-01154, U.S. District Court for the District of Columbia, filed June 14, 2017, https://www.theusconstitution.org/wp-content/uploads/2018/01/Blumenthal_v_Trump_DDC_Original_Complaint_Final.pdf; and *D.C. and Maryland v. Trump*, Case 8:17-cv-01596, U.S. District Court for the District of Maryland, filed June 12, 2017.

13. Jessica Gresko, "Supreme Court: Trump can use Pentagon funds for border wall," Associated Press, July 27, 2019, https://apnews.com/article/mexico-donald-trump-ap-top-news-courts-supreme-courts-5d893d388c254c7fa83a1570112ae90e.

14. Matt Zapotosky, "Prosecutors have 'concluded' Michael Cohen campaign finance probe, judge says," *Washington Post*, July 17, 2019, https://www.washingtonpost.com/national-security/prosecutors-have-concluded-michael-cohen-campaign-finance-probe-judge-says/2019/07/17/733391a0-a8b1-11e9-9214-246e594de5d5_story.html.

15. Amber Phillips, "More than half of House Democrats support an impeachment inquiry. So, why isn't there one yet?," *Washington Post*, August 2, 2019, https://www.washingtonpost.com/politics/2019/08/02/more-than-half-house-democrats-support-an-impeachment-inquiry-so-why-isnt-there-one-yet/.

16. Laure Hernandez, "Activists interrupt Pelosi award ceremony in San Francisco, demand she take action to impeach Trump," *San Francisco Chronicle*, August 21, 2019, https://www.sfchronicle.com/bayarea/article/Activists-interrupt-Pelosi-award-ceremony-in-San-14369487.php.

CHAPTER 6: THE RUNAWAY CHAIRMAN

1. Norman Eisen, *A Case for the American People: The United States v. Donald J. Trump* (New York: Crown Publishing Group, 2020), 98–99.

2. In re: Application of the Committee on the Judiciary, U.S. House of Representatives, for an Order Authorizing the Release of Certain Grand Jury Materials, Case 1:19-gj-00048, U.S. District Court for the District of Columbia, filed July 26, 2019, 30.

3. CNN, *Erin Burnett OutFront*, Transcript, August 8, 2019, https://transcripts.cnn.com/show/ebo/date/2019-08-08/segment/01.

4. Nicholas Fandos, "Is it an impeachment inquiry or not? Democrats can't seem to agree," *New York Times*, September 11, 2019, https://www.nytimes.com/2019/09/11/us/politics/democrats-house-impeachment-inquiry.html.

5. Sarah Ferris, Heather Caygle, and John Bresnahan, "'Feel free to leak this':

Inside the Pelosi-Nadler impeachment schism," *Politico*, September 18, 2019, https://www.politico.com/story/2019/09/18/pelosi-nadler-schism-impeachment-1501755.

CHAPTER 7: WHISTLEBLOWER

1. Caitlin Emma and Connor O'Brien, "Trump holds up Ukraine military aid meant to confront Russia," *Politico*, August 28, 2019, https://www.politico.com/story/2019/08/28/trump-ukraine-military-aid-russia-1689531.
2. John Bolton, *The Room Where It Happened* (New York: Simon & Schuster, 2020), 445.
3. Bolton, *The Room Where It Happened*, 445.
4. Adam Entous, "Will Hunter Biden jeopardize his father's campaign?," *New Yorker*, July 1, 2019, https://www.newyorker.com/magazine/2019/07/08/will-hunter-biden-jeopardize-his-fathers-campaign.
5. Tim Lister, "Giuliani's case rests on two Ukrainians with checkered pasts and suspect motives," CNN, October 5, 2019, https://www.cnn.com/2019/10/05/politics/guiliani-ukraine-shokin-lutsenko-intl/index.html.
6. Ron Johnson, Letter to House Republican ranking members Jim Jordan of the House Committee on Oversight and Reform and Devin Nunes of the House Permanent Select Committee on Intelligence, November 18, 2019, https://www.ronjohnson.senate.gov/services/files/E0B73C19-9370-42E6-88B1-B2458EAEEECD.
7. Bolton, *The Room Where It Happened*, 416.
8. "Graham: Trump a 'race-baiting, xenophobic religious . . . ,'" CNN, December 8, 2015, YouTube video, 03:34, https://www.youtube.com/watch?v=2bkDykGhM8c; and Donna Cassata, "Senator on GOP backing Trump: 'Party has gone batshit crazy,'" Associated Press, February 26, 2016, https://www.seattletimes.com/nation-world/nation-politics/senator-on-gop-backing-trump-party-has-gone-batshit-crazy/.
9. "Lindsey Graham chokes up talking about Joe Biden," *HuffPost* video via YouTube, July 2, 2015, https://www.youtube.com/watch?v=kLMYW8jFPHg.
10. Adam Schiff, *Midnight in Washington* (New York: Penguin Random House, 2021), 203.
11. Rudy Giuliani, Twitter post, June 21, 2019, 11:04 a.m., https://twitter.com/rudygiuliani/status/1142085975230898176?lang=en.
12. President of Ukraine, official website, "Volodymyr Zelenskyy had a phone conversation with the president of the United States," News release, July 25, 2019, https://www.president.gov.ua/en/news/volodimir-zelenskij-proviv-telefonnu-rozmovu-z-prezidentom-s-56617.
13. House Foreign Affairs Committee, "Three House committees launch wide-ranging investigation into Trump-Giuliani Ukraine scheme," News release, September 9, 2019, https://foreignaffairs.house.gov/2019/9/three-house-committees-launch-wide-ranging-investigation-into-trump-giuliani-ukraine-scheme.

14. Michael Atkinson, Inspector General of the Intelligence Community, Letter to Adam Schiff, Chairman, and Devin Nunes, Ranking Member, of the House Intelligence Committee, regarding "urgent concern," September 9, 2019, https://intelligence.house.gov/uploadedfiles/20190909_-_ic_ig_letter_to _hpsci_on_whistleblower.pdf.

CHAPTER 8: THE MESSENGERS

1. Greg Miller, Ellen Nakashima, and Shane Harris, "Trump's communications with foreign leader are part of whistleblower complaint that spurred standoff between spy chief and Congress, former officials say," *Washington Post*, September 18, 2019, https://www.washingtonpost.com/national-security /trumps-communications-with-foreign-leader-are-part-of-whistleblower -complaint-that-spurred-standoff-between-spy-chief-and-congress-former -officials-say/2019/09/18/df651aa2-da60-11e9-bfb1-849887369476_story.html.
2. Ellen Nakashima, Shane Harris, Greg Miller, and Carol D. Leonnig, "Whistleblower complaint about President Trump involves Ukraine, according to two people familiar with the matter," *Washington Post*, September 19, 2019, https://www.washingtonpost.com/national-security/whistleblower-complaint -about-president-trump-involves-ukraine-according-to-two-people-familiar -with-the-matter/2019/09/19/07e33f0a-daf6-11e9-bfb1-849887369476_story .html.
3. "Giuliani contradicts himself over Ukraine probe of Biden," CNN video, 01:15, September 19, 2019, https://www.cnn.com/videos/politics/2019/09/20 /cuomo-rudy-giuliani-ukraine-biden-sot-cpt-vpx.cnn.
4. Emily Davies, Rachael Bade, and Laura Hughes, "House Democrats in Trump districts resist liberal pressure on impeachment," *Washington Post*, August 31, 2019, https://www.washingtonpost.com/politics/house-democrats-in-trump -districts-resist-liberal-pressure-on-impeachment/2019/08/30/97254710-ca7c -11e9-8067-196d9f17af68_story.html.
5. Julian E. Barnes, Michael S. Schmidt, Kenneth P. Vogel, Adam Goldman, and Maggie Haberman, "Trump pressed Ukraine's leader on inquiry into Biden's son," *New York Times*, September 20, 2019, https://www.nytimes .com/2019/09/20/us/politics/trump-whistle-blower-ukraine.html.
6. Karoun Demirjian, "Trump's freeze on Ukraine aid draws new scrutiny amid push for Biden investigation," *Washington Post*, September 20, 2019, https:// www.washingtonpost.com/national-security/trumps-freeze-on-ukraine-aid -draws-new-scrutiny-amid-push-for-biden-investigation/2019/09/20/f22f0a98 -dbd3-11e9-ac63-3016711543fe_story.html.
7. Alan Cullison, Rebecca Ballhaus, and Dustin Volz, "Trump repeatedly pressed Ukraine president to investigate Biden's son," *Wall Street Journal*, September 21, 2019, https://www.wsj.com/articles/trump-defends-conversation -with-ukraine-leader-11568993176.
8. Nancy Pelosi, "Dear Colleague" letter to House Democrats, Washington, D.C., *Politico*, September 22, 2019, https://www.politico.com/f/?id=0000016d -5d62-d53d-affd-fdf6182f0002.

9. Gil Cisneros, Jason Crow, Chrissy Houlahan, Elaine Luria, Mikie Sherrill, Elissa Slotkin, and Abigail Spanberger, "Opinion: Seven freshman Democrats: These allegations are a threat to all we have sworn to protect," *Washington Post*, September 23, 2019, https://www.washingtonpost.com/opinions/2019/09/24 /seven-freshman-democrats-these-allegations-are-threat-all-we-have-sworn -protect/.

10. Kyle D. Cheney, Twitter post, September 23, 2019, 8:30 p.m., https://twitter .com/kyledcheney/status/1176292762867634184?s=11.

11. "Pelosi says Congress should pass new laws so sitting presidents can be indicted," NPR, September 20, 2019, https://www.npr.org/transcripts /762594886.

CHAPTER 9: A PERFECT CALL

1. "Press gaggle: Donald Trump speaks to the press before Marine One departure," Factbase video and transcript, 13:14, September 22, 2019, https:// factba.se/transcript/donald-trump-press-gaggle-marine-one-departure -september-22-2019.

2. Karoun Demirjian, Josh Dawsey, Ellen Nakashima, and Carol D. Leonnig, "Trump ordered hold on military aid days before calling Ukrainian president, officials say," *Washington Post*, September 23, 2019, https://www .washingtonpost.com/national-security/trump-ordered-hold-on-military-aid -days-before-calling-ukrainian-president-officials-say/2019/09/23/df93a6ca -de38-11e9-8dc8-498eabc129a0_story.html.

3. Kevin Sullivan and Mary Jordan, *Trump on Trial: The Investigation, Impeachment, Acquittal and Aftermath* (New York: Scribner Books, 2020), 224.

4. Kyle D. Cheney, Twitter post, September 24, 2019, 2:48 p.m., https://twitter .com/kyledcheney/status/1176569188195930113; and Kyle D. Cheney, Twitter post, September 24, 2019, 12:17 p.m., https://twitter.com/kyledcheney/status /1176531204314677249.

CHAPTER 10: IMPEACHMENT BY ANOTHER NAME

1. David A. Fahrenthold, "Trump recorded having extremely lewd conversation about women in 2005," *Washington Post*, October 8, 2016, https://www .washingtonpost.com/politics/trump-recorded-having-extremely-lewd -conversation-about-women-in-2005/2016/10/07/3b9ce776-8cb4-11e6-bf8a-3d2 6847eeed4_story.html?tid=a_inl_manual.

2. Peter Baker, *The Breach* (New York: Scribner, 2000), 101–2.

CHAPTER 11: "THE DYNAMITE LINE"

1. White House, Memorandum of Telephone Conversation between President Donald Trump and President Zelenskyy of Ukraine, July 25, 2019, 9:03– 9:33 a.m., Declassified by order of the President, September 24, 2019, https:// www.washingtonpost.com/context/official-readout-president-trump-s-july

-25-phone-call-with-ukraine-s-volodymyr-zelensky/4b228f51-17e7-45bc-b16c
-3b2643f3fbe0/.

2. Greg Miller and Philip Rucker, "'This was the worst call by far': Trump badgered, bragged and abruptly ended phone call with Australian leader," *Washington Post*, February 2, 2017, https://www.washingtonpost.com/world /national-security/no-gday-mate-on-call-with-australian-pm-trump-badgers -and-brags/2017/02/01/88a3bfb0-e8bf-11e6-80c2-30e57e57e05d_story.html.

3. Charles Schumer, Letter to Senate Majority Leader Mitch McConnell, Washington, D.C., September 23, 2019, https://www.democrats.senate.gov/imo /media/doc/SCHUMER%20Whistleblower%20Letter%20to%20Sen.%20 McConnell.9.23.2019.pdf.

4. Ben Terris, "Mitch McConnell doesn't care what you think. He just wants to win," *Washington Post*, January 24, 2020, https://www.washingtonpost.com /lifestyle/style/mitch-mcconnell-doesnt-care-what-you-think-he-just-wants -to-win/2020/01/23/e8acc1d4-3deb-11ea-8872-5df698785a4e_story.html.

5. Abraham Lincoln, "II. In the First Debate with Douglas," in Great Books Online: *The World's Famous Orations*, 1858, https://www.bartleby.com/268/9/23 .html.

6. Sarah Ferris and Heather Caygle, "Vulnerable Democrats fear impeachment messaging stumbles," *Politico*, September 25, 2019, https://www .politico.com/story/2019/09/25/democrat-impeachment-vulnerable-freshmen -congress-1510587.

7. Norman Eisen, *A Case for the American People: The United States v. Donald J. Trump* (New York: Crown Publishing Group, 2020), 164.

CHAPTER 12: THE RISE OF SCHIFF

1. Jon Meacham, Timothy Naftali, Peter Baker, and Jeffrey A. Engel, *Impeachment: An American History* (New York: Modern Library, 2018), 73.

2. Philip Bump, "How America viewed the Watergate scandal as it was unfolding," *Washington Post*, May 15, 2017, https://www.washingtonpost.com/news /politics/wp/2017/05/15/how-america-viewed-the-watergate-scandal-as-it-was -unfolding/.

3. "Senate Select Committee on Presidential Campaign Activities (The Watergate Committee)," U.S. Senate Historical Office, January 23, 2022, Washington, D.C., https://www.senate.gov/about/resources/pdf/watergate -investigation-citations.pdf.

4. James R. Dickenson, "Sen. Sam Ervin, key figure in Watergate probe, dies," *Washington Post*, April 24, 1985, https://www.washingtonpost.com/wp-srv /national/longterm/watergate/stories/ervinobit.htm.

5. Meacham, Naftali, Baker, and Engel, *Impeachment*, 89–90.

6. Tim Naftali, "The secret plan to force out Nixon," *The Atlantic*, December 17, 2019, https://www.theatlantic.com/ideas/archive/2019/12/when-house -republican-leadership-wanted-oust-nixon/603706/.

7. Madeleine Conway, "Schiff: There is now 'more than circumstantial evi-

dence' of Trump-Russia collusion," *Politico*, March 23, 2017, https://www
.politico.com/story/2017/03/schiff-russia-trump-collusion-236386.

8. ABC News, *This Week*, Transcript, May 27, 2018, https://abcnews.go.com
/Politics/week-transcript-27-18-sen-marco-rubio-rep/story?id=55444994.

9. Robert S. Mueller III, *Report on the Investigation into Russian Interference in
the 2016 Presidential Election*, Volume I (Washington, D.C.: U.S. Department
of Justice, March 2019), 9, https://www.justice.gov/archives/sco/file/1373816
/download.

10. "Russia's International Influence," C-Span video, 02:54:46, March 28, 2019,
https://www.c-span.org/video/?459258-1/house-intelligence-committee
-examines-russian-election-interference-tactics.

11. Adam Schiff, *Midnight in Washington* (New York: Penguin Random House,
2021), 18.

12. Todd S. Purdum, "The 2000 campaign: California; emotion and spending
run high in one close House contest," *New York Times*, September 17, 2000,
https://www.nytimes.com/2000/09/17/us/2000-campaign-california-emotions
-spending-run-high-one-close-house-contest.html.

13. Matthew Rosenberg and Emmarie Huetteman, "House Democrats ask
Devin Nunes to recuse himself from Russia inquiry," *New York Times*, March
27, 2017, https://www.nytimes.com/2017/03/27/us/politics/devin-nunes-house
-intelligence-committee-white-house-wiretap.html.

14. Ben Terris, "Adam Schiff once wanted to be a screenwriter. Can he give the
Trump presidency a Hollywood ending?," *Washington Post*, November 1, 2019,
https://www.washingtonpost.com/lifestyle/style/adam-schiff-once-wanted
-to-be-a-screenwriter-can-he-give-the-trump-presidency-a-hollywood-ending
/2019/10/31/07cb9594-f748-11e9-ad8b-85e2aa00b5ce_story.html.

15. Donald J. Trump, Twitter post, "Tweets of September 29, 2019," compiled
by the American Presidency Project, University of California, Santa Barbara,
https://www.presidency.ucsb.edu/documents/tweets-september-29-2019.

CHAPTER 13: "KEEP YOUR POWDER DRY"

1. Gary Martin, "Nevada lawmakers want Trump investigations to continue,"
Las Vegas Review-Journal, September 27, 2019, https://www.reviewjournal.com
/news/politics-and-government/nevada-lawmakers-want-trump-investigations
-to-continue-1858504/.

2. Humberto Sanchez, "Amodei on Trump impeachment inquiry: 'Let's
put it through the process and see what happens,'" *Nevada Independent*,
September 27, 2019, https://thenevadaindependent.com/article/amodei-on
-trump-impeachment-inquiry-lets-put-it-through-the-process-and-see-what
-happens.

3. Neil Vigdor, "Mark Amodei is first House Republican to support Trump
impeachment inquiry," *New York Times*, September 27, 2019, https://www
.nytimes.com/2019/09/27/us/rep-mark-amodei-impeachment.html.

4. Peter Baker, *The Breach* (New York: Scribner, 2000), 67, 101–2, and 125.

5. Todd S. Purdum, "Kevin McCarthy and 'the other California,'" *Politico Magazine,* October 8, 2015, https://www.politico.com/magazine/story/2015/10/kevin-mccarthy-bakersfield-213230/.

6. Dorothy Mills-Gregg, "Before Kevin and Devin, there was Bill," *Capitol Weekly,* March 1, 2018, https://capitolweekly.net/kevin-devin-bill-thomas/.

7. Josh Dawsey and Robert Costa, "Kevin McCarthy relishes role as Trump's fixer, friend and candy man," *Washington Post,* January 15, 2018, https://www.washingtonpost.com/politics/kevin-mccarthy-relishes-role-as-trumps-fixer-friend-and-candy-man/2018/01/15/a2696b4e-f709-11e7-b34a-b85626af34ef_story.html.

8. NPR, *PBS NewsHour,* Marist Poll, *Impeachment Inquiry,* September 26, 2019, https://maristpoll.marist.edu/npr-pbs-newshour-marist-poll-results-9/.

9. Jennifer De Pinto, Anthony Salvanto, Fred Backus, and Kabir Khanna, "CBS News poll: Majority of Americans and Democrats approve of Trump impeachment inquiry," CBS News, September 29, 2019, https://www.cbsnews.com/news/trump-impeachment-inquiry-poll-cbs-news-poll-finds-majority-of-americans-and-democrats-approve/.

10. U.S. Congress, House of Representatives, House Judiciary Committee, *Resolution of Inquiry,* 93rd Congress, 2nd sess., February 6, 1974, H.Res. 803, *Washington Post,* December 10, 2021, https://www.washingtonpost.com/wp-srv/politics/special/clinton/stories/hres803.htm; and U.S. Congress, House of Representatives, House Judiciary Committee, *Resolution on Clinton Impeachment Inquiry,* 105th Congress, 2nd sess., October 8, 1998, H.Res 581, December 10, 2021, https://archive.nytimes.com/www.nytimes.com/library/politics/100898clinton-gop-text.html.

11. Baker, *The Breach,* 115.

12. U.S. Congress, House of Representatives, Kevin McCarthy, Letter to House Speaker Nancy Pelosi, October 3, 2019, via Kevin McCarthy, Twitter post, October 3, 2019, 11:20 a.m., https://twitter.com/gopleader/status/1179778155340603392.

13. "31 Democrats defect, support impeachment inquiry," CNN, *AllPolitics,* October 8, 1998, https://www.cnn.com/ALLPOLITICS/stories/1998/10/08/defect/; and Alison Mitchell, "Impeachment: The Overview—Clinton Impeachment; He Faces a Senate Trial, 2d in History; Vows to Do Job Till Term's 'Last Hour,'" *New York Times,* December 20, 1998, https://www.nytimes.com/1998/12/20/us/impeachment-overview-clinton-impeached-he-faces-senate-trial-2d-history-vows-job.html.

14. James M. Naughton, "House, 410–4, gives subpoena power in Nixon inquiry," *New York Times,* February 7, 1974, https://www.nytimes.com/1974/02/07/archives/house-4104gives-subpoena-power-in-nixon-inquiry-judiciary-panel-is.html.

CHAPTER 14: SPIN FACTORY

1. Kurt Volker, WhatsApp messages, as compiled by the House Foreign Affairs Committee, the House Committee on Oversight and Reform, and the

House Permanent Select Committee on Intelligence, October 3, 2019, 5, 9, https://foreignaffairs.house.gov/_cache/files/a/4/a4a91fab-99cd-4eb9-9c6c-ec1 c586494b9/621801458E982E9903839ABC7404A917.chairmen-letter-on-state -departmnent-texts-10-03-19.pdf.

2. Andrew Howard, "McCain Institute head Kurt Volker steps down as US diplomat," *State Press*, September 27, 2019, https://www.statepress.com/article /2019/09/sppolitics-mccain-head-steps-down.

3. U.S. House of Representatives, Permanent Select Committee on Intelligence, joint with the Committee on Oversight and Reform and the Committee on Foreign Affairs, *Interview of Kurt Volker*, Transcript, Washington, D.C., October 3, 2019, 11, 36, 46, https://docs.house.gov/meetings/IG/IG00 /CPRT-116-IG00-D007.pdf.

4. U.S. House of Representatives, *Interview of Kurt Volker*, 69–70, 73, 80, 115, 123, 129–30.

5. Katherine Faulders and Conor Finnegan, "'Crazy to withhold security assistance' to Ukraine for political campaign: Top US diplomat," ABC News, October 3, 2019, https://abcnews.go.com/Politics/top-diplomat-ukraine-crazy -withhold-security-sasistance-political/story?id=66039011; and Connor Mannion, "'It's crazy': Fox News obtains texts between US diplomats discussing Trump pressuring Ukraine on Biden," *Mediaite*, October 3, 2019, https://www .mediaite.com/tv/its-crazy-fox-news-obtains-texts-between-us-diplomats -discussing-trump-pressuring-ukraine-on-biden/.

CHAPTER 15: "THE ONE-WAY RATCHET"

1. Caitlin Oprysko, "Trump says China should investigate the Bidens amid impeachment furor," *Politico*, October 3, 2019, https://www.politico.com/news /2019/10/03/donald-trump-china-should-investigate-bidens-024697.

2. Elijah Cummings, Adam Schiff, and Eliot Engel, Letter and Subpoena to Acting White House Chief of Staff Michael Mulvaney, Washington, D.C., October 4, 2019, https://oversight.house.gov/sites/democrats.oversight.house .gov/files/documents/2019-10-04.EEC%20Engel%20Schiff%20to%20 Mulvaney-WH%20re%20Subpoena.pdf; and Dareh Gregorian and Alex Moe, "Impeachment inquiry turns to Vice President Mike Pence," NBC News, October 4, 2019, https://www.nbcnews.com/politics/trump-impeachment -inquiry/impeachment-inquiry-turns-vice-president-mike-pence-n1062646.

3. Aaron C. Davis, Josh Dawsey, Michelle Ye Hee Lee, and Michael Birnbaum, "'Disruptive diplomat' Gordon Sondland, a key figure in Trump impeachment furor, long coveted ambassadorship," *Washington Post*, October 14, 2019, https://www.washingtonpost.com/investigations/disruptive-diplomat -gordon-sondland-a-key-figure-in-trump-impeachment-furor-long-coveted -ambassadorship/2019/10/14/c5afb950-ec3f-11e9-9c6d-436a0df4f31d_story .html.

4. Shane Harris and Aaron C. Davis, "With revised statement, Sondland adds to testimony linking aid to Ukraine investigations that Trump sought,"

Washington Post, November 5, 2019, https://www.washingtonpost.com/world /national-security/with-revised-testimony-sondland-ties-trump-to-quid-pro -quo/2019/11/05/3059b3b8-ffec-11e9-9518-1e76abc088b6_story.html.

5. Pat Cipollone, Letter to House Speaker Nancy Pelosi, Intelligence Committee Chairman Adam B. Schiff, Foreign Affairs Committee Chairman Eliot L. Engel, and Committee on Oversight and Reform Chairman Elijah E. Cummings, Washington, D.C., October 8, 2019, https://www.washington post.com/context/letter-from-white-house-counsel-pat-cipollone-to-house -leaders/0e1845e5-5c19-4e7a-ab4b-9d591a5fda7b/.

CHAPTER 16: REVENGE OF THE DIPLOMATS

Kevin McCarthy's spokesman Matt Sparks denies that he cursed at the White House aides or demanded that they leave. However, his pushback, which came more than two years after the incident, stands in contrast to what others in the room told us happened just months after it occurred.

1. Hill Staff, "The Hill's review of John Solomon's columns on Ukraine," The Hill.com, February 19, 2020, https://thehill.com/homenews/administration /470700-trump-defends-yovanovitch-attack-i-have-freedom-of-speech; Donald Trump Jr., Twitter post, March 24, 2019, 12:12 p.m., https://twitter.com/ DonaldJTrumpJr/status/1109850575926108161?ref_src=twsrc%5Etfw; and John Solomon, "Top Ukrainian justice official says US ambassador gave him a do not prosecute list," TheHill.com, March 20, 2019, https://thehill.com/hilltv /rising/434875-top-ukrainian-justice-official-says-us-ambassador-gave-him-a -do-not-prosecute.

2. Juliegrace Brufke, "House Republicans voice concerns about White House's impeachment messaging," TheHill.com, October 2, 2019, https://thehill.com /homenews/house/464153-house-republicans-voice-messaging-concerns.

CHAPTER 17: DEFENDING THE INDEFENSIBLE

Jaime Herrera Beutler disputes the description of what she said in Steve Scalise's impeachment information session. She believes she asked, "Why would anyone support this?" However, this exchange—specifically her challenging leadership on why they should oppose an impeachment inquiry—was described to us by multiple sources in the room, including one who took notes. Two specifically mentioned to us that her comment set off a chain reaction to press GOP leaders to do more to get moderates like her in line.

1. Rishika Dugyala and Melanie Zanona, "Can the Republican Party save one of its last Latina congresswomen?," *Politico*, December 11, 2019, https://www .politico.com/news/magazine/2019/12/11/can-the-republican-party-save-its -only-latina-voting-congresswoman-076693.

2. Lauren Dake, "Herrera Beutler rejects Trump for president; will write in Ryan,"

The Columbian, October 8, 2016, https://www.columbian.com/news/2016/oct/08/hererra-beutler-rejects-trump-for-president-will-write-in-ryan/.

3. Calley Hair, "Herrera Beutler calls for impeachment vote," *The Columbian*, October 11, 2019, https://www.columbian.com/news/2019/oct/11/herrera-beutler-calls-for-impeachment-vote/.

4. "GOP Rep. Fred Upton on Trump impeachment inquiry: 'I want the answers to the questions,'" *Detroit Today*, Transcript, October 2, 2019, https://wdet.org/posts/2019/10/02/88688-gop-rep-fred-upton-on-trump-impeachment-inquiry-i-want-the-answers-to-the-questions/.

5. Julian E. Barnes, Michael S. Schmidt, and Matthew Rosenberg, "Schiff got early account of accusations as whistle-blower's concerns grew," *New York Times*, October 2, 2019, https://www.nytimes.com/2019/10/02/us/politics/adam-schiff-whistleblower.html.

6. Glenn Kessler, "Schiff's false claim his committee had not spoken to the whistleblower," *Washington Post*, October 4, 2019, https://www.washingtonpost.com/politics/2019/10/04/schiffs-false-claim-his-committee-had-not-spoken-whistleblower/.

7. Rachael Bade, Mike DeBonis, and Karoun Demirjian, "Republicans echo Trump in suggesting whistleblower complaint is politically motivated," *Washington Post*, September 20, 2019, https://www.washingtonpost.com/politics/republicans-echo-trump-in-suggesting-whistleblower-complaint-is-politically-motivated/2019/09/20/10d1e602-dbdc-11e9-adff-79254db7f766_story.html.

8. Adam Schiff, "Dear Colleague" letter, Washington, D.C., October 16, 2019, via J. M. Rieger, Twitter post, October 16, 2019, 6:59 p.m., https://twitter.com/RiegerReport/status/1184604895514628096/photo/1.

9. Jaime Herrera Beutler, Twitter post, October 17, 2019, 7:15 p.m., https://twitter.com/HerreraBeutler/status/1184971165418295297.

CHAPTER 18: "GET OVER IT"

1. "White House whistleblower comes forward in Oversight Committee investigation of security clearances," U.S. Congress, House of Representatives, Committee on Oversight and Reform, News release, April 1, 2019, https://oversight.house.gov/news/press-releases/white-house-whistleblower-comes-forward-in-oversight-committee-investigation-of; and U.S. Congress, House of Representatives, Committee on Oversight and Reform, *Corporate and Foreign Interests Behind White House Push to Transfer U.S. Nuclear Technology to Saudi Arabia*, Second Interim Staff Report, July 2019, https://oversight.house.gov/sites/democrats.oversight.house.gov/files/Trump%20Saudi%20Nuclear%20Report%20July%202019.pdf.

2. Meredith Cohn, "Rep. Elijah Cummings had a rare cancer. That he survived it for 25 years might be more rare," *Baltimore Sun*, November 13, 2019, https://www.baltimoresun.com/health/bs-hs-cummings-rare-cancer-20191113-rg2kailg4vd7vbgrxfbcxwzd2u-story.html.

3. Lindsey McPherson, "Fines? Jail? Democrats leave all options on the table for enforcing subpoenas," *Roll Call*, May 1, 2019, https://www.rollcall.com/2019/05/01/fines-jail-time-democrats-leave-all-options-on-the-table-for-enforcing-subpoenas/; and Todd Garvey, "Congressional subpoenas: Enforcing executive branch compliance," Congressional Research Service, March 27, 2019, https://sgp.fas.org/crs/misc/R45653.pdf.

4. Eric Swalwell, *Endgame: Inside the Impeachment of Donald J. Trump* (New York: Abrams Books, 2020), 185.

5. Kevin J. Hickey and Michael A. Foster, "The emoluments clauses of the U.S. Constitution," Congressional Research Service, January 27, 2021, https://crsreports.congress.gov/product/pdf/IF/IF11086#:~:text=The%20purpose%20of%20the%20Domestic,to%20exert%20influence%20over%20him.

CHAPTER 19: THE PRICE OF PRINCIPLE

1. Water Resources Development Act, Public Law No. 115-270 (2018), Secs. 1308–10.

2. Alex Rogers, "Francis Rooney is the rare House Republican open to impeaching Trump," CNN, October 19, 2019, https://www.cnn.com/2019/10/19/politics/francis-rooney-florida-republican-trump-impeachment/index.html.

3. CNN, *Newsroom*, Transcript, October 18, 2019, https://transcripts.cnn.com/show/cnr/date/2019-10-18/segment/03.

4. Emily Cochrane, "Francis Rooney, G.O.P. lawmaker who won't rule out impeachment, is to retire," *New York Times*, October 19, 2019, https://www.nytimes.com/2019/10/19/us/politics/francis-rooney-retirement-impeachment.html.

5. "'Asset' Utah Ad," Club for Growth, October 16, 2019, YouTube video, 00:30, https://www.youtube.com/watch?v=-iuEIJRjbt0&t=30s.

6. White House, "Statement from the Press Secretary," News release, October 6, 2019, https://trumpwhitehouse.archives.gov/briefings-statements/statement-press-secretary-85/; and Lindsey Graham, Twitter post, October 7, 2019, 12:48 p.m., https://twitter.com/LindseyGrahamSC/status/1181249892527808512.

7. Rachael Bade, Mike DeBonis, and Seung Min Kim, "Growing number of Republicans struggle to defend Trump on G-7 choice, Ukraine and Syria," *Washington Post*, October 18, 2019, https://www.washingtonpost.com/politics/growing-number-of-republicans-struggle-to-defend-trump-on-g-7-choice-ukraine-and-syria/2019/10/18/20e56612-f1b8-11e9-89eb-ec56cd414732_story.html.

8. Seung Min Kim, Rachael Bade, and Josh Dawsey, "Trump opens up Camp David as an 'adult playground' to woo GOP lawmakers during impeachment," *Washington Post*, November 22, 2019, https://www.washingtonpost.com/politics/trump-opens-up-camp-david-as-an-adult-playground-to-woo-gop-lawmakers-during-impeachment/2019/11/22/ec6e7810-0c6f-11ea-8397-a955cd542d00_story.html.

9. Maggie Haberman, Eric Lipton, and Katie Rogers, "Why Trump dropped his idea to hold the G7 at his own hotel," *New York Times*, October 20, 2019, https://www.nytimes.com/2019/10/20/us/politics/trump-g7-doral.html.

CHAPTER 20: GET TOUGHER

1. White House, "Remarks by President Trump in Cabinet meeting," Transcript, October 21, 2019, 11:42 a.m., https://trumpwhitehouse.archives.gov/briefings-statements/remarks-president-trump-cabinet-meeting-15/.
2. U.S. Congress, House of Representatives, Office of the Clerk, Roll Call 568, H.Res. 647, On Motion to Table, October 21, 2019, 6:57 p.m., https://clerk.house.gov/Votes/2019568?Date=10%2F21%2F2019.
3. Igor Derysh, "White House: Taylor's testimony was part of 'coordinated smear campaign' from far-left and radicals," *Salon*, October 23, 2019, https://www.salon.com/2019/10/23/white-house-taylors-testimony-was-part-of-coordinated-smear-campaign-from-far-left-and-radicals/.
4. Eric Swalwell, *Endgame: Inside the Impeachment of Donald J. Trump* (New York: Abrams Books, 2020), 194–96.

CHAPTER 21: "MORE LIKE NIXON"

Both Daniel Goldman and the House Intelligence Committee categorically denied that a Schiff staffer said, "Fuck Donald Trump." We had multiple sources recall the interaction, so we stuck with our reporting.

Daniel Goldman, the House Intelligence Committee Democrats' investigations director during Trump's first impeachment investigation, also disputes that he ever said "Jerry Nadler? With him, *everything* is negotiable." Goldman believes he instead said: "With your committee, everything is negotiable," referring to the Judiciary Committee of which Nadler was chair. His comment, Goldman said, was based on past experience of the two committees negotiating with the team of former special counsel Robert S. Mueller III for his public testimony in the summer of 2019. Our reporting is based on multiple sources, who stuck by what they heard when challenged with Goldman's assertion.

Adam Schiff, the House Intelligence Committee's Democratic chairman, disputed some aspects of the exchange between himself and Judiciary Committee chairman Jerrold Nadler on October 29. "Chairman Schiff's position was that the president should get due process, and would get due process," his office wrote to us. "However, Trump should not be allowed to game the system by withholding witnesses and documents from the Intelligence Committee's investigation and then cherry-pick certain documents and present them in the Judiciary Committee that would mislead the Congress and the public. In federal court, a party is not allowed to do so, and the same due process should be used by Congress—empowering the chairman to prevent this kind of abuse." Schiff's office also disputed our reporting about Harvard professor Laurence Tribe, stating: "Professor Tribe in fact agreed that Congress could define the appropriate due process as it had the sole power of impeachment."

We explained Schiff's position on the impeachment rules in the chapter, and we stand by our reporting of this exchange, which is based on multiple firsthand sources and notes of people in the room.

1. Laurence Tribe and Joshua Matz, *To End a Presidency* (New York: Basic Books, 2018).
2. U.S. Congress, House of Representatives, House Judiciary Committee, *Resolution of Inquiry*, 93rd Congress, 2nd sess., February 6, 1974, H.Res. 803, *Washington Post*, December 10, 2021, https://www.washingtonpost.com/wp -srv/politics/special/clinton/stories/hres803.htm; and U.S. Congress, House of Representatives, House Judiciary Committee, *Resolution on Clinton Impeachment Inquiry*, 105th Congress, 2nd sess., October 8, 1998, H.Res. 581, December 10, 2021, https://archive.nytimes.com/www.nytimes.com/library /politics/100898clinton-gop-text.html.
3. U.S. Congress, House of Representatives, Directing certain committees to continue their ongoing investigations as part of the existing House of Representatives inquiry into whether sufficient grounds exist for the House of Representatives to exercise its Constitutional power to impeach Donald John Trump, President of the United States of America, and for other purposes, 116th Congress, 1st sess., October 31, 2019, H.Res. 660 and H. Report 116-266, https://www.congress.gov/bill/116th-congress/house-resolution/660 /text/eh.
4. Andrew Napolitano, "Judge Andrew Napoliano: Trump's call with Ukraine president manifests criminal and impeachable behavior," Fox News, October 3, 2019, https://www.foxnews.com/opinion/judge-andrew-napolitano-trump -attacks-presidency.
5. "Trump attends fundraiser for House Republicans," Associated Press, October 29, 2019, https://apnews.com/article/3da2475a7b004804b418ce54f2 c243b4.
6. Rose White, "Fred Upton was one of 4 Republicans who voted to condemn Trump's tweets," Associated Press, July 16, 2019, https://www.wzzm13.com /article/news/fred-upton-is-one-of-4-republicans-who-voted-to-condemn -trumps-tweets/69-afb5db2a-e76e-418e-a83d-7ba66b2045de.
7. Melanie Zanona, "Inside Trump's roast of House Republicans," Huddle, *Politico*, October 31, 2019, https://www.politico.com/newsletters/huddle/2019 /10/31/inside-trumps-roast-of-house-republicans-487560.
8. Tim Alberta, "Who will betray Trump?," *Politico Magazine*, November 8, 2019, https://www.politico.com/magazine/story/2019/11/08/trump-impeachment -republicans-congress-229904/.
9. U.S. Congress, House of Representatives, Office of the Clerk, Roll Call No. 604, H.Res. 660, October 31, 2019, 11:27 a.m., https://clerk.house.gov /Votes/2019604?Date=10%2F31%2F2019.

CHAPTER 22: PLANNING AHEAD

1. Procedure and Guidelines for Impeachment Trials in the Senate, S. Doc. No. 93-33, 99th Congress, 2nd sess., 61 (1986), https://www.govinfo.gov/content /pkg/CDOC-99sdoc33/html/CDOC-99sdoc33.htm.
2. Michael C. Bender, *"Frankly, We Did Win This Election": The Inside Story of How Trump Lost* (New York: Twelve, 2021), 70.
3. Peter Baker and Nicholas Fandos, "Show how you feel, Kavanaugh was told, and a nomination was saved," *New York Times*, October 6, 2018, https://www .nytimes.com/2018/10/06/us/politics/kavanaugh-vote-confirmation-process .html.

CHAPTER 23: MISSED OPPORTUNITIES

1. John Kruzel, "Judge fast-tracks case over former White House official's refusal to testify in impeachment inquiry," TheHill.com, October 31, 2019, https:// thehill.com/regulation/court-battles/468424-judge-fast-tracks-case-over -former-white-house-officials-refusal-to.
2. Dareh Gregorian, "Bolton knows about 'many relevant meetings and conversations' on Ukraine that lawmakers might be unaware of, his lawyer says," NBC News, November 8, 2019, https://www.nbcnews.com/politics/trump -impeachment-inquiry/john-bolton-s-lawyer-says-he-has-new-relevant -information-n1079036.
3. Andrew Desiderio and Sarah Ferris, "Vulnerable Democrats seek impeachment guidance from Pelosi," *Politico*, September 26, 2019, https://www .politico.com/story/2019/09/26/democrats-impeachment-guidance-nancy -pelosi-1515591.
4. John Bolton, *The Room Where It Happened* (New York: Simon & Schuster, 2020), 294–97.
5. Philip Bump, "Nearly a third of the days he's been president, Trump has visited a Trump-branded property," *Washington Post*, December 30, 2019, https://www.washingtonpost.com/politics/2019/12/30/nearly-third-days-hes -been-president-trumps-visited-trump-branded-property/.
6. Dan Managan, "Trump wins appeal in case where Democrats sued him for allegedly violating emoluments clause," CNBC, February 7, 2020, https://www .cnbc.com/2020/02/07/trump-wins-appeal-of-emoluments-clause-lawsuit-by -democrats.html.
7. Simon Shuster, "Exclusive: How a Ukrainian oligarch wanted by U.S. authorities helped Giuliani attack Biden," *Time*, October 15, 2019, https://time .com/5699201/exclusive-how-a-ukrainian-oligarch-wanted-by-u-s-authorities -helped-giuliani-attack-biden/.
8. Devlin Barrett, John Wager, and Rosalind S. Helderman, "Two business associates of Trump's personal attorney Giuliani have been arrested on campaign finance charges," *Washington Post*, October 10, 2019, https://www .washingtonpost.com/politics/two-business-associates-of-trumps-personal

-lawyer-giuliani-have-been-arrested-and-are-in-custody/2019/10/10/9f9c101a
-eb63-11e9-9306-47cb0324fd44_story.html.

9. Caroline Kelly, Jim Acosta, and Jeremy Herb, "Mick Mulvaney refuses to comply with House subpoena and doesn't show up for impeachment deposition," CNN, November 8, 2019, https://www.cnn.com/2019/11/07/politics/mick-mulvaney-subpoena/index.html.
10. Tamara Keith, Ayesha Rascoe, and Franco Ordonez, "White House officials decline to appear for closed-door impeachment inquiry," NPR, November 4, 2019, https://www.npr.org/2019/11/04/775861308/trump-impeachment-inquiry-turns-focus-on-national-security-councils-eisenberg.
11. Pamela Brown, Rene Marsh, and Paul LeBlanc, "All four White House officials scheduled for House inquiry depositions Monday won't testify," CNN, November 4, 2019, https://www.cnn.com/2019/11/03/politics/officials-testify-impeachment-house-inquiry/index.html.
12. Reuters Staff, "Pompeo not complying with impeachment probe subpoena: lawmaker," Reuters, October 6, 2019, https://www.reuters.com/article/us-usa-trump-whistleblower-pompeo/pompeo-not-complying-with-impeachment-probe-subpoena-lawmaker-idUSKCN1WL0CI; Lauren Egan and Courtney Kube, "Defense Secretary Mark Esper will no longer comply with impeachment inquiry," NBC News, October 16, 2019, https://www.nbcnews.com/politics/trump-impeachment-inquiry/defense-secretary-mark-esper-will-no-longer-comply-impeachment-inquiry-n1067226; and Anthony Adragna and Ben LeFebvre, "Rick Perry won't comply with subpoena in impeachment probe," Politico, October 18, 2019, https://www.politico.com/news/2019/10/18/rick-perry-subpoena-impeachment-051335.
13. Joaquin Castro, Twitter post, October 28, 2019, 11:33 p.m., https://twitter.com/JoaquinCastrotx/status/1189022382008291328; and Danielle Wallace, "Dems may pursue perjury charges against Sondland: Welch," Fox News, October 23, 2019, https://www.foxnews.com/politics/gordon-sondland-perjury-charges-ukraine-controversy-impeachment-testimony.
14. Brian Stelter and Jeremy Diamond, "John Bolton lands a book deal. It will publish before the 2020 presidential election," CNN, November 9, 2019, https://www.cnn.com/2019/11/09/media/john-bolton-book deal/index.html.

CHAPTER 24: SHOWTIME

1. Leon Neyfakh, *Slow Burn: Watergate, Slate* podcast, Season 1, Episode 3, "A Very Successful Cover-Up," December 13, 2017, https://slate.com/news-and-politics/2019/09/slow-burn-season-1-episode-3-transcript.html.
2. Taylor, Walter, "Watergate caper: Cash withdrawal revealed by U.S.," *Washington Evening Star*, June 24, 1972, 10, via NewsBank Inc.'s *Washington Evening Star* archive, Washington, D.C., Library system; and Carl Bernstein and Bob Woodward, "Bug suspect got campaign funds," *Washington Post*, August 1, 1972, https://www.washingtonpost.com/wp-srv/national/longterm/watergate/articles/080172-1.htm.

3. Carl Bernstein and Bob Woodward, "FBI finds Nixon aides sabotaged Democrats," *Washington Post*, October 10, 1972, https://www.washingtonpost.com/wp-srv/national/longterm/watergate/articles/101072-1.htm.

4. Lawrence Meyer, "Last two guilty in Watergate plot," *Washington Post*, January 31, 1973, https://www.washingtonpost.com/politics/last-two-guilty-in-watergate-plot/2012/06/04/gJQAQQdHJV_story.html.

5. Geoff Shepard, "Annotated Watergate chronology," Shepard on Watergate, January 20, 2022, https://shepardonwatergate.com/detailed-chronology/.

6. "Chronology of Watergate developments in 1973," in *CQ Almanac 1973*, 29th ed. (Washington, D.C.: Congressional Quarterly, 1974), 1014–53, https://library.cqpress.com/cqalmanac/document.php?id=cqal73-867-26366-1225636.

7. Alicia Shephard, "The man who revealed the Nixon tapes," Opinions, *Washington Post*, June 14, 2012, https://www.washingtonpost.com/opinions/the-man-who-revealed-the-nixon-tapes/2012/06/14/gJQAsEZUdV_story.html.

8. John A. Farrell, "James McCord: The Watergate burglar who cracked," *Politico Magazine*, December 29, 2019, https://www.politico.com/news/magazine/2019/12/29/james-mccord-watergate-burglar-obituary-086480.

9. Leon Neyfakh, *Slow Burn: Watergate*, *Slate* podcast, Season 1, Episode 4, "Lie Detectors," December 20, 2017, https://slate.com/news-and-politics/2019/09/slow-burn-season-1-episode-4-transcript.html.

10. Amanda Reichenbach, "Watergate and public broadcasting," in *"Gavel-to-Gavel": The Watergate Scandal and Public Television*, American Archive of Public Broadcasting, December 11, 2021, https://americanarchive.org/exhibits/watergate/watergate-and-public-broadcasting.

11. *Time*, "Senator Sam Ervin," Cover illustration, April 16, 1973, http://content.time.com/time/covers/0,16641,19730416,00.html; and Mark Simon, "One view of mess in Washington/'Sam Ervin Fan Club' founder is pessimistic," *SFGate*, October 6, 1998, https://www.sfgate.com/politics/article/One-View-Of-Mess-in-Washington-Sam-Ervin-Fan-2987179.php.

12. U.S. Congress, Senate Historical Office, Washington, D.C., "Select Committee on Presidential Campaign Activities (The Watergate Committee)," December 11, 2021, https://www.senate.gov/about/powers-procedures/investigations/watergate.htm.

13. Andrew Kohut, "From the archives: How the Watergate crisis eroded public support for Richard Nixon," Pew Research Center, August 8, 2014, republished September 25, 2019, https://www.pewresearch.org/fact-tank/2019/09/25/how-the-watergate-crisis-eroded-public-support-for-richard-nixon/.

14. "A look back at the Senate Watergate hearings," *PBS NewsHour*, May 17, 2013, https://www.pbs.org/newshour/politics/a-look-back-at-the-senate-watergate-hearings.

15. Robert D. Luskin and Kwame J. Manley, Letter to Adam B. Schiff, "Re: Sworn Testimony of Ambassador Gordon Sondland," November 4, 2019, in *Deposition of: Gordon D. Sondland*, 376–79, https://docs.house.gov/meetings/IG/IG00/CPRT-116-IG00-D006.pdf.

16. Scott Clement and Emily Guskin, "Americans are split on impeachment,

just like they were before the public hearings," *Washington Post,* December 3, 2019, https://www.washingtonpost.com/politics/2019/12/03/americans-are-split-impeachment-just-like-they-were-before-public-hearings/.

17. Joseph Wulfsohn, "ABC News political analyst hits Elise Stefanik in controversial tweet sparking 'sexism' backlash," Fox News, November 13, 2019, https://www.foxnews.com/media/abc-matthew-dowd-elise-stefanik.

18. NCPR News, "Timeline: Rep. Stefanik often sharply critical of Trump, but backs his agenda," North Country Public Radio, August 10, 2018, https://www.northcountrypublicradio.org/news/story/36791/20180810/timeline-rep-stefanik-often-sharply-critical-of-trump-but-backs-his-agenda.

19. Elise Stefanik, Twitter post, November 21, 2019, 9:52 p.m., https://twitter.com/EliseStefanik/status/1197709454445334529.

20. Kevin Sullivan and Mary Jordan, *Trump on Trial: The Investigation, Impeachment, Acquittal and Aftermath* (New York: Scribner Books, 2020), 343.

21. David Brennan, "Fox News guest John Yoo accuses Vindman of 'espionage' ahead of testimony to Trump-Ukraine impeachment investigators," *Newsweek,* October 29, 2019, https://www.newsweek.com/fox-news-john-yoo-alexander-vindman-testimony-trump-ukraine-impeachment-1468355.

22. David Crary, "Trump impeachment inquiry heads to live TV coverage," Associated Press, November 11, 2019, https://apnews.com/article/6f36c34ab6b845bf8b279db3ac559897.

23. Michelle Mark, "The number of Americans watching Trump's impeachment hearings on TV pales in comparison to Nixon, and some are worried it could spell trouble for the Democrats," *Business Insider,* November 16, 2019, https://www.businessinsider.com/trump-impeachment-tv-viewership-comparisons-2019-11.

24. Nicole Goodkind, "Robert Mueller hearings had lackluster viewership, millions more watched James Comey and Brett Kavanaugh," *Newsweek,* July 26, 2019, https://www.newsweek.com/robert-mueller-ratings-testimony-congress-russia-1451350.

25. Douglas E. Kneeland, "Dean at witness table: A calm and cool 'David,'" *New York Times,* June 27, 1973, https://www.nytimes.com/1973/06/27/archives/dean-at-witness-table-a-calm-and-cooldavid-dean-at-witness-table-a.html.

26. Editorial Board, "Opinion: Sondland has implicated the president and his top men," *New York Times,* November 20, 2019, https://www.nytimes.com/2019/11/20/opinion/sondland-impeachment-hearings.html.

CHAPTER 25: "BUILD A BETTER CASE"

1. Mike DeBonis and Toluse Olorunnipa, "Democrats sharpen impeachment case, decrying 'bribery' as another potential witness emerges linking Trump to Ukraine scandal," *Washington Post,* November 14, 2019, https://www.washingtonpost.com/politics/pelosi-calls-trumps-actions-bribery-as-democrats-sharpen-case-for-impeachment/2019/11/14/0ee9a202-0702-11ea-b17d-8b867891d39d_story.html.

CHAPTER 26: THE CLIENT

1. Gregory Lewis McNamee, "Ted Cruz," *Encyclopedia Britannica*, January 14, 2021, https://www.britannica.com/biography/Ted-Cruz.
2. "Lindsey Graham roasts Trump, Cruz in D.C. speech," CBS News, January 8, 2022, YouTube video, 01:45, https://www.youtube.com/watch?v=e6AW 3IzaP1Q.
3. Todd J. Gillman and Matthew Adams, "The Donald Trump–Ted Cruz bromance, from 'Lyin' Ted' to 'total endorsement,'" *Dallas Morning News*, October 22, 2018, https://www.dallasnews.com/news/politics/2018/10/22 /the-donald-trump-ted-cruz-bromance-from-lyin-ted-to-total-endorse ment/.
4. Adam B. Lerner, "Ted Cruz: I wasn't attacking Mitch McConnell 'personally,'" *Politico*, July 27, 2015, https://www.politico.com/story/2015/07/ted-cruz -i-wasnt-attacking-mitch-mcconnell-personally-120684.
5. Marianne Levine, Burgess Everett, and Meridith McGraw, "White House backs full Senate trial if House impeaches Trump," *Politico*, November 21, 2019, https://www.politico.com/news/2019/11/21/white-house-backs-full-senate -trial-if-house-impeaches-trump-072578.
6. Jenna Portnoy, "A Republican state lawmaker joins the race to challenge Rep. Abigail Spanberger," *Washington Post*, November 18, 2019, https://www .washingtonpost.com/local/virginia-politics/a-republican-state-lawmaker -joins-the-race-to-challenge-rep-abigail-spanberger/2019/11/18/5aedb6be-0a1f -11ea-8397-a955cd542d00_story.html.
7. Michael Kruse, "The town hall that impeachment blew up," *Politico Magazine*, November 27, 2019, https://www.politico.com/news/magazine/2019/11/27 /mikie-sherrill-impeachment-tearing-apart-her-district-074097.
8. Kate Sullivan, "Michigan Democrat confronted over support of impeachment inquiry at town hall," CNN, October 5, 2019, https://www.cnn.com/2019/10/05 /politics/michigan-democrat-confronted-town-hall-impeachment-inquiry /index.html.
9. Michael Barbaro, "The freshmen: Elissa Slotkin confronts the impeachment backlash," *The Daily* podcast, *New York Times*, October 9, 2019, https://www .nytimes.com/2019/10/09/podcasts/the-daily/house-democrats-elissa-slotkin .html.
10. American Action Network, "AAN launches $7 million television and digital ad campaign opposing impeachment," News release, November 18, 2019, https://americanactionnetwork.org/press/aan-launches-7-million-television -and-digital-ad-campaign-opposing-impeachment/.
11. National Republican Congressional Committee, "Impeachment advisory: Attend coffee with Elissa Slotkin," News release, October 2, 2019, https:// www.nrcc.org/2019/10/02/impeachment-advisory-attend-coffee-with-elissa -slotkin/.
12. *No B.S. News Hour*, No Bullshit News podcast, November 24, 2019, https:// www.nobsnewshour.com/no-bs-news-hour-november-24th-2019/.

CHAPTER 27: NADLER'S LAST STAND

1. Peter Baker, *The Breach* (New York: Scribner, 2000), 148–49.
2. Douglas O. Linder, "The Impeachment of President William Clinton: A Chronology," *Famous Trials*, December 11, 2021, https://www.famous-trials .com/clinton/881-chronology.
3. Peter Baker and Juliet Eilperin, "Defense: Impeachment is not warranted," *Washington Post*, December 9, 1998, https://www.washingtonpost.com/wp-srv /politics/special/clinton/stories/impeach120898.htm.
4. Norman Eisen, *A Case for the American People: The United States v. Donald J. Trump* (New York: Crown Publishing Group, 2020), 162.
5. Pat Cipollone, Letter to House Judiciary Committee Chairman Jerrold Nadler, Washington, D.C., December 1, 2019, via *Washington Post*, https:// www.washingtonpost.com/context/dec-1-letter-from-white-house-counsel -pat-cipollone-to-house-judiciary-committee/6ca5316a-72b9-4859-96f7-9f7f8 ec89e17/.
6. Rachael Bade and Mike DeBonis, "'The president gave us no choice': Pelosi resisted Trump's impeachment, now she's the public face," *Washington Post*, December 5, 2019, https://www.washingtonpost.com/politics/the-president -gave-us-no-choice-pelosi-resisted-trumps-impeachment-now-shes-the-public -face/2019/12/05/56f31916-1774-11ea-a659-7d69641c6ff7_story.html.
7. Seung Min Kim, Mike DeBonis, Rachael Bade, and Karoun Demirjian, "White House gears up for aggressive effort to defend Trump in Senate as House moves toward impeachment vote," *Washington Post*, December 4, 2019, https://www.washingtonpost.com/politics/white-house-gears-up-for -aggressive-effort-to-defend-trump-in-the-senate-as-house-moves-toward -impeachment-vote/2019/12/04/e596a606-16b1-11ea-a659-7d69641c6ff7_story .html.
8. Ella Nilsen, "House Democrats have passed nearly 400 bills. Trump and Republicans are ignoring them," Vox, November 29, 2019, https://www.vox .com/2019/11/29/20977735/how-many-bills-passed-house-democrats-trump.

CHAPTER 28: COLD FEET AND A DEFECTION

1. Rachael Bade and Mike DeBonis, "House Democrats brace for some defec- tions among moderates on impeachment of Trump," *Washington Post*, De- cember 11, 2019, https://www.washingtonpost.com/politics/house-democrats -brace-for-some-defections-among-moderates-on-impeachment-of-trump /2019/12/11/8698a398-1c29-11ea-8d58-5ac3600967a1_story.html.
2. Sarah Ferris and Melanie Zanona, "Small group of Democrats floats censure instead of impeachment," *Politico*, December 10, 2019, https://www.politico .com/news/2019/12/10/democrats-censure-impeachment-080311.
3. Peter Baker, *The Breach* (New York: Scribner, 2000), 165–67.
4. Laurence Tribe, "Opinion: Impeach Trump. But don't necessarily try him in the Senate," *Washington Post*, June 5, 2019, https://www.washington

post.com/opinions/impeach-trump-but-dont-necessarily-try-him-in-the
-senate/2019/06/05/22d83672-87bc-11e9-a870-b9c411dc4312_story.html.

5. Chris Franklin and Bill Gallo Jr., "I would have won if people didn't call me a racist, GOP House candidate says," NJ.com, November 8, 2018, https://www
.nj.com/news/2018/11/without_distractions_2nd_district_gop_hopeful_says
.html.

6. John Bresnahan and Heather Caygle, "How Trump and McCarthy wooed Jeff Van Drew to switch parties," *Politico*, December 16, 2019, https://www.politico
.com/news/2019/12/16/trump-mccarthy-jeff-van-drew-switch-parties-086249.

7. Mike DeBonis, Rachael Bade, Paul Kane, and Josh Dawsey, "Rep. Jeff Van Drew, anti-impeachment Democrat, expected to switch parties after Trump meeting," *Washington Post*, December 14, 2019, https://www.washingtonpost
.com/powerpost/trump-urges-rep-van-drew-anti-impeachment-democrat
-to-switch-parties/2019/12/14/b201bb4a-1ea0-11ea-8d58-5ac3600967a1_story
.html.

CHAPTER 29: IMPEACHED

1. Justin McCarthy, "Trump approval inches up, while support for impeachment dips," Gallup, December 18, 2019, https://news.gallup.com/poll/271691
/trump-approval-inches-support-impeachment-dips.aspx.

2. Eric Swalwell, *Endgame: Inside the Impeachment of Donald J. Trump* (New York: Abrams Books, 2020), 279.

3. Raoul Walsh, director, *They Died with Their Boots On*, Warner Bros., 1941, 2h 20m. Also: Norman Eisen, *A Case for the American People: The United States v. Donald J. Trump* (New York: Crown Publishing Group, 2020), 192.

4. Eisen, *A Case for the American People*, 185.

5. Donald J. Trump, Letter to House Speaker Pelosi, Washington, D.C., December 17, 2019, via *Washington Post*, https://www.washingtonpost.com
/context/letter-from-president-trump-to-house-speaker-pelosi/fc9b1b07
-c534-454a-afe3-8333910c9c87/?utm_campaign=the_daily_202&utm_medium
=Email&utm_source=Newsletter&wpisrc=nl_daily202&wpmm=1.

6. Mike DeBonis, "Pelosi says House may withhold impeachment articles, delaying Senate trial," *Washington Post*, December 18, 2019, https://
www.washingtonpost.com/politics/some-house-democrats-push-pelosi-to
-withhold-impeachment-articles-delaying-senate-trial/2019/12/18/6e25814a
-21c5-11ea-a153-dce4b94e4249_story.html.

7. Eisen, *A Case for the American People*, 192.

CHAPTER 30: "MUTUALLY ASSURED DESTRUCTION"

1. Charles Schumer, Letter to Senate Majority Leader Mitch McConnell, proposing trial structure and subpoenas for documents and witnesses, News release, December 15, 2019, https://www.democrats.senate.gov/newsroom
/press-releases/leader-schumer-in-letter-to-leader-mcconnell-puts-forward

-structure-for-a-fair-and-honest-bipartisan-impeachment-trial-in-senate
-schumer-proposed-trial-structure-would-require-specific-documents-and
-testimony-from-four-key-witnesses.

2. CNN *New Day*, Twitter post, December 16, 2019, 8:48 a.m., https://twitter
.com/NewDay/status/1206571692971249664?ref_src=twsrc%5Etfw.

3. Eric Pooley, "A wizard casts his spell: Wily Al D'Amato is fighting for his
political life against the strongest opponent he has ever faced," *Time*, October 26, 1998, https://www.cnn.com/ALLPOLITICS/time/1998/10/19/damato
.ny.html.

4. Adam Nagourney, "The 1998 elections: New York State—the Senate;
Schumer uses D'Amato's tactics to win Senate election handily," *New York
Times*, November 4, 1998, https://www.nytimes.com/1998/11/04/nyregion/1998
-elections-new-york-state-senate-schumer-uses-d-amato-s-tactics-win-senate
.html.

5. Richard Cohen and Charlie Cook, "Chuck Schumer," in *The Almanac of American Politics 2020* (Bethesda, MD: Columbia Books and Information Services,
2019), 1210.

6. Emily Heil, "Chuck Schumer and that 'most dangerous place' joke," *Washington Post*, April 1, 2015, https://www.washingtonpost.com/news/reliable-source
/wp/2015/04/01/chuck-schumer-and-that-most-dangerous-place-joke/.

7. Noah Bookbinder, "The Senate has conducted 15 impeachment trials. It
heard witnesses in every one," Perspective, *Washington Post*, January 9, 2020,
https://www.washingtonpost.com/outlook/2020/01/09/senate-has-conducted
-15-impeachment-trials-it-heard-witnesses-every-one/.

8. U.S. Congress, Senate, *Impeachment Trial of President William Jefferson Clinton, Volume III: Depositions and Affidavits*, 106th Congress, 1st sess., S. Doc.
106-4, 13, February 12, 1999, https://www.govinfo.gov/content/pkg/CDOC
-106sdoc4/pdf/CDOC-106sdoc4-vol3.pdf#page=13.

9. Manu Raju, "Can Schumer and McConnell just get along?," *Politico*,
June 15, 2015, https://www.politico.com/story/2015/06/senate-schumer-and
-mcconnell-just-get-along-118994.

10. Paul Kane, "Gorsuch vote makes McConnell-Schumer relationship look bad. It
might get better," *Washington Post*, April 6, 2017, https://www.washingtonpost
.com/powerpost/gorsuch-vote-makes-mcconnell-schumer-relationship-look
-bad-it-might-get-better/2017/04/06/cddadaf4-1ac0-11e7-855e-4824bbb5d748
_story.html.

11. Manu Raju, "Chuck Schumer's man cave," *Politico*, April 21, 2015, https://
www.politico.com/story/2015/04/chuck-schumers-workout-a-little-bike-a-lot
-of-schmoozing-117170.

12. Paul Kane, "'We don't dislike each other': McConnell, Schumer make nice
on eve of immigration debate," *Washington Post*, February 12, 2018, https://
www.washingtonpost.com/powerpost/we-dont-dislike-each-other-mcconnell
-schumer-display-unity-on-eve-of-immigration-debate/2018/02/12/a4a5811e
-100d-11e8-9570-29c9830535e5_story.html.

13. Seung Min Kim, Paul Kane, and Rachael Bade, "Senate Republicans look
to hold short impeachment trial despite Trump's desire for an aggressive de-

fense," *Washington Post*, December 11, 2019, https://www.washingtonpost.com
/politics/senate-republicans-look-to-hold-short-impeachment-trial-despite
-trumps-desire-for-a-raucous-show/2019/12/11/b55f7da8-1c58-11ea-9ddd
-3e0321c180e7_story.html.

14. Helen Dewar and Peter Baker, "Senate sets rules, defers witness issue,"
    Washington Post, January 9, 1999, https://www.washingtonpost.com/wp-srv
    /politics/special/clinton/stories/impeach010999.htm.

CHAPTER 31: THE MODERATES

1. Sean Maguire, "Murkowski 'disturbed' by McConnell's vow for 'total coordination' with White House for impeachment trial," KTUU Alaska, December 24, 2019, https://www.alaskasnewssource.com/content/news/-Murkowski
   -disturbed-by-McConnells-vow-for-total-coordination-with-White-House-for
   -impeachment-trial-566472361.html.
2. Richard Cohen and Charlie Cook, "Lisa Murkowski," in *The Almanac of American Politics 2020* (Bethesda, MD: Columbia Books and Information Services,
   2019), 77–78.
3. Lisa Murkowski, "Murkowski statement on Don't Ask, Don't Tell," News
   release, December 8, 2010, https://www.murkowski.senate.gov/press/release
   /murkowski-statement-on-dont-ask-dont-tell.
4. Lisa Murkowski, "Op-ed: Murkowski shares thoughts on marriage equality
   with Alaskans," *Commentary*, June 19, 2013, https://www.murkowski.senate
   .gov/press/op-ed/op-ed-murkowski-shares-thoughts-on-marriage-equality
   -with-Alaskans; and Charlie Savage and Jeremy W. Peters, "Bill to restrict
   NSA data collection blocked in vote by Senate Republicans," *New York
   Times*, November 8, 2014, https://www.nytimes.com/2014/11/19/us/nsa-phone
   -records.
5. Nathaniel Herz, "Murkowski: Decision on Trump was 'instantaneous' after
   seeing video," *Anchorage Daily News*, October 9, 2016, https://www.adn.com
   /politics/2016/10/08/u-s-sen-lisa-murkowski-in-interview-said-decision-on
   -trump-was-instantaneous-after-seeing-video/.
6. Phil McCausland, "Murkowski and Collins: The two women who helped sink
   Obamacare repeal," NBC News, July 29, 2017, https://www.nbcnews.com
   /news/us-news/murkowski-collins-who-are-two-women-gop-senators-who
   -helped-n787711.
7. U.S. Congress, Senate, *On the Nomination (Confirmation Brett M. Kavanaugh, of
   Maryland, to be an Associate Justice of the Supreme Court of the United States).* Roll
   Call Vote No. 223, 115th Congress, 2nd sess., October 6, 2018. https://www
   .senate.gov/legislative/LIS/roll_call_votes/vote1152/vote_115_2_00223.htm.
8. Josh Dawsey, Twitter post, November 7, 2019, 10:56 p.m., https://twitter.com
   /jdawsey1/status/1192652129485426688?lang=en.
9. Liz Ruskin, "Alaska senators circumspect after release of Trump's Ukraine
   transcript," Alaska Public Media, September 25, 2019, https://www.alaska
   public.org/2019/09/25/alaskas-senators-uneasy-after-release-of-trumps
   -ukraine-transcript/.

10. Jordain Carney, "Murkowski, Collins say they won't co-sponsor Graham's impeachment resolution," TheHill.com, October 28, 2019, https://thehill.com/homenews/senate/467842-murkowski-collins-say-they-wont-co-sponsor-grahams-impeachment-resolution.

11. Eric Levenson, "Donald Trump rips Mitt Romney as 'one of the dumbest and worst' candidates ever," Boston.com, February 25, 2016, https://www.boston.com/news/politics/2016/02/25/donald-trump-rips-mitt-romney-as-one-of-the-dumbest-and-worst-candidates-ever/.

12. Lisa Riley Roche, "Mitt Romney: Trump is 'a phony, a fraud,'" *Deseret News*, March 3, 2016, https://www.deseret.com/2016/3/3/20583951/mitt-romney-trump-is-a-phony-a-fraud#mitt-romney-former-governor-of-massachusetts-shakes-hands-after-addressing-the-hinckley-institute-of-politics-at-the-university-of-utah-in-salt-lake-city-on-thursday-march-3-2016-regarding-state-of-the-2016-presidential-race; and Pamela Engel, "'Like a dog': Donald Trump impersonates Mitt Romney 'choking' in the 2012 election," *Business Insider*, April 13, 2016, https://www.businessinsider.in/like-a-dog-donald-trump-impersonates-mitt-romney-choking-in-the-2012-election/articleshow/51803206.cms.

13. David M. Drucker, "Mitt Romney: Insurgent and insider," *Washington Examiner*, May 1, 2018, https://www.washingtonexaminer.com/news/campaigns/mitt-romney-insurgent-and-insider.

14. Gabriel Sherman, "'Romney is the pressure point in the impeachment process': Mitt won't primary Trump—but he's trying to bring him down," *Vanity Fair*, October 7, 2019, https://www.vanityfair.com/news/2019/10/mitt-romney-wont-primary-trump-but-trying-to-bring-him-down-impeachment-2020.

15. Mitt Romney, Twitter post, October 5, 2019, 4:50 p.m., https://twitter.com/MittRomney/status/1180586045961691136.

16. "'Asset' Utah Ad," Club for Growth, October 16, 2019, YouTube video, 00:30, https://www.youtube.com/watch?v=-iuEIJRjbt0&t=30s.

CHAPTER 32: TRUMP WHISPERER

1. U.S. Senate Committee on the Judiciary, "Chairman Graham introduces resolution condemning House of Representatives' closed door impeachment process," News release, October 24, 2019, https://www.judiciary.senate.gov/press/rep/releases/chairman-graham-introduces-resolution-condemning-house-of-representatives-closed-door-impeachment-process.

2. Meredith McGraw, "Escape to Mar-a-Lago: Trump gets a post-impeachment mood lift," *Politico*, December 22, 2019, https://www.politico.com/news/2019/12/22/trump-vacation-impeachment-mar-a-lago-089499.

CHAPTER 33: PRE-TRIAL POSITIONING

1. U.S. Congress, Senate, Impeachment of President William Jefferson Clinton: Constitutional Provisions; Rules of Procedure and Practice in the Senate When Sitting on Impeachment Against President William Jefferson Clinton;

President Clinton's Answer; and Replication of the House of Representatives, 106th Congress, 1st sess., Document 106-2, 3, January 13, 1999, https://www .govinfo.gov/content/pkg/CDOC-106sdoc2/pdf/CDOC-106sdoc2.pdf.

2. Noah Feldman, "Trump isn't impeached until the House tells the Senate," Opinion, *Bloomberg*, December 19, 2019, https://www.bloomberg.com /opinion/articles/2019-12-19/trump-impeachment-delay-could-be-serious -problem-for-democrats.

3. Nancy Pelosi, "Dear Democratic Colleague," Letter, January 10, 2020, https:// www.speaker.gov/newsroom/11020-0.

4. Kate Brannen, "Exclusive: Unredacted Ukraine documents reveal extent of Pentagon's legal concerns," Just Security, January 2, 2020, https://www.just security.org/67863/exclusive-unredacted-ukraine-documents-reveal-extent -of-pentagons-legal-concerns/.

5. "Federal judge says Lev Parnas, indicted Rudy Giuliani associate, may give records to House," Associated Press, January 3, 2020, via *Los Angeles Times*, https://www.latimes.com/world-nation/story/2020-01-03/lev-parnas-judge -records-ruling.

6. Chris Kahn, "Let them speak: Most Americans want witnesses in Trump impeachment trial—Reuters/Ipsos poll," Reuters, January 22, 2020, https:// www.reuters.com/article/us-usa-trump-impeachment-poll/let-them-speak -most-americans-want-witnesses-in-trump-impeachment-trial-reuters-ipsos -poll-idUSKBN1ZL33O.

7. Colby Itkowitz, "Democrats increase pressure on Susan Collins as Trump impeachment trial begins," *Washington Post*, January 21, 2020, https://www .washingtonpost.com/politics/democrats-increase-the-pressure-on-susan -collins-as-senate-impeachment-trial-begins/2020/01/21/15289d60-3a17-11ea -bb7b-265f4554af6d_story.html.

8. Demand Justice, "Demand Justice announces release of new, six-figure digital ad campaign holding Collins accountable for Kavanaugh vote," News release, January 21, 2020, https://demandjustice.org/demand-justice-announces-new -six-figure-digital-ad-campaign-holding-collins-accountable-for-kavanaugh -vote/.

9. Matthew Chapman, "Collins calls out Schumer's support for her 2020 rival as reason for backing McConnell's trial rules," *Salon*, January 8, 2020, https:// www.salon.com/2020/01/08/collins-calls-out-schumers-support-for-her-2020 -rival-as-reason-for-backing-mcconnells-trial-rules_partner/.

10. Dareh Gregorian, Kasie Hunt, and Leigh Ann Caldwell, "McConnell makes last-minute handwritten changes to Trump impeachment trial rules," NBC News, January 21, 2020, https://www.nbcnews.com/politics/trump-impeachment -inquiry/mcconnell-makes-last-minute-changes-trump-impeachment-trial -rules-n1119511.

CHAPTER 34: SCHIFF'S LECTURE HALL

1. Paul Kane, Twitter post, January 26, 2020, 11:13 a.m., https://twitter.com /pkcapitol/status/1221466219519320064.

2. Burgess Everett, "Jerry Nadler 'stunned' Susan Collins into writing a note to John Roberts," *Politico*, January 23, 2020, https://www.politico.com/news/2020/01/23/susan-collins-impeachment-note-john-roberts-102826.

3. Ted Barrett, "GOP Sen. Lisa Murkowski was 'offended' by Nadler's comments, her spokesperson says," CNN, January 22, 2020, https://www.cnn.com/politics/live-news/trump-impeachment-trial-01-22-20/h_a37b4df7f867cbb66af91d7a5287f975.

4. "Trump dismisses impeachment as 'a hoax,' says Senate trial will 'work out fine," *Washington Post*, Washington Post video, 00:31, January 21, 2020, https://www.washingtonpost.com/video/politics/trump-dismisses-impeachment-as-a-hoax-says-senate-trial-will-work-out-fine/2020/01/21/5f5d2ada-e8b6-4b93-a201-87d17759838c_video.html.

5. Annie Karni and Maggie Haberman, "Angry Trump says focus should be on a trade deal, not a 'hoax,'" *New York Times*, January 16, 2020, https://www.nytimes.com/2020/01/16/us/politics/trump-impeachment-reaction.html.

6. Philip Bump, "Trump's second-heaviest Twitter day mirrored the heaviest: Lots of feedback about things on TV," *Washington Post*, January 22, 2020, https://www.washingtonpost.com/politics/2020/01/22/trumps-second-heaviest-twitter-day-mirrored-heaviest-lots-feedback-about-things-tv/.

7. CNN Wire Staff, "Impeachment trial of federal judge gets under way in U.S. Senate," CNN, September 13, 2010, http://www.cnn.com/2010/POLITICS/09/13/judge.impeachment/index.html.

8. Ryan J. Reilly, Twitter post, January 22, 2020, 10:17 p.m., https://twitter.com/ryanjreilly/status/1220183835205341185.

9. Norman Eisen, *A Case for the American People: The United States v. Donald J. Trump* (New York: Crown Publishing Group, 2020), 214.

10. Ted Johnson, "Impeachment viewership: An estimated 9.3 million tuned in on Monday," *Deadline*, January 29, 2020, https://deadline.com/2020/01/impeachment-ratings-donald-trump-1202845451/.

11. Mariam Khan, "Democrat Schiff's 'head on a pike' comment draws outrage from GOP senators," ABC News, January 25, 2020, https://abcnews.go.com/Politics/democrat-schiffs-head-pike-comment-draws-outrage-gop/story?id=68527054.

CHAPTER 35: BOLTON'S BOMBSHELL

1. Maggie Haberman and Michael S. Schmidt, "Trump tied Ukraine aid to inquiries he sought, Bolton book says," *New York Times*, January 26, 2020, https://www.nytimes.com/2020/01/26/us/politics/trump-bolton-book-ukraine.html.

CHAPTER 36: MITCH'S PRESSURE COOKER

Pat Cipollone disputes ever telling Mitch McConnell that the White House would seek an injunction to prevent John Bolton from testifying in Trump's

first impeachment trial if the Senate subpoenaed him to do so. However, this
conflicts with the recollections of others privy to their conversations.

CHAPTER 37: THE MUSK OX CAUCUS

1. Sean Maguire, "Murkowski 'disturbed' by McConnell's vow for 'total coordination' with White House for impeachment trial," KTUU Alaska, December 24, 2019, https://www.alaskasnewssource.com/content/news/-Murkowski
-disturbed-by-McConnells-vow-for-total-coordination-with-White-House-for
-impeachment-trial-566472361.html.
2. *National Federation of Independent Business v. Sebelius*, 567 U.S. 519 (2012),
Opinion of the Court.
3. Mark Sherman, "Roberts, Trump spar in extraordinary scrap over judges,"
Associated Press, November 21, 2018, https://apnews.com/article/north-america
-donald-trump-us-news-ap-top-news-immigration-c4b34f9639e141069c08cf
1e3deb6b84.
4. Joan Biskupic, "John Roberts presides over the impeachment trial—but he
isn't in charge," CNN, January 21, 2020, https://www.cnn.com/2020/01/21
/politics/john-roberts-trump-impeachment-trial-strategy/index.html.
5. Brian Fallon, Twitter post, January 28, 2020, 12:01 p.m., https://twitter.com
/brianefallon/status/1221840749936959488.
6. Demand Justice, Twitter post, January 27, 2020, 11:57 a.m., https://twitter
.com/WeDemandJustice/status/1221839536751349760.
7. Demand Justice, Twitter post, January 30, 2020, 10:47 a.m., https://twitter
.com/WeDemandJustice/status/1222909315431968769.
8. Paul Kane, "Senate to emerge from impeachment trial guilty of extreme partisanship," *Washington Post*, February 1, 2020, https://www.washingtonpost.com
/powerpost/senate-to-emerge-from-impeachment-trial-guilty-of-extreme
-partisanship/2020/02/01/c4886b80-44b9-11ea-aa6a-083d01b3ed18_story
.html.

CHAPTER 38: AUTOPILOT

1. Peter Baker, *The Breach* (New York: Scribner, 2000), 330.
2. Ali Zaslav, "Undecided Democratic senator calls for the Senate to censure
Trump," CNN, February 3, 2020, https://www.cnn.com/2020/02/03/politics
/joe-manchin-censure-trump/index.html.
3. Zeke Miller, "News of Bolton book sends jolt through impeachment trial," Associated Press, January 27, 2020, https://apnews.com/article/ap-top-news-john
-bolton-joe-biden-politics-donald-trump-c5f9cc7070a1d3a0e6afc945036811ae.
4. Cameron Peters, "3 Democrats walked out of Trump's State of the Union
in protest," Vox, February 5, 2020, https://www.vox.com/2020/2/5/21123942
/democrats-walked-out-trump-state-of-the-union-protest.
5. Jeffrey M. Jones, "Trump job approval at personal best 49%," News release,

Gallup Poll, February 4, 2020, https://news.gallup.com/poll/284156/trump-job-approval-personal-best.aspx.

6. Toluse Olorunnipa, Annie Linskey, and Chelsea Janes, "Buttigieg and Sanders take lead, Biden fades in partial results from marred Iowa caucuses," *Washington Post*, February 4, 2020, https://www.washingtonpost.com/politics/buttigieg-and-sanders-take-lead-biden-fades-in-partial-results-from-marred-iowa-caucuses/2020/02/04/0ff44134-4758-11ea-bc78-8a18f7afcee7_story.html.

CHAPTER 39: "POLITICS WILL BREAK YOUR HEART"

1. Joe Kildea, "Club for Growth launches TV ad on Romney siding with Democrats on impeachment," Club for Growth, News release, January 29, 2020, https://www.clubforgrowth.org/club-for-growth-launches-tv-ad-on-romney-siding-with-democrats-on-impeachment/.
2. Kerry Picket, "Conservative group pressures Mitt Romney to oppose Trump Senate impeachment trial witnesses," *Washington Examiner*, January 30, 2020, https://www.washingtonexaminer.com/news/conservative-group-pressures-mitt-romney-to-oppose-trump-senate-impeachment-trial-witnesses.
3. Katie McKellar, "Utah lawmakers filed bill to allow recall of sitting U.S. senator," KSL.com, January 30, 2020, https://www.ksl.com/article/46711309/utah-lawmaker-files-bill-to-allow-recall-of-sitting-us-senator.
4. Benjamin Wallace-Wells, "George Romney for president, 1968," *New York Magazine*, May 18, 2012, https://nymag.com/news/features/george-romney-2012-5/.
5. Grace Segers, "Susan Collins will vote to acquit Trump, saying he's 'learned' from impeachment," *CBS Evening News*, February 4, 2020, https://www.cbsnews.com/news/susan-collins-will-vote-to-acquit-trump-saying-hes-learned-from-impeachment/?ftag=CNM-00-10aab8a&linkId=81760957.
6. Norman Eisen, *A Case for the American People: The United States v. Donald J. Trump* (New York: Crown Publishing Group, 2020), 219.

CHAPTER 40: "THE IMPEACHMENT THAT WASN'T"

1. Toluse Olorunnipa and Mike DeBonis, "Trump lashes out at Democrats in cheering his acquittal as Pelosi declares him 'impeached forever,'" *Washington Post*, February 6, 2020, https://www.washingtonpost.com/politics/trump-lashes-out-at-democrats-in-cheering-his-acquittal-as-pelosi-declares-him-impeached-forever/2020/02/06/2148e47a-48f3-11ea-b4d9-29cc419287eb_story.html.
2. Gillian Brockell, "After impeachment acquittal, Bill Clinton was 'profoundly sorry.' Trump not so much," *Washington Post*, February 6, 2020, https://www.washingtonpost.com/history/2020/02/06/bill-clinton-impeachment-apology/.
3. John Gramlich, "Looking back on impeachment, a quarter of Americans say Trump did nothing wrong," Pew Research Center, March 17, 2020, https://www.pewresearch.org/fact-tank/2020/03/17/looking-back-on-impeachment-a-quarter-of-americans-say-trump-did-nothing-wrong/.

4. Pew Research Center, "2020 Pew Research Center's American Trends Panel, Wave 62 Pathways & Trust in Media Survey, Final Topline," February 18–March 2, 2020, https://www.pewresearch.org/wp-content/uploads/2020/03/Pathways-Feb-2020-ATP-W62-Topline.pdf.

5. Peter Baker, Michael S. Schmidt, and Maggie Haberman, "Republican senators tried to stop Trump from firing impeachment witness," *New York Times*, February 8, 2020, https://www.nytimes.com/2020/02/08/us/politics/trump-vindman-sondland-fired.html.

6. Peter Baker, Maggie Haberman, Danny Hakim, and Michael S. Schmidt, "Trump fires impeachment witnesses Gordon Sondland and Alexander Vindman in post-acquittal purge," *New York Times*, February 7, 2020, https://www.nytimes.com/2020/02/07/us/politics/alexander-vindman-gordon-sondland-fired.html.

7. Shane Harris, Ellen Nakashima, and Josh Dawsey, "Responding to news of Russian interference, Trump sends chilling message to U.S. intelligence community," *Washington Post*, February 22, 2020, https://www.washingtonpost.com/national-security/responding-to-news-of-russian-interference-trump-sends-chilling-message-to-us-intelligence/2020/02/22/1c63faec-5502-11ea-929a-64efa7482a77_story.html.

8. Melissa Quinn, "The internal watchdogs Trump has fired or replaced," CBS News, May 19, 2020, https://www.cbsnews.com/news/trump-inspectors-general-internal-watchdogs-fired-list/.

9. Ayesha Rascoe and Colin Dwyer, "Trump received intelligence briefings on coronavirus twice in January," NPR, May 2, 2020, https://www.npr.org/sections/coronavirus-live-updates/2020/05/02/849619486/trump-received-intelligence-briefings-on-coronavirus-twice-in-january.

10. Kyle Cheney, Heather Caygle, and Sarah Ferris, "Democrats wrestle with how hard to go after Trump's scandals," *Politico*, June 23, 2020, https://www.politico.com/news/2020/06/23/democrats-trump-scandals-336560.

11. John Bolton, *The Room Where It Happened* (New York: Simon & Schuster, 2020), 305.

12. Reality Check Team, "US election 2020: Fact-checking Trump and Biden on Covid," BBC News, October 27, 2020, https://www.bbc.com/news/election-us-2020-54248080.

13. "Presidential Election Results: Biden Wins," *New York Times*, November 3, 2020, https://www.nytimes.com/interactive/2020/11/03/us/elections/results-president.html.

14. Carol Leonnig and Phil Rucker, *I Alone Can Fix It* (New York: Penguin Press, 2021), 340.

15. William Cummings, Joey Garrison, and Jim Sergent, "By the numbers: President Donald Trump's failed efforts to overturn the election," *USA Today*, January 6, 2021, https://www.usatoday.com/in-depth/news/politics/elections/2021/01/06/trumps-failed-efforts-overturn-election-numbers/4130307001/.

16. Rosalind S. Helderman and Elise Viebeck, "'The last wall': How dozens of judges across the political spectrum rejected Trump's efforts to overturn the

election," *Washington Post*, December 12, 2020, https://www.washingtonpost
.com/politics/judges-trump-election-lawsuits/2020/12/12/e3a57224-3a72-11eb
-98c4-25dc9f4987e8_story.html.

17. Jonathan Karl, *Betrayal: The Final Act of the Trump Presidency* (New York: Dut-
ton, 2021), 170, 173.

18. Michael Balsamo, "Disputing Trump, Barr says no widespread election
fraud," Associated Press, December 1, 2020, https://apnews.com/article/barr
-no-widespread-election-fraud-b1f1488796c9a98c4b1a9061a6c7f49d.

19. William P. Barr, *One Damn Thing After Another* (New York: William Morrow,
2022), 16.

20. Tim Kephart, "Trump calls Ga. secretary of state 'enemy of the people,'"
CBS 46, November 27, 2020, https://www.cbs46.com/news/trump-calls-ga
-secretary-of-state-enemy-of-the-people/article_917de492-30c5-11eb-a89b
-6f888a101160.html; and Stephen Fowler, "'Someone's going to get killed':
Ga. official blasts GOP silence on election threats," NPR, December 1, 2020,
https://www.npr.org/sections/biden-transition-updates/2020/12/01/940961602
/someones-going-to-get-killed-ga-official-blasts-gop-silence-on-election
-threats.

21. Amy Gardner, "'I just want to find 11,780 votes': In extraordinary hour-long
call, Trump pressures Georgia secretary of state to recalculate the vote in
his favor," *Washington Post*, January 3, 2021, https://www.washingtonpost.com
/politics/trump-raffensperger-call-georgia-vote/2021/01/03/d45acb92-4dc4
-11eb-bda4-615aaefd0555_story.html.

22. Zachary Cohen and Paula Reid, "Exclusive: Trump advisers drafted more
than one executive order to seize voting machines, sources tell CNN," CNN,
January 31, 2022, https://www.cnn.com/2022/01/31/politics/trump-executive
-orders-seize-voting-machines/index.html.

23. Leonnig and Rucker, *I Alone Can Fix It*, 437.

24. Karl, *Betrayal*, 166.

CHAPTER 41: SHATTERING THE GUARDRAILS

A note on the timing of the fateful Trump-McCarthy call on January 6: Due
to the GOP leader's refusal to discuss anything related to January 6, there
were still ongoing questions about the exact timing of McCarthy's call with
Trump upon publication of this book. One Republican close to McCarthy
told us he believed it happened on the way to Fort McNair. As such, we have
included the call there in our book.

1. "Pence," The Lincoln Project, December 8, 2020, YouTube video, 00:38,
https://www.youtube.com/watch?v=HxBPqCHFCcc.

2. Jonathan Swan, *Off the Rails* podcast, Episode 7, "Trump turns on Pence,"
January 20, 2021, https://www.axios.com/off-the-rails-trump-pence-048fcbc8
-54dc-43bc-8832-46950ffd6fd5.html?deepdive=1.

3. Bob Woodward and Robert Costa, *Peril* (New York: Simon & Schuster,
2021), 229.

4. Woodward and Costa, *Peril*, 198.

5. Peter Baker, Maggie Haberman, and Annie Karni, "Pence reached his limit with Trump. It wasn't pretty," *New York Times*, January 12, 2021, https://www.nytimes.com/2021/01/12/us/politics/mike-pence-trump.html.

6. Mike Pence, "Dear Colleague" letter, Washington, D.C., January 6, 2021; also shared via Twitter post, January 6, 2021, 1:02 p.m., https://twitter.com/Mike_Pence/status/1346879811151605762?s=20.

7. Dalton Bennett, Emma Brown, Atthar Mirza, Sarah Cahlan, Joyce Sohyun Lee, Meg Kelly, Elyse Samuels, and Jon Swaine, "41 minutes of fear: A video timeline from inside the Capitol siege," *Washington Post*, January 16, 2021, https://www.washingtonpost.com/investigations/2021/01/16/video-timeline-capitol-siege/.

8. Karoun Demirjian, Carol D. Leonnig, Paul Kane, and Aaron C. Davis, "Inside the Capitol siege: How barricaded lawmakers and aides sounded urgent pleas for help as police lost control," *Washington Post*, January 10, 2021, https://www.washingtonpost.com/politics/inside-capitol-siege/2021/01/09/e3ad3274-5283-11eb-bda4-615aaefd0555_story.html.

9. Dalton Bennett, Shawn Boburg, Sarah Cahlan, Peter Hermann, Meg Kelly, Joyce Sohyun Lee, Elyse Samuels, and Brian Monroe, "17 requests for backup in 78 minutes," *Washington Post*, April 15, 2021, https://www.washingtonpost.com/investigations/interactive/2021/dc-police-records-capitol-riot/.

10. "Day of rage: How Trump supporters took the U.S. Capitol," *New York Times* video, 40:32, June 30, 2021, https://www.nytimes.com/video/us/politics/100000007606996/capitol-riot-trump-supporters.html.

11. Carol Leonnig and Phil Rucker, *I Alone Can Fix It* (New York: Penguin Press, 2021), 466.

12. Woodward and Costa, *Peril*, 248.

13. Jamie Gangel, Kevin Liptak, Michael Warren, and Marshall Cohen, "New details about Trump-McCarthy shouting match show Trump refused to call off the rioters," CNN, February 12, 2021, https://www.cnn.com/2021/02/12/politics/trump-mccarthy-shouting-match-details/index.html.

14. Ashley Parker, Josh Dawsey, and Philip Rucker, "Six hours of paralysis: Inside Trump's failure to act after a mob stormed the Capitol," *Washington Post*, January 11, 2021, https://www.washingtonpost.com/politics/trump-mob-failure/2021/01/11/36a46e2e-542e-11eb-a817-e5e7f8a406d6_story.html.

15. Woodward and Costa, *Peril*, 249.

16. Kevin Breuninger, "Jan. 6 panel recommends contempt for Meadows, reveals panicked texts from Trump Jr., Fox hosts over riot," CNBC, December 13, 2021, https://www.cnbc.com/2021/12/13/jan-6-panel-votes-for-house-to-hold-trump-aide-mark-meadows-in-contempt.html.

17. Jennifer Haberkorn, "Sheltering in a Capitol office, California lawmaker sent text and got impeachment ball rolling," *Los Angeles Times*, January 13, 2021, https://www.latimes.com/politics/story/2021-01-13/sheltering-in-a-capitol-office-a-california-lawmakers-frantic-text-got-the-impeachment-ball-rolling.

18. Jonathan Martin and Alexander Burns, *This Will Not Pass* (New York: Simon & Schuster, 2022), 187.

19. Emily Cochrane, Luke Broadwater, and Ellen Barry, "'It's always going to haunt me': How the Capitol riot changed lives," *New York Times*, September 16, 2021, https://www.nytimes.com/interactive/2021/09/16/us/politics/capitol -riot.html.

20. Leonnig and Rucker, *I Alone Can Fix It,* 471.

21. Demirjian, Leonnig, Kane, and Davis, "Inside the Capitol siege."

22. White House, The Daily Diary of President Donald J. Trump, January 6, 2021, https://www.washingtonpost.com/wp-stat/graphics/politics/jan-6-call -logs-white-house/daily-diary-of-president-donald-trump.pdf.

23. Hannah Knowles, "Democrats take control of Senate as Jon Ossoff defeats David Perdue," *Washington Post,* January 6, 2021, https://www.washingtonpost .com/politics/2021/01/06/georgia-senate-election-results-live-updates/#link -C2JKNKKHIVFJHBQOQJ3UAUAHCU.

24. Kerri Kupec, Twitter post, January 6, 2021, 3:55 p.m., https://twitter.com /Kerri_Kupec/status/1346923256989802498; Mick Mulvaney, Twitter post, January 6, 2021, 3:01 p.m., https://twitter.com/mickmulvaney/status/13469 09665423196162; and Lloyd Grove, "Ann Coulter blames 'gigantic pussy' Trump for MAGA riots: 'I hate him,'" *Daily Bears,* January 6, 2021, https:// www.thedailybeast.com/ann-coulter-blames-gigantic-pussy-trump-for-maga -rioting-i-hate-him.

25. George W. Bush, "Statement by President George W. Bush on insurrection at the Capitol," George W. Bush Presidential Center, News release, January 6, 2021, https://www.bushcenter.org/about-the-center/newsroom /press-releases/2021/statement-by-president-george-w-bush-on-insurrection -at-the-capitol.html.

26. Lisa Mascaro, Ben Fox, and Lolita C. Baldor, "'Clear the Capitol,' Pence pleaded, timeline of riot shows," Associated Press, April 10, 2021, https://ap news.com/article/capitol-siege-army-racial-injustice-riots-only-on-ap-480e95 d9d075a0a946e837c3156cdcb9.

27. Aaron C. Davis, "Timeline: How law enforcement and government officials failed to head off the U.S. Capitol attack," *Washington Post*, February 18, 2021, https://www.washingtonpost.com/graphics/2021/national/national-security /capitol-response-timeline/.

CHAPTER 42: IMPEACHMENT 2.0

Kevin McCarthy denies that he turned to Liz Cheney for advice or that he had reservations about the amicus brief his members were filing to the Supreme Court. However, that stands in contradiction to multiple sources in his office at the time.

1. Sarah Ferris, Twitter post, January 8, 2021, 1:01 p.m., https://twitter.com /sarahnferris/status/1347604326525644801?s=.

2. Jack Healy, "These are the 5 people who died in the Capitol riot," *New York Times*, January 11, 2021, https://www.nytimes.com/2021/01/11/us/who-died

-in-capitol-building-attack.html. Later, a bipartisan Senate report determined that a total of seven people had died in connection with the Capitol riot—information that was not known at the time. Chris Cameron, "These are the people who died in connection with the Capitol riot," *New York Times*, January 5, 2022, https://www.nytimes.com/2022/01/05/us/politics/jan-6-capitol-deaths.html. Also Peter Hermann and Spencer S. Hsu, "Capitol police officer Brian Sicknick, who engaged rioters, suffered two strokes and died of natural causes, officials say," *Washington Post*, April 19, 2021, https://www.washingtonpost.com/local/public-safety/brian-sicknick-death-strokes/2021/04/19/36d2d310-617e-11eb-afbe-9a11a127d146_story.html.

3. Tom Jackman, "Police union says 140 officers injured in Capitol riot," *Washington Post*, January 27, 2021, https://www.washingtonpost.com/local/public-safety/police-union-says-140-officers-injured-in-capitol-riot/2021/01/27/60743642-60e2-11eb-9430-e7c77b5b0297_story.html.

4. Chuck Schumer, Twitter post, January 7, 2021, 11:48 a.m., https://twitter.com/SenSchumer/status/1347223560302034945.

5. Bob Woodward and Robert Costa, *Peril* (New York: Simon & Schuster, 2021), 259.

6. Jamie Raskin, *Unthinkable: Trauma, Truth, and the Trials of American Democracy* (New York: HarperCollins, 2022), 192–94.

7. Maggie Haberman and Zolan Kanno-Youngs, "Trump weighed naming election conspiracy theorist as special counsel," *New York Times*, December 19, 2020, https://www.nytimes.com/2020/12/19/us/politics/trump-sidney-powell-voter-fraud.html.

8. Woodward and Costa, *Peril*, xix–xxii.

9. Jon Meacham, Timothy Naftali, Peter Baker, and Jeffrey A. Engel, *Impeachment: An American History* (New York: Modern Library, 2018), 73.

10. Jacob Knutson, "McCarthy joins 125 House Republicans in backing Texas lawsuit challenging election," *Axios*, December 11, 2020, https://www.axios.com/house-republicans-texas-lawsuit-election-a33e2081-89fa-442a-b1f6-eb1fcf9f4b16.html.

11. Paul Kane, "McCarthy's failure to lead House Republicans started before Jan. 6," *Washington Post*, April 22, 2022, https://www.washingtonpost.com/politics/2022/04/22/mccarthys-failure-lead-house-republicans-started-before-jan-6/.

12. Douglas MacMillan and Jena McGregor, "Lawmakers who objected to election results have been cut off from 20 of their 30 biggest corporate PAC donors," *Washington Post*, January 19, 2021, https://www.washingtonpost.com/business/2021/01/19/gop-corporate-pac-funding/.

13. Jonathan Martin and Alexander Burns, *This Will Not Pass* (New York: Simon & Schuster, 2022), 202.

14. Harry Enten, "How Republicans pulled off a big upset and nearly took back the House," CNN, November 14, 2020, https://www.cnn.com/2020/11/14/politics/house-republicans-elections-analysis/index.html.

15. Jonathan Swan, "Trump falsely blames Antifa for Capitol insurrection,"

Axios, January 12, 2021, https://www.axios.com/trump-falsely-blames-antifa -for-capitol-riot-bab4943c-d465-4d05-ae36-1e8d1437f168.html.

16. Woodward and Costa, *Peril,* 288.
17. Jeremy Herb, Manu Raju, Lauren Fox, and Phil Mattingly, "Republicans begin backing impeachment in 'vote of conscience,'" CNN, January 12, 2021, https://www.cnn.com/2021/01/12/politics/republican-reaction-impeach-vote /index.html.
18. Howard Altman, "15,000 National Guard troops now in DC for inauguration in eerie calm before the feared storm," *MilitaryTimes,* January 17, 2020, https:// www.militarytimes.com/news/your-military/2021/01/18/15000-national -guard-troops-now-in-dc-for-inauguration-in-operation-named-joint-task-force -district-of-columbia/.

CHAPTER 43: SPEAK REPUBLICAN

1. Tim Alberta, "How Donald Trump came between Mike Pence and Jeff Flake," *Politico Magazine,* January/February 2018, https://www.politico .com/magazine/story/2018/01/03/mike-pence-jeff-flake-republican-party -friendship-216208/.

CHAPTER 44: PEER PRESSURE

Chuck Schumer's office pushed back on suggestions that the leader or his staff sought to pressure the managers into a short, witnesses trial—particularly any charges of bullying. Schumer's counsel at the time, Mark Patterson, said in a statement for the book that Raskin's managers "enthusiastically" signed off on the rules, which allowed for the ability to call witnesses. He also argued that their advice was a success, given the broad bipartisan vote on the impeachment rules, saying it kept GOP senators open to voting for conviction rather than repelling them.

"Both before and during the trial, I made it very clear to the Managers, on behalf of Senator Schumer, that the decision of whether to call witnesses was entirely up to them," he said in a statement. Patterson also insisted that his pushback to having Harris break a tie to enact rules the impeachment managers wanted stemmed from his fear that a party-line, 50/50 roll call would lead to the trial being "denounced . . . as unfair from the get-go, making it impossible to attract Republican votes for conviction."

Five members of the managers' team said that even if Schumer's office at some point told the team the leader would support their calls for witnesses, he made his desires very clear and they did feel pressure. We stuck with our reporting.

1. Mitch McConnell, *The Long Game* (New York: Sentinel, 2016), 35.
2. Ian Duncan, Michael Laris, and Josh Dawsey, "Transportation secretary Elaine Chao resigns, saying she is 'deeply troubled' by violence at the Cap-

itol," *Washington Post*, January 7, 2021, https://www.washingtonpost.com /local/trafficandcommuting/elaine-chao-resigns/2021/01/07/7fcbe17a-511f -11eb-bda4-615aaefd0555_story.html.

3. Tara Palmeri, Rachael Bade, Ryan Lizza, and Eugene Daniels, "Republicans feel the squeeze on impeachment," *Politico Playbook*, January 25, 2021, https://www.politico.com/newsletters/playbook/2021/01/25/republicans-feel -the-squeeze-on-impeachment-491510.

4. J. Michael Luttig, "Opinion: Once Trump leaves office, the Senate can't hold an impeachment trial," *Washington Post*, January 12, 2021, https://www .washingtonpost.com/opinions/2021/01/12/once-trump-leaves-office-senate -cant-hold-an-impeachment-trial/.

5. "Madison Debates: Friday, July 20, 1787," Avalon Project, Yale Law School, accessed April 7, 2022, https://avalon.law.yale.edu/18th_century/debates_720.asp.

6. Hannah Knowles, "Sen. Lindsey Graham labeled a 'traitor' by pro-Trump hecklers at airport," *Washington Post*, December 19, 2021, https://www.washing tonpost.com/politics/2021/01/08/lindsey-graham-airport-confrontation/.

7. Seung Min Kim and Paul Kane, "McConnell breaks with Trump, says he'll consider convicting him in Senate trial," *Washington Post*, January 13, 2021, https://docs.google.com/document/d/17qrOuyYKzAnjYK_LQ7iE0BVGU jq9Z6aJy8r4oWmXkdI/edit#.

8. Manu Raju and Ted Barrett, "GOP senators warn McConnell could face backlash if he votes to convict Trump," CNN, January 20, 2021, https://www.cnn .com/2021/01/20/politics/gop-senators-warn-mcconnell-backlash/index.html.

9. McConnell, *The Long Game*, 35.

10. Ryan Lizza, Rachael Bade, Tara Palmieri, and Eugene Daniels, "The Washington Trump leaves behind," *Politico Playbook*, January 19, 2021, https:// www.politico.com/newsletters/playbook/2021/01/19/the-washington-trump -leaves-behind-491443.

11. Jonathan Martin and Alexander Burns, *This Will Not Pass* (New York: Simon & Schuster, 2022), 204.

12. Roxanne Reid, "House Minority Leader Kevin McCarthy & Sen. Mark Warner talk Pres. Biden & Trump impeachment," CW, *Full Court Press with Greta Van Susteren*, January 23, 2021, https://www.fullcourtgreta.com/2021/01/24 /full-episode-house-minority-leader-kevin-mccarthy-sen-mark-warner-talk -pres-biden-trump-impeachment/.

13. Alayna Treene, "Kevin McCarthy's rude awakening," *Axios*, January 24, 2021, https://www.axios.com/kevin-mccarthy-criticism-trump-impeachment -295d5309-8f5a-40ce-a97b-5aee436db191.html.

14. Jordain Carney, "Schumer: Impeachment trial will be quick, doesn't need a lot of witnesses," TheHill.com, January 25, 2021, https://thehill.com/home news/senate/535812-schumer-impeachment-trial-will-be-quick-dont-need-a -lot-of-witnesses.

15. U.S. House of Representatives, Kenneth Starr, Referral from Independent Counsel Kenneth W. Starr in Conformity with the Requirement of Title 28, United States Code, Section 595(c), 105th Congress, 2nd session, House

document 105-310, September 11, 1998, https://www.govinfo.gov/content/pkg
/CDOC-105hdoc310/pdf/CDOC-105hdoc310.pdf.

16. Andrew Glass, "Secret Service agents ordered to testify in Lewinsky scandal, May 22, 1998," *Politico*, May 22, 2018, https://www.politico.com/story
/2018/05/22/judge-orders-secret-service-agents-to-testify-in-lewinsky-scandal
-may-22-1998-599428.
17. Jamie Raskin, "House impeachment managers request former president Trump testify under oath next week," News release and letter, February 4, 2021, https://raskin.house.gov/2021/2/house-impeachment-managers-request
-former-president-trump-testify-under-oath.
18. Jeremy Herb and Mani Raju, "Trump quickly rejects impeachment managers' request for testimony at impeachment trial," CNN, February 4, 2021, https://www.cnn.com/2021/02/04/politics/impeachment-trial-trump-testify
/index.html.

CHAPTER 45: TRIAL TAKE TWO

1. Karoun Demirjian and Tom Hamburger, "'One down, 44 to go': Inside the House impeachment team's uphill battle," *Washington Post*, February 17, 2021, https://www.washingtonpost.com/politics/interactive/2021/impeachment
-managers-trump-trial/.
2. Demirjian and Hamburger, "'One down, 44 to go.'"
3. Amy B. Wang and Felicia Sonmez, "'Disorganized, random': Several GOP senators criticize performance of Trump's lawyers," *Washington Post*, February 9, 2021, https://www.washingtonpost.com/politics/trump-impeachment
-republicans-senate/2021/02/09/2d5d57ac-6b2d-11eb-9ead-673168d5b874
_story.html.
4. Kyle Cheney, "Tuberville says he informed Trump of Pence's evacuation before rioters reached Senate," *Politico*, February 11, 2021, https://www.politico.com
/news/2021/02/11/tuberville-pences-evacuation-trump-impeachment-468572.
5. Seung Min Kim and Karoun Demirjian, "Republican senators show emotion, but little evidence of changed minds," *Washington Post*, February 10, 2021, https://www.washingtonpost.com/politics/republican-senators-show-emotion
-but-little-evidence-of-changed-minds/2021/02/10/25b4810c-6bc2-11eb-9ead
-673168d5b874_story.html.

CHAPTER 46: THE *OTHER* JAIME

Mark Short, through a Mike Pence spokesman, said he did not recall any conversations on February 12 about whether he would comply with a trial subpoena or fight it in court.

Charles Cooper also recalls the events of February 12 somewhat differently. He does not recall having discussed Pence's team going to court or refusing to do a proffer that morning with the managers, but thinks this may have been discussed earlier—even the night before. He believes the call that morning focused more on whether the managers should subpoena Kevin McCarthy. However, that account was disputed by multiple people in the managers' room on February 12, and the phone for the Raskin-Cooper call was at one point put on speaker, where others heard the conversation.

John Katko said that he offered to testify in the Senate trial if subpoenaed and disputes that he told Raskin that Jaime Herrera Beutler "is all you need" that Saturday morning. This runs contrary to at least five Democratic managers' team sources who were well aware of Raskin's effort to find anyone who would step forward.

Schumer's office and his counsel Mark Patterson again refuted suggestions that they in any way leaned on the managers team to end the trial early. "I did not pressure the Managers to accept this proposal," Patterson said in a statement. "They in fact immediately saw the advantage of the idea because it admitted the Herrera-Beutler account into the record, but avoided any rebuttal testimony from Rep. McCarthy, who nobody on the Democratic side believed would be willing to incriminate President Trump on a witness stand."

Barry Berke, the impeachment counsel for Jamie Raskin, denies that he wanted to subpoena GOP witnesses on February 13 without knowing what they would say. The deliberations, however, were described by three people present for the conversation.

1. Jamie Gangel, Kevin Liptak, Michael Warren, and Marshall Cohen, "New details about Trump-McCarthy shouting match show Trump refused to call off the rioters," CNN, February 12, 2021, https://www.cnn.com/2021/02/12/politics/trump-mccarthy-shouting-match-details/index.html.
2. Chuck Cooper, "The Constitution doesn't bar Trump's impeachment trial," Opinion, *Wall Street Journal*, February 7, 2021, https://www.wsj.com/articles/the-constitution-doesnt-bar-trumps-impeachment-trial-11612724124.
3. Chris Sommerfeldt, "Schumer says Senate will call witnesses for Trump's trial—if impeachment managers want them," New York *Daily News*, February 11, 2021, https://www.nydailynews.com/news/politics/ny-impeachment-trial-schumer-20210212-5tdn5xrmxvdwlhvtfwfr5qcdx4-story.html.
4. Jaime Herrera Beutler, Twitter post, January 6, 2021, 9:23 p.m., https://twitter.com/HerreraBeutler/status/1347005938318848001.
5. Barry Holtzclaw, "Herrera Beutler works hard to spread facts about Jan. 6, says her decision was personal not political," *Daily News*, January 17, 2021, https://tdn.com/news/herrera-beutler-works-hard-to-spread-facts-about-jan-6-says-her-decision-was-personal/article_07c75c39-59df-5f59-b9ef-fd50ba6104f2.html.
6. Burgess Everett, Heather Caygle, and Marianne Levine, "Inside Democrats' witness fiasco," *Politico*, February 13, 2021, https://www.politico.com/news/2021/02/13/senate-democrats-impeachment-witnesses-468992.

CHAPTER 47: FALLING SHORT

1. Jonathan Martin and Alexander Burns, *This Will Not Pass* (New York: Simon & Schuster, 2022), 227.
2. Jeff Field, "Mitch McConnell 'absolutely' would support Trump if GOP nominee in 2024," Fox News, February 25, 2021, https://www.foxnews.com/politics/mitch-mcconnell-absolutely-would-support-trump-if-gop-nominee-in-2024.

EPILOGUE

Kevin McCarthy and Jaime Herrera Beutler jointly dispute details of the meeting on February 25, 2021, dismissing the reporting in a statement as "wrong" and "dramatized to fit an on-screen adaptation." However, we stand by the reporting, which includes a primary source who relayed quotes. McCarthy also boasted about this meeting to other lawmakers, who first told the authors about it.

For transparency's sake, here is their statement: "The alleged reporting of a February 25, 2021 meeting between the two of us is wrong. Beyond multiple inaccuracies—it is dramatized to fit an on-screen adaptation, not to serve as a document of record. We know it's wrong because we were the only two in the room for this conversation."

1. National Commission on Terrorist Attacks, *9/11 Commission Report: Final Report of the National Commission on Terrorist Attacks Upon the United States* (Washington, D.C.: U.S. Government Printing Office, 2004).
2. Karoun Demirjian, "GOP senators block Jan. 6 commission, likely ending bid for independent probe of Capitol riot," *Washington Post*, May 28, 2021, https://www.washingtonpost.com/national-security/january-6-commission-senate/2021/05/28/54e9f692-bf27-11eb-b26e-53663e6be6ff_story.html.
3. "State party censures in response to Trump impeachment, 2021," Ballotpedia, https://ballotpedia.org/State_party_censures_in_response_to_Trump_impeachment,_2021.
4. Geoffrey Skelley, "9 of the 10 House Republicans who voted for impeachment already have primary challengers," FiveThirtyEight, March 17, 2021, https://fivethirtyeight.com/features/9-of-the-10-house-republicans-who-voted-for-impeachment-already-have-primary-challengers/; and Mark Weiner, "Rep. John Katko to retire from Congress, ending bid for 5th term," *Syracuse Post-Standard*, January 14, 2022, https://www.syracuse.com/politics/2022/01/rep-john-katko-to-retire-from-congress-ending-bid-for-5th-term.html.
5. "Voting Laws Roundup: December 2021," Brennan Center for Justice, December 21, 2021, https://www.brennancenter.org/our-work/research-reports/voting-laws-roundup-december-2021.
6. Brittany Shammas, "A GOP congressman compared Capitol rioters to tourists; Photos show him barricading a door," *Washington Post*, May 18, 2021,

https://www.washingtonpost.com/politics/2021/05/18/clyde-tourist-capitol
-riot-photos/.

7. Keith Alexander, "Prosecutors break down charges, convictions for 725 arrested so far in Jan. 6 attack on U.S. Capitol," *Washington Post*, December 31,
2021, https://www.washingtonpost.com/politics/2021/12/31/capitol-deadly-attack
-insurrection-arrested-convicted/; and Zoe Tillman, "'Justice for J6' says
they're rallying for nonviolent offenders. Most alleged Capitol rioters in jail are
charged with violent crimes," BuzzFeed News, September 18, 2021, https://
www.buzzfeednews.com/article/zoetillman/insurrection-defendants-jail-rally
-political-prisoners.

8. Jennifer Agiesta and Ariel Edwards-Levy, "CNN poll: Most Americans feel
democracy is under attack in the US," CNN, September 15, 2021, https://
www.cnn.com/2021/09/15/politics/cnn-poll-most-americans-democracy
-under-attack/index.html.

9. Shane Goldmacher and Rachel Shorey, "Trump has built war chest of more
than $100 million," *New York Times*, July 31, 2021, https://www.nytimes
.com/2021/07/31/us/politics/trump-donations.html.

10. Eli Yokley, "Most GOP voters want Trump to run again, but among those
who don't, Pence and DeSantis are the leaders," *Morning Consult*, October
13, 2021, https://morningconsult.com/2021/10/13/trump-2024-pence-desantis
-polling/; and Gabriela Schulte, "Poll: Just under half of voters support Trump
running in 2024," TheHill.com, October 18, 2021, https://thehill.com/hilltv
/what-americas-thinking/577199-poll-just-under-half-of-voters-support
-trump-running-in-2024.

11. "General election: Trump vs. Biden," Real Clear Politics, https://www
.realclearpolitics.com/epolls/2024/president/us/general-election-trump-vs
-biden-7383.html.

12. NPR Staff, "Rep. Liz Cheney read text messages she said Mark Meadows
got during the Jan. 6 siege," NPR, December 13, 2021, https://www.npr
.org/2021/12/13/1063955835/rep-liz-cheney-read-text-messages-she-said
-mark-meadows-got-during-the-jan-6-sie.

13. Melissa Quinn, "Supreme Court rejects Trump request to shield release of
records to January 6 committee," January 20, 2022, https://www.cbsnews
.com/news/trump-supreme-court-january-6-document-release/.

14. Ann Marimow, "Biden administration, House Democrats reach agreement
in Donald McGahn subpoena lawsuit," *Washington Post*, May 11, 2021,
https://www.washingtonpost.com/local/legal-issues/donald-mcgahn-subpoena
-lawsuit-settled/2021/05/11/8c445dfe-b2ab-11eb-ab43-bebddc5a0f65_story
.html.

INDEX